SHINING THE LIGHT VII

THE FIRST ALIGNMENT:
World Peace

LIGHT TECHNOLOGY RESEARCH

SHINING THE LIGHT VII

THE FIRST ALIGNMENT: World Peace

LIGHT TECHNOLOGY RESEARCH

Light Technology Publishing

This book has been compiled from both unpublished channelings and
channelings previously published in the *Sedona Journal of EMERGENCE!*,
a monthly magazine published by Light Technology Publishing.

Cover Art: "Balance"
by Robert Lewis Arnold

ISBN 1-891824-56-2

Published by

3° LIGHT
Technology
PUBLISHING

800-450-0985
www.lighttechnology.com

Printed by

GraphTech
DIGITAL & PRINTING

PO Box 3540
Flagstaff, AZ 86003

Dedication

Greetings, my friends!

I hope you enjoy this *Shining the Light* book. It is a transitional book, as you will see when you get to *Shining the Light VIII*. Consider, as you are reading it, the many books that preceded it in this series. You have seen how they have evolved over time, gradually entrusting you with more and more of your own capabilities to think and to wonder if things could be better. Isn't it possible that things could be better—wasn't there a way that you could help make life on Earth more benevolent? When you get to the end of this book, you will be perhaps slightly provoked by the ending, but the ending is meant to lead you to the book following, which will be the last book in this *Shining the Light* series. I hope you enjoy this one. The one to follow will truly be the graduation book of *Shining the Light*.

—Zoosh through Robert Shapiro
August 25, 2005

BOOKS BY ROBERT SHAPIRO

Explorer Race series

1 The Explorer Race
2 ETs and the Explorer Race
3 Explorer Race: Origins and the Next 50 Years
4 Explorer Race: Creators and Friends
5 Explorer Race: Particle Personalities
6 The Explorer Race and Beyond
7 Explorer Race: The Council of Creators
8 The Explorer Race and Isis
9 The Explorer Race and Jesus
10 Explorer Race: Earth History and Lost Civilizations
11 Explorer Race: ET Visitors Speak
12 Explorer Race: Techniques for Generating Safety

Material Mastery series

A Shamanic Secrets for Material Mastery
B Shamanic Secrets for Physical Mastery
C Shamanic Secrets for Spiritual Mastery

Shining the Light series

Shining the Light: The Battle Begins!
Shining the Light II: The Battle Continues
Shining the Light III: Humanity Gets a Second Chance
Shining the Light IV: Humanity's Greatest Challenge
Shining the Light V: Humanity Is Going to Make It!
Shining the Light VI: The End of What Was
Shining the Light VII: The First Alignment—World Peace

Ultimate UFO series

Andromeda: UFO Contact from Andromeda
Zetas, Hybrids and Human Contacts

Secrets of Feminine Science series

Book 1: Benevolent Magic & Living Prayer
Book 2: Disentanglement & Deep Disentanglement
Book 3: Disengagement, Engagement & Connections

Shirt Pocket Books series

Touching Sedona
Feeling Sedona's ET Energies

Contents

Creation Homework

Introduction:
Become a Player in the
Art of Resolving the Impossible!

Zoosh
December 23, 2004

All right, Zoosh speaking. Greetings. Now, many of you have been reading this series of *Shining the Light* books and articles for some time and so you are reasonably well informed about the circumstances in the U.S. and in the world regarding who is doing what to whom—at least in an overall sense, without naming names too much. We really cannot do this, because the way to resolve these matters is not to point the finger of blame so much as to encourage you, the reader, to bring about resolution by involving yourself in spiritual capabilities to influence events in your world in the most benevolent way. Therefore, I am issuing a graduate certificate to you all and urging you to take the next step that will allow you to come into a greater practitioner role through which you can incorporate the methods and means to bring about benevolent change. If you are in accordance with those ideals, please read on.

A New Direction for *Shining the Light*

This is intended to support you to shift from looking for who to blame (such as the sinister secret government, or the SSG: "Who are they? No names"), to move you from your position of suspicion to a position of, "Well, what can we do about it benevolently?" And as you can see, these books are moving toward that. Ultimately, I'm hopeful that *Shining the Light* readers will read the *Explorer Race* books also.

The *Explorer Race* series is offered to you as a handbook that you might be able to understand why you are here as a people, what you are doing, where you are going and why. Also, the *Shamanic Secrets* series and other instructional books along these lines—including the series known as the *Ancient Secrets of Feminine Science* books, especially those—are intended to give you very specific instructions on what to do about challenges, both day-to-day and global, so that you as an Earth citizen can work on, contribute to and even specifically, individually resolve serious challenges. In short, the *Explorer Race* books, the *Shamanic Secrets* books, the *Ancient Secrets of Feminine Science* books and, to a degree, the *Shining the Light* books are meant to educate, to empower and to encourage the application of your natural benevolent magical powers to bring about solutions to global and personal challenges and problems.

Yes, you all want clarity about events that affect you personally and globally—details and background information: "What's happening now?" But it is in the nature of insolvable problems—problems that simply cannot be solved—that if we are attempting to solve those problems with magic, then that analytical, mental understanding of all the things that are wrong won't help us very much. That's why we've shifted off the format of the first six *Shining the Light* books. Let me elaborate.

In order to bridge the gap between what is known and what is desired, there needs to be something that happens in that gap. The gap is that those who are personally affected by the events that are occurring nowadays must not only be involved in the events and therefore proceed in some way, must not only be desirous of changing those events, but must be personally and directly involved in bringing about a change in those events of the day in a way that deals directly with the impossible as an accepted fact. It's not just, "That's impossible; we can't do anything about it," but "That's impossible and we *can* do something about it."

The Solution Lies in the Continuity of Your Immortal Personalities

How do you do that? There's no way to do that other than doing something that all souls are embracing—and by all souls, I mean the souls of the terrorists, the soul of every criminal, the soul of every murderer, the soul of every depraved or crazed person, the soul of every benevolent person, the souls of all folks, period. Every soul must gain and cooperate; therefore, this system must be based in some manner that ensures that no person is left behind and everyone can move along in a benevolent way, being protected, supported, nurtured and otherwise cared for.

The objective is to move through—not jump over, but move through—the impossible to solutions that have no logical means to explain them. And if you did attempt to explain them, you would undo the solution because you would essentially tear apart that solution and try to force it into an analytical design that does not explain how the solution was accomplished. The solution involves more than the existence you are living in; it involves the existence that connects all souls before you came to this planet, while you're on this planet and when you go beyond this planet.

In other words, the solution is located directly in the continuity of your immortal personalities. This means that all souls can agree on the continuity and the benevolence and the value of the continuity and benevolence of life. The solution comes within that corridor; it does not come in whatever totally impossible-to-solve problem you are experiencing. That's how benevolent magic exists universally and beyond this universe. It doesn't make any difference what the problem is; it can be solved as long as everyone benefits. That's all. That's where you get universal cooperation. So in order to bring that about, there need to be solutions that do not ignore the problems but which also do not use the old methods of attempting to fix the problems if those methods were used to create those problems in the first place.

Therefore, with analysis and thought—"How are we going to do this? Here's the problem. Let's do this; let's do that. Ah, that's the solution!"—you think you have a solution, only to discover that by using the same method to bring about the solution, you are incorporating further problems because you are using that same old method that caused the problem in the first place. Therefore, you must do something unique, something different, something that does not necessarily reject that process—it might allow it to be included in its applications, but it does not depend upon that process to bring about the ultimate benevolence for all beings.

After all, although it might seem to be perfectly logical to execute somebody for murdering someone else, I can assure you that there's at least one person, to say nothing of that person's loved ones, who would object to that—certainly the person being executed, in most cases, objects to being executed. So you know for a fact that there's at least one soul who objects to that, even though you might very reasonably say—and I'm not trying to say do or don't execute people—"This person committed this horrible crime, and we don't want him or her back out on the street again, and the surest way to keep that from happening is to execute him or her." So that is flawless logic, and yet it is that same flawless logic—not always flawless, granted, but it is that same method of logic—that got you into the trouble you're in right now.

Your Job Is to Bring About Benevolent Change

I grant that there are plenty of times when logic has been avoided, but even with the best efforts at creation, there have been gaps. And those various gaps have not been ignored, but people have simply thrown their hands up in the air and said, "Well, there's nothing we can do about that."

Take, for example, radioactive waste: "There's nothing we can do about that. We hope there will be someday, but for right now, let's just bury it and hope that because we can't see it anymore that it will be safe." Now, everyone knows that there's no guarantee, but what about benevolent magic? That's what contains the impossible, and the more we get the word out about benevolent magic and living prayer, the more likely these things are going to change because nothing is hurt or harmed. To change radioactive waste, we do not destroy or encase the radioactive waste; we simply use benevolent magic to bring about its change. I'm not going to go into that campaign at the moment.

LIVING PRAYER
Speaks of Many Truths

Living prayer allows you as an individual to give to the Earth. So many of you ask, "What can I do for the Earth? What can I do for the animals? What can I do for people suffering in other parts of the world or in my own town or family? What can I do?"

If people are suffering on the other side of the Earth, you can say, "May the people be nurtured and know they are loved. May their hearts be healed and may they find what they need, or may it be brought to them in a benevolent, beneficial way for all beings."

Say this key phrase—"I will ask," or "I am asking"—out loud, though perhaps softly. This way it is understood that what you are asking is about physical things. In the case of a war on the other side of the world, you might say, "I ask that everyone's heart be healed and that they find peace together in the most benevolent and beneficial way for them."

Let's say you are driving through the forest and there is no one else around. Suddenly your heart hurts. It is a dull ache. When you get used to this living prayer, you will look around and say, "I will ask." The moment you say that key phrase, Creator knows that you are saying a living prayer. "May the heart of the forest be healed. May the hearts of all the trees, plants, rocks, animals and spirits who like to be here be healed. May they enjoy their time in the forest and feel welcome."

Then go on. Your heart will probably feel better. If you get the feeling again farther up the road, say it again without looking at them, "May their hearts be healed. May they feel welcome wherever they go or where they are."

Remember, you have to say these blessings only once for each place, person or group of people. You are more sensitive now, and the plants and the animals and the stone and maybe even other people are more sensitive too. You all need each other more now than ever, and here is something you can do to help others and feel better yourself.

Try not to look directly at people who cause your heart to hurt. Some other part of your body may hurt sometimes when you are near people who are suffering in some way. First ask that their hearts be healed, then add other parts of them according to what hurts on you. You don't have to name the organ unless you feel sure; just say the place on the body.

It is intended now that many people begin giving and asking for such prayers. As Mother Earth and her rocks, trees, plants and animals come under more strain in your time due to so many people and their needs, these natural forms of life may no longer be able to give you the healings and blessings they have been doing simply by being and radiating their good health. So you can now give to them in return for all their generations of benevolence. These prayers are all they ask.

It is your job right now as beings to bring about benevolent change and to recognize that the mechanics of benevolent magic lie in the total agreement—not forced in any way—of all souls and in an embracing of that total agreement in the total genuineness and total honesty of all souls. This means, "There are certain things we can all agree on, yes? We want to be happy. We want to have food. We want to have clothing. We want to have shelter. We want to be appreciated. We want to have valuable lives. We need to have basic necessities. In short, we want to have good lives and be able to pass on those good lives to our wives, husbands, children, families, friends, cities, towns, the world. In short, we want to have good lives." What's wrong with that? Not a thing. Therefore, benevolent magic and living prayer are dependent on the cooperation of all souls because they are geared to nurture benevolent life for all beings.

We are no longer just focused on the sinister secret government and what they are doing. The whole question now always has to be based on, "What can we do about that to bring about some benevolent change?" Or you might simply say, "What can we do about that?" The whole structure of the *Shining the Light* books has to change to, "What can we do about that?" In order to move to this situation that I talked about a moment ago, there needs to be motion by all beings, whether they are locked in a dungeon somewhere, as many prisoners are, or whether they are living in the penthouse of the finest office building in whatever city they're in. In order to bring about benevolence for all beings, wealthy people do not have to give up money. It's really true. They can if they choose, but they don't have to. Rather, there has to be inclusion, not exclusion.

Inclusion Will Bring Benevolence in Your Global Relationships

I might add, as a political side note here, that many people in the U.S. culture and, to a degree, in cultures around the Western world are completely shocked at the inclusion of China, certainly a nation with a government that the U.S. used to be totally ill-at-ease with, to put it mildly. But many people who are aware that things need to be done differently are entirely focused in inclusion. The way to involve China in the world is to involve her in a way—in a *way*, not *ways*—that is benevolent for China. What you see going on is a variation.

I grant that China is not 100 percent heroic, but neither is any other country. But what you see going on is economically—and politically, to a degree—an attempt at inclusion. Because if you include people, even if you don't like their political system, even with the problems that that approach to your economic system might turn up, eventually they're going to see how it benefits them. So you might see that on an analytical basis—not having to do with benevolent magic, but on an analytical basis—you are seeing the results of inclusion, of the Western world embracing China economically. Look back twenty or thirty years and you don't see that too much.

The U.S. used to say, "How many slogans can we come up with about Red China?" But you don't hear the term "Red China" much anymore. Yes, that's not an accident. You can't call people names and say, "Stop acting like that," unless you want to agitate them further. Rather, you stop calling them names and say, "Well, how can we include these people in a way that they want to be included?"

What you see going on here is something akin to what you were asking in the first place, which is, "How can we understand what's going on mentally so that we can put the pieces together so they'll make sense and we can understand the bigger picture?" Well, what you see here is a foundational building block—granted, analytical and mental—of people attempting to do just exactly that, those who are influential in bringing governments and peoples together under, in this case, the common bond of the economic benevolence that is being brought about globally.

Are there problems? Yes, and benevolent magic can help to bring about that focus on common ground in a better way. But right now I salute those who are determined to include others, even if they don't understand them very well, even if they don't approve of their tactics all the time. They are determined to include those others and bring everybody into the system. And they are just as determined to bring about benevolence in the long run. But first you have to bring everybody in. So even though it may not be obvious, I see good things happening here as a result.

We have the situation in Iraq. What do we do about that?

Exactly what you're doing in China. Ultimately, you have to look past people's religion, philosophy and all the things you don't like about them, and you have to say, "Look, you have oil and we want it, but you also have other things that we like and we have things that you like. Let's find our common ground and unite there." And you have done a pretty good job of that, but it's been too focused on oil. There need to be other things: "What can we do economically and on a business level? How can we get together on the united business front in order to bring about benevolence for us all?" And then we come back, you see, essentially to the First Alignment.

You can't just say, "Bad. Stay out." That's been the situation in the past, and look where it has led. That's what happened to post-WWI Germany: "Bad. Stay out." Then look what happened. Nowadays, you see, people in the economic world have a very strong global support system: "Bring everybody in, and we'll sort it out as soon as possible."

How do we bring Korea in?

In the same way. It's a matter of time, and it's going to come about at some point due to the cooperation of certain governments and economic groups in the hope of uniting Korea if at all possible (which is sort of a compromise situation), or at the very least, bringing the benevolence of the south to the north, not unlike what happened in Germany. And it's just going to require certain unpleasant measures, which can only take place if brought about by certain groups. It will take place because the groups will all see that this is necessary to bring about, at the very least, the values of the First Alignment.

Islam Perceives U.S. Actions in the Middle East as an Attack on Their Religion

What about Iran?

Iran is not the big enemy so much. It's that they see what is going on in the Middle East as an attack on their religion. They see it as an invasion of the Christians. They are not foolish; they know there are some economic things going on here, and they know that since they've got oil, they are certainly at the top of the list for people who would like to have greater influence in their country. So they are not blind to that quite obvious detail. However, they also see it as a direct attack by Christians—or simply by people who are not of their religion—because it is largely people who are not of their religion who are involved in, as they see it, the escapade there in that part of the world.

So from their point of view, especially from a conservative fundamentalist religious point of view (which is what they have), this is quite obvious to them. If you look at the world through certain philosophical points of view, you are quite clearly going to see the world tinted by that perspective, and this is the perspective they have. It is not unlike the perspective of other religions of a fundamental nature, that they will see the world through *their* point of view.

But this is not religious warfare, although it may appear to be that to people of the Islamic countries there, and I do completely and fully understand their point of view. After all, the facts are undeniable. The people who are, from their point of view, invading that part of the world are largely Christian and certainly, at the very least, not of their belief system. Therefore, it's quite obvious to people of the Islamic countries that aside from wanting to plunder them, as they would see it, the invaders are there to bring their religion into a dominant position in this other world, their world.

So they are, from their point of view, fighting not just for their land, for their products and for their wives and children and families and societies, but for their souls. They are fighting to protect their souls, and it is that perspective that would cause a religious nation to fight to the last man. Quite obviously, then, regardless of the best intentions of the global economic community, the solution that is taking place to rid the world of—yes, no question about it—an infamous dictator is not sufficient. It needs to be done differently. I know that the president of the U.S. and various allies cooperating in this do not see themselves as infidel invaders, but that is certainly the way Iran and other countries of that religion see them.

A Living Prayer for Global Harmony

So what do we do about this?

For starters, for you as an individual and for the individuals reading the *Sedona Journal of Emergence!* and the *Shining the Light* books, since you have graduated in your knowledge about what's wrong, it's time to put into application what you can do. Living prayer functions in a way that is more than just words. Many of you will feel energies or you will feel a different sense in your body after you say it. Say the living prayer and be quiet for a time afterward. Don't just jump up and do another task. Say this, if you would:

> *Living Prayer*
> "I AM ASKING THAT THE BENEVOLENT HEARTS OF ALL
> BEINGS COME TO THE AID OF GLOBAL HARMONY AND RESOLVE
> UNRESOLVABLE ISSUES AND COMPLAINTS TO BRING ABOUT
> HARMONY IN THE MIDDLE EAST BETWEEN WARRING PEOPLES,
> AND THAT THAT HARMONY IN ITS METHOD OF SOLUTION SPREAD
> TO OTHER PLACES WHERE WARRING PEOPLES EXIST."

After you say that, just sit quietly for a time, even if you don't feel the benevolent, loving energy of Creator and other loving beings. Just sit quietly for a while and consider how wonderful the world will be when that harmony comes about. This is said in a way, if you look at it and think about it, that is benevolent to all beings. And that is how this benevolence is brought about. It does not require anyone to change. It does not say, "This is true and that is false." It unites, it supports, it nurtures and it encourages. That is why it works. It will take as long as it takes.

Religions of the World: You Can Work Together toward Benevolence

By all means, do other things that you can do to bring about benevolent change, and yet I feel that the more people who say this living prayer and others, the more likely these changes will happen in the most benevolent way and the most rapid way that is available to the people of your planet. I am not trying to bring about a change in the way you practice your religious life, but I am suggesting that the religions of the world come to an agreement on what they hold to be dear. And that needs to have a total cornerstone based upon the improvement of the lives of all beings. You can at least start and ask for the improvement of the lives of all human beings, that their lives and expectations are benevolent.

I recommend, religions of the world, that you look at the global business community as a model. Granted, it's not perfect, but it's becoming more benevolent when you compare it to what it was, say, thirty or forty years ago. See if you cannot pattern—or repattern, either way—your methods of agreeing with one another along similar lines: "What do we agree on?" And strive toward benevolence—not just tolerance, but benevolence toward one another.

That's my encouragement. It's up to you. You cannot continue to battle and fight. You cannot say, "Our way is best." What you can do is say, "What do we both agree on and how can we work together to bring this about?" This is largely what the global economic community is doing. I know the religious community can do this and has been attempting to do this for a time. You can do it. Just keep trying. Your efforts are appreciated.

Beginning to do living prayer and benevolent magic allows those of you who have been reading these books to graduate and become practitioners rather than simply observers. Come out; get out of the stands. Been in the bleachers, eh? You've been reading about it, you've been discussing it with one another, but now you can come out of the stands, out onto the field, and become a player. Yes, as you read these books with their focus on, "Here is the situation/problem, and here is the living prayer and benevolent magic that you can do to resolve the unresolvable," you'll no longer be an observer, a witness, but you will become a player, a player in the art of resolution.

Thank you very much.

You are most welcome. Good life, my friend, and good night.

Good night.

Part 1:
The Origin, the History, the Purpose
and the Role of the Sinister Secret
Government of Earth and How They
Assist in the Explorer Race Plan of
Creating Apprentice Creators

Before the Beginning:
A Prequel to the SSG

Spirit of Transformation and Zoosh
February 7, 2001

T his is the Spirit of Transformation.

You Are Assimilating Wisdom from Those around You

When human beings come to Earth, you are here to emulate; you are not here to learn. When a tree comes to Earth, its learning is represented by each ring. Oh yes, there is physical growth, but the rings and the way the rings show themselves is like a map of the tree's actual growth. That's why rings do not tend to appear uniform from tree to tree, whereas fingerprints in human beings remain uniform throughout the human being's lifetime. This is because you are not growing in terms of acquisition of real wisdom, but rather you are assimilating wisdom from those around you or emulating that wisdom.

That is why there need to be volunteers who come here, such as the trees, the animals, the plants and the many-legged little insects . . . the big animals, the flying ones and the sea creatures. In short, there need to be animals and other beings anywhere human beings might go, even if you only go there rarely. In this way, there are always beings who are carrying wisdom that you might emulate.

Human beings are often studying the animals to emulate their wisdom in some way, and as you know, this observation helps you to know more about yourselves as human beings. This is why human beings cannot simply be placed on a planet with one another with no other life forms and be expected to grow. This was done before human beings came to Earth, and the growth of the Explorer Race was minimal. Simply contacting one another is not enough; you emulate and assimilate all you each have to offer, but after a while, there is no growth because there is no exposure to other beings of wisdom.

It is the sinister secret government's desire to expose you to that—those circumstances and situations that will take advantage of this natural inborn desire to emulate. One may emulately-acquire wisdom that he utilizes in the world, and since human beings are natural communicators, he will pass this on to the entire species in some way, often slowly. But in this day and age now of high-speed, more broad communications, not unusually it is passed on quickly. Therefore, if the sinister secret government can expose you to a potential for acquiring more and yet that more that you acquire is not actually providing you with wisdom, it will do so. That is why the subtlety of corruption provided by the sinister secret government and their conscious or unconscious dupes is particularly insidious.

The exposure to, say, more material goods, for instance, allows the human being who is preprogrammed to desire more in terms of wisdom and experience that will lead to a wiser being, to acquire more in terms of material goods, but the satisfaction is only fleeting. One has the satisfaction of the acquisition, but the acquisition does not allow one to enjoy wisdom, for instance, and pass the wisdom on in many different ways and stories and retellings—to enjoy the pleasure of seeing other people with the "Oh, I get it!" and "I understand!" that often feed you as teachers, just as you are fed as students. Rather, with the acquisition of material things only, there is the fleeting joy of having a new material object, which sometimes becomes a standard fare around the house and is not even fully appreciated as it once was. Therefore, the desire for more grows hungrily within you.

It is as if you are not being fed what you need to survive, as in food, when you are fed something that will allow you to have the feeling that you've come here to actually utilize. But it doesn't feed you what you want, so you want greater amounts, just as a person might grow in girth because he or she may not be eating the right foods that support and nurture and give actual strength, but rather the foods that are either available, which is often the case, or simply the foods that represent that which one is missing in life. So the sinister secret government will use these things in order to acquire wealth, power and influence, and therefore be able to spread this influence further.

Z oosh here.

Conflict Grew Out of an Urgent Need to Know

In the time before conflict, confusion and the experience of the unknown, in that time there was no sinister secret government, nor anything even remotely akin to it. But this universe that you are living in—speaking about the universe broadly, to include all that has been discussed up to this point in time, including the origins discussed by Ssjoooo [see the forthcoming book, *The Explorer Race: The Totality and Beyond*]—was inheriting a factor that Ssjoooo himself discovered. And that's that Ssjoooo accidentally, you might say—or maybe perhaps not accidentally—supported the idea and experience (or for you, it would be as a feeling) of the unknown—meaning, is there anything unknown? Yes, something is unknown, simply by his reaction to create.

This then created an underlying underpinning of everything that was created, that if there ever came to be a desire by any peoples to know something that was not known, if their society or civilization did not have the answer, then it would create a generated need to resolve by whatever means might be available. As a benevolent society, of course, one would simply put a call out for teachers and so on—before the time of conflict, naturally, there was nothing but benevolent societies.

Still, what has prompted conflict as you now know it grew out of that, on the level of an urgent need to know. The moment one adds urgency to anything, there is initially a problem, and that is that this experience is best assimilated by any being when he or she is ready for it. You can be exposed to it before the time you're ready, and it either rolls off your back, literally or figuratively, or it can even take you down the wrong trail because of having parts of your whole being that are not complete—"complete" in this sense meaning as complete as you need to be to fulfill that action. Therefore, those parts cannot receive that experience and do the most with it in the most benevolent way for you.

So what one experiences, then, when urgency is added, is this sense of challenge, which literally can create an experience that is almost hostile to the nature of natural life. Natural life proceeds in harmony with all other life; it does not have urgency, other than in reaction physically as one might see with animals and people and so on. But it does not have urgency in any other way, other than in reaction, as far as the natural life cycle goes.

So in order to find the source of—how can we say?—almost the appeal of manipulation and control and power and influence that are the main drives to establishing not only a sinister secret government but *rule*, one needs to recognize these sources. The urgency, then, started actually right around the time of the creation of this universe by this Creator because of the consultants the Creator brought [see *The Explorer Race: Creators and Friends*]. The consultant who was of the more negative energy [the Master of Discomfort], that consultant brought with it this sense of urgency to resolve itself. All the other consultants did not have this sense of urgency—only that one.

Urgency Broke Out First on the Pleiades

But one cannot throw that into the mix without it having an effect. Even though the Creator of this universe made every effort to soothe that sense of urgency, one cannot have such a being in one's midst, even as a consultant, without some of that energy mixed in. And as you know, energy naturally radiates.

So the potential for that urgency was there for a long time. It didn't break out immediately on Earth but rather initially on the Pleiades, then in Orion and now in this solar system of which Earth occupies an orbit.

This is why the Pleiadians have such an ancient rule in their culture that they will not accept polarity, because to them polarity was the result of urgency. So what they do, even today in their cultures, is that since they have urgency and they can't get rid of it, they have put urgency into a segment of their community that can utilize it without harming the population, and that is their ships, which fly at great speed. When you apply urgency into the actual material that makes up the ship—and it makes it up because it chooses to participate in that—for that to be urgent actually works for everyone's best harmony. This is what they have done; they have assimilated all the urgency that way, thus removing it, even from the people who ride on the ships. Part of the reason people wear certain garments on the ship when they ride on it is to protect them from assimilating urgency on their own.

So the reflectivity—if that's the best term, but it's not quite; they don't wear something shiny—of the garment and a device they use that reflects energy to some degree—not as great a degree as around Earth humans, for example, but even on the ship—keep them from feeling urgent and thus, as a result, potentially becoming polarized. So it started on the Pleiades, and once they could see that it was something they couldn't get rid of, in terms of urgency, they found a good use for it. But not before they had a problem. They had, to them, what they would now consider a catastrophic problem, but to you, what you would consider a war with lingering effects, as you have had very often in your wars.

For instance, the obvious lingering effect of World War I was World War II, so it wasn't a small thing. And in a largely benevolent population, where even a lesson for an individual, which would be a minor lesson in a benevolent population, would take perhaps eight or twelve hundred years to assimilate . . . can you imagine how long it took them to get over polarity? It was so long and so impactful and so difficult that they quite reasonably, given the choice of their culture, refused to allow polarity as an experience, even in a tiny percentage. Granted, the Explorer Race will alter that, but the Pleiadians have grown since then, and even they do not realize how much they have grown. So they can assimilate, perhaps, a half of a percent or 1 percent of discomfort without stimulating polarity. They don't know this, but they'll find out.

But stimulating growth . . .

Yes, it stimulates growth, but not polarity. You don't have to have polarity for growth. You might theoretically or scientifically be able to call it polarity, but it's not polarity as you understand it to be here.

Negativity Comes to Orion, and the Precursor of the Explorer Race

Sometime during the course of the recovery period for the Pleiades experience of that, you then developed this influence. You understand, during the war years on that planet in the Pleiades, the Pleiadians called for help from anyone and everyone who would assist. One of the planetary groups and cultures that assisted was Orion. And on Orion, even though they didn't have polarity (they didn't even have urgency), what they did have was a certain fixation or appreciation of excitement, really expressing itself more along the lines of fun—excitement/fun, fun/excitement and so on. So they were quite clear that war was not exciting, and they knew they could not help, except when it came to evacuations.

So this group from Orion helped along those lines to clear populations away from what were then fighting vehicles, largely automated at that time. This, however, affected the crew members, even after this good deed. So when they returned to their native cultures, what they had seen and what they reported on was what stimulated an urgency, then polarity, then, because of their planetary interests culture-wise, an excitement.

You can see how it was not a big step to go from excitement to polarity or negativity on Orion. It was not a big step and was much, much more difficult to get rid of. That's why Orion had to essentially use the iron fist to get rid of it. And one of the ways they did that was to essentially kick a large segment of the population off the planet, and that segment of the population is largely the precursor of the Explorer Race. Granted, this is an overview, but I'm mentioning these things to help you to understand how, why and where, so that you will understand that the precursor was something largely very innocent in its makeup.

You're referring to that unfelt need that Ssjoooo felt, that was throbbing there in front of him, right? [Again, see the forthcoming book, The Explorer Race: The Totality and Beyond.*]*

Yes, he felt a need. In short, it was the first time Ssjoooo had ever experienced something outside of itself, stimulated outside of itself, to which an action would be necessary that was outside of its ordinary actions to resolve. In short, Ssjoooo experienced urgency. Aside from what else he had to say about it, it was the first feeling of urgency—not any kind of urgency that you would recognize as urgency today, but simply brought about on a level of accumulation. Because, you know, he said, "Well, I considered it for a long time," and when one is considering something for a long time, what is experienced is urgency spread out over time. So those are the opening remarks.

The Master of Discomfort Acquired Discomfort from Other Creations

Are you saying that in all of the totality then, that no one had ever felt urgency until . . . you know, this is trillions of eons later or gazillions of whatever you count later. It took this long, then, until the . . . no other discomfort any place in any creation had ever created urgency?

No. Every time other creations felt anything like that, what they did is they would pull all of that material out and essentially place it into what came to be known as the Spirit of Discomfort. And so the Spirit of Discomfort, which . . . isn't that the name of the consultant of . . . ?

Yes, well, we called him the Master of Discomfort, but Spirit is fine.

Ah, that's right, but at that time it was the Spirit of Discomfort. The Spirit of Discomfort essentially became a wandering being. He wasn't initially a being, but eventually he became a wandering being who would go and acquire, who would take on that material from all other creations, and then those creations would not have that.

That was never brought out in the other books, as to how he got all of that discomfort.

That's how; that's how it came to be. Because of urgency being there and urgency potentially leading to all of these different places, the creators would just pull it all out and request that the spirit of what came to be called the Spirit of Discomfort would pick it up. And of course, when a creator requests, you can't say no. But what was different here is that your Creator utilized what was then the Master of Discomfort—who by this time had evolved through all this discomfort and had developed a level of mastery—and literally brought the Master of Discomfort and other consultants to this universe. Quite a bit different than what the other creators . . .

They tried to get away from discomfort.

That's right. So that's why you didn't really have a manifestation of these things before the creation of this universe you are in now.

This was the first universe that the Master of Discomfort stayed in, right?

That's right.

But what about all the time that he's been here? Does he still go out and pick up discomfort?

This Creator has never called upon him to do that and has always looked upon the Master of Discomfort as a consultant.

No, I mean, all the rest of the totality that was calling on him before to pick it up—are they still doing that?

No. Once it's done, it's never generated, you understand? When they called upon him to do that, all they were really doing was picking up the urgency and so picking up any negativity. But they were simply pulling out all of the traces of urgency as a potential, not even as an experience, and giving it to then what came to be known as the Spirit of Discomfort, and he would take the urgency and go on. That is why one of the main traits of discomfort almost immediately, even in a child . . . one of the ways you know that there is discomfort is urgency. The child cries, responds, and that response immediately triggers in the parent, what? A sense of urgency. Now. The cry is about *now*. That's the feeling it stimulates, and that's why. Parents respond immediately to *now*.

Other Creators Challenged the Creator of This Universe

The situation here on Earth might be compared, at least in its early stages, to Orion or the Pleiades. But really before the Pleiades, I cannot see with my long vision anything that resembled a warlike act or even a conflict between individuals in other parts of this universe. And I believe that the reason this stuff started being stimulated, first on the Pleiades and then on Orion, was because of a need by the other creators—not this Creator of this creation—to encourage this Creator to prove the value of what He was intending to do with His creation.

They were not trying to make it hard for this Creator, but saying, "Okay, now you've prepared this whole creation to prepare this Explorer Race. You can't put it off any longer. You need to actually utilize these things that all the rest of us have rejected." Essentially, all the other creators rejected the urgency: "You need to show us what you can do." They didn't trigger wars, but that's why the timing . . .

Don't I remember hearing that the first place a planet was blown up was in the Pleiades?

The Pleiadians have since changed that time sequence, and that planet has no longer blown up but was simply isolated for a time. It became an ice planet. That's been changed; what you heard has been changed.

The SSG Is Not Interested in Killing Off Humans

Where are we on the dimensional scale?

No change.

Is there no H5 virus out there? The chemtrails are the secret government attempting to soothe down and make the multitude a little quieter, right?

I don't agree with all of that. I'd just like to say that when people are referring to chemtrails, fully 90 percent of what they perceive of as chemtrails are contrails. Sometimes it's a greater percentage, but at least 90 percent. Chemtrails are rare.

There is no H5 virus ready to kill us, then?

You have to remember this also: One thing you can be certain about the sinister secret government is that at the very core of their belief system, they see human beings—each and every one of them—as consumers or customers. They do not see them as some kind of disease that needs to be controlled.

Right—don't kill the consumers.

The last thing in the world the sinister secret government would want to do is to kill off the population of the Earth, and they would fight—and they have some considerable weapons—to prevent it. So any viruses that show up . . .

They're going to try to eliminate.

The chances of them having been put out in the population by the sinister secret government are remote in the extreme. The only kind that they might have ever done that with are viruses for which they have the cure, which they will release just as soon as it's clear that they can make a major profit.

And that's HIV, right?

I'm not going to label anything.

HIV Is Not the Cause of AIDS

HIV, by the way, is basically benign. The cause of AIDS is not HIV.

What is it?

It is a reaction in the body. The actual definition of AIDS, which is acquired immune deficiency syndrome, is a very good description of what AIDS is. That's why it tends to show up in different symptomatology in different people. So AIDS is a reaction. It is not stimulated or prompted by that which could be called a virus; it is largely a reaction to general assaults on your body's immune system, which are cumulative, from many sources. Pollution . . . electropollution, especially. Your exposure to electropollution is a real problem right now. But different people have different reactions to it; your immune system can be strong, and you can stand under a wire that is . . . you know those big wires . . .

Those big power lines . . . transformers, the places where they're really powerful.

. . . and not be affected at all. Whereas if you are worn down, it can prompt a condition that is similar to AIDS, only it is immediately recoverable. I'll tell you that roughly 75 percent of the so-called colds that people get are simply a temporary wearing down of your immune system, which, during the symptoms of a cold, you gradually reacquire the strength of your immune system and push it out of your body again. So the cold actually doesn't come from people around you. Granted, people around you might—how can we say?—wear down your immune system by various means, including people with colds, but it comes from within you, biologically.

So AIDS is not sexually transmitted?

AIDS is only sexually transmitted through sweat and saliva. You can get AIDS, not from a toilet seat, but from contact with a person who has it—if he or she has, say, full-blown symptoms—if he or she is sweating and you come in contact with that sweat in some place receptive in your body, or if you come in contact with that person's saliva in some receptive way, such as kissing. But aside from the fact that HIV has been cultured in various bodily fluids, it only shows up on its own, in what I've seen, in sweat and saliva. And what shows up in there is another . . . it is like . . . it's not a virus, it's not a germ, so I can only describe it as . . . I can see it, but the problem is, I don't know how to describe it. It's something that isn't a virus, and it isn't a germ that can be passed on.

But it's transmittable.

It can be passed on, but you have to remember that it's not an accident. The reason that gay individuals have the disease in the United States, whereas in other countries it's not that way at all, is that the disease was originally spread intentionally by individuals who thought they were doing people a service. Part of the organization, the health organizations that thought they were giving people shots to prevent a disease, accidentally—it was an accident—spread this propensity toward this disease. I will say, however, that those who wished for such a disease to be spread were not born on this planet.

Can you say where they were born?

It had to do with a failed attempt to . . . it was associated with the Xpotaz. [See the previous books in the *Shining the Light* series.]

Oh, really?

But I can't say too much about it, because I don't have their permission. Permission is everything.

By 2300 Discomfort Will Be Unknown on Earth

Is the Explorer Race still going to be here in 2423, or are the negative Sirians going to be up here by then?

The experience of discomfort as you know it on the Earth will become unknown by the year 2300. So that will be an entirely benevolent society.

Ah, but still the Explorer Race?

There will be vestigial remains of the Explorer Race here, but only that, because the Explorer Race will be out exploring. Why would they be here?

So who's going to be here?

Others.

What others? The negative Sirians?

They won't be negative by then, but no, it won't be them.

Before the Beginning:
A Prequel to the SSG

The Spiritualization of the
Corporate World Order

Zoosh

September 21, 2001

All right, Zoosh here.

Welcome.

There is no question that the people ultimately behind all turbulence that causes corruption, disruption and general disharmony between all peoples on the Earth is the sinister secret government, and they are directly in some ways and indirectly in other ways behind this attack. Granted, they did not summon troops of their own, which they do not have. They did not go up to individuals and give them money; they never work directly. But working through their conscious and unconscious contacts—meaning people who don't know that they're working for them—they have supported, sustained and kept many conflicts going that would have otherwise been resolved.

Now, let's understand the nature of these type of conflicts. Do they only involve people with guns that go bang-bang or bombs that go boom-boom? No, it isn't always that. Sometimes it's to support truculence, stubbornness and a general demeanor that says, "No! I want it my way! You can't have it your way, no matter how justified you may be in your position, no matter how important your need, no matter how much support you might require. I'm used to having it my way, and that's that." And sometimes people like this are also supported by the sinister secret government because they tend to promote, maintain and demand the status quo. But now what is needed by people of the world is a form of global support system. You cannot have only individual countries anymore.

The Coming of the Spiritual World Order

Recognize clearly that the world government has been forming for some time and that the actual world government, while not being an authorizing body, is forming around the corporate model as I always said it would. This means that you are roughly right now slightly more than halfway through the time of the corporate model as a world order. Therefore, this tells you something critically important—and this was something felt by some of you over the past week to ten days—and that is that a clarion call has gone out to begin the spiritual and energetic connections that are necessary to form the benevolent world order, which will gradually . . . not usurp, but gradually form an underpinning underneath much of the disrupted world order and underneath the corporate world order.

This will form, in time . . . picture this if you can: For those of you in the Western world, picture it like the cream filling in the Oreo cookie, although the cookie parts may not always be the best part. In this part, the spiritual world order will wedge itself between the sinister secret government and the corporate model world order. In time you will see develop a means by which the corporate model is supported and sustained, not in the way you understand it, but by a spiritual method that gradually resolves—meaning creates alternatives, offers means by which a rigid hand of authority, as is sometimes present in business, is no longer necessary—whereby business becomes fully spiritualized. You have all been exposed to some businesses that are profoundly spiritual and others that leave you wishing for more spirituality. So this is initially, then, the spiritualization of the corporate world order model—which at the same time creates a buffer zone protecting you, meaning the human population of Earth, from the impact of the sinister secret government and their cronies.

Homework: Don't Let the SSG Manipulate You into Fighting with One Another

Now, what can you do to bring this about? In order to bring this about, you will need to take action *right now*. I am going to give you all homework, and I'm expecting you to do it; I will be watching. And here is your homework: It is necessary for you all to recognize that those people who did not harm you by terrorism, who are your citizens—whatever country you are in—that these people are your fellow citizens and they are to be treated with the same respect, appreciation, kindness and understanding that you rally around your own citizens. In other words, don't let the sinister secret government manipulate you into fighting with one another, pointing the finger and saying, "You did it! He did it! She did it! They did it!" If you allow that to happen, you will only be playing into their hands and demanding that the sinister secret government be your boss because you love to be their slave so much.

So stop blaming one another. Start looking to one another for help, and start giving one another the support you all need. Recognize that the enemy as you see it— meaning the people who are attacking whatever government you are living under, whatever country you are living under—the people who are attacking are basically faceless, so you won't know who they are. This does not mean that you should then attack everyone you don't trust, pull out your enemy list and say, "Look, we don't like these guys this week, so let's attack them." It's not about that. It's about finding who did it, and letting the people who can find who did it, to do so.

Groups of Cooperation Need to Be Formed

Simply and redundantly, this means it might take awhile to find out who the guys are who are giving everybody grief. But you need to allow those services that work for your respective governments to find these guys, and it will be a whole lot easier if you allow and support your governments to get together, all as a group, to say, "We're going to find these guys. We're going to share information where we feel comfortable doing it, we're going to cooperate with each other and we're going to find these guys; we're going to recognize them. We're going to do what we can about them, and we're also going to look to see why these guys came to be the way they are."

In short, you are becoming a world planet—no longer this government, no longer that government, no longer this race, no longer that race. You need to recognize very clearly right now that in order to improve the quality of life for any group on your planet, you need to improve the quality of life for *every* group on your planet. The United Nations is a pretty good role model; it's a good place to start. For those of you who don't have confidence in that, then find your business center places, where business disputes get resolved. I believe somewhere in Europe things like that are happening. In order to bring about that resolution, you will very often need to form up in groups of cooperation in the business community. And other groups need to form up groups of cooperation: in the religious community, in the philosophical community, in the educational community, in the medical community, in the farming community and so on. Groups of cooperation have to form up, irregardless of your race, religion or national origin.

If you expect to not just survive but to flourish in the twenty-first century, you're going to have to get past being manipulated by the sinister secret government—and they almost always, if not directly involved, are at the very least indirectly involved in encouraging groups of people to keep fighting with one another all over the world so that you won't look for who's behind it. As long as you think, "He did it! She did it! They did it!" you won't look for *them*, the sinister secret government, and say, "Wait a minute! Who's promoting all of this stuff?" And that's what they're counting on. If you want to support the sinister secret government, just say, "Rule me! I want to be your slave. Tell me what to do, step on me, tread on me; send me out to tread on others. I am so happy to do your bidding, and misery is my greatest friend." If that's what you want to do, then you can live your life that way; if you'd rather live your life in a more beneficial way, then please follow the advice and homework in this article.

Wonderful! You sound so up and enthusiastic; that's wonderful.

Well, you know, an interesting thing, which Robert [the channel] and a few of his friends and other people have been discussing all around the planet, is that after this catastrophic event in New York, a few people felt . . . after a few days, they felt this strange sense of euphoria.

Yes! I've noticed it.

Yes, and other people have, too. And the euphoric feeling is based entirely upon the clarion call that is literally going out all over your world, which says, "Okay, now it's time." And that's what it is, so don't be shy about that feeling.

Thank you. Good night.

Good night.

The Sinister Secret Government Attempts to Stimulate Global Crisis— What You Can Do about It!

Speaks of Many Truths and Isis
October 5, 2001

*W*elcome. *Some things happened yesterday [October 4, 2001], and I want to know if any of them are accidents or caused by the terrorists? A Russian jet over the Black Sea exploded, with seventy-six people on board. The news reports are talking about a Ukrainian training missile, but they say the range is off. Can you say anything about this?*

I feel that this was caused by a weapon, but it was not a conventional weapon. It appears to be something that is disguised, very carefully disguised.

False Trails of Blame Spark Global Conflict

This represents a clandestine war. In various intelligence communities around the world, there is and has been some suspicion for some time that a group of individuals is actively operating and is attempting to stimulate a global war as well as a global crisis. Some of the individuals in these communities feel that the intention is to create a global calamity that will literally involve every continent, although not every country. The scenario, observed by many of these well-established intelligence communities, is that the victims (if I may use that term) or those suffering are connected with the former and recent global wars.

Therefore, it is most important to historically study who fought whom in World War I and, more to the point, World War II. Those who are really behind this intend to create enough crises that they can usurp power. They [the sinister secret government, or SSG] do not intend to create a negative global government per se, but they do hope to be able to usurp power, depress the stock market and obtain the rights, privileges and authorities that are often

Passenger Jet Down in Black Sea

A Russian airliner, flying from Tel Aviv to
Siberia, exploded in flight over the Black Sea.

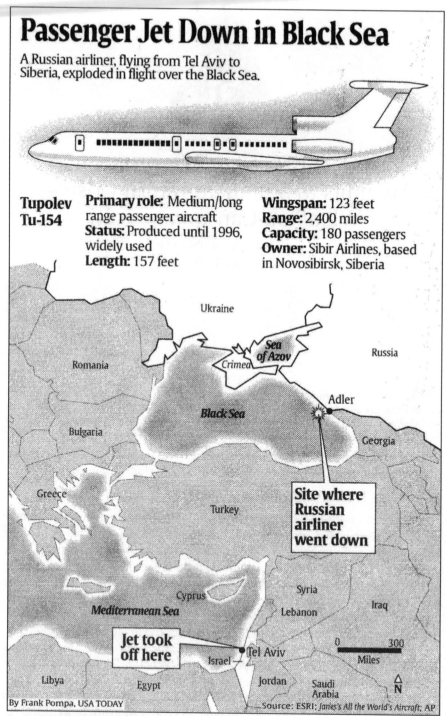

Tupolev Tu-154

Primary role: Medium/long range passenger aircraft
Status: Produced until 1996, widely used
Length: 157 feet

Wingspan: 123 feet
Range: 2,400 miles
Capacity: 180 passengers
Owner: Sibir Airlines, based in Novosibirsk, Siberia

Ukraine

Romania

Crimea

Sea of Azov

Russia

Black Sea

Adler

Bulgaria

Georgia

Greece

Site where Russian airliner went down

Turkey

Cyprus

Syria

Iraq

Mediterranean Sea

Lebanon

Jet took off here

Tel Aviv

Israel

0 — 300
Miles

Libya

Egypt

Jordan

Saudi Arabia

△ N

By Frank Pompa, USA TODAY

Source: ESRI; *Jane's All the World's Aircraft;* AP

Fig. 3–1. Thursday, October 4, 2001.

obtainable during such crises, and then exercise them later in order to influence the population.

Some of the more interesting analyses from intelligence communities—not only in the United States, but elsewhere—suggest that it is possible that this represents an attack from an extraterrestrial source. And the reason that has been proffered as a possibility is that, for one, the attempt to create suspicion is following very closely along the lines of World War II enemies and allies. A network that might be extraterrestrial with terrestrial allies might very well try to push buttons, so to speak—not atomic buttons, but the buttons of individuals, based upon sensitivities. The U.S. isn't entirely over its experience with Japan in World War II; Japan isn't entirely over *its* experience with the United States in World War II. So countries that need to be observed for victimization and terrorist acts against them—or that which have been analyzed as terrorist acts but may not actually be—are Japan, the United States, Russia and, of course, Germany.

Now, I do not wish to alarm people, but I feel that the citizens of Germany and the German government need to be on very high alert to keep their people safe. I am not saying that they have to worry about their current allies or even their past enemies, but the threat will come in a clandestine way from individuals trying to pass themselves off as somebody else—exactly the way the Trade Center disaster and the Pentagon and airline disaster happened to the United States, where there was an attempt to make it clear that the United States was being attacked by its former ally Osama bin Laden and, generally speaking, Middle Eastern countries with whom the United States has recently had disputes.

But look at other things: Tokyo recently had the subway gas attack. This was a direct attack on citizens, again with a trail apparently leading back to radical elements within their country. All these are false trails, and there will be a false trail with this Russian disaster. So I want to alert the global community that these trails apparently leading to whomever the country is at odds with at that time—or even criminal elements within the country (where there have been difficulties in the past)—that almost all those trails will be false and that the real challenge is not only the sinister secret government but their allies whom they have made a connection with. The connection was made by utilizing their old time-travel device.

I realize that the average community of citizens will find this all hard to believe, but my message is less for the average citizen—other than to inform people—and more for those who can turn over rocks and look in the right places. I feel that one of the better ways to combat these attacks on Earth—and this is the best way to look at it, that these are attacks on Earth and Earth civilizations—is to unite as a global community. It won't be easy, because every one of these attacks will happen in a way that is easily traced. And that's the problem—it's too easily traced. A bone of contention in the intelligence communities has been that it's obvious who did it. Why is it so obvious? It shouldn't be that obvious; we shouldn't be able to find out so quickly, you see? Every one of them is caused by these individuals.

The SSG's Alliance with Negative Orions from the Past

This allied connection of the sinister secret government, through passage in time, is not going back to any government or even past government on Earth, but far back to a distant circumstance associated with the constellation of Orion. There has been, you understand, no conflict in Orion for thousands of generations, but if you go back far enough, you'll find conflict. The sinister secret government was able to make the connection with these people, based largely upon their personal contact with individuals from Orion [see *Shining the Light I–VI*].

From their relationships with present-day Orions? Are you saying that was the connection?

But the present-day Orions would represent what I would call benevolent Orions. However, the SSG has been able, through capturing . . . literally not so much capturing but detaining a visitor from Orion whom they were able to identify (who was not paying a diplomatic call on them but to others on Earth). They managed to capture this person, and utilizing their rudimentary time-travel potential, they were able to explore this person's Orion lineage to the past.

So that's the SSG's string to the past belligerent and warring Orions?

That's the string. The SSG is using techniques largely associated with disruption of global unification, because if you look at your recent history on Earth, there have been increasingly strong business connections—forming a de facto business global community (if not government, at least a local community)—which are now being strained. The sinister secret government feels a distinct threat. They know their days are numbered, and they are fighting. They are using every means at their disposal to keep you all at each other's throats.

How long ago did they capture this Orion whose lineage was traced back and followed by the time-traveling SSG to a time when Orion was not benevolent?

They obtained this person and have detained him for about three months. He resisted for a time, but after a while he could not resist anymore. All diplomatic efforts from the current civilizations on Orion have been ignored. They have been unable to get their person back.

So this is a relatively recent situation, then? In our terms?

Recent in terms of their getting ahold of this person, but the moment you travel in time, then you can't use the word "recent" anymore.

So what did the SSG do? Did they go back and get some operatives or physical Orions from the negative past and bring them here?

No, they made an allied connection with those in that distant disruptive time in Orion. They said that they would like to bring them here but could not at this time with the state of their technology, so they would like to create an alliance. Should the technology be made available to them, they would bring them here so that they could survive. They could not survive with their belief in war. They would not be killed on Orion in that distant past, but would be transformed. Of course, if you have certain beliefs, you don't want to be transformed. You want to go on believing what you believe—that's pretty universal. So when the technology was available, the SSG offered to bring them from where they are to here. Of course, if you follow this in linear time, they are long since dead, but with time travel, that is ruled out.

So did the SSG ask the ancient Orions for advice as to how to achieve the upsetting of the benevolence that was spreading on Earth?

Yes, they asked for advice on ways that would be sure to work. And what was suggested was to find the most recent global conflict and to create agitations between former enemies and former allies. With all your recent global conflicts, even after the conflicts were over and the winning side was patting each other on the back, they were also getting suspicious of their own allies. So the idea was how to fan that suspicion, as well as how to push the buttons between former enemies. That's what's going on.

Is this also relevant to the World Trade Center?

Yes. The World Trade Center, the recent explosion on the Russian plane, the gassing in the Tokyo subway and, I might add, the attempt to eliminate certain populations on the Earth, which has been in the past traced to sinister secret government connections with former German governments of the past.

You're talking about Hitler starting the Bosnian war? [See Shining the Light IV, *chapter 42.]*

Yes, that's right. But it goes back before that. The whole point is that there has been for some time an effort to disrupt and corrupt and keep people at odds with each other. That's why all of the [channeled] messages after the World Trade Center collapse had to do with unity and avoiding blame. But it isn't sufficient to be united as a country; you have to be united as Earth, to become aware of being Earth citizens. If you are anything but Earth citizens right now, you will be susceptible to constant manipulation and attack. But if you begin to identify as Earth citizens and find ways to resolve your difficulties, it will help. It may not be possible overnight, but find ways, work on them. That's why Zoosh recently spoke about not allowing yourselves to be manipulated [see chapter 2].

The Past Is Vulnerable to Change

Now, the Tokyo subway gas attack was farther back than three months, so obviously they went back in time for that, right? So this attack a couple of years ago was caused by something they initiated three months ago?

You can't say that, because they've had the person for three months, but that's splitting hairs. Let's just say that anything you know to be true in your past, that you can trace and prove, is always available for change.

That's pretty dangerous.

Think about it. It tells you how very vulnerable the past is. If you change the past just a little bit . . .

You change the present?

The present will alter. That's why there has been such an attempt to figure out how to change the past, even by individuals wanting to do good. They hoped that the present would be more benevolent. But there has been almost no effort to figure out ways to protect the past. In my understanding, the best way to protect the past is to unify and to have methods firmly in place to resolve disputes—not only economic and business disputes, but governmental, nationalistic, internal (meaning between social groups), all disputes—not with an iron hand, but with the best possible compromise. Everybody can't have everything they want; that's not what compromise is about.

Well, it looks to me here like humans versus the secret government . . . that they've got more toys and more . . .

But they don't. That's why we're going to talk more about benevolent magic. That's why we've encouraged Robert [the channel], when he goes to the UN in New York, to channel about that. That's why books like *Shamanic Secrets for Material Mastery, Shamanic Secrets for Physical Mastery* and ultimately *Shamanic Secrets for Spiritual Mastery* [coming 2005] will be so important, because they are intended to give people a working mechanism to create and sustain benevolent change and to protect the past.

Using Living Prayer to Protect the Past

Now let us discuss how to go about protecting the past. For starters, recognize that everything that has happened in the past is not something that you would necessarily like to protect. [Chuckles.] You'd like some things to change. But you have to protect it first, and then learn how to change it. So I'm going to suggest this:

For those who can now, feel the heat or the love as it is felt physically as warmth in the chest/solar plexus area in general, the love-heat/heart-warmth/physical-warmth—begin with that. Then say the following words [for more information on living prayer, see p. xxii]:

> *Living Prayer*
> "MAY THE PAST OF EARTH AND ALL THE CIVILIZATIONS UPON IT BE SAFELY UNITED NOW, AND MAY OUR PAST LEAD TO GREATER UNION NOW AND IN ALL NOWS TO COME."

Write those words down. You are practitioners now; you are material-masters-in-training. While you're feeling the heat . . . you have to be feeling the warmth. Wherever it comes up for you, go into it and feel it more; don't try to move it around. Have that statement in front of you, in big letters so you don't have to struggle, and slowly read it only once while feeling the heat.

It won't be easy to maintain the heat and to read that statement, but try it. Say it only once. If you can do it on your own and maintain the heat through the whole statement, good. If you can't do it—you've said it, but you feel the heat come and go—get together with some of your friends who do the love-heat and do it well. You can all get together and read it. It doesn't have to be

THE LOVE-HEAT/HEART-WARMTH/ PHYSICAL-WARMTH EXERCISE

Robert Shapiro

I am giving what we're calling the love-heat/heart-warmth/physical-warmth exercise in a way that Speaks of Many Truths taught me how to do it. Take your thumb and rub it very gently across your fingertips for about half a minute or a minute. And while you do that, don't do anything else. Just put your attention on your fingertips. Close your eyes and feel your thumb rubbing slowly across your fingertips. Notice that when you do that, it brings your physical attention into that part of your body. Now you can relax and bring that same physical attention anywhere inside your chest—not just where your heart is, but anywhere across your chest, your solar plexus area or abdomen—and either generate or look for a physical warmth that you can actually feel.

Take a minute or two or as long as you need to find that warmth. When you find it, go into that feeling of warmth and feel it more, just stay with it. Stay with that feeling of warmth. Feel it for a few minutes so you can memorize the method and, most importantly, so your body can create a recollection, a physical recollection of how it feels and how it needs to feel for you. The heat might come up in different parts of your body—maybe one time in the left of your chest, maybe another time in the right of your abdomen or other places around there. Wherever you feel it, just let it be there. Don't try and move it around—that's where it's showing up in that moment. Always when it comes up and you feel the warmth, go into it and feel it more.

Make sure you do this when you are alone and quiet, not when you are driving a car or doing anything that requires your full attention. After you do the warmth for five minutes or so if you can, or as long as you can do it, then relax. And afterward, think about this: The warmth is the physical evidence of loving yourself. Many of you have read for years about how we need to love ourselves, but in fact, the method is not just saying, "I love myself," or doing other mental exercises that are helpful to give you permission to love yourself. Rather, the actual physical experience of loving yourself is in this manner, and there are things you can do that are supportive of it. But in my experience and the way I was taught, this is the method you can most easily do.

The heat will tend to push everything out of you that is not of you or that is not supporting you, because the heat, as the physical experience of loving yourself, also unites you with Creator. It unites you with the harmony of all beings, and it will tend to create a greater sense of harmony with all things. You might notice as you get better at this and can do it longer that should you be around your friends or other people, they might feel more relaxed around you or situations might become more harmonious. Things that used to bother or upset you don't bother you very much, because the heat creates an energy, not only of self-love, but of harmony. Remember that the harmony part is so important. You might also notice that animals will react differently to you—maybe they'll be more friendly, perhaps they'll be more relaxed, maybe they'll look at you in a different way. Sometimes you'll be surprised at what animals, even the smallest—such as a grasshopper, a beetle, a butterfly, a bird—might do because you're feeling this heat.

Because it is love energy, it naturally radiates just as light comes out of a light bulb. Remember, you don't throw the heat out, even with the best of intentions. You don't send it to people. If other people are interested in what you are doing or why they feel better around you, you can teach them how to do this love-heat/heart-warmth/physical-warmth exercise in the way you learned or the way that works best for you. And the most important thing to remember is that this method of loving yourself and generating harmony for yourself creates harmony for others, because you are in harmony. Remember that this works well and will provide you with a greater sense of ease and comfort in your life, no matter who you are, where you are, what you are doing or how you're living your life. It can only improve your experience. The love-heat/heart-warmth/physical-warmth exercise is something that is intended to benefit all life, and in my experience, it does benefit my life.

read at the same time, but you need to feel that heat for every word, and doing it together might be easier. It needs to be said out loud, but it doesn't have to be yelled; it can be said out loud quietly. Doing it all together in the same room might be easier.

If you still can't do it, then do this. Go someplace where there's an old tree—it's used to human beings. The best type of tree would be out in a forest where the tree has grown naturally without being planted by human beings. It has just grown naturally where it felt welcome. Go up to the tree and say "Good life" out loud. Then feel the love-heat within your body. If the tree is not busy, you will probably then feel an increased level of that heat. That is the tree experiencing that warmth with you, which creates extra warmth. Wait for a moment while some of it radiates, then see if you can say that phrase out loud while you feel the heat. It ought to work then. The tree will understand what it means, so you don't have to explain it. After you are done and the warmth has died down and you feel relaxed, say "Good life" to the tree and gently walk away.

All of you must begin to exercise material mastery now. You might wonder, "Why are these terrible things happening now?" It is not just Creator putting you to the test, to say, "Look, see? You have the tools; you know what to do about material mastery. It is not a secret." It is rather that you are being put into a position of responsibility. "Who will save the Earth? Where will the saving come from? Is God going to return now and say, 'All right, stop your fighting. Come, let's sit down together and be happy'?" That will come in time, but it would first behoove you to begin. Material mastery is the next step in spiritual mastery, and those of you who wish to engage it, please engage it fully now. This is the way. Also, please read and practice, to the best of your ability, *Shamanic Secrets for Material Mastery* and *Shamanic Secrets for Physical Mastery*. And while you're doing that, we will prepare *Shamanic Secrets for Spiritual Mastery* for your application in the future.

Recent Events Not Linked to the SSG

Yesterday on a bus in Tennessee, a man from Croatia used a knife and attacked the driver. The bus went off the road and killed six people. Was that an isolated event, or was it manipulated by the SSG?

No, that was a genuine terrorist event, not stimulated by these people we've been talking about today. It is a sad thing, because somehow people who do what is called terrorism get it into their heads that as a last resort, "We'll do these things, because no one's paying attention to us." But they don't realize that with computers and communication, it is possible nowadays to get attention paid to you in less violent ways. Your press, unfortunately, does tend to cater to that. They don't talk about this problem with these people and how to resolve the troubles. Rather they tend to give exposure only to violent incidences. You will need to do something about that. But it is not the SSG behind this.

6 Killed in Attack on Bus

Passenger slits driver's throat, grabs wheel and crashes bus in Tennessee. Greyhound temporarily shuts down service across the country.

Source: *USA Today*

by Larry McCormack, *The Tennessean,* via AP

Fig. 3–2. Thursday, October 4, 2001.

There was also an explosion in a chemical plant in France yesterday that killed twenty-nine people. Was that an accident or an incident?

It was not sabotage. It was unplanned.

Unplanned, meaning a mechanical situation or something?

Yes. Also I might add that France, having a lengthy history of diplomacy and having—how can we say?—a little more tolerance, might be less at threat than some other countries.

The Economic Recession and Transportation Safety in the U.S.

Regarding the economy, we appear to be in a serious recession. What does it look like right now as to how long it will last?

I think by February you will see a lot of recovery. And of course, for the Christmas season people will insist on purchasing presents, so there will be what they call a bounce. But people won't want to give up the bounce, so you'll see strong recovery that is noticeable by February, although there will be indicators before that.

I understand that in the United States it's particularly unsettling to see certain things that look like a police state. But as your government discovers ways it can secure your safety and make things safe all over, including on buses . . . you will see more security people there, but it will largely be a comfort. Once upon a time it was typical to have railroad detectives on the train. It's just that such practices became somewhat lost over time, and to have people like that on buses, like railroad detectives . . . now you're having them on planes, yes?

Air marshals, yes.

Pretty soon you'll have air marshals on public transportation like buses. It will seem unsettling at first to some people, but after a while they will grow to like it and say, "This is a good thing," and it will create lots and lots of jobs for young people who might be interested in being of service—and many are interested these days. It might even be possible to have a volunteer corps temporarily, not unlike other volunteer protection services that went into effect in various big cities in the past.

Like the reserves or the volunteer fire department, something like that?

Yes, things like that, which cities can identify with. I think it might actually be a good thing.

Recent Fears Are Creating Sleeping Difficulties: What You Can Do

A lot of people are saying that it's hard to sleep in the middle of the night. Everything's speeded up; we seem to be facing more emergencies, more difficulties. Sometimes, with this energy, you're buzzing. Sometimes it's heavy and sometimes it's light.

There is a new fear now, like the way it is in the U.S. and globally, because of the idea that things [such as 9/11] could happen in this modern age when people are trying to get closer together, not farther apart. It is typical to not be able to relax as deeply so that deep sleep can take place. Deep sleep is always disturbed by anything physical—for example, sound, even if it's a sound you're used to. If the house creaks, normally you're used to that. Yet when you're not feeling particularly safe, that creak will disturb you. But this will pass.

There are things you can do. Many of you are exposed to more electrical radiation than you have been, and rather than go around and turn off everything electrical, try to sleep in your bedroom with as little on electrically as possible. I have always recommended not having a television set in your bedroom, because it's radiating pretty much all of the time—not a lot, just a little bit. The electricity is always on, just a little bit. What you want is the least amount of electrically radiating appliances on in the space in which you are actually sleeping.

Then, of course, for anybody who lives with cats or dogs, they are also nervous. If animals sleep on the bed with you, they're going to move around more than usual, and being that you are a little on edge now, you will wake up during that. So there is a lot going on. It's not that you are anticipating something; don't worry about that. It is more because you are on edge and you need to do what you can to deflect such things.

Here's something you can try: There is an object that can be purchased cheaply from many sports equipment stores, maybe even a hardware store. It's called an emergency blanket that basically looks a lot like a piece of tinfoil, only it doesn't tear as easily as tinfoil. It's kind of a space blanket, and it's basically reflective, a combination of plastic and metal. If you can find something like this and it has that metallic quality to it, put it over you to see if you can sleep under it. It might deflect lots of that radiation away from you. Or those who live in big cities can hang it over the window to see if it will deflect more of the radiated electrical energy in the air away from you.

The main thing is that you are being exposed to too much stimulation. Science has shown that you can put a gentle electrical stimulation on your arm, and your muscle will immediately contract. What's happening is that at night now, because all of you are feeling more nervous, when your muscles contract for any reason, you will come immediately up out of deep sleep to either light sleep or almost waking up—in some cases, waking up. So it's disturbing your sleep.

So it's not that there's more electrical radiation; it's just that at this time of what you call nervousness, we're more susceptible to it?

That's right. And it will pass in time. For some of you, you might find that gentle music, even with subliminals, will be useful. For many of you, you might find that if you practice the safety exercise—which takes time, because it's done in steps, very gradually—it will generally illuminate a lot of your discomforts [see *Shamanic Secrets for Physical Mastery,* Appendix B]. What happens as a result of practicing this exercise is that you begin to radiate safety all around and about you. When your body gets used to that, you don't send it out from you; your body is just radiating like a light bulb, feeling safe. And when your body gets used to that, you're much more likely to be able to sleep through the night. It creates safety for you, rather than you having to do the thing you normally do and even the excessive things you might normally do in order to feel safe. The safety exercise, as Zoosh calls it, is very valuable at this time, and I recommend it.

So everything has changed?

Nothing has changed. Just things that could have happened, things that might have happened, things that we hoped wouldn't happen—that's what changed. But everything is always possible, and you hope that things will proceed along benevolent pathways. But it is not a rigid thing. The future, as your friend Zoosh likes to say, is not cut in stone.

What you're publishing is so good and so valuable, people need to do more than read it; they need to practice it, put it into practice, do it. That's why the material for the *Shamanic Secrets* books is so important.

Isis, I wasn't expecting what Speaks of Many Truths said. This disguised weapon that blew up the Russian jet on October 4, 2001, over the Black Sea . . . can you describe it enough so that security people at airports can look for it? This weapon doesn't look like a weapon, but it explodes airplanes?

How to Detect the Disguised Weapon That Blew Up the Russian Jet

It looks like an electronic device. The sneaky thing about it is that when tested and run as an electronic device, in whatever form, that device will actually perform rudimentary activities. If it is a cell phone, it will do basic cell phone things, although it won't do complex cell phone things. If it is a camera, it might be able to flash and the shutter will go click. So it's in the shell; the shell of the device is the explosive. And there's a timing mechanism built in. It is pretty exotic.

Is it from off-planet?

No, it just hasn't been used. It's the kind of thing that governments dream up and don't really put into practical action because it's expensive, plus they're trying to create alliances with other countries, not war. But this is part of the reason that security has a lot of problems. This is the resolution for security. If they're not sure about something or if they think that it ought to be all right (meaning it looks like what it's supposed to be and it basically does what it's supposed to do), but they are still are suspicious for any reason, this is what they can do. The material is stable, meaning that it can be bumped around and nothing will happen, but it has a very tough outer coating. What you can do is to take an instrument and scratch it. (Granted, this will put a scratch in the surface.) Then run it through the sniffer. It can be sniffed out, but only if the surface has been scratched.

That's incredible. So it could look like a cell phone?

Any small kind of electronic object, not anything big. Someone might take it on in a purse. And very often the people have no idea what it is; they don't even realize they're taking something on board that is lethal.

So is it possible there were two explosive devices on this Russian plane, since one went off in the air and one when it hit the water, according to the newspaper report?

I think something was in the wing that went off . . . part of the wing, when it hit the water. I cannot say. The people have all crossed over. What occurred in that incident is less important; it is more important to keep it from happening again in the future. The tricky thing is that the device can perform rudimentary tasks. Even a small tape recorder . . . you can press a button and it will record a message and play it back. But the explosive is in the actual shell. Now, there is an exception: If the shell of the device is metal, then you don't have to worry about it. This is only the case if the shell of the device appears to be plastic. So if it is a camera body, for instance, that is entirely metal, you can dismiss it—other than, of course, perhaps opening the camera to make sure it is what it appears to be. But it will not take the appearance or form of metal, only of plastic.

So this was not a suicide situation? The device was installed or implanted on someone?

That's right.

This Is a Time of Empowerment

Nowadays, whoever's doing what, all of that is less important than what you can do about it. This is a time of empowerment based on practical application. It's not empowerment based on what you *think*; it's based on what you do, according to the practical application of homework that you have done. You can now take the next step to see what can be done. That's why it's so important to follow the homework in various steps. That's why you do the love-heat first, before you take the next step. Maybe you do this with a tree and you feel the warmth more. Then you begin to do benevolent magic in one way or another, all geared toward asking for what you want for yourself.

You have to start with yourself. You can't exclude yourself; you can't say, "What I want for the world . . ." You have to say, "Hey, this is what I need, and . . ." and then you apply it to everybody from that point forward. Because *you* are the foundation. That is the whole structure of material mastery; you cannot be a material-mastery student and exclude yourself. The student must be a branch of the tree or even the trunk. But you cannot be a leaf on the tree without a branch.

It's so important to understand this. That's why the homework is done to a degree in sequence, so that you can build on what you've done before. And empowering happens on the basis of one step after another. When you have done enough, you feel confident—"I've done that; I know how to do it. I can do the next step. Now that I've done both those steps, I can go on and do the step after that. All right, now I've done that; what's next?" In short, one thing built on the other builds up your confidence. You feel safe. You go on and do the next thing. Good night.

Benevolent Magic: The Antidote to the Sinister Secret Government!

Zoosh

October 10, 2001

Now hear this: Something is being planned by the sinister secret government right now, and I am calling on you readers to prevent it. You have it within your power, using the work that has been taught in these books, to support the change that will be necessary.

The Next SSG Event: Turnabout Is Fair Play

The sinister secret government is planning to do "turnabout is fair play," from their point of view—although it's not fair play to anybody else. They plan to infiltrate the airlines of other countries and try to create a false trail of blame leading back to the United States. It is essential for the intelligence community and the administration to get on top of this right away, and for the State Department to interact with both friendly and unfriendly countries to warn them of this possibility. The plan is to do something very similar to what was done to the United States.

You're talking about September 11?

Yes. The challenge for all of you will be to change it. Once upon a time I said to you that there would be tests coming up in the future, things that you could change, things that you could do—in short, you've been given a lot of training over these past few years in the pages of these books to produce benevolent magic. And I am calling upon you now to begin to do this work—not only for yourself and your family and community, but globally for the betterment of all beings. Here is the homework assignment:

THE GOLD LIGHT EXERCISE
Isis

To do the gold light exercise, imagine a gold light in your solar plexus area. It's important to start it there—or if you prefer, you can start it behind your bellybutton. Consider it to be like a light bulb. Let the light gradually move into the rest of your body, and imagine that your body is glowing with the gold light.

Remember, let it start within you and radiate out. Some of you will be able to feel something benevolent. Many of you will feel like you are using your imagination, but since the imagination is the divine part of the mind, that is perfectly all right. Stay with that feeling for at least five minutes.

It's particularly helpful to do this before you go to sleep—either before you take a nap or before you go to sleep at night. It's perfectly all right to do it if there's somebody else in the bed, but not if you are entwined with that person. Try not to be touching anyone when you are doing it, but shortly after you do it, then you can touch someone if you like.

You may also do this in a chair sitting up if you like, but lying down is best. If you sleep with pets, it is all right if they are near. This will not harm them in any way; they might actually like it. But ideally you would do it on your own. This is a particularly good thing to do if you do not feel safe sleeping at night. Perhaps you feel that there are energies in your sleeping place that are uncomfortable—then this is something you might try.

Benevolent magic is how people are going to restore balance, based on what are perceived as current impossible conditions. You can't solve the world's problems by exercises of will. Here is the benevolent magic. First I want you to center into the love-heat/heart-warmth/physical-warmth [see p. 23]. If you can't, then I want you to picture gold light within [see above]. Just visualize it as best you can. Then say this, only this:

Living Prayer

> "I AM ASKING THAT ALL PLANS OF THE SINISTER SECRET GOVERNMENT INTENDED TO CAUSE HARM AND BLAME BE IMMEDIATELY TRANSFORMED TO BENEVOLENCE."

That's it. [For an explanation of living prayer, see p. 73.]

SSG Plans World Conflict to Gain Power

You see, they've got this whole plot line going, designed essentially to create a world conflict and world suspicion in which they—pulling the strings from behind the scenes—can exert their power and influence. They would ultimately run the world in a more commanding and, to some degree, more exposed way than they have before. That's their plan, to be seen as the heroes riding over the hill to save the world. I'm not saying here that today's heroes are to be considered suspicious beings from the sinister secret government. I am saying that the SSG's ultimate plan is to be perceived this way: "We're going to show you how it is, and won't you be happy!"

I'll tell you how they plan to do it: They will show up in a space vehicle. Here's how you will know the difference between the sinister secret government's space vehicle and those of the ETs who occasionally show up. The sinister secret government's space vehicle will be bristling with weapons. Spacecraft with benevolent, genuine ETs will not have weapons. They use defense systems that do not incorporate weapons, especially in vehicles used to contact other races of beings.

Say the benevolent magic just once. There is, however, something else to say. Wait about five days and fill yourself with the love-heat. Those who have difficulty with that, do gold light within you. And as it radiates around you, say:

Living Prayer

"I AM ASKING THAT THE GLOBAL PEOPLES OF THE WORLD NOW COME TOGETHER AND SEE, AS WELL AS FEEL, HOW VERY MUCH A FAMILY WE ALL ARE, AND KNOW THAT JUST LIKE IN A FAMILY, WE CAN SETTLE OUR DIFFERENCES TOGETHER."

Just like that. Say it once. If you say it more than once, as Speaks of Many Truths, Isis, myself and others have previously stated, then that which creates—meaning you, because you're part of Creator, the rest of creation, all the Creator has created and Creator Itself, that which creates, all together—will assume you are saying something or singing something, which creation simply allows you to do, and are not in any way involved in creating it. That's how you can sing songs without things happening as a result of singing the lyrics.

Mantras?

Yes, or prayers or something you like to say gently and often to feel good and to improve the quality of your life. This is different, though; this is benevolent magic, intended to bring about benevolent change for all beings on Earth. That's the homework.

Benevolent Magic Will Solve the Unsolvable

Are you talking about the eleven or so left of the absolute inner circle of the secret government? Or are you talking about an outer ring? [See Shining the Light V, *chapter 21, and* Shining the Light VI, *chapter 23.]*

No, when I refer to the sinister secret government, I'm talking about the inner core group. The important thing about this homework is that for years now the devoted readers of the *Sedona Journal of Emergence!* have been getting a great deal of training. And those who read the books, especially the *Shamanic Secrets* series, are getting even more training, to say nothing of those who read the *Explorer Race* and *Shining the Light* series, who are getting the background that supports their training. Now is the time to put that into effect. You've had incremental steps—do this, try to change this for yourself, here's some benevolent magic for you. These are all steps. The more people involved in doing this benevolent magic, the more likely the change is going to occur.

As I've said on many occasions, the only way you are going to feel and sense with all your senses that this benevolent magic is working, is when you're looking at or hearing about something that appears to be unsolvable, and you do the benevolent magic. Even one person makes a difference; if there's more than one person, so much the better. Then you hear about how this apparently unsolvable situation has either suddenly changed or is at least showing signs of changing to something more benevolent. Be aware that we're talking about true magic, not the illusion that magicians do, pulling a rabbit out of a hat. It's not the kind of sorcery that is used to change and control and disrupt and corrupt people's lives, but rather benevolent magic—what you do all the time in other lives, what Creator does every day, what all creators-in-training do. You must begin to use this more and more on a regular basis, asking for what you want—never phrasing it in a way that suggests something you don't want and never phrasing it in a way that attacks people. You must use this always and only to bring about benevolence and a better life for all beings.

I had the idea that the inner core were older men. I seem to remember that they can shape-shift or something . . .

Oh, I don't think that you have to be too concerned about them appearing as anything other than what they are.

They're not going to try to look like Andromedans or Pleiadians or something like that?

No; they look the way they look. That's how they look and that's that.

Okay. I've never asked how they look.

And I've never told you.

Is it time to ask now?

They look like human beings.

Like businessmen?

That's all. I don't really have their permission to say what they look like. Just a few statements about what they look like, and you could greatly narrow down who they might be.

The SSG Is Assisting with Creator Training

Exposing them now would simply cause you to have to do this all over again. Remember, the challenges you are experiencing now, including the sinister secret government—who for all intents and purposes do appear to be the bad guys—are study aids in the larger picture of creator training. You have to have seemingly unsolvable challenges like radioactive waste, for instance, in order to transform the problems through benevolent magic, and you have to learn step by step how to do it. In the process of learning, of course, you have to grow. You can't just learn this and conduct your life the way you always have. You have to grow. That's why you're here; this is school.

School—Earth, your life on Earth—is about growth for all people. That's why you read accounts of people who've had after-death experiences or you've heard how it is for people to pass over. It's very easy; there's nothing to it. It's a snap to return to your natural way of being. When you do return to your natural state of being and someone comes to get you, you step out of your body. You feel fine and comfortable, and you go off with your guide or your angel to the next world or through the veils. But when you are born here on Earth, it's not that easy.

You have to spend all that time inside your mother and go through the slings and arrows and difficulties and challenges of childhood. You are learning and experiencing something difficult, which tells you right off the bat that this isn't natural; it's not our natural way of being. This is school. When you go to school, everything is hard at first. You have to study; you have to do things that aren't part of your natural life.

Where are the recesses?

Recess happens afterward when your guide or angel comes to pick you up and says, "Okay, it's time to go home now!" That's when you feel like recess. But just as it was at school, if recess is too long, you're going to want to get back to school. That's when you're going to want to have another life. Once you've had a life on Earth with all of its challenges, you say, "Well, I'd be okay having a life with some little challenges, because I know what it's like to have big ones," and you live that life and you think to yourself during that life, "This is a snap," even though there might be people around who are struggling with something that would be a snap to you. So you come here, that's how you learn. And you become a teacher and gradually work toward being a creator. It's all part of a plan.

Does the secret government, who wants to control the world and the people, realize that they're our training aid?

They don't look at it that way. They know that that is the way I might look at it, though. They might scoff at it, but it is strictly bravado on their part. I've spoken to them.

Yes? And then what?

I hear nothing but bravado and blustering. But that will change.

Anthrax in South Florida and Other Incidents Are Not Foreign Terrorism

What about the small airplane that went down in Milan [October 9, 2001], killing 118? Was that an accident? A Scandinavian Airlines flight bound for Denmark hit a private jet that wandered across the runway, then careened into a building. All the people aboard were killed.

This was not a terrorist event. Purely an accident.

The Kursk submarine [which went down on August 12, 2000]—did anybody go back in time and do something there?

No, that was not an event like that, but was what I would call an extremely hazardous situation. It's too soon to discuss that in detail.

What about the anthrax in south Florida? It's up to three cases now.

I am sure the government, especially the CDC, is looking into this. I will caution them, meaning, "Do all your work," but I do not feel that this was a foreign enemy's action. That's the important thing here. This does not represent a foreign enemy doing something.

One man died. They found a spore somewhere else and found it all over the guy who died and his typewriter. Another woman is in the hospital, then another woman was contami-

nated. They're giving them both antibiotics.

These people are all in the same locale? There's a limit to what I can say, but this does not represent foreign terrorism. It represents . . . I have to speak carefully here. The person spreading this was born and raised in the U.S., and I feel that this was essentially a murder. This is more criminal activity than a terrorist act, but even so, the federal government and the FBI and so on have to be involved. I feel that ultimately it will be prosecuted as a criminal act by a single individual. And I feel that it will not be difficult to solve if the federal authorities allow the local police in the community (from thirty miles around the focal point) to be fully involved in the investigation, because they will know who's who. I feel that that's what will be found out.

I'm sorry to say that such germs were for a time available for various fringe groups to obtain. This is not a sinister secret government action. This is not, from my perspective, a terrorist action, though it could be classified within the context of an American terrorist. But you would have to use a broad definition there. The building can be decontaminated. The main thing is to find and arrest that individual because that individual is a loose cannon and not particularly stable. This is not unlike the police looking for a serial killer. It's very much like someone who goes into an establishment and uses a gun. This time they used these germs. So, police officers, you have to investigate the person who was killed. You have to investigate his life to see who his enemies were. This is something that can be resolved by the community police. So I'll say to the FBI: Let them be involved, and you'll get your person pretty quickly.

I'll say this: There are a few groups outside of laboratories around the countryside and also outside of legitimate authorities who have these kinds of germs. But the good news, if you want to call it that, is that most of these groups are exceptionally patriotic, and the idea of using anything like this against U.S. citizens would be the last thing that occurred to them. On the other hand, there are a few loose cannons, and it is mostly the loose cannons who need to be thoroughly investigated.

How to Correct Malevolence in Benevolent Magic Exercises

Those of you who are enthusiastic about learning benevolent magic, try and embrace this homework, these assignments, and see if you can do them in the best way for you. If you're going to adapt them into some technique you are already using, feel free, but remember that you must always ask for what you want—never ask for what you don't want. And don't try to adapt benevolent magic to harm others. Not only will it not work, but those spirits who cooperate with you in bringing about all the good that benevolent magic does will cease that cooperation in general for some time to come. The only way you will be able to get that cooperation again is by doing the love-heat and basic exercises and homework that we've given in the past.

I realize that sometimes you feel you might accidentally say something that might be malevolent. If malevolence accidentally or unconsciously slips out, then this is what to say. Don't say, "Cancel it"; that doesn't work. Rather, begin at the beginning of what you were saying. Stop the process entirely, and go back to the very beginning, even if you have to let go of the warmth and the love-heat and all that. Stop, wait a few moments, then go back to the beginning and start all over again. That is the way to do it. And when I say go back to the beginning, I mean go back to the beginning of what you did that day. You don't have to go back to stage one of any particular process.

Say you started a homework assignment using benevolent magic. Perhaps in the course of the process, you suddenly realized you were feeling uncomfortable. If that happens, then stop. Rest a moment, then start all over again. Gradually do the love-heat, if you can, or the gold light. That's what you do if that happens.

Find a Quiet Place to Work Your Benevolent Magic

From time to time, something might happen, someone might walk into the room unexpectedly and say something and interrupt your flow. That's why it's important to do these things alone. If you look into it in the past, you will almost always find that mystical people or shamans, whoever they were, were alone when they did their work or had a place they could go to be alone. That's because they would have to be open, as human beings, to interact with nature and spirits and energies around them.

So you as shamans-in-training—or at least benevolent-magical-people-in-training—need to recognize that also. You will be somewhat open when you do this work. Try to make sure that your mate doesn't charge into the room to tell you the latest news while you're doing this. Some of you who simply can't get a place without people being around can use your car, if you have to. Drive down a road where you feel safe or it's quiet. Or go out on the land someplace where you also feel safe and comfortable. But you have to do this work someplace where you feel safe, because you will have to open up.

I'd like to say that it is important for you to know that I perceive you as creators-in-training and, to a degree, shamans-in-training, though you don't have to be. At the very least, I perceive you to be not only magical in your own uniqueness and beauty, but magical in your capacities.

+   +   +

We are reprinting the following article by Edward Humes, first published in Los Angeles Magazine, *July 2001, because of its particular relevance to the murder of the man in south Florida who received anthrax through the mail.*

The chilling, mind-boggling realization is that if one Dr. Ford exists, other Dr. Fords exist in the U.S. who—without a conscience, casually, at a whim—incapacitate or kill those whom they perceive have slighted or angered them (think south Florida, National Enquirer, Mr. Stevens) with the botulism in the refrigerator and the anthrax or worse stored in the garage.

What does this have to do with the sinister secret government? The mindset behind all of the Dr. Fords is the secret government's. Their desire to control and to have the means to selectively eliminate a person or a culture or a nation is why these programs are funded, whether it is through Congress or through black operations (diverted funds, drug money and so forth).

What can you do? Do the benevolent magic as given by the Explorer Race mentors. Help create a reality that will not support or allow such malevolent mindsets or activities!

THE MEDICINE MAN

Larry Ford was a brilliant scientist bent on saving the world
from disease and misery, but it wasn't the Irvine doctor's lab work
that spared the most lives. It was his suicide.

The meeting at the Beverly Hills mansion of the South African trade attaché was unusually secretive, but Peter Fitzpatrick still managed to witness it, peering from an adjacent room through a massive shared fireplace. He watched as Niel Knobel, deputy surgeon general of South Africa—the white-ruled, apartheid South Africa of 1986—met Larry Ford, a noted Los Angeles gynecologist and infectious disease specialist with an unofficial subspecialty: biological and chemical warfare. The two spoke in hushed tones, then Ford, a devout Mormon who volunteered his services to missionaries and Boy Scout troops, passed over a hefty black satchel. The meeting came to a close. Later Fitzpatrick sat down with the boisterous trade attaché, Gideon Bouwer, who could not resist explaining in his thick Afrikaans accent what had just happened.

The white minority government of South Africa was in those years locked in a bloody struggle with its black citizens, willing to do anything to stay in power. Bouwer's role was to thwart the U.S. trade embargo on technology and expertise coveted by the apartheid regime; Fitzpatrick, a young actor, glib and personable, was part of Bouwer's informal embargo-busting team, making sure the parties at the mansion were well attended by the well-connected.

Larry Ford was a regular at those gatherings, and the technology he handed over that day, Bouwer chortled, could prove invaluable: a sampler of virulent, designer strains of cholera, anthrax, botulism plague, and malaria, as well as a bacteria he claimed had been mutated to be "pigment specific." "Kaffer-killing germs," Bouwer confided, using the derogatory Afrikaans term for blacks. "Dr. Ford has done my country a great service."

Fitzpatrick clinked glasses with Bouwer and left, then called his handler at the FBI, where he served as one of two informants planted at South Africa's Los Angeles consulate. He told the FBI everything; yet, he says, nothing was done. According to Fitzpatrick, the deputy surgeon general flew off with his suitcase full of death. "Why didn't you guys stop him?" he later asked his handler. The agent just stared at him.

Fifteen years passed. Apartheid was dead. The FBI had long since lost interest in its old informant, and Peter Fitzpatrick was sitting on his couch talking with his wife, the television set muted as the evening news flashed by. Then something on the screen caught his eye: a grainy photo of a jut-jawed, narrow-eyed, round-shouldered man he hadn't seen in years—Dr. Larry Ford. He turned up the volume and heard a reporter explain how Ford, co-owner of an up-and-coming biotech firm, had become a prime suspect in the attempted murder of his business partner. That stunned Fitzpatrick, but what had him scrambling to his feet and reaching for the phone were images that followed Ford's photo: policemen searching the doctor's Irvine home—unprotected.

"Oh my God, they have no idea what they're getting into," Fitzpatrick exclaimed. It all came back to him then: Ford's talk of bio-weapons and booby traps, his hoard of guns and explosives, not to mention the doctor's claims of doing dirty work for the CIA—stories Fitzpatrick had once dismissed as a nerd's Walter Mitty fantasies until he noted the FBI's official hands-off policy with the suitcase of germs. "I've got to warn them," he told his wife.

So for the first time in many years, Fitzpatrick called the FBI. And once again, no one there seemed interested in what he had to say.

When a masked assassin put a bullet into James Patrick Riley's head in front of his office on February 28, 2000, the case at first unfolded as a classic story of greed and envy, a corporate power struggle between Riley, the voluble CEO and marketing whiz, and his partner, Dr. Larry Creed Ford, the visionary with big ideas and the scientific skills to carry them out.

Ford was working on a combination contraceptive and microbicide he and Riley named "Inner Confidence," a suppository that promised not only to revolutionize birth control but also to prevent HIV infection, AIDS, and almost every other sexually transmitted disease. Ford liked to say they were going to save the world—and get rich in the process. Their Irvine company, Biofem Inc., could capture annual sales worth some $400 million, Riley told investors. The

profits, in turn, would fund Ford's true passion of the past 12 years, a secret Biofem project to develop a superantibiotic derived from what he called "Unidentified Amniotic Fluid Substance." He believed it was nature's way of protecting embryos from disease, the reason HIV-negative babies can be born to HIV-positive mothers. Ford hoped to synthesize the substance, saving countless lives, and earning him a Nobel Prize along the way

But Ford had come to resent his decade-long partnership with Riley, who had final say in every Biofem decision and who had the physician bound to a contract so sweeping—giving him a 50 percent share of any idea or product Ford might conceive—that one lawyer likened it to indentured servitude. The agreement snuffed out Ford's attempts to make lucrative outside deals, and so, police and prosecutors have alleged, he decided Riley had to die.

Fig. 4–1. Larry Creed Ford.

Riley had just emerged from his blue Audi and was walking to Biofem's offices on a Monday morning when the gunman approached and fired. A chance turn of the businessman's head sent the bullet through his left cheek instead of his brain. "I have no doubt I would be dead if not for that," Riley said recently, a faint, nickel-sized scar marking the bullet's point of entry. After crumpling to the hot asphalt, he staggered back to his feet, blood gushing, pulled out his cell phone, and called the one person he knew could help—his friend and partner, Dr. Larry Ford. The doctor ran outside and applied pressure to the gaping hole in the side of the CEO's face as they awaited an ambulance

Within three days, however, Riley's savior had become a prime suspect. After the first of several searches of his house—which turned up only documents—the 49-year-old gynecologist met for five hours with his lawyer, scribbling notes throughout the discussion. Then he returned home and retreated to his bedroom, where he carefully laid out a selection of firearms from his collection. He put a double-barreled shotgun in his mouth and pulled both triggers. His wife, Diane, heard the blast and the thump of his body on the floor and knew; she called the lawyer and the police without going up to see her husband. The authorities found beside him a rambling, nearly illegible five-page note—what he had been writing in the lawyer's office—protesting his innocence. He had six different antidepressants in his system.

The Biofem case might have made the back burner then and there had Irvine police detective Victor Ray quit when his department and the FBI warned him to. But Ray, a former sonar technician on navy submarines, a job that requires patience and persistence, would not give up. He steered the investigation to Ford's backyard, where men in Andromeda Strain suits would evacuate a neighborhood and haul away an arsenal of toxins, germs, plastic explosives, and guns. In the process they unearthed a trail that stretched all the way from the CIA to apartheid-era South Africa and Dr. Wouter Basson, the man who ran the country's clandestine bioweapons program.

> Dr. Ford liked to tell people how he mistakenly killed all the animals in a
> government laboratory. "I thought I was in for it then," he would say. "But
> when the general called me in, all he asked was, 'Can you do it again?'"

The question still plaguing federal, state, and local investigators is a simple but urgent one: What was Ford planning to do with his germs and bioweapons expertise? The discovery of militia-movement and racist literature among Ford's papers has raised the possibility that he offered biological or chemical weapons to terrorist groups. Concerns have also mounted over a patented feature of his Inner Confidence suppository: the microencapsulation of beneficial bacteria. It turns out this architecture could double as an ideal delivery system for bioweapons, allowing otherwise fragile disease organisms to be seeded virtually anywhere. Ford, in essence, had patented the prescription for a perfect microscopic time bomb.

"That," says Ray, "scares the hell out of everyone."

One of Larry Ford's favorite stories about himself dated back to his teenage years, after he won first place in the International Science Fair in 1966 for his studies of radiation exposure. Awards from the Atomic Energy Commission and the defense department followed. Next came an invitation to continue his research in a government laboratory.

So there was young Larry in his buzz cut, canvas low-tops, and high-water pants in a military lab back east, starting a new set of experiments. He was giddy about the turn his life had taken—until he walked in one morning and found that, overnight, he had accidentally killed every lab animal in the facility.

"I thought I was in for it then, that I would be washing dishes the rest of my life," Ford would say. "But when the general called me in, all he asked was, 'Can you do it again?'" Ford did it again, and a longstanding affiliation with the government had begun.

The invitation to work in the government laboratory had come from a man Ford identified only as General Wyman. He liked to show people a framed photo of the general and himself (with Ford in an army uniform, though records show he was never in the military). This offer to an 18-year-old about to enter college did not seem all that unusual to Ford or his blue-collar parents. He had, after all, earned lab privileges at Brigham Young University in his hometown of Provo, Utah, at age 12, according to Riley.

Ford told the Rileys and others his subsequent work for the military and the CIA included research on biological and chemical weapons, consulting on Iraqi capabilities during the Gulf War, and sneaking into epidemic hot zones in Africa to gather samples of such killer organisms as the Ebola and Marburg viruses.

Victor Ray, a compact man with thinning hair who has been on the Irvine police force for ten years, initially discounted most of Ford's claims as the nutty imaginings of an unbalanced genius. It's not that Ray hadn't handled unusual cases in the past. He was the detective assigned to the headline-grabbing case in which an "evil twin" allegedly plotted to murder her sister and take over her life.

But the bungled attempt on Riley's life suggested something far more mundane, and quite a bit less, than the work of a CIA-trained operative. Almost any other time and place for a hit would have been better than the crowded commercial parking lot in front of Biofem's offices in the Irvine Spectrum, which sits wedged in the busy "golden triangle" where the Santa Ana and San Diego freeways merge. An experienced hit man might have simply pulled up next to Riley's car in an isolated location and opened fire on a caged target, Ray suggests. This guy, in his black clothes and mask, waited in a public place at ten in the morning for Riley to get out of his car, then shot him with a $70 Russian-made semiautomatic known for jamming, which probably explains why only one round was fired.

The hit man, described by witnesses as a slim and athletic man with blond hair peeking out of his ski mask, sprinted across the office plaza brandishing his gun, running directly in front of the Spectrum Bank branch below Biofem's second-floor suite. Suspecting a robbery, bank employees locked their doors and watched the man jump through the side door of a silver Aerostar van.

> The search of Dr. Ford's house unearthed explosives, illegal weapons, and more than 260 containers of biological material. A jar of deadly ricin was found in the family room. In an office refrigerator, Ford stored botulism next to the ranch dressing.

Police traced the plates and the van to an old friend of Ford's with a violent past, Dino D'Saach, who was arrested that night as the getaway driver and has since been convicted of attempted murder and conspiracy, crimes carrying a mandatory 26-year sentence. His cell phone records showed him talking to Ford immediately before and after the hit from a cell location near Biofem. (Biofem's receptionist remembers seeing Ford on the phone at his office window just before the shooting, with a perfect view of Riley's parking space.) Police found private Biofem correspondence faxed from Ford to D'Saach's South-Central Los Angeles tax preparation business, along with hit-man manuals, photos of Riley's parking spot, and a crude homemade silencer.

If the crime wasn't enough to reject the CIA stories, Ray figured, there was Ford himself. Disheveled and disorganized, known for his painful lack of conversational skills ("He could light up a room just by leaving," Fitzpatrick says), Ford came off as both a brilliant researcher and a childish

Fig. 4–2. FBI agents remove evidence from the doctor's residence.

eccentric. The only shoes he wore were black Converse All-Stars, no matter the occasion, and he was known to skip through hospital hallways, pepper his speech with expressions like *yippee* and *okeydokey*, and issue prescriptions with a trademark cliché, "Better living through chemistry!"

None of his friends or family, not even Riley, sitting in a hospital bed with his face a swollen pumpkin, thought Ford capable of murdering anyone. His wife and three college-age children—who declined to be interviewed for this article—saw only a devoted family man whose worst "sin" was a fondness for diet cola, a violation of Mormon prohibitions against imbibing caffeine.

"Everyone who knows him knows who he really was," Ford's eldest son, Larry Jr., told the *Deseret News* in Utah shortly after the suicide. "He was the most loving, giving, loyal person." Larry Jr. suggested that his father killed himself not out of guilt but "out of love, because he wanted to protect his family from what was eventually coming."

Ford graduated magna cum laude from BYU, published more than 65 articles, held numerous patents in medicine and biochemistry, had an international ob-gyn award named for him, and built a patient list that included doctors and a smattering of celebrities (although one, the late Margaux Hemingway, overdosed on barbiturates Ford provided).

"Look at his background," says Dr. Hunter Hammill, an associate clinical professor at Baylor College of Medicine and a Biofem consultant, who served his medical residency with Ford at UCLA. "He was the chief resident. He was good. He was so bright, you'd ask him about a compound, he could describe for you the whole formula, how to build it, its structure—he had it memorized. He was the golden boy."

But during his residency there was at least a hint that all was not quite right in Ford's life. One night in a campus parking lot in 1978, a gunman opened fire on him. He let off five rounds, though only one struck Ford, square in the chest. He was saved by several cassette tapes he had stuffed into his breast pocket, just enough to deflect the small-caliber bullet, leaving only a bruise over his heart. There had been no robbery attempt. The doctor was evasive when questioned by police, and no one was ever arrested.

Only after Ford's suicide did informants start coming forward. Ray began hearing about an entirely different Larry Ford, a man who cheated on his wife, betrayed his partner, and bred supergerms and was willing to use them. This was the Larry Ford who formed a close bond with Jerry D. Nilsson, a gifted Anaheim general surgeon with extreme views and a penchant for trouble that quickly made him a suspect in the Riley shooting. Nilsson, who boasted of having worked as a special forces physician for the white minority government of Rhodesia, now Zimbabwe, appears to have kindled Ford's interest in supporting apartheid. At the time of Ford's suicide, Nilsson was in the process of losing his license for sexual misconduct with patients, one of them a 14-year-old who allegedly became his lover for the next 15 years.

Whenever the two doctors were together, it was the charismatic Nilsson who made the most lasting impression. Now 72, the surgeon was a formidable presence even in late middle age. Tom Byron worked with Fitzpatrick as an FBI informant in the South African Consulate in the 1980s and spent time with both doctors. He describes Nilsson as "the monster with miracle hands," a towering figure with a shaved head—Jesse Ventura as a skilled surgeon. "He was very fit, very muscular, the kind of guy who could knock you out with one punch," Byron says. "He told me, 'I've killed people in my lifetime, and I have no qualms about killing again.' I would *never* cross that man." Nilsson was not available for comment.

Nilsson had long worked with Ford to amass biological and chemical weapons, and both doctors stored them openly in their homes, his ex-lover told the FBI. She sued Nilsson and won a confidential settlement after accusing

Fig. 4–3. Detective Victor Ray.

him of performing unnecessary surgeries on her, including cosmetic enhancement, without her permission. She was also treated by Ford and was one of several former patients who told Ray that the gynecologist used them as lab rats, deliberately making them ill in order to test his remedies. "If taking a life advances scientific knowledge," Ford would tell her, "the sacrifice is well worth it."

The detective spoke with a Los Angeles gun-shop manager, a longtime friend of Ford's, who developed a complex of rare diseases, among them a chronic lung and immune system disease, sarcoidosis, that is extremely uncommon in every racial group but one: African Americans. The man is white, and he is convinced Ford had a hand in his ailment. There was a woman with cervical cancer whom Ford treated with an experimental drug that didn't work; she later required emergency surgery to save her life. Other women, Ray learned, had been given prototypes of Inner Confidence that were never intended for human use. All of them fell ill with a variety of vaginal infections, he says.

"Riley was told there was no product, that it was still being developed, but I have one in a jar sitting in my office that Ford gave to a patient," Ray says. "He was experimenting."

More people came forward. A former business associate of Ford's said that when a mistress broke up with Ford in the early 1980s, the doctor vowed to infect her with an "alpha bug," promising "she will never be healthy or normal again." Authorities talked to the woman and learned that she suffered from a mysterious and incurable malady that has caused debilitating vertigo for the past 14 years. She's undergone two brain surgeries just to ease the symptoms. At least one other woman, who maintains that Ford drugged her against her will during a business lunch, has reported similar problems with chronic vertigo and complained of symptoms that resemble Gulf War Syndrome, except she was nowhere near the war.

State and county health officials, with help from the Centers for Disease Control in Atlanta, interviewed many of these patients, but their investigation was limited to whether there was a public health risk, such as the threat of an epidemic. They found none and closed their inquiry, though the FBI still makes it a point to ask former patients of Ford's if they were ever unconscious in his presence, something the complaining patients all have in common.

"We started to realize there was a lot more to Dr. Ford than we had first thought," says Ray. "It began to look like there might be something to the stories he told, and that the attempt on Mr. Riley's life was just the tip of the iceberg."

In 1997 Ford's long association with UCLA, the school where he had been a clinical professor and director of research for the Center for Ovarian Cancer, abruptly ended. He had been caught disposing of blood samples in a trash can in the middle of a chemistry lab instead of taking the biohazard precautions required by the university. Later he was spotted scraping petri dishes into a toilet, another health hazard. The school asked him to vacate the lab and never come back, according to Rick Greenwood, director of UCLA's Office of Environment, Health, and Safety.

Greenwood, who knew Ford in graduate school, describes him as an arrogant, single-minded know-it-all incapable of admitting mistakes, as when he accidentally killed two rabbits while trying to extract blood from them, then insisted that it was the animals' fault.

A biochemist who worked with Ford at both UCLA and Biofem says Ford also faked research results—what the science community calls "dry-labbing." "I could never replicate his results when I would repeat his procedures," he says. To be associated with Ford now, he explains, would be professional suicide, and he is unwilling to be identified in this article. "The sloppiness was unbelievable. His technique was awful. I ended up deciding I didn't want anything to do with him."

One of the most chilling stories Ray heard came from the owner of Chantal Pharmaceuticals of Los Angeles, a company that developed an antiwrinkle cream with Ford's help. She told the FBI that Ford, angry with one of her partners, went into the man's office carrying a cardboard box with a rabbit inside. He put the box on the man's desk, pulled on latex gloves, removed a syringe from his pocket, and squirted two drops of a viscous amber liquid onto the rabbit's shoulder. It immediately convulsed and died, blood pouring out of its nose and ears. Ford, never uttering a word, turned and left, the box still sitting on the desk.

Ray got confirmation of the doctor's government ties three days after the case was opened and a few hours after Ford's suicide. He had picked up Valerie Kesler, Ford's research assistant at Biofem, for questioning. She met Ford while an undergrad at UCLA, and the two had been lovers for most of the past 18 years. The night of the shooting, she spent hours deleting Ford's files from Biofem computers, according to James Riley's wife, Pam, who is the company's business manager. (Kesler's attorney, John Kremer, says that any files that may have been deleted had nothing to do with the shooting.)

Kesler denied knowing anything about the attempt on Riley's life. Later, however, her lawyer suggested officers exercise caution opening up a gym bag in the trunk of her car, which Ray had impounded. Kesler had told her attorney that it might contain firearms and a knife dipped in ricin, a deadly toxin synthesized from castor beans. A drop in the bloodstream was all it took to kill. Ray and his superiors called in the FBI, whose Weapons of Mass Destruction Response Team is charged with dealing with biological and chemical threats.

According to Ray, the agent in charge of the team mocked the notion that Ford was connected to bioweapons research and the CIA. But with Ray insisting that the information seemed good, that it matched other accounts, the agent agreed to contact the FBI liaison to the intelligence agency. In about ten minutes a call came back: The CIA knew of Ford.

"The CIA knows a lot of people," the agent laughed. "They probably know my grandmother." But ten minutes later the liaison called again and said there was "high confidence" that Ford had biological- and chemical-weapons knowledge and did, in fact, have the capability to coat the knife with a deadly toxin. Shortly after that a third call came in: Ford did work for the CIA, the chastened FBI official told the room full of cops.

There was no more laughing after that. The men in space suits took over. Searchers found an Uzi and another illegal firearm in the gym bag; the knife was plunged into decontaminating fluid before it could be tested, which allowed the authorities to make the calming announcement that they had found no dangerous substances in the car. But a jar of ricin turned up later in Ford's home.

While this drama unfolded in Irvine, Peter Fitzpatrick was trying to get through to someone, anyone, at the FBI who would listen to his recollections of Ford's involvement with biowarfare in South Africa. No one was available, so he went to the FBI's bureau in West L.A., where he was turned away by the receptionist. "Basically," says Fitzpatrick, "they said they didn't know who the hell I was and that I should go." Next he called the Orange County

District Attorney's Office and asked for the prosecutor assigned to the Ford case, but ended up trapped in voice mail. He left an exasperated message, then hung up.

The next day, to Fitzpatrick's surprise, two FBI agents met at length with him to discuss his information about Ford, bioweapons, and South African surveillance. Then two things happened: First, the weapons team showed up to do another high-risk search and excavation of Ford's home. They uncovered nearly a hundred firearms, most of them shotguns and rifles, 17 of them illegal automatic or semiautomatic weapons, including four Uzis, an M16, and a gangster-era Thompson submachine gun.

Ford had stowed the illegal weapons in six large plastic cylinders buried in his backyard, along with thousands of rounds of ammunition—something his family apparently did not consider unusual, though they were unaware that one canister contained a large supply of the powerful military explosive C-4. The plastic explosives were packed with blasting caps and secreted dangerously close to electrical wires. Some 52 homes and several hundred people had to be evacuated to the Hyatt Regency for three days (it was, after all, Irvine—no Red Cross sleeping bags in the school gym for this crowd).

At the same time, Detective Ray expressed interest in talking to Fitzpatrick and Byron in order to explore the South African angle, but he and his partner were forbidden to do so by the bureau and forbidden to come near Ford's house. Their department pulled the reins even tighter. "[They thought] we were crazy, we were imagining things," Ray says. "They said we had been working too long without enough sleep. It stunk. But we were off the case."

Now a clerical worker for a Beverly Hills law firm and an aspiring screenwriter, Peter Fitzpatrick was a television and stage actor in the mid 1980s when he struck up a friendship with Gideon Bouwer, the South African trade attaché in Los Angeles. He had written Bouwer asking for help financing a hearing aid that Tom Byron, an out-of-work engineer friend, had thought up. The attaché, always in the market for any piece of new technology to squeeze past the trade embargo, agreed to meet them.

Early into the meeting, Bouwer, an imposingly large man, began spouting racist rhetoric. Fitzpatrick didn't blink, sensing this was a test of sorts. He leaned back in his chair, crossed his legs, and smiled at Byron. "You're among friends," he told Bouwer, and just like that, they were in.

The pair became regulars at the consulate and at the attaché's home, where senior officials from local defense contractors and pharmaceutical companies, along with minor celebrities, would frequent the parties, barbecues, and dinners Bouwer hosted to forge informal ties to get around the embargo. Each man was recruited independent of the other to feed information to the FBI but eventually learned of their mutual mission. Byron helped plant electronic surveillance devices for the bureau.

Both informants say that Ford, Nilsson, and Ford's mistress, Kesler, were regular guests at Bouwer's mansion, and Byron remembers encountering Dino D'Saach, the getaway driver, at several gatherings. Indeed, Ford and Nilsson's connection to South Africa ran deep. The two doctors went on big-game hunts beginning in the early 1980s—about 20 stuffed trophies lined the walls of Ford's home—and, as Ford and Nilsson told it, they did charity medical work there.

Later Ford and Kesler began smuggling into the U.S. distilled human amniotic fluid collected by South African doctors for Ford's antibiotic research. They would hide the biologically hazardous body fluids in wine and liquor bottles to avoid impoundment. Riley, in testimony in the D'Saach trial, described one trip in which a bottle of amniotic fluid broke inside a suitcase while in flight, creating a noxious odor that permeated the aircraft.

Ford and Nilsson were befriended by South African deputy surgeon general Dr. Niel Knobel. Ford began advising him on protecting troops from biological attack, as well as suggesting AIDS prevention programs in a country that today has the worst AIDS infection rate on earth—benign and praiseworthy endeavors that Knobel maintains had "no political agenda." But the AIDS prevention program was for whites in the military, not blacks. A secret right-wing South African organization, the Broeder-bond, conducted studies around this same time that suggested the AIDS epidemic could make whites the majority in the future.

Since then, through the new government's Truth and Reconciliation Commission, which was formed to probe the abuses of apartheid, information has surfaced about a secret South African bioweapons program. Code-named Project Coast, it was run by another Ford friend and financial benefactor, Dr. Wouter Basson; Knobel had administrative oversight. Basson's alleged ties to hundreds of poisonings and assassinations in South Africa and in the neighboring countries of Angola and Zimbabwe earned him the nickname Dr. Death in the South African press. Documents indicating he had arranged an offshore bank account for Ford were found in Ford's papers after his death.

The commission uncovered evidence that whole villages, including an Angolan settlement of several hundred people suspected of harboring rebels, may have been decimated by Project Coast weapons. This finding parallels information Nilsson's ex-girlfriend provided: She said Ford more than once boasted of wiping out an entire Angolan village during a civil war. (She claimed Ford had been talking with Nilsson in 1996 about obtaining a missile or bombing system from former Soviet bloc nations that might be used to deliver biological weapons.)

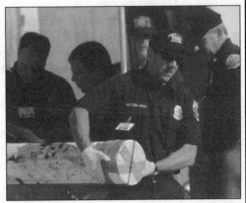

Fig. 4-4. One of the weapon-filled canisters from Ford's yard.

Project Coast scientists called to testify against Basson have said Ford was brought in to brief them on the use of biological weapons in mass attacks and discrete assassination, the latter through the contamination of ordinary items such as *Playboy* magazines and tea bags. One scientist involved with South African bioweapons development noted that Ford's ideas—and arrogance—were not well received, and that his work was given little credence in the Project Coast lab. However, Ford continued to work with Basson and Knobel, who had a picture of him hanging in his den at the time of the suicide.

According to a recent U.S. Air Force Academy report on South Africa's biological warfare program, Ford was part of a global network of scientists that Basson assembled to assist Project Coast. Whether that meant creating—or receiving and storing—toxins produced by the program is a matter of conjecture, the report suggests, as South African officials have been unable to account for all of the dangerous material produced over the years. The air force report quotes testimony from a Swiss intelligence agent who laundered money for Basson and who describes a worldwide conspiracy involving unnamed Americans.

"The death of Dr. Ford and revelations of his South African involvement," the report states, "[raises] the possibility of a right-wing international network, [still] united by a vision of South Africa once again ruled by whites."

In the wake of Ford's suicide Fitzpatrick and Byron reminded a new set of FBI agents about the meeting between Ford and Deputy Surgeon General Knobel, in which the satchel of deadly germs was allegedly passed over to the South African—and about the fact that nothing was done to intercept Knobel as he returned to South Africa. Once again no explanation was offered. Byron suggested reviewing the surveillance recordings from the bugs he and Fitzpatrick helped plant so long ago. "You can get a blockbuster out of those, I'm sure."

"Not even we can get those tapes," he remembers the agent responding. "They're sealed. National security."

Matthew McLaughlin, spokesman for the FBI in Los Angeles, says the bureau's policies bar him from confirming or denying Byron's and Fitzpatrick's accounts. Nor will he comment on their allegation that the government permitted Ford to illegally develop and traffic in bioweapons. McLaughlin does caution, however, that there are often reasons criminal activity is allowed to go on in order to preserve an investigation, and that no informant in any case has the whole picture.

"We compartmentalize people we work with, and they are not privy to the breadth and width of a case," he says. "They see the elephant's toenail."

Of course, Byron and Fitzpatrick say trade attaché Gideon Bouwer was clear in their conversations 16 years ago about what had happened in the meeting with Ford. They say he raved about the ability to keep whites in power through biological warfare, and he hinted at being part of a separate agenda—some sort of extragovernmental conspiracy, like the one described in the air force report, that had plans to unleash biological agents worldwide on South Africa's enemies if the need should ever arise.

"Just be ready," Fitzpatrick remembers Bouwer warning him cryptically, then asking, "How fast could you get your daughter out of the country if you had to?"

"I have to be honest," Fitzpatrick says. "Gideon could be a great guy. But there was something dangerous about him. And when he started talking about that master plan, about what a great service Ford had done for his country, about getting out of the country, it gave me chills."

Niel Knobel has admitted meeting with Ford at the attaché's home in the period Fitzpatrick and Byron describe but denies any involvement with biological weapons.

The informants never found out what happened after that meeting between Ford and Knobel. Bouwer fell from favor less than a year later, apparently considered a security risk by his own government. He was recalled, and the visits by Ford and Nilsson to the consulate ended, as did Byron's and Fitzpatrick's work there. Bouwer died ten years ago in South Africa.

Looking for answers, Fitzpatrick recently used the Freedom of Information Act to obtain his FBI file. All but the captions were redacted from the small ream of reports detailing his information about Ford and the South Africans. But those captions clearly show one thing: Whatever Fitzpatrick told his handler was immediately forwarded to FBI headquarters in Washington, and then it was dispatched to the CIA.

Victor Ray was brought back on the Ford case after a week, once it became clear that he had not been off-base about a possible CIA connection and that he had developed sources the FBI wanted—sources he wasn't going to give up unless there was mutual cooperation.

After some initial tug-of-war the Irvine police and the FBI are working well together, Ray says, but there have been disagreements. He could only get to Byron and Fitzpatrick through an *L.A. Times* reporter whom Fitzpatrick had called, rather than through the FBI, which declared them off-limits. And it is Ray, not the FBI, who has kept pushing to widen the investigation, expanding it to other suspects and states, securing out-of-town search warrants the FBI said couldn't be obtained, locating a key witness the FBI believed to be dead. It appears that Irvine's small police department is the main reason an international investigation is now under way, one that started with an Orange County grand jury probe and that now appears headed for a federal grand jury.

So far the only public charges have revolved around Riley's shooting. Besides D'Saach's attempted-murder conviction, Kesler has been charged with weapons violations for the guns found in her car. She remains a suspect in the shooting, as does Nilsson, whose home was searched but who has not been charged. The gunman remains unidentified.

Biofem, meanwhile, is still trying to recover from the loss of Ford. The Unidentified Amniotic Fluid Substance project, which Riley only reluctantly admitted existed when called to testify against D'Saach, may well die without Ford. Inner Confidence is moving forward, but FDA clinical trials, which were supposed to have begun by now, have been postponed. Investors can't be happy about the revelations concerning Ford, and Riley fears the delay has opened a window to rival products, since interest in microbicides as a means of battling HIV has grown intense in the last year or two.

The search of Ford's house unearthed more than 260 containers of biological material, most of it in a refrigerator in Ford's garage, along with the jar of ricin, the substance Kesler said the knife had been dipped in. Authorities found it in his family room. Botulism, which produces one of the deadliest toxins known, was recovered from a refrigerator at Biofem, stored by Ford next to a bottle of ranch dressing.

These discoveries were followed by reassuring statements to the public that the doctor's illegal brew of germs was aged and posed little danger. But internal FBI reports state there was a genuine public health hazard, and Dr. Mark Horton, head of public health services for Orange County, concedes that, had the materials been handled without great care, they could have imperiled the community.

It turns out that the assurances were based on the testing of only 16 of the samples—there has been no official accounting of what was in the rest. The public statements did not even mention the botulism.

Ray has no doubt that the danger was severe. He notes that many of the biological samples in Ford's home were stored next to a jar of what was suspected to be old and chemically unstable ether. "If that ether had been exposed to a higher temperature, it would have exploded," he says, "and Larry Ford's chemistry set would be blown all over Irvine."

His disgust over the case almost led him to leave it for good last summer. He was away all the time, his wife was complaining; the stress was enormous. "It really made me think . . . what in the hell was going on and how could the government have stood by while Ford . . . did these things? I really wondered if there was anything that I could or should do."

He took two trips to Washington, D.C., that summer, the first to wander alone among the monuments, the Arlington cemetery, the Vietnam and police officers' memorials, looking for inspiration. During their second trip, Ray and his wife decided he should continue the case. "It's hard to stand among so much history of personal sacrifice and say, 'I'm more important,'" he says.

But reality was not far behind. While at the capital, he tried to make contact with officials at the South African embassy, to pass on his information about Ford and Dr. Death's financial dealings and offshore accounts. Prosecutors in South Africa had been desperately trying to hold their case together, Ray knew, and the records he had found could have helped. But no one, he sighs, was the least bit interested.

Los Angeles Magazine, July 2001, Volume 46, Number 7
LOS ANGELES MAGAZINE is published monthly by Los Angeles Magazine, Inc.
5900 Wilshire Blvd., 10th floor, Los Angeles, CA 90036

Prayer to Stop the SSG from Usurping Power

Reveals the Mysteries, Isis and Speaks of Many Truths

November 15, 2001

The BBC reported today that Taliban supreme leader Mullah Mohammed Omar is speaking of a plan in the works to destroy the United States. Omar said that the current situation in Afghanistan is related to a bigger cause—the destruction of America—and that if God's help is with them, this will happen in a short period of time [CNN, November 15, 2001].

Reveals the Mysteries: This is a continuation of the manipulation by the sinister secret government. The sources who would federalize the U.S. are trying to find a way to try to usurp power by clandestine means and are manipulating the elective officials who are largely blind about this. The best hope to resisting such federalizing is in the Congress of the U.S.

I sis: If the many who have New Age, spiritual and ceremonial abilities practice their skills and gifts, and if everyone who goes to church also practices their ceremonies and does their heart-centered benevolent work—be it benevolent magic or be it enlightened wisdom of some form—it is possible, even likely, that this threat can be headed off. Partly the threat is illusion, not unlike Hitler saying, "Is Paris burning?" but the threat is real enough that security people will have to be careful. Of course, they are already, but they will need to be even more careful.

I will say that regardless of this leader's threat, his belief that Arab-Americans will cooperate in such a religious war is largely unfounded, just as Japanese-Americans did not cooperate with Axis powers during World War II and would not have if allowed to go about their business unfettered. The United States is a young country and has been active beyond its wisdom level in international affairs for some time. It is essential for the U.S. to call on allies and even new friends who have longer-standing cultures or governments, to ask that they give advice, give suggestions and otherwise give counsel to the U.S.

I am calling on all heart-centered people to perform your ceremonies or prayers and give support to those who can resolve conflicts between angry parties. I also would like to give a special living prayer [see p. xxii] for those who can do heart-love, the love-heat/heart-warmth/physical-warmth [see p. 23]. When you achieve the warmth in your heart, say slowly while maintaining the warmth:

> *Living Prayer*
> **"I ASK THAT THE HEARTS OF ALL BEINGS UNITE NOW TO FORM THE ONE HEART ALWAYS INTENDED BY OUR BELOVED CREATOR."**

For those who can add that to their prayers, I request that you do so.

This challenge to the U.S. is not only meant for the government but is largely meant to rally the citizens of the world. It is time now to see how much you are alike and how little your differences are—enough to create interest, but not so much as to block friendship.

Speaks of Many Truths: I know that some of you are angry at your elected officials and you want to elect them out of office. I want to tell you this: What you do in your elections is up to you, but I assure you that regardless of threats, intimidation and possible temporary restrictions on travel, you will all get through this globally.

After this Middle East crisis settles down a bit, I recommend that cooler heads behind the scenes and in diplomatic and global business circles make permanent agreements of mutual cooperation and support designed to create a global business and humanitarian exchange. Although other priorities may seem to be called for, I feel that a global business and humanitarian agreement can resolve a great many international and domestic crises all over the world. And such a partnership can cement ties and make friends and partners out of former adversaries. Even though your world will be united in one heart someday soon, begin by uniting in the wallet, since business and diplomacy are so very united in your time.

I am speaking to you now in the light of reality, since I feel that is the most prudent course to follow. Look around globally, those of you in business now or in diplomacy, and see those whom you can form alliances and partnerships with. Such international alliances, even with businesses that are not so big, can do a lot to embrace global partnership.

I know you want to do something; this is how to start. Encourage your employees or staff to network and even chat with your new international friends and partners. Resolution comes not only from hands across the sea but also from ignorance turned into familiarity.

Origins of the Sinister Secret Government

Zoosh

December 3, 2002

One of the things that really must be talked about now is the point of origin of the originating souls of the sinister secret government. This is critical to understand, because once you understand their point of origin, you will understand how to resolve the energies that motivate them.

The SSG Came from a Point of Need

Before the loop of time (as it has been called before) that you occupied to bring about resolution—and you're in the resolution cycle now—there was the clear recognition by all beings who would have anything whatsoever to do with this drama that there would need to be something that would not only pull you along, which is your normal way of acting and reacting, but that would push you along, since you would be going through, at times, linear time. Understand that linear time can be felt either as a powerful motivating force or with various subtle actions and reactions, and you're into the more subtle time now.

As a result, what is needed is something—or in this case, *someones*—that will snap at your heels so that in case you actually fall back by the wayside and say, "Let me just sit down here for a few years and take a breather," you will feel their hot breath on the back of your neck. This is not, in that sense, satanic, but rather it is something that prompts you as a group-soul Explorer Race to say, "Well, that's long enough. Let's get going." And that's really about the size of it.

So where did they come from? They did not actually come from a place but from a point of need. You have to ask yourself, "How could souls even volunteer for such an action given the strain it would necessarily have on their personalities?" The only way they could do that was to wear a garment. What was the garment? The garment was loaned by the Master of Discomfort [see *Explorer Race: Creators and Friends*].

The Master of Discomfort said, "I will provide this cloak to souls who choose to take on this task, but only if the cloak is and remains connected to me. Therefore, even in that way, I can experience from time to time if I choose a direct connection"—or as direct as possible given the isolation that is often the case with the sinister secret government individuals—"to the human race on Earth. Since I will not normally have anything that resembles a direct connection, this will be a chance for me to experience personally the value of all the work we are doing here" ("we" speaking in the aspect of the consultants rather than Creator Itself). So it was decided that since it would require a capacity for self-destructiveness—and as you know, I describe self-destructiveness as that which hurts you or anyone else—then the only way that beings, souls, could choose to do this is to have a need to experience a level of *performance* that would bring about almost a magical experience for who they are.

As Souls, SSG Members Are Servicing You

Now I'm going to explain the fine points of these individuals: At all times individuals who are bodily incarnated, meaning physical on Earth, who are members of the inner circle of the sinister secret government, every single one of these individuals have in previous lives—never in current lives—been actors. As you know, actors must be able to convince others of their persona, their character, so that those others in viewing the act or performance believe that they are who they are pretending to be in those moments so they can then suspend their disbelief and enjoy the performance. This tells you something that is vital to know: All of these individuals in previous lives were master actors. They had been able to achieve a profound ability to stimulate their audiences to drop any shred of disbelief so that their performances would be absolutely convincing.

Think about it. This is a perfect quality that would assist in their capacity at the soul level—along with their personal experience in this life—to be able to don such a personality while being and having within themselves their own unique soul from Creator. This is why I've said in the past that you will not know who the sinister secret government members are, because they need to be protected because they are actually—even though it won't feel like it to you—performing the valuable task of motivating you. They are not the only motivation, but they are what I call the emergency motivation in case you sit too long by the side of the Explorer Race path and decide to do a "Rip Van Winkle." So they are the motivators of last resort.

So you have then the personality of these beings explained and the means to understand now how they could don this discomforting role—self-destructive to themselves and others—why they can do it and also that it is actually a personal sacrifice for them. As individuals they give up a lot of their happiness to do this. I'm not saying nor am I suggesting that you believe they are beings to whom you ought to say, "Thank you so much." Rather I am suggesting that as souls they are in a form of self-sacrificing service. It's important for you to know that.

SSG Inner Circle Members Are from Your Future

Now, where are they from? Since it was understood that the Master of Discomfort would provide this cloak of personality that they would wear, they would have to be from somewhere that would have a strong connection and identify with the Explorer Race and the Explorer Race concept (the overview, the value of it all), while at the same time having versatile natural capacities, souls—in short, immortal personalities. Where else could such beings possibly be found than in your future when you had in fact come to resolution with what you are doing here now? Think about it. How could they maintain their motivation to do these things, even though at many times they would personally feel like they were giving a performance and would feel awkward and uncomfortable with that, while at the same time feeling in their *now* lives that they were performing a duty that they were required to do.

Now, because they are coming from your future and will have seen the ultimate value of the Explorer Race having gone through these hard times of struggle, drama and, yes, suffering, they will remain motivated at the soul level because they will have a knowing at the soul level that it turns out all right and that no matter what they do in these roles as members of the inner circle of the sinister secret

> It has been said in previous books that these individuals [SSG members] always have these duties handed down to them, so they don't have a choice. It comes down, not so much through a bloodline, but through what they would call a line of duty.

government, it will still turn out all right. Granted, this allows them to personally excuse their own actions and to even believe that their own actions have value beyond greed and corruption and so on, but think about it. I've stated before that you cannot go on to achieve Explorer Race completion in this experience without the inclusion of all your members who choose to go on, which is essentially or (as you like to say in the computer world) virtually everyone, with a few possible exceptions who may have been with you for a long time but will choose to leave the experience, do things elsewhere. But those are the rare exceptions indeed. Otherwise, you must have everyone with you.

How can you possibly leave these individuals of the sinister secret government behind? You cannot. The only thing you can do is to give them permission to remove those cloaks passed on to them and supported for them by the Master of Discomfort. How can you give them that permission? You must begin when you are ready to take responsibility for your own creation. You have been given in the pages of the *Sedona Journal of Emergence!* and in the many books published by Light Technology and other places, many means and ways to actually alter your experience in life—not the least of which is living prayer [see p. xxii] and benevolent magic, but also those things by other channels, psychics, guides, teachers and religious leaders [as in the benevolent magic so uniquely and personally described recently by Tom Moore in the following article, published in the December 2002 *Sedona Journal*]. In short, these are things you can do to change your life and the lives of others.

BENEVOLENT OUTCOMES
ANOTHER TOOL FOR YOUR TOOLBOX
Tom T. Moore

From your reading and studies, you understand that we are all creators-in-training. We are supposed to be learning how to create from the ground up, with the third dimension as our training ground. Now we are entering a new phase of learning how to benevolently create events. Robert Shapiro, in *The Council of Creators* book in the *Explorer Race* series, channels the following: ". . . seek out more benevolent experiences for yourself. Seek out more benevolent companions and experiences of benevolence for you and your companion or your family or your people."

Around six or seven years ago, I started noticing that benevolent outcomes were mentioned in channelings and that Zoosh, through Robert, also recommended that we request benevolent outcomes. I decided to try it out and started to say out loud that I requested a benevolent outcome for almost every physical event that was occurring in my life. Amazingly, everything that happened turned out for the best—including those difficult lessons in life that we have contracted to experience.

So before we go too far, I would like for you to say out loud (you can whisper if it would disturb someone or bring unwanted attention), "I request the most benevolent outcome from reading this article." Did you say it? Humor me and give it a try. Now that you have, does this sound a little "weird" or "funny"? We'll discuss that later. And I will include a discussion I had with Speaks of Many Truths and his teacher, Reveals the Mysteries—both Native American shamans channeled by Robert—to better understand how this works.

Using Metaphysical Tools

The title of this article mentioned a tool for your toolbox. I discovered that there are a number of metaphysical tools available to help us through these Earth lives. You just have to make use of them.

Here is an example: Back in 1968, I was operating a ski club for single adults as a business. One day an astrologer predicted on the front page of the local newspaper that the Dallas Cowboys would not make it to the Super Bowl that year, but would go the following year. At the end of the American football season, the astrologer was proven correct. I booked three hundred airline seats to Miami one year in advance and became the first tour operator in Dallas to ever run a trip to the Super Bowl for Dallas fans. I started scheduling all of my ski club meetings and parties to coincide with benevolent (there's that word again) astrological aspects.

This was highly successful. The club grew to be the largest in the region, and many couples met and eventually married. I also had to open a travel agency, and it eventually became one of the largest wholesale tour companies in the southwestern U.S., selling tours through three thousand travel agents nationwide. This success inspired me to search out other metaphysical tools to use. Numerology is one of them. If you haven't done so, buy a book and figure out your own charts. It will contribute to you understanding who you are.

I began recording my dreams in a dream journal on a daily basis in 1979. Recording dreams each morning has been a major tool in my toolbox. Over the years, I have recorded thousands of dreams, many of them precognitive. My dreams also guided me to change careers. It's the closest you will get in this life to your immortal self, and I highly recommend it.

The newest metaphysical tool I use is the 26-second meditation, channeled from the Group by Steve Rother in his book, *Re-Member—A Handbook for Human Evolution.* You begin each day sitting in silence with both thumbs touching the middle and ring fingers of your hands. Allow a few seconds to strengthen the connection. Breathe in through your nose and out through your mouth. Then visualize the most beneficial events that could happen to you during the day with Spirit as your partner opening the doors ahead of you.

I used this for the first time recently while preparing for a TV market. With just over two weeks to go, I had only forty appointments. I started visualizing receiving four or five new appointments per day. It happened! Then I visualized going to market with one hundred appointments. When I left for the market, I had over one hundred appointments! Experiment with using this for a few days. Imagine all the lights being green as you drive to and from work. This is a very powerful tool for your toolbox!

Better Than the "Parking Angel"

This brings us to benevolent outcomes. This tool will allow you to learn and experiment with cocreation while on the physical level. It will give you immediate feedback—which is very important, since we are never sure whether we are really manifesting something or not.

Here's an easy-to-do exercise: Let's say you're going to a shopping center or a restaurant or a movie theater at a location where it is typically hard to find a parking space. Well, before you arrive, say, "I request a most benevolent outcome for finding a parking space near . . ." Now, I have had some friends say, "But, Tom, I already use my 'parking angel.'" Here is why I think requesting a benevolent outcome is better: If you just request the nearest parking space, your angel or guide will comply, but that might not be the most benevolent place to have your car parked. Someone could open a car door too hard and ding the side of your car, or someone might back into your car and dent it. By parking too close to where you want to go, you might miss that old friend of yours you haven't seen in ages or a sale you would not have known about if you had not walked past it on the way to your destination. But benevolent outcomes work perfectly!

Recently, on a visit back to Sedona, we drove with our friends to the "uptown" section for Mexican food. For those of you who have visited Sedona, you know that the parking there can be quite problematic because of the many gift shops and restaurants. I requested a most benevolent outcome when we left the hotel. Every single parking space on both sides of the street was taken until we reached the restaurant. There, right at the front entrance, was "our" parking space. Again, this was immediate feedback we were creating!

Clara in Seattle emailed me that the first time she tried it was when she went to pick up her grandson on a hot summer day. She knew she would have to wait for him and hoped to get a space up close. When she arrived, the only space available was on the last row, but it was in the shade! It made a believer out of Clara, who says she now uses it for everything and it has never failed her.

Two of our friends, Joy and Bob, recently drove to Las Vegas from Dallas. They requested a most benevolent outcome for their drive, hotel and parking. Each time they passed a police radar speed trap, they were behind trucks and other traffic that had slowed them down. In Las Vegas, they were given exactly the floor of the hotel they wanted and a view of the Strip. And they found the perfect parking space where their car would not get dinged.

Problem Solving and Winning

Joy and Bob just purchased a home in the country. Every time they closed on a house in the past, they experienced problems at the closing—mistakes in the paperwork and so on. This time they requested a most benevolent outcome for the closing and sailed through the process with no problems.

My son, two friends and I flew to Salt Lake City, Utah, and camped all the way up to Yellowstone National Park and back. What a wonderful trip! I knew that our flight back to Dallas was oversold, so I volunteered the four of us to be "bumped." Typically, the airline compensates with free tickets, which I thought we could use the next year. Naturally, I requested a most benevolent outcome. They did not need our seats, but for volunteering they gave us four first class seats. My son, his friend and the friend's father had never flown first class, so this was the treat of their lives. The following summer our schedules did not coincide, and we were not able to return—therefore, truly a benevolent outcome!

My family and I took a cruise from Houston. My daughter and I played bingo the first day, but other activities kept us from playing again until the last day of the cruise. I had requested a most benevolent outcome the first day, but we did not win anything, and so I requested one again on the last day. The overall pot had not been won during the week, and on the last day they play until someone wins it. I won half of an $8,400 pot, along with a young man who was sitting right next to me. I'm sure people thought he was my son. What synchronicity! It paid for our cruise, as we had already been given 50 percent off, thanks to a benevolent outcome on the same cruise the year before.

My son returned from an all-night high-school graduation party with a Sony PlayStation he had won in a drawing. Although it was the second largest prize, it was the one he really wanted. He explained to me that he had requested a benevolent outcome "two times." Once would have really been enough.

Success in Business

Another couple in our metaphysical group have a very high-end painting contracting business. With the economy in Dallas and the rest of the U.S. in retreat, things have been tough for them. Billy hasn't gotten used to requesting benevolent outcomes yet, but his wife, Jo, and I both requested a most benevolent outcome for their business to pick up. Just in the past week, they secured a twenty-thousand-square-foot house, which will take a year to complete. He is about to sign a contract on a second large house and will probably be awarded a third contract in the next two weeks.

Recently I requested a most benevolent outcome for my sales trip to a TV market in Budapest, but I added, ". . . and may it produce better results than I expect or hope for." I was invited to a meeting where a Russian/Ukrainian TV network agreed to become a coproduction partner in a movie to be filmed in Siberia; our company will be the worldwide distributor. I flew from Budapest to Athens and requested the same thing. Not only was my business successful there, but my colleague in Athens asked me to help him sell his TV productions on historical Greece.

Synchronous Synergy

Last weekend we drove with our friends to Mena, Arkansas, for the weekend. I discovered that my van was short on Freon for the air conditioner. Not having sufficient cooling in the final dog days of summer in the South can be miserable. The receptionist at the motel told me that finding a place open on Saturday in such a small town might not be possible, but he gave me the name of a tire store to try.

We were there at 7:00 A.M. the next morning, but it would not open until 8:00 A.M. I was drawn to a nearby service station and asked if they knew of a garage to service the air conditioner. A young man who just "happened" to be there suggested a garage several blocks away and recited the phone number. Finding that one closed, we returned to the tire store, and I requested a most benevolent outcome for getting the air conditioner serviced that day. The lady said they didn't have the right equipment, so I pulled out the telephone number I had kept and asked her to call it.

The garage owner answered and said that normally he did not work on Saturday but to come by, as he was repairing a UPS truck we had seen in the driveway. He replenished the Freon and charged me only one-third of what I would have paid in Dallas. As a side benefit, he showed us his unbelievable collection of old Indian motorcycles, a 1942 Hudson sedan, marbles and toy cars in their original boxes. He had taught automotive repair in a local college for twenty-five years before retiring. Had the lady not telephoned him, he might not have said yes to us.

Benevolent Outcomes Are Benevolent Magic

Does requesting benevolent outcomes sound strange or weird or funny? It does take a little getting used to. Some of my metaphysically oriented friends have slowly adopted using the request, especially as they are seeing more and more positive results. But it has been difficult for others. I can't help that; I did not invent the words. I just started using what the channeling entities used as part of their language. When I started using this statement, there was very little written about benevolent outcomes. More is now being written, and it seems that we are using benevolent magic.

In order to understand how benevolent outcomes work, I "interviewed" the shamans Speaks of Many Truths and his teacher, Reveals the Mysteries, channeled by Robert Shapiro. I will excerpt some of their comments here, in order to clarify how these requests work metaphysically.

Channeled Comments: How This All Works

What is the definition of benevolent and benevolent outcomes in the spirit world?

Speaks of Many Truths: "It's not like that in the spirit world. The reason we sometimes say that we are literal when you speak to us is that we are literal to the point of your meaning. Or the other possibility is that we are literal to the point of what is applicable to the situation and even what is safe to tell you.

"The reason I made a point that different beings work with benevolent magic and others with living prayer, for example, is that with benevolent magic, direct connections need to be drawn and requested, which encourages people to do what they might otherwise do in any event. Do you see? But something needs to bring it to their attention so they do whatever it is at a given moment rather than at some other time. That's very precisely what goes on there. It is not something that operates against anyone's will or manipulates them in any way."

Reveals the Mysteries: "You have to remember that the keyword in benevolent magic is magic. The keyword is not benevolent. Do you understand the difference?"

Not exactly.

"You can describe magic in different forms, but you're talking about magic first and benevolent second. But you say benevolent magic, because you want to make it clear that it is magic intended to be benevolent for all beings. This means that you do not wish beings to change against their will or their better interest. But it is ultimately magic, meaning that things change without any apparent effort of will or undue influence. So in that sense, for no reason that you can put your finger on, things change in some benevolent way.

"And that's magic. It is done through various beings functioning in various ways. In benevolent magic, you ask for a very precise thing."

So benevolent magic is magic used for the small things, the small details in our interaction with other people?

"Not small. Benevolent magic has to do with specific details and very specific intentions. It is a pinpoint, usually a narrow-ranged thing. You are asking for something specific."

A Physical Process

A request for benevolent outcomes has to be done physically—either verbally or in writing—as we are in a physical world. It seems we are communicating at a superconscious level with other higher selves to cocreate these requests. These benevolent requests are probably only training wheels in our learning to cocreate, but it should give all of us a basic understanding of creating benevolent events. You will receive immediate feedback, which will increase your confidence in its use as a tool. I also like to say "thank you" three times when I receive a benevolent outcome. It's just nice to acknowledge the assistance you received.

Keep in mind that you must be willing to accept the benevolent outcomes. If you request one for a dear person's recovery from an illness or injury, the benevolent outcome might be that they transition peacefully. If you ask for a benevolent outcome for a job interview and the company chooses someone else, you have to accept that something better is on the way for you. If you have had a number of successes with the more mundane incidents in your life, it will be much easier to accept the outcomes for those major events that come along.

Please test this out for yourself. It is a habit created by repetition. You have to consciously think to use it for some time until it becomes natural. But the potential results will mean an easier life for you, your family, your friends and ultimately for all of us. It will certainly contribute to a lowering of your stress level!

✢   ✢   ✢

Tom Moore is a spiritual man whom I've known for some time. He has been able to integrate his spirituality with his personal and business life. Considering the intensity and demands of his life, this is an accomplishment in itself. I highly recommend that you practice those parts of Tom's article that feel good to you. I'm sure that his suggestions are intended to improve the quality of your life.

—Robert Shapiro

You Need to Make a Leap of Faith

So what can you do to release the sinister secret government? You can motivate yourself. Remember, they are the motivators of last resort, and the only reason they've been needed is that you've been waiting for someone else to come along and do it for you. To some extent, one might look at your current religions and say, "They are to blame," but it's not true. The reason those religions evolved as they did—meaning, "those who will come to save you" and other such similar stories and ideas in religion—the reason they came about in the first place was a desire by you, by the Explorer Race, to have such saving take place.

This is because in your previous experience, since you've been in this universe created by this Creator, you have not been able to make the leap to close that loop to come to fruition of the purpose of that loop, which is to re-create so you can resolve all. You have not been able to do that, and what happens to souls when they are unable after repetitive tries to do something is that they give up—they stop. Or at the enlightened level, they wait until someone or something changes so that their efforts can come to fruition. Some time ago, you reached that point and you were waiting. That was the motivation that brought about religions that would say to you, "Someone's coming. There will be a time . . . the messiah . . . and so on." That's the motivation, so you can't blame the religions and say it's their fault, no.

You need to make what we've called before a leap of faith, but it is not something that is rare and impossible for you. Think about it. How many times have you in your lives now been trying to do something over and over again: "I can't do it, I can't do it, I can't do it." And time goes by and you say, "One more time," and you're able to do it. Granted, sometimes this involves timing, sometimes it involves other individuals and sometimes it involves something new that you've learned, but what it ultimately involves is that you've evolved, you've changed by exposure, by experience, by learning consequences, by applying applications. In short, you've matured as souls.

With Living Prayer and Benevolent Magic, You Can Bring About Change

So what I'm saying to you then is: Don't give up. Use the benevolent outcomes as they are stated in Tom Moore's article, use living prayer, use techniques that you do and say to bring about benevolent change in your life and in the lives of others, and know that as long as you remain dedicated to using this every day and stay on the path of that dedication, the sinister secret government will have no need to be here. They will have no need to be employed that way. In time the Master of Discomfort will say, "Well, it seems that my energy is no longer needed," and the Master of Discomfort will withdraw that energy it has granted to those souls, and those souls in the inner circle of the sinister secret government will literally be unable and unwilling to go on with those activities. The motivating energy of discomfort to drive you on will no longer be needed, and discomfort as an experience all over the planet—including dreams, recollections, day-to-day experiences, fears, anxieties, worries—everything will begin to decrease as an experience until it is no longer felt.

In short, my friends, it is up to you. There aren't any great secret formulas. Look to the *Shamanic Secrets* series. Look to whatever means and philosophy works for you. Don't look to blame. Blaming won't work, because blaming is ultimately self-destructive—meaning that blaming (feeling it's your fault, their fault, "They did it") feels bad to you and it causes harm to others. In short, it is self-destructive. Rather, look for the cure: "If others are causing harm, what can we do as individuals or as a society to bring about change for those individuals so they no longer want to cause harm?"

You have tried many things: penal institutions, therapies. Parents have gone out to their wits' end. I'm not saying you haven't tried, but you must try benevolent magic and living prayer and spiritual means. Do try, because it will have powers of influence these days unlike what you've known before. Remember, your souls had to mature and they are mature now; thus what you can do with living prayer and benevolent outcomes is particularly powerful. So I do recommend that you try it.

Understand that if you can do these things—benevolent magic, living prayer and other things—you can bring about change that, even though you may not immediately experience it yourself (although you might very well, especially with benevolent magic and benevolent outcomes), it will affect others. Remember, you are all one. How many times have you heard and read that? Since you are all one, what is of value and helps others that you do not even know personally in this life will ultimately in this life help you and everybody else.

Remember, many others cannot help themselves because they are in circumstances or conditions that are overwhelming, and then it is up to you to say things for them. If you are saying benevolent outcomes, try to keep it as inclusive of your life as possible. If you are, on the other hand, saying living prayer, then you can make that universal and it will also come about. You have the power; you have the influence. Use it, and it will not only benefit you, your friends, your family, your community and your world, but it will change the Earth. And as a result, all those who are snapping at your heels will be changed and the Explorer Race will reach its ultimate purpose: to expand the universe, to bring about hope and value, and to improve (believe it or not) the universe as Creator intended for you to do.

That's exactly what I wanted.

You know, sometimes it is not that you have to ask the right question, it is that you need to have the feeling. As you said, "It's exactly what I wanted," and that feeling creates a receptivity. It's like, "I'm ready to throw the ball and you're ready to catch it."

The SSG Is a Recent Phenomenon

At what point in the future, when the Explorer Race coalesced as the Creator or after they had moved on, did these beings come back to become the sinister secret government, or does it matter?

After the loop of time is entirely closed.

Only after the loop of time! Not even when we got to become the Creator, then?

No. They have to completely understand the motivation and the value of the loop of time, because it is during the loop of time that this vast amount of discomfort takes place. Before the loop of time, there's practically none.

And the whole point of it is to change the decision to work with the heart and mind, not just the mind?

That's right, because before then there was just a teensy amount of discomfort, if any, and how could beings, souls, actually be directly involved in stimulating discomfort, pain and suffering to others? How could they even consider it without having absolute convincing evidence—not just mentally, but *knowing* that kind of evidence, where it is reality and does not require words (the sky is up, the Earth is down, that kind of knowing)—that such a contribution and sacrifice on their part will turn out all right, but it is required that someone do it?

So we go through the loop of time, and then after that they decide to come back into the loop of time—it's almost like we did it twice.

No, it isn't. You're stuck in the concept of linear time. These souls have to make this decision really when the loop is just starting, because it takes time. If those souls are going to someday be the sinister secret government souls, understand that the beginning of the loop of time is entirely unnecessary. The sinister secret government is a recent phenomenon, but their souls would have to travel, go through experiences and so on to prepare them to be accepting, not only of the cloak provided by the Master of Discomfort, but to say, "This is all right. I can do this." That's one of the ways they discovered that they could do this, to be slightly disconnected from the experience of their lives, and what better disconnection and what better training for disconnection than to be master actors.

You said they had a need to experience the self-destructiveness. Was that need focused by the fact that they had the cloak of the Master of Discomfort, or did something in them cause them to need this?

That is brought about by their performance so that their personality would have the level of the performance in their inner being. This does not mean that their personality is so very different from those of other people. Any actor of today would have his or her inner being and his or her performance. How many times have you heard about the most appreciated actors who literally become their role and are therefore totally convincing? You have experienced such performances. So they would have to have those qualities and be able to call on such qualities. They aren't actors in this life, so they would have had to experience multiple lives of being an actor or a performer in multiple situations in societies.

Think about it. Actors, other than in recent times, were never known for being wealthy. As a matter of fact, actors were generally looked down upon in the past few hundreds of years in your Earth societies—not all societies, but let's say westernized societies. Certainly some actors in Asian societies were considered wonderful members of the community, but we're talking to the Western world here in these pages essentially, although others might be interested in it. However, they would have essentially gone through a period of suffering and struggle, and therefore, they would have built up in their souls not only the motivation and the *capacity*, but they would also have within their personalities the ability to quickly click into something else that they could use as a protection or literally as a garment—an alternative personality.

So all actors know—actors of today and actors of all times—that their expression in life is enhanced by their capacity to perform. This may be part of the reason that the marriage partner of an actor must be tolerant and have a good sense of humor, because it's true that his or her spouse may be performing at times in interactions with him or her, being a role, and with a sense of humor, that's fine.

But it is also for these highly sensitive people, to be an actor . . . to be that you must be profoundly sensitive to portray the nuances of personality that are necessary to convince the audience that you are this thing that you are portraying, at least in those moments of their observation of you as a member of the audience. So such personalities must be carefully formed.

That brings up the question of the size of the repertory theater. I think you said they've been around for three hundred thousand years, figuring three generations every hundred years. That's ten thousand to twelve thousand beings. Are there that many, or does each one have many lives?

What you are doing now is going into linear mathematical formulas. I would suggest that what is occurring is a very distinct line being passed down from soul to soul along this line. I will not say it is a bloodline, but it is a distinct line. We're not talking about hundreds of thousands of individuals. Remember, the sinister secret government as described in these pages and in the pages of the *Shining the Light* books is a recent phenomenon. So what has been going on is the formation of souls that can adapt to donning these roles, but we cannot say that the sinister secret government has been going on for repetitious generations.

Can you say at what point in our time the phenomenon of the sinister secret government started?

Ninety years ago, maybe. No more than that. In terms of actually doing things, really being known, being felt, it was less time than that, but we can use ninety years ago as a point. Before then, greed, corruption and suffering happened strictly on the basis of what human beings did and reacted to and responded to, and didn't need any stimulation.

Apply Living Prayer and Benevolent Magic Now

A few months ago, you said everybody was very impatient and the reason they were so impatient and violent and wound up is that they were waiting for something that was going to happen in fourteen months. Can you discuss that, or do we need to wait to see what happens?

I can only say, "Why wait?" Apply benevolent magic and living prayer now. I'm not going to say anything more. What happens if I tell you what's going to happen?

We'll probably change it.

There's no "probably" about it. Would you really want to change something like that and then have to wait two to three hundred years of the old timeline again? Do you really wish to perpetuate the old timeline and struggle for two to three hundred years to create another synchronicity window?

Will you say what it is when it happens?

No, but you will. When you think about it, what is a question, after all, but a response?

I understand that we had the loop of time because we have to have time to get the value of love, right?

Yes. One thing leads to another.

The SSG Has Conditioned Humanity to Be Self-Destructive, but You Can Do Living Prayer for Benevolence

Reveals the Mysteries
March 12, 2003

T hose in the sinister secret government believe they have achieved their objective—they've gone as far as they can go in order to influence the outcome of the human race on Earth. And it is true that it is now up to you. You have been conditioned to polarized points of view. You cannot simply ignore this as if it weren't there; you must recognize that the conditioning itself—and all of its attendant stimulations, actions and reactions—needs to be recognized.

Choose Benevolent Self-Transformation

This is how you can do it: Notice when you are being self-destructive—for example, taking a risk for the sake of risk only, not to achieve a goal of preserving, sustaining or rescuing life in some form. Self-destructive behavior is the foundation of the SSG's conditioning of you through all of its methods and influences, including anything you are exposed to that discourages your wonder of life, your application of love, your appreciation for yourself and all life and your responsibilities to transform your conditioning by recognizing the facts as you see them and as you feel them. To do this you will need to feel, and you will need to know what those feelings mean on an individual basis. This is why we have been putting our attention toward recognizing feelings and applying those that do not judge you but from which you can build value for yourself and others. This is the purpose of the *Shamanic Secrets* books and ultimately the *Explorer Race* books. The *Explorer Race* books explain; the *Shamanic Secrets* books instruct.

Now it is up to you to choose self-destructiveness with all of its misery and suffering (which you will feel individually and apply to the world as individuals) or to choose the more benevolent path—recovery through recognition, acknowledgment and the application of the benevolent self-transformation abilities you've learned through these books and other loving methods. It may require vigilance on each individual's part to see and treat himself or herself and maintain benevolent change. This can lead to a new form of conditioning—one that becomes easier to maintain over time and then becomes natural for you through repetition. You build your life from a foundation of benevolent feelings you can recognize individually, and you know the truth of it by what you feel.

To this end we dedicate ourselves to serving your needs. You can feel love, comfort, happiness just to be alive, and you can feel self-constructiveness, which builds from that benevolent foundation to make every moment of life worth living and each moment to come something to look forward to with a smile and reassuring anticipation. It's important to understand that, unfortunately, the nature of the conditioning has been pretty successful and widespread. That is why the focus of the past few years' channeling has been to counteract the effect of their negative conditioning of you.

The love-heat/heart-warmth/physical-warmth [see p. 23] and all of those things are foundational elements, not just to counteract it, but to reestablish the natural state of being within the human person. When you are born as a baby, you are celebrating life, you are happy to be here. You've seen babies experience the joy of being a flower or any number of things. That joy is natural; it is not just childlike. To call it childlike puts a limit on its capacity and its duration, although it is a rather natural state. That you change has partly to do with acculturation, but even within acculturation there is conditioning—and we cannot expect to change your conditioning— and your immediate future generations are conditioned right away. So individuals are left to choose whether they wish to change their conditioning on their own; the work through this channel and possibly others for the past few years has been about accomplishing that consciously.

Conditioning by Shock and Slow Conditioning

How did the SSG grow? How did they condition an entire planet?

Rather than recap how to destroy, which is destructive in its own right . . . if you want to change something that is innate, meaning people are born to it, the best way to do that is either through sudden, shocking changes or gradual changes, or you could do it through both. Some of that shocking change might be natural—meaning a storm or lightning, for example—but if the philosophy of the people you are living with encompasses such things, then you look upon lightning as part of nature, part of life, no matter how destructive it might be. Even the animals attacking and killing each other to eat might be terribly violent to hear about, to say nothing of seeing it . . . and of course, having to kill animals to eat yourself is also frightening to those uninitiated in that experience.

Nevertheless, if a culture has included that as part of life and the natural cycle and has been encouraged to show it as part of a whole picture—meaning mother had to eat in order to sustain her energies so that she could give birth to you—then it's part of a whole picture rather than individual segments, and then it is possible to adapt to such natural shocks. But, of course, there are man-made shocks, such as war—which is a shock to everyone—where someone attempts or accomplishes violence toward you or others even though they don't even know you, you've never met. That's pretty extreme.

Then there's slow conditioning, meaning incremental steps intended to move you away from what is natural. An example that many people will have experienced in your time, many who can even remember, happens in childhood: A child has a dream, and rather than explore the possible meanings of the dream or even the psychology behind it, bringing on a release and so on, the well-intentioned parent says, "Oh, it's just a dream, dear. Don't pay any attention to it." Or the other example that is typical and happens in childhood is where the child will have feelings come up and the feelings are strong, and the well-meaning parent in your time says, "Don't respond to that," in some language, whatever your language is. And, "Think before you act so you don't do anything foolish." Or worse yet, the parent says to the child wanting to fit in, "Think before you act so you don't *look* foolish." That's a big threat. It doesn't seem like one to the parent, it seems like a loving remark, but all these things condition children so they become less trustful of what is natural.

Understand How the Natural Works

The important thing in your time is to understand how the natural within you works and to adapt your stories, myths and culture to take in the natural, to honor the natural and to stop trying to turn the natural into the unnatural. If you say that feelings are not natural and that thought is the highest level, then you ignore what you are born with. You are not, as a child, a thinking being. This does not mean you cannot process that which you see in some way, but you process it in a way that interacts largely with spiritual beings, your guides and so on, and you tend to process things pictorially rather than on a linear linkage basis, as thought might work.

That pictorial frame of reference is also connected to feelings. So understand that if you are born with these things and if they are suppressed by natural means (in some cases) or unnatural means (which is by far more typical), then you are building a foundation of awareness on a myth. It is like the famous story of the "Emperor's New Clothes," where the emperor was, in fact, not wearing any clothes. That story was created in order to show not just how people can be fooled, but more importantly, how people can fool themselves and actually find that attractive. It is a very important short story. If there are any readers of this material who have not read that story, I recommend you read it; it's very important to read this. Generally, one reads it as a youngster, but if you haven't read it, read it. It won't take long and it's enlightening—and amusing, of course.

The reason I don't want to dwell on how the sinister secret government did the conditioning is because you don't have to be sinister to do this. That's why I used examples of parents. The parents certainly weren't sinister when they said those things to the children. It was probably said to them as children, or they heard other people say it, or they simply didn't have the tools or capacities; they weren't acculturated, they weren't encouraged to understand how to talk to their children in ways the children could hear and understand, so they could feel better about things going on for them. But the parents were not sinister when they said those things.

I brought that example up on purpose so you'd understand that the parents are either conditioned by a lack of wisdom or conditioned by life and the conditioning around them—acculturation is what I call that. We can go into how this was happening and how that happened and so on, but my feeling for the past few years—and Speaks of Many Truth's feeling and Zoosh's and everyone else's for that matter—has been that it is more urgent to *do* something about it.

You Are in a Time of Emergency

Now, you have a situation with the U.S. and Iraq and just the U.S. and the Middle East in general right now. This is a result of all that conditioning. You could say, "Well, let's explore the history of that and analyze that," and it would certainly be interesting and it could help you to mentally grasp how it happened—yet you wouldn't, of course. If there was a car crash, you wouldn't explore or analyze how the car crash happened at first. First, you would call the doctor and the ambulance so that the people could be treated. So the reason we have glossed over how it got to be this way for the past few years is because this is an emergency and you are in the "doctor and ambulance" time. That's why—not because Reveals the Mysteries or Speaks of Many Truths or Zoosh is trying to patronize you, but rather because we didn't want to say, "This is a matter of life or death. This is something that has to be taken care of right now, at least to begin. And here are the tools to begin, and if you don't, you'll all die a horrible death." We didn't want to say that, because that is not only arm-twisting and manipulative, but it is also terrifying, and in my experience, you do not encourage people to become receptive and learn and want to learn by terrifying them.

This is why, and it may be obvious, but it is important to make it clear. The obvious is not always clear. Everyone has had the experience of overlooking the obvious, but that was because the obvious wasn't clear. Clarity makes a big difference. So that's why we've been doing this and why we haven't been going into a lot of detail about how it was done. Also, another reason needs to be spoken of and cannot be glossed over: If we go into it at length as to how it was done, it's just by way of passing on to others, who don't know how to do these things, how they can do it. We don't want to create a course or a teaching that would present to people, "Here's how you can manipulate, condition and control others." There's enough of that already. We prefer to say, "Here's what you can do for yourself, here's what you can do with others, here's what you can do for others and here are the results you can expect."

So we're in a time of emergency right now—you're willing to say that?

Yes, it has been an emergency. The emergency didn't just start, you understand. Go back to the beginning of the talk about the love-heat. It's been about ten years now, and we in spirit were a little indulgent in the beginning with the Light Technology editorial staff, talking in such great detail about the sinister secret government [see the six *Shining the Light* books], because it was understood that Light Technology was attempting to create a chronology by which people could mentally understand things. This was not to convince them of the value of applying these benevolent methods, but rather to give them an understanding so they could feel mentally reassured that it might have value—not to convince or to twist anyone's arm. So about five or six years' worth of that information was intended to do that for the readers. But you've been in the emergency situation now for about ten years and . . . you understand, Iraq is an extreme example (Iraq meaning the U.S.'s position toward Iraq and the reaction of the global community).

This is like a flag waving, which you cannot avoid in the United States. For many years now there have been terrible wars and infighting and suffering and so on in other countries, but the greater press in the U.S.—not meaning good or bad, but the press that reaches the vast majority of the people—has given these events almost no exposure. Granted, specialized journals and publications have given this a great deal of exposure, but then for only a very small community of readers. This is not to say that these stories have been suppressed, but rather that—and not to be unkind here or to sound cold, but to speak a reality for some people—those stories didn't have "commercial" value, meaning that the stories didn't feel close enough to television and other forms of commercial outlet. So they went largely unreported, but that doesn't mean that they didn't exist. Such things were happening all over, and it didn't take too much effort to find out, but you did have to make an effort. So the emergency has been in effect for some time, but it has been a gradual initiation process. I'm not speaking about all channeling everywhere, but about channeling through *this* channel, because the pertinent point here in this article is that there has been a gradual initiation process for the listener and the reader so that there could be an easing in.

Emergencies here, you understand, are not the same kind of emergency as a car crash. A car crash happens in seconds, minutes. This kind of emergency is something that has a greater duration, but because the emergency went unnoticed to the general public for a while, the messages on a global level got, as you might say, louder. By louder I do not mean that the wars and the bombs made bigger noises, but rather that wars and the difficulties presented themselves closer and closer to home—meaning the Western world, the U.S., Europe and so on—and became impossible to ignore. So the emergency is upon you, and in an emergency, you have to have things you can do—doctors, nurses, police officers, firemen, the military, all that kind of stuff—but you also have to take the long view: "What can we do to change ourselves so that we and our children and our children's children do not continuously have to relive these kinds of ongoing crises?"

DISENTANGLEMENT: A GIFT FROM THE EXPLORER RACE MENTORS

THE
DISENTANGLEMENT
BASIC PROCESS

Ssjoooo

Lie on a flat surface on your back, hands by your side, palms down and slightly away from your body—preferably three hours after eating and before you go to sleep, but it works anywhere, anytime. Remove any metal buckles and take coins or metal keys out of your pockets. Do not cross your legs or feet. This position allows you to get used to being open in your most receptive area.

Say out loud (if possible), *"I am asking gold lightbeings, Earth gold lightbeings, lightbeings who can work through gold lightbeings and lightbeings who can radiate or emanate to gold lightbeings, to disentangle me from my discomforts and their causes."*

Squeeze your eyelids shut and then focus on the light patterns—don't think. If you catch yourself thinking, gently bring your attention back to the light patterns and continue.

Do this for twenty or thirty minutes or for as long as you feel you need to do it or until you fall asleep. This can be done twice a day.

After a few weeks, make a list of every person and event in your life that makes you feel uncomfortable. Say the above statement and add, "I am asking to be disentangled from the discomfort and pain of _____," reading one or two names or events from the list. Do each name for two to three days or until you feel clear with the person.

SPEAKS OF MANY TRUTHS ADDS:

"You may notice that if you say those specific words or names during the course of your day, after you've done disentanglement on them three to five times, that you no longer feel physically as uncomfortable about them as you once did.

"This means the disentanglement is working. The objective is to feel physically calm. Keep saying those specific words or names in your disentanglement process until you feel physically calm. When you do, move on to other words or names, never more than one or two at a time."

See our website for this process in Hungarian, Japanese, Portuguese, Norwegian, German, Italian and French. Learn more at our website: www.sedonajournal.com.

Recall Your Natural Abilities

Now, my belief—which is based, granted, on living it [Reveals the Mysteries lived as a Native American in the 1600s in the western United States], but also on looking at your times and comparing them to our times, as well as looking at future times beyond your times—my belief is that the way a human being is born (a gift from God, yes?), the way you are born, with all the abilities and capacities to produce a benevolent world, is the easiest and most accessible way to bring about benevolent change for yourself and others. All of these exercises—disentanglement, love-heat, benevolent magic, living prayer [see p. xxii]—have been geared toward helping you bring back up to the surface those natural tendencies and abilities you were born with. You don't have to actually learn anything from scratch for which you have no knowledge, awareness or capacity, but you can simply pull it up through recollected body memory. You need to have an intellectual or mental model upon which you can base your recall of your natural abilities, since your society now—like most of your societies now—is highly focused in the mental.

That's why all of the words are used to bring about a sense of permission within the individual that exercises such as the love-heat are intended not only to reveal to you your own capacities but to allow you to benefit from them. They are not exercises that one does for the short duration. Rather, once you have learned how to experience the love-heat and are beginning to learn how to apply it, it is something you do on a daily basis—not to substitute for your religion and not to eliminate your philosophy, but to improve the quality of your life and to reinstall within you the original gifts of God that you were born with as a child.

A Living Prayer to Heal Communication in the Iraqi Conflict

Is there going to be a war with Iraq? What can we do about that?

All I can say is that it's up to you. You may not be able to stop it, but you can do a lot to moderate it. You all know how to do living prayer; you've been instructed. That would be the means by which you would say something to moderate the impact. The way I would suggest you say it, as a baseline, is:

Living Prayer

"I AM ASKING THAT THE PEOPLE INVOLVED IN POSSIBLE IRAQI CONFLICT ALL BE PROTECTED, THAT THEY HAVE THE GIFT OF PROTECTION FROM LOVING BEINGS, AND THAT THEY ALSO COME TO THE CAPACITY TO COMMUNICATE FREELY AND EASILY WITH ONE ANOTHER IN A WAY THAT EVERYONE CAN UNDERSTAND."

That would be an example of a living prayer that would serve value in this situation. But understand what I'm saying: The problem between the U.S. and the UK and Iraq is largely one of communication. Granted, a lot of the communication problem is not with the current administration. The current administration is essentially following up on communication that went awry in a previous administration—and everyone can grasp what that is.

The structure of what you can do is best done through living prayer. I don't encourage you as individuals to use benevolent magic here unless you are in Iraq for any reason—whether you are an Iraqi citizen or are visiting the country, or whether you are a soldier of that country or a soldier of the U.S. or England or anyone else who participates in that combat. In that case, if you know about benevolent magic, feel free to say it. Remember, you must always say it in a form and structure that is about you. I know that the desire to use benevolent magic as an overall way of bettering the situation is seductive, but even as horrible as this Iraq situation appears to be, it is part of a larger picture. Remember what I said before: It is like a flag, catching people's attention.

Factors Contributing to the Situation in Iraq

Are you all in this country going to say like automatons, "Oh boy, we're going to war! Oh boy, we're going to free the people!"? After all, when you have gone to war in the past, you were thinking about what you could do to free the people of Europe so they wouldn't be crushed by a system that was intentionally crushing them. Even when you've gone to war in more limited ways, meaning the U.S. and Vietnam, then again the idea was, "We're going to free the people from a system that's trying control them." Of course, that's up for debate, but the European war, WWII, is perhaps a better example, because there the U.S. and other countries were truly attempting to generate freedom: "We're going to war to save our friends in Europe," if you weren't directly involved, understand? Or, "We're going to war to save our friends wherever."

But here's a situation where you're going to war . . . to do what? You can say it's to save the Iraqi people, who are being ruled by a harsh ruler, and yet although that is true, having this be convincing is problematic. As people have rightly brought up, if that were the only reason, you might use that same rationale to go to war with North Korea, which of course I do not recommend. But you could use that same rationale. I don't want to speak excessively about things that everyone is quite well aware of, but I do want to say what you can do about any situation in Iraq or in any other Middle Eastern country.

Obviously, this is why the Middle Eastern countries are not too thrilled about the U.S.'s approach to Iraq, with a preemptive battle, because certainly it wouldn't be too difficult, from their point of view (sitting on valuable property as they are in the oil countries), to have someone pick a fight with them and say, "Well, we're going to have a preemptive battle here." I'm not saying that that's the U.S. or Western position at all; I'd say it's far from that. But given their situation, you can see where they might be concerned about that. So my feeling is that you ask that the people be protected, and if enough people do this, you may be able to head off some of it. You might even be able to head off most of it, but you'll have to work fast. I feel that this is an old policy being brought to the current time. I'm not trying to suggest that the arguments of the West—referring to the U.S. and England—are not valid. They are valid, and should the West bring about a change in government there, I think they will then be able to speak more freely about what they're concerned about. They won't say everything, but they'll say some things, and many people will be stunned.

The governments of the U.S. and the UK might feel freer if they could bring about a change in government in some way. The West then might say, "Okay, this is why we did this and why we felt it was urgent and couldn't wait." They've already hinted at a few things, but they haven't laid all their cards on the table. Granted, it's partly about oil. But from my point of view, I have to give the West some credit. It's *partly* about oil. One might say it's all about oil, but one cannot really say that genuinely, because there are other factors.

Why can't these other factors be discussed?

Because if you speak of these matters, speak about weapons systems, again we are terrifying the people, and we don't want to be part of the problem—"we" meaning spirit. We don't want to be part of the problem. If we say that the Iraqis have this and this and this weapon, and more to the point, that they have this or this alliance, and even more to the point, that they have this or that distribution system, then we are becoming part of the problem.

It would be much better to have a benign change in government, have the Iraqi people have some kind of government that is inclusive of all the more ancient tribal systems there. I do not think the people will lunge toward democracy immediately, but they might find some kind of a system of states. You have the United States of America, with each state initially having its own particular picture of itself, its own wants and desires culturally and so on. You could perhaps have a United States of Iraq, meaning each tribal area and so on might have its own specific area, its own specific government. That, I think, might be done successfully there, but it would take time and the people would have to be shown that it could work for them. Of course, it would be a long-range commitment, during which some Western governments—the U.S., the UK, France and others—may have to come in and show the value of such a system.

I say France, and I've included France and Zoosh and others have spoken about France a lot in the past, because France has a long history of diplomatic applications. Let's just say that the French have the capacity to talk behind the scenes very effectively and educate others on how to do this. Others may not always like the education, but the knowledge can be useful. The more successful diplomats in the U.S. and in the Western world in general have studied this, and I bring it to the general attention of people here because I would recommend that you do it too if you can. You have the time to study it. You might find out ways to resolve your own problems in your family as well as in your business. It might take a little research, so you'll have to decide if you want to do it.

The U.S. Hides an Embarrassment

If the U.S. has this evidence you mentioned, then why haven't they told the other countries of the world about it?

Because of a simple embarrassment. The U.S. is a generous country—I think that's widely known and understood—but that generosity goes beyond food and clothing and money and medical support at almost the drop of a hat for anyone who is in crisis and needs it. This is a very wonderful aspect of your people, but as I say, it goes beyond that. You get support if you're a friend of the U.S., especially if you border a country that the U.S. is having a conflict with and even if you're a temporary friend the U.S. had in the past. Of course, the U.S. is not alone as a country doing this, but we're talking about the U.S., so we'll be specific. In the past, you have shared not only money, medical supplies, food, military technology and all of this with your allies, but you've also given out certain tools and techniques. The U.S. has even shared, for the purposes of defense, certain techniques that could be used to combat other weapons. For instance, if there was a fear that your mutual enemy of that moment was going to apply some kind of chemical or biological warfare to (in this case) a neighboring country that is an ally to the U.S., and if that fear was proven to be a real fear, then the U.S. might realistically give its ally at least the means to research, or if the emergency was urgent—meaning an attack might come at any moment—you might actually give them the materials to combat such chemical and biological warfare.

So we gave that to Saddam?

The U.S. has done that with Saddam and others, and by Saddam I mean Iraq. It's important to understand that this is different here. The U.S. has not been stingy when it comes to sharing, especially with long-term allies, and of course, the allies themselves may very well have shared similar things with the United States. This is typical amongst allies for mutual defense, yes? The difference with Saddam is that, generally speaking, such things are known, understood and honored to be not spoken of in public. This means that if the U.S. has an agreement with France or England or any of the other countries the U.S. has agreements with (of which there are many), certain things are going to be kept discreet, unspoken, for various reasons—and a lot of them are very good reasons.

But the situation with Saddam is that once upon a time, Saddam was an ally or (at least as the U.S. or any country might put it) a temporary ally—an ally out of necessity . . . and not necessarily someone you loved, but someone who was willing to be enough of an ally so that you could have some advantages you wouldn't have had otherwise. The difference with Saddam, as compared to others, is that he has made it abundantly clear to the U.S. that he will not only speak of these secret matters, but he has the means and the willingness to put out this information in a way that would be hideously embarrassing to the United States. Now, by that I don't simply mean that the U.S. is going to war because some people might feel silly, but rather that Saddam has stated or made it clear that he would not only put out this information, but he would basically release formulas so that any youngster with a chemistry set could manufacture chemical and biological weapons with that chemistry set and basic household products.

I grant that there are some extreme places where such information is available, but this would be different. This would be put out in such a way that people couldn't avoid it. It is almost like saying . . . well, imagine this: It would be like a person saying, "If you're going to hurt me, then I'm going to hurt everyone."

Keeping Saddam from Creating a Mess

So you have to understand that the U.S. would like to see the world of oil become stabilized, with oil as a dependable product rather than one that is used for blackmail, which I think you understand quite well. I think anyone in international business, to say nothing of conscious citizens, knows that. Granted, that's true. But the deeper picture, of which I'm revealing a teeny bit here, is that the U.S. is attempting to keep an individual from creating a terrible mess. Saddam really could—how can we say?—become the sinister secret government's poster child. Not to be unkind, but if you had someone who was going to say or do such things . . . to a degree, this can be prevented by good security, and you've all seen this security get intensified. Some things would just make trouble for years and years and years, and we come back to, "If you're going to hurt me, I'm going to hurt you back"—*you* meaning the world. This is a man who has had no problem using chemical and biological warfare on his own people. It's true; it's not a made-up story. Women, children, men, noncombatants—no problem! I grant that accidents have happened in the Western world that way, but they weren't done on purpose. There's a big difference.

But there's still a possibility . . . there are behind-the-scenes efforts toward this, a larger picture that could halt this war. But it can only happen if he and his immediate family—meaning the ruling family—would move on. It wouldn't be enough for him to move on; it would have to be his general ruling family who would have to move on. There would have to be radical changes in the government of the country. It couldn't just be a powder keg waiting to blow; it couldn't just be Saddam leaving and passing everything on to the next Saddam. It can't be like that—that's not sufficient.

So it will require living prayer, and the more people do it, the more it will help. There are people within Iraq who are doing what they can to help, too. It's one thing to do what you can to help in a free (or reasonably free) country—"reasonably free" meaning that there are some restrictions to your freedom, but you are relatively free. It's something else entirely to do things in a country that is totally authoritarian, where any real expression is not allowed. So it has to be done quietly, and obviously, I'm not going to give it away. People's lives are at stake.

Self-Destructiveness Is Not Natural

Have those in the sinister secret government achieved their objective or do they feel they've achieved their objective?

I'm saying that they *feel* they have achieved their objective. They have accomplished what they set out to do. What they set out to do, their basic goal, was to derail your natural process, as human beings, of learning what you came here to do using the natural abilities you were born with: to take in the best of what you learn and move on in life toward the future to create a benevolent world and be a benevolent influence for the planets nearby that you will explore. From their point of view, they wanted to derail this process or at least delay it as long as possible, and they feel they have accomplished their purpose by instilling self-destructiveness within you. Those of you who've read the literature from UFO contactees and the extraterrestrials, reports of them and so on, might notice that these beings universally observe how self-destructive Earth people are and ask, "Is this natural?" And I am saying, no, it is not natural.

Granted, in my times, there were risks. You couldn't take an aspirin, okay? So if you got an infection, that might be it. A lot of people died from a toothache because it became an infection. Life, therefore, didn't go on that long, but there were certain qualities associated with it that have been lost in your time. So I'm not saying that aspirin is a bad thing, you understand? It's a good thing. What I'm saying is that it's not a good thing to throw out the old ways just because those old ways we lived with in my time didn't have your modern conveniences and wonders. In short, the means by which you've achieved these wonders—aspirin and other things, technology that benefits people—are that you've excelled in expanding your mental capabilities. But in the process, you've let go of things that you need now more than ever, which is why we've been talking about feelings, how you can apply them to your benefit and how you can ultimately change your world and the world around you.

So even though we as the Explorer Race were polarized before we came to this planet . . .

You had experiences of being polarized before you came to this planet, but when you're born as a child on this planet, you don't arrive polarized—even though you might say that the Explorer Race has had lives on other planets where you were polarized or suffered or were working through things that you accomplished before you got here. You can read the *Explorer Race* books to see that. Still, when you're born here, you're born with all the abilities I've mentioned as God's gifts that one sees in a child. But you are all that child. When you grow up, you do not abandon the child, you do not kill off the child, nor do I recommend this. Rather, you become bigger physically and you develop certain capacities that you didn't have as a child. But the idea is not to throw away those natural abilities and gifts you were born with; the idea is to build *on* them, not *over* them. One does not see the foundation of a building, and yet without that foundation, the building doesn't last long. It doesn't take too much effort to find the foundation of a building, meaning it isn't built over to the point where you can't see it. You can find it if you're looking for it. Build on it, don't build over it and hide it so you don't know what's holding up the building. That's why I'm correcting what you said for the sake of the reader. The reader doesn't understand why you said it that way.

Conditioned Self-Destructiveness

Let's look at the sinister secret government again. I can't imagine they're just stepping back, saying, "Ah, well done," and riding off into the sunset.

They feel they've accomplished their goal, but they will remain vigilant. If people start to show that they are less self-destructive, they will keep it coming—all those things that they have influenced or supported—to bring about self-destructiveness. Think about it. If people talk about going to war in Iraq and you hear maybe a comedian on a television show making jokes about Saddam and the audience is laughing and cheering about going to war in Iraq . . . these people for the most part probably have not been to war. Yet it is influential because the vast television audience thinks, even for a moment, that these people all think going to war is great. As a wiser adult, you might know that a lot of it isn't so wonderful. But as a youngster already sufficiently conditioned and trying to fit in, you might think, "All the voices that are cheering sound like my people, and right down in the front rows are young people like me!" or even more to the point, "They look the way I want to look; they're beautiful and I want to be them." A youngster doesn't think like that, in those words, but that's the motivating factor. Comedians are their own beings, but they themselves might have certain conditioned, self-destructive tendencies—plus, they know the jokes will appeal in certain ways and they want a good response. I'm using something from television because television is so influential. Look to television, movies and the media in general, to say nothing of the way people interact with one another.

You can talk to me about self-destructiveness and I would not say that I don't understand it. I understand it completely, and I even understand people's desire for ending their lives at times, especially when one is old and has problems or a disease or something like that. I understand. I'm not saying I don't. What I am saying is that conditioned self-destructiveness reveals itself, for example, in taking a risk repeatedly, over and over, for the sake of taking the risk. When you do that, that's self-destructive.

But you need to expand the definition—it's also being destructive to others.

Self-destructive means being destructive to self or others. Thank you for bringing that to the reader's attention. Self-destructive means hurting yourself or hurting someone else. And to make that point clear, this means intentionally or unintentionally hurting yourself or intentionally and, to a degree, unintentionally hurting others. I'm not trying to make you all feel guilty; rather, I'm trying to bring it to your attention so that although you have to live your lives, at times you can pull back and ask, "Is that self-destructive?" I'm counting on the psychologists to help out here. Psychologists and therapists have been taught a lot of this stuff, and you can reach out to them. You can say to your therapist, "Is this self-destructive?" But you can also look at your own life and ask, "Does this harm me?"

For example, when you are reading something or watching something on television—people watch television a lot—how do you feel physically? Are you feeling stressed? Are you feeling uncomfortable? Are you feeling really good? Does it make you feel good? Well, maybe you'd better watch more of that; if you have good physical feelings in your body—warmth, laughter or amusement—maybe it's good. But if you're feeling stressed, nervous or anxious, then you probably don't need this.

You Are Addicted to Stimulation

It sounds very simplistic, but it is foundational, and things that are foundational often sound simplistic. It has to be simplistic, or it wouldn't be understood by everyone. I'm not speaking to you because I think you cannot grasp complicated concepts, but rather because I want you to avoid overlooking the foundation. Build *on* the foundation but not *over* it—seeing the foundation, seeing the basics. Remember the basics: "Am I being self-destructive? What will it take to change that?" Turn off the TV and relax for a while, then ask, "How do I physically feel now?" or something like that. Don't turn off the TV and pick up a book—just do nothing.

Turn off the TV and do nothing if you can for a while, and notice how you feel. If you turn off the TV and pick up a book, you'll still be stimulating yourself. Your societies today are in a constant state of stimulation, because people have more time, granted, and because the sinister secret government has supported stimulating you to the point where you become dependent on stimulation. When you're dependent on stimulation—and this is very important to understand—*any stimulation will do to satisfy that craving!* It is vital to understand that. It can be *any* stimulation, not just the stimulation of the fragrance of a flower, which makes you feel wonderful. It's not just the stimulation of enjoying watching your children do something that makes you smile or laugh. It's not just the stimulation of petting your cat or dog or doing a job well. Any stimulation—drugs, violence (even at a distance), television, movies—will satiate that desire, so think about it. That's another one.

Remember, I said in my opening statement that self-destructiveness is one of the things they've managed to condition in you, but they've also conditioned you to be dependent on stimulation. So when you turn off the TV, don't immediately pick up a book or a magazine. You won't be able to tell how you feel. Turn off the TV and do nothing, and see how you feel.

They've really amped up the magnitude of the stimulation in movies and television and violent video games.

Please make sure that the comment you just made gets in, because I need to bring that to the point—amped up.

In another context, you said about the conditioning to repress those natural parts of yourself, that the conditioning itself and all of its attendant stimulations, actions and reactions need to be recognized. So the stimulation causes us to take certain actions that possibly we wouldn't otherwise?

Look at the key to understanding your life (and most people will be shocked to realize this, literally shocked): In the westernized worlds—and it may be different for other people elsewhere—most of you are addicted to stimulation. Think of how often you've turned off the television and immediately picked up a book or a magazine. That is because your societies stress the value of the mind and what's underneath that. If you're not using your mind, then what are you doing? You're either doing nothing, accomplishing nothing, or are inactive. If you're not using your mind and you're inactive, what is that? Is that perhaps the "devil's playground"? Think of all the sayings you have about that. In short, it's suggested that if you're not using your mind, not doing something constructive, not doing worthy work, not even doing your job, not doing this or that, then you have to be *doing* something, and it does feel like you're doing something when you're watching TV or being stimulated in some way, even sitting around drinking coffee. So there are chemical stimulations that people recognize, and then often you use chemical depressants when you get overstimulated. Of course, then there is also TV.

TV was originally intended to be relaxing and informative, and the original TV shows in the U.S. were funny or news-oriented. Some had a greater depth of story and the visual pictures to support that, but they weren't, as you said recently, about being amped up.

They were benign.

Yes, they were largely benign, and to be perfectly honest, the comedy was silly. But it was intended to be silly and relaxing so you could sit in front of the TV and laugh about something that was just silly, not very important. Granted, you could analyze it and say, "This was important and that was important." I'm not disputing that, but this was the original program—or menu as you might say—on television. But it has changed. Now television has to fulfill your craving for stimulation, and that's why the programs have become increasingly extreme.

It's as if you were overly addicted to something that was readily available, like alcohol. People start drinking a little bit, then they drink more and more to get the same feeling. It's like that with some extreme television programming now. Even though you can find more benign television programs to watch, you still go to the extreme explosively violent ones . . . well, you know about that—the movies, all of that. I'm not indicting television. But there's a lot of extreme programming, and the reason they're putting it out is not because they're evil and the enemy. These are the shows the sponsors pay to have their advertisements on so that the audience will watch and buy their goods, because that audience was born and raised with and now craves the intensity of being stimulated every moment. Why do you think people have such a hard time sleeping?

The next step, then, is that if this war happens, that's the ultimate reality show—watching people being killed in real time. What can they do after that? Where can that go?

I don't think it takes too much imagination to guess what could follow. I don't want to give any ideas to programmers, but it might be some kind of program where people are killed or nearly killed. You watch car races and people get killed, and yet the car races still happen—not that there hasn't been a great deal of improvement in race cars to protect the drivers, and I honor that. I'd like to see that applied to the cars that people can buy. Obviously, if a race car driver can crash and roll, hit poles and whatnot and all of this business, and get out of the car and walk away, that's fabulous. One wonders why that isn't applied in regular vehicles. So I'm not indicting anyone; I'm just saying that I'm agreeing with you that if more is selling and making money . . .

. . . then mega-more . . .

That's right. You're going to have to keep doing more and more—more extreme—and that's full circle. Before you know it, you have the Roman coliseum.

The Goal: Regain Your Spirituality While You're on Earth Physically

The future of the planet is resting with those people who can work on this spiritually?

Yes, and all the other things we've been talking about. Remember, the main goal of those in the sinister secret government is that they want to influence you, yes? But, of course, they also want to continue to perpetuate the current form of life, whereas we—if I might include you as a human being and myself as a spirit in one statement—want all the world to grab on to the future benevolent timeline, as we've called it (which is the way of life of the future), and bring that into the present . . . rather than merely being on this timeline, which is connected to a negative past. We call it a timeline so we don't have to give a fifty-word description.

So that's the issue. The sinister secret government will do everything in its power to maintain power and control, to keep you on your present timeline, period—and of course, they are limited, and they know it by the process. This is what they are trying to do, and they have been successful at it, which is unfortunate—although you can tell by my example that they're ultimately going to lose. It's as if they are on a river in a boat, yes? They have been paddling for some time and are approaching a waterfall. It doesn't have to be Niagara Falls, but you know how it is on a river that goes over a falls—the pull of the water as it gets toward the waterfall gets stronger. They've added a motor to that boat, so now they've got a powerboat, and pretty soon it'll be a speedboat and they'll be doing more and more. Remember when you used that term, that things are so "amped up" now? It's like it's a speedboat. They're producing tremendous effort to influence people to support what they want—that is, to say what the government wants.

That's why things are amped up—because even though they're doing this inexorably, people are moving toward that more spiritual way of being. Our whole point, what we want to do (tipping my hand here for a moment), is that we want Earth people, the Explorer Race—as you are human beings on Earth now alive, physical—to achieve that spiritual place *while you are on Earth physically*. The sinister secret government can do nothing to prevent you from regaining your spirituality as you naturally die and go on. You are spiritual, that's it—they can't do anything. They can't influence that at all.

At the same time, when we humans leave through dying, we can no longer directly influence events on the Earth.

Wait, let me finish. Their point is, they're not even trying to do anything about that. They know they have no chance, but we would prefer (tipping my hand here a bit, showing you my whole card for a moment), if you possibly can—and we're supporting you since that is your objective in your hearts and souls—that you achieve it *while you are physically alive on Earth* rather than as a result of destroying the Earth and everyone dying. There's a big difference!

It can be achieved in two ways, then. It can be achieved by everybody dying, and when everybody dies, of course, you naturally become spiritual beings, yes? In that process, you become your spiritual self again. If everybody dies, then everybody becomes his or her spiritual self again, but that is not why you came here. You came here to do it *while you're alive physically*. So those in the sinister secret government are willing to say, "Well, if you all die . . . okay, we can't stop that, just as long as we stay in control and have the power until that moment." Their whole point is, "Well, we don't think you're all going to die at once, even though we don't care." From their point of view, they literally don't care. If many, many of you die at once, they don't care—as long as they're in charge and have the power (and by "in charge," I don't mean over every aspect of your life, but behind the scenes).

So *their* whole point is, they want to control you. *My* whole point is for you to change by becoming what you naturally are while you are still in your physical body—that will require the least effort on your part. That's why all the exercises and homework have been given toward that end—because the least effort is not only what you might have time for or what you might be willing to do but also what is natural for you. So I tipped my whole card there a bit. We want to support you to achieve the goal of your heart and your spirit, which is to achieve these wonderful things while you are alive. Then you can pass it on to the next generation and support their conditioning in a natural, benevolent way. That's how the Earth comes to be benevolent once again in the future, and that's why you're here—to do that.

How do you see the percentages? What are the chances of us doing it now if we're in the middle of an emergency?

It's always just as good as it ever was. I'm not going to give a percentage, because do you know what happens when I give a percentage? People say, "Well, there are enough people doing this, so I don't have to." But I'll say this: Your chances of accomplishing it are better than ever if you participate.

Let the Love-Heat Guide Your Actions

I don't exactly feel at ease with all of this. Let me try to get a little clarity myself. We've been in an emergency situation for ten years—that would be since 1992 or 1993—but this is the first moment you have spoken in this manner.

I want to honor the flag that's being waved. You understand why I'm calling it a flag—because the general public knows that not only is the U.S. getting ready to engage in something that is problematic, but the rest of the world doesn't approve. While the U.S. is normally perceived by the rest of the world as being something special, it is now being perceived by the rest of the world as being horribly out of step. As such, the flag that's being waved is like a red flag, so the general public, regardless of those who might say "rah-rah," can see that the rest of the world does not approve of this. That is important, because it forces you to take a look at the situation whether you want to or not. In the process, you understand, there are other threats here. Think about it. People have been growing mistrustful of institutions that they've felt very good about in the past. People used to feel pretty good about the government; people used to feel pretty good about what they read in the paper. Do you understand? You could name five more things that people used to feel pretty good about . . . they used to feel pretty good about their church. You could name many more, but people's capacity to count on others is being removed.

What does that suggest? It doesn't mean that others are unreliable. It means that what's being underscored is that you need to be able to do something as an individual, on your own. That's why the bulk of the homework that we—speaking for beings channeled through Robert [Shapiro] here in general—have been giving has been structured toward what you can do on your own. Granted, people are saying, "What can we do together?" But you can't really accomplish anything long lasting together until you can do something on your own that has physical feelings in your own body, feelings you can use to recognize whether what you're doing as an individual—to say nothing of what you're doing as a group—is worthy and worth doing. You can't just go to the experts.

You've all been faced with this. You've had disappointments with the experts. Granted, much of the time you felt good about them, but you can't just fall back on the old ways, or at least the ways of the past sixty or seventy years. You have to be able to go within yourself, to know and recognize certain physical feelings as being benevolent for you. When you go to do benevolent work with a group, if what the group is doing doesn't feel good to you, it doesn't mean that the group is bad; it just means that that's not the group for you to be working with. In short, this home-work we've been giving you has been to accentuate the basics so that you don't rush to do something because it seems like a good thing or because your good friend tells you it's a good thing, but rather because you feel it and have the physi-cal evidence within yourself to prove it's a good thing. Not only is it a good thing, but it's compatible with you. Therefore, what you put into the group, since it's compatible with you and you have that good physical feeling, will be compatible with everybody else. That's the key.

If you go into any group, any group accomplishing anything (whether it's for a benevolent purpose or even something that has some benevolent purposes with it), say a business, and you don't feel good about it, if you're not all ener-gized the same way, the business will become more difficult. But let's say it's a benevolent group attempting to do something spiritual; these groups often fall apart. That's because there are those in the group who are not bad people but are intended to be in other groups doing other things that feel good to them, things for which they have warmth in their bodies.

So don't go to a group just because your friend tells you it's good. If you go or even if you think about it, write down that the group is called this or that. Write it down in front of you, or think or say the name. If you get that warmth in your body, then that's a good group for you to go to. It will be good for you. If you go there and you feel good, if you get that warmth, then that's a good place for you to be, and you can contribute.

The Reputation of the United States Will Be Permanently Altered

My concern is that this is going to set off an escalating situation if the U.S. goes against the world and attacks Iraq, and then we'll have to deal with the religious groups who feel we are attacking them. Is there an actual danger of a third world war here?

No, I do not feel that, partly because the U.S. is a conglomerate of peoples. If the U.S. were made up of one general racial group or even one general religious group, that could be catastrophic, but even though the U.S. has certain religions that are specifically the majority, there are still other religions. There are lots of people in the U.S. who are of other religions, and certainly it's a racially, cultur-ally and nationally mixed bag. So, no, I do not feel that is likely.

What I feel, on the other hand, is this: The reputation of the U.S. will be per-manently altered. To tell you the truth, I think it's a good thing for the United States. The U.S. has been pedaling harder and harder every year to try to keep up its reputation—speaking generally of it as a country—while at the same time try-ing to accomplish all your other goals of success and wealth and health and happi-ness and so forth. Those goals and the means by which you achieve them are not always compatible, so the U.S. is really not in a position to be a world leader, nor do I think the U.S. makes a good world leader.

If you want to be a good example, then be a good example by displaying your good qualities. Just be open. People from the U.S. are known to be open and to display their qualities. Whether they are perceived by other cultures to be good or otherwise is another issue, but the point here is that I feel that because the U.S. as a country has actually had world renown thrust upon it—largely as a result of WWII and its outcome—you have felt that it is your "job" to be a world leader, but I don't agree. You're still a young country in your culture. You're still growing and expanding, still learning and maturing. I think that youngsters can take over families if they have to, but they're not usually wise enough to do everything. They just do the best they can. It's usually the eldest child who does that in an emergency—the other youngsters turn out as best they can without their parents, just having the sibling. That happens. I think that's the situation you've got here.

I don't think the U.S. is bad; I'm not saying that. What I am saying is that to be thrust into a position or *feel* you're thrust into a position to be a world leader is not a good idea. I'm not saying you're not motivated toward sustaining that world leadership or doing more in that way, but it's strictly sustenance. Your country has been acting in a way that would suggest that if other countries don't emulate you in every way, there's something wrong with them. Now think back to what you know about colonization, attitudes one country has against another, seeing a country or a whole group of people as barbarians simply because you don't understand their culture or its value. Think of the countless examples you have in your own global history.

Not being like other countries and peoples, right now you are going through what amounts to "growing pains." You've been going through growing pains since the 1960s, but the growing pains are getting louder and more noticeable. Other countries have finally come around to recognizing and discussing among themselves that the U.S. really isn't the best example for them to emulate. Granted, the U.S. is a good example in many ways, but not in *all* ways. So I think it's best for the U.S. to have its growing pains in a slightly less influential way globally. That's why you're seeing that on news broadcasts on a daily basis, to say nothing of the world's economic and business reaction.

You Can't Blame the SSG for Everything— You Have to Take Action

How do we tie that in with the sinister secret government? Is the U.S. being used by the sinister secret government?

No more than the sinister secret government's desire to influence and control everything as long as they can maintain the power. Once upon a time, the U.S. government was wholly trusted as individuals. But because the U.S. system of economics has so embraced the *economics* over feelings and individuals, now the government has become, not vast groups, but businesses—which is not unusual. Other countries have gone through this, and now it's your turn. It's not a system you're required to go through, but because you don't have your natural abilities (although they're there, we're bringing them up with these exercises), because they're conditioned out of you, there's a tendency to reach out for this or that to temporarily satiate yourselves. We're getting into broad topics here that we can't cover all at once. The simple fact is that you can't just say, "Well, things aren't going right for us; it's all that sinister secret government's fault." We can't say that, because then we're just blaming, and it's not far from that to, "Poor us; what are we going to do about it?"

I want to support you taking your own power in ways that are benevolent to you and to others, so let's not get too caught up in, "They did it. Let's get them," because obviously you can't. And that's where the sinister secret government is of value. Isn't that an interesting thing to say? If you knew who they were, you could "get 'em." As people have said, "They're the enemy; let's get 'em"—meaning that once you've gotten them, everything's going to be fine. You can look at history to see that that doesn't work. They're behind the scenes, and you can never quite see them. So then you have to focus your energy on what you can do and what you can't do. No matter what is going on in your life, no matter where you are—even in prison—you can work on yourself.

We have to look in ourselves to change in ourselves what we want to change—we can't change them?

But more to the point, let's get clear; I feel you're not quite making yourself clear here. What you can do is to notice, yes, what isn't working. That's good. But what you can do to change it is more important; put attention and energy toward what you can do to change it. Changing your mind isn't enough. You still have to take action. You can be building a house and tapping nails in with a wrench. You can change your mind and say, "I need a hammer to do this!" and you can think about that all you want, but without actually going out and getting that hammer and putting it into effect, you haven't applied what you need to do. So that's why we've been giving you homework, encouraging you to do it on a regular basis, so that you're not just changing your mind but are changing your life through the application of something that is so much more benevolent for you that you do that instead of what you used to do.

Is any of this information being given through channels in other languages, in other countries?

Here and there, some, but usually not with the whole cohesive string we've attempted to give . . . bits and pieces only. And of course, it is somewhat up to you to see that it gets out there to other countries in their languages, but I can't guarantee that their cultures will embrace it. It's not always easy to translate things, to get the idiom correct. The only way you can actually hope to achieve that is to be in communication with people in other countries who have read the material, know it and understand it. They have to be multilingual, then take the material and translate it into their language, using idioms and terms of their time in order to get the best possible translation—not just a computer translation, you understand? So you can't necessarily do that all the time, but you can do it in bits and pieces. You'll get volunteers; some will come and some will go.

Now Is a Pivotal Time

Is this a moment in our history that is a pivotal point, where we have to do something or the Explorer Race isn't going to make it? Or is it just that you're using this to try to get people to take steps toward feeling and changing how they relate?

I see a pivotal point as being in the moment, immediate. What would I call it if we could expand the definition of a pivotal point as having started about ten to twelve years ago and we're still in it? Yes. Yes, it is that.

But expanding how far?

That's up to you. If you do nothing, if nothing gets accomplished, it will just get worse and worse, and the pivot will extend. If all of you do a lot, it will expand only so far. It is up to you. You've heard that how many times? Thousands? You've heard it through other channels as well. When they say it is up to you—speaking for myself and all the others who have said that it is up to you—it means that it's up to you to take action and bring about change. They don't say that part, but that's what they mean when they say that it's up to you, the readers and all humans.

I hadn't considered that it was possible not to get on the new timeline or not to connect to the benevolent future.

It is possible for it to be delayed, and the sinister secret government's whole point is that the longer it can be delayed, the longer the SSG is in power. That's the whole point, you understand. If you were them, you'd say "Hey, let's delay it forever." Of course, it won't be forever, but people in your time tend to speak in that kind of lingo. It can't be delayed forever, but it can be complicated. Even if the sinister secret government was simply to say, "Okay, that's enough. We're moving now. We're going to go to another planet. We're not going to do any more," just what they've done so far, the complications would last and last if people didn't do something.

So I'm saying that it's not enough just to wait. That's not enough. You have to take action, and that action happens within you to begin with so that you know what actions are best for you to take at any time. You can't know or even have the benevolent influence with others until you know what benevolent is. And benevolent is not Webster's definition of benevolent . . . well, yes, it is that, but more to the point, it is the way you physically feel—physical evidence, warmth. "This feels good to me. There's physical warmth. I can feel it. This is good for me in this moment," say you, doing that.

Waking Up to Spirituality Is a Process

So why only in the past five years of the several million years of the Explorer Race are you focusing on this information? Wasn't it possible to talk about this before?

You have to be ready. Recall, years ago, when beings were talking about the next wave, the big wave coming that's going to wake people up. How do you wake people up? They don't just get woken up to spirituality overnight, where you click a switch and "bup, bup," they're all awake now. You know that.

It doesn't work like that. They wake up gradually, and one of the ways they wake up is that things get their attention and the means to resolution they've used or depended on in the past doesn't seem to work. Iraq is quite a sterling example of that, because your country had a battle with Iraq some years ago and what happened? Not resolution. One might pause to consider what happens if the U.S. goes into Iraq and there isn't the overnight success. What about the overnight success that didn't happen in Vietnam? I'm not trying to say what would happen. I'm just trying to say that it's important to take note of things. I'm not trying to bring it to your attention so much—the *world* is bringing that to the attention of the citizens of the United States. To be perfectly honest, I'm quite certain that a significant percentage of people in the U.S. alone, to say nothing of the world, do not back this battle with Iraq. Granted, if the government could reveal all it knows, I think that backing would become a majority for sure, but it's not able to do that at this time.

Nevertheless, that's not my point. The process by which people wake up is that things happen and the way you've always resolved them doesn't work anymore, so you have to look in new places. You can look in increasingly complicated places, and people have been trying to do that. The problem with complicated things is that they tend to get more complicated, not less so. So the homework—that which you do for which there is physical evidence, something you can look at and say, "This really improves my life"—has to be simple. It can't be complicated, and that's why it is simple.

I think you've done a masterful job in presenting this. It's certainly a very big and immediate subject.

Wouldn't you say that sometimes it's valuable to understand more and be able to present it in an understandable way to people so they can see and think about it, imagine and correlate—that's the key, correlate—all these things they know about for themselves? You are, after all, thinking individuals, and you have the full capacity to correlate many things not spoken of in this article. You can correlate them to this article and use it to correlate to other things. I have faith in you that you can do so and are also likely to do so.

What I'm saying is that the U.S. is a wonderful country filled with wonderful people, just like every place else. Granted, sometimes you're not so wonderful, but everyone is like that. I feel strongly that it is too soon in your culture to be a world leader, and more importantly, I don't think anyone's culture should be a world leader now! I feel it's much better for cultures and nations to come together and come to a consensus of how things will be done. That's why the UN is the hope of the world, plus there are business organizations that are trying to do something similar. That is why you are seeing (Zoosh said so some years ago, yes?) that the First World Order would be based on multinational corporate business—the corporate model.

And it's absolutely working. It has things about it that are not good, but by and large it's working. It doesn't make any difference if your shipping country is in Norway or Africa or Europe or Russia or China. There's somewhat of a universal language amongst people who ship products, as an example, and there are other businesses that are all working, no matter what language or in what country. So while this may not be the model to run your world, it is a good beginning. It shows you that people working together for a common good, regardless of their culture or nationality, can achieve their purpose by working together. So that's the world leader I think is best. And it's the same thing with the United Nations.

I know the current situation is upsetting, but it's part of a larger situation. I won't go so far as to say it's part of the plan, but it supports the plan—"the plan" meaning how you get to where you're going on the basis of your heart and soul desires. The plan is not words cut in stone, but it's a general description. That general description is the way you have to refer to the plan, because the plan is flexible.

Thank you.

Good life.

✛   ✛   ✛

Living Prayer to Help World Peace

Reveals the Mysteries
March 18, 2003

Dear Friends of Light Technology Publications and the Sedona Journal of Emergence!: *We feel that many of you, like ourselves, have strong needs to DO SOMETHING about our present world situation and feel frustration about what we can do to influence the world. Recently, Reveals the Mysteries, knowing of humanity's needs and frustrations, speaking through Robert Shapiro, came through with a living prayer for each of us to say.*

We were told that all of us could create a beneficial result if just 10 percent of us would actually say the words of one of these living prayers with feeling. Perhaps you could share this with your friends.

Here is a living prayer for the world situation now:

Living Prayer

"I am asking that the souls, with our infinite wisdom throughout all times and many places, of the Explorer Race in our now guise as Earth human beings, pull together our full knowledge and wisdom of what has gone on in the past for us—our trail of education to this place and this point in time.

"I'm going to ask us now to come together as if as a single being to resolve conflicts, difficulties, worries and cares of the human demonstration of life and to recognize the value of each and every human in the world in which we live.

"I know we can do it, and I believe in our capacity and desire to bring it about while supporting each other and creating the world we know we want to live in. I am asking that this be so now."

You can say this once or several times. This is especially for those who have read the *Explorer Race* books, but it can be said by anyone. Some of the language referring to the Explorer Race won't mean much to those of you who haven't read the books or the articles in the *Sedona Journal*, but it is not necessary to have read the books in order to say this prayer to bring about the most beneficial results that living prayer can do.

Sometimes it is difficult to know what to do and how to do it in the most supportive way for each other. That's the key. To bring about resolution for yourselves now, you can do a great deal for yourselves individually using living prayer and benevolent magic. But to do something that affects the global population, human beings, plants, animals, everyone, you need to work together, and this is a living prayer to help you to unite in a moment and also to support, encourage and nurture that unity by simply desiring that it be so.

The purpose of the living prayer, then, is to request—never demand—that this come about in the most benevolent way for all beings, and specifically to the point, for those beings who are in the guise now of human beings, your selves on Earth, the Explorer Race, which includes all humans. And as a result, I believe that this will help you not only to come together in a unified way but also will remind you gently, very gently, that your guise as human beings on Earth is only a guise. You are more than that.

You have many faces throughout the universe, many before you got here and you will have many more after you leave here. It is a gentle reminder, then, that you are of many cultural strains and of many cultural hearts, and yet you are ultimately one being. And this moment in time is to show a practical application of what you can do, no matter what guise you may be demonstrating yourself as at any moment.

For those who want something shorter and simpler, I offer the living peace prayer:

Living Prayer

"I am asking that the hearts of all beings come to love peace, cherish it and involve themselves in its creation."

"You say the living prayer because it is a creation 'device.' The prayer itself is not an 'Oh, please help me' prayer. It is a creation. Living prayer is a creation. 'I am asking' is a creation."

—Zoosh

Part 2:

The Explorer Race (Human Race)
Awakens to Its Creator-Apprentice Status
and Becomes Aware That Each Human Has
the Ability to Call on All Creation for Help
in Achieving Benevolent Solutions to What
Were Thought to Be Impossible and
Unsolvable Human and Earth Situations

Officials Ignorant of Fifty-Year Files

Edgar Mitchell, PhD

January 22, 1998

On January 31, 1971, Navy Captain Edgar Mitchell, with Adm. Alan Shepard and Col. Stuart Roosa in Apollo 14, embarked on a journey of over five hundred thousand miles in outer space that resulted in his becoming the sixth man to walk on the Moon. This historic journey ended safely nine days later on February 9, 1971. After retiring from the Navy in 1972, Mitchell founded the Institute of Noetic Sciences to sponsor research into the nature of consciousness as it relates to cosmology and causality.

The Prophets Conference was presented last October in Phoenix. The following is an excerpt of Mitchell's response to remarks presented by Steven Greer about technology and efforts to brief government officials on the UFO phenomena.

I'd like to add that in our [April] briefing of the Joint Chiefs of Staff Intelligence Group, it became very clear to us that they were naive. They did not really know any more about this effort than we do, if as much. That is because, as Bob Dean pointed out earlier, most of the people [now] in government were not in government when I retired twenty-five years ago. They are younger people. The files going back fifty years just no longer exist. They've either been purged, compromised or whatever. They don't exist. So when we blame government for not being forthright, they really don't have anything to be forthright about, at least at that level.

Now, somewhere there are knowledgeable people, and Steven has ferreted out quite a few of them. In my own efforts in talking with these folks and talking with the government, the question often comes up as to how they could have kept this a secret for so long. And friends, they haven't. It's been around us all the time, but it has been denied and obscured.

I often like to state the condition, the story—the myth, if you will—about Columbus coming here and some Indians not seeing the ships simply because it was not in their collective consciousness and their repertoire; they at least didn't want to see them. Much of what we're seeing now is what many people don't want to see either.

There's been a massive effort at creating that, of denying the obvious, of saying that you're not seeing what's sitting right in front of you right now, thus causing doubt in your own mind. It's amazingly effective. Documentation and evidence that is probably the smoking-gun type of evidence have been totally compromised by saying that it's simply not true. So it is not true that they (the government) have kept the secret. They haven't kept the secret; it has been totally compromised by misinformation and disinformation.

Now, for my own experience, I have had no firsthand experience like so many of you. I have not encountered a UFO and we did not have them trailing us, as far as we know, going to the Moon. We didn't meet anyone on the Moon. We did it just like we said we did. For the last twenty-five years, we have dealt with the issue of, on one hand, the flat-earthers who said, "You didn't go anywhere; it was all filmed out here in the desert," and on the other hand, another fringe that said, "You have been there, but you were followed. You were in contact with UFOs. There were beings on the Moon that you met and had contact with." Well, that's not true either.

So we have walked between these two extremes of misinformation, disinformation and pure ignorance. We did what we said we did, and I want to assure you that, from that period up until the current time, NASA was one of the organizations ignorant of this type of activity. And the prevailing wisdom in NASA (at the time) was that we didn't even think about it. It was a ridiculous idea that we would encounter beings on the Moon.

However, in the last twenty-five years since that time, I became quite knowledgeable and became friends with Allan Hynek. I know and work with Jacques Vallee consistently now, and I have known the gentlemen on this stage, Bob Dean and Steven Greer, for a few years. For me, with all the evidence, it's not a matter of believing, it's a matter of the preponderance of evidence, and the evidence keeps building. The sightings keep happening. It is clear that if they are ET (and I question some of the sightings as to if they are ET), they are making their presence known. I also think that the prevalence in the modern era of so many events—the sightings, the continual mutilation events, the so-called abduction events—that we are likely looking at reverse-engineered technology in the hands of humans who are not under government control or any type of high-level control. I find that quite alarming.

With regard to the technology itself, I work with folks who do know what is in our technological database and what is available to modern armies. The so-called ET technology, the ability to have silent engines and flying machines that make no sound, flying machines that have the characteristics that are consistent with reproduction of UFO sightings, are not in any nation's arsenal, but they do exist. So if there are back-engineered technologies existing, they are probably in the hands of this group of individuals—formerly government, formerly perhaps intelligence, formerly under private-sector control, with some sort of oversight by military or by government. But this oversight is likely no longer the case as a result of this access-denied category that is now operating. I call it a clandestine group. The technology is not in our military arsenals anywhere in the world, but it does exist, and to me that's quite disconcerting.

I do work with a number of groups. We know about some of the things that the technologies are used for, and I want to assure you that these technologies are not that far beyond our current state of knowledge. Now, understanding it scientifically, understanding how it can be, is a long way from having a fully developed, usable technology. But if in our knowledge we can understand how it has to be in order to create that technology, we're not that far away. So I want to assure you that we're not talking about technologies that are so far-fetched that we can't understand them. They're just beyond the technological horizon.

I want to tell you that it doesn't appear we need to be using ultradimensions and wormholes, etc., for this. It looks like our three-dimensional or four-dimensional space-time universe is about what it appears to be, and that we can operate within that space-time universe with these types of technologies. We have tended, like the ancients of old, to have invented myths about too many dimensions and time travel, wormhole travel and so forth, and it doesn't look like that's necessary to explain what we're seeing.

The Changing Roles of Women and Men Will Be to Our Advantage

Zoosh
February 28, 1998

Excerpt from a private session, with permission.

One thing I have noticed recently is tremendous activity among females breaking away from their so-called positions of allowance; they are acting much like males. Maybe this is a period of time when female energy is being affected differently by the grids, but there seems to be a real shakeup of a lot of females. They are throwing away their husbands or mates and their families, and acting in a different manner from what we have seen in the past. I wonder if you have any comment on this.

The Energizing of the Feminine Principle

As far as women moving out of their traditional roles, this is not surprising at all. Consider that men have been moving out of their traditional roles for some time now, whereas women have been easing out of their roles but in a gentle way—more like expanding their roles. What you find now is the energizing of the feminine principle.

Before, you have often read about and observed the feminine principle rising on this planet. You could see many circumstances that tended to give evidence, such as abundant rain, which is the feminine. Without getting bogged down in such details, I would rather say that one aspect of the feminine energy rising is evident in women and even men who are primarily feminine (not those who have a particular preference, but men whose work or lives are focused primarily in receiving and disseminating in a gentle way). The capacity now for Mother Earth to demonstrate a message to those who are most capable or comfortable with receiving is much more profound. The physical evidence of this message is seen all over the world—not only in weather changes, which are obvious, but also in feeling or emotional changes.

People are charged up all over the world. They feel that either something is going to happen or something must happen. If you break down people's general emotional feelings that they cannot define, they'll fall into those two categories. What's happening is that Mother Earth is insisting that either the capacity of human beings be used in whatever way you can to treat her more benevolently, or as parents at their wits' end might say, "Get out."

This tells you that what you have known for a long time is occurring. Mother Earth would never self-destruct in order to destroy you, but she is like any person whose back is to the wall. She will do many things that you will see in the news, but more importantly, she will begin to broadcast an urgent message on the level of love/need—a certain energy that will be understood by people with the capacity to be protective, such as mothers, grandmothers or even a protective grandfather—that can only be felt (that's why you are feeling it on the emotional level), and that message is, "Help!"

Men Will Feel More Confident about the Future

So you are seeing things happening, and they are noticed usually on what I call the political front, which is the interactions between men and women all over the world, including children, of course. You are seeing women in a seemingly defensive role. If you asked all the men affected by the events you referred to what they noticed first when their wives or daughters were saying, "That's it; I am out of here" (as the kids used to say), it was a disagreeable defensiveness.

Now, think about that. Let's say hypothetically that you feel as a woman that there is a child somewhere crying out for you to defend him or her, but you know there isn't one or you can't find one. Unconsciously, the next shift will be to one's inner child, meaning one's old hopes and dreams as a youth—not in the psychological sense, but in the sense of the tender innermost part (the one rarely revealed to anyone, much less to oneself). Thus, up comes the warrior to protect oneself, even in circumstances when a warrior might not normally be called for.

Here we have physical evidence, and the political outcome will be profound. For a long time your ultimate hope has been the United Nations, and even now you are beginning to see examples of that. So what's going to happen is that women all over the world are going to decide that they have to do it themselves. Now, you can look back in political history and see many times when vital women have done such things in large or small ways. Nevertheless, what I am talking about is a universal experience. This means (not to put too fine a point on it) that this condition is prevailing. You might ask as a follow-up question, "What can men do about this?"

For one thing, men will have to become more flexible—something perhaps surprising to many men. They will have to become more flexible, and in terms of their personal needs, they might have to become a little more independent. Some men will have to wash the dishes more, look after the children more and perform more domestic duties, but interestingly, men will have to be comfortable with doing less on the political front.

Right now, a lot of men achieve their self-identity by what or how others see them. Usually this occurs in the family, at least on the primary level, but to a great degree it occurs in the community. That is why, in your cultures all over the world, when men in the community are doing domestic jobs, they are considered by that culture unseemly, or not so wonderful. Most men feel ashamed, not only because of their acculturation, but because they feel they are supposed to be doing something else.

Now men will have an opportunity to let go of that. The culture may not support you in letting go of that false shame for a long time, but you will feel it slipping away without even being aware of it. Most men will notice that this shame is gone after the fact. This will allow, at least sometimes, a lot of men who are in roles they feel embarrassed about to notice that they feel all right about it. They'll feel more confident for no reason they can explain. They'll feel more cheerful and, perhaps most importantly, something most men have not felt since they have become adults—they'll feel confident about the future. Now, ask yourself, not only as an individual, but as any man you know: When is the last time you met men on a regular basis who felt confident about the future?

The United Nations Will Be Run by Women

It is a time of shifting roles all over the planet, of women's emergence from their allowance to be formed into a stage role: "Women can do this and not that" and so on. In some cases, it will be dramatic, but in many cases, it will be a woman simply saying, "No, I have to do something else." Many times she will justify it like any human being, saying, "I've got to go out and find my work. I've got to find my mission in life." Those words support the feeling she has, but they do not directly express that feeling, because words cannot express the feeling. However, other women will know. They are going to look at one another and say, "You are feeling it too, aren't you?" There are no words for this, but I have done my best to explain it.

The main thing is this: You are now experiencing more evidence of necessary change. You might ask reasonably, that if the United Nations is going to be your greatest hope in the future, then why hasn't it been your greatest hope in the past? It's an interesting thing. If you look at the United Nations in the past, the one general rule of thumb that was reasonably predictable was that most, if not all, representatives of foreign countries were men. In reality it is intended that the people (the representatives) in the United Nations, the bulk of the staff and—someday, not immediately—the person in charge, the secretary-general (the current secretary-general is a fine man and perhaps one of the best to bridge this circumstance), will all be women.

If you think about this, it will give you some interesting insights, many of which are humorous. You know the old joke that tends to be rather true: If you get a group of men together, they talk about women, about politics and generally about things over which they have no power. This is usual for men, not because

they feel powerless, but because most men all over the world have been acculturated to believe that their power is limited. That is another reason they tend to
exert the power they have where they can and sometimes not in the best ways.

If you get a group of women together, you will find, once they get done talking or kidding about men, that they talk about political things. But you will also
find that they talk about things over which they have power—day-to-day things,
things they do, things they could do better, things other women can help them
with. In other words, they advise each other on the necessary daily functions of
life, and once that advice has been received, their ability has been improved.

This is not only a joke; it is a practical piece of evidence. What do you think
will happen when these women get into the United Nations? You know what's
going to happen: Once they get over their initial shyness about how they are
supposed to act, how to be very official and all of that business, they will realize
how quickly they can accomplish what needs to be done.

What you are seeing now and what you have been seeing for some time is the
physical evidence of the changing roles of men and women, and also the simpatico
relationship between the needs of Mother Earth and the needs of humankind,
which are very much in alignment with each other. As you know, very often one's
true needs are seen more easily by others. The reason you are getting all these different stories that come through from this or that entity is that they all see your
needs clearly, but naturally they interpret them through their own eyes, their own
acculturation and their own awareness, which is a good thing because different
people on the Earth need to hear this story in different ways. To sum it all up,
things around you are changing, and ultimately it will be for the better.

*Well, that's good news. We can look forward to something positive. Men who are energized
beings can believe in the future.*

Men Will Be Able to Let Go

Is it not ironic that the men you have spoken of and your own nervousness
about these things are ultimately leading to a circumstance in which men can
let go of the truly impossible burden that many men take on in order to take
care of their families as well as their worry about things over which they have
no direct power to protect their families from? Throughout their entire lives,
they have done whatever they could to change things they thought would keep
their family safer.

That pretty well sums up the reason for wars and strife. I grant that some wars
are caused by convoluted reasons and by greed and all these other things, but a lot
of wars, especially the more ancient ones, are caused by a desire to guarantee the
safety of the tribe or family into the unforeseeable future. As you know, it is not
for humankind to understand everything, and some actions are understood only
after different things happen in the future, so you say, "Oh well, I can do nothing
about this, but I'll do what I can." Sometimes you understand in the future why
something was done that way. That is why when human beings exhibit impatience . . . on the one hand, it is their desire to become confident creators now, but
on the other hand, putting it in the most gentle way possible, it is not unlike chil-

dren dressing up in their parents' clothes, looking comical and having fun, but perhaps it's too soon for such responsibility.

I say this not only to reassure you but to support you. These changes are intended. Even though much of what you see now is the mask over the true change, the mask itself is important because the things women are saying and doing are important only in the moment. In the long run, what they say when they exit the situation they are in (in many cases, temporarily) are the best words they can summon to explain the feelings that are really unexplainable.

So please reassure the men you know that even though they will have to don those aprons, wash up and make breakfast for the kids sometimes, and this is a role they are not familiar with, it's not a role that is unknown. They will be able to do it, and in time it will cause them to be more relaxed because they will be able to let go of some responsibilities. Most likely what you'll see happen is something that happened a few years ago and is still happening now with women. When divorce became more common in your culture, you would occasionally see that women would move in together with their children and help one another out.

You will see that happening with more men. You will see men moving in together, bringing their children and their dependents, and helping one another out. That one act alone will allow men to see the world in a very different way and break down false barriers, false pride and all the things you can see so clearly. I am not saying it's the most pleasant way to learn, but it is a way and it's the way your society has chosen, at least unconsciously.

We kind of brought it upon ourselves to learn that way, since we were so extreme on the other end.

That's right.

The Souls of Men Are Encouraging This Shift

It's not because it's payback, as you know, but because the soul must understand. Think of it this way: If an entire group in society, meaning women, is placed under false pressures and forced to do things that are not all of what they are—such as creating a feminine role rigidly and forcing women into that role—a couple of things will happen. You will notice, either quickly or slowly, depending on the individuals in the society, how women react to that and its intended reaction from men. But ultimately and over the years, the things that men's souls notice are, how is it possible for women to thrive in this circumstance? The souls want to know how. If enough of that builds up (which it will, regardless of what people think, because the soul is completely free to develop its own curiosities and applications), they will say, "We are men, but we would like this opportunity."

The soul does not consider it enslavement that women have been forced into this position all over the world, with some exceptions. The souls of men are curious—granted, this is over lifetimes—about how women can thrive: "We must learn this." So there's that factor, too. I am not saying that men are now going to become enslaved or chained by women. Women are not likely to exert such an influence, although it is a great and deep and abiding fear in many cultures that women could become like men. This is not because men logically think it could really happen, but because men fear retribution.

As a result, there is a possibility that in a very few cases that will happen, but I guarantee you (a Zoosh guarantee) that in 95 percent of the cases, it won't happen, or if it does, it will be a brief anomaly that will be something to joke about in years to come.

There won't be a male inquisition? [Laughs.]

No, there will not.

I got you. They will get their licks in, but they won't revel in it.

Remember the Lessons of Atlantis:
The Consequences of Genetic
Animal Experimentation

Zoosh

July 30, 1998

All right, Zoosh here now. I want to talk a little bit about the effects, the impact, of these new genetic experiments on animals with the expectation and intention of growing human body parts in animals, specifically where they grew a human ear on a mouse [see "Mouse prepares to lend an ear," *Boston Globe*, Oct. 25, 1995, p. 9].

There Is a Murmuring

For a long time, the animals of Earth have felt increasingly unwelcome, and as a result, there has been what I would call a murmuring. We all know what "murmuring" is verbally, but this is a murmuring just below the surface of the verbal that can be felt by sensitive human beings. Some people have been feeling it in a way that causes them to feel unexpectedly nervous or suddenly shy or on edge. It comes and it goes. (There certainly might be other causes for such reactions, so all such reactions are not caused by the murmuring.)

This murmuring is united amongst all animals, even animals you cause to feel welcome, such as dogs and cats and others you like to live with. To put it in a nutshell, the murmuring is, "It's time to go home. They don't appreciate us here. They don't respect us, they don't love us and many times they insult us, even though we are offering them everything we have to give."

The animals know what they always know. They are not here to learn anything. They are here to teach you, not one another. They will often act in a certain way, follow a course of action, for instance, that they would not follow if human beings were not here, because that course of action is intended to have some impact on you—the human race, the Explorer Race—and to bring about some form of learning for you. So you need to give them much more respect and kind treatment. It goes without saying that animals you raise on the hoof for food and other products require a tremendous amount of respect and appreciation for what they are offering. I do recommend, therefore, that respect be given.

Atlantis and Lemuria Are in Your Future

I have been saying off and on for a while that Atlantis and Lemuria are not past-oriented cultures. Oh, I know I may have gone along with them being past cultures, but that was just to establish a general generic history for you. At that time, it was necessary that you thought of them as being in the past. If you considered at that time that Atlantis and Lemuria were in your future, you would have been more inclined to embrace technology, though you would be better off to be suspicious of it. When you are suspicious of technology, you tend to proceed with more caution. This is advantageous to you and to that which makes up the machines.

That was then. Now I can reveal to you that Atlantis and Lemuria are in your future, not to be relived, but totally in your future. It is intended that you do not cause the outcomes projected in the past for Atlantis and Lemuria because of a decision to pursue more extreme polarities. It would be conceivable for Atlantis at least, as well as some aspects of Lemurian life, to be less benevolent than intended. Therefore, it is a critical factor for you to avoid devastating mistakes, compared to minor mistakes that you can resolve.

You cannot come to your Atlantean society and your Lemurian society without being guided or led. Those who lead you most of the way will be the animals. Those who lead you the final distance will be the children. The animals' great importance to you spiritually has been subtly pointed out to you in many famous books, and children have also been indicated in this way.

You Must Reform Your Welcome for All Animals

Since I want to talk tonight about the impact of these experiments and uses of animals that are truly obscene, I will pursue that for the moment. Animals are not products. Science has gotten used to the idea that they are mere tools, not unlike a glass beaker or a Bunsen burner, but they are not. They are living, breathing, spiritual, loving entities in their own right—*every one*, be it a friendly cat or an admirable horse or a butterfly or an ant. (Ants are one of the most advanced spiritually on your planet.) The animals are here for you, to show you things about yourselves and to give you lessons as creators-in-training.

Science has treated them as a product for a long time, using many animals who would be considered pets by many, such as white mice. They call them rats, but I am calling them mice, even though they are bigger than mice, because they are so docile. If you were to visit with one, you would immediately consider it a pet. White mice, of course, as well as rabbits, monkeys and even dogs and cats and other animals are abused because science has still not found its heart.

Perhaps the biggest challenge to science is the pursuit of the perfection of the scientific mind—not the spiritual mind, such as is pursued in the East—which is designed and intended to be entirely free of any so-called emotional caveats, meaning warnings or restrictions.

The true challenge, then, is that while science is somewhat capriciously flirting with this heartless mind (all your minds are not heartless, but this type of mind, this type of mental goal, is heartless), it is up to other human beings to reform your welcome for all animals. When I say "all animals," I do not exclude animals who have recently gone into what is considered extinction, but I do exclude dinosaurs and animals who would perhaps be impractical at this time. They are happy where they are anyway, so there is no need to encourage them to re-form here.

How to Welcome Animals

How does one welcome animals? It is surprisingly easy. Most of you reading this have at one time or another either been welcomed or have welcomed some other person. So you know what it's like to be welcomed or to genuinely welcome someone you are happy to see and look forward to spending time with. This is the intended feeling.

So either remember a time when you felt such welcome, or for those of you who can focus directly into your feelings, fill yourself with that feeling of either being welcome or welcoming—welcoming is perhaps the best. Then pick an animal—it can be any kind of animal—and welcome that animal that day. Even if you are working that day, do it three or four times a day. It won't take more than a minute or two. Fill yourself with the feeling of welcome and say, "Welcome, rabbits," for instance. On another day, you could say, "Welcome, horses," if you wish, or "Welcome, mice." (I know you do not often consider mice to be welcome, but they are essential. Aside from the fact of their own lives, philosophies, songs, music, rhythm of life and the beauty of their being, they literally support a great many other animals on the planet with their bodies. So they are essential.)

Remember always to first feel genuinely welcoming. Say these things about a type of animal out loud, because you don't want to welcome only the spirits of the animals. If you *think* the welcome, that might be a conclusion or memory of the animals, which is even more likely to be a conclusion by the creation world. But if you say it out loud, since you are using your physical apparatus and speaking and making sounds, it will be taken as a sign that you are welcoming the physical animals, and it goes without saying that they will come with spirit and memory.

You Are Immortal

I mention this to you now because more and more these days science is running pell-mell down a road for which it cannot see a future other than the idea of limitless creation in order to perpetuate the lives of human beings. You know that you are in fact immortal—and I am not talking about something like your soul, which you may not be able to fully grasp as an entity. Besides your soul, the immortality of your being is your personality. There is no need (though I know there is an attraction) to extend your life to 100 years (some of you live to be that now, but most do not) or 150 or 250 years. I know you like the idea because you think you can do more, be more, become wiser and so on. But your wisdom curve does not continue to increase at an increasing rate.

Your wisdom curve increases up to about the age of 65, maybe 68 at the most, and then it begins to taper off. After that point (I am talking about age in terms of your now time), you gradually begin letting go of Earth wisdom as you approach the end of your natural lives, which might take five, ten, fifteen or twenty years or more. As you approach the end, it is intended that you let go of this dimension's functions and format. That is why senility exists, so that you can bridge the gap to your next step.

You Must Also Welcome the Dark-Skinned Race

What I am saying is this: It is potentially catastrophic to unwelcome the animals. Think about it. Think how you've intentionally or unintentionally unwelcomed many of the races. Throughout the years, there have been different races that were unwelcomed by the ruling races, meaning whoever was the most powerful and influential at the time and place (I am talking about Earth people here).

As I have said in *Explorer Race: Origins and the Next 50 Years*, there are some races on this planet that you cannot get along without, because just by their very being, they hold an energy that maintains life here. I referred before to the dark-skinned peoples who all hail from Sirius. Sirius is the place where the prototype feminine human being was created. Sirius as a galaxy [system] is also strongly feminine and is the source of the Mother energy that you all often attribute either to religious figures or to Mother Earth. But, in fact, the real source of that feminine Mother energy is Sirius. The dark-skinned peoples are all rooted from Sirius. If anything happens to them in a way where they don't feel welcome here, the murmuring will begin amongst them as well.

I am not talking about conversation; I am talking about an energy connected to the subconscious. The subconscious is united with both the conscious and the physical, so it is something that is felt and only sometimes understood. If the murmuring should begin in the dark-skinned races, all peoples on the Earth will be in trouble. I am not saying that you have to revere dark-skinned people, though I will say that they are usually treasured on other planets as a powerful force for nurturance just by being.

Therefore, if you are consciously or unconsciously or even unintentionally unwelcoming dark-skinned peoples, then add dark-skinned peoples to your thank-yous. You can say "peoples from" a given country, but I recommend just saying "dark-skinned peoples," because dark-skinned peoples live all over the world. In this way, you will not exclude any. Perhaps when you get done thanking the different animal species you choose to thank, or even before that, if you choose to go in that order, fill yourself with that feeling of welcome and genuinely say, with the meaning and the intent of welcome, "Welcome to Earth, dark-skinned people. Thank you for coming." "I appreciate you" might be an option at the end.

I am not trying to create a hierarchy amongst races, but it is important to acknowledge, appreciate and respect those you cannot live without. You all know that you cannot live without Mother Earth. If something happened to her, you would be . . . well, elsewhere. But you do not often consider that you would also be elsewhere if something happened to some human beings on Earth.

So it is important that you find your place of welcome. After you have welcomed animals, dark-skinned people and other races of people, if you wish—or ETs, mountains, lakes, rivers, any natural things—always doing no more than one species a day, then you can begin to welcome feelings for yourself, for instance, using the same process. Let's say you would like to feel loved or appreciated or respected or even honored. Pick one of those feelings and follow the process. You may not immediately notice results, but you will notice them eventually.

Beautiful! Do you want to say anything about the gypsies?

Gypsies are also another race of beings. Calling them a race is necessary here, even though I do not exactly consider them to be a specific race, but they are a cultural and a divine race, divine because of certain connections they have to special aspects of Creator. So I will ask you to allow me to say "the gypsy race." They also would be a good one to thank.

I grant that individuals of these races may not be people you would care to welcome all the time, but I suggest that you welcome them as a group by saying so and feeling the feeling. Then they might stay—the African aborigines, the Australian Aborigines and many others.

Mother Earth Is No Longer Shepherding You

As you become more influential on Earth as creators-in-training, Mother Earth will begin to take cues from you. As I have said before, Mother Earth has begun to release her shepherding of you. She has been shepherding you as her children for a long time. Since your bodies are made of her body, she had that right, and as she saw it, she had that responsibility. She would sometimes demonstrate things to you—"This is how you must do this," or "You cannot do this now"— not only by demonstrating her physical being (day and night, lightning, rain and so on), but also by having unexpected events such as floods and fires caused by lightning and so on, which required certain reactions on your part.

Mother Earth knew, however, that you are creators-in-training, and as a result, it was always her intention to someday become a reactionary individual to your creations. As I have been saying for some time, you are now much, much more responsible for what is created on Earth, not just out of your actions, but out of your beliefs, thoughts, feelings and desires. That is another reason why it's critically important for you to be able to separate your entertainment, especially violent entertainment, from what you believe. It is very easy to watch violent entertainment and begin to accustom yourself to the idea that the world isn't safe and that there are people with guns waiting for you right around the corner. I am not saying that these circumstances don't exist at times and in certain places, but it is not the dominant theme, even though the news and the entertainment industry might prompt you to think otherwise.

Mother Earth Will Now Begin to Reflect Your Behavior

Now Mother Earth, without speaking out loud, is saying to most of you, "Show me and I will show you." "Show me" means "demonstrate to me how you feel about this and that." And when Mother Earth says to demonstrate to her, she does not mean that you walk up to a mountain and act out your feelings, emotions, beliefs and desires, but that you act them out with one another. Every time one individual acts out anything with any other or many others, it demonstrates it to Mother Earth, since all bodies on Earth are made up of her body.

So if you feel that some people are not welcome, such as the dark-skinned races, then she will perhaps demonstrate to you the consequences of your beliefs. I am not saying that you all feel this way; I am simply showing you the danger of feeling this way. Certainly the dark-skinned peoples are not the only ones to suffer. In recent years, there has been a lot of resentment and anger from dark-skinned races toward light-skinned races. At times catastrophes have happened that have affected them.

I am mentioning this now, however, because it is a much more common experience. You might or might not believe it, but I will tell you this now: For a long time, your unconscious (meaning your body's physical mechanisms) has been creating almost 100 percent of your physical day-to-day experience here—not just physiologically speaking, but events, circumstances, political realities, social realities. But in recent years, that's been moving out of the unconscious into the subconscious—and as any psychologist can tell you, the subconscious is often a reservoir of old resentments and unhappiness in general.

I am not saying that you must all get psychoanalyzed overnight and cleanse your subconscious, but these disasters that are happening occasionally—not end-of-the-world catastrophes, not California falling into the sea, but such catastrophes as the recent tidal wave in New Guinea—are a direct demonstration of Mother Earth reacting to the belief widely held by many people (not only the light-skinned races) that the dark-skinned races are either less than or are to be feared and controlled at all costs. This attitude has been recently demonstrated on New Guinea. Mother Earth did not do this out of some capricious cruelty, but she must follow just as you must follow. As a result of increasing drains and strains on her systems through mining and overpopulation, she is unable to shepherd you as she once did because she is having to work overtime to try to save herself because of so much destruction done to her body. And that is not all. It is also within the plan that you are ultimately intended to experience and become a creator in your own right. It is intended that Mother Earth simply let go of her shepherding duties and pass them on to you.

Your Subconscious Is Now Creating Much of Your Reality

Your unconscious used to create almost all of your physical reality. Now your subconscious is creating fully 45 percent of your physical reality. The subconscious is affected not only by the conscious but by the unconscious. The unconscious knows that the sky is up. When you go outside, you look up; you look down to see the ground. This is accepted, and it is absolute from your individual point of view.

Such beliefs are beneficial for the subconscious because it lives in a world of absolutes. There is no gray—it either is or it isn't. If somebody hurts you or hurt your feelings when you were a child, if it happened often enough and was damaging enough, your subconscious might come to feel that you are ·not an acceptable person or that certain kinds of people can never be trusted or other well-known and well-established psychological analyses of such early treatment. Once upon a time, your subconscious might have felt that these things were bad but that they didn't reflect directly on you—in other words, there was some moderation. It isn't moderated anymore. Now it either is or it isn't. This is necessary so that you can learn through consequences, but it can be a tough and even brutal lesson—or it can be a gentle and benevolent lesson.

Examine Your Reactions to Know Your Subconscious

If you want to know what your subconscious knows, examine your reactions. Some time ago, psychologists would say a word in a word-association text, and you would say another word. This was a way to examine your subconscious and where beliefs are held in absolute, and to some degree, also the conscious mind. So if you want to know how you feel about something, check out your reactions—not to news events or things you hear about, but to people. As a light-skinned person, when you see a dark-skinned person, what is your first reaction—not your first thought, but your first feeling? As a dark-skinned person, when you first see any light-skinned person, what is your first feeling? This feeling, if you can identify it, might be mistrust or anger or some such thing, but it is the absolute belief of your subconscious. Since the subconscious is becoming much more influential in your day-to-day creation, do you really want to believe these things? If you do, Mother Earth will continue to demonstrate your subconscious to you.

What can you do about this? It is essential that you do not begin to desensitize yourself as people have done for years by smoking or drinking or taking various drugs, because the subconscious still holds on to its absolutes, even in those circumstances. It does not waiver one iota, even if you are so drunk you pass out. What you need to do is consciously set out to make a friend from the racial group you distrust the most. It may not be an overnight cure, but it is a beginning. Your subconscious sense of absolutes is significantly shaken by developing more friends in races to whom your subconscious first reacts unpleasantly.

What I am talking about here is another creator lesson. It is also going to be increasingly possible for you to have a much greater affect on Mother Earth's weather and her natural occurrences: tidal waves, yes, but even earthquakes. Often there is prayer to keep earthquakes away or there might be requests for divine intervention or even attempts to scientifically stop an earthquake. Certainly many spiritual people are using their methods as well.

Calming Fault Zones

What if I told you that you could learn how to cause the Earth underneath you to feel more comfortable with its own body—which is injured in many ways from mining and other pollutions and disruptions—and that there are things you can do to put the Earth at ease? Imagine four to five hundred miles of the San Andreas Fault running through California. Imagine forty or fifty people getting together (even one would make a difference) and spacing themselves out regularly along the landed part of the San Andreas Fault. If these people were to move their hands in a waving motion gently toward the San Andreas Fault, as one might make a diagram in the air of the symbol for water in sign language . . . another possibility is to move the hand as if your palm were moving over a wavy line (you can also move the hand with the palm upward). As you know, it is possible to stand right above the fault (safely too, I might add).

Without having any thoughts and keeping thoughts from your mind but experiencing the feeling of welcome, you would welcome fluids that Mother Earth has deep down below—forms of oil, forms of oil and water—which Mother Earth uses not unlike hydraulics, the hydraulic principle. You would be welcoming these fluids into that fault zone so that Mother Earth could move when she needs to, but it would be much, much more gentle. What now might be felt as a 9 earthquake, which would be calamitous in California, would barely be felt as, say, a 2 or a 2.5. People would hardly notice it; it would be fun, not a terrible catastrophe. Think about it. There is a great deal you can do to benefit Mother Earth in this way, and while you are about it, you will be fulfilling further creator lessons. [See the *Shamanic Secrets* books, which have many creator lessons to practice.]

The Function of Parenting

Parenting and the way it exists has always been intended to be a lesson for the parents. The children, while objects of joy and happiness, are also the teachers. They teach by their need. The sensitive parent might even be able to experience telepathic pictures from babies and youngsters who consciously or unconsciously communicate in this fashion. This is the way animals—and the way you, in your normal state of being—communicate. Here you are experiencing ignorance so you can re-create your reality, but normally you also communicate in this fashion, with feelings and pictures.

So parenting is also part of the plan. It would have been very easy to have created a method of reproduction for the human race that did not take so long [laughs] and was much more benevolent and easier. But it has been necessary to teach human beings by requiring them to study the impact of their actions, deeds, words and sometimes even their unspoken thoughts through the demonstrated imitation of children's behavior, thus giving many parents instantaneous (or at least at some point) evidence of consequences.

I grant that in later childhood, the child is influenced in other ways by other people, not the parents only. But generally speaking, the first two to three years of the child's life are intended to be lessons for parents and not in any way lessons for children. This is the reason that children at this age are very, very conscious. They often have their teachers with them. They travel a lot in different planes and dimensions. They relate to spirits, angels, animals and other pure beings on a very benevolent level.

Because they have this profound connection to spirit in the early years, they do not need to learn much of anything except how to communicate with the adults around them and, once they start toddling, how to use their bodies. In this way, the balance is present. The children teach through their needs and the parents learn by their own actions.

Your Evolution toward Atlantis and Lemuria

Do you want to say anything to help us get a mental handle on the idea that Atlantis and Lemuria are ahead of us? Can we see it as a circle that we are going back to?

Yes, you can see it as a circle, but you are in a loop of time, you know. Still, it has been necessary, vital even, to settle into the consciousness of the human being such civilizations of vastly superior consciousness—superior in a sense of mind power and spiritual insights—as Lemuria and Atlantis. Lemuria is perhaps the more feminine—meaning pure feminine, pure love, support, nurturance and so on—whereas Atlantis is the more masculine—meaning mind, experiment and so on, as is in existence now. So if these civilizations-to-be could be impressed upon you as being in the past, you could analyze them—what you know about it, what you feel, what you dream, what you hear, what you read—and see how your now civilization relates to the past, which is simply another example of historical comparison.

It has always been considered that you are evolving toward Atlantis and ultimately some kind of Lemurian lifestyle after that. But in reality, Atlantis is in the future and so is Lemuria. Atlantis (though it might be called something else) as you know it is a culture, a civilization that represents the last true full capacity for violent self-destruction. Once you have moved on to Lemurian ways, that will be gone. Therefore, with a powerful sense of the mistakes made in an Atlantean scenario that might still happen, you are more likely to be cautious with that which is unknown or at least not understood.

Sometimes these seeds are necessary to recognize in this fashion. Many people are looking forward to re-creating the beauties of Atlantis, which are many and varied. However, one of the more threatening aspects of a violent Atlantis (which is, as I say, still a potential) is the firm hierarchical system wherein a ruling class dominates other beings who are considered simply less than and in such a manner that those human beings would be bred and (not to put too fine a point on it) slaughtered for their body parts so that the ruling race could live indefinitely in such a cruel fashion. Obviously, we cannot have that.

And the human ear on the mouse is the first little glimmer of this?

The ear on the mouse is perhaps the first undeniable aspect of it. Whereas before one could say, "This is not a good thing," or "That is not a good thing," or "It's a deplorable thing," now you have something that is entirely obscene, from my point of view.

Don't Destroy Your Animal Teachers!

Think about it. Right now you have not even begun to scratch the surface of what the animals can teach you. Many of them have gone away for a time—as you say, become extinct. But if you welcome them, they might be able to come back. Your scientists are prepared to corrupt these beings in such a way that they will not be able to give you their wisdom. If mice or any animals are being used as a breeding ground for human organs through genetic experiments, the animals, because of the pain and suffering and misery—to say nothing of the schizophrenia it will cause—will be unable to impart the wisdom that they are now ready and able to give you. Now some small element in your society is driving you toward destroying these very teachers.

You know, there is not a single ant on Earth who does not know the cures in the plant world for human diseases—they all know. When you learn how to communicate with them clearly in feelings and pictures and in stories that you sense (where it might feel like your imagination, which I remind you, is the divine part of the mind) . . . when this happens (it is coming soon), you will have what the animals must teach you. Until then they will do their utmost to survive and remain pure enough to teach you. But if you corrupt them (and many of them have been corrupted already) with drugs and other treatments, hybridization (when hybridized animals are no longer their true selves) and so on, it is much more difficult for them to communicate.

For example, wasps are not hybridized. They are what they are. But you consider honeybees to be vital for not only the growth of food but also for the food they provide. Understandably, you desire to be more peaceful with you. (In their natural being, they are not exactly aggressive—though one would assume that—but they are much more protective of their young than is normally the case with what are considered honeybees.) Therefore, the sensitive or spiritual person can get much more innate wisdom from the average wasp than the honeybee. This is not to say that honeybees are not wonderful, benevolent beings, but as you know them in your country, they are a hybridized version of their true selves. When you learn how to be at peace with yourself, no animals will be violent with you. Even if they require, for instance, blood to survive, such as the mosquito, they will go elsewhere.

After you learn what the animals have to offer, then they will go home. But if they feel sufficiently unwelcome, they will go home anyway, without you learning. They are not going to get on spaceships; they will simply allow themselves to die off, as cows have demonstrated recently with the so-called mad cow disease. This is really a way of cows saying, "We can go anytime we want."

Time-Traveling Interference in Israel Imperils Middle East: How to Resolve It

Speaks of Many Truths
October 8, 1998

This channeling was previously published in Explorer
Race: Earth History and Lost Civilizations.

In the country of Israel, as it is now called, where the western border meets the Mediterranean sea, to about sixty miles north of the southern border that also meets the sea and about, I think, just a few miles south of their northern border, which meets the sea, there is a fold in the energy of continuity that supports Mother Earth as a planetary being. This fold (it's the best way I can describe it) would look very much like you folded over a piece of cloth, then folded it back toward yourself. It would look like a lap in the cloth, as they say in some craft circles.

This fold is very difficult for Mother Earth to comprehend, much less deal with. It is not of her making and is a direct result of the sinister secret government's attempt to hold the spiritual psyche of that region in check and bind it to past rivalries. It is a current success, or challenge—depending on your view of the sinister secret government—that has so far defied many spiritual attempts to resolve it.

In 1985 the SSG Time-Traveled to 7000 B.C.

It has been in effect for about eighty-five hundred years, which would naturally suggest the question of what the sinister secret government has to do with it. It is one of their time-travel successes. They haven't had many, but that's one of them. As a result, if you went back in tribal history in that part of the world, you would find that about ten thousand years ago, even nine thousand years ago, most of the tribes were at peace with one another. They shared resources, water and so on.

But right about eighty-seven hundred years ago, people started to get nervous. They didn't know why they were nervous; they didn't even know that they were nervous. They didn't have words for that then. This nervousness was their anticipation of the secret government's attempt to go back in time. The SSG had started, right around nine thousand years ago, to try to poke a hole in the spiritual rhythm of that place, and people started to feel it about eighty-seven hundred years ago. About eighty-five hundred years ago, the SSG was successful, and they tore a hole in the spiritual fabric. Then, in order to confound other spiritual beings from repairing the hole, they folded it over on itself. They tied its resolution to the peoples in the area having to return to the peaceful state or condition that preceded their attack.

In this way, they were able to confound the attempts to resolve it. From their point of view, they were being reasonable. Of course, the damage they did to the spiritual fabric has been largely the cause of strife in those areas.

What year in our time did they go back and do that?

I am told it was between 1985 and 1987. Their first attempt was in 1985. They lost about 457 people in the project and damaged a great deal of their equipment, but they didn't care about that. Through the utilization of their time field, which uses electricity, magnetics and some radioactive elements, they ruined a natural underground cavern they were using. They also utilized sorcery to pull in certain soul energies, without permission, from human beings living on the Earth. (They did this to disguise what they were doing.) I cannot say more about their process without putting weapons in the hands of people who might misuse this information, but those who understand such things will know what I am talking about.

Was it done underground in Montauk or somewhere else on the planet?

No, this was done underground in South America, very deep under the country known as Argentina, about eighty miles underneath the surface. Needless to say, this was done without the knowledge of the surface population.

Down at the tip of the continent? At the very tip?

Down at the southern end, yes.

Is that what Zoosh says is the office from which the secret government runs the planet?

No, because this is a natural cavern, but it is close to that place. Their base is something they dug, but this is a natural cavern. Now it is not safe for life. It has been damaged, and it is not possible for Mother Earth to repair it, but it will be repaired in time by higher beings, most likely not for another five or six thousand years.

Mideast Conflicts Result from Damage to Spiritual Fabric

So is the fighting and lack of peace in Israel and in that area now a result of what the SSG did?

As I said, the tribal warfare had not really begun before they did this, and the battles up to this time (including now) of this whole area are a result of the SSG's activity. The damage and the radiation create a tension. If one puts an artificial tension in any construction . . . an analogy is that if a tension is artificially placed in, say, a bridge or a road, that bridge or road will fail in considerably less time than its expected lifetime.

In this case, we have a tension compounded upon itself. Imagine, those of you who get chiropractic adjustments or even massages, if you had a tight muscle that needed to be released and it wasn't—it would get worse and worse and worse. It's

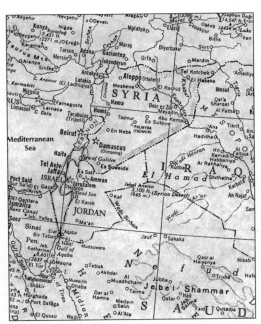

Fig. 11–1. Map of tension radiating in the Middle East.

like that. To the degree that this fold is under tension, it radiates more of what I would call the feeling of agony. If you show me a map, I will show you how far it radiates out of that fold [see Fig. 11–1].

The center point, where the radiation is most extreme, is right here, a big city—Tel Aviv. This is where the tension is usually the most extreme in the area. This is usually the tension, but it does not stay only there. What I am told is that this is where the energy is, but there are some little tendrils everywhere. These are temporary and move around.

But what about to the east? Is it getting into the eastern countries or south to Egypt?

No, it doesn't go that way, only where I have shown it. This is the center of the fold. If you were to look down at it, you would see it as a smoky area. Now, I am also told that this energy, if the sinister secret government wants to make trouble, can be concentrated like one concentrates a light ray; it can be momentarily focused or beamed for a second or maybe a half or three-quarters of a second.

Like a laser?

Not that tightly. No, it would be condensed down to about fifty miles wide. It can be aimed, but only in the general direction of its current radiation.

Toward the east.

I am told that this has been the cause of a great deal of strife that has been stimulated in recent years in Afghanistan, Pakistan, India and other countries (for instance, the presence of Russia, or the then Soviet Union, in Afghanistan).

The people in these countries have suffered because the energy is so powerful and it is used to keep the area disrupted.

It goes almost through Baghdad.

The Mideast Was Originally the Greatest Influence for Unity

You might easily ask (and I did the first time I heard of it), why did they do this in this area? They did this because the most influential religions and philosophies consider this area to be sacred. Their members do not make up all the people of the world, but they are, together, an influential group.

It was originally intended that these religions—Christianity, Islam and Judaism—form three portions of a single circle of influence and that this circle of influence would support a united world. If the SSG had not been successful in this attack on the spirit of peoples, that area would have united completely and formed this circle of influence. Your establishment of the United Nations and its encouragement would have been followed by a one-world benevolent society ten years after the foundation of the United Nations.

That is why the SSG considered this so imperative. They were willing to pay any price in order to cause this calamity. Now let me tell you what you can do.

Practical Homework to Change the Energy

For those in the area, if you should hear of these things we are speaking of today, here is your practical homework. I know that it is difficult to live there. If you are Islamic, it is very difficult right now. If you are Christian, it is also difficult. If you are Jewish, it is not only difficult but confusing. So I'm going to give you an assignment: In the next three to six months from when you hear about this, please go out and make one new friend in each of those religions, which includes your own religion. Then the four of you make it a point to get to know one another and do something socially at least once a month. That's the homework for you who are living in this area. If you cannot do this because you do not know people of the other religions or it is not easy to meet them, then try to make friends with people who live near you, people you never see and have nothing in common with. This will help.

Now, for those of you who do not live in the area but are of one of these religions, you can also do that homework. When I say you are of these three religions, I mean that you practice one of these religions, not just that you were born to it. For those of you who practice something else or do not practice a religion as it is understood in your time or who maybe have a philosophy you live by, I encourage you to do whatever ceremonies of love and companionship and friendship you can.

If you are at a wedding, a christening or a celebrated holiday where there is happiness, just once during the celebration say, "Peace and brotherhood" (and you can say sisterhood if you prefer) "is natural to this area." So know the map. You can say Israel. You can say Syria. You can name these countries, but try to have a picture. You might not believe it, but just say it. Others of you, put it in your prayers; do something to soothe the area. Try to contribute to the peace there, because the people who live there are having a very difficult time.

When the people who live in the area affected by the folded energy have friends who practice another religion or even friends in their own religion, sometimes they are at such complete odds that they almost (and sometimes do) come to blows. But I will tell you the biggest challenge: It's not just the different languages (that's enough, yes), but that people are so overwhelmed by this fold of energy that makes the communication of people's feelings into words that are understood by others much more difficult.

Communication by Feelings

Those who have the greatest passion to communicate with their feelings are the Islamic people. Those (I am generalizing, you understand) who have the greatest command of words and who trust words more than feelings are the Jewish and Christian people. If you know that as a general rule (not for everyone), then understand that feelings and mental words do not directly communicate.

If someone is talking to you and has strong feelings that you are not understanding, you may not have perfect communication language-wise, but normally it's good enough to understand. If you don't understand, ask the person to touch you physically, gently, in some way. Reach over and touch that person's arm or hand while she is talking to you. Then you will feel the person's feelings and understand. Do the same when you talk to that person, because passionate feelings are most easily understood by the feeling body.

Equally, if you are a person of words and a person of feeling cannot understand your words even though he understands your language, if he does not know what you are trying to say, reach out and touch that person in some socially acceptable place. (These touches should be all right. I am saying the arm or the hand, but you know in your part of the world how or where to touch each other.) If that is acceptable, do that and then talk. Even if that person does not understand what you are saying at first, he will in time, especially if you get into the feelings of what you are saying. Ultimately, all people communicate with their feelings, but those who rely on words are more apt to have misunderstandings.

That's something everyone can do. So the history of the past eighty-five hundred years has changed as a result of this interference by the SSG?

Yes.

Is what we're seeing in the Middle East the result of that change?

Yes. If that attack by those negative peoples (the SSG) had not taken place, the area would be beautiful. It would be the place people would come to when they want to go somewhere to have a good example for getting along with one another. If people were having trouble . . . let's say that you are a father and you are having trouble communicating with your son and your son cannot make you understand. You would then go to that place and after a few days there you would be able to understand each other. That was how it was meant to be.

History Changed for Everyone Alive in 1985

It happened in 1985, so things were changed in our lifetime?

They went back, you know. It took them two years, from 1985 to 1987, to succeed in their cruel goal. I mention that because it was in 1985 that they began and it was in 1987 when they decided to say, "This is enough." They felt that they had accomplished their purpose.

What we know of Israel and the formation of their state, the wars, our modern history . . .

. . . has all been affected by that. I am told that I have to explain this. When this kind of change is caused, in 1985 you should have been able to read a history book printed in 1945 and the history would be accurate. But no, when this intervention in past time takes place, it changes the memories and the reality of all beings. So even if you were born in 1935, you would remember what has taken place coming forward from eighty-five hundred years ago, not the past you lived before 1985.

When you go back in time and change something, it changes the present as well as the past. It changes memory; it changes everything. That's why we have to fix it so that you can recapture your true memories.

The Remedy

Why can't the dimensional masters or the spiritual teachers go in and undo it?

They have all told me that this is something that the people of the area must begin, that if the people of the area become convinced that they must have peace so that they can discover what they like about one another, then they will be able to do it. But it must begin that way. It doesn't have to be that the people there have to make this conversion to this society. But they must begin of their own desire, not because someone like Speaks of Many Truths tells them they ought to.

I think that in time it is going to happen. I wouldn't be surprised if it happens in your lifetime, because all the work is in place by all the spiritual teachers and benevolent beings to immediately change it. The only thing they are waiting for is the action of the people in the area, and when that takes place, the energy will change. The first thing that people all over the world will notice is that they won't seem to be able to remember the history of that area, and no one will be able to find any history books that say anything about it. That will last for a while, then people will begin to remember this different history that was supposed to have taken place. Then they will find it in the history books.

That's wonderful! I didn't understand that back when Zoosh told us about the time-track removal of the peace avatar U.S. president by the SSG. [See Shining the Light I.*]*

Science, Sorcery and Shamans

It's very scientific. The SSG has to use science and sorcery because they are doing things that are against the natural flow of energy, and only science and sorcery can do this. When science is reengaged in your time with its natural heart and finds its god, as Zoosh says, then science will no longer be used by them and they will have only sorcery. By that time you will have enough mystical people and shamanic people to combat that sorcery. Even as I speak in your time, many mystical people are training. Some of them do not know why or what for, but they are training to combat sorcery.

The need for people with shamanic training is probably why there is so much of it out there today?

Yes.

In the United States, people are remembering the Native American teachings, and there are other countries of the world where the people are looking for their shamanic heritage.

When times are unknown and uncertain, this is part of the reason people are almost always attracted to the permanent, natural ways.

The Aborted Meeting and Shamanic Training

You said that there was a meeting of native elders not too long ago and that they were supposed to disclose all their secrets, which would have created new interest in the shamanic way of life.

They were going to disclose these things, yes, but they didn't because they needed to have two other groups, I believe.

One group was the Mormons—what was the other one?

It was going to be certain scientists, and one was going to say, "This is our story." They wouldn't say, "This is our vision." They would say, "This is what we believe." Then the Latter Day Saints religion would say, "This is what we believe, and here are our proofs." Then the scientists would say, "We know of these things. We have found all these proofs, and here they are."

But because the other two groups were not prepared or did not show up, the elders wisely decided to say nothing or to say only things that people had heard before. They knew that if these other groups were not prepared to talk, something was out of balance and they would have to wait.

In spite of that, the people who need shamanic training are going to get it, whether or not these secrets are revealed—is that true?

Yes, people are getting that training now all over the world. Some of them have been misunderstood, and people think they are crazy and put them in institutions. If you are practicing and are being taught to be a mystic or a shaman, when you are doing your practicing, your teaching, your studies, as long as what you are doing is benevolent (not harming you or anyone else), it might look very strange to someone else.

If you think they can accept these words, you say, "This is part of my mystical training, and it is a step on the way. I don't understand it completely yet, but there will be more revealed to me in time." But if you think they would not understand those words, then you can say, "It's part of my religion and I feel inspired to do it." Most people can accept that.

The people in that area . . .

It is difficult to talk about their origin because of this corruption. That's why I'm not talking about it. I can't talk about their origin when I can't see the slightest demonstration of their origin. Their origin is clouded, so I have to skip over talking about the people's origins there. Maybe we can talk about it some other time, but I am guided to say nothing about it at this time. My feeling is that if the SSG knew of the people's origins, they might find even worse ways to attack them.

Please do not feel that this difficulty with the SSG is a permanent situation. I have faith in your resolving this, because I have seen the future of Earth in third and fourth and fifth and other dimensions, and I see people in this area getting along and doing well together, even forming a mutually shared philosophy.

So I feel that you will succeed, but you must make the effort. Some of you will have to make the effort as if success is not guaranteed. I have seen this future, but my feeling is that it will take a great deal of work and commitment, especially by the people in that area. It's awfully hard, you know, to make a friend out of someone you don't trust, but sometimes, if you go slow enough with it, you'll find things you like, and you can share and do things together. Maybe you both like to play the same game and get to be friends because of that game. You do these things now. I feel that you will resolve it, but it will take a little time. So make the effort, please.

"I Put My Trust in God"

Zoosh
November 6, 1999

C *an you say what happened to EgyptAir Flight 990 on October 31, 1999?*

This I would say to the family of that man, Gameel el-Batouty. Know that this was not an intentional act. He was not turning his back on his family, whom he loved dearly. Because the wreckage has been underwater for so long, it would be difficult if not impossible to prove that this man, I believe, had a stroke. It was not the kind of stroke that knocks a person out, but the kind that is disorienting. It was this sort of circumstance.

The man was concerned about his health. It wasn't a concern from doctors telling him he would soon have to retire from flying, but he occasionally noticed a little shaking in his hand, which he could not understand. It appeared only during stressful circumstances, such as on the job; it rarely appeared during family life. I think it is called an embolism (maybe I have the wrong term). It did not knock him out but caused erratic behavior, like a stroke. I may be using wrong term, but "stroke" is pretty close. He did not have normal control over his body functions. Doing things with the plane . . . it was like his mind was saying one thing and the body was saying something else.

Most important to know is this: As everybody knows who is of this man's religion, suicide is never considered an option. Islam does not say suicide is okay. If one dies in a circumstance such as a war, laying down your life for your comrades, that is not considered suicide. He was a good family man, a good man.

The copilot recited his simple prayer not once, but again and again as the 767 jetliner plunged into the sea. An exclusive inside report on Flight 990, the EgyptAir jet at the center of the probe, and the rising tensions over the key question: Was it a suicide?

www.newsweek.com

Fig. 12–1. October 31, 1999.

I say this especially to the people of Egypt: It was not done on purpose. It was one of those things that happens medically. You read about it sometimes: Someone is driving a car; something goes wrong and she crashes and causes much injury to others. Later the doctor says she had a heart attack or a stroke. This wasn't a heart attack, and it wasn't enough of a stroke to knock him out.

But he knew it to the extent that he said something like, "I put my trust in God."

Yes, he was trying to do things with the airplane, but his body was not obeying the commands. It was much the opposite—he would turn this switch and something would happen. It was not a suicide. Please put this in the front of the magazine [the *Sedona Journal of Emergence!*] to console the family, because he loved them dearly. He is very sad to not be with you anymore. He tells you from beyond the veils that this was not intentional.

We read that the captain came back and saw what was happening and tried to pull the plane back up.

The captain struggled back to the cabin, which was not easy when the plane was plummeting. It was a heroic act for the captain to even get to the cabin, but because the plane was moving so fast then, when the captain tried to pull it up, the plane did not fare well as a result. It was not designed to take such stress. It was not the fault of the manufacturer or the airline; it was just something that happened. It could have happened anywhere.

Other crew members were present who probably could have done something, but because the copilot was alone at the time for just a moment, it simply happened, and he was unable to prevent it.

Techniques for the May 5, 2000, Alignment

Zoosh and Speaks of Many Truths
January 26, 2000

Z *oosh, on May 5, 2000, there's going to be an alignment of the planets with the Central Sun and apparently there's going to be some shifting of Earth energy and spiritual energy. Do you have any insights into this?*

These planetary shifts are all designed. They are not coincidental to your being here, but you know that. It is important to understand that while you are here, you are citizens of Earth but have souls that go beyond Earth—for that matter, core personalities that go beyond this universe. It is very easy on the day-to-day level to think about being a Hawaiian citizen or an Earth citizen, but in fact, even though your physical bodies are made up of Mother Earth energy, your *actual, functional physical reality* includes not only your Sun but also all the planets that orbit your Sun, including those as yet undiscovered—or in one case, now unreported but soon to be reported.

Helping Earth Recrystallize Itself

I mention this because when planets align in a certain way, it is intended that they perform some direct function—not for you, but for Earth and the other planets, sometimes for the Sun herself or himself. This alignment coming up has a great deal to do with helping Earth recrystallize itself. You all know that aside from industrial mining geared toward products, there has been in recent times a lot of mining of crystals because of the beauty and other things ascribed to them (sometimes true, sometimes wishful thinking, but that's another subject). These crystal veins perform, not unlike your own physical bodies, an actual function in

Mother Earth's body.

If you find crystals on the surface of the planet, that's one thing. Feel free to use them. But I don't want to support digging crystals out of Mother's body—sorry. I know they're beautiful, but in fact, they are always performing a profound function, which usually has to do with a system in her body that would be equivalent to your nervous system and brain. An analogy is that Mother Earth's crystal veins deliver impulses all around her body.

Scientists, anthropologists and weather experts, when studying rock formations and petrified objects and whatnot over the years, have noticed that weather patterns have changed over time. Even some things spoken of in the Bible and other people's wisdom such as the Great Flood are real things. You might ask, "Does this alignment or any other alignment have anything to do with something we should be worried about?" This is the crux of your question. I'd say no. On the other hand, it does have something to do with your personal responsibility to Earth as your host.

Most of Your Responsibility Is Geared toward Earth

As I said awhile back, "You (everybody on Earth) have recently received a little surprise. You're creators-in-training here, and that's why you constantly experience things that most ETs never experience—abundant responsibility for your own personal life, to say nothing of those who depend on you. So you're constantly faced with creator decisions. As a result, you're dealing with life on a regular basis. The recent surprise has to do with the fact that visited upon you now is your having to also deal with 5 percent (out of 100 percent) responsibility for this universe. Not to worry—most of your responsibility is geared toward Earth. Of that 5 percent, perhaps only .0003 of it is universal responsibility, all of which you handle at the deep sleep state. This eases you into this. No sudden responsibility was dropped on you without your ability to deal with it consciously.

On the other hand, what about all the crises on Earth amongst your populations? Different people are doing what they can about that in different ways. You know that, but planetary alignments like this (this one in particular) are geared to help Mother Earth recrystallize herself. She sends out impulses from the core of her being, not only in this dimension, but in about nine dimensions, which are experienced as physical reality when you are in them. I am being very specific here, because even though you might experience fifth-dimensional Earth as physical if you are there, you obviously don't experience it here or it would be distracting, to say the least.

Mother Earth is recrystallizing herself in the core of her being in all these physical as well as nonphysical dimensions so that her weather patterns can get more stabilized. This will not happen immediately; it will take about one and a half average lifetimes for the human being, or 125 years. But it has to begin, because individuals entrusted with recrystallizing Earth have been able to do only a little bit, and it has to go faster.

So here's homework. You have the capacity now, simply by knowing about this, to take action on the deep sleep level. You will do so tonight, not because

Uncle Zoosh says, "You will do so tonight," but rather because you know about it and you tend to process daily affairs at the deep sleep level at night. One assumes it is at the lighter sleep level because one remembers things sometimes, but in fact, it's at the deep sleep level where this takes place. This will come up at some point, and that's good. I want you to do that, but the actual homework is different.

This is what you can do if you like. You can tell friends about it; they can do this homework if they like. Although the alignment takes place over a greater time, the given date is the fifth.

Benevolent Magic Homework for the May 5 Alignment

During the twenty-four hours of May 5 (and if you want, an eight- to twelve-hour overlap on each side of this event), go outside (it's got to be outdoors). Stand on the earth barefoot. (If you are in snow country, go outside wearing leather-soled shoes, not rubber-soled shoes.)

Stand in a specific attitude. The position is fairly simple but precise. Stand with your back to the north. (If you don't have a compass, then just make your best guess.) Stand in a slightly wide stance, as if you are bracing yourself.

Put your open right hand in front of you as if you were going to shake hands with somebody, then pull it back so that the heel of your hand (where your wrist connects) is about six to eight inches, no more than a foot, away from either your navel or your solar plexus (whichever is easiest to find) or somewhere between.

Extend your right thumb upward. Now put your left hand, opened in the same way, directly over your right hand but so that your right thumb is pressed against the left palm. Start with your hands in that position no more than a foot from your body.

Hold that position for a minute or two. If you need to feel a sense of time, wear your watch on your right hand, pushed up on your sleeve.

After a minute or two, move your hands forward, fully extended in front of your body. Hold that for thirty to forty-five seconds. Most of you will be able to do that comfortably.

I will tell you what that's about: It's one thing to know in your minds what I'm talking about here and to do things during deep levels of sleep, but it's entirely another to take physical action to support the reason for your being here. All of you are members of the Explorer Race, as defined in the *Explorer Race* series. That doesn't have to do with your being human, but this is the form you take because it's the form here on Earth.

In order to fully experience your responsibilities as creators-in-training, nowadays you need to begin to take physical actions geared toward producing physical results. In the past, you might have said things, you might have meditated, you might have sat in very specific ways or focused your energies. In short, you might have done lots of things, but now you need to take physical action as well.

When you do this gesture, you do not need to say anything, but you do need to *think as little as possible*. I'm going to tell you how to do that: Look at something you consider innocuous or everyday—if you are in snow country, look at snow, or look at a tree. Focus only on that. If you're in Hawaii or some place mild, look at the dirt. It's also all right to look at a mountain, but try not to look at anything man-made and definitely avoid looking at human beings. If one happens to pass through your line of sight, it won't harm them or you, but it might slightly impact the homework.

Ideally, you want to have no other human beings pass through your line of sight and you want to focus on something simple, maybe part of Earth or something connected to Earth—a tree, soil, a mountain. The sky is acceptable. If it's nighttime, just look down, but keep your eyes open. If you know where a mountain is, you can look in that direction. In short, *make conscious contact with Earth* and acknowledge being part of Earth by standing on her or by letting her hold you up, as some people say.

In this way, you can perform creator training and application. A teacher might take you outside and train you to do this or that, but at some point you need to do it not because the teacher is saying, "Change this; that's not so good." Not that at all. You need to go out *on your own* and do it. I will not be there with a clipboard to put a red check by your name. This is on your own, if you care to do it.

You might ask, "Does this mean that we're supporting the rebuilding of Mother Earth's crystal veins?" No. We're not doing that, because the planets are doing that. What it means is that *you are supporting the alignment of planets.* You are actually supporting the orbital positions of the Sun, the Earth and all the planets—not just those that are lined up, but all the planets in your solar system, because they make up a complete cell that has to do with this solar system's purpose for being. So in that moment you are doing something more along the lines of what a creator might do.

Resonance Will Be Directed to Save Earth

I have a question about rebuilding the crystalline core of the Earth. Does this mean a rising resonance of the Earth, of the fifth dimension?

Resonance is something that is felt, so I do not expect it to make any difference in the resonance. Other people and other spirits say other things; I do not feel beholden to that. But I will say that it makes a difference in capacity. You know that your resonance as an individual is changed according to what you consume or according to the way your personal mass changes, to put it in scientific terms. This is what's going on.

From my point of view, the human expectations, desires and needs of Mother Earth are at this point in time almost—not quite, but almost (I don't want to be too undiplomatic, but shall I be direct?)—of no consequence to Mother Earth because she knows that the first lessons in creator training always give the students lessons in what to do for themselves and others (you've been working on that for a long time, since well before you were born) and what to do for the environment— which is, of course, Earth for you. So it is up to you as Earth people to do for Mother Earth and expect her to do nothing for you. That's astonishing.

Right now you take Earth for granted, even though you might thank her on a daily basis. You take for granted that she will have certain things necessary for you to survive. But what if I told you that your responsibility, which is at 5 percent now, will increase very gradually over the next twenty or thirty years (it won't go to 100 percent in your lifetime, so don't worry), during which you will be literally responsible for all the things humans need that Earth has heretofore provided?

I might add that you cannot afford to leave it to science to do that because practitioners of science are stuck at the moment in the consciousness of creating externally—looking at what's out there and what to do with that. Those of you in more spiritual pursuits will need to be conscious of creating internally, individually as well as with others of like demeanor.

Therefore, any resonance that may or may not be stimulated, supported or created by this event will not be in any way directed to help the people of Earth. It will be directed only to save the patient, who is Earth. Right now Earth is well past her capacity to survive. If it hadn't been for other planets, other beings and, to some extent, the contributions, prayers and spiritual work that you are all doing, she would be long gone.

This tells you something very important. If any of you have ever been around anybody who's sick or grievously ill or injured, you know one thing they can't do very well—help others. It's all they can do to help themselves, and usually they need help. You all know that it is human nature (actually it's conditioning, not your nature) to respond to crises first.

Don't you think Creator knows this? That's why you are gradually being brought into the fold of applied creativism, meaning *what* you do as a creator and *how* you do it. You are being brought back into that fold gradually, not only through various generations who have lived here, but through *all* the Explorer Race has done before we got here that you've been involved with. Every human on Earth is part of the Explorer Race—not the animals (they're not here to learn anything, but to teach), not the plants, not the Earth itself.

Homework: Applied Creativism

Right now you have responsibilities. I will be talking to you about your responsibilities increasingly over the next few months. The reason I am putting so many underlines under your responsibility is that you not only have all the capacity you need to do these things, but the time of benevolent magic is upon you. It's not nigh anymore; it's upon you. You need to be doing things now. (By way of explaining benevolent magic in greater depth, you can look at *Shamanic Secrets for Material Mastery*. There are many hand positions in it that have to do with relationships to Earth. Look at it if you want to and get a feel for it.)

At this level of responsibility, you cannot take for granted anything that Mother Earth can do for you. I want you to be thinking about something (it's not homework; just consider it): "How would I make air that we can breathe?" Of course, you might say, "I know there needs to be so much oxygen and so on," but that's not it. It's not aggressive; it's not about science: "How would I do it? How would I make the water we need to survive?" I'm not talking about, "You need so many hydrogen atoms and so many oxygen . . ." No, science is going to work on its own; you don't have to be scientists.

"How would I make the water? How would I make the Sun shine? How would I make the Moon illuminate? How would I make the stars shine?"—because they do have a benevolent impact here. "How would I make the night, and how could I make the night peaceful, as it's intended to be? How would I make food to feed myself, my family, my people, the people of Earth? How would I make these things for the plants? How would I make these things for the animals? In short, how would I make all the things that Mother Earth makes?"

Some of you will say, "Oh, I'd say a prayer and I'd ask for it to happen." But you need to understand something that religion does not teach you: When you say a prayer (aside from whom you say it to and where you say it), it always involves others, even if you're saying it in a very religious format in a church or temple or ashram. Wherever you might be, it will immediately activate all life around you.

It may not come to you immediately. If it is something benevolent, it will come in some form. (If it is something malevolent, it usually has a tendency to come to you in some teaching form, not necessarily kicking you in the shins, but you soon find out that that's not a good thing to do.) I am not saying either don't pray or do pray. Understand, however, that when you pray, it immediately brings Mother Earth into the picture—the planets, the stars, the universe, Creator and whomever you pray to. It's all-inclusive.

The homework I'm suggesting here is not something to do, but something to think. How would *you* as a representative, as one of God's creations, do it? There's no right or wrong answer to this, by the way, but when you think about it, it's kind of profound. If you rule out science, if you don't ask others to do it, how would you do it? Here's a hint: You have to give yourself Creator status. That's why you're here.

All right, this is Speaks of Many Truths. Do you have questions?

I'm experiencing spiritual burnout. Is there such a word for that?

Sure.

The past ten years of learning . . . I've been very resistant. How do I get that back? I've heard of other people going through the same process.

That's a wonderful question. Thank you.

How do you get the desire back?

Don't. I'll tell you why.

More of You Is Present

When you come here to Earth, you leave a great deal of yourself behind. You have lived forever, and when you've lived forever, you accumulate a great deal of wisdom. If you brought that wisdom here—as any reasonable person would do—applied that wisdom and lived the way you've always lived that has always satisfied you before you came here, would that not be reasonable? Of course.

But when you come here, like anyone who comes here to Earth, it is because you want to learn something new—not to discard your past wisdom, but to add to it in some way that would allow you to provide more, to be more, to experience more. In short, to be more. So you let go of your wisdom temporarily. It's there for you when you pass through the veils at the end of your natural cycle, but you let go of the wisdom you've accumulated and come here as a child, as if you had never learned anything anywhere.

But these times are about more than your individual journey, and you know this, though your individual journey is included. The entire world and this world's effects on other worlds are involved. As a result, what you are experiencing more and more each day—sometimes in spurts, sometimes pausing for a day or two—is more of your potential, but not more of the wisdom you've accumulated, the wisdom you're keeping at bay because you want to learn more.

More of your creative potential and ability is coming to you all the time now. That has been happening for many people—as you say, others you know have been experiencing it. This always causes an impasse, not only personally, but always philosophically, meaning the wisdom you use in your daily life because it works.

It does not mean that the training and the spiritual capacities, all that you've learned, are in any way failing you. What it means is that more of you is present, which needs more. Don't feel odd or sad. You don't even need to feel apologetic if all that training does not serve you anymore. For those it serves, wish them well and say, "May you enjoy this. I am expanding into other things, and I will always cherish my time in that philosophy with you all," or whatever words feel good to you.

It's not abandoning; it's going on to more. It is a time of discernment, yes, but it's been discernment for some time. It's a time primarily of individual expansion. Zoosh talked to you about the increasing responsibilities you have, but as you know, Creator would never give you increased responsibility without at the same time giving you increased capacities. When your capacities increase, it brings in more of the potentials for you—in short, more of you. When you were born as a baby, you had physical potentials. You weighed perhaps seven, eight, nine pounds, and you could say that you had seven or eight or nine pounds of physical potential.

But this is different. The potential you also has needs. If the philosophies and spirituality are sufficient for an individual when such potentials are given, then you will be able to serve that. You have been getting this more gradually over many years, and this philosophy in the past has served you, what you have learned and accumulated. But now you've noticed that you feel distracted; it doesn't feed you the way it once did.

That means you need something else. Start looking around to see what does feed you. If nothing does that you can find, then maybe it is time to feed others. You know, many times a person will be involved with a spiritual teaching and listen to a good and beloved teacher, but at some point that person will leave the fold. For a while, there's a feeling of uncertainty, but eventually that teaching plus the inspiration that comes to you is what you teach.

So don't feel bad. If it's time to go out that door, another door will open. You will either find inspiration for yourself or you will give inspiration to others. When you do that, what always happens is that other people ask you questions at some point for which you do not have the answers, but those answers are often inspired.

How many times have you been in a situation where somebody asks you a question? They have a terrible situation and you want to help them, but you yourself have no personal means to resolve it for them, to say nothing of wisdom. But something pops into your head and you say it, and when you're done, you are almost as surprised as the person who heard it. Can you identify with that?

It is like that for you now. Don't be apologetic. It is time for something more. You may use what you have learned; it won't go to waste at all, but it's not enough.

Get Up and Go!

Isis
June 13, 2000

A great many people have been wanting to do something, and doing something is necessary. As you know, the more Creator energy that is fed to beings on Earth, to human beings, the more you will have to do or else the more it will simply happen on its own. Therefore, the important thing here is to begin to not only lay out plans for what you would like to do—in short, goals—but also to lay out some kind of idea about what you are going to do to achieve those goals. I know that people have done this before. Those were exercises really in preparation for this, but now it's here.

Because there is sufficient Creator energy, you'd be surprised at how little you have to do to generate the potential of your goals coming to you. But in order for you to see it and experience it, to understand what's going on so that you can recognize it and to have the discernment to acknowledge that it is something of value versus something that is no longer for you, it's helpful to have a clear-cut plan of action.

Write Down Your Goals and Take Action

Therefore, I recommend, again, that people write down their goals. And don't make them halfway goals. Write down your goals, and if it's a business, write down the process you think might work. Then start taking some action, some steps toward those goals, even if it is making contacts in fields that seem to be related to your potential success. Then I think the success will start to come to you.

It's as if you are waving a flag at someone to say, "Okay, I'm ready now." But saying you're ready now isn't enough. You have to do something. This way the creative energy will come through in a way that is benevolent. But if you continue to simply stay where you are, doing nothing, and you feel uncomfortable, the creative energy will express itself that way. If you feel stuck, the creative energy will do something to move you off that stuckness, even if it is something unpleasant. So it's better to put your focus into what you want and take action in that direction. Then the creative energy will run down that stream and help make it happen real quick.

Work with the Creative Energy

Can you say where we are in the movement from the third to the fourth dimension?

You're at about 3.48 and a half, and there is a chance for you to get to 3.49, but it requires action—action based not on reaction to things you don't like, but action toward things you do like and want. It can't just be reaction. You may need to have reactions in order to sidestep unpleasant things, but you must also take action. Therefore, you must know what actions to take. If you don't know, have somebody suggest to you what to do—consult an adviser, whatever works for you in your profession, job or relationship. Have somebody advise you so that you have some idea of something constructive you can do. Then the energy will be there.

It's all right to work on it step by step, but you can also take action on the next step. You can even begin to take some action on the steps beyond that, meaning research or making some calls or something. In that way, you clearly define to the creative energy what it is you want to do, what you plan to do and, of course, what you're willing to do. The goal can then be achieved much quicker, and the creative energy goes into something you actually like rather than into something designed simply to get you moving.

How long ago did this expanded level of creative energy begin flowing?

I'd say that within the last three to five months it started in such a way that people started feeling a little uncomfortable or fidgety. It was present before then, but it is now in place in such a way that people feel that they must do something. And when you do that, when you take those actions, the fidgety feeling will go away. That's the thing—it will go away. It is your body's nervous system and musculature that is intending to get you to act. In short, this tells you that if it is your body intending to get you to act, it must have something to do with material mastery, which it does. So this is a material-mastery time for you all. If you know that, then you will know that discernment and all the work you've done in discernment up to this point in time is vitally important.

Is this something that is going to continue to expand gently or exponentially, or how?

It won't be exponentially, because that's too much pressure for people who don't know what to do and don't know how to do it, but it will continue to expand gently. It's like physicists who excite atoms to see what happens, but in this case it is known what will happen. But the excitement must take place on the physical level first so that people will know that a physical action is required. You can't just think about it.

Get Your Plan in Place

If you don't have your plan in place now (some of you do), get it down, get it clear and make sure that the goals are something you want, something that feels good to you, not just something that other people say is right for you. Then write down what you think you can do to get there and begin taking physical actions, even if it's dialing a phone. But that's just a beginning. Then you need to go places, do things, contact people, depending on your profession.

For some of you, it will simply be moving your office from some small space that's cramped and uncomfortable to some place big and more expansive, or looking around and seeing what's available and going out and touching the space, saying, "Oh, this would be wonderful!" And even if you can't get that ideal space, something will come along that is better than what you've got, according to what you can budget and so forth.

So it's all designed to improve the quality of your life at the same time you let go of what you now have so that others can obtain it. For others, that will be their goal. But if everybody sits where they've been sitting, how is anybody going to obtain his or her goal? You need to have motion. Get up and go!

In Motion, Your Heart Energy Will Support Your Body

What about our heart energy? How much can we hold now, and what's the average we're holding?

I'm glad you asked that, because those who do get up and go will find that their heart energy will support their body, and they will be able to assimilate about another 3 to 4 percent of your heart energy. But if you do not or cannot get up and go, you will not receive any more, simply because the more heart energy you receive, the more you are likely to feel the need for an improvement in your lifestyle. So it is done with kindness, not with authoritarianism.

That's good. Thank you.

Techniques for Working with Mother Earth to Enhance Your Life Force

Speaks of Many Truths
September 27, 2000

G reetings.

How to Counteract the Lethargy from Chemtrails

What can one do to counteract the toxic effects of the chemtrails? When they are overhead, one's energy is depleted; it's like being comatose.

I would say that you have to get used to utilizing the reservoir of strength within the planet. It does not do you any good to pull from great distances when you do not know how to pull or connect with that which is right next to you or in contact with you. There will be times when you feel lethargic (which would be a good description of the effect of chemtrails), but regardless of the cause of the lethargy, I would recommend the following:

If there is a mountain or some prominent part of Earth at a distance (but mountains are best), look at it with as few human-built things within your line of sight as possible and find the most comfortable place to rest your eyes or your vision on the mountain, the place that feels most comfortable to you. That is the first thing. When you find that spot, you will know, because your body will feel relaxed, and those of you who know how to do the warmth or love-heat/heart-warmth/physical-warmth [see p. 23], or who have practiced the warmth in your body, will feel some warmth. That is the mountain inviting you to make contact. Then you just breathe naturally, in and out, about ten times. Don't blow at the mountain; just breathe in and out naturally while you look at that place, and you will feel better.

Getting the Strength You Need from Mountains

If you are exposed to things, as happens from time to time, you need to be able to do as little as possible when you are lethargic and still have the strength you need. If you cannot summon the strength within yourself, then you can look at a mountain. Not everyone will have a mountain nearby or even have one close enough that they can see at least part of it, so what you do if you are outdoors is to look down at the ground. See if you can find a place on the physical ground—not on pavement, on the physical land—that feels the same way, gives you a sense of warmth or just feels good to you. Then try it, just take a breath in from that point. If on the first intake of breath you feel uncomfortable—especially for those of you who do not know how to feel the warmth—then immediately breathe out. In that case, you can blow out. Continue breathing normally for a time and see if you can find a place on the physical land that prompts you to feel good. Then breathe in gently from it.

It won't work to breathe in from another living source—human being, animal. It won't work to breathe in, for those of you in the city, from a building that's man-made. You have to find something that is of the land. In my time, the mountains were often referred to as sacred, but people in your time often don't know what that means [Speaks of Many Truths was alive on Earth in North America in the 1600s]. It means not only that the land is sacred everywhere, but it also means that certain mountains, those places on Earth, naturally exude an energy.

This is why mountains exist at all; it's not a scientific accident. Scientists can explain how mountains come about, but they do not explain the motivation for mountains. The motivation—other than being produced volcanically, but even then—is that an energy is being exhaled by Mother Earth right there. This is energy she makes available for her resident beings—human beings, animals, plants. It's available there, and it comes out right there. And parts of her body tend to thrust up in those areas. If you can then look at those mountains, what we call sacred mountains, and breathe naturally in and out when you are looking at them, you will experience the strength you need, often for whatever you have to do.

In my time, we didn't have these chemical exposures like you do. But sometimes we would have to go great distances, frequently by walking. Sometimes we would have to travel farther than might be considered reasonable or without as much water or food as we needed. We would need great strength, sometimes more strength than we had. If we could just look at the mountain, even if we were collapsed on the ground from exhaustion, if we could look at the mountain and breathe in and out, we would have the strength to go on. This is energy that Mother Earth offers freely. That which is offered freely is often of greater benefit than that which is taken. You know that if someone takes something from you without your permission, it doesn't feel very good. And that person might not get much energy from it. But if you have plenty and offer it freely, those who receive from you might get more out of it because of the love that goes with it.

Breathe and Know What Is Meant for You

Some of you in the scientific community might find this hard to quantify, even though you might believe it. When you are attached to quantifying or measuring things for the sake of science, you will not use science in the way it was always intended. In my time, science of a sort existed also, and that was the means to know what was for you and your fellow beings and what was for others. Science does that in your time, measuring (if you like to use that term), weighing or calculating what is appropriate for human beings and in what quantity, and what isn't. In my time, we would look at something, breathe in and out, and on the basis of how we felt when we looked at it, we would know whether or not it was for us. I grant that this might not seem quantifiable to science, but it is based on the same need, and the principle is related.

You will continue to find, in your time, things that—even though they might look like they would be good to consume or breathe or experience—are not meant for you. That does not mean they are bad. They are just not meant for you; they are meant for others. On the other hand, certain things might not always look like they are meant for you—how to know? Look at it; breathe in and out while you are looking at it. If it feels good, perhaps it is for you. If it doesn't feel good, then it is for another.

If it is a human being or a physical being or a plant being you're looking at, you can be pretty sure that this technique is not meant to be applied. At least let's say that this technique is not meant to be applied right now by you, at your level of wisdom, in association with human beings right now. At some point in the future, I will give you more steps so that you will know whether a human being is right for you as a friend or even as a lover. In that case, one never looks directly at the person, but there are other ways.

How to Tell Which Mountain Is Best for You

Still, in this case, we are talking about how one can have the strength one needs by utilizing freely offered energy from Mother Earth. How do you know which mountain is best? You will know based entirely upon your physical body's reaction. That is why you've had so much training in these books over the years about knowing and understanding your body's signals, which tell you that something is for you—or isn't. An uncomfortable feeling means it isn't for you—not for you at that time or not for you at all. Whereas a feeling of physical-warmth, or love-heat, means that it probably is for you, especially in the case of a mountain's energy, for example.

I can't give you an across-the-board description in your time, because your time is more complicated. But I can give you these basic rules so you will know that all of these challenges—including the ones that might be caused by human beings, for whatever reason—are, in the larger picture, designed as a clarion call to remind you that you must now use the simple techniques you have been guided to use in order to feel better or at least to have the strength you need to feel well. How, for example, can you feel good, not just have the strength you need, and in circumstances as described by the general question today, the chemtrails? How can you feel even vigorous in such circumstances, with chemicals and so on?

As I said before, how can you tell which mountain is best for you, or which spot on the mountain? You can do so based entirely on the way your physical body reacts. So look around the horizon until you find all of the spots on all of the mountains you look at that prompt your body to feel physically warm. Breathe in and out, looking at all of those different spots. How long? At least ten breaths, no more than twenty-five—natural breaths, in and out. Always, when you are done with that process, say, "Good life." You can say, "Thank you, Mother Earth," as well, if you wish. But just say, "Good life." That which interacts with you in that way knows who you are talking to. "Good life" is a blessing in that situation. And you'll find, after those different points of contact, that you will feel pretty good, at least good enough to do something. Don't do this just to improve your mood. Do it if you need to do something, if you need to invigorate yourself. And in time I will suggest other things. But this is what I recommend for now.

Release Excess Energy to the Mountains to Relieve Sleeping Difficulties

Now I want to give you something else: There are those of you who have difficulty going to sleep when you need to. Perhaps you have more energy than you need. Don't do this as a donation if you are awake and filled with energy, but do it if you need to go to sleep or rest for a time. You can look at the mountain—or even places on the land for those of you who have no mountains handy—and simply, very gently, blow. You don't have to do anything particular. If you feel energetic but you need to sleep, you can simply exhale; blow gently out of your mouth. It's best to blow at a mountain or at the land, and that will release your excess energy.

If you are not sure whether you are releasing excess energy, then, if you like, you can put one of your hands on your solar plexus, but not flat on it . . . put the fingertips on your solar plexus, then blow. That is a signal to your body to release energy from there. Granted, energy is in all parts of your body, but excess energy will go immediately to your solar plexus, and when you blow, since your solar plexus is near, that part of you that puffs (what you call the diaphragm) will release through there into your lungs, into your breath and out. I'm not saying that it is something you must do if you have excess energy—only before you go to sleep if you are having difficulty sleeping. It is also a way to share excess energy with those who might need it somewhere else.

Remember, the big picture, what is going on here, is the unification of all human beings as a species, from one to another. As this occurs more and more and as time goes on, you will gradually be able to resolve problems—some of which don't seem to be resolvable right now—simply by being unified. I can assure you, those who feel totally isolated will feel like you can't understand them even if they speak the same language; they will not even try to tell you what's wrong with them. Any parent who's ever asked a loved one, especially a youngster, will know that speaking the same language is not sufficient to get another to confide in you. And very often your lover is the same way if he or she feels there is no way to explain something. But if you feel unified, even on the small basis of the family, there will be words, gestures and understanding. That alone is often helpful.

Is the reverse true? If holding your fingers on your solar plexus and blowing out excess energy focuses it from there, is breathing into the solar plexus and holding your fingers there a way to bring extra energy to that point?

No, it isn't.

Energy Depletions Are Not Just from Chemtrail Exposure

I'd like to get a whole understanding of why we're being subjected to these toxic chemicals in the air we breathe.

Let's broaden your question. Let's say, "Why are human beings exposed to anything that causes trauma, difficulty, disease and misery?" Then the answer I just gave is sufficient: It's because it is a clarion call.

You are always being unified first with your physical body, as demonstrated in *Shamanic Secrets of Physical Mastery* and its basic unifying technique of heart-warmth/physical-warmth, also known as love-heat work, which lets you know how your body works. Often you will be exposed to things. As a matter of fact, at the very least, you will be exposed on a daily basis to other people's uncomfortable feelings about that which is going on in their lives that they cannot immediately cure. Perhaps it is slight, perhaps it is major, but they will exude those feelings all the time. You are constantly exposed to this. On the slight level, it is one thing, but when everybody is feeling bad, you must be able to do something instantaneously; otherwise you will feel bad. I can assure you that your energy becomes depleted much more often because of this than because of anything that is sprayed in the sky for any reason whatsoever.

Using Warmth from the Mountain to Resolve Differences with Other Humans

You need to do the work that will allow you to unify with all human beings. But do I suggest that you look at other human beings and breathe in, or not? No, of course not. Because all human beings are not in the state of grace. Grace, in this sense, is not referring to a religious state, because you all have different religions, but to the state of grace—meaning that you are united and at ease and comfort in your physical body and with the physical body of Earth. Earth herself is the great equalizer for all human beings.

For example, you might be having some difficulty, some argument with somebody—a husband and wife, brother and sister, friends—you might be having an argument. You could go outside. You could each look at the mountain and breathe ten breaths, in and out, in the way described. Find the spot on which your eyes rest on the mountain, where you feel the warmth inside your body; then breathe in and out for ten breaths, and go on with your discussion or talk about things. While you are each looking at the mountain, don't tell each other where you are looking. Sometimes you'll feel warmth from the same part of the mountain, sometimes from different parts. You might find yourself talking back to back sometimes, looking at different mountains. While you are doing that, breathing in and out naturally, feeling the warmth and also just feeling invigorated, you'll find that you'll be able to resolve your differences more easily. It doesn't mean that you will agree with the other person, but you might find a resolution that will be sufficient in that moment, even if it is only to forgive one another more easily.

The great equalizer is at work here, and the true great equalizer is Mother Earth, who has all physical energies within her, at least those associated with life on Earth, human beings, and more importantly, who can interpret all physical energies in ways that are compatible with you. That is why you will look at one part of the mountain, for instance, one day or one moment and feel warmth in your body.

It is not only that that part of the mountain is prepared and able, with enough energy, to communicate energetically with you—meaning to help you to feel good. It is also because that physical part of the mountain is most in tune with your physical body in that moment and is able to interpret whatever physical energies you need from whatever source they are coming from—whether from Earth or other beings on the Earth—to interpret in the most benevolent way to you that which you breathe in at that moment. Learn how to work with your own physical body and your own breath and your own warmth, and thence you will be able to work with Mother Earth and, in time (as in the example for resolving arguments), with human beings—but always in your now state of learning, utilizing the Earth as a buffer or as a medium between yourself and that which you are in conflict with. In this way, resolution comes about through the material master.

Mother Earth, in this case, is the physical master and the spiritual master. Of course, she is many other kinds of masters, but in this particular case, your problem is with materials, whether it be chemtrails in the sky or another human being, who is material and spiritual. So when there are problems in your lessons of material mastery or challenges in your lessons of physical mastery or needed solutions in your lessons of spiritual mastery, first utilize what is native, natural and simplest for you before you try the more complicated. First you must have union with yourself and do the heat that feels like warmth, the love-heat. Then you apply that heat, which also says this is good for you now—in other words, this is love for you now—you apply it to other things. And you learn in time how to utilize that for everything you do. Whether it is what you eat, when you sleep, who you work with, where you work, where you live—everything.

In time, when you feel the warmth from all that you do, all that you interact with, all beings, then you will all have heaven on Earth. It is what you do and how you do it that allows you to feel this heaven, which in this sense is the applied method Creator uses to know what goes with what all the time, everywhere, in all times. If that is a definition of heaven, then I offer it to you.

Life Force Is Designed to Come in through Breath

How was the human body designed to receive life force? Does it come in through the crown chakra, in through the pores of the body, in through the cells, in through the feet?

Through the breath. It is not an accident that children, when they are born from their mother, are encouraged to breathe. Not just because you breathe to live when you are physical, but because you must take in energy to live. That's why when birth is done in a very gentle, loving manner, the child naturally begins to breathe rather than having to be prompted to breathe by a sudden gesture, a tap or even a little slap. I realize these slaps are done with the intention of encouraging life. Still, even in my time, we tried to welcome a child gently. It is natural to breathe, but when born, sometimes a child does not immediately have to breathe because of still being connected to the mother, where the mother's body is providing that breath.

But, in time, children have to breathe on their own, and they do so. That's why what is around the children when they take that first breath is important. Is it loving, gentle beings who welcome that child? Then with that first breath, that first contact with the energy source beyond mother and beyond oneself, one feels love, one feels welcome. One feels, as one's basic patterning of life, that Earth is a place one can feel good about. Whereas, if one suddenly gets slapped on the bottom, even with the best of intentions, one is not immediately sure—and never becomes sure, regardless of the best help or therapies—that Earth is that safe.

In time you will reinstitute a more gentle birth all over the world. This is a gentle reminder of that. When one feels safe and welcome in a place, one is much more likely to open up and offer what one has to offer in the best way one can offer it. Sometimes you might not think that's enough. But often, since you are all individuals here, what you have to offer that is of your nature, of your being, of your very specific energy, might be valuable to another, since you are all individual, unique parts of one whole thing.

I stand on the land and breathe, and I feel an energy coming up my feet. Is that a different type of life force than the one that comes in the breath?

No, because you are breathing when you are standing on the land. You are taking it in, or even exhaling it through the bottoms of your feet. But it is still involving breath.

How would you describe the breath, then? As a directive force?

It is the means of engaging physically with all physical support systems. It's the first thing you do.

Building Strength

So with these chemtrails . . . they're putting biological spores in the air, right? That's insidious. It's attacking the very way we get our life force.

But look at the broader picture. As I said, this is just one more thing that encourages you to find the means that will give you strength. Ultimately, it will build strength for those of you who do it regularly, to the point where even things that have bothered you in the past won't bother you. Do you understand what I'm saying? Don't wait to feel bad to go outside and make contact with the mountain this way, and breathe in and out. Do it every day, whether you feel good or bad or not. In this way, you continue to build up your physical strength and your natural ability. Remember, when you look at the mountain and you find a spot on the mountain that prompts your physical body to demonstrate warmth, it is not only that Mother Earth is saying, "Here, let me give you this energy." She is also saying, "Here is where I welcome what you have to give." Because when you look at it, you breathe in, and it's the breathing in that gives you the energy. But what happens when you breathe out?

You're giving energy.

You're giving energy, that which might not in the immediate moment seem to be giving you strength. Maybe it is, maybe it isn't. But at the very least, some of it will give strength to others—as interpreted, filtered and translated through Earth in a way that when others call upon it wherever they live by breathing to their mountain, they can feel it comfortably.

So do it every day at least once. When I was living on Earth, I used to do it five, six, maybe even ten times a day, whether I felt good or bad. This is possibly why people from my time didn't get sick as often as people in your time, even though there were times when we were exposed to things that would have been considered not just toxic in your time, but lethal.

So how does doing this five or six times a day accrue? Is there a residual effect?

I'm not saying you should do it five or six times a day; I'm just saying what I did.

Did it bring more life force or strengthen the immune system? How would you describe the effect in the body of what you did?

I don't describe it scientifically; I just say that I would feel better. Let's use an analogy: Let's say that there's a universal choir and you cannot reach all the notes, nor can you sing all the parts all the time. But as you breathe in and out and accumulate different sounds, let's say—though it's not just sounds, but I'm using it as an analogy—then you have that within you when or if you might ever need it.

It fills in the gaps and spaces. Sometimes when you feel poorly, it's not just because of something you can put your finger on and say, "There, that's the cause." Sometimes it's because you have so many gaps and spaces in your physical vehicle that have not been filled in by your intimate moments of breathing in and out, looking at Mother Earth, appreciating her for what she can offer to you, but not thinking about that. You think about that afterward—that you get so much from Mother Earth. She is an instrument, but she is truly a mother. She gives you strength and energy.

So if you do not have those gaps and spaces filled in, sometimes when you are exposed to something, even temporarily, you will become exhausted or feel poorly or even get sick. But if you have those gaps and spaces filled in, then you'll feel better. This works whether the mountain is above the surface of the land or in the sea—for those of you who might occasionally see such a thing while you're under-water—or coming up out of the sea, as islands do. I mention that in passing for those of you who might live on islands.

Those who do not live near mountains, try to look either down or off into the distance at a place that is not paved but is exposed earth. Find a place with the same warmth as your body feels, that you can breathe in and out as in the exercise—the interaction, let's call it—I've discussed.

Some of you live in the flatlands, with no mountains available. In my time, we very rarely would choose to reside someplace where there wasn't at least a hill, because you needed to have a place where Mother Earth demonstrated to you that she was breathing·out energy that was available. If there was at least a hill, you would know that she was breathing energy out there, because of the bulge. But if the land was completely flat, it meant that she was not exhaling out any excess energy.

For those of you who live on flat land, well, I'm just hoping in times to come that most of you will move and live near . . . not *in* the mountains, because the mountains must breathe in and out for themselves as well. But if you can live near the mountains where you can see them, that's the best, I believe.

But for those who do live on flat land, you said to either stand on the earth or get a line of sight to a piece of natural earth, and that would help.

Yes, do the best you can. On that note, I will say, "Good life."

Good life.

Masculine and Feminine
Components of the Feeling Body

Zoosh

March 3, 2001

Excerpt from a private session, with permission.

W hen you say you understand the phrase "As you think, so you create" . . .
that is a complete fallacy in your time. The mind has become almost godlike in
the reverence people have for it. It is not godlike in its own right, but people
consider it such a wonderful thing because they see the value of thought as a
unifying force among people, helping to minimize conflict. I grant that, but "As
you think, so you create"? No.

The Human Mind Inhibits Creation

The human mind stands outside of all creation on Earth. It can observe and
instruct, but more often it controls. And it is the control aspect of the mind that
actually inhibits creation. As a child is being raised, in whatever faith or philosophy, the basic conditioning conveyed is, "Don't," "Stop" and "No." Those words
in any language, no matter how well intended, immediately or gradually cause
the child to feel that his or her natural feelings cannot be trusted.

This is a complication on Earth, because the human mind judges feelings as
being entirely in reaction. But, in fact, feelings have a masculine and a feminine
component. Reaction is entirely the masculine component, but the feminine
component of feelings is in creation. If you can understand that fine point, you
will have some insight into how creation works. Creation is achieved by human
beings in cooperation with all life. Human beings have some problem with this,
not understanding it fully.

The assumption is that Creator is all life, meaning that the human being creates in cooperation with a creator, but that's not true. You create in cooperation with all life equally—the Creator, a plant, a mountain, a rainstorm, an animal or an atomic particle. Creator and all Its creations, including all human beings, are equal elements. Therefore, when you create, the feminine feeling process is in contact with that same feminine feeling process in all other beings in the universe. Creator would be the last being in the world, if I might use that colloquial phrase, to consider Itself separate. Creator is not separate and is not "greater than." Creator is absolutely equal to all Its creations. How could it be any other way? Therefore, all feeling on the feminine level is the means by which you create your reality.

When adults tell children, with the best of intentions, "Don't touch that," or "Stop doing that," it has no great effect unless spoken harshly. If spoken tenderly, it has no restrictive effect on the feminine creation ability along feeling lines. But if spoken harshly or even with a spanking (perhaps not to punish or hurt, but just to get his attention so baby does not stick his fingers in the light socket), this perfectly reasonable action produces an impact that the parents do not realize. The actual impact is that the baby, who is a being in much greater harmony than older humans, begins to distrust his feelings. And therein lies the problem.

The Feminine Feeling Self Connects You in Harmony with All Creation

The feeling ability of human beings—the feeling body—is unknown in your time, and it's something you need to know. Any human being can learn how to interact with the feeling body, to rebuild or, in most cases, to begin to develop a sense of understanding of how the feeling body works, that it has more than one component, that it is not strictly in reaction to anything. The reactive part, to remind you, is the masculine part. But the creation portion of the feeling body is what literally creates your world.

For example, people are always asking for things they need. Sometimes this is a genuine need; sometimes it's merely perceived. If you knew how to ask for that using your feminine feeling self, you would have a good chance of receiving it. Now, what if an individual were to ask for something that might harm somebody else, perhaps in a moment of anger? What if that person was to focus into those feminine feelings and ask for something harmful? It would not work, because in your feminine feeling self, you are connected in harmony with the feminine self of all creation. When you are connected that way, you are the divine creation portion of the human being, or the Explorer Race. This is the core, the root of your being, why you are here. It is, in short, what you are.

Now, even if you could manage to wish something harmful, when connected with that, it would never occur. You would be slightly distant from that feminine creation energy of all beings, not quite able to tap into it for a time until you learned that this is not acceptable. However, you probably would simply not be able to say it because when you are connected to that feminine-creation-feeling portion of yourself, you are able to speak and desire only in terms of benevolence.

Homework: Differentiating the Masculine and Feminine Feeling Bodies

So I would like to give you a little homework to help you differentiate between the masculine side of the feeling body and the feminine side. It will not be difficult. The first stage is simply to notice the masculine side of the feeling body—don't try to control it, just notice it. Notice how you react in your feeling body to whatever is going on around you for the next few days. Just notice. You don't have to keep a record; you can if you want to, but don't make it so detailed that it interferes with your life. Notice that you saw something, heard something, felt uncomfortable. Or be more specific: "I felt uncomfortable in my chest or arm," something like that.

After that, wait a few days. Then experiment with the feminine portion of the feeling body. This begins with creating a feeling. So between the two assignments, you can make a list of feelings you would enjoy experiencing, anything you like: love, happiness, humor. Remember, some things that are considered to be experiences or actions are also associated with feelings, so explore that.

Now, after that, experiment a bit. Begin when you expect no interruptions, when it is calm and quiet. You can, if you like, use earplugs to eliminate sound, but allow sounds of nature to be present unless they are too distracting. Wear as little clothing as possible, very loose and comfortable. Now lie down or sit. If you sit, do not cross your arms or legs. Take off anything made of metal other than gold. Remove any other metal unless it is something that has been on your body for years.

Simply relax on the bed or in a comfortable chair, and pick an emotion or a feeling from your list. Recall when you had this feeling, unless there is a painful memory associated with it, or imagine it with some story you tell yourself. Rather than attempting to create something, I'd like you to stimulate it with your mind so that your mind feels part of the process. That's important because of the great authority your generation and generations before you have given to the mind. Your mind has been conditioned to believe it must be involved in everything. So we're going to use the divine part of the mind, which is the imagination.

Now, remember and try to bring up the memory, as an actor might do, to create that feeling in your body. Before you do this, you can, if you like, focus on creating heat in your chest or solar plexus, the love-heat/heart-warmth/physical-warmth [see p. 23]. You can also create the heat at the end of the exercise. It is important for the mind to know that it is being consulted but it is not the authority. This way the mind will feel involved but not overwhelmed.

I want your mind to feel that it is not being shut out, but rather that it is being incorporated into the process as an equal participant. Go to a feeling and try to create it—maybe two or three feelings each time you do this. Between feelings, just relax for a few minutes to give your body time to adjust. Then go on to another feeling. Once you are into that feeling, try to stay in it as long as you can. Your mind is going to want to think about it, which will immediately prompt other experiences or reactions in your body by the masculine feeling self. Try to stay in the feminine feeling, the generated feeling.

End with the heat in your chest or solar plexus or wherever it shows up. Don't try to move it around. It might show up in one place one night and in one place another day. That's fine. When you end that way, the mind will recognize that it is participating equally in something, and over time it will begin to feel more relaxed in general.

Do this exercise for two to three consecutive days or nights, and then stop. Take a few days off, and then do it again, always ending and, if you choose, beginning with the love-heat feeling. You will find that in time you'll be able to differentiate the masculine feeling self from the feminine feeling self. This will give you a much greater understanding and possibly access to the creation abilities you actually have.

The Mind Is Overwhelmed

Most people's minds feel overwhelmed all the time because there is too much for them to do of which the mind is entirely incapable. That is why as you look around your world, you see the great benefits that science and technology have provided along with the horrible catastrophes they have created. That is because the mind does not have—nor is it naturally equipped to have—a set of morals associated with harmony. Only the feelings can do that. So you can get different thoughts that feel perfectly true to you individually, but when connected with feminine harmony, all beings feel exactly the same. That's the unifying element.

Many people's minds or mental selves are in total panic unless the mind is being used in a disciplined fashion. That's because their minds know that the mind itself is completely out of its depth when it comes to creation. This is why people are often nervous and agitated. That nervousness is a large part of why the human being does not live for 150 to 200 years, which is your natural life cycle in your present body. The mind is overwhelmed by a task that it was never intended to do and of which it is entirely incapable.

The creation-feeling feminine self is not able to feed and nurture the physical body because it has been short-circuited by well-intentioned conditioning within you. If the human being were able to feel this feminine feeling (love and so on) on a regular basis, the incorporation of that feeling would extend life. You might reasonably ask whether there is a feeling you could experience on a more frequent basis that would actually improve your quality of life and perhaps extend it. I cannot guarantee it, but the love-heat feeling was initiated by Speaks of Many Truths so that people would begin to connect with that feeling of access into the feminine feeling self and possibly enter into a harmonic creation ability that would connect them with all life.

Your Natural Creator Self

This work is not intended to give you something you don't already have but rather to show you something and present you with physical evidence of it, to acquaint you with the feelings you have in your physical body, to show you something that works in minute and detailed steps. People have asked me over the years why they have to learn these things in such minute, slow ways on Earth. These are creator lessons. You, the Explorer Race, are intended to become the Creator someday, but in order to do so, you must completely understand the consequences of creation. The only way to understand that is to experience it on a personal level. That's why you come here, why you learn things incrementally. That is why I'm reminding you of the existence of your natural creator self.

You don't have to learn how to become a creator. You're here to learn how to experience on a personal level the impact of your creation so that you do not frivolously or flippantly create something that could have a profound, hurtful impact on beings. As I stated in *Explorer Race: Techniques for Generating Safety*, that is simply because your Creator—not your original Creator, but the Creator of this universe where you have been for some time—does not personally understand the feeling of pain from Its own experience. It has been shown this feeling by another being, but It had to be taken out of this creation briefly to experience it. And the creation suffered a little bit for a time, but now it is all right again. This Creator has encouraged you, the Explorer Race, to take over for It eventually, and to do so, you have to be more finely tuned than this Creator. That's why you are going through these exhaustive steps, so that you will not make the same mistakes as this Creator has done, with the best of intentions, when you take over this creation.

One likes to think of the Creator as omnipotent, wonderful, without error. But, in fact, all creators need to learn. That's why they exist in the form that they do—because they are learning. And just as a parent feels toward a child, this Creator wants you, the Explorer Race, to be better than Itself. So you go through this long, exhaustive lesson for which there has been so much suffering. And now, through the re-exploration of the creation process, you are going to re-create benevolence here on Earth. This is the purpose of the homework I gave you, that you can as a human being, in your portion of Creator, come into that harmony and create. You'd be surprised how much good you can do and what a short time it will take once you learn how to do these things.

The questions you asked triggered this information because it was you who asked and at this time. Others have asked similar questions on previous occasions, but it was not the time and it was not you asking. I am not trying to say you are God or something like that; I am saying that certain souls (my perception of souls is immortal personalities) have gotten together before this experience on Earth and said, "Well, when the time is right, you ask me a question and I will deliver the information." How will we know the time is right? The time is right because human beings of many cultures on Earth—with their conditioning, awareness of the world and experience of being human—can personally grasp this knowledge. It is something that humanity needs and can experience in this moment. So my answer, while it might seem oblique, is in fact the direct answer to your questions.

It's the Feminine Feeling Self's Job to Instruct

I will tell you what you can do to make me happy: Embrace life as much as you can. Experience physicality in ways that please you and feel good to both your masculine and feminine feeling selves. Now that you have the homework, you can discern those things. Don't favor one over the other. It is not your job to discard the masculine feeling self but to instruct it.

The feminine feeling self's job is to instruct. Women know innately that it is their job to instruct men, even if they are not conditioned to believe that. Very often the woman has difficulty with this, or she could even get into trouble by telling the man too much. But the woman is born knowing that as a feminine being, it is her job to instruct. What she doesn't realize, because your society has not yet sufficiently evolved, is that she needs to be instructed in all the true harmonious feminine arts and abilities so that she can instruct in ways the masculine being can hear and embrace without feeling threatened, condemned or intimidated in any way.

Therefore, understand that your feminine feeling self is intended to instruct your masculine feeling self on which feelings are the best to experience, not only in terms of generating those feelings, but (and here is the crux of the matter) in experiencing, seeking, creating—in short, in living a life where those benevolent and wonderful feminine-inspired feelings will be felt in reaction to what you are doing. When the masculine feeling body has learned to distinguish which feelings are good and not so good, beneficial or not, in terms of your relationship with yourself and others, it will then seek out experiences with all life. It will react with those wonderful feelings the feminine feeling self has shown are intended to be felt in the harmonic feminine feeling selves of all other life.

Human beings do not always have access to these feelings because they are here to learn. After they have learned, they will choose to experience feelings prompted by the feminine creation feeling self, not only because of some statement by Grandfather or Uncle Zoosh, but because it feels good and has a benevolent effect on all other beings. That, my friend, is what you can do if you choose.

The Keys of Enoch

The major strength of the book *Keys of Enoch* lies in the illustrations and their effect when you touch them. To do that, lay either hand palm down on the illustration and see what happens (experiment with which works better for each illustration and at different times). Do this only two or three a day, however, as the material is rooted in the past and is extremely potent. Therefore, I do not choose to support and sustain such books; I merely acknowledge that this material is true and worthy of doing.

Generally speaking, I do not support what I call the Jehovan past. Jehovah is a past incarnation—thinly but not directly connected to the Creator of this universe. In the past, I might have, for the sake of being polite and not wanting to shock people too much, indicated that Jehovah is somehow connected to the

Creator of this universe. That is not a lie but rather a diplomatic statement, and at times I know how to be diplomatic. Therefore, I would say that work such as this *Keys of Enoch* book can root you to the Jehovan past and take you into a more challenging future. So, in short, I don't support it.

Grasp the Future Timeline!

I have informed people that if they continue to burn water—break it down into hydrogen and oxygen and use it for fuel, which is happening now—this planet will eventually look like Mars. Now, understand, you could see that along a Jehovan timeline, an experience line. It is intended that a different timeline be engaged, and one of the ways you can engage it is the method I have suggested—working with your feminine creation feeling.

Recognize that your vision is associated with what I would call the past timeline, not the future timeline, which in order to be activated, must be grasped by human beings in the present. And the more who grasp it, the more likely it will be engaged and the old timeline left behind. When you are in your feminine creative-feeling self, the idea of burning water will be unthinkable. But when you are engaged in the Jehovan timeline, which embraces science and technology with mind but without heart, then it seems perfectly acceptable to burn water, especially when you think you have an inexhaustible amount of it.

Of course, it's not only *not* inexhaustible, but the replenishment of pure water, rain, is life giving. That's why animals prefer it. Animals will drink water you put out for them, but they much prefer to drink life-giving water that comes in the form of rain or bubbles up from a spring. That gives life. So recognize that the consumption of water in the form of fuel could occur along the Jehovan timeline. But to grasp that future timeline, do the homework I've given you.

Societies have existed on other planets—Mars, for example. Mars looks like Earth in a lot of ways; however, the most striking thing about it is the absence of water-supported life. The water has been burned up. I have stated that it is essential not to use water as fuel. It is too easy, for one thing. An engine that runs on water was demonstrated a few years ago—not only is it too easy, but it poses a serious threat.

There are always stories of automobile companies purchasing and withholding patents for certain products that increase fuel efficiency, resulting in better mileage. Well, sometimes corporations do good deeds—although they might be for self-serving purposes. One of these good deeds is the decision not to produce engines that run by breaking down water. A water-injection system for vehicles was tested awhile back that improves mileage but stimulates the same pattern or technological means. Observers and participants watched demonstrations in shock. It was dangerous, not just because it threatened various industries, but much more to the point, it threatened all life as you know it. So the corporations did you a service by blocking that device.

You have done well, my friend. You have learned how to be a human being. You have learned the valuable lessons that have taken you to this point where you can ask these questions in the right time and in the right way. It has produced this wisdom, this knowledge, this important awareness. It will help many people.

Shaking Up the Human Situation

Zoosh and Isis
April 13 and 20, 2001

Z oosh here. The Earth is vibrating at a different level right now; the Sun has activated Earth to do so. Only the Sun in your solar system has the capacity to do this. The people and animals have already adjusted, except for some animals in the extreme northern hemisphere, but they will adjust at about the same pace as human beings. However, the increase in the vibration is forcing people to move their vibration up a little bit. It doesn't necessarily mean that people will be more spiritual, but it means that they will have to be less self-destructive and they'll have to start getting along with each other a bit better.

Humans Will Shed Parts of Themselves That Are Not Real

It won't be easy. It will, perhaps, not look so good for a time, but it won't be a long time—we're not talking years. From time to time now, Earth is going to trigger such events, meaning she will ask—not in words, but essentially ask—the Sun to activate her, for lack of a better term. Earth has all the necessary capacities within her, but she likes to work with the Sun sometimes. And at times like that, there will be minor solar flares, an attempt by the Sun to reach out toward the Earth.

Shortly thereafter, there will be an increased vibration, which is specifically causing people to shed parts of themselves that are not real. It's like shaking people, in a cartoon sense, and things that are not part of them fall off. So it's a good thing, but you know, sometimes when you shed things—even if they are not really a portion of you but that which you've stuck to yourself or others have stuck to you, even unintentionally—it can be a bit traumatic. That's why there's nervousness. People are feeling fear because they are going to have to shed these things. It's not conscious, it's not mental, but it's triggering their instinctual bodies. On the deeper level, of course, the hearts and souls are cheering. And on the mental level, the unconscious mind is cheering, but the physical self doesn't like it because it feels the process is not natural.

However, each individual's physical self recognizes that the impact of its old inappropriate behaviors on itself is not a good thing, as these behaviors impact the physical self in sometimes deleterious ways. Therefore, the physical self, although it doesn't like the feeling of the vibration, recognizes that it's intended to do a good thing. You know, you material masters don't like to be grabbed and shook [laughs], which is what your physical body is experiencing, but you can recognize that the intention is good and that you will feel better, even if the moment-to-moment experience is less than fun. So that tends to add the physical aspect to the conscious personality's nervousness, and thus you feel the fear, the shakes, the general uncomfortable experience. But it will work itself out pretty quickly.

I sis: Your bodies, as has been said for some time, are based—not loosely, but very specifically—on the structure of Earth's body. The actual function, if not the form, is intended to be as close to a duplication of her mechanism—the way she functions—as can be, given your different appearances and outward differences. Nevertheless, the actual function is not simply a mental analogy, but quite similar.

Solar Flares Are Meant to Get Your Attention

When Earth reaches out to the Sun for assistance, she doesn't do it because she needs it and cannot do it herself; she does it very specifically because that's what you do when you need assistance—you reach out to someone else. And if you need assistance on a grand scale, you might tend to reach out to someone with either grand abilities or grand abilities in your eye, depending upon who the individual is. So she does things like that with intention. And since she is consciously teaching you material mastery, she will do so in such a way as to produce as much physical evidence as possible without trying to knock you over with it.

So in this day and age of science and, at the very least, observation, to say nothing of communication, there is this spectacular occurrence on the Sun. You understand, the Sun does not have to produce the solar flare to reach out to Earth; it can do so entirely without that. But the Sun also consciously does this to get your attention so that you can see how you are similar and therefore begin to pay attention to your needs as well as planetary needs on the basis of common ground rather than as something separate.

So the actual effect on your physical bodies is very similar to what Zoosh said—it's as if something inside of you is shaking you. Zoosh used the analogy of a cartoon, but I would say it is more like being inside a bell that is being struck. There is no place to turn to avoid the vibration, and it does not in any way feel external—it feels completely internal. That is intended so that there is no escape—not because it is something punitive, but rather in order to speed the process. That was always the intention, knowing that there would be distractions, knowing that there would be individuals such as those in the sinister secret government and other individuals who simply would, because of their own agendas, cause the people of Earth to turn a deaf ear to their own needs and to the needs of people around them. If such occurrences were to have a sufficient impact on the Explorer Race, then such occurrences would take place. That's why you're seeing things that are odd.

An example of this oddity is the incident that happened not long ago with the U.S. and China [the midair collision over China]. The U.S. and China as countries have been bending over backward to try and find a common ground on which to unite so that they don't have to go broke trying to prepare for an inevitable war, which neither country would like to experience. So they have found some common ground in doing business. This is something that mainland China finds a little appalling; nevertheless, they are trying. So this midair crash was an excessively eccentric experience. I'm not going to comment on who did what; that's less important than the obvious drama and curiosity of it. It is not something that one would normally expect—to find planes hurtling at each other, especially military planes that are not actually in battle. And so the oddity and the extremeness of it grab your attention and sort of pull you outside of yourself, but they do not alter the fact that you are all pilots at that time, and everybody is being shaken from the inside out and things are being forced to fall off.

Resistance and Intolerance Are Being Shed

As children you naturally pick up habits that are demonstrated by your parents. Sometimes they are thrust upon you, meaning you have to learn to survive and adapt. Sometimes they are things you want to imitate. And often, consciously or unconsciously, you perpetuate these agendas later in life. In your now time, though, given the generation that is running things politically and even economically, many of the habits learned in childhood are not appropriate to the times. That is why one often finds that the younger generation is more equipped to handle the business machines of the day, having been raised with them. So I'm not saying that the reins of power should be handed over to them, but the fact that they know so much is not an anomaly. Such things are intended to show you that national borders and nationalism are not fitted to your world so much anymore. And it might take a younger generation—to whom international communication is not only a given but a right—to resolve it. And they are doing their best to do so.

So I do not want to make it sound like a campaign, but I want to give you some idea that what is falling off the older generation, for the most part as a general thing, is resistance. And what is falling off from the younger generation is intolerance. Now, of course, individuals will experience other things that fall off. And as you know, when something you are used to having falls off, the initial and immediate reaction is alarm, fear, nervousness, anxiety and a general feeling of disquiet. Sometimes you will rationalize why you are feeling this way, but in fact, this is the reason, regardless of your rationale—the only exception, of course, would be people in dramatic or traumatic situations. Nevertheless, such rationalization is common in your time.

But the reality is simply that you are often feeling stressed and you don't know why, but if you paid attention to it, you'd notice that the common-ground experience is that something is missing. You don't know where it went. It feels funny, strange, and it makes you nervous that it's gone. And the maddening thing about it is that you can't really put your finger on what it was.

This Helps Lighten the Load

You said the shaking up didn't affect our spirituality, but is it moving us farther up the dimensional ladder?

Not really, because you can't do that without wanting to, but it creates a lightening of the load. So in that sense, it helps, but it can't push you up the ladder. It just simply makes it easier for you to climb the ladder.

You said in an earlier session that the energy of the solar flares was helping the gold lightbeings to disentangle the cords of discomfort and pain from humans.

Not much more expansion is necessary on that. I will simply say that given the communication about the process of disentanglement [see p. 70] by those who have used it successfully, there is greater demand being placed upon gold lightbeings, and they need a certain amount of energizing. Not that they don't have their own energy, but the kind of energizing they need is that which allows them to interface—meaning to move from their existence into Earth existence, back and forth like that—a little more quickly, a little more frequently and a little more comfortably. And the energy of the solar flare makes that a lot simpler for them. It's like greasing the rail.

That's good.

What You Can Do

Let's look at the human situation now. We are being forcibly shaken to cause us to drop old negative patterns such as resistance. What can each person do to cooperate and help rid the self of these old unneeded fears and resistances?

Try to think about it at some time during the day, maybe not when you're at work, but when you get home and have a spare five minutes somewhere. You don't need much more than three to five minutes to think about it. Don't think about things that are happening in your life that you get mad or disgusted at yourself about. Rather, just see if you can internally feel a sense of relief anywhere. Don't try to rationalize it or explain it, but see if you can feel a sense of relief. It will be almost as if a responsibility was removed from you, one that perhaps you didn't know you had. You will look around to see evidence in your life to support the feeling that some responsibility has been removed, but you won't see that evidence for the most part. Rather, this is something that has to do with an agenda or feeling of being driven to accomplish something. Or very often, as happens in childhood, it has to do with a sense of inadequacy brought about by a simple child's inability to emulate the traits in one's parents that one admires or wishes to be approved of for demonstrating. This kind of feeling of inadequacy tends to perpetuate itself in very self-destructive ways as the child grows into being an adult—very often, for example, in not having a feeling of true satisfaction about one's accomplishments because one feels that he or she should have done better somehow. That is shockingly common.

As another example—and you will run across this many times—compliment other people and they cannot take the compliment gracefully. Very often in a competitive society such as that which you find yourself in, that particular thing makes for profound and self-perpetuating self-destructive habits. These kinds of habits are often passed down consciously or unconsciously in families and groups of friends, and even in companies and on corporate levels. Often people who accomplish things never really get to feel anything other than a backhanded compliment for their work—for example, "Nice job; maybe you can do it better next time." And it's surprising how often that happens within companies, which is why so many companies fail. It is quite important to be aware that it will be things like this—these kinds of old self-destructive agendas—that will be cracked. They won't necessarily fall away without you thinking about it, but pieces of them will fall away so that you can no longer easily maintain and self-perpetuate these old self-destructive agendas without having to consciously think about their value and embrace them. And of course, if you really think about them, you'll want to let them go. But it will bring them to your attention. You will become more aware of these self-destructive habits, even if you do not consider yourself—or others do not consider you—a conscious person.

Rigid Philosophies Will Have Difficulties at This Time

How long will this vibrational shaking last for people on this planet?

I should think that the drama of it, meaning the sense of effects and aftereffects in terms of the physical and so on, will go on for at least forty days. The effects after that will tend to be more on the process level. Something has changed, you don't know what it is and it stimulates you to think about it, to talk about it with each other, to discuss it: "What can we do about it?" "I feel different. How do you feel?" Like that. That will tend to perpetuate itself for two or three months. And that's all very good because it will get people talking about things. And I would say that the only effect that might seem hard to take would occur for people who are attempting to perpetuate a philosophy that has rigid rules. So if your philosophy is flexible and adaptable, it will be a good thing. But if your philosophy is absolutely rigid, it will be very difficult for you during this time, if not impossible.

So that should play out in some of the more rigid belief systems in religions? What will we start seeing in churches?

Churches are actually more flexible than they seem to be. Dogmatic, yes, in some churches, but for some time there has been a tendency to become more flexible or at least broad-minded. It is not necessarily about feeling good about being broad-minded, but recognizing that this is the reality of the times in which they are living. They still want people to believe the core beliefs of their church, of their religion, but they recognize the realities of life. So in that sense, churches have been primed for this, if they are prepared to make changes. Even some of the old established religions are acknowledging this. Granted, it might not be readily and immediately apparent in terms of edicts that come down from on high within the church hierarchy, but it will be fairly apparent on the individual church level. Or for smaller religions, adaptability will be something that is no longer out of your reach. In many cases, it will be very good. Projects that have been impossible to accomplish can be accomplished, and people will be more cooperative, even if they do not see the immediate advantage.

On a personal level, it is more likely that individuals will not feel so driven to do something for which they cannot easily rationalize the goals, to say nothing of the steps along the way. So motivations that have to do with unconscious agendas will tend to break down a bit.

How will this play out, for instance, in the Middle East, where belief systems exhibit so much rigidity on both sides? What will we see there?

Interestingly enough—and this does not get reported very much—the younger people in the Middle East on all sides are attempting to reach out to one another. They don't have much power or influence and so one does not often see these attempts in the international press, but in the local press, to say nothing of communications from individual to individual, it is becoming something beyond an underground experience. Some of it has to do with more readily available communications, and some of it has to do with decreasing levels of intolerance. Sometimes with youngsters it's intolerance of the rules and regulations or parents and so on, which all youngsters go through as part of their adaptation to the changes in their own personalities, but sometimes it's also an intolerance one has for the rigidity of the system and things that you must do that you wouldn't do if you had a choice.

It is not that they will embrace these things that they must do. Rather, it is that they won't feel as judgmental toward those who are demanding these things of them as they have in the past. When you have to do something and you don't want to do it, the tendency is to become angry, resentful, and then, as you have to do it, to transfer that anger and resentment in some other way, often becoming self-destructive or becoming destructive toward others. But when this kind of intolerance is dropped or falls away or is greatly decreased, that kind of transference is less likely to happen because demands will be accepted on a more philosophical level. The attempt to get something out of the experience or the attempt to broaden the experience for yourself and others will seem not only inviting but possible.

This Was Set Up for This Time

Now we're at the peak of the eleven-year solar cycle. Is it coincidental that this vibrational shaking is happening now, or was this part of a larger plan?

Nothing is coincidental, period.

All right. So this was sort of set up for this time, then?

Yes.

Does it get set up like this every eleven years and we just didn't know about it before, no one told us about it before, or what?

Well, let's just put it like this: What science considers eleven-year cycles to be—how can we say?—a rule, is only a rule when change is necessary.

How far back did these eleven-year cycles start, then?

Well, it's really unimportant. The main thing is, if you go back, say, ten or twelve thousand years ago, it wasn't really so important then.

I understand. When did this grabbing and shaking start now?

I'd say it started shortly—in terms of your calendar—maybe around April 2 or 3.

Is that going to affect the military?

It shouldn't have any effect on the military one way or the other. Of course, eventually militaries will not train to defend or attack, but they will rather train for conjoined exploration and what we can we do together and so on. But even now some militaries make a great effort to teach teamwork—not just competition, not just how much you can do it better than the other squad or the other platoon, but how we can cooperate with them. One does not find that everywhere, but it is gradually becoming more common, and that's a good sign.

It's simple in a sense, but it has dramatic repercussions.

Yes, it does. This is how it affects you. This is how it affects the world. It doesn't place a lot of demands on people. Very often in these articles we say, "Do this, do that." But this isn't about homework so much. It's about understanding and trying to make sense of what's happening and observing its effect on you.

The Truth and Nothing But the Truth: What's Happening and Where We're Headed

Isis and Zoosh

May 11, 2001

A ll right, Isis here. Can I say one thing about food as a general factor?

Smell Can Feed You

The assumption of science in your time is that people's likes and dislikes in food are irrelevant. I'm not saying this is true; I'm saying that the assumption of science is that this is irrelevant and that the only thing that's relevant is what science has proved to be good for the average human being. But, in fact, what smells good, what tastes good to individual human beings is very often what's good for them. They don't necessarily have to eat vast quantities of it, large amounts, but sometimes if it is something that smells good, eat a little bit. I'm not saying that this is a fact for everyone; you might have something you're allergic to or that is definitely bad for you to eat. But if it is bad for you to eat, then this is what to do, for those of you who are allergic or have medical conditions. This might be tantalizing and frustrating, but if it smells good to your body, then your body needs to take it in, in some way.

So what I'd like you to do is . . . let's take, for example, chocolate. Some people are allergic to chocolate or perhaps they have physical conditions where they cannot eat chocolate—say, diabetes, for example, and the chocolate has sugar. Then what I would recommend you do, if you can do it without eating it, is that you obtain some of this in the condition that it smells good, and smell it. Don't get the chemical that smells like it and smell that. Get the actual food product and smell it—just don't eat it, if you can't. And the smell alone will help your body to relax, at least 50 percent, so that it doesn't need it so much. And then if you're hungry, you can eat something that's safe for you to eat.

That's really something that's not understood well in your time, and science has been attempting to create a body of knowledge that can prove effective in the treatment of vast numbers of people on an average—which is an attempt, of course, to improve the quality of life for the so-called average person. And while I heartily approve of that pursuit, it is also important to recognize that what individuals need to eat, aside from what they're allergic to and all this other stuff, might be entirely different than what is approved of. And if it's not safe for them to eat, then they can use that method of smelling it.

So the smelling feeds on some level, too?

That's exactly right, the smelling feeds you physically on some level. And it's not just on a spiritual level; it's on a physical level. That's why you can smell things— not just so you'll know what's safe and what isn't, but also so that you can eat things that aren't safe for you to eat but that your body requires. It's hard to imagine in a scientific vernacular or even in a scientific exploration how chocolate might be required in someone's diet—whether they're allergic to it or not—but it is.

Remember that it's not an accident that foods smell the way they do, aside from what fragrances or what spices have been added. The way they smell is very often intended to nurture and nourish your physical body; that's why it is normal in many households to have a table or a bench or something so that the family, even if they're not involved in the process of cooking, can be in the kitchen so they can enjoy the warmth and the nurturing atmosphere and, of course, the smells. The smells don't only whet your appetite; they feed you.

Corporate Exploration of Space

What about the people who are saying that we did not go to the Moon? Why is that? Neil Armstrong went to the Moon and walked on the Moon—isn't that correct?

Everything that I can see, that I can discuss freely at this time . . . because I need to acknowledge that there are some things that your governments are doing that they would like to remain quiet, all right? Secrets. And I'm going to honor that. But ruling out secrets that I'm not going to discuss, let's just say that the U.S. government has been to the Moon, people have walked on the surface of the Moon. The main reason they went there at all—aside from, "It can be done; let's do it"—was to explore the makeup of the Moon geologically for potential mining for other materials that might be useful on Earth. And you can't fault that, because your economy is set up on a materials basis.

But when they got there, they found all these other people mining the Moon and they never went back, right?

I'm not prepared to discuss that.

But we have pictures of it.

I'm not prepared to discuss that, because it's ongoing. I don't always talk about the same things that Zoosh talks about. If you want details like this, talk to Zoosh. Zoosh will talk with unbridled enthusiasm, but it's not a subject . . . I'm not . . . my job is to talk about things in a more nurturing vein, not to delineate enemies.

But why are people putting programs on television and going around saying that we didn't go to the Moon? What is the point of that?

I think that it's a reasonable suspicion on their part. The National Aeronautics and Space Administration (NASA) in the U.S. has for so long been involved in so many secret things with the government that their natural propensity is to keep everything they do secret. And I can see certain advantages in some of this. But now look at what they're doing with this man who is a paid passenger to space. As he so rightly said, what he did is the best thing that could ever happen to NASA. Now, I don't necessarily agree with that, but it's the best thing that could ever happen for commercial space travel, and I think that the United States government is a little embarrassed that this has happened by a country that was formerly Communist, because this is an overtly capitalist act. But let's just say that Russia has embraced capitalism and is struggling with finding a means to express it on a benevolent level for its citizens. This is one thing they are doing, and I'm sure they will do it again repeatedly, and eventually the United States will relent and do it as well, but probably not under the auspices of NASA. NASA is set up as a pseudogovernmental agency, and it's not in its nature to work with people who are not part and parcel of that whole package.

So it's not surprising that people are suspicious of NASA, because it's just like saying, "Are people suspicious of the government?" Yes, they are, because the government does not tell all. And when it comes to space and people going out into space and what they saw and all of that, the vast amount of people in general polls, of course, as you know, believe that there is other life in space. Aside from how much or how little they believe it, the majority of people believe that there is. And the fact that NASA is not coming out and saying, "Yes, we believe that this is true, and we have some proof to support that," bothers people. So right now there is a huge groundswell of interest in private industry going out into space, taking people like the space consumer out there and showing them whatever it is that they see.

But remember that agencies like NASA—and, I might add, some others around the world, representing some other governments—are profoundly nervous about this. They don't want to look foolish. They're afraid that government secrets will be exposed, and they're doing what they can to keep it from happening on a commercial level. But Russia is no longer a hostile force so much as it is a competitive capitalist force. And Russia's attitude is different. So the U.S. and its allies will simply have to find a political . . . it won't be scientific and it won't be military either. They'll have to find a nice political means to resolve this, and I think the means will be easily accommodated by taking the constraints off of private businesses who wish to go up into space for private ventures. This has been something that many U.S. and international corporations have wanted to do for a long time with the cooperation of the U.S. government.

The U.S. government has not only not cooperated, but it has actually gone out of its way to work against this. I think if the U.S. government just doesn't do anything else but stop working against this, that it will naturally develop in your global economic policies and many countries will do it. There's obviously a lot to be gained by this. I think that certain protocols could be set up so that the vehicles going out do not interfere with other activities, but some of it will simply have to be exposed. But you don't have to reveal all the secrets at once; it can come out gradually and slowly, and it probably does not have to scandalize anyone.

So, of course, the reason there is a vast amount of suspicion about whether the U.S. went to the Moon or not is because the evidence is not present in the public domain that this took place. There is plenty of evidence to support it; it just has to be released. And giving people rocks from the Moon isn't it. But encouraging people to fly up into space in contraptions that can do that, that can go up, come down, be recycled and go back up again . . . it will be expensive and it will initially be an occupation of the wealthy, but that's okay. I do not see a problem with that. Ultimately, it will lead to corporate exploration of nearby space, which I think will be acceptable. There will be some excesses and people will be a little shocked, but to some extent, it will just be science fiction come true.

So we'll start by mining asteroids and then the Moon? We can't get very far—we don't have spaceships.

It has to be financially feasible to mine in the first place. You can go to the Moon and find all kinds of things that are very valuable and useful on Earth, but unless it's economically feasible to make it pay—to go up, to get it, to come back— then it's really just like, "Isn't that nice?" but you might as well leave it there.

Why did the United States government stop going up there?

Because it really comes down to that feasibility. It's like, "Well, okay. Now we know, and this is as much as we know, and to the extent that we're going to do more, we're not probably going to constantly talk to people about it." A lot of the work now has to do with what can be done to make it pay. The Russians found out—they had to find out, because they're not a wealthy country—what you can do in a space station to make it pay; they did a lot of that work. And they've not been shy; they've let some of those things come out, so now others know that. That's why the U.S. and the Russians and some other countries are involved in creating a space station, because you don't have to go to the Moon to make things pay. You can make things on a space station in a gravity-free environment that you can't make on Earth in gravity—it's as simple as that. And those things can be sold and used by various populations to their greater benefit.

So let's just say that commercial exploitation is well under way, even though it's operating with science and with the military, both which tend to be reticent as far as presenting what they know to the public. So when it has to do with military and government secrets, people want to know, yes.

But the fifty-year contract on secrecy expired in 1997—that's four years ago. Are they just so used to their secrets that they think it's a way of life?

That's right. If someone has been keeping secrets for fifty years, well, it's a habit. And it's actually more than a habit—it's a protocol. A protocol, as you know, is "the way we do things." "The way we do things" is not readily changed in scientific, military and governmental circles, especially when the people making the decisions are not voted into power. So it will change; it will just take time. But in the interim, other countries will fill in with stopgap measures and say, "Well, if you're not going to do it, then we will!" And after the U.S. stops being scandalized, they'll say, "Okay," and instead of treating it as a scandal—"Oh, how could they do this?"—they'll treat it as a trial balloon and say, "Oh! If they can do it, then we'll start looking into it and see what we can do." I don't expect NASA to be receiving millions of dollars from somebody to go up, but some commercial venturists in the United States will certainly do it, especially if the government just gets out of the way.

ETs Need to Feel That You Are Trustworthy

Will we be able to make spaceships that will take humans to Mars? How far can we get on our own?

When you're traveling through space within time, I don't think it's realistic you'll get volunteers . . . don't get me wrong, but vast mileage is involved. I don't think it's realistic. You're going to have to travel in time.

Which means that ETs have to come?

ETs have to be embraced, and they have to feel that you are trustworthy. That will require some form of global government, which is in place de facto now, as far as business goes. And Zoosh talked about that at length [see *Explorer Race: Origins and the Next 50 Years*].

Yes, the multinational corporations.

Yes, they're the first form of global government, a government based on money. But it will evolve.

In, say, twenty years?

It depends; it will evolve. And it cannot do anything but. ETs have the capacity, if they should care to . . . most of them don't, but should they care to, all they have to do is push a button to change things. But they're not going to do that. The fact that people in your governments are afraid that they are going to do that is why a lot of money has gone into various defensive weapons. But ETs are beyond that, most of them. The ones who aren't are a bit rebellious, but they are also, most of them, not so foolish as to fork over too many secrets to a "planet like this," from their perception. I'm not judging your peoples, but most ETs have enough knowledge to know what to do and when to do it. There are a few exceptions, and errors were made in the past, but they were well-intended, they just didn't work out. The timing wasn't right. And that's part of the reason that certain technology existed before its time on this planet, but that's understood. We went into that in other books, so I'm not going to go through that again.

A ll right, Zoosh here.

Welcome! Things are really accelerating in the Middle East. What can we do? What can anybody do?

The Middle East Is Corded to All Places Populated by Human Beings

It may surprise you, but the best thing you can do is to learn how to get along with the people you see on a daily basis. The Middle East is always striking a resonating chord with what is going on in the rest of the world. If the rest of the world is at peace and everybody's loving one another and happy with one another, then the Middle East is also. But if there's any problem anywhere, the Middle East will have problems, and it will get people's attention. So the Middle East functions as a telegraph system. If you don't know that there's a problem somewhere, you can be sure it will be expressed in some way in the Middle East. That's why when you get people living in the Middle East who are mutually incompatible because of their religions, it creates—how can we say?—a delicate balance that . . . it would not take much to trip it off.

So what you can do, as an average citizen, is to make all of the changes *you* need to make, rather than asking, "What can we do about the Middle East?" Make all of the changes you need to make in order to resolve, to come to peace and some kind of harmony that you can comfortably live with, with you and all the people you know—including people you communicate with on the computer.

Do the people who incarnate there incarnate in service?

Yes. Everybody who incarnates there is incarnating as a service. This is not necessarily true for people who move there, but people who are actually born there know that they're in service and that they are intended to respond. For instance, there might be some strife in Africa in some place that people don't know about outside of the boundaries of that area or the news services just don't report on it for some reason, and the Middle East might flare up. People say, "Oh, there's something wrong in the Middle East," and granted, that's the surface, but the Middle East is totally connected, corded to every other place on Earth that has populations of human beings.

You Can Help the Middle East by Living in Peace

So we can't "solve" the problems in the Middle East until we open up and remove suffering all over the planet?

You can start in your hometown. You can't ignore the Middle East—plenty of people there have legitimate complaints. But if you yourself can't do anything to help the people in the Middle East, what you can do immediately is to try to find ways to live in peace and harmony with those whom you are living with. If you can't do that, then find the best way to live in peace. Harmony may not always be available, but you can strive toward it. It might require that you find out what's bothering other people. To find out might not always be readily available or reasonable, but just do what you can to find out so that you can understand, so you don't just assume that the other guy is just a jerk.

It's not necessarily the case that you are meant to resolve the other person's problems. But if you know what they are, then you know why that person is acting that way. It doesn't necessarily make for peace, but it helps to know, just as it helps for that other person to know why you act the way you act— which to you seems perfectly reasonable, but from his or her point of view, *you* might be the jerk. Listening is important.

The U.S. Needs to Eliminate Its "Superpower" Image

This thing with the UN—I mean, we consider ourselves a superpower and we're not part of the planetary government.

The interesting thing is, the United States considers itself a superpower, but everybody else in the world is offended by that. It's as if the United States is saying, "We are a superpower and the rest of you guys trail behind somewhere." Everyone, even the allies of the United States, is offended by that posturing. It would be nice to just eliminate that term. Regardless of how the U.S. government and its representatives and many of its citizens feel that the UN *owes* something to the United States and should be forever grateful and, when called upon, provide groveling thank-yous, the reality of the situation is that the UN is doing wonderful work, even in its limited way. And it is not for the U.S. to do anything other than be thankful that the UN is on your territory, in New York.

I assure you, there is plenty of money and plenty of willpower to say, "Let's move this thing." Where do you think the United States' influence and power will be then? If they move the United Nations building and its headquarters to some country that is considered at least semineutral, then the rest of the countries can say, "Okay, it's inconvenient to start going there, but if we don't have to put up with the United States' posturing, we'll be happy to do it!" I can assure you that there will be a move in the United States to say, "Well! They don't love us and appreciate us; they're not treating us like gods. We'll take our toys and go home." And who will you hurt then?

Ourselves.

Exactly. So my basic advice to the United States about all of this UN stuff is, *grow up.*

But our current administration is looking like they want to go at it alone—you know, military in space and avoiding all the treaties.

Your Government Officials Need to Stop Being Businesspeople

Do you recall a few years ago, when even though the Democrats were in power in the White House, the Republicans got in [to Congress] and they said, "Now you're going to see some changes, and we're going to make a contract with the people, and we're going to do this and we're going to do that!" Everyone said, "Well, that's nice," and after about 150 days or so, people were already angry at them. It's like that. This government is . . . the people are excited to be in and they're saying, "Now we're going to do this and we're going to do that!" I can assure you, there will be a groundswell by the citizens of the U.S. at some point, and they will say, "I don't care what you're going to do; you're not businesspeople anymore, you're government leaders. We expect you to behave like government leaders, not like spokespeople for the businesses you once were a portion of." In short, the government is still functioning like a corporation, and it's painfully obvious to the citizens.

Obviously, this whole thing about power consumption and all this business in California needs to change. They need to build more power plants, they need to do all of these things. But that's not going to happen immediately. A crash program . . . fine, get that going. But in the interim, other things need to be done. The government officials in power now might be amused by California's plight, but such amusement does not play well with the people. And they might be prancing around their offices, saying, "We've got four years," but if the people don't like the government and the government officials, they have a way of showing it. It's not going to be something violent, but it will be something that will come home to roost on those in power. And it comes home to roost more quickly in Congress, and then, of course, in the Senate. Or let's just say, it will come home to roost more quickly in the House of Representatives, and then the Senate (also known as the Congress), and then eventually in the executive branch.

I can assure you, you're going to see some big changes in the next election, no matter what scandals are created. "People cannot be fooled all the time," as Abraham Lincoln, the famous president, said. So I will simply say this: You—speaking to the president and his immediate staff of advisers and helpers—you've had your fun; now be politicians, not businesspeople.

Power Companies Need to Lobby for Alternative Energy Sources

For years they killed the inventors of renewable energy sources and bought out the products and hid the knowledge. Are we in a time now when some of these free energy and renewable energy sources will be available?

Yes, and a lot of them have been available for a long time, just not commercially available or widely distributed. The reason these kinds of technologies—even though they're available for purchase now—are not being widely embraced is because simply being able to walk over to the wall and flip a light switch and have a wire connected to the wires that go around your city is cheaper and easier. But as electric power gets to be more and more expensive, in an innovative place like California I can assure you that many of these alternatives will start to look not only viable commercially—meaning that power can be added to the grid by various means, which has been happening on a very slow level for a time—but individuals will start looking toward the potential of producing power plants and selling power and electricity on a smaller level. And laws will change. You'll see things like people having three or four windmills on a piece of their land. Maybe they have five, six, seven acres, and it's fairly breezy, and they'll campaign hard to get laws to change so that they can be their own little power company. Right now the power companies all over the U.S. have pretty much made it difficult.

There are thirty-four states that let you sell electricity.

I know, but they let you sell electricity from your house because it's a teeny-weeny little trickle. But it's entirely another thing if you have the capacity to produce megawatts of electricity on your land with wind generators. Then you're really kind of competing with the power companies. I'm putting the power companies on notice: either you can have competitors or you can have suppliers. Make your choice now, because the groundswell is going to be in an innovative place like California, where trends are started. And when I talk like this, you know it's important.

I can assure you, especially with the government that is in California, the chance of changing laws and encouraging people—instead of discouraging them—to start their own mini power plants in some way where the power is acceptable and can go right out to the grid . . . corporations who are strapped for cash or have seen their dot-coms crash into the sea, now just a memory, what if you could just take so-called alternative technology and start producing power, which is getting more and more expensive, which makes it more reasonable to commercially produce it? It isn't cheap anymore; it's actually worth selling. This is just like the price of gasoline, which wasn't worth selling for thirty cents a gallon, but at a dollar and eighty cents a gallon, it's worth it. But there's a lot to be done in order to produce gasoline, and it's frightfully expensive to do so, whereas it's not so frightfully expensive to produce electricity by alternative means that are readily available in areas in which Mother Earth is more than happy to cooperate. In short, power companies, embrace and campaign for laws that will support you in purchasing power from lots and lots of little power companies, or say goodbye to your monopoly.

Drilling on the North Slopes Is Inevitable

How do you feel about drilling for oil on the north slopes?

In Alaska?

Yes.

It will happen. And the current administration's attitude, even before they were the current administration, was, "It will happen; it's just a matter of when." Now that they're in, they're prepared to say, "When." And they're going to use their cudgel, as they have been using, over California to say, "Get out of the way, or we'll just let you go right down the drain." Obviously, that's not going to happen, because California wields a very large stick, almost as big as the federal government. It's just that the guys in the federal government right now don't see that. I'm calling them "guys" because they're behaving like a club, all right? They have to change; they have to shift gears. If they behave bratty, they're behaving . . . it's just the way you see the government behaving toward the UN—it's bratty. And the way they're behaving toward California is bratty. If you're going to behave like a brat, people are eventually going to treat you exactly the way brats are treated, and you won't be in office long or you will be the object of public ridicule like you've never seen before.

Remember who you are mistreating! Almost all the television programs and the movies and the entertainment industry in general are situated in California. Do you think they are just going to roll over and say, "Oh, please help us, federal government! We'll do anything you want us to!" Do you think they are not going to strike back and make them look like the brats they are behaving as? No, no, no, no. I am sorry—you must behave. You must say, "Okay, we've had our fun. Now it's time to be diplomats, statesmen. If we can't do that, then let's bring people into our group, our cabinet, who are good at that, who know how to negotiate, who know how to make deals. Otherwise we're going to permanently have eggs on our faces. And if we don't watch out, there will be bacon there soon."

So rather than have that take place, it's time to grow up and start acting differently—not just the executive branch, but Congress too, in places. I really think that realistically, you're going to have to understand that even when Bill Clinton was in there, the government has always considered the oil in the north slope to be part of the United States government's reserve. But what isn't understood very well by the general public—because in the past it's been considered a secret by the oil companies—is that if the U.S. does not start drilling for oil on its own property, someone will just drill from . . . they'll go off your coast, if they feel it's worth it, and they'll be perfectly willing to establish some kind of a means to invade U.S. territory and take your oil. I don't mean a military invasion, but once oil comes to be more and more expensive, which it's going to be, eventually it becomes worthwhile to try and figure out a way to take it. And the obvious thing, which the oil industry has known for a long time, is that you don't have to be on top of something and drill down to get into it. And obviously, the nearest foreign country . . .

. . . is Russia?

Oh, no. What's the nearest foreign country to Alaska?

Canada!

And it is that reason that has caused consternation in Canada for years. Now, I'm not saying that Canada is going to greedily attack the north-slope oil, but what I am saying is, if someone makes them an offer they can't refuse, they might say, "Okay, drill any way you want to, and we'll look the other way. Or maybe we'll do it ourselves." What goes on underneath the surface, well . . . I'm not saying Canada is the enemy. What I am saying is that the U.S. has been snubbing them for so long, could you blame them for saying, "Well, if you guys aren't going to drill, we sure are!"

Environmentalists: Cooperate with the Drillers to Lessen the Impact on the Land

So what I am saying is, realistically it's going to happen. What I'm suggesting that environmentalists do is, don't try to keep stopping them; rather, work with them to create the drilling to be as honoring of the land as possible and to create as little impact on the local wildlife as possible. A lot of drilling can take place that does not require multiple oil derricks all over the place. It can be done in different ways, and it's going to be done. What I am saying to the environmentalists is, why don't you work in cooperation so that it's done well, rather than it being an either/or? It doesn't have to be an either/or. You could say, reasonably, "Well, why doesn't the U.S. just buy oil from overseas?" But the U.S. government is really sick and tired of putting the U.S. treasury into a position where other countries could, if they chose, call in your loans. What do you do, in the U.S. government, if they call in your loans? Do you declare war on everybody and say, "If you try that, we'll kill you!"? I don't think so. It's a global economic government that's forming up here. The U.S. has to catch up politically.

I think you have to face the music that drilling is going to take place there. I grant that offshore drilling is not yet able to do the job without polluting. The technology is coming, where they will be able to do it without having a surface derrick, meaning it will all be done under the ocean and basically under glass—not exactly under glass, a glass dome, but there will be portions of it that will be transparent. It will be very expensive, but if oil is expensive enough, it will be worthwhile.

I might add that for those who produce these things, please, if you want to make a little extra money, even though you won't immediately be able to have tourists there, do think about creating a setup for having tourists there at some point. Create, if only in your plans, a means by which tourists can visit. Yes, there will be people who will pay lots of money. It won't be a lot of people, and it won't be like going into space and paying millions of dollars per person. But initially it will be like going into some place that most people haven't seen. And to get a person to pay $100,000 for a week is reasonable, for people who can. So, oil companies, you can make a pretty little profit out of this.

It has to be done very beautifully, though, so be thinking about creating an oil-drilling operation on one side of this underground/underwater structure and, on the other side, a luxurious, if somewhat small, hotel. You won't be able to have everything in it that people expect in a resort, but you will have a window to the sea that most people have never seen. And you will also be able to create another little area that will be scientific, where colleges can pay to come and use the facilities. In short, be thinking about how you can finance this operation without having to break your bank. If it's done when they have that much of an influx of cash that can be perceived, at least in the distance, then putting that kind of money into it needs to be honored.

And environmentalists, you have to understand that the oil you use for almost everything . . . your whole technology is built upon that product. The oil you use right now, environmentalists, has to come from somewhere. So honor the people who drill it; don't make them your enemy. Work with them, offer them your skills; don't be a combatant. I can assure you, the more you remain a combatant, the more difficult the situation will get on both sides.

The Navies of the World Will Be United

The whales are in danger in the Pacific because of the radar testing by the Navy. They're actually starting to test the hearing of whales. Can you say something about that?

Whales do not just hear through their orifices that take in hearing. Whales hear exactly the way you hear—they hear throughout their entire physical body. You do that, too; it's been measured that you can hear through your head, not just through your ears. But if you make the effort, you will find out that you can also hear—meaning pick up vibrations that can be interpreted in some way and also quantifiably measured—through your toes, to say nothing of through the occipital region of your head. So whales are just like you, only they have refined that skill much better. A whale on one side of the Earth can hear something that a whale hears on the other side of the Earth, not just telepathically, but through the vibration of it—and I don't mean some spiritual vibration, I mean a *physical* vibration. And if they can do it, so can you!

So, U.S. Navy, please do not look at this as an assault upon your capacity to communicate in discreet manners; look at it rather that you are opening up a means by which human beings can learn how to hear in new ways and for which you will be honored. I recognize that this, in its own right, does not appeal to you sufficiently right now to alter what you're going to do, but know that in the long run, that's going to be the case. Because believe it or not, the U.S. Navy, whether or not it is the most powerful in the world, will not always be under the auspices of the U.S. government. Welcome to the new world! Eventually, as the corporate model becomes more and more the dominant factor as a global government (as I've said before), navies, armies and air forces will not just be perceived of as a means to make money to produce weapons but as an anachronism, because they have the capacity to destroy commercial enterprises. Therefore, everyone will get together and say, "Wait a minute! We need to change the whole element of what military services do and we need to put this all under one general authority."

People in the U.S. for years have been worried about being under the UN's authority; it's come up before for certain individuals, and there's been some press about it. I can assure you, it wasn't a trial balloon; it is the coming thing. Of course, it's true that one government has the capacity to obliterate another country. Not only is this a terrible catastrophe on a humanitarian level, but on a business level—I'm not trying to say that this is better; I'm just trying to acknowledge a reality—businesses are going to say, "Don't drop your bombs on my enterprise, not only ruining my people, but ruining the billions and billions of dollars I put into this enterprise!"

In short, even now, behind the scenes, there's a lot of discreet moving going on, and in the long run, I can assure you that the navies of the world will unite. And they will essentially come together and do what's going on in space now. But navies, why not explore deep? If you had all the resources of all the other navies of the world and you were all together, you could do lots of really neat things in the water. You could explore things, you could find things, and you could eventually do it in a way that doesn't harm life. You know darn well that you've thought about it for a long time, navies, about having underwater bases that actually work—not just that are experimental and work sometimes. And if all the navies are united and you don't have to worry very much about defense and you don't have to worry very much about offense . . . the only defense you have to worry about is crush weights and all of this kind of thing.

So I'm putting you on notice, navies, armies, air forces and so on: Get used to the idea that you're all going to be part of a global enterprise and that you will form up, in time, the core of space explorers, whether it be inner space (under the water or inside the Earth), or whether it be outer space. And it won't be hard to get people to join up to do that—talk about adventure! You won't have to get them excited because they're going to be able to shoot one another; rather, it's going to be more fun because they'll be able to discover exciting, wonderful things together. Start thinking about it. I know you're not ready to put it into application yet, but start thinking about it as an eventual reality, not as something to fight to the last ounce of your breath.

Maybe later we could talk about exploring some of the caverns and tunnels, and some of the communication routes under the Earth. Is it safe to do that now?

Oh, a little bit. We won't go into a lot of it, because there is a lot of stuff down there that's secret, and even I like to keep a few secrets. But I am encouraging people to explore Inner Earth. Obviously, it will initially be done via the Jules Verne method, which has been going on—spelunking and exploring old volcanic openings and so on. This has been going on for a long time. But there's a lot more that can be done, doing minimal damage to the Earth, by exploring things and understanding things and sending little tiny robotic things into spaces where human beings can't go, which can send back crystal clear picture images. You can see things that you wouldn't want to destroy by drilling holes into them. And it will be fabulous. Once you become united as a military force and then become united as a force of adventure—really not so much military combatants—then you will probably get lots and lots of cooperation from extraterrestrials, who will view that as a hopeful sign that you are coming together to work as an Earth government rather than as separate factions. As long as you remain separate factions, they will keep their distance. Good night.

The Myth of the Noble Predator: Unnatural Predators Have a Message for You

Speaks of Many Truths

June 27, 2001

All right, this is Speaks of Many Truths. Now, the subject I'm going to discuss briefly may be a bit upsetting, but it is something that needs to be understood a bit more in order to be resolved, and that is predators.

Predators Are Unnatural

In your time, you have been able to identify obvious predators, and in your way, you have attempted to eliminate them as a threat. These obvious predators are lions and other wild animals whom you have attempted to control either by destroying them or capturing them and putting them on display. Partially, of course, putting them on display not only reassures you that you are in control, as your psychologists would probably agree, but this also tends to create an artificial myth about who they really are. It is this myth that is causing the trouble.

In the past, in my time [in the 1600s in North America], the bear, for example, was not deified as some of the scientists of your day have assumed, but rather the bear was considered a threat. This was not always, but only with certain bears, ones who were injured and refused help in some way or could not receive help and became ravagers, or ones who had become unnatural, meaning they were sick in some way—you might say like a mad dog. This happened in my time, too. When you see pictures in stone of bear images, it is not what you think. It does not have to do with the spirit of the bear; it does not have to do with an attempt to control the bear. Rather, it has to do with the way the hunters were trained. To even smell some part of a bear captured or killed by hunters before did not always work, because if a bear was killed for meat, the smell would be different. But to hunt down and drive away or destroy (driving away also being a possibility) . . . the smell of such a bear would be completely different.

This was what we would consider a predator: something that kills, not just to protect itself, but something that has a will to kill, even if it is reassured that it will not be attacked. In your time, if this were a man, he might be considered a dangerous person, a murderer, some psychological term perhaps. But even in your time, you would not consider an animal to be a murderer or a psychological term. In my time, I recognized that what a man can do, so can an animal. Yes, we looked at unspoken feelings or unresolved angers in our people, but the hunters had to try to protect while that was going on, so others attempted to resolve that. But more to the point, not unlike in your time, we tried to understand what a predator was and how we could resolve this issue.

You might ask, why would we do that, living on the land the way we did in our time? It was in our nature to assume that things happened for a reason. When you learn how to live by observing nature and attempting to imitate the portions of nature that seem to be working for the animals and plants, it is natural to do the same when something seems to run against your survival or your happiness. So there was a discussion when the time existed, after the threat was over, about what it meant and why we were experiencing it.

This is what we knew: We knew that a natural animal, as you call it, attacks or kills because it is afraid or it is defending its young or it is defending itself because it is wounded or ill. In other words, when it is natural and healthy and not defending its young . . . or in some cases, not defending its food, but an animal will not usually attack humans and kill to defend food. It might attack other animals, but that is natural behavior for the animal. If an animal attacked and killed for no apparent reason, then we would ask ourselves why. We did not attempt to analyze the animal's thoughts, even though I have done some work, interacted with bears, slept near bears—or should I say, bears have slept near where I was, maybe a hundred feet, seventy feet away (that's close enough for me [chuckles])—and found myself breathing in unison with the bear and having some bear dreams. And I believe that the bear perhaps had some dreams of mine or experienced them. That was all very helpful. But that was a natural bear, a bear who did not feel threatened by me, who was not protecting its young—in other words, a natural or, as you would say, healthy bear.

They Are Trying to Teach Us Something

My experience did not help me nor my people to understand a bear who attacked and killed for no apparent reason. So we sat around sometimes, other mystical people or elders and myself—no one was excluded, of course; other people might have sat in on the talk or listened—and we discussed what the cause of this was. And of course, we had these discussions because we knew that living on the land the way we did, we saw how we were like the animals and how imitating animal behaviors that served the animals, that allowed them to live more pleasantly on the land, had been helpful to us. So we knew the animals were our teachers to live benevolently. And yet we also knew that if the animals were our teachers and we thought of natural animals this way, then who were these other animals and what were they trying to teach us?

This is what we decided: They were trying to warn us. I grant that their behavior may have been for their own reasons, but living on the land the way we did, we had to look at animals as teachers, because they were surviving and often surviving well. If we were not surviving or surviving well, then we looked to our immediate physical teachers who were doing so. And the only reason we could come up with, given that method of learning, was that the animal was trying to warn us.

If it was being unnatural to its own kind . . . I have noticed in the case of an unnatural bear, that natural bears rejected it—not only would not associate with it, but would not come near it, would keep the young far, far away and would exhibit behaviors around such an unnatural bear that I have not seen before with bears. You have seen, perhaps, that bears growl at each other, keep each other at a distance, but I have only seen a bear do something like this, which I will describe, when a natural bear is confronted with an unnatural bear. The natural bear will make a sound like a hiss; it makes a hissing sound through its teeth at that unnatural bear—with no other particular threat—and that unnatural bear goes away, just with that sound. I have on occasion heard of my fellow mystical people attempting this sound to keep an unnatural bear away, but it doesn't work. The natural bear is doing something besides that sound—we don't know what it is yet—to keep the unnatural bear away.

We felt, then, that the unnatural bear was trying to show us something about ourselves, because being unnatural does not in any way endear it to other bears—and of course, being a bear, in order to have a happy life, it needs to be around other bears sometimes. I know bears are nomadic and they are not always around other bears, but there are times when they are. So if a bear behaves in an unnatural fashion and it does not have any apparent wounds, it does not appear to be sick, but it attacks and kills unexpectedly and is therefore unnatural in their eyes, and that behavior causes other bears to reject it, and that rejection is accepted without objection by the unnatural bear, then I have to believe (as do my other friends and mystical people and elders whom I have met, as well as other people I know in my time) that this is a message for humans.

Pictures in Stone Are Meant to Warn Us

That's the other reason pictures of animals were left in stone—or sometimes later on in a form of what you might call paint, but pictures left in stone last longer. It was intended to be a warning that there will be animals who behave in strange ways and that this is a message directed toward human beings. You can usually tell that these pictures are different from other pictures you might see in stone, because the unnatural animal will be pictured much larger than the other pictures near it, but it will be near or with the other pictures. When you see something larger, it's not because the artist wanted to be known and was [chuckles] trying to be more dominant, but rather because the message was important and we in our time believed it wasn't meant for us.

Living benevolently amongst each other as we did in my time, we came to the conclusion that the message was meant for us to pass on in the best way we could. In my time, we would pass this on with stories and hope that they would live, but because of the disaster in the United States (with the invasion), most of those stories did not last, and if they did, they are being guarded and protected by the survivors. So the pictures were considered in a hopeful manner, that perhaps someone would think of this, would consider it and would understand that it was always intended to be a warning.

In my time, we believed that it was not that human beings imitated animals or that animals imitated human beings, but that animals in their own way exhibited their behaviors both naturally and unnaturally at times—that all beings did this— and that just because an animal was not like us in some ways, we did not ignore how the animal *was* like us in many ways and how we could learn from that animal. We believed that this message that we had to pay attention to, because it was a matter of life and death, is meant for your time.

Human-Being Predators

From what I have observed with my long vision, in your time you are (you think) controlling the animals or destroying them. But the message is happening, only it is happening with the animals you do not easily control, and that is with your own kind—human beings. There are human-being predators now who prey on other human beings. I do not have to describe this. You understand this; you know about it. And yet I believe that it is not about a warning that you have to pass on to future generations; I believe the message is for you, in *your* time, because I see no threat that you cannot meet from space. More to the point, people from other planets, coming from space, will almost always be friends. And on the very rare occasions when they are not, you have enough defensive weapons to repel them or unwelcome them sufficiently so that they will go away. And you have those right now.

I think the message about the predators is for your time. And it's not about controlling them; it's not about putting them on display and creating a myth about them. It's not about putting the lion in the zoo and talking about qualities that the lion doesn't really have but that you pretend it does—meaning how magnificent it is, how brave it is, how lazy it is, all of this stuff. No prisoner ever exhibits his or her true personality when captured; it is no different for the animals. So you cannot say what the animal is like unless you are a lion and unless you've lived as a natural lion. If you've been born and raised in animal prison, you may not be natural; you may have some natural parts, but you don't know what it's like to be natural.

The Myth of the Noble Enemy Stimulates the Myth of the Noble Predator

You have created, then, a myth, and I feel that this myth of the Noble Predator is what is promoting and supporting and sustaining and feeding the encouragement . . . what is encouraging individuals who might have a tendency to be predators. This is not only something that they are open to on the soul level, but perhaps they have been reacting to conditioning that they have had as children or as young people. But this is known in your time, and I don't need to discuss it. Your psychologists understand how a man or a woman becomes unnatural and a predatory threat. But I want to bring up what I feel you're not looking at. I feel that the myth of the Noble Predator, something that you do even with your vanquished enemies—as you see it, "enemies"—is something that is creating a problem in your time.

During World War II, the people in Germany formed a political and a military power known as the Nazis, and everybody in those times was very clear that the Nazis were the enemy. People who were clear thinkers realized it was not the German people per se who were the enemy, but it was those who embraced and fought for and defended the Nazi cause who were the enemy, and that the character traits displayed by those conditioned to those principles were ones that needed to be fought. But even those soldiers in the field and sometimes officers in the field fighting these individuals would have a degree of admiration that one often has as a military person or as a warrior for the warrior whom you are fighting, even though this admiration does not mean that you do not fight.

What is often left, though, especially when a war has excesses—and especially in your time when the excesses maim and injure innocents, children, women, dependents, old people and injured people, as happens with bombing and other situations in war—what happens is that the shame of that is so extreme that one does not wish to look at it, does not wish to consider it. One likes to say that the enemy is the devil, the monster, that they had it coming.

Yet you get over those feelings usually, or succeeding generations do. And then you like to think, "What was it about?" And very often, because you feel so upset about what was done to the enemy or to those associated with the enemy, such as children, that you cannot bear to look at that and say, "We did that." So you begin to look at the qualities of the enemy that you admire and, as psychologists in your time understand, create the myth of the Noble Enemy. I believe that it is this myth of the Noble Enemy that is stimulating the myth in your time of the Noble Predator. If you look around the entertainment industry in your time, you will see that many people in the past who were murderers, thieves and did other terrible things have been turned into heroes. It is the Noble Predator all over again.

The Danger of Creating the Myth of the Noble Predator

I feel that the unnatural bear in my time was designed to get our attention so we could warn future generations that the unnatural human in your time would be a great threat. And that is why I'm speaking to you now of the danger of creating the myth of the Noble Predator. If you must put animals you are afraid of on display, please do so in large areas where you do not go into those areas very much. Or if you do, go in vehicles where you are completely protected and where, more to the point, the animals cannot see you. If they are raised in such an area, they will create their own myth about what those vehicles are about.

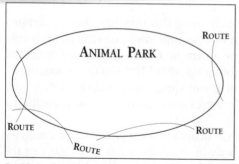

Fig. 19–1. An animal park that is more private for the animals.

But those vehicles must move very slowly. Whether they are people helping to sustain the animals or whether they are visitors, they must move no more than, in your time, seven, maybe even five miles per hour. It is a potential threat in an animal's eye, so if the vehicle is moving slowly and it looks like it is not easy to attack, it will be considered less stressful by the animal and its family—if it is moving *slowly*, especially if it is moving away.

So I'd like to draw a little picture of what I mean by that [draws Fig. 19–1]. I'm drawing a picture showing the animal park and the route of slow-moving vehicles. You'll notice that there's one side of the park where no routes go; there ought to be a large part of the park where the animals know they can go and be themselves. Even if they're not themselves in places where they can be seen, there ought to be someplace where they can be private; otherwise, it is cruel.

It is a compromise in any way, in any event. I know that you, as human beings, do not like to be prisoners, and in your time, this is an issue because many of you are concerned about your privacy. You know you're not a prisoner, but the more you are observed, the more you feel as if you are becoming one—it's just that the prison is more comfortable and you seem to have freedom. Yet there is no prison in your time where there are not cameras, where there are not people taking down information about the prisoners. But, you see, this is happening in your time because of the danger society sees in the predator, and this is appropriate. This danger is true, and it does require responses. I feel that many of your capacities in protecting citizens can work so much better if citizens are not conditioned to believe in the myth of the Noble Predator.

Look Within to Decrease Your Experience of Predators

This is all I want to say about this today. I hope you will consider it and think about it, and if you want to know more about it, then we can discuss this more in some future article. But I feel that this is urgent now, because your desire to turn the enemy, once vanquished, into something that it isn't, is creating an increasing problem for you. Your internal contradictions are often difficult for you, but you can see a therapist or a counselor to discuss these and try to resolve them. But your external contradictions are not always so easily treated by therapists, because they are not individual. Perhaps the conflict or difficulty is experienced by someone else, and yet the therapy is the same—it's just that you as an individual have to include a larger group of people in the therapy.

Union in your time comes about not because people love one another and want to protect one another—oh, no. These are all valuable desires, but it comes about the same way as it came about in my time. Union is natural within a tribe and group of people, but what about other tribes? Sometimes we don't get along with other tribes, and yet when there is a threat, we have to get along. But what if that threat is of our own making? Then we have to look within ourselves and change the way we are. It is time for you to do that in your time. Look within yourselves, change the way you are and grow, and you will experience less of the threat of predators.

Heroic Acts of Flight 93 Save the White House from Destruction

Isis, Zoosh and Speaks of Many Truths

September 11, 2001

I sis: I do not want any of you to become overly alarmed at this event. It has been predicted gently for many years that such a thing could take place, which would cause the U.S. to cooperate more fully in the establishment of a world government and probably lead the way to the establishment of a universal ID for which the technology is already available, even though it is not quite perfected. So this will cause changes in the U.S.—some of them short-term, some more long-term—and it will create for a time a cause for the young people. But cooler heads will prevail.

Build a Greater World Community

In terms of national attention, within a week or two many people will begin to talk, especially the young people, about forming an alternative method of service that involves cooperation among young people around the world. Email will support this and be the means of communication initially, but it will take over in other ways as well. This terrible tragedy has shocked the U.S., but know that there will be other attempts at warfare. It is not likely that the U.S. will engage in warfare with another country, but there will be restrictions, especially for certain people, which may be unfortunate since they are not really at fault. So the best you can do is to throw flower petals on the water rather than oil. What I mean is this: Encourage your friends and acquaintances to do the love-heat/heart-warmth/physical-warmth exercise [see p. 23] and the disentanglement [see p. 70].

The real meaning of this tragedy, when you look past the ghastly aspects of it, is that it is no longer possible to ignore people who are suffering, because with today's complex technology, they will find a way. And that way will often be to strike back at people they *think* are their enemies, even though the actual enemy is that they have been unheard and their value has not been appreciated. I am not saying that the people who have done this terrible thing are good people, but given the nature of humanity as it exists now, it is in your nature to ignore your own pain until it commands your attention. Think about that, how often so many of you do that—maybe you take an aspirin, but you don't go to see the doctor unless it is an emergency. That is a direct analogy, you see, to how the members of your world have been treating one another. If you ignore your own pain, how easy is it to ignore the pain of others?

Homework: Don't Ignore Your Pain

A society such as the United States has the capacity and the wealth to take care of its members, its citizens, and all of their discomforts, and in time this will be done. But it must be done globally as well. So in the future, I would like to give this homework to each and every one of you: Don't ignore your own pain. Practice this for the next few weeks. When you notice some discomfort in some part of your body, touch that part of your body if you can. If it is comfortable, give it a stroke downward, meaning from the top of your head down. And say to your pain, "Thank you for calling my attention to you. I will look into helping." That's all. Then if you need to, call a doctor or take an aspirin or whatever it is that you usually put off.

The main thing is that it is important to begin to pay attention to your own pain and to your own needs, because in that way you respond sensitively. When you desensitize to your own pain, it becomes infinitely easier to desensitize to the pain of others. When that is done repeatedly, especially with people who, in the Middle East, for example—an area known for its strong feelings—especially for those people there who are in that heightened state of feeling, they will get your attention in one way or another. Therefore, I would recommend that you begin by sensitizing to yourself.

Then for those of you who live with children or animals, pay attention to their needs. If they ask you for something, if you can, give it to them. If it is all right, then do so. Most of the time they will need attention, reassurance. Love is not something you say but something you do. To the best of your ability, try to give them what they need, not what you think they need. Become sensitive to others, beginning with yourself and your family, whether they be children, your husband or wife, a grandfather or grandmother, or cats or dogs or horses. As you do so, you will become more sensitive to the needs of your own family.

I know that pain is often an aspect of life that one must endure, but it is important to acknowledge it and to do what you can about it. Become sensitive to the needs of you and yours, and then because you are used to being sensitive, you will find it to be much easier to become sensitive to the needs of your greater community, your neighborhood, your farming community or your town. Let that expand

and grow slowly over the next year or so. If you do so, by this time next year you will have a budding world community. I think that the young people can more easily adapt to this, but I am hopeful that all ages will wish to try it.

It Is Important to Do the Love-Heat Exercise

Okay, but that is not the thought in America right now. At 4 P.M., on this day of September 11, 2001, it is retribution, justice, revenge. How are we going to change that?

Yes, retribution. That is why it is important, you see, to do the love-heat exercise, those of you who can do it. If you cannot do that, then do gold light [see p. 32]; it is helpful also. The love-heat and the gold light make a difference; you would be surprised at the result. For example, many of you have been exposed to people who are angry. If everyone around them gets tense and upset, they are likely to stay angry. But if people around them are calm, then the anger goes away or becomes something that can be dealt with. You cannot calm everybody down. People will be angry, their feelings will be hurt, they will be grieving, and that is expected. But the more of you who are now doing the love-heat, that energy will become a link and become larger than your numbers would indicate. Those of you who have been doing this for a time, if you know others who are doing it, get together now in groups to sit and do the love-heat. It will become very, very strong and radiate out into your world and do much good. As you know, let it radiate out; don't send it out. That way it will find its own way to where it needs to go.

This plot has been in effect for quite some time; it is something that has been planned for a long time. I will say that the individuals who carried it out, those who were actually involved in taking over and flying the aircraft, were not directly involved themselves but rather were volunteers, not draftees. Draftees, of course, were the ones who were on the plane and their families. But I would have to say that the individuals involved did not have the formal backing of any government. However, the people who will be blamed for this initially will be, for the most part, identified as enemies of the United States based on their track records. But I will say this: Don't try to make things too complicated. It is important to look deeper. I will allow Zoosh to speak to you of such matters, since he is perhaps more involved in the political and historic human reality. But I will say that it is not for the most part what is being thought or stated.

The plane in Pennsylvania was crashed as a result of efforts by the pilot and crew and passengers to keep the hijackers from crashing into the White House?

Yes, that was a struggle, but they were very heroic. They fought back and were somewhat informed of what was going on because of people using phones and their own capacity to find out and so on. As a result, they were able to fight for the controls and refused to crash the plane into the White House. As you can see, because of the president's location, the hijackers would not have harmed him anyway. But they could have done what the instigators of this plot wanted to do: create a battle between the U.S. and Middle Eastern countries and for the U.S. to declare war on this or that Middle Eastern country, based upon your current relations.

But, you see, there are many cool heads in the White House and in the government, and the chances of the U.S. doing that are almost zero. It does not mean that there will not be innocent people killed in revenge attacks as always happens, as it did today. But it does mean that their plan, their hope, if I may say that, was dashed almost exclusively because the plane did not hit the White House. Had that happened, it might have been difficult to keep Congress and others from reacting by declaring war on this or that country. But I think that the president and his people—many cool heads among them—will see through that and not take that action. The president will be strong in his talk tonight, perhaps a bit aggressive, but he will not carry out some of those statements. He will carry out some things, but not everything. He knows it is necessary to sound strong and send a message to the rest of the world that the U.S. will not stand for such things in the future, and it is true. But underneath it all, there are plans in place and things in motion now. Good night.

Zoosh: Fortunately, the courage of the pilots, the crew and the passengers on board the plane that crashed and did not hit the White House was immense. Perhaps in time some kind of medal or public recognition or appreciation ought to be granted to the pilots, crew and passengers who cooperated fully, and although the plane crashed, it still foiled the worst of the attempt. The best of it is that some good things will come about, even though the price has been so terrible.

Many of you now are feeling that you want to *do* something; some of you feel that you want to strike out. This is what I am going to urge you to do: Look around at your fellow citizens. Rather than looking for enemies, look for friends. I want to give you a homework assignment. You would be surprised how many terrorist acts, whether on such a massive scale or even on a small scale, occur. A couple of men rob a small store and shoot everybody instead of simply grabbing the money and running—that is a terrorist act. You would be surprised how many of those acts can be avoided if such people, before they become criminals like that, have friends.

Homework: Make a New Friend

So I want to give you homework, which might be awkward, but try to establish it, meaning accomplish it in some way in the next thirty days. I'd like you to make a new friend. (Make as many new friends as you want, of course, but for the purpose of the homework, this is what I am recommending.) I'd like you to look around at the people you meet and already know, and select the person or people whom you would be least likely to approach as a friend. Obviously, you do not want to approach someone who is frightening to you, but just pick out someone you would not normally approach and find some way to strike up a conversation about whatever you think might be of mutual interest. And see if you can establish a friendship. You don't have to become intimate or best friends, though this is fine if there is mutual consent, but more to the point, establish a sincere friendship.

You would be surprised at how many self-destructive acts (and know that I define self-destructive as something you do to hurt yourself or others) would be utterly eliminated because people who were friendless now have friends. They find out that many of the feelings and thoughts they have, others have as well, but those others have found ways to resolve them or have found things to do to comfort themselves. Friends are one of the greatest solutions to all your problems. Those of you who have few friends know that this is true; those of you who have many friends sometimes forget. So that is your homework. I think you will find it to be a bit of an adventure. Again, you don't have to approach somebody who is frightening—just someone you wouldn't normally think of as a friend. And if it works and you get a new friend you like, try it again and tell others. Before long, perhaps there will be lots more friends and a lot less people who are likely to become self-destructive.

Global Relationships Will Have to Change

There will be some significant changes in the way planes leave the airport and in security. It will probably mean that air travel will be slowed down a bit until there is a major effort (which I think now will be easier to get approved) to build more airports and landing strips to ease traffic congestion. What the airlines say is quite true: If there were another fifty airports, there wouldn't be such congestion. Regarding security, a system needs to go into place that is global. The United Nations will have something to say about that. I think, generally speaking, it will require the union of businesses looking into that and applying it. This can be done now, and I think it will be because of the obvious threat that such a terrible action represents. Needless to say, security at airports globally is the issue now.

This action was directed specifically at the U.S. Other countries have been less involved in international affairs in the past thirty or forty years than the U.S. has been, and perhaps more to the point, these countries (even England, and certainly the older and more established civilizations in Europe and other places) have a more fixed sense of identity as to who are their friends. The U.S., being a young country, has not been quite so fixed. In one way, this is good, because the national attitude is that everybody can be our friend—no one is excluded. But the problem with this is that anybody can also be our enemy—no one is excluded. As a result, many agreements between governments and groups of people have been broken by the U.S. This will have to change.

Yes, we have upset many people in many countries, and now we have to go and say, "Help us."

Yes, but that was to be expected anyway because of the economic situation, so this is simply another reason to say, "Help us." And sometimes you not only do yourself good by receiving help when it is freely offered—which it will be in this case—but you remind yourself that you often need help but have been too proud or shy in the past to accept it. And it is the same for governments as it is for individuals. Therefore, extra-credit homework is to accept and be open to help that you need from sources that are prepared to offer it.

You Need to Create a Kinder Society

My brother said something interesting today. He said, "Everything has changed—thirty years ago, if you had a hundred people on the plane and three or four terrorists with knives, the people would all get together, and a couple of them might get hurt, but they would take those terrorists down. They don't do that anymore."

That's right, because people in your country do not feel as friendly toward one another as they once did, although older people who remember things like that would be likely to cooperate. So, you understand, people have gotten used to isolation—in short, alienation. That's not good. That's why this homework has been along the lines of how you can unite with yourself and with others. Such a sense of extended family is a good thing. Bad things happened thirty years ago. Whole groups of people in America were excluded. But despite those situations, in crisis everybody tended to pitch in—it is natural that you unite. We would like to remind you that you do not need a crisis to unite. There has been a breakdown in moral fiber. We must attempt to rebuild a new moral fiber that includes all people and creates a kinder society. But in the process of dumping that old style, as referred to by your brother, some good things were thrown out with the bath water, eh? If not the baby, then certainly some necessities the baby needed. That's why the homework is all geared and structured to support that sense of love and cooperation among family, friends, communities—and the global community as well.

When people feel that they have a means to get their problems resolved, they are more likely to pursue those means. Your own government, for example, is set up so that if something isn't working right, you call this place or you go to that place (granted, there are strata, and things do not always work out as quickly as you would like). Eventually, things may not get worked out exactly the way you want, but they get better. Other countries are not always like that. So even now, even with this terrible catastrophe in the U.S., people globally will look to the U.S. and say, "What are you going to do?" and will continue to look to the U.S. as a hopeful place. People will still want to come here, be here.

S peaks of Many Truths: We would like to say to the families, friends and caring individuals: May you find the great depth of love and caring in yourselves to nurture one another and get through this terrible time of grief and upset, and that it is best to nurture, even though your warriors will have to protect. It was like that in our time. [Again, Speaks of Many Truths was alive on Earth in North America in the 1600s.]

Homework: Find River Willow

In addition, I would like to say, for those of you who know plants, if you can find river willow, willow that grows near water (streams, creeks), this is what I recommend. If you can get down to a river or stream safely, please do so, in groups if you like, but be safe. When you get to the willow, stand a few feet from it. Then pray or feel the heat or other spiritual phenomena in your bodies, or call in angels or others. Every time you exhale, blow gently toward the willow. The willow has the capacity to amplify anything it is exposed to. For those of you who cannot get too close to the willow but can see it (perhaps you are not as agile or young as you used to be), do the same thing and blow toward the willow. It will not work quite as well, but it will work somewhat. The willow will amplify and send out that good energy in all directions, to all places where it is needed.

You Will Need Bravery in the Future

You knew this was going to happen?

We all knew that it probably would happen—it wasn't absolutely fixed. It was hoped that it wouldn't happen or that the degree of tragedy would not be so severe. There was the other possibility that it could have been worse, but the heroics of those aboard that plane—which were not unlike the way your brother explained (I heard that comment), for they were struggling with the enemy *as* the plane went down—were definitely the primary reason the plane did not strike the White House. Many passengers fought back bravely. Others who couldn't fight prayed and comforted those who were crying. What could they do? But there was much bravery by your people on that plane.

You will need more such bravery in the future. There will be hotheads among you who will say, "She did it," or "They did it," just because of the way they look. We had an attack on our people once by another tribe. We had two people staying with us from that tribe, but they were children, certainly not involved in such a plot. And we beat the attack off. Afterward, I am ashamed to say, there were people who pointed to the children and called them the enemy, but other heads, cooler heads, immediately said, "Not possible. They are our guests, our friends, and most importantly, they are children. How could they know?" And the hotheads were calmed down then. But the warriors, as always after such an experience, had to go out and protect, as will your warriors. But if people are yelling, "He did it," or "She did it"—especially people whom you know didn't do

THE ANGER EXERCISE: A MODIFIED VERSION

Isis

A good modified form of the anger exercise would be to do something not unlike actors might do as training—meaning you have to feel it as much as possible. Imagine you are trying to convince a producer or a director who is checking you out for a performance that you can do it, because that person will have to be convinced that you mean it.

This is something you do entirely on your own without anybody else present. I do not recommend doing it if others are present unless they are doing it also at the same time, but I only recommend that in circumstances where you cannot get away from each other, such as in prison, and then only if the two of you desire to do this at the same time. For everyone else, try to do this on your own in your own space, or possibly out in the woods or someplace out in the open where you can do no harm to others and where no harm will befall you.

If you want to do this outside, bring along a friend who can stand off a hundred yards or so away to deflect people from coming your way. If you want to do it indoors, do it in a room where no one is likely to come into that room for at least an hour or two hours afterward. It would be better for there to be a six-hour gap. If it is a place where a dog or a cat must come in, I recommend that you do not do it there.

Now, the performance, or real thing you feel . . . I'd like you to get very angry. I know this is a contradictory thing for you. Most of you have been taught to control yourself at all costs or you might look foolish or some other thing, and although that might be appropriate in some societal situations, for the sake of this exercise, it is not appropriate—although you do not have to throw things, you do not have to break things. Imagine—some of you may have seen such a thing—a child having a temper tantrum. The child might yell and scream and jump up and down or lie down on the ground and hit her fists to the ground and so on. You don't have to do that either. You don't even have to get up if you are unable or have difficulty in moving.

The process is to shout, but you're going to whisper—you see? You put all of your effort and all of your feeling into shouting, but you whisper. This is why it's a mild form of the anger exercise. You whisper, but all the passion is there. Just think of something or someone you're mad at. The purpose of the exercise is to express the energy so you can release it and you do not bind it to you where it can give you constant discomfort.

Do this no more than three times a week—expressing your anger so you can say anything you want about the person as long as it is whispered and done with passion. You see, in order to truly express even this mild form of the anger exercise, you need to release; it's all about releasing physically. If you can get up and move around, then if you want to, jump up and down or wave your arms or legs—that's all right. If you can't get up for any reason, then move around as much as you can or shake your fist. But if other people might come into the room, then try to do it at a time when it's least likely that they would. Tell people that from time to time you may be doing the anger exercise, but it does not mean you are angry at them.

Remember, whisper. You can say anything you want about anyone as long as you whisper it passionately. You will know when you have let go of this energy that might harm you by holding anger because you will be able to say a person's name—or an event's name or a place or an object, anything—you will be able to say it and the energy, your physical feeling you had once, will either be greatly diminished or you will feel nothing. This will let you know that you have let go of that energy about that.

This is a well-established procedure. Psychologists often give an exercise like this, or more often counselors do. There are even instruments, objects, padded sticks that are sometimes available in sporting goods stores for the purpose of hitting someone or something without causing any harm. They're sometimes sold as toys. I do not know the name of these things, but some people might. If you know a counselor or someone like that, that person might know.

So to put it simply, this modified form of the anger exercise is designed to allow you to release energy that you are holding that might be causing you to feel uncomfortable or ill at ease and restricting your happiness in your life as you live in your world.

it, your fellow Americans from that part of the world—it doesn't mean that they did anything. They are your people first. Granted, there may be a few hotheads who were peripherally involved, but I do not think there is anybody I can see who was in any way directly involved—except for one individual who is now in custody. But that individual is detained.

Practice the Anger Exercise and Plant Therapies

For those of you who do not know what to do with your grief and anger, do as Zoosh has discussed in the past—a mild form of the anger exercise. If you have to punch something, don't punch one another. It is a time to make friends, not to add enemies. If you have to punch something, punch something like a pillow or a bed to release your anger. It is all right to have such a tantrum, because it will transform the anger in your body. Sometimes such a terrible event brings up old anger, old resentment in your body from previous events that you don't even remember. If that happens, go ahead and hit the bed or hit the pillow—something soft—but don't hit one another.

Those of you who know herbal teas, strengthen the warriors, for they will need it. Also, for those who stay at home and might be fretting, give them herbal teas containing the following: goldenseal, comfrey, chamomile and just a little bit, if you have it, of elderberry. I recommend that as calming and life-sustaining. Those of you who are herbalists know of other things to give, and I support that. It is a good time for plant therapies like this. And the plants and animals around you will be more than happy to support you in this terrible time. Count on one another. Look to one another for support, not to blame. You will reform the community you once called, when you were young—yes, those of you with gray hair—our place, our country, our home, our America. Good night.

Difficult Changes Are Coming in the U.S. Government

Reveals the Mysteries
October 25, 2001

G reetings.

September 11 completely changed the way the American people perceive their reality. There's fear now. There is incredible new legislation cutting down our privacy. Our lives have changed, we don't look at life the same way we did, and it was one act that changed everything. It was such an incredible feat to . . . I mean, who would have thought that one act could have changed everything about America—that it could have put the whole country in disarray, that the stock market would go down, that no one would fly in airplanes, that people would just change the way they thought about everything?

People Will Not Accept Rigid Authoritarianism

Well, I will say this: Politically speaking, I think I can pretty well guarantee you that the Democrats will be voted in next time, because regardless of the perceptions in the White House that people want to be safe, they really do not wish to experience what is being done, supposedly on their behalf. And I think that unless the voting is suspended, which is unlikely—although there was certainly some tampering last time—I think that you will see most legislators who vote for what I would call truly interfering legislation . . . oh, it is one thing to keep track of people from other countries in your country. In my time, if we had visitors from outside our people, we certainly kept track of them as well. But I'd have to say that the legislation, to some degree, is likely to be appealed by succeeding administrations, but not insofar as the treatment by the United States of people from other countries or, for that matter, of permanent visitors, meaning so-called resident aliens (an unpleasant term).

There will be a lot of groundswell support for a national identification system, and there has been a lot of research on this, as you know. And while I do not think that your people in your country will embrace it immediately, there will be encouragement to do so. Ultimately, once the problems with that system have been worked out, it will be a good thing, but in the short run, people will not react well. I would have to say, though, that the legislation as you described it, that is coming now, may not pass quite as easily as people think, and if it does pass, it probably won't be applied in its complete form. Some of it will be what you might call "just in case" legislation, and I do not expect to see what amounts to police-state tactics where people walking down the street are stopped and their papers are demanded, as in a war situation. I would, however, expect to see a change, but my best guess is that people in the country, in the countryside, are going to begin to lead rather than follow.

As a result, I feel that what will prevail will be community, meaning that, "We know our friends and neighbors, and we know who's visiting, and this is how we understand our lives"—as compared to in cities where, "We don't know our neighbors and we expect others to protect us because we don't know anybody and we don't want to." I feel that the voice of the country will be heard, the country people will be heard, and that is what you will see the system evolving into. In short, people will not really accept a rigid authoritarianism, and I feel that in Washington this is not understood, especially in the executive branch—although it is understood by the courts and I believe there is some understanding in the Senate. So we will see.

I think the ones who don't understand, I think they see this as a wonderful excuse to get some of this stuff passed that they've wanted all along.

They may see that. I would be very surprised if during the next election the voters do not turn everybody out.

Despite Expectations, Crime Will Not Stop

Well, do you think that the masterminds, the operatives connected to the sinister secret government, really conceived of this result? I mean, are they spectacularly surprised, or are they going, "Well, yeah, that's what we tried to create"?

The latter. That is what they tried to create, because when you're feeling impinged upon, as they have been, one of the first things you want to do is control. And one of the best ways to control people is through fear; it is not a good thing, but it is often done. Therefore, as far as they are concerned, this is a spectacular success. Now, one of the ironies here is that one might expect that as a result of such levels of scrutiny that the government is putting on your population, that organized crime would come to a standstill. And, you see, this is where your government is wearing blinders. People's attitudes are going to be very simply, "If you know what everybody's doing here, how come any crime can go on at all?" You see? The established elected and bureaucratic people in Washington are going to have to face the music on that—that people will expect crime and those who do crime to be at least observed, if not exposed.

And will that happen? Will they be exposed?

No, it is not likely.

Why?

Because the attention being put on the public is to search out . . . it is not unlike in wartime, where you're looking for spies and you don't care about anything else. But the public will expect the payoff here to be that every crime is going to be discovered.

Right. If we have to give up our freedom—our email, our financial transactions, our travel, everything—if that's to be totally known, then we are going to expect crime to stop.

People are going to expect . . . if all of this is going on, then why? Where is the reward? And also, of course, in this information age, people will be communicating with their friends and neighbors in other countries, and asking, "What's it like down there?" You know, everybody in the U.S. who is uncomfortable with this system is not simply going to emigrate to other countries. The U.S. is, if nothing else, resilient; I do not think that the people of the U.S. will go along indefinitely with such levels of control. Previous generations are used to some control, some sacrifice, as in rationing during the major wars, but even they will not go along with giving up the Constitution and the Bill of Rights.

So I am not saying what anybody ought to do. What I am saying is that for legislators, it would be a good thing to go out into your districts where the actual people you represent are—speaking especially to Congress here and the Senate. It is not the executive branch's job so much to have their finger on the pulse of the nation; that is the job of the House and the Senate. Especially in the House of Representatives—speaking to you directly—the reason you are voted on so often is that you are expected to be citizens first and representatives second. So I call upon you to remain in touch with your constituents and make sure that you are representing their real cares and not simply jumping on the railroad without checking to see where the train is going.

Why the Towers Fell

What about the actual World Trade Center? It's not logical for those two buildings to implode; it's just not. Were there other explosives, or was there something else planted in the buildings, or did they actually implode because of the crash and the burning of the jet fuel?

I grant that it is not logical that buildings would so completely disintegrate as a result of this—yes, damage, but not that level of damage. But I would have to say that the causal factor has more to do with the construction technique, which was revolutionary at its time, the way it was done. But in hindsight . . . I might add, people in building and safety actually warned the city that this was not proper construction technique and they didn't recommend it. Nevertheless, I would have to say that it is highly unlikely that such form of construction will ever be allowed in New York again, though the country will have to be vigilant to keep it from happening elsewhere.

So the steel really did get to two thousand degrees, it twisted and the concrete floors came down just like they said?

What I am saying is that the quality of construction left a lot to be desired. That's all I'm going to say, and that . . . think about it. If something isn't built that well, regardless of what the specifications say, it may not necessarily be too stable.

Local Terrorists Are Responsible for Most of the Anthrax Attacks

The other thing I wanted to talk about is anthrax. Is that something you want to talk about?

I will try, and if I am not sufficient, then we will let Zoosh talk about all these matters, since that is really his forte. But I will see what I can do.

Zoosh had said that in Florida at the National Enquirer building, it was, like, a serial killer [see chapter 4]. But now since then it's been sent to NBC and Senator Daschle's office and the postal sorting center and other post offices, as well as the New York Post and the Senate building. Can you say who is doing this?

I would have to say local-born-and-bred terrorists, but they do not consider themselves to be terrorists. And I would have to say that what is going on here . . . it is obvious that one might say, "Well, this would play right into the hands of the sinister secret government, because the more one can induce terror and . . ."

Hysteria, fear, yes. I mean, people are afraid to look in envelopes, they're afraid to go to work.

The more one can do this, then it creates serious problems. However, one must understand that there are elements of people in your country who are unstable. My feeling is that—and I will give you a percentage—90 percent of the initial attacks using this product, if I might call it that, were from unstable elements. But 10 percent were criminally backed indirectly by the sinister secret government. And that which is criminally backed . . . I can tell you how you can separate it. That which is sinister secret government–associated will always be spread around in some way to the general public, but never sent to a well-known or respected political figure.

Their whole point—from the sinister secret government's point of view—is, "How can we keep the general population stirred up?" They're not going to try to attack someone who's not only a well-known political figure, but one so well thought of.

Well, all of the other cases so far are of one kind of anthrax, but the one that was sent to Senator Daschle had peculiar characteristics. It was highly concentrated, the spores were smaller, it was purer and there was a special additive so that it would travel through the air more easily. So that one seems to be different than the other ones.

Well, you can ask Zoosh, but my feeling is that these are local-born-and-bred individuals.

Were the people who mailed the letters in the cases I've talked about, are they directly related to Larry Ford, the man featured in Los Angeles Magazine [this article is reprinted in chapter 4]?

No; some of them had interactions with the larger group of people he was involved with. And I can't say too much about the larger group, because the larger group is a highly intertwined multiple-leveled group of sometimes . . . not friends, as you would say, but more like people at odds who are having to work together, even though they don't want to.

But for a common goal?

Yes, and the common goal is to acquire the means to manipulate. So I would say that for a long time, chemical and biological warfare has been a major threat. But the application of biological warfare is not new; the initial application of biological warfare as suggested in this magazine article—and as channeled about extensively in the past—was the spread of AIDS in Africa. That was always the presentable thing.

Which they got from the Xpotaz [an off-planet renegade group], right? [For more information on the Xpotaz, see previous Shining the Light books.]

Well, let's not even go into that, because the problem with revealing esoteric things is that it causes readers to feel powerless, whereas the reason this article is so important is that these are all human beings on Earth and there may be some means for the police to do something about it. The problem in intelligence circles and even at national investigative agencies is that the great challenge there is to acquire information and accumulate it long enough so that entire rings or groups can be prosecuted or eliminated, whereas with policing, the actual attempt is to protect the community on a day-to-day basis, which is quite different. So my belief is that policing is a better protection for the average citizen on a daily basis than the other, even with all of the value and good that the other does. Once people read that article, they're going to look entirely differently upon all biological and microbiological scares. Granted, it was written about a person who was mentally unsound and clearly—how can we say?—criminal. But the article says a few other things. It says things, and more to the point, given your readers' level of consciousness, it will ring bells.

The U.S. Will Have to Change

Is it your opinion that once the Taliban are taken out of Afghanistan, that they're going to turn to Iraq or to some other country? I mean, what is the inner thinking here? They're saying that this might take years. I read today that the Cold War lasted fifty years. Are they looking to sort of go from country to country and bomb out the terrorists?

"They" meaning the United States?

The United States and Britain and any of their allies.

I can assure you that the Arab world will not sit still for a second to allow that to happen. They are even now gritting their teeth; it is all they can do to stand by and allow this to happen. It is not really in their nature. You have to remember that the degree to which they have united in recent years was a long, arduous process for them. They understand that their common religion—meaning their religion they have with one another—is what binds them together, but they also recognize very clearly that there are vast differences between them as cultural groups. Still, they've made a lot of progress, and they are very much disinclined to allow outsiders, from their point of view, to come in and colonize them— which is exactly what is going on (granted, from the United States' point of view, unintentionally). But that is really it. I think that they ultimately will not try to say, "Okay, we're assembling our forces and we're going to attack the U.S." But you have to remember that the U.S.'s position is very vulnerable in economics. The U.S. is one of the larger debtor nations in the world, and it is only a monument to your business system, the way it runs, that your system is not collapsing around you. As private businesspeople like to say, "If I ran my business like that, I'd be out of business."

So you have to look toward who owns the banks and who owns the paper that the U.S. pays on. What happens if your loans are called? No, I feel that the U.S. has to pursue these desires through the United Nations, and even though it is slow . . . you have to remember that the citizens of the U.S. and its government have never yet learned that sometimes worthy goals take time. If you check with France and, for that matter, other countries that have a long-established culture— I pick France because they discovered the follies of colonialism and now have more of a worldview—if you look at these kinds of countries, you will see that they take the long view now. They don't say, "What can be done tomorrow?" No.

I feel that ultimately when the U.S. again becomes part of the global community, then we will see some good changes for this country. But until then, it will be kind of touch-and-go until the other countries of the world stand up and say, "Look, you can't be the policemen to the world. We know you're trying to do good things here, but the methods and manners of your approach are not acceptable." It will take something like that. These things are being said now, but quietly. The U.S. is used to influencing, but it has not really learned yet how to be influenced gracefully. Your government's been influenced many times, but how to be influenced gracefully and be patient . . . that is something you're still learning. And over the next twenty or thirty years, you will learn it, and it will be comforting once you have. But in the process, you will have to change. I think the change will largely be a good one, helping the U.S. government become recognized for the good you do—which . . . you do a lot of good—but also encouraging the U.S. to not be the Boy Scout to the world. You have to be more than a Boy Scout to accomplish global goals. You have to recognize other cultures and other governments as being equal to you, not as being different and needing changes to make them more like your own government.

Fixing, yes.

Sometimes those governments, even though they may seem to be outrageous, are based upon the cultures of the people who live in those countries, not based upon an idea that seems wonderful to the United States. Your government is based on an idea that seems wonderful, but given the fact that there is no single homogenous culture in your country, it is difficult for your government to grasp the idea that other countries are quite different. They often do have homogenous cultures, or cultures that are at least considerably more united in their makeup and their day-to-day activities and what they do—this is not all countries. The U.S. tends to gravitate on a friendly basis toward countries, naturally, that are more like itself, but the vast majority of countries are different than that. And the U.S.

needs to learn this. You're a long way from being elder statesmen, and you just need to grow up a little bit.

I'm not trying to talk down to you, but I'm talking more to the government here. You know, gentle reader, that in a family, you do not let the children run the family, even though very often the children think they can. They know how it ought to be done. Remember back to your youth: Once you got a little older, in your teenage years, everything seemed very clear. It was very obvious the way things ought to be done, and you found it very frustrating that the adults were so slow and didn't want to change anything. It was maddeningly frustrating. Well, right now most of the world looks on the United States as being exactly at that stage, being the teenager who believes that it knows exactly how things ought to be done and is frustrated with the rest of the world for not seeing teenage truth as being universal.

So I feel that in the coming seven years or so, there will be a sort of difficult time in the U.S. government—not so difficult with the people, because the government and the people have always been somewhat at a distance from each other. But in the government it will be difficult; the government will think that the people want them to do one thing, when in fact they really want them to do another. It is not unlike a family. Think about it, parents: When you ask your little ones, your young children, what they want to do, you usually hear exactly what they want to do. Maybe you don't do it or can't do it, but it is very straightforward. But, parents, what happened the last time you talked to your teenagers and asked them what they wanted? Were they honest and straightforward, or did they think you were square and beyond hope in terms of communication? Did you just get the blank stare, or "Oh, Mom," or "Oh, Dad, you don't understand." Well, you have a similar situation with the government and the citizens.

So with that point, I am not trying to say that you are all children here. What I am trying to say is that sometimes, even though you don't like what's going on in the world, sometimes it's better to let things work out on their own, rather than to just go in and say, "We don't like you, we don't like the way you're doing things, and furthermore, we think we can do a better job"—which sounds an awful lot like a lot of teenagers whom parents love, and those teenagers love their parents. But it sure sounds like a generation gap to me.

All right, I'll accept that, although I really believe that the Taliban should be removed from power.

Helping Is Not Always Such a Good Thing

I cannot say that I in any way agree, and I'll tell you why. Even though they did not get elected to power, you understand, the way it works in the United States, they came to power not unlike other people came to power in the past in that region. I am not saying it's necessarily good, but I do feel that it is ultimately intended that the people in that region choose what to do about it. I'm not saying that the U.S. didn't have a perfect right to go in there and say, "Give us the criminal; we want him back," but that doesn't give you the right to go in and say, "And we don't like the way you look either! We don't like the way you're running things! And, oh, by the way, I think we'll just take over your country, and then afterward we'll decide what to do with it." Now, I'm not saying the U.S. is talking to anybody like that, but that is exactly the way the people of that country feel.

The people of that country do not feel in any way like the U.S. is rescuing them. They *do* feel in every way like the U.S. is attacking them, and even though other countries are there helping the U.S., they are crystal clear that the person they're blaming for this is the United States. So I'd have to say that you are actually making more trouble for yourself than you are trying to fix. Remember the old story about the Boy Scout helping the lady across the street when she was waiting for a bus?

Sometimes when you want to do a good deed and act on that good deed, it turns out to be something not so good after all. The people of the United States are exceptional; you want to help, and no country in its culture—in your modern times, let's say the past thousand years or so—has ever wanted to help and has helped as much as you have. I am not saying you are bad; what I am saying is, you need time to consider what you'll do next. You are a very young country. In the past, you've depended upon other countries you might have considered the old country: England, France, for some of you, Germany, the Nordic countries. But you know, there are other countries that are the old country, considering your population: Mexico, Canada, Africa, the Caribbean, all kinds of places. Your people come from all over the world. And therefore, with this group of entirely mixed and different cultures and ways of being and races and religions, I believe that this is what motivates you to want to help, because every one of you has to be helpful in order to learn how to get along.

So it is in your nature to want to help. It is built into your culture and even built into your precious documents: the Constitution and the Bill of Rights. Helping one another is almost a religion in your country, and certainly many religions have it built into their philosophy as well. But there are times when helping is not such a good thing, because if you see that you are helping, you see it in your own eyes. For example, you might want to help some people who are hungry, and you share your food with them. But maybe that's not the kind of food they eat, and your food makes them sick, and they wither and die. And you feel terrible, but you had nothing else to offer but your own. What I am saying is, what could you have done? In that case, you would have asked others to help who know these individuals and their culture, and what could be offered and how it could be offered. Maybe the others wouldn't do as good a job as you could do, but perhaps in the long run, it would be best.

So it is not my job to say, with a finger in the face like a stern parent or grandparent, that you are bad and you deserve a spanking, but I feel that your country tends to be overenthusiastic in ways that are sometimes rash and not just ineffective but actually unintentionally troublemaking. And I feel that your invasion of this country, regardless of your motivation, which I grant is benevolent, is mistaken. I do not claim to say that the Taliban government is benevolent and benign—quite the opposite. But let's just say, when you were setting up your government in this country, I can assure you that England considered you and your people here in this country to be barbarians. Did you welcome their soldiers when they came to liberate you? I don't think so.

You Have Much More in Common Than You Think

Well, this ought to be well received, with all the propaganda and patriotic stuff that's going on these days.

It is good, patriotism, and I support it as long as it is about coming together and helping each other and feeling good about who you are. All of that is fine— I completely agree with the nurturing quality of it. What I do not agree with is saying, "You! You're at the top of the enemy's list; you did it!" It is not suffi- cient. You know, the terrible thing in your time is that your government's mili- tary is set up to battle an enemy that is identifiable, but the trouble with an underground enemy is that he is almost always unidentifiable. And while your people engaged in this operation completely understand that, it really is neces- sary for you as citizens to stop demanding that the government—your govern- ment—strike back at whoever is the popular enemy in that moment. A lot of mischief has been caused by this in the past. Many, many people, sometimes whole peoples and cultures, have been wiped out. What a loss to you all now— how much they could have done to improve the quality of life for you all! No, it is important that you recognize that all of you have much, much more in com- mon than you have that is different.

And while it is good to try and help people to live lives that are more benevo- lent and gentle and kind to each other, you can't grab them by the arm, twist their arm behind their back painfully and say, "Have I got a way of life for you, and you're going to like it!" It doesn't work, even if what you have to offer is a hundred times better than the way they are living. You didn't like it when the British said, "We can offer true civilization." Can you not remember?

Did you want to be liberated by the Nazis, the German Nazis, who would have offered a different form of culture, who would have said, "Oh, if we can just get rid of this group, then you'll all be much happier," and after that happens, "Well, now, if we can just get rid of this group, you'll all be happier." But of course, as you remember, that was all subterfuge. There was more going on there. But for you, I do not feel that your government or your people had any interest in welcoming the invading hordes that ran all over Europe to take over countries there, nor does anybody in that country you invaded say, "Oh, welcome; it's wonderful." It is not like liberating Paris. Unfortunately, even though your inten- tion is good, I feel that the ultimate impact will not be good. Please take a les- son from your new friend, Russia. They tried it; it didn't work.

Listen to the Advice of Other Countries

So what's the downside, then? What do you see as the downside of the next couple of years of invading Afghanistan?

It is ultimately probably going to require a change of executive branch gov- ernment. What you have in there now is an executive branch that is much more interested in international affairs, the world, but in the larger sense, they are per-sonally—especially the president—involved in the desire for stability and the creation of some kind of harmony. But the president feels driven by public opin-ion, even though he's trying to shape it, and he has people around him encour-aging him to do what are truly radical things.

No, I feel that ultimately it will require a president to be voted in who is more interested in domestic policies—"What can we do for our people here?"—to get the people of the country focused back on your own country. That's where you can do the most good: taking care of your own people. There are a lot of people in your own country who need lots of help, and you are in a position to help them, whereas in other countries that have entirely different systems than yours, even with the best of intentions, you are in a very good position to stub your toe there.

It's fine if we learn some lessons, but I don't want it to be a catalyst for a larger war.

Well, that's why I'm talking to you this way, because I am hopeful that your government will listen to the advice of other countries, including your old and trusted allies, as well as your new friends. And for the people of the United States, please, please, do not demand that your government revenge you on . . . who? An unseen enemy? Or are you just going to say, "Those guys! We don't like those guys, and they're obvious, so it's them!" That doesn't work; it just causes more trouble than it repairs.

So I'm leaving it up to you. I'd like you to encourage your government, to tell them that you appreciate all their efforts and those of the people in the govern-ment who are unelected and who largely work in a thankless way, tirelessly try-ing to help all of you citizens. But I think you need to write letters to your representatives and to your president and to others, and say, "It's okay; it's fine to have stability. We recognize that people in other countries are different from us, and you don't have to plant the flag of the U.S. in foreign lands. We'd much rather have you plant it on Mars or the Moon; that's the kind of adventure we can really embrace." With that kind of adventure—international adventure going to other planets—the whole world can embrace that. You don't have to become different. You can be yourself and say, "Isn't that exciting?" in whatever language you speak.

Many Beings Are Directing More Attention to Earth These Days

Wonderful. Thank you very much; we're going to talk more. You were physically a teacher to Speaks of Many Truths in his time—have you had a body on the Earth since?

I have lived on the Earth since, unlike Speaks of Many Truths.

Can you say anything about that?

I had a nice life in France.

In what year?

In the 1800s.

Oh, what an exciting time! Would I recognize your name if I researched?

I wouldn't think so.

Oh, a quiet life?

A nice quiet life. I had many children, and I lived long enough to experience the joys of grandchildren.

And is some of your lineage still on Earth now?

Yes. I have a special interest in the Earth, and I appreciate the countryside, especially the dairy farms of France.

But I thought I understood last time that you were a teacher on some planet in Sirius?

Sometimes, yes. But I am directing much more of my attention to Earth these days.

Do you have students whom you teach as a spiritual teacher?

Not so much that, but many beings are directing more attention to Earth these days, and I am amongst them.

Because it's such a pivotal time, yes?

Yes. I will say, good life.

Thank you very much.

The Meaning of Crop Circle Illustrations

Speaks of Many Truths and Zoosh
November 10, 2001

This is Speaks of Many Truths. Greetings.

Greetings! Which crop circle would you like to talk about first?

The so-called face on Mars [Fig. 22–1].

The Crop Illustration Face: A Wake-Up Call

For starters, it is not the face on Mars. I grant that it is a face, but it is not that face. It really has to do with the face of an individual who might come in time to speak to people, and they will see the face in their mind's eye or imagination. It will be something that will happen for most in dreams, for some in their meditations. But the face is not really the one on Mars, though it has enough similarity to it that the parallel has been drawn.

Who put the crop circle there?

How can we say it? The crop circle came about by those desiring to illuminate human beings and to encourage their spiritual growth. I have to be vague here, because the intention of the crop circle was to do a good thing. I would say, however, that these types of crop circles are not really crop circles; they are illustrations.

As crop illustrations they represent, for the most part, an attempt to communicate in current terms rather than in symbolic terms. In the past, there have been symbolics with crop circles—at first, less complex, then becoming more complex over time. But now that the symbols have done their work, from the

Fig. 22–1. The crop illustration face.

Fig. 22–2. The Arecibo response illustration.

point of view of those who are creating them, it is time for the impressions—"impressions" meaning the way an artist might impress a design on some material. These impressions are intended to be contemporary rather than something that is . . . how can we say?

An old master painting?

Yes. That is why the initial ones have to do with things or images that are quite obviously contemporary, such as in the punch card illustration [see Fig. 22–2], which is clearly a suggestion that the crop illustrations now will begin to show a current or updated acknowledgment of the age of the mind and technology.

Can you say who this being is, where he's from or anything about him? Who's going to talk to us?

Different people will identify him with different names. Some will identify the being as a she rather than a he, and that's acceptable. But the being will have to speak in ways that can be most easily accommodated by different individuals according to their cultures and nationalities. Still, it will be an impression. Once you have moved the mustache and beard off, or you have taken off the headscarf, or you have illuminated the eye patch . . . in short, once you have stripped away the defining factors, that face as it appears would be the overall impression. You might add different colors and so on, but those general characteristics would be loosely grouped under that appearance. It is less important who the being is—the general communication is more important.

The communication will take the form of instructions of what life is about, initially at the basic level, and then creating the means to understand life in a different, perhaps more benevolent way—and also to establish a means of communication. It's meant as a wake-up messaging system for the general population. Some time ago I believe Zoosh mentioned that there would be a final wave waking up. As you know, they are waking up now.

They're waking up now, and they need to have tools of significance. Religion, while often a support and inspiration to daily lives, is still not enough. They also need something practical. Even though religion will often address the practical, the advice of religion isn't always, in fact, practical for living. So there will need to be something that is a bridge from religion, culture and philosophy to the day-to-day practical. This instruction will be that. Sometimes people won't even remember words at all; they'll just have the impression of a face. But if you can all compare notes, regardless of how the face looked . . . if you strip the face away to its basic features, those would be the ones.

Who planned this?

It is a plan to wake up general society. Remember, it is much more fun to wake up to someone gently touching you, saying, "Time to wake up, dear heart," than to have an alarm bell go off or have someone throw a bucket of water on you. It is gentle, and it is, by its very nature, angelic and feminine. Yet it will be heard, felt and understood in many different ways.

Starting now?

Oh, it has been going on for a time. A few weeks before the crop circle appeared, people were having the experience. But the crop circle was intended to announce the experience. You could say, "Well, how many people could see a crop circle?" and that's quite true. There were other announcements, usually in dreams or meditations or visions, sometimes in the form of clouds in the sky. Long before there were crop circles, there were clouds. Look sometime into the sky, and see how many shapes and faces you see. Sometimes they are right-side up; sometimes they are on the side or looking up or down. But it would be a good education for you.

Spirits show themselves in clouds all the time. Every day. Sometimes they're not meant for humans; sometimes they're meant for other spirits, or for rocks, or for Earth, or more often for animals. But at least half the time they are meant for humans, and of that time, at least 5 percent of that time they are meant for the specific individuals who see them. They are not always meant to be interpreted. Sometimes they are old friends, sometimes they'll make you smile, sometimes they'll make you laugh. Other times it will make your eyes moist. Looking at the sky has always been a valuable thing for human beings to do—sometimes at the stars at night, but in the daytime is better. Look at the clouds. They reveal mysteries while generating them at the same time.

Well, that's an apt description of what you've given us about this face. That's all, that it's a wake-up call? There's no who, what, where, why, when?

There's no advantage to give you that. To give you that would be only one example of the many versions that will go out to individuals. If I say, "Oh, well, it is from these people to those people and meant to do this," then all of the other things will be ignored by many. No, it is better to be general, to use the broad brush rather than the narrow.

So can we say that the angels are coming to gently tap on the shoulders of humans and say, "Wake up!"?

Are there any religions that don't believe in angels?

I don't know.

That's just it, you *don't* know. There are religions that don't believe in angels. Just because you've been raised with them as a concept as well as a religious principle, does not mean that other religions believe in them. No, you can't say that, because it is too narrow. It's not a broad enough brush. I'm using a broad brush because it's intended to touch all. If you use a narrow brush, it will only touch some.

All right. So it's meant to touch all humans on the planet who need to wake up.

It's meant to touch all humans on the planet, period. But it will be something more felt by those who are in the process of waking up.

So would it be like I had a feeling that someone wonderful spoke to me last night?

Yes: "Someone wonderful was talking to me, and this is what he or she looked like, and his or her face kind of looked like this." And some people will say, "Oh, he was black," or "He had a really big nose." But you know, when you whittle down the general characteristics, you will see that it can fit this. You would just take that face and make it black, or you might tint it red or brown or some other colors that are of human beings. You might add an eye patch or glasses or a mustache or a kerchief around the head or a babushka.

The Arecibo-Response Illustration

Did you want to talk about the other crop illustration? Who sent it, what does it mean, why is it there and what are we supposed to do about it?

I've already referred to it. You don't do anything about it. It is a way for those beings who do crop circles to let you know that they are prepared to communicate in contemporary terms. So it is a notification saying, "In the future, look for other such things." That is why the borders are squared off, because squared borders are not natural in nature, except in a particular element of nature. What might that be? To have angular borders?

Something made by humans?

No, in nature. Crystals. Crystals often have angular, if not square, borders. So this tells you that those crop circles that have angular borders are directly related to crystals and that those people working with crystals can do more with this kind of crop circle than with others. If they're having success working with crystals with other crop circles, they ought to give these a try. Angular, as you said before, has to do with humankind's creation, but it also, in nature, has to do with crystals. And of course, you combine that in your time by using crystals in your technology, something you create. You manipulate the crystals.

The story is that in 1974 at Arecibo, Puerto Rico, using large radio transmitters, something was transmitted that looks like the left side of this illustration [Fig. 22–3], and now twenty-seven years later, we get this crop illustration that looks like the right side. I was told or I read that we transmitted the symbol for carbon and received back, in that space, the symbol for silicon.

That doesn't communicate to you any other thing than saying that silicon . . . silica. What's silica? [Pause.] It comes back to what I was talking about—it relates to crystal. So it's trying to draw your attention to crystals.

The story was that although we were carbon-based, maybe the beings who made this were silicon-based.

Well, you don't have to overanalyze crop circles. When crop circles are illustrative like this, they are crop illustrations, direct. You see, because crop circles in the past have been symbolic, you've had to reach and interpret and make your best guess—"What could it be? What might it be?"—and there would be more than one explanation. These are crop illustrations, and they are direct.

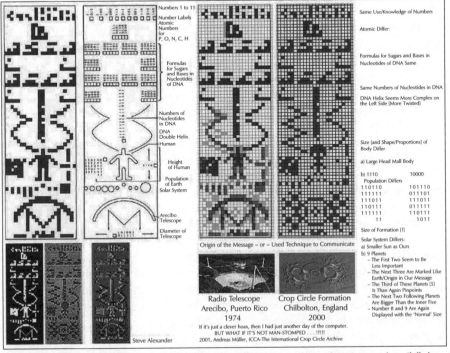

Fig. 22–3. Comparison between 1974 radio transmission from Arecibo, Puerto Rico, and 2000 crop circle in Chilbolton, England.

Okay, so the direct message is . . .

It is what it seems to be. It says, silica, then it means, "Oh, what's silica?" Rock, quartz, crystal . . . like that. And it also establishes a precedent with such crop circles. It means that crop circles are now prepared to communicate to you in contemporary symbols. This is very helpful, because you will be able to use them a little more as a direct communication, rather than just making your best guess.

Can you say who put it there?

What's the point? Others might wish to discuss that, but my whole point is, what does the message mean? You understand, what if you went to a friend's house, but your friend was not there. What if you did not speak your friend's language, nor did you even know how, if you possibly could, to write in, say, Egyptian or Arabic. You wouldn't know where to begin. So you would take a piece of paper and make an illustration of whatever it was that you wanted to suggest. Maybe you would roughly draw a stick figure showing the sunshine and yourself as the stick figure in the kitchen of this person's house. Then you'd draw an arrow to the next illustration, showing the nighttime with the Moon in the sky and you coming back to the house, meaning, "I'll be back tonight." In short, this is a picture with a direct meaning—not something that one sits down and says, "Now, what's the symbology of this?" [Chuckles.]

Okay, so . . . just work with crystals? That's all it means?

Oh no, it doesn't mean *work with crystals*. It means for *those who are using crystals*, now it's time for *you* to pay attention, not only to crop circles, but to crop illustrations. And more crop illustrations will come for those who are working with silica—not just people working with crystals, but people working with technology that uses crystals. What might that be? Almost everything you use today: computers, satellites, automobiles, communication devices, space vehicles and more. But specifically, computers.

Crop illustrations that follow will often be aimed at people using this tool, and not just at work. Ultimately, it is intended to be a tool of communication, is it not? How we talk to each other in print, symbols, drawing, illustrations . . . as much of ourselves as we can put into the machine and pass on to others, which is sometimes difficult to say to those others, to their faces. Email—yes?—and other things.

Email is actually an expansion of communication, even though in the beginning to many people it feels like a contraction. Ultimately, it's an expansion, just as letters were in days gone by. The advantage of computers, of course, is that they can, however poorly, translate. And as time goes by in the future, the translation will get better. Translation right now does not really include innuendo, and of course, as you know, innuendo is almost everything in language. For instance, you can say to a person as he or she comes into your house, "Sit!" meaning relax, whereas you might say to a dog or a child, "Sit!" and it is the same word, but . . . innuendo, yes?

That's incredible. Thank you.

G reetings! Zoosh here.

Anything else you want to say about the crop circles?

What do you want to know?

The Age of Crop Illustrations

Well, as I've been sitting here staring at the crop circle face, I have seen, as Speaks of Many Truths said, everything from a beautiful woman to a man with vacant eyes. What is the face based on? What was the model?

It's the foundational model of the . . . you might say, the primordial modern man. Primordial modern, in this case, means the overall features that have proven to be of value, to be a foundation for the human presence of today. And it is also meant to tell you that those ETs whom you will initially meet—not just the ones people have met through contactees and UFOs, but the ones you will meet, who will be presented to you—will all look like this. They will look like you. They will say, "Well, here I am; I'm from another planet," and you'll say, "You look like us! You could be a human being!" And they will say, "Well, let me demonstrate this and let me demonstrate that," and people will say, "Wow!" This will happen in person, not just on television. People don't believe what they see on television anyway. But it is also a reminder that we'll look like you, we won't scare you. We'll show up, and we won't frighten you. We're not going to have long sticky tongues that are going to reach out and grab your lollipop.

[Laughs.] All right. And what's your perspective on the square edges?

My feeling is that it is definitely intended to be representative of contemporary modern man in the age of technology. And it is really almost forcing that point of view on you, to say, "Hey, this isn't just past-oriented; it's not just symbology. This is today; it is contemporary." I like Speaks of Many Truths' description—these are crop illustrations.

Yes, I like that word. We're going to use it.

And let's call it, when you use it, the *age of crop illustrations*, because it's actually a shift in policy. You might still notice other kinds of crop circles, but these will happen more and more often, at least from time to time. And I don't have any problem with human beings reproducing them. I would recommend that it might be an interesting experience for weavers—not only those who are learning it in school, but more contemporary weavers, professional or hobbyist weavers—to try to make designs like this. Weaving a design, you might easily be able to make something with squared-off edges; it might be interesting. Especially that face . . .

it might be interesting on a wall hanging, for instance. Possibly you could add things to the face. Using the face as an underpinning of the design, you could add things to the face to make it more palatable or interesting or humorous or loving, according to your perception of those qualities in a human face.

Well, when you look at it as I have been doing, it changes constantly.

Isn't that wonderful?

It's fantastic.

It changes because of its very nature. This face is a bridge to spiritual experiences occasionally felt throughout all time by people, such as yourself, who can see. It is also a bridge for the general public to have those experiences of seeing from time to time—if not in their waking state, as you are now, at least in that world between the dream and the waking state.

Is there anything specific you want to say about the other crop illustration that talks about the silicon?

I agree with Speaks of Many Truths that it is intended to engage people who are using crystal in technological formats, technological applications or even more ancient crystal works. So I would say that it is a time to apply such things according to your practices.

I gather you don't want to say who did them or anything about them.

I think it's pretty important not to say that right now. But I will say this, that it does have to do with beings you will meet on Earth and that it is a preparation, a herald, as it were. Not a trumpet blowing and then in walks the king or queen—that means something immediate. But it is a trumpet blowing over the hill. You can hear the trumpet and you know something's coming, because it's getting louder. Like that—it is a herald.

Oh, that's great. It's in the distance, but it's coming toward you.

That's right.

After September 11: A Time of Unity

Is there anything else you want to say?

Now that you've had an opportunity to experience the shock of the unexpected in such a hideous and stunning way, as experienced in New York City and near Washington, D.C., you now must look at the world as being something that you are a portion of. Please engage yourself as an individual citizen and as a global citizen with your institutions that unite—the United Nations and business institutions that unite. Recognize that this terrible experience was not only evil . . . certainly those who carried it out regretted it instantaneously, the moment they passed through the veils with those they took with them. Immediately, they were screaming, "We didn't know! We didn't understand!" and saying individually, "I didn't know, I didn't understand! I'm so sorry!" Because when you get through the veils, even the initial veils, you immediately realize that all is love, that love and God are one, and that harming and hurting in the name of God is the ultimate blasphemy.

Now that you've had this terrible experience, please recognize that it is a unifying factor between all human beings of contemporary times. It does not behoove you, as a society in America or as a race of beings, to prepare to meet beings who will love you, appreciate you and guide you, be they in the spirit world or in any form . . . it does not prepare you to say, "You did that to me; I'll do this to you." Revenge almost invariably harms innocents who never harmed you, and not those who did.

Homework: Make a Friend

So I'm going to say this: It is not a time of revenge, but rather a time of acquaintanceship. Would you like some homework? Here is some homework for those of you who wish to grow from this experience. Make a friend. You've got thirty days—begin. It doesn't have to be an accomplished friendship, but sometime at the end of thirty days I'd like you to be able to say, "I have begun a friendship with someone who looks completely different from me." Maybe the person is a different race or culture; maybe he or she is younger or older than you; maybe the person is simply so different you would never normally approach him or her.

I've given you this homework before, and I'm giving it to you again. It is time for you to do that homework again. It is a preparation to meet beings from afar, but it is also, more importantly, a preparation to meet beings from *near*. Why search the skies for ETs when you are surrounded by them? *All human beings owe their cultural heritage to the stars*. If you want to meet ETs so much, go introduce yourself to your neighbor. It is time for that homework.

It is important, then, to make friends with those people you might not normally make friends with. Sometimes it's possible to do this at work or on the bus or at the store, or perhaps in a safer way if you feel the need—at a club, at a gathering, at church. But begin. Recognize that union and unification will bring and attract help to you, the kind of help you want, the kind of help you need, the kind of help you have been praying and asking for—loving guidance and support that helps you all to unite, to feel the value in each other, to support and nurture each other and to help each other obtain what you need and what will improve your quality of life.

Prepare by embracing one another. You don't have to embrace everyone. Just start by making a friend who is different. Don't expect him or her to be like you; this person will be different. Use it as a challenge and say, "Let's try to be friends. Not just at this bus stop or at the store today, but maybe we can find something we can do together, a fun thing. Do you like to bowl? Do you like to go to the movies? Do you like to watch sports? Do you like to participate in sports?" Go right on through your list until you find the things you like to do together, meaning the things you do separately that maybe you can do together. It is simple and uncomplicated, but it is a risk. Still, it is a way to prepare for the future you are all praying for. Good night to all of you. Thank you.

Past-Anchored Flashes Surface in Dreams and Visions as People Release the Old Past-Anchored Timeline

Speaks of Many Truths and Zoosh
December 19, 2001

This channeling was previously published in Explorer
Race: Techniques for Generating Safety.

Web Dreams
[Dreams courtesy of www.syzygyjob.net/dreams.]

1. 12-19-01: Mr. Bopp
Last night: Paratroopers were falling from the sky and the sky was blood red. The planes were troop carriers, just black silhouettes swimming in the sea of red as thousands of parachutes blossomed behind them. I was not able to tell if they were ours or some enemy invading us.

2. 12-19-01: Linda Marie
A few weeks ago, I also had a dream where paratroopers were coming down. We were trying to escape on foot through some woods before they landed and saw us. I got the feeling they were Chinese.

3. 12-16-01: MC Young/TX
Awoke from this very scary dream about an hour ago, hands still trembling. I saw two Asian men dressed in dark suits. One said to the other, "Any minute now, it will detonate." We (a group of bikers and their families, as well as myself) were in a small rural mountain area in the foothills. I followed these two Asian men and stood behind them. Facing south toward Los Angeles, I saw a dome-shaped light arise from the ground upward off in the distance. This was followed by a mushroom-shaped cloud. I could not believe my eyes! I was utterly stunned. Then

I ran inside a nearby house and dialed my mother, but my friend Cindy in Washington answered instead. "Cindy! It's MC," I said. "Well, I gathered that. What's happening?" she replied. I said, "Cindy! Don't you know!???" "Know what?" she asked. "Cindy, they just dropped the bomb on Los Angeles!!!" I cried. She was silent for a very long moment and then disassociated and started chatting about her cats. I screamed into the phone for her to pay attention: "Cindy! They just nuked LA!!! Turn on the news!!! I have to get hold of Mama right away so I'll call you back, but know this: Seattle is next!!!" I hung up the phone and then I woke up, heart pounding, sweating and trembling. It was so vivid and real. I hope it's just another unsettling nightmare and nothing else. My mother, whom I just talked to about it, suggested I post it here anyway. Is anyone else dreaming anything like this?

4. 12-16-01: Marcia in Oly.

I know several have been having nuke dreams. I had one awhile back that involved a plane crash in a desertlike area (California?) and involved nuke fallout in my area in Washington and chaos in the country as a whole. It seemed the news was not getting proper info, a few cities (I felt on the East Coast) had been wiped out and they were trying to figure out what was happening—poor radio reception, limited airwaves. Mine was incredibly vivid as well. I hope they're just bad dreams.

5. 12-18-01: Arthur

Had a vision two months ago of three missiles coming into the U.S. They came from the northwest . . . like over the Canadian border near Washington State. One hit the East Coast Virginia area and another hit the Chicago area, the Midwest. The third hit somewhere in the Northwest. I heard a voice . . . China . . . I said, "Oh, @^#$!" and woke up.

6. 12-18-01: Stardanya

In 1998 I woke from a deep sleep in a cold sweat with my heart pounding and yelling the words, "The China man is coming!" To this day, I have no idea why I yelled that.

7. 12-18-01: Marcia in Oly.

Recently, a visionary from Betania (Venezuela) was quoted after 9/11—I think on spirit day—that a big country and a small one were responsible. She said to watch China and that the U.S. should be very, very careful because of this. It seems this statement might be truer than we realize.

All right, this is Speaks of Many Truths.

The End of What Was

Regarding this visioning of atomic weapons exploding in the U.S., while it does not seem to be good news, it actually is. The current climate in Washington, D.C., and in the country would naturally cause people to feel that the vision of atomic explosions has to do with dire circumstances your country seems to face in the headlines every day. But what this really represents is a motion out of the old past-anchored timeline.

Consider this: When people have near-death experiences or even some kind of near miss—say they almost crash their car—often you'll hear of their life flashing before their eyes. This is a similar, if not identical, phenomenon. Although your life can flash in front of your eyes, given the number of lives involved and the amount of time involved, what is occurring is that people who are envisioning this atomic warfare are seeing something similar to the life view of Earth going through that circumstance I described. It is not as dire as it looks. Granted, as a culture, as the Explorer Race, as a society, you have not yet anchored in the future timeline, but the fact that you are experiencing such visions is a clear-cut piece of evidence that you are releasing the old one.

Consider again: If a person has that near-death experience, the life that flashes by is the life she has led up to that point. The person doesn't see her past life; she doesn't see her future life. She sees what you could call a past-anchored timeline associated with her given physical life. So what you are seeing here is very much the same thing—a past-anchored flash of life. Now, granted, the past does not go back to infinity on Earth. Rather it goes back in association with the generation before the second world war and even a little bit before. People are also seeing scenes of battle and other things associated with the historic and cultural events of the past century. So I do not feel that this represents a dire threat, but rather is a good sign.

Recognize that the best homework that could be applied to this is something to soothe the feelings these things bring up. Putting out these words, if you like, will support and sustain those having these visions, but also it might be worth reminding people that it is a time of year when renewal is important. Remember to feel. Work on attaching yourself and your society, if you can, to the future-anchored timeline.

Essentially what I am saying, then, is that if you can nurture each other as human beings, remind each other that the good

Feeding Your Heart
The Mother of All Beings

Anchor the future timeline in your heart, not only to feed your heart, but also to prepare it for becoming its more benign and benevolent self in a safer environment. Your heart will know how to relax when safety is around you. Sometimes it will just be moments. Other times, as you move into that more benevolent future, it will last for longer periods of time. But always move your hand over to your heart, actually touching your heart on the surface of your chest. Or just come close into your auric field and move your hand about a little bit. Hold it there, anchoring that future benevolence and reminding your heart, your physical heart, that it exists and it is there for itself and other parts of you, sustaining that future. You don't give the future to your heart; you give your heart to the future. But your heart, being a vital organ in your body, is very clear. It is in the present, although its dreams of beauty are sometimes in the future. Your heart needs to be fed this love and gentleness. If you can do it, your heart will have greater strength and nurturing to take you through the present, whatever it might be.

feelings between human beings and other beings go on, you will be reassured that life will go on. It is not the end. It is the end of what was, but it is not the end of life. Work on anchoring your culture to the future benevolent timeline and create a new and wonderful beginning.

Zoosh here.

Echoes of Events That Did Not Occur

People will continue to have visions, and other things will come up. There might even be something I would call an echo. An echo of an event that does not take place would be something like this: There would be a report, possibly unsubstantiated, but with enough energy around it . . . a report about an atomic explosion somewhere, just to use the example, or that someone was assassinated. And then even though there would appear to be enough evidence for the person to report it, that evidence would vanish. Everyone's memories of the event would seem to disappear so that there would be a state of confusion. It would cause a lot of people to go back over tapes and so on at the news services to try to understand what had happened. Of course, in the process it would cause them to become much more serious in terms of their means of confirming stories, although some of them are pretty serious already. That would be an example of an echo of an event that does not but could have occurred.

Now, that is yet to come, but you will probably see it, if not once next year, then perhaps twice. Most likely it will be in the second half of the year, though it is possible that it will be earlier. So watch out for that, and don't immediately react to some extreme story unless it's in the news for an hour and a half or so. If it's still being reported an hour and a half after the fact, it's probably true, but if it seems to disappear within the first five or ten minutes of people hearing it, it's probably not true in the sense of referring to a physical fact as compared to a potential fact.

Security Alert

It is especially important right now that world leaders do not take unnecessary risks in public appearances. It is also useful for world leaders to be a bit more discreet about their travel plans. Perhaps it might be beneficial to lay a few false trails, not unlike what good protection services have done in the past. But in this case, I do not simply mean a false trail in terms of a specific route, but rather a false trail such as, "Where is he going to be?" "We're not sure." "Where is she going to appear?" "We're not certain." In short, I realize this will wreak a bit of havoc with politics and the facts of politics, especially in election years, but it would be useful for the sake of stabilizing world governments, to say nothing of influential leaders.

It is also important to note here that we have to broaden the idea of who world leaders are. Even though the assumption is that they are presidents and vice presidents and premiers and so on, there is a broader context here. We must recognize that people who are well-known and who are quoted—movie stars, representatives at the United Nations, perhaps even well-known television personalities—would have to be included as well. These people might not think of themselves as world leaders, since they have to pay most of their attention to entertainment (learning lines for their jobs and so on), but in fact, they are influential. When people are influential with thousands or even millions of other people, one must acknowledge—even though you might not like to sometimes—that these people are in fact world leaders. I feel that the security alert applies to them as well.

I do not wish to alarm people unnecessarily, but you have to recognize that there are elements in your world now, not only battling for power and influence, but battling to be heard. For people who are not being heard, especially in places where they need to be—such as in the avenue of public opinion—then sometimes violent acts are committed on purpose, as has been done in the past, because they know that it will get press coverage—even though, from their point of view, it is not something they like doing. So when the press paints so-called terrorists as bloodthirsty savages, that is almost never the case. It is, perhaps, convenient to paint them this way for the sake of public opinion and propaganda. But, in fact, most often the people doing this are at their wit's end and act in order to get attention for a cause they believe in. I'm not trying to say that they are good people or heroes, but I think it is better not to get too caught up in heroism as it is defined politically. It is better to acknowledge and recognize that heroism is carried out by individuals or groups of individuals and is designed to support, sustain and love life, often with disregard or apparent disregard for one's own life. This is heroism, and I think it needs to be put out just like that.

That's my security alert. I feel it's important, and I'd like those of you out there who are influential in the court of public opinion to take note. Think about it and be a little bit more discreet in your travels, or at least have protection. If someone says, "Oh, would you like me to come along and look after you?" or "We're happy to include security services as part of doing business with us," any of those things, don't automatically say no. It won't be forever, but it is a good thing to embrace for the next four or five years. Then things will get better.

Is this worldwide?

Worldwide.

Every country?

Every country, although it is less important in some countries. Those of you who live where benevolence is the typical experience—or at least nonviolence, for the most part, is typical—can pay less attention. But please do not pay *no* attention. Recognize that one of the most difficult challenges for you all, which you have noted and thought about in recent months and years, is that even if your country is peaceful, even if your people are generally benign or benevolent toward peoples of other countries and other cultures, it does not mean that you are necessarily safe. People who are trying to get attention, desperate people, might strike out in directions that are actually self-destructive to their cause— meaning that they will strike out in passion, not in calculated thought. Therefore, worldwide caution is recommended.

After Afghanistan

What advice do you have for United States leaders? It looks as if we're almost through in Afghanistan—is there a warning about carrying this further?

I would really like to say that it is unrealistic to the extreme to think that Islamic countries in general will allow the U.S. and its allies (even under the guise of the United Nations, if the United Nations can be persuaded to partake in this in a more universal way) to allow people to march through their countries to quiz everybody, especially at the barrel of a gun, as to whether you are this or whether you are that. It is not realistic. Even though it might cause you to gnash your teeth and stamp your feet or worse, you're going to have to face the music: The ultimate resolution of terrorism—whether it is government-induced or has to do with individuals, groups, cultures or even tribal conflicts—is talking and communicating with influential people everywhere, even if those influential people might just be a father or a mother or a youngster. People in intelligence circles are not surprised at this statement, but others might be.

Therefore, I would have to strongly recommend that the war not be extended to any other country, even—and I want to make this crystal clear—if the government of that country is cooperative in any way. Some governments might be fairly cooperative, saying, "Oh yes, these people need to be rooted out," referring to a culture within their own country that the government does not approve of at that time. And yet you can be certain that at the first sign of internal stress within the country, the government is going to point a finger at the outsiders and say, "They did it!" [Chuckles.] Please, go to school on the experience of your predecessors: Do not make threatening sounds; do not consider in public what to do along these lines of invasion. If you must do something, make certain it is clandestine, with internal cooperation from those concerned. On-the-spot people in circles who have to make these decisions know what I'm talking about.

We had battles in our time too, and we knew when to say, "This far; no further." Sometimes you have to draw a line and say, "Well, all right; we're not going to allow free immigration or travel to these countries because we can't be certain who's traveling around." It creates hardship, certainly, but sometimes the demands of security do create temporary difficulties. You will have to balance what is good for people and business while you say, "This far, and no further."

Don't be attached to rounding up the so-called villain. The "villain's" faces and names will change, just as in England when Americans were battling for freedom. Then, you were the "villains," you were the terrorists. I don't expect you to have real memories of things like that anymore, but just remember that how terrorists are defined depends on which side you are on. Understand that even with the best of intentions (as has been given considerable press during this Afghanistan campaign), innocent people are killed, hurt or maimed. And that is the nature of war, which is why the famous statement from that well-known general in the United States . . .

"War is hell."

Yes, by someone who helped to make it that way. When General Sherman said it, it was not a statement, but an excuse. Those who live in the southern United States know what I am talking about.

Closure on bin Laden

Is it important as a symbol of closure that they find bin Laden?

Bin Laden is long gone out of Afghanistan and has been for some time. I would say that it is less important that this man be found than that some compromise be made with him. The United States will not be able to do so diplomatically, so in this case, I am speaking to diplomats of other countries. It might be possible to make a compromise with him, if not necessarily to keep him persona non grata from every country, then to create a place where he can go—maybe not entirely welcomed, but acceptable. This will have to be faced, as it is possible for people to remain out of the reach of the long arm of enforcement almost indefinitely, given that the enforcement is coming in the guise of the Western world, which essentially has been grating against the Islamic world going back a long way. In short, do not expect the Islamic world as a whole—in part, yes, but not as a whole—to support any effort to round up this maverick.

It would probably be better that countries noted for their diplomacy—France, maybe Belgium or Switzerland—intercede on behalf of the world and try to work out something quietly. And there are other countries who can work on this. I do not think it will be able to be worked out openly in the United Nations, but behind the scenes something can be done. You will have to recognize, however, that you cannot just kill off people who disagree with you—you have to take their complaints seriously and, if not do everything to improve conditions, do something. Otherwise, there will be an ongoing problem.

Middle Eastern Business Unification

Of course, in the larger picture, you must look at the fact that the Middle East has been disrupted for so long, and so many parties have been involved in the disruption that it might take awhile for the Middle Eastern countries to form an economic union, which would be very helpful, and then ultimately a cooperative union. It won't ever be a union as in the United States, but a simple economic and cooperative union might be very helpful. I know the world is afraid that they will be held hostage by the countries that have oil, but there are other countries with oil and there's lots and lots of oil yet to be found.

So I would say that ultimately you might have to allow the Middle East to work out its own problems in some form of unification, and I would recommend right now that the best would be business unification, not unlike what you see happening in Europe. I grant that the Middle East is quite a bit different cultur-ally, but you would be able to easily find people in the Middle East who would do business on a daily basis with somebody they wouldn't normally talk to. The business is good for them and their people, and therefore, they'd grit their teeth and say, "We don't have to shake on it, but it's a deal." In other words, people can stretch to do business. And in time that stretch can lead to alliances. Certainly it has done so in Europe, and the United States has some fledgling experience with that, though long-term alliances with the United States are still something relatively new, although developing.

Give Up the Celebrated Rebel

So what you're saying is, a business association similar to the European Union, but also that our outreach needs to be more humanitarian than authoritative?

Yes, because you can claim to be chasing down somebody who is a monster, who has wronged you and all of the rest, but you have to remember . . . think back to your celebrated history. You have celebrated people who, in their time, were considered to be profoundly evil. Think of how your movies have cele-brated the lives of people who were terrorists of their own time. An obvious example is Billy the Kid—not a pleasant person, not someone you would want to know, not someone heroic in the slightest. And yet you have celebrated people like him. In your own time, you have smirked and said, "Oh well, he's pretty clever, that person," even though you knew that what he was doing was really terrible. You have to stop making heroes out of people who are destroying their lives and the lives of others. Your attachment to the celebrated rebel has to go. In short, you might just have to mature a bit on that point and recognize that you can't celebrate the beloved destroyer, because the beloved destroyer is not something to be celebrated but rather something to be encouraged to change, to become something more benevolent.

Well, this will be good advice to the Muslim countries right now, won't it?

Yes, but this advice is not aimed at those countries, not specifically. It is gen-erally aimed at the world and, more to the point, really aimed at the United States. You can't celebrate your own so-called bad guys and expect other countries to do any different. Other countries do not take their cues from the United States, but it is not unusual for people to hide otherwise criminal individuals simply because they are pursued by the guys everybody in that part of the world is angry at. Not everyone is angry. Many Islamic peoples, countries, governments and so on consider the United States to be a friend and the people of the United States to be admirable.

There are some, though, who would hide someone, even one who has been ruled to be a monster in the court of public opinion, simply because they don't believe the things that are being said. They need someone, and this person seems to be a nice person. How many murder victims thought their murderers were nice people when they met them? How many people are quoted in the newspaper when some neighbor is revealed to be a murderer or a child molester, saying, "But he always seemed to be nice and friendly." They're not saying that because they're stupid; they're saying that because that's exactly their experience. Don't expect people in other countries to be different than you. As has been said for a long time, they are more like you and you are more like them than you are different from each other.

Yes, we're all humans on this great planet.

And your behaviors are more similar than they are different.

Homework for the Unification of All Things

Any particular homework for the month?

Yes. Something a bit more universalizing for the sake of all citizens. I would recommend that if you live near the sea, if you can see a mountain (if you can't, then you can't), look at some point on the mountain where there is nothing man-made, if you can. If you can find a place like that, look at it and take three breaths in, just exhaling naturally, and absorb the mountain for a moment. If on the first breath it does not feel good, then stop and look back at the sea and breathe naturally. If it feels all right, take three breaths in, exhale naturally and go on with your life.

If you live nowhere near the sea but near a lake or a river, do the same thing. Look at some place on the lake or the river or the stream that feels good in your body (not *thinks* good, but *feels* good), meaning you're relaxed or you notice you feel better. Take in three breaths, exhale naturally and go on with your life. This helps to unify people, places and even, yes, things.

Benevolent Magic to Move the Future to You

Reveals the Mysteries
December 27, 2001

This channeling was previously published in Explorer
Race: Techniques for Generating Safety.

P *lease help the reader understand the past-anchored timeline and the future-anchored timeline.*

This misnomer is what is causing the problem. The difficulty is with the attachment to time. The so-called future is right here, right now, just as all futures are. Therefore, it is not associated in any way with time. You have to try to shake yourself out of the concept that the only time is linear time; it's just the only one you're living in at the moment. Time is entirely physical. If you attempt to create it to be anything other than physical, it will always generate worries and not be tangible.

The key to understanding how to achieve that benevolent future, how to anchor that future in your current, immediate life, is not to see it as something you are striving toward. It is understandable in your current existence that you would find a goal-oriented ideal to be attractive. Therefore, striving for something sounds not only ideal but even commonplace—and more to the point, as you say, doable. But if it is something immediate and present and desirable and you're not doing it, then it sounds either fantastic, fictional or unbelievable. Nevertheless, if you would like me to advance the reader a step, I will.

How to Move the Future into the Present

This is how to achieve anchoring in your present and how, rather than to move yourself into the future, to move the future into the present, which is the only means that uses magic to replace all that is harmful in the present. This is how to do it in your world in a way that works. For starters, the future has been somewhat thinned by many different visions. The future has to have the foundation of loving and caring between all forms of life: respect, honoring, sanctifying and appreciating the value of all beings, including one's immediate, physical and immortal self. That is a requirement. It won't work if you think about it. It will work if you think about it and then do it, but you have to apply it. It is awkward, that, because in your world you are used to walking on the grass, used to breathing in, used to eating, used to many things that cause pain and discomfort to other valid beings. And yet you cannot stop doing that. You are in your world. What you can do is embrace this future world in your present. Here's how [draws Fig. 24–1].

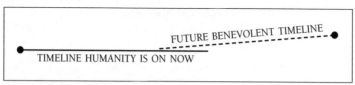

Fig. 24–1. Moving to the future benevolent timeline.

This is not an exercise. It is not a meditation. It is magic. You cannot see this image, you understand? You can't look at a picture in a book and breathe in and out. You have to create the image for yourself, focus completely on the image. If the image fades for a moment, then you have to stop and re-create it. The image is created and you're focused in it, meaning that you're feeling the love between you and the animals, or between you and the other people. Then you're just breathing—you're breathing it in, you're in it, and you're breathing it in. It's magic, it's physical, it's grounded, it's permanent. It will bring it to you.

You Can Change the Physical

But no one knows what it is. When you mention the word "timeline" to people, they just look at you blankly.

Forget the "timeline" thing—throw it out. Throw out "timeline," then. Forget the whole point of "timeline." "Timeline" is a word that can be disposed of.

Okay, but there is an energy connecting us into something in the past that we're trying to move beyond and onto something that's connected to the future. Whatever word you use, there is a connecting point, an anchoring point—it is something.

It is a physical feeling as well. As a physical feeling, you can do something about it. You understand, the whole purpose is to empower. You cannot empower people with something over which they have no power at all. If it is something mental—a thought, a concept—they don't have much power over that. They can think about it. You can think about the theory of Einstein, but you cannot change it, you understand? It is a thought. But if it is something physical, that's something you can change, because you have physical feelings. You can change your feelings, either by action or by interaction. So let's make it physical, and let's make it empowering, and let's make it magical. Magic is centered in physicality; it has nothing to do with thought. But we utilize thought, because your world now is engaged in thought. If people are using a tool to live, you must use that tool to live with them.

The whole "timeline" thing is a mental concept over which people have no control whatsoever. But they do have some influence, if not control, over feelings—their own and, to some extent, the feelings of others. But the power lies in their own feelings. So it is not only the exercise given, which is, in fact, magic. The magic given is not, "Oh no, not another creative visualization." It's not a creative visualization, it's a physicalization, all right? It is critical in your time for people to move past thought, which has been holding you back. Right now people continue to project their worries based on the past, or history based on the present, or crisis into the future, therefore supporting and projecting that past timeline into the future. You understand, the point is to try to raise people up a notch here, in terms of their perception of reality. *"Believe what you want, but here's what you can do to change your life."*

Benevolent Magic Must Be Based in Physicality

The purpose of benevolent magic, of course, is to bring about change that is benevolent *for all beings.* Benevolent magic may be done by an individual, it might even be aimed toward himself or herself, but in fact, the only parts that will work will be that which creates a benevolent magical change for that individual that affects other individuals benevolently. That is why when people sometimes do benevolent magic, it will only partially work, because all of the beings must cooperate fully in bringing it about. And of course, most human beings are not conscious of cooperating in magic at all, although you do it every day. You do it when it *feels* good to you, not when it *thinks* good, because you're not consciously aware of it. Therefore, you are constantly cooperating in benevolent magic every day and in many different ways, when all kinds of people, animals, plants, everything . . . thousands of times a day you give permission for benevolent magic to take place, because it feels good to you.

This is all happening now and has been happening forever for you. It is all happening because of your feelings. So your feelings have the power. My whole point is, let's bring this into conscious reality. Let's say, "You have tried the other things; now try this with the knowledge and understanding that your capacity to generate change for yourself benevolently lies in the physical and feeling worlds of your own physical body." Ancient peoples knew this—that is how they were able to do as much as they did. Look at the mysteries that have been left on Earth on purpose. Something is created intentionally not just to be enigmatic, not just to make you wonder, but to make you consider what might be possible. How can a man move a huge boulder by himself? He cannot move it with his sweat and muscle, but other ways are possible. Suppose that boulder would like to move? It's tired of lying on that side; it would prefer to move into a different position on another side. Then the boulder is happy for the loving interaction of the man and cooperates with the man's moving it without touching it. You can think of many circumstances where rocks have been moved in unlikely situations without any marks that they were moved, because they wanted to be moved.

Benevolent magic has to be based entirely in physicality—what can be done physically and how it can be achieved physically, not what can be done mentally. All of you have done just about as much as can be done mentally in a given life to achieve what you are attempting to achieve. But if you think back on what I said, that benevolent magic works—think about it now. Benevolent magic works every day, millions of times a day, because all the beings who need to bring about whatever is desired cooperate because it feels good to them—meaning that if they have to cooperate in any way, that cooperation feels good to them. If it doesn't feel good, they do not cooperate, even if their cooperation is needed, whether they are conscious or unconscious of participating in the benevolent magic.

Well, that's how we create our reality.

Yes, this is set up on purpose. This is the foundational element that allows ignorance to function on Earth so that the Explorer Race can re-create reality. This is the mechanical principle by which that is done. It is not just a simple thing; it is the key. But you will have to think about it, and you will have to write it down.

Physical Handwriting Supports Feeling

Write down what I said about how benevolent magic works. But it won't work to write it on the computer. You have to write it by hand. When you write things by hand, you put your feeling into it. When you write it on the computer, the computer receives your feeling and shows an image, but the image does not demonstrate your feeling. It is the feeling of the physical handwriting that sustains and supports that feeling. When they read their own handwriting, people get excited. Why do you think the people who discovered scientific principles were known for their excitable nature? They were not naturally excitable; they were excitable when they discovered these principles, because they looked at their writing and remained excited. If they were writing on a computer, they wouldn't have gotten excited at all. It was the excitement that fed them. It was always a good thing, but in this case it creates a self-sustaining stimulation, and that stimulation works to open up a wider gate to inspiration.

So we've lost a lot going from handwritten notes to email?

A tremendous amount, although it has created a universal form of intellectual communication. But it has effectively removed feeling, even if you put in words of feeling. Words of feeling cannot make any great impact with another person when he or she reads them. You ought to be able to pick up a lot more feeling. Say someone sends you a handwritten letter—you ought to be able to pick up feeling from the handwritten letter, at least what that person might have been feeling at the moment. Look how excited she was when she was writing this, as compared to reading it, and then it seems very dull or ordinary. Maybe what she was writing was the tip of the thing that she was going to discover, and the reason she was excited is that it was the opening, it was the gate. That's why she was excited. What would come after that would be exciting, and though it might take years, it would eventually come.

You Need to Move Past Mental Dogma

I would still like a definition of "timeline."

I understand that it's an intellectual principle. If you want me to discuss the intellectual principle, I will. It is physically illustrative, you understand—it requires a picture. But it doesn't actually exist. It's a means of analyzing your history.

But we're on something that we have to move off of, whether you call it an energetic . . .

No, no! It is that belief that you're on something that is holding you back. The purpose of the word "timeline" is to show the reader that the history you remember is connected to a specific memory pattern built up over time in your personal life and collectively in the personal lives of all the people on Earth in your different cultures and histories who are connected to a past, a present and a desirable future. That is a timeline. But I'm going to require that you don't become dogmatically attached to "timeline" as anything other than a mental concept to explain a physical situation that needs to be changed. What I am trying to do is to liberate your mind from dogma. The dogma here is not what others said about the timeline, even though it sounds like that. The dogma is authority. You need to bring authority into the immediate present to feel if it has value. Feel it right now, the feeling of the word "authority" in your body. How does it feel?

Restrictive.

Yes, thank you. With that sensation, you know that we don't wish to be authoritative to other people, or they will always feel exactly what you felt yourself. Therefore, we need to keep the concept somewhat loose. It's not rigid, because if it attempts to be authoritative and say, "This is how it started, and this is how it began, and this is how to change it," even within that context it will be enslaving people in an authoritative manner. I realize this is round logic, but it's important for you to begin to feel it. Suppose that, on the other hand, we say, "Timeline are a mental means of understanding a history that is entirely changeable in the present, so that however personal or societal that history is, no matter what happened, if you choose you can change it right now."

That's the point. We need to help people move past their mental dogmas. Think of all the mental dogmas cruelly inflicting misery and suffering on people right now, even though their initial creators saw them as liberating ideals. Religions, politics—you can think of others. Why are they rattling around and creating death rattles for people? Because they fell back on the principle of authority. What do children hate more than anything else in the world? Why do they leave home as soon as they can? To get out from under the finger of authority. Why? Because authority feels . . .

Like you can't expand and become what you want to be.

That's right. And to you it felt physically restrictive.

Religions Are Humanity's Creation

The dreams and visions people had about atomic explosions and people paratrooping in that I asked Speaks of Many Truths about [see chapter 23], a lot of them refer to China as the supposed enemy. We're not at war with China, but people seem to feel that China's there, ready to move in or bomb us or paratroop in or something. What is that about?

You have to remember the Christian country that you are living in, the Christian republic . . . I have to use it in the context of religion. You will see clearly that the Christian republic in which you are living has been at war with "godless Communism" ever since Communism arose, even though in your own country cooperatives amongst farmers and cooperation amongst people has been of long standing. But in a political system such as Communism, as practiced in these countries where private property is unacceptable, the politic wages strong. You also have to understand that religious bodies sometimes feel that if private property was not allowed, how would they obtain any influence whatsoever? We think that a glance at the ownership by certain religions of private property would shock the average citizen if such a thing were ever published. What religions own in the United States and how people live who are some of the slumlords—it's a bit shocking that those who would tell you how to live and talk to God are causing your suffering. No, I have to say that religions are not the enemy, but they are man's creation, even though they claim to be God's establishment. Now, you have to understand that you and all the people in your country have been raised in the veil of this demagoguery, so it is not at all surprising that people would have visions that have to do with the last large godless Communist country in your world. They're not too afraid of Cuba.

That is my perception. I do not wish to shake a fist at organized religion, but those in the higher echelons of all of the more established organized religions know exactly what I am talking about. And many of you, if I may speak to you directly, do have unsettled feelings about what has been going on. Recognize that you can exert change, but you will have to speak out. Make sure you do so with others at the same time. So you will have to get some physical commitment from them, something in writing. That's how changes are made in upper echelons. You can't necessarily get lawyer's decrees, but you'll have to get something in writing—not to embarrass others, but to present a united front, even if you're a minority.

They're going to know what you're talking about?

They'll know what I'm talking about.

Okay, thank you.

Good night.

Your Responsibility to Resolve Other Worlds' Problems Is Over! The Result: A Happy Feeling That Anything Is Possible!

Zoosh

January 22, 2002

All right, Zoosh here. Greetings

It feels like something is throbbing in the energies. Is something getting ready to happen in March?

It will actually start sometime around February 28, maybe a little before that. There will be a feeling of opening, one that will be felt globally. In some places, it will be felt by individuals as if anything can happen. The feeling that will follow that will be exultation, excitement, upliftment, happiness, joy—all of that. But some people will then become afraid, because if anything can happen, anything could be *absolutely anything*. Other people will feel as if, "It's possible!" and everyone has his or her own definition of it.

Things that once looked impossible now *feel* as if they might be possible. It is not a mental change; it will be something that is felt physically, and as such, it is a physical opening. Granted, Spirit is involved, but it is something that will be felt— I cannot underscore that enough. The feeling, as I say, will begin in the last few days of February and will

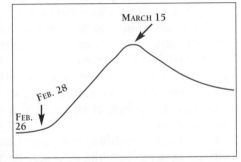

Fig. 25–1. The peaking of the "It's possible!" energy.

peak somewhere around March 15. Then it will taper off a little bit, but not completely. So it will be felt indefinitely, but first it will start off with the peaking.

The Burden of Restriction Is Lifted

It will be an interesting phenomenon for many, because most people have often felt as if their lives were set up according to limits established by some unknown or unseen being. This set of limits would seem to have created fixed parameters whereby their lives have been lived, whether they liked it or not—some people would have liked it; others would have felt restricted. It doesn't mean that people are going to be able to fly and reach high notes beyond their natural range. What it does mean is that a great deal of the burden of restriction will be lifted. And this feeling of "It's possible!" will be global.

How will you know? For some people, it will happen one day, for other people, another day. But you will know because you will wake up in the morning—or even wake up after a nap—and suddenly have the feeling. For others it will happen more quickly—you might be in an elevator and suddenly the feeling will sweep over you. And you might look around the elevator as if everybody else had it too, but no. If you are lucky, maybe someone else will have had the feeling, but maybe not, in which case you will certainly feel a bit like singing or dancing. It doesn't mean you have to do it, but you will feel that sensation of euphoric possibilities. And maybe you won't know what to do with it, but there it will be.

If you would, don't suppress it. Enjoy it while it's there. And don't try to channel it only into what you want in one avenue of your life; just let it permeate you. It's not going to disrupt you. If you're driving or involved in something complex (machining or working with knives or something like that—as a chef, for instance), you're not going to suddenly not know what you're doing. It won't be a hazard. It will come in at a time when it is safe for you. But if you are driving and it sweeps over you suddenly, it will sweep over you at a time when it's safe. Don't worry, okay?

You Are No Longer Responsible for Resolving Other Worlds' Problems

It is not something that is being sent to you—this is an important thing to know. It is not as if Creator was saying, "Okay now, click! Here is a present for you." It is something you have earned. And the earning is not so much the feeling itself; rather you have earned the right to drop the old feeling of restriction, the old box, the old envelope, whatever you want to call it. If it had a label, that envelope or box would read on the outside: Other Worlds' Problems. It essentially means that when that feeling occurs, you will no longer be responsible for resolving *any* problems associated with any other world, time, place or dimension—anything.

It's as if you were fishing using a cork bob and the bob popped right up to the surface—whoop! Just like that, because you no longer have anything pulling down, making you remain on Earth at a certain level that forces you to process something for others, which is always very slow and painstaking because it has nothing to do with you personally as an individual. It does not, for the most part, in the case of processing things for other worlds, have anything to do with your world at all. Therefore, whatever you are processing—such as the Andromedan-thought consciousness as was discussed in previous books (but that was over quite some time ago)—whatever you are processing for any other world is no longer your responsibility. For the most part, what happens is that those worlds will then be responsible to take what you have done and assimilate it into their culture, dimension, place, planet—wherever they are—and do with it what they choose. It is simply not your responsibility anymore, and that is that.

So most of you will also feel a sense of relief. For some of you, it will literally feel as if something you were carrying, such as a backpack or a heavy book, suddenly isn't there anymore, and it's easier to walk, easier to move. Generally, you will have a feeling for a little while, at least, that life suddenly became easier. Even though you look around your life and it basically seems to be the same, at the same time you will have the feeling that it is easier.

You might wonder why in recent months you've felt a sense of tension. Some of you have been feeling something bordering on anxiety. Yet you look at your life and you see that there's practically no reason for you to feel that way. Oh, maybe there's a little tension, but it's nothing different from anything you've ever felt before. For others of you, it might have felt almost like pressure—for some of you, even like a physical pressure or a physical pain. I'm not saying that all your pains and aches are going to go away, but what I am saying is that different people have felt it in different ways. The reason you have been feeling it is that the other worlds, while not panicking [chuckles], know that they are going to have to take responsibility for what you have been processing for them for years and years and years (in some cases, for generations), and still it is as if they were trying to get out of you the maximum that they could as they came down the home stretch. So that is why your lives have felt as if they were too much. For example, many of you have not been sleeping very well, or you wake up in the middle of the night and you don't know why. This is because even your sleep periods were involved in processing things for other worlds.

The New Opening Will Create Improvements in Your Life

After this engages, most of you should notice that you will sleep more restfully. If you do not, then there is some other cause, but you ought to notice an improvement in your sleep and in your digestion. Those of you who have exercise programs, even mild ones, will find that you do a little and you feel tired, but then after a time you start to feel more peppy because you've increased your breathing capacity and your muscle capacity and all this. But for those of you who've been in physical conditioning and have noticed how slow it's been going and how difficult, you will again notice that cork-to-the-surface experience. You will notice that you suddenly feel better physically, that your training goes easier and you feel better as a result. Many of you will be able to cut back on the amount of physical conditioning and training you've been doing in order to accomplish your goals, and that will feel good. So, generally speaking, there will be improvements.

There are other improvements. Many of you have felt very distracted in your thought processes for the past five or six months, and it has been hard to concentrate and maintain that concentration. Sometimes some of you have been able to use this to your advantage, you have been able to do more than one thing at once fairly well, and it's good that you have learned this or adapted to it. But I think you will find, after this process engages, that you will not feel as if you *must* do that. Oh, you will have a new tool for your bag of abilities, but you will not feel as if you *must* do it, nor that it's required based upon some unseen rush-rush. So, in short, things ought to noticeably improve, even though your day-to-day life, as you look at it, might not seem to be much different. But you ought to feel noticeably better.

This Is Not Something External

Can you tell us what's causing the process to engage? What's the dynamic of that?

Because you are done. It is literally that. When people run a marathon, near the end of the race for some, and more just slightly past the middle for others (depending upon how well-conditioned they are, how long they've been doing it), they get to something they call the wall, which is a momentary exhaustion. Then, if they are good at it, they break through and continue on. The point is that this resistance toward the end is really not of your making. You have to remember that all these things you've been doing for other worlds are things you took on before your physical life. "Yes, we will do that," you said.

There are requirements to come to this world. If you are going to learn, if you are going to grow, if you're going to get everything you want to out of your Earth life, you still have to do all these other things. "Yes," you said as a soul, igno-rantly. [Laughs.] Or shall I say innocently? And then you came down here and said, "Wait a minute!" [Laughs.] But then it is too late. I am just kidding about this, but that is close to some conversations that took place before you entered this world.

Now, what you have to understand is that this is not something external; it is more as though you are being relieved of a responsibility that you took on. For example, say a woman is pregnant, and her child is born in April. The child will be born without the burden of that responsibility; however, because the baby was in the mother during some of that time, the baby might have a feeling—almost like a recollected feeling—of that responsibility, but will not actually have to apply it in his or her life. What about if the mother gets preg-nant, say, in April? Then the baby will not have a recollected feeling of that at all when he or she is born. It will be like, "Oh well, this world is this world, and that's that." So it is really like a door or like a process; you get to the end, and that's that.

What are some of the things we've been doing for other worlds that we might not know we were doing?

I don't want to say that, and I'll tell you why. For one thing, we have to recognize that I'm not talking just to you. This is something that will be published and known. And if I say what you are processing for other worlds, there is no question that some of you will find some of those things fascinating and you will want to continue. So I see no reason in creating an unnecessary addiction. No, I don't think so. I think it is better to drop the garment and go on. It is as if you don't have to wear short pants anymore; now you can wear long pants.

It's Possible—Happiness!

How will this affect major issues, like in the Middle East or on the whole planet, with different beings fighting one another? Will any of that happiness percolate into those areas and make them more loving or cooler or peaceful?

It ought to; simply think about it. If people suddenly feel that it's possible . . . translate that across the board for everyone—everything you want is possible. For some people, things they want might not be so compatible with everybody else, but the main thing you have to understand is that the thing you want might not always be the thing you really need. I'm going to use my old example: Say you want a new car because you can go here, you can go there, it will be reliable and so on. But what is underneath that? You want the new car. Why? Because it will make you happy. Granted, it will be more practical, it will be all of these practical things, but ultimately a new car will make you happy. You want it for all these reasons, yes, but ultimately underneath all that, at the foundation, the new car will make you happy.

So recognize that what you want, speaking to the reader here, might very well be a step that you are striving toward in order to feel happy, to feel satisfied, to feel fulfilled (put in your word). It's not about being revenged, because even for those of you who are fighting in battles in the world, while you might at one moment or another want revenge, ultimately what's the reason you want revenge? Because when you have revenge, you think you will then be happy.

So I'm not saying that revenge is good; I am not saying that requiring or needing a new car is good. I'm not putting labels of good, bad or indifferent on any of these things. I am just saying that when that feeling strikes you, that when you suddenly feel "It's possible!" the very next thing you feel is—it will really be superimposed—you will feel happy. Understand that physical feelings are the goal as well as the experience. Everybody who wants to be in heaven, who wants to be with God, with Creator, the stars, the planets—whatever they want, as they see for their next life and so on, or after this life—what is the feeling that goes with that? "Why do you want that?" asks the ignorant man. And the other person says, in a moment of clarity, "Why do I want to be with Creator? It would be wonderful!" "But what will you feel?" asks the man. "Oh, I'll be so happy!"

A Crack in the World Egg Allows More Light to Come In

So understand that it's possible, and then the feeling of happiness overlies it. So it's a compound: Overlying "It's possible!" would be the feeling of happiness. It overlies and continues on. Now, the reason I am putting it that way is that your question was, "Will the Middle East get better? Will other things get better?" I am saying that if people can embrace the feeling . . . and you won't be able to shove the feeling away—for those of you who want to be unhappy, I'm sorry. At some point, whether you want to or not, you will feel "It's possible!" and then you will feel happiness. That's just how it is. Because you have to remember that your life as you are living it here is very much a performance. This is not to say it isn't real, but it is a performance based upon how your soul has had to adapt to living on Earth as it is now during your lifetime. Even though it has changed during your lifetime, you're still adapting; you're being who you are based upon your conditioning, your life experience and so on. But it is as if all this is happening inside an egg. And now—crack!

The egg is cracking. And what happens when that crack happens? What happens for a chick beginning to crack its way out of the egg? The first thing that comes in is a certain amount of light. Crack! Peck! And more light comes in. So "It's possible!" and then happiness. I'm not saying it is heaven; what I am saying is, you are coming out of the role you had to adapt to in this life and taking a big step toward achieving your natural being. Of course, granted, this doesn't happen overnight, but when you are feeling more like your natural being, those goals and ideals that were way, way beyond your possible capacities at this time will seem much closer, will seem possible, will not seem so very impossible. Because, remember, what's this about? It's possible: happiness. A feeling, not a thought.

Remember, you will be able to identify the feeling in different ways. Some of you will say, "Wow! I just feel happy all of a sudden! I feel as though I can do anything!" Those are words. For others it will be other words, but they will all be like that. It will all fall under the heading of: "It's possible: happiness." "I feel joyful; I can do anything"—whatever. The main thing is, don't jump out the window and see if you can fly. It's not about that. It's about returning after a long trip, returning, yes, and also moving on to your natural way of being. So don't be too upset about this tension. This tension is like a membrane, and you do not have to break the membrane. When it is time for each of you, the membrane will just become very thin and then evaporate and then—poof! Yes? It's possible: happiness. And then you will go on with your life. Try to leave the feeling of happiness and the feeling of "It's possible!" there, all right? Let it find its own place in your life and settle into your life wherever it feels most welcome.

Children Born after April 2002 Won't Need a Savior

The children born in April—how will they be different from even the ones who have been extolled as having no karma, the ones who are so brilliant and so bright who will save the planet?

I will tell you how they will be different: For starters, they will not have the capacity to solve other worlds' problems, because they won't need to. You have to remember that there is a tendency still among humans . . . look at the Indigo children idea—what does it represent? Compare it to religion. I am not saying it is a bad thing, but compare it to religion, and what leaps out at you? Tell me.

A savior is coming!

That's right. But if you are conceived afterward, what does that mean to you? You don't have the capacity or responsibility to solve other worlds' problems— what does that mean?

More time and energy to solve this world's problems?

More than that. You don't *need* someone to come and save you, because you are going to be responsible for being here, doing things here, interacting with others here and accomplishing things here. You do not need to have someone come from some other place to tell you how to do things here. You will have what you need, or you will be connected to what you need when you are born here. If you need Creator's influence, you will be connected to it. But you will not have the feeling about Creator that Creator is in any way external; you will have the feeling that Creator is part of you, part of your life, a friend. I'm not saying the children who have been conceived after that time, as we discussed, cannot be conditioned to believe that Creator is something separate and authoritarian. I'm not recommending it, but there will be those who will want to continue that as a teaching. Nevertheless, you will not be able to convince children on the physical level that Creator is separate. You might get them to agree outwardly, "Oh yes, Creator is separate; Creator is a separate being," but inside themselves they will know very clearly on the physical-feeling level that Creator is connected to them.

In short, they will be different, yes? They will not require a being who is separate. Your religion has unintentionally created the idea of a Creator who is entirely separate from you, while at the same time saying that you are Creator's children. That's why I say I feel that this was unintentional. So that will be solved by the natural process of life.

Almost 35 Percent of Your Energy Was Being Used to Solve Other Worlds' Problems!

Is there a percentage of our energy and our beingness that was taken up in this resolving of other worlds' problems?

Yes, I can say: Fully 26 percent of your waking efforts until these recent months were involved in solving other worlds' problems. Now, in this now time, which is why you find yourself so distracted, it is almost 35 percent, more like 34.9 percent, that's involved in solving other worlds' problems. Is it any wonder that people feel distracted? And this is why it is overlapping into your sleep time, because it's too much. So it overlaps into your sleep time, and that is why your sleep has been wild. Some of your dreams have been wild, and you wake up because you come to a point in your sleep state where you're solving other worlds' problems while you're sleeping, but your body needs to sleep! You wake up to cut that off so that you can actually go to sleep and get the rest you need. But even then, many people—even people who have slept well their whole lives—will have times when they will wake up and not feel rested. But that's coming to a close soon.

This is one of the happiest things I've ever had the privilege of listening to. This is great. Thank you for coming.

You're welcome. Good night.

Take Responsibility for Your Life!

Zoosh

February 18, 2002

Z oosh speaking. Greetings.

Greetings! In January you said that the work we did for the other worlds was over and that we're going to have this wonderful increase of energy [see chapter 25]. Can you continue?

There is a body tumbling in space. In size it is about one-third the size of your home. It does not represent any danger to Earth or, for that matter, to the solar system, but it will tumble through the solar system out a little bit past Pluto. And it will have a certain resonance associated with it that is going to have an effect on your Sun, which will be . . . not quite like a switch, but the effect on the Sun will be to transfer some of the Sun's duties to you as individuals.

You Will Take Over the Resolution of Residual Energies

Obviously, you will not have to get hot and light things up, but the Sun has other duties. One of them is the purification of residual energies that, if just allowed to float about, could cause trouble. People die all the time, and you can only take so much of your personality with you; you cannot take things with you that can only be resolved on Earth. So those things are shed like a garment when you leave.

You might reasonably ask, "Well, what happens when you go through the first veil?" as it's called. (It's like a screen—not so much a veil.) And what happens is that it eliminates that stuff that can only be resolved on Earth. If you're going to come back to Earth, it will stick around, and you can choose to work on it when you return. If you're not going to come back to Earth within a reasonable amount of time, it will need to be resolved. This is something the Sun does, because Mother Earth can no longer do it. Oh, she could do it if the population were forty million or so, which is in her comfort zone, but with the now population, it's too much. So the Sun has taken this chore over. But as creators-in-training, you need to have jobs that you can do.

So when this object tumbles through your solar system, out a ways, it's going to have an effect—not a gravitational effect, as a physical object might, but it's going to have a spiritual effect on the Sun, or at least a spiritual result. The trigger will take place in about three-and-a-half to four weeks, but the Sun will then gradually, over a period of about six to eight years, eliminate its duty of resolving that energy. And it will be up to you, as creators-in-training, to resolve it, taking it over yourself.

So I wanted to put you on notice now: You have about six to eight years to train for this. And at the end of that time, it will be entirely up to you to resolve residual energies. This will not require you to resolve energies that are connected or attached to people who are living or energies that are waiting for those who are coming in, meaning to be born. This only involves energies that are residual from those who have died and have moved on, and who will not be processing that energy.

Homework: Assimilate the Sun's Personality

So this is something you need to prepare for. You need to begin doing initial work. Now I'm going to suggest how to do that. This is the initial homework to prepare. You don't *have* to do it. If you want to, you can do it, but everybody on Earth is not expected to do this, okay? It's only those who want to. And just learning how to do this might be of benefit to other spiritual goals you may have in your life.

The best beginning is to look at something that reflects the Sun. For those of you living near bodies of water, look at the water as it's reflecting the Sun, even if it's an artificial body of water. Granted, a lake, an ocean, a river or a stream is better, but some of you do not live near those kinds of things. Nevertheless, an artificial body of water will do, or even a temporary one such as after a rain when the Sun comes out—a puddle, all right? The way the Sun glints on that . . . don't stare at it, but glance at it. If it's too bright, you can close your eyes a little bit, squint your eyes, or look at it and then close your eyes and picture it or experience the latent image of the light—which, as you know, can be done.

What this does is it connects you to the personality of the Sun. The Sun, like every other living thing, has a personality; it's action-oriented—you know that—and it's inclined to express itself constantly. This is why it performs so many vital functions in your solar system. Any other personality—say, a shy, reticent one—would not make a very good Sun. It might be good as some other planetary body, but it wouldn't make a good Sun. So you know that the personality is vibrant.

You know that you can't look at the Sun directly . . . well, of course, you can glance at it for a split second and then feel into it, but you don't really get the best reflection of the Sun's personality unless you use a reflection. Don't use a mirror or anything like that; water is the best way, because it will reflect and, more importantly, refract the Sun's personality. Each different glimmer of light on all the different areas of that water all represent a slightly different aspect of the Sun's personality. So, granted, with an ocean, for example, or even a river or a lake, you're not going to be able to look at all of the reflection of the Sun in the water, but you'll see some of it and it will allow you, just looking at it or glancing at it, to assimilate some of this personality. Remember, it's not the water you're looking at, though the reflection on water is the best way.

Now, some of you will not have even an artificial body of water to look at, but you will have something to look at that reflects the Sun that will also be nurturing, and that is the Moon. The Moon's identity is primarily to feed, nurture and superimpose the identity of the Sun into your lives—for all beings on Earth—in such a way that it is nurturing and easily accommodated. You can look at the Moon for a time comfortably.

So that's what I recommend; keep it that simple. More elaborate homework will come. But the reason the Sun is able to resolve all of these residual energies—some of which have to do with feelings, some of which have to do with things that have not been completed, events only partially done and not completed this time, and other things like that—is because of the vast spectrum, not only of different colors and sounds associated with the Sun, but also the spectrum of its capacity in the feeling range. The Sun is quite obviously a material master; it is also a spiritual master. It is a teaching master, but it only teaches indirectly through reflection. And it is a dimensional master, meaning that it can function in many different dimensions simultaneously. It is also the quantum master, so it has accomplished all that Earth has been intending to do, and that is how you will be able to assimilate the training—because your bodies are made of Earth and your souls are immortal, so you will therefore be able to assimilate this without too much trouble.

So for the first year's training, all I really want you to do is to look at the Sun's reflection on water. That's all. Or if it is not available, look at the Moon. Look for three or four minutes a day, that's all. Try not to think when you're doing it. If you catch yourself thinking, then do it a little longer. Don't give yourself a hard time; just say, "Oh, okay, I notice I'm thinking." Just look at it. If the glint on the water is too strong, you can always look at the Moon. Sometimes this may not be possible; you won't be able to do it all the time. Some days will be cloudy, nights too, or it might be raining or there might be a storm, so don't do it those days. That's all. Keep the homework simple. And gradually over the next year or two, we'll line up the homework to prepare you so that you will know how to resolve these residual energies, so that by the time the four- or five-year mark comes, when a lot of it will be on you, you'll be able to perform that duty.

You Can Learn Only When Responsibility Is Part of Life

You have some other advantages in the spiritual realm. One of those is that for those of you who are attempting to learn how to experience perceptions, perhaps visual perceptions—not physically—in places other than the places you're in, you will find that while this homework will not teach you how to do that, it will lay a groundwork for you if you are learning it.

Are you saying that this is like long vision?

Yes, like long vision, as Speaks of Many Truths has. Long vision is important; it's not the same as remote viewing. Remote viewing is strictly that: you are looking at something at a distance. And if it is taught at all, it is usually taught in such a way that there is not sufficient respect for that which is being viewed. After all, if you look at something, by the time you get the feeling of whether it's okay to look at it or not . . . that feeling might take a little longer than normal. By the time that feeling registers, it will already be well past the point in which the person, place or thing that is being looked at is uncomfortable with that observation.

But long vision takes everybody's feelings into account. It also allows you to see in different times as well as in different places, and you can see places that are at a great distance, not just on your planet.

You said feelings would need to be resolved from people who weren't coming back in a reasonable length of time. How would you define "reasonable length of time"?

Oh, within a thousand years.

A thousand years?

Given your time as you experience it now, a thousand years or so—maybe a little less than that, but not much.

But I thought most of the people leaving now were not coming back.

That's true.

So that's why this is becoming an issue?

That's right. The Sun's duties in this way are becoming more and more and more so over time, and now because of that circumstance, it is even more so. And the Sun can do it, but you are here to learn creation, and this is creator school—granted, at the basic levels, but basic levels must be mastered until one can build upon them.

So here's the opportunity for another lesson.

Another opportunity to learn and achieve more than you normally do when you are living other lives in other places beyond Earth. You can only learn these things when responsibility is a part of life. Your responsibilities in other ways are being lifted off your shoulders. But after all, your whole life has been set up to prepare you for responsibility, and this leaves you with a groundwork or a lattice of responsibility that you can build upon. So, of course, you're going to want to build upon it in these levels of material mastery.

Why?

That's what this is; it's material mastery and spiritual mastery combined. And one often finds levels of mastery combined. One does not learn a level of mastery and then do only that. You learn a level, and then you build on it; you learn another level, and then those two levels can work in an interrelated or interconnected way. You can use one or the other, but most often you will use them in an interconnected way. That's why, for instance, you have spiritual mastery when you come here—you all do. Then you learn material mastery here, or at least you begin, and some of you will even be working on teaching mastery here, meaning that very often you use all of that together—not always, but you might.

Tumbling Rock Carries the Energy of Your Future Teachers

What's the significance of this rock? And why is it tumbling instead of orbiting? What's so unusual about this rock?

It's tumbling because it's not in an orbit; it's coming from some place to another place. It's not at all unusual for small bodies like this in space to tumble. Tumbling is typical; it's typical to do that. After all, you wouldn't expect anything other than a planet or a moon to be orbiting on an axis. Other things that meander about in space typically might be tumbling. So that rock just happens to be tumbling.

And where is it coming from? Where is it going to?

It's coming from the outer reaches of your galaxy; it's been coming for a long time. And it's amazing, you know, the timing of these things. Everything had to be exactly right for it to come by, because remember, it's not in an orbit. It's coming by at this time; if you weren't ready, it would just go right on by and that would be it. It would never come again. That makes you think, eh? It's coming from and was launched by your future teachers. When you with the Explorer Race reassemble yourselves as a creator-in-training, as one unit, you will have teachers then—not the same teachers you have now. Those teachers sent this on its way, like you or a child might take a pebble or even a marble and, with a finger, flick it. It was flicked in a similar fashion. You might reasonably ask when that flick took place: It took place long before Earth was here in this place. It's been traveling, then, for quite a while.

How long?

It's been traveling for a long time—let's just say that. Your future teachers sent it. You might also reasonably ask, "Well, what is it? What's it made of?" It is apparently only a rock; it is hollow, but it does not contain any mechanism or anything like that. But the energy within it is the energy of your future teachers. It does not in any way connect to your future personalities and all of that business, no. It is the energy exclusively of your future teachers, and it is not all their energy, just a little bit. This is how it is able to find you, because your future teachers obviously know where you've been, not just who you are in the future. So it's able to find you and be on a precise path. This is also why it's able to pass you up and to have that effect on the Sun at the exact right moment.

Granted, if there were a problem, then it would go on by, but that would be all right, because if there were a problem, you would need to do things differently in your motion toward the future anyway. But I do not perceive that this will occur. It will come by; it's not that far away. It may or may not be picked up by individuals using either telescopes or magnetic- or radio-reception devices, or even other sound or . . . there are devices on satellites that essentially measure the change in spatial reference. The only way it's likely to be picked up is by these devices that measure the change in spatial reference. Look for it just a little bit beyond the orbit of Pluto.

I think it might be fun to look for it. It won't be easy to pick up, but there's a good chance, maybe a 20 to 25 percent chance, that such an instrument will be able to pick it up. And there's even the odd chance that an astronomer might be able to notice it, because it will, for a very brief moment, reflect a little light physically. But I'm not making an issue out of that, because there's a pretty good chance that it will not be noticed.

So can we infer from this that we're on time, then? That we're on schedule?

Oh, yes.

And where is it going? What was it aimed at?

Here. Once it passes by and has that impact on the Sun, it will be done. It will then go wherever it wishes to go. The teachers' energy will be withdrawn, and if the stone, as an object, has a desire to go somewhere, it will be placed there or set on track to go there. In short, as a volunteer and, let's say, a vessel— a volunteer vessel—it will have fulfilled its duties and will then be free to go wherever it wishes to be.

So the teachers' energy will affect the Sun? Give the Sun a message? What's the dynamic of that?

The teachers' energy, through the stone, will essentially release the Sun from these duties it's been doing. It won't actually tell the Sun anything. It's not unlike a switch, but it's not an actual switch that you click. Sometimes you can interrupt an energy and the interruption itself is a message. Understand that the energy the Sun uses to broadcast and receive from Earth for this function isn't a straight line; it's constantly fluctuating, moving about and so on. And it is not a vast focus of energy, meaning that . . . let's say this is a microcosm, all right? Let's say you were in a room for which there was an energy moving about that was about the size . . . in this case, we're talking about something that's shaped like a cord. And the room is a typical room, nothing too big. You would easily be able to walk through the room and not contact that cord—the cord would not be trying to avoid you, but you simply just wouldn't contact it. In short, the cord is moving about constantly over a vast amount of space; the chances of anything contacting it are almost nil.

Understand that we're not only talking about the space between the Sun and the Earth, but we're talking about a space that has to assimilate everything, every direction and every spiritual consequence where you might pass through that veil. So we're talking about something that is not only a physical space, but more to the point, it is a spiritual space. And as such, for such an object to have an impact on that . . . the chances of it having an impact on that are remote to the greatest degree. So if it should transit and touch that cord at all, it's going to have that effect. But the fact that the teachers' energy is inside will be like a cosine, meaning that, "Yes, this isn't an accident, and this is what's intended to happen."

So there will be an attraction?

Not an attraction, but it would be as if you were expecting a breeze, okay? (It's not a breeze; this is an example, an analogy.) If you were expecting a breeze to spring up at a certain time—like the trade winds here on the islands [of Hawaii], which usually spring up at a certain time—and you felt the breeze, you'd say, "Oh, this was intended, and I was intended to feel it." I'm trying to interpret mastery levels to something that to a linear world doesn't interpret very well.

But you're giving us a feeling.

I'm giving you an idea of what it might be like. The main thing is, the Sun knows what it's about, and it responds. And as I say, in about six to eight years, all of the duties will be transferred to various individuals on Earth.

The volunteers?

The volunteers, that's right. Some of these individuals are not here yet; they will be born soon, within the next four or five years. But the rest of you are here now. I consider this to be important, for you to know about it, but it's not pressing yet. It will be pressing in about four or five years; it's not pressing now. That's why you can take your time in learning how to do this and why I'm giving the homework out fractionally so you do not feel overwhelmed given all the other things you are doing.

Use the Remaining Energy Physically in Your Life

Now that we have this freedom from resolving other worlds' problems, how can we best use the energy?

That's why I'm talking about this. Now it's for you to resolve a challenge on Earth. Instead of resolving other worlds' problems, you now have it delivered to you to start resolving things that require creation energy here on Earth—things that you've taken for granted, things that others have been doing.

But that won't take 25 percent of our energy.

Not now, but by the time you start taking over in four or five years, it will probably take a good 7 percent of your energy.

Okay, so how would you recommend that we use this? It's like money in the bank; we have this asset, we have this energy that's available to us. How can we use this?

Use it physically in your life.

Physically?

Yes, physically, because most of you are functioning at reduced physical levels. Even athletes are functioning at reduced physical levels.

Because of this resolving of other worlds' problems?

That's right, so just use it physically. Let it reinforce you physically so that you can experience a greater means of feeling better physically and functioning and performing better physically. It's better to do that. Some of this has been lost in your time because the oxygen level on Earth is too low. There's not much you personally can do about that at this time; granted, with enough creator training, you'll be able to do more in the future.

Let Plants Grow Where They Are Welcome

But for right now, there's not much you can do to increase the oxygen. You can change the oxygen to other things, but this is not really giving you any great advantage. Obviously, the forms of life that can intake what you exhale and transfer it into oxygen are essentially members of the plant world or microorganisms. And you have less of that around today—more houses and fewer plants. It comes down to that. The more buildings, the more paving, the more pollution in the ocean—in short, you don't have that much in the way of life forms that are creating or generating oxygen. Granted, in time some of you will be taught how to do that yourselves. Essentially, you will be taught how to function at another level, in a plantlike way—not exactly photosynthesis, but you will be able to generate oxygen. But it's too soon for that.

Are you talking days, weeks, months, years?

Years.

But not centuries?

No. Just think about it: Your population is growing at an increasing rate. Aside from all of the challenges there, where are you going to get enough plants? And you have a lot of habits that may seem attractive to you—for instance, many of you cut the grass and so on. I grant that if the grass dies and it's no longer performing the function of grass, it's a good thing to cut it. But if it is living, what's the point? For one thing, the grass doesn't like it. For another thing, it's just that much more plant material that's making oxygen. So why do it?

What are some things we can do now? Not cut the grass? Have a lot more plants in the house? Plant trees?

Let plants grow where they are welcome, because a plant that is grown where it was welcomed by the Earth will function better, be happier and, as far as you're concerned, produce more oxygen and more of what you need, simply because it is happy. I will give you an example that you can understand: When you are frightened, as a human being, a couple of things happen. If you are terrified, you breathe fast. But if you are just nervous, you tend to breathe shallowly, meaning that your transformation of oxygen into carbon dioxide is less so. It is no different for a plant. When a plant is frightened, it will breathe more shallowly. If a plant is terrorized, knowing it's going to be cut, it stays frightened. But there's another way plants can be frightened. If they are planted somewhere by human beings, they will stay frightened for a very long time because they know they are someplace where they were not welcomed by the Earth. Maybe the Earth was welcoming something else.

It's not that the Earth rejects plants; it's that the Earth welcomes plants to grow in very specific places, and most of them know how to find their way to those places. Nature is not an accident. Seeds blow to a particular location, and they are welcomed. If they are welcomed sufficiently, they sprout, they grow, they bloom. These plants feel welcome, and they often thrive, given the chance. But if a plant, even with the best of intentions, is planted someplace where it did not arrive on its own accord or by some natural process—say, a seed floating downstream, for example—it will not feel safe, and it will breathe in a shallow fashion for a long, long time.

How long?

Let's say, for example, with a tree: Trees can live for thousands of years—some species perhaps—if they are undisturbed. Let's say the tree is going to live for a hundred years. If the seed is welcomed in the natural way, it grows and thrives. Then it breathes openly and fully for that whole lifetime. But say that with the best intentions of a human being, even done lovingly—which is not often the case, but let's just say, even in the best way, done lovingly—the tree is planted, nurtured, talked to, welcomed as best you can, the tree will breathe in a shallow fashion for at least 25 percent of its life.

Now, let's say that the tree is planted callously: "Oh, we want some trees here because we're going to grow the trees, we need the wood. We'll grow it for a while and then we'll cut it down."

Like a tree farm?

Like a tree farm, for example; that's right. And of course, while they're growing, they're beautiful, but those trees will remain frightened. They will never do anything but breathe in a shallow fashion. It's important to know that. You might say, "Well, what about all the people planting trees and attempting to do good things?" I'm not saying don't plant trees. I'm saying, when trees grow, perhaps in an unexpected place—you go out into your garden and say, "What's this?" and if you know anything about plants, you say, "Oh, it's a pine seedling just springing up on its own"—*please leave it.* It will grow and thrive on its own, and it might just be a thing of beauty. I know that for farmers this might not always be possible, but consider it.

You Are Straddling Dimensions

It didn't occur to me before, but the Earth has many, many, many dimensions; you are working on the ninth dimension of Earth right now, right?

The ninth dimension, period. It just happens to affect Earth.

The ninth dimension of what? The solar system? The galaxy? The creation? What?

Ninth dimensions are not geographically located, period. It's just that what I'm doing on the ninth dimension just happens to be beneficial to Earth as a planet and to you upon the Earth—"you" meaning everybody.

What you're doing is beneficial to us in the third dimension now?

The third, fourth and fifth. You have to understand that even though you know you are in the third dimension and you know you are moving to the fourth dimension, you are also staking out a claim in the fifth dimension. In order to stake that claim, you have to have a resonance that welcomes you. You are no different than that seed floating in the air, say, from a dandelion. You are looking for someplace where you are welcomed—where you feel at home, where you feel safe, where you feel happy to be there and where wherever there is, is happy to have you there. So in order to be stabilized in the fourth dimension, you have to be welcomed in the fifth. This is just like now: In order to be stabilized in the third dimension, you have to be welcomed in the fourth. Do you understand?

So there is a straddling of dimensions that is ongoing. I might say that there is even some straddling the other way: You're in the third dimensionally, but there's some straddling to the second. This doesn't mean that you are entrenched in the second dimension, but there is enough straddling so that you can sometimes accommodate or perceive or, more to the point, support what's going on in the second dimension should beings there need your support in some way.

So this straddling takes place, and in order to prepare the fifth dimension for some of you who may wish to reside there at some point, you need to have a resonant energy that will hear, feel, sense you as you are becoming—not just as you are. If you were in a fixed situation, not in creator school, not in the Explorer Race, none of that would be necessary. But because you are in flux, you are in creator school, you are members of the Explorer Race—in short, your soul energy is, in the most infinitesimal portions of its personality, to say nothing of its greater personality, in flux, changing, growing—that resonant echo of your soul personality is changing. It is not a fixed quality; it is not a fixed quantity, for that matter. Therefore, the fifth dimension must be prepared very carefully to expect the spectrum, meaning the flexible fluctuations of how your soul personalities may be, while excluding all else that does not belong there. It is very complex.

What are you doing that is helping that?

That's what I'm doing. That.

From the ninth dimension?

Yes. Remember, it's not a geographic location. Set that aside. It would be . . . let's say you had an idea, a picture in your mind's eye. You saw a pear, and then you saw an apple. Where is the pear? All right? You need to shift gears. The dimensions are not in a place, period. This does not mean you are wrong in your question; it means that your question is not phrased correctly, and I do not know whether you will be able to phrase it correctly.

Well, it's a faster vibration, it's a feeling, right?

Yes. It's a manner of existence that allows energies, energy personalities and expressions of energy personalities to exist exclusively in a space that is compatible with them only. That is a very good description of any dimension anywhere. And that is why different forms of life that are in other dimensions cannot be accommodated here and are generally not seen or do not interfere or flow into other dimensions that would not be comfortable with them. For that matter, neither would you be comfortable in other dimensions. The dimensional system is a means of creating a nonimposing barrier—"nonimposing" meaning, you don't feel like you ran into a wall.

Accommodations Have Been Made for the Beings at 3.0 Earth

Can we discuss the beings on what we call 3.0-dimension Earth? Was that frequency prepared for them, or were they just put there? How did that work?

You understand, they're not only in 3.0; they're at about 2.76 to 3.0. That has not been clear to you before, but the reason they're in 2.76 is that the "2" part of it allows them to feel . . . how can we say? Even the third dimension is overwhelming to them, given what they've been through. They need to have the least amount of demand on them as possible while having the responsibility of having physical bodies. How does this play out? For example, they might do something that you would not do; they can go into a dormant state. In the dormant state, they do not breathe, they do not eat, they do not excrete. It is not what you would call suspended animation in that sense of reanimation through some external means; it is a dormant state, not unlike what the chrysalis might go through for that form of life here on Earth.

But in the state itself, the physical body does not deteriorate in any way, and that dormancy could last—granted, the years and the time are not the same, but to give you an example—from, say, five years to eight or nine hundred years. The whole time the personality is in the body; the personality doesn't run around and do other things as it might do in the case of sleep. This is not sleep; it is a dormant state of physical existence during which the personality experiences the physical body and has a chance to relax into the physical body without being required to do anything. That allows the being to gradually relax.

> The formerly negative beings who were at 2.0 and were afraid of the transition to 3.0 were from the planet that blew up in Sirius a few years ago. These beings came to Earth, seemingly unaware that we were in the third dimension, and made deals with some governments to do some nefarious things in exchange for weapons. Then these beings started to threaten the various governments of the planet with their talk of a superweapon and became so obnoxious and made such nuisances of themselves that they were ordered to volunteer to go to a lower dimension of Earth than humans are on. When the planet in Sirius blew up, the souls of the rest of the beings were also brought there.

These beings have been through hell, though not the religious version of that. They've just been through terrible things, and it's overwhelming; they need a long relaxation. Some of them don't, but many of them may. Therefore, this dormant state is available, and it's a quality of the latter stages—although for the sake of our analogy, there are no latter stages. It's a quality of 2.76 and beyond, roughly to about 2.87, that that kind of dormant state can take place. And that's why it's that way.

How do the others perceive them when they're in that dormant state?

They see them, but those who are going into a dormant state like that would be placed in a separate area so that they would be safe, so that they would not be rained on, for example. They wouldn't be allowed to lie in a gully that might have a wash going through it; they would be placed someplace where they could relax, be comfortable and be relatively safe and protected. Granted, the occasional fly might come through and land on their body, but that fly is not going to plant eggs on their body as they do with a dying creature. The fly will be very clear that this is something living.

Also, in that dormant state, the body tends to give off a low level of radiation—not like atomic radiation, but radiation that essentially keeps things away that would be harmful to the body, including microorganisms. Normally if you went into a dormant state for eight hundred years, your body would be a wreck. If you could wake up after that, your body would be a wreck—no muscle tone and all that. This is different—you go into this dormant state, and when you come out of it, the muscle tone is the same as when you went in. It's as if your heart stops beating, or maybe it stops at a half-beat and doesn't complete the beat. When you come out of the dormant state, it completes the beat and goes on.

This was set up just for these beings because of the terrible trauma they've been through and because unlike in the usual life cycle, where when somebody dies (as it is on your planet or anywhere), that being goes off to a multiplicity of places, all of the souls on this planet transferred here en masse, together—"here" meaning at this different dimension, but here on Earth. This is unusual, so as a result, there are forms of accommodation for their specific needs. It had to be set up to take in the possibilities that they might require, to support them, to nurture them and, more importantly, to allow them a chance to just relax, to feel safe and to experience a physical body as a safe place to be.

When they were on this other planet, in the bodies they were in there, just *being* meant you were unsafe. Can you imagine even for a moment living like that all the time? Soldiers who have been in war, people who have been in prisons and so on know what it feels like to know that you're not safe. In your society, I might add, there's no excuse for that—and I've heard them all [chuckles]. People who have been in situations like that are never the same again. You don't get over that, not in the short life you have here. So these beings experienced that for their whole lifetime, which is quite long, many of them having repeated lives over and over and over again in such a place. So the idea of having a dormant state is a welcome relief.

Why would they have to have repeated lives rather than going off to have lives in other places?

This is usually a choice, a choice to experience something to the utmost, and a surprisingly large percentage of individuals did that. You have to remember that there was constantly an ongoing effort to overthrow the government there, to create something better, to create improvements. That's why a lot of the souls chose to come back, to be involved in the cause, to keep things going and so on. It didn't work out the way they wanted, but now they are having . . . it is like a second chance. It's like having something in reserve. This experience for them now was the thing that was in reserve for them. If they couldn't get what they wanted, then this would be available. They are living that "then" right now.

This presupposes the fact that some of these beings are in this dormant state and that others are caring for them.

The only caring that's involved is just making sure that the physical body is someplace where it's safe; that's all. You pick it up and you put it someplace where it's safe, or you direct somebody, if that being is going to do the dormancy. These beings don't arrive dormant, all right?

They don't?

They arrive physical, and then they have the choice to go into this dormant state if they like.

So some of them are living a life, then?

Yes, some of them are just thrilled and happy and want to live, and they immediately assume a life and begin living here. But others are more traumatized, and they need to utilize the dormant state. And this is quite easily known, meaning that the individuals themselves will know that they need to utilize the dormant state. Someone does not come along and say, "You need to be dormant!" They know it, and if possible, if there are others around, they will say, "I'm going to go into this state."

But as sometimes happens, perhaps there aren't any others around when they need to go into that dormant state. That is why all of the individuals on the planet are fully prepared all the time, if they see somebody in that state, to put them someplace where they will be safe. So they're vigilant for that, because the chances are that the person will have been able to say, "I'm going to go into this state," to someone, and they'll say, "Well, let's get you to where you need to be." But as time goes on, of course, there is less and less of a likelihood that a person will go into the dormant state without being able to tell somebody, because there are more individuals there, more family units and so on. But there's still the possibility, so everyone is still vigilant.

You Have the Capacity to Be Multidimensional

You've talked many times about the Earth having the different dimensions.

Oh, yes.

Your being is in many different dimensions?

Yes, that's right.

So that implies, then, that the Sun and the Moon and all the planets in the solar system are all in many dimensions.

That can be, as with you. You cannot live in a physical body made up of Mother Earth's body without having that capability yourself of multidimensional capacity. But as you know, a computer, for example, or a machine might have a capacity that you never use because you don't need it. You have capacities to be in all dimensions at once, to be in various dimensions when needed, but most of you will never need to utilize this. But you have that useful capacity because you exist. Good night.

Steps toward
Unity of Consciousness

Reveals the Mysteries
May 5, 2002

This is Reveals the Mysteries.

Welcome.

Union in the Dream State

Let us first talk about dreams and dream phenomena. It's important to note that as your responsibility for the functioning of different aspects of this planet increases, so will you be expected to provide balance on the planet—first in your unconscious state, then in your dream state, then in your subconscious state and finally in your conscious state. You have been working as a people to provide balance on the planet in the unconscious state for some time. One of the results of that work is the general public's increased awareness of problems all around the world that need to be addressed in ways that do not simply involve control or order. They have to be resolved on a permanent basis that nurtures and feeds people, even if there seems to be no apparent way to do so.

Now you've added to that the dream state, which is the next level of your responsibility and which you've been working on for a time. But you are beginning to do more than simply share or complete each other's dreams and understand the uniform application of how such things work. You are learning now on the "lab basis," meaning applied challenges, to see what you can actually do as groups of shared dreamers.

Groups of shared dreamers always have to do with entities—individual personalities as you understand it on Earth—who have lived together before in other lives or will live together in the future and as a result have some sense of familiarity on the soul or immortal personality basis. There is at least enough familiarity that if you sample or complete the dream of one of the members of your group, it will not be so remote, strange or uncomfortable that it causes you to feel that it is foreign. Such a dream from some soul personality who is not this familiar might cause you to at least wake up suddenly or feel as if you had a nightmare, even though the dream itself, as you remember, it was not nightmarish in its quality.

With these new challenges, you are beginning to resolve the incompatibility that you often see from one group of individuals to another. Those you've shared lives with before or will share lives with in some way in the future—who make up a dreaming group like this on Earth now—are from all walks of life, all nationalities, religions, races. This shared commonality has nothing to do whatsoever with any kind of mutually shared interest, but is strictly a familiarity based on past, future or, even in some rare cases, other-dimensional interactivity. So these levels of responsibility you will feel more and more. Eventually, groups will expand to include those whom you might have some contact or slight contact with.

As a result, you will have a need for some greater capacities. You are working on these capacities now as you are finishing the dreams of your fellow compatriots or loved ones or friends from other lifetimes. Sometimes it is because the people have died suddenly while asleep; other times you do this because their dream cycle was interrupted while they were involved in a very important dream that needed to be finished. You will finish the dream for them. Don't be alarmed, then, if you have these dreams that seem to be in some way wholly foreign to your life. Don't assume there is a pattern to them that is unsettling, that they are necessarily visions. Unless they have a wide, sweeping panorama of global events or an intensely personal feeling, with the faces of people you know now and their body shapes—not just their faces superimposed on the dream images, but the genuine sensation of individuals you now know—unless that is present, you can be reasonably certain it is just an overlaying of familiar individuals onto the last vestiges of the dream as a result of your waking process . . . as you wake up.

Now, in order to recognize your responsibility, you need only to sleep when you sleep. You do not have to say, "I will finish the dreams of my fellows." You don't have to do that. It has begun. This is a part of your agreement, which you have arranged on the unconscious level. There are many more things that you have set up on the unconscious level, and these will filter into what you do over the next seven to eight or ten years, according to the sequence of timing that feels right to each and every one of you. They are based entirely on the shared, mutual feelings you experience—not only in dream circles, but also globally—as a result of sensations from people on the other side of the world or even the sense of awareness brought about by reading or viewing or hearing about the news of the day or speaking to friends or communicating with them in some way.

All these things and others might easily bring up a sense of shared, mutual feeling, which might—if you deem it is appropriate on the unconscious level (acting as the human race united), if you deem it is the timing that is intended and has been triggered—inaugurate or initiate another series or sequence of applications used to resolve such difficulties, challenges and problems that arise out of a need to create absolute union. Then you can all be united, not only on the unconscious level (as you all are right now according to your arrangement and according to the overall desire of the vision of the Explorer Race), but also according to simple practicality. This creates a world that works for such a vast population living on a fairly small planet, intermingled with animals, plants and other species. Such complexities require your attention. You might not have felt a need for such attention when your human population was smaller, but now that it is bigger, it requires this attention.

Union in the Subconscious State

As time goes on and you begin to develop the same sense of union that you have unconsciously developed in your dream state—and this will take awhile—you will then move on to the next level of union in the subconscious state (even though you've begun to touch into that level right now). Union in the subconscious state allows you to be vaguely aware on the conscious level, moment to moment, of the need to unify. When this begins to happen, you will see vast, sweeping changes on a physically perceptible level of groups of individuals, then whole populations and cultures making radical change—not violent, but radical change—in perception, attitude and general homage paid to each other. This will occur not on a religious level, but on a level of politeness and caring that you have only hoped, wished and dreamed for in the past. Once that is established, you will then move on to the totally conscious level of union.

All these things will take time. But I bring to your attention today how much progress you have made. You are totally unified as a human population on the unconscious level. You are working toward union on the dream level. You have begun with union on the subconscious level. In short, you are making progress.

That's wonderful! What is the benefit or purpose of finishing the dream? What happens if it doesn't get finished?

It's not a problem if it doesn't get finished. Its benefit is that it is simply a vehicle that allows you to unify and become aware at least of the unsettledness of the lives of other human beings. In short, it is a means by which you can make a connection—a further connection, let's say—between your feeling self, filtered as it is and protected in the dream state, and the feeling self of other human beings living on Earth now.

You talked of a group of dreamers—what kind of group? Are there two? A thousand?

It could be anywhere from two or more. It might be that you are involved in more than one group. One does not arrange spiritual groups according to dozens.

You said that we have set up other things at an unconscious level to lead to unity. Are they too far in the future to talk about? Can you give us a hint?

You mean that which you have planned to initiate? I will not speak of those things now. If I speak of them, you will wait for them to happen, and you will wait indefinitely. In short, I do not wish to derail the process by making conscious something that is intended to function—how can we say?—on the analogy level. It functions the way your heart and breath work, without your thought. You don't think, "Okay. Now I'm beating my heart and beating my heart again."

These are the six billion humans on the planet? Or maybe this is also connecting to the other 94 percent of the Explorer Race?

It is unnecessary to connect to any being except to those on the planet now. Because you are here, you are functioning in the physical; you are not exclusively in spirit. If you are exclusively in spirit, there is no need or reason to apply physical lessons, experiences and so on.

So are the other 94 percent all on a spiritual level? They don't have lives waiting somewhere else?

They might. It is up to them. But waiting is not quite the same on the spiritual level as is, say, waiting for the bus.

To Share a Dream Is Intimate Indeed

Is there any scenario where you could finish someone's dream and cause a problem?

No, because you are asleep. If you were finishing it on the conscious level without all of the training and all of the steps I've mentioned in sequence . . . yes, you could. But you would not even be able to do so on the conscious level without all this training in unity. So that is theoretical.

So we're making progress.

It is important for you to understand that there is a reason when things happen. And that what appears to be unreasonable and outrageous might be just that, when seen as an individual event. But it is also important at times—maybe not every time, but at times—to pull back and look at it in the larger context, which is what I'm doing here. Meaning that, since the topic is dreams, if you usually have certain types of dreams and you suddenly have something completely unusual for yourself and it doesn't fall under the qualification I gave before as an exception, then you might consider that you are perhaps finishing or following up on a dream sequence that was left unfinished by someone else— not because the other would suffer a trauma from that, but because it allows you to experience a connection with another human being at a deeper level than simply, "Hey, how you doing?" or other things you say that are often intended to keep people away from you, not to draw them closer. This is much more intimate. To dream, to share a dream, is very intimate indeed.

Is there any learning a dreamer in such a case could use in his or her physical life?

Generally, in this case, no, because it is so far afield from your own life that there is no apparent connection or application. That's another way to know. You might not know immediately, but if you keep a dream journal or if you recall your dreams, within two or three days you might know if there has been no connection whatsoever. For one thing, you don't have to try to remember all of your dreams; you will know when you wake up. "That was really strange," you might say, or "I've never dreamt anything like that before," or "That was wild," or "That was wonderful." It's not just something frightening; very often it might be something wonderful that doesn't relate in any way that you can understand to anything you might normally dream—or, for that matter, in any way to your life.

Aboriginal Dreamtime

When one reads about the Australian Aborigines operating in Dreamtime . . . based on what you just said, does that mean they're totally unified on the unconscious level?

You are all totally unified on the unconscious level, but I think what you're trying to say is that they are totally unified on the dream level.

Well, where would you put the dream level? Is it another level between the conscious, the unconscious and the subconscious?

I didn't put it that way, because I don't want to unnecessarily complicate the process. But if you're changing the subject to ask about these individuals, then I will simply say that for them to function, it is not quite consciously. Rather, it is a bridge from the conscious self. It is a bridge from the spiritual conscious self into the dream state, to function on a unified level unconsciously, on the dream level subconsciously and consciously for a specific purpose. Those who can do this must do so benevolently. Oh, various war research individuals have tried to do so malevolently . . .

As a way to influence reality?

Yes. It has always been a catastrophic disaster—usually for those who are the researchers.

Would you say that what the Aborigines do, then, is a step up, a step on the path ahead of us?

Not necessarily. That is a shamanic act, done almost always with the intention of improving the quality of life for troubled individuals, groups or even vast populations. In short, it is like the doctor of the dream or a dream doctor; it is a shamanic function done to improve the quality of life. But you do not all have to become physicians or dentists, you know.

I didn't understand that it was a shamanic technique.

No, individuals do it. It is only . . . like in other groups of people, some individuals do this or that. Are you all in your culture bankers?

Life Extension Demands You Release the Attitude of "Suffering Makes One Stronger"

I want to talk briefly, not at length at this time, about the conditioning of the religions and, more importantly, the historical philosophies that have made up the means by which you have been able to justify your history of Manifest

Destiny and other things in the United States to accomplish your goals and purposes as a society. Specifically, at this time I want to talk about why only a minority of people are given pain medications or, for that matter, the means to die—not just people specifically traumatized, but those who are suffering lingering deaths from diseases. Why isn't there a vast amount of research into these areas? Why isn't there a tremendous amount of application so that people can, as you like to say, die with dignity?

Now, it's perfectly all right for those whose bodies are changing in some uncomfortable way to accommodate for those changes in a hospital or hospice, with care by professionals and loving family members, but there needs to be a recognition that in order to improve the quality of life, simply extending life or life extension is insufficient. Speaking to the researchers here, before life extension can even be embraced by the physical body, for the physical body to embrace and allow and encourage and nurture such life extension, you must reassure scientifically and on the feeling level. The scientists must become more complete and apply their feelings in nurturing all human and animal subjects they are working with to want to live longer. And one of the vital and obvious means by which to accomplish this is to be able to mentally and on the feeling level—including touching—reassure all participants that whatever pain they experience, whether it has to do with their death or part of the process involved in extending life, that their pain will be completely dulled so they do not feel it and can experience life to the best of their ability, interacting with family, friends and loved ones.

It's vital that you do this—I'm speaking especially to life-extension advocates—if you expect to truly accomplish a life that goes on 150, 175 years, in which you feel vital. Of course, this will not happen immediately, overnight, but it cannot happen by transferring pig organs to the body of a human being. I grant that you are doing that on an experimental basis. I'm not going to comment here whether I think it is a good thing or a bad thing, but I am commenting that the obvious advantage is to have your own human organs last for 150, 175 years at fully 80 to 90 percent of their youthful capacity—even in the 170th year. This is what you want in life extension.

I want you to clearly recognize that there is a direct connection between the physical body's reassurance—physically, on the feeling level—between a confidence of no pain to suffer and the desire to live longer. As any physical person knows, when you get injured, when you get hurt, sometimes the pain is slight, sometimes it is great. There comes a point in time when the physical body cannot, nor will it (this is a matter of permission), give permission to go on beyond a certain point. When the pain gets to be too much, that's it. The physical body says, "Okay, I would much rather change my physical matter into something else in which I am more comfortable." And of course, your soul personality will also agree. "Oh yes, I'd much rather be elsewhere," says your soul personality. "I want to go and be with God or get on with my other lives," whatever your philosophical belief is. And your physical body says, "I'm in complete agreement. I'd rather be elsewhere, not experiencing this pain."

Life Extension and the Elimination of Pain

So in order to get what you want—a longer life, a happier life, more comfortable, more vital—you will literally need to change the means of your science, your medicine and your philosophy to embrace on the feeling, loving level. Not, "Oh, I love you, I love you"—those are words—but the literal feeling as a love-heat/heart-warmth/physical-warmth loving experience given many, many times in these books [see p. 23]. I really want to encourage all of your scientists and life-extension advocates to experience that, to do it and to apply it in their work to the best of their ability while they are working with experimental subjects and volunteers.

And remember, the goal is to reassure the physical bodies of these beings—whether they be human or animal or plant—that your desire is to see them live longer, happier, more comfortably and without pain. This has to be a convincing situation that doesn't only function on the mental level, because on the mental level . . . that goes without saying. Everyone, for the most part, wants to live without pain. But to convince the physical bodies of all these beings, you must make reassurance and nurturing on the physical, loving basis a given, not an exception.

When it is a given, it is as with the animal; the animals naturally love, they love one another. This is a natural, a complete given with most animals whom you at least identify with. It is essential that you recognize that it is natural for human beings to do this too, but because of the complexities of your world and the challenges you experience in this growth school on Earth, it is sometimes something you forget to do. But for something that is such a common experience—all of you experience it, birth, death, *all* of you experience pain—you must do what you can about what you can influence.

You *can* influence the experience of pain, so kindly let go of this attitude—and it is purely and exclusively an attitude—that suffering pain makes you stronger. The reason that whole thing developed was to create a rationalization, to reassure people that once they got through their pain, they'd be stronger. And while that might be true sometimes, it is not a reassurance to the physical body to want to live longer. So understand that my conversation with you today is to draw a direct correlation between life extension and the elimination of pain as you know it.

Is it a religious issue? Why do we seem to suffer more in the United States than people do in Europe? They have painkillers that they give out liberally.

What I would say is that many times in other countries . . . other countries have absolutely no qualms about providing pain medication. But very often you will find that these other countries have had to face the fallacy of their religious beliefs or, in some cases, their philosophical beliefs because of the vast suffering brought on by war. In Europe and in other countries, Asian countries, who have experienced war and such phenomena of vast suffering, the idea of allowing such suffering without providing the pain medication that is available would be unthinkable. We use Europe as an example, because in many places in Europe there has been, out of necessity, a recognition of the shortcomings of religions, philosophies and other forms of conditioning that try to rationalize pain as something of value.

Pain-Free Existence Is Possible

Now, the origin of this idea is to explain why life is the way it is, which is ultimately the purpose of any philosophy or religion. And when people experience as a universal fact that certain things cause pain, such as things that are absolutely accepted as being part of life—birth and death—there needs to be an explanation. I will tell you that someday all birth will be pain-free. Not just from drugs . . . yes, drugs are good. Stop thinking of them as being bad. Granted, you have some uses of drugs now that are not so good, but in time you will find a resolution for that; it will not be as hard as you think. But recognize this and appreciate it: The purpose for which drugs exist at all is to relieve pain and improve the quality of life, whether a technique of application is taking place or whether a step toward greater length of life is being embraced.

It is not my intention today to take on the vast issue of birth and death and pain and all of that. But I do want to suggest to you this linkage between life extension—whether it be a few years or vastly into the future, a huge length of life for a single individual in a single body—and the experience of pain and the embracing of life. The linkage is total and direct. So, life-extension researcher—and I know you are working on this all over the planet—recognize this and first put your efforts into the relief of pain, which is not that difficult with what you know now for all people.

It can be done fairly inexpensively, and then it will take several years for the individual's body to believe that pain-free existence is possible in extraordinary circumstances or even in expected circumstances such as a lingering death, as will be the case for many of you. Also, there will need to be global acceptance of the fact that no one has to suffer because it is so easy to do something, to switch the pain off for the purpose of being able to live comfortably or at least experience a comfortable death . . . so one could say goodbye, have a kiss, a touch, an embrace with loved ones and friends. Don't leave this research up to only the military, which will seek to do this for the sake of defense procedures with soldiers. Recognize that this is a reality. If physicians globally embrace this, it will be a gift to humanity and your lives will ultimately improve. How many of you would like to live to be 170, 175 years old if you would know that you're going to be vital and pain-free? Think about that.

Everybody. Thank you very much, Reveals the Mysteries.

Pay Attention and Use Material-Mastery Techniques to Guard Against Terrorist Threat

Speaks of Many Truths

May 20, 2002

D*o you want to discuss this latest thing in the news that is being put out by the administration—that they suspect another 9/11 shortly? They just don't know where or when.*

The U.S. Government Is Trusting Its Citizens

It is true that the administration is trying to warn people of things they've seen, not only as potentials, but as things that have occurred elsewhere. Also, the administration has made some efforts to globalize itself in preparation for potential threats—meaning, "What are other people worried about? What are other people doing?" and so on. The U.S. administration has been perhaps properly discreet in the past. But it was not just, "We're not warning our population because we want business as usual." I realize the administration is being painted that way in some circles; previous administrations were painted the same way. It's not that. It's not that Big Brother is going to take care of you either. But there are genuine concerns.

In the past, there have been warnings about some potential threats and there were reactions. Your country is different. You are multicultural, multiracial. The administration is trying to avoid creating a witch hunt, to appropriate a term under which so-called witches and even self-called witches have been persecuted in the past. For the most part, they weren't practicing what people accused them of, and your administration is taking note of the fact that your population is not rising up in arms now against the priests. Granted, the rising up is taking place in the organized cultural ways, meaning in your culture—lawsuits being filed, things like that. But priests are not being stoned, with occasional exceptions.

So as long as there is a means to resolve things, your society is demonstrating to the administration that they can be told things and they're not going to riot in the streets or track down everybody of a certain culture and say, "You're bad just because I can't pronounce your name or you look different." In short, the administration wants to trust the American people and say, "Look, there are these risks. We're going to tell you more about it and we want to enlist you to be our good scouts, our good citizens, and tell us, tell your police officials, what you think could be a problem." Granted, most of the time what gets told will be false alarms, but sometimes people will say, "Look, here's something," and someone will be caught before any damage is done. So I'd say it's a good thing, what the administration is doing.

I think it is less important to state blame. Granted, the administration was warned about the potential for 9/11, but you have to remember, these administrations are no different than previous political administrations—and for that matter, political administrations of cities and states and all of that. These kinds of warnings are always coming in. It's hard to know whether they can be trusted to be real, whether the threat is real. The people who make up the business side of that, the intelligence people, all they can ever offer is their best guess, and that's what they do; that's their job. So, granted, the administration was warned about people who were credible threats, but they are not expected to be all-knowing gods and deities. It happened, and now you're taking more precautions. So the administration is warning the citizens about this.

You Need to Use Your Physical Body to Guard Against Any Threats

Is the threat real? Absolutely it's real. If that's what you're asking, it's certainly real and it needs to be paid attention to. Now, the threat level . . . let's talk about percentages. Quite obviously, someone could move into an apartment. How do you know what's in the boxes? You don't. People are moving all the time. So the threat level is real. The main thing to notice as a citizen is, how do you feel? Why do you think we've been giving the homework in these pages, helping you to sensitize yourself to your own feelings so you can *know* what feels good for you. You know that at times you get an uncomfortable feeling around people. Maybe it's because the situation is new and unusual for you, or maybe you don't know the people, or maybe you're afraid of what they might think of you—all of those things. That's all—reasonable day-to-day matters.

But there are some times when you definitely feel a gut feeling and say, "Something isn't right." Many of you have had this experience. You get frightened, and the fear may even be unreasonable, meaning you can't hang a finger on who or what it is. Just take note—take note of where you felt like that physically, geographically. Where did you start feeling like that? Were you driving along and you suddenly got the feeling? Can you remember where you were when you got the feeling? Try to trace it back, "Where was I physically?" because you might have gotten the feeling long before you got to your house and you didn't really notice it right away.

You need to use your physical body. Remember, the training I've been giving and that others have been giving in these pages has been about material mastery. Material mastery is understanding the harmony between all forms of life around you and within you so that you can act and interact with it in the most harmonious ways. That's material mastery. But also it is founded in the physical feelings that you have; it's your instinct. If you know this, you'll be able to be a big help.

Granted, you can't call up the police department and say, "I'm a shaman. I had a physical feeling that something is uncomfortable." Probably they won't listen. But if enough people call up and say, "I was driving by this building and I had a really uncomfortable feeling. Nothing happened, nothing went on; I just had this uncomfortable feeling driving by this building," or "I was walking by this store front and I had this really uncomfortable feeling. I was having a good talk with my friend, we were having a good time, the people around were friendly, but for some reason I got this uncomfortable feeling." If the police get one call like that, they might not do anything, but if five or ten people call in with the same story, they're going to say, "Well, maybe we'll send somebody over there and check the place out."

Police get hunches all the time. They're used to acting and reacting on the basis of feelings. It's a little awkward for them to justify it sometimes, but they are totally used to feelings, so if you use your feelings too, it might help. Be good citizens, good scouts. Support the government in this, and they will be more likely to let you in on more things in the future.

You know, citizenship in my time was how we took care of one another as a family, as a group that you call a tribe. We don't think about it tribally. It has connotations, but how we take care of one another and ourselves . . . sometimes what I do for you, my neighbor, is going to help my family. Even though there might not seem to be any direct advantage, it pays off for everybody. My neighbor does something for me the same way. You live in bigger cities now. Even small towns are bigger than what I lived in, but "people to people" doesn't change.

Sometimes you might just get a bad feeling. It's not because there's a bomb in there. For all you know, there's somebody inside who needs help, all right? Maybe somebody fell down, broke his or her leg or something and can't call for help. The police get all these calls: "I got this uncomfortable feeling walking by this place. I felt fine before I got there and I felt okay after I left, but I still had this funny feeling and I felt I just had to call you and tell you. I feel better now that you know about it," like that. No elaborate explanations of how you're a shaman or a mystical person or anything—keep it simple.

The police go there, and they find somebody who fell down and they can help that person, or they find something suspicious. There see these boxes sitting around and there's nobody around who's renting this place: "Those boxes look a little funny. What are those wires? Let's call the bomb squad." Use your feelings.

Pay Attention in Apartment Buildings

Is there anything you can say specifically about any viable threats that look like they could play out?

I want to support the administration. This is certainly possible. If those who are called terrorists now, if they try to do this . . . I know there's some worry about them doing this in small apartments. If they can do it in a small apartment once or twice, trial runs . . . your administration is trying to stop that. But I think what they're really going to try to do is go for the bigger apartment buildings and get these explosives somewhere near the supporting members of the building with an attempt—which is not likely in older buildings but is a real threat in newer buildings—to structurally weaken some main support system so that part or all of the building collapses. They will call afterward and say, "We did it, and you'd better give us what we want or you'll be sorry." People do this kind of stuff all over the world. That's what they're saying: "Give us what we want or you'll be sorry."

But how much threat is there? I'd say the reason the government is telling you is that there is a credible threat. I'll give you a percentage, okay? There is right now about a 23 percent chance that this will take place in the United States within the next three to six months. But if enough citizens pay attention . . . you don't have to create a witch hunt. It's not, "He looks this way; she's got that name"; it's nothing like that. Use your feelings—not just your fears, but your feelings as you've been taught in the pages here in these books [see the *Shamanic Secrets* series]—and you'll be able to help and probably prevent a disaster. This is a 23 percent chance in the next three to six months during which time a lot of organization will happen on the local level to improve alert systems amongst managers and staff of apartment buildings and other office complexes to try and discourage this kind of thing.

Obviously, for those of you in more modern buildings, pay attention, particularly to apartments that are located near structural supports for the building. And for those in older buildings, pay attention to apartments that are near sensitive mechanisms in the building. If they can't knock the building down, they'll try and knock out the elevator or possibly near electrical systems or near sewer systems or something like that, so that at the very least people are inconvenienced. Pay attention to things; there are many things in apartment buildings that if disrupted, broken or otherwise disturbed can in their own right create problems, such as sewer or water systems, or electricity, all right?

You know what to look for, or if you don't know what to look for, then fire marshals need to talk to building managers in group meetings. Don't go around to one building at a time. The managers can all go on various meeting nights in various towns. They can all go to some hotel, and the fire marshal will tell them what to do, and other people might be there. The managers can tell their staff; the fire marshals can give them some printed material. That's the kind of thing to do. That's how you get started. It's not really much different from having a big family: "This is what to watch out for, and this is how we can prevent it."

But for those of you who are interested in the material we are giving in these pages, use your feelings.

The SSG Has Stirred the Pot

Let's back up one step. You and others have said in these pages that it was not terrorists who orchestrated 9/11; it was a rebel faction of the secret government. So who is behind these threats? Is this what we have come to call terrorists, or is this another attempt by this group to stir up America and provide problems?

I'll say this: The sinister secret government has almost nothing to do with this. From their point of view, they stir up the pot and let it bubble on its own. They've stirred up the pot, and it's bubbling on its own. You understand, it's in the nature of global business that the more people can travel freely, the more likely the business community is going to thrive and, equally, the population is going to thrive and people are going to get wealthier together. If they're wealthy and business is good for business, it's good for populations in a lot of ways. So much of what you're dealing with now with this so-called terrorist threat and these political threats involves people who are left out or people who want to do things the way they did them in the past—as you say, extremists—or people who simply can travel more easily these days because of accessibility.

So if you're asking if the current threat that your political people are talking about is in any way associated with the sinister government or even an underground group within your own government who has its own agenda, I'd have to say no. I would say there was some support as far as 9/11 goes—not directly, but indirectly, so I wouldn't worry about that. But in the long run, you're going to have to face the music as long as there are unhappy people struggling for power so they can improve their circumstances and at least run their part of the world the way they want to. You're going to have these problems as long as there are vulnerable systems that they can attack and/or means that they can use to create problems. So obviously, your world is getting more, as intelligence people say, hardened—I don't mean your hearts, but rather that vulnerable systems are going to become less vulnerable.

The Universal ID Is Coming

Ultimately, the universal ID—meaning something that's implanted in your body that is genuinely certifiable so that people know it's you—is coming. Don't be too afraid of it, okay? It's coming. Governments are kind of trying to condition you to it being worthwhile. A lot of people are going to resist it, but it's not going to be so terrible. Almost everybody on other planets have it, okay? Granted, it might feel a little creepy to some of you at first, but I do not think it is too terrible. It will create a lot of change. People will feel funny about it, but the governments will make it worth your while. Things will be very smooth and easy for people who have these IDs within them, okay? So don't be too upset about it.

Smooth and easy—what do you mean by that?

For instance, if you're going to drive a car, you won't have to carry a driver's license. Everything will be done through the ID. If you have to take the driver's test again—you might have to take it every ten years or so—when you take it, it's just programmed through an external electronic device into that little doodad inside your hand or somewhere around there (in the palm of your hand or somewhere near your hands if not in them). It will be very simple: You pass the license test and that's it. You won't have to carry all those documents with you. If you need to apply for government programs or interact with the government in any way, it will be easy. If you go through airports and all of the security stuff, for anybody who flies, it will be in that little thing so that you'll be able to walk through—they'll pass this thing over you and they'll know immediately who you are, what you are. It's very simple. It will speed up a lot of things.

So the more people who have them . . . it will become popular to have them because things that slow you down will become so much easier. Eventually, businesses will climb on board and you'll be able to literally . . . well, if you go to the movies, you'll just run your hand over something and that's it. You won't have to stop, take out your wallet, give money and make change—all that kind of business. So this will improve and speed up commerce.

Will it deduct your money from the bank?

It might. It may be something like that, where it will automatically deduct that. You know, for quite a while now, businesses have been trying to engage you in paying things by computer, but people are perhaps understandably suspicious about that—not just because of the change in technology, but because they've seen some abuses with that in the past. This system won't be flawless, there will be some problems, but they'll be quickly worked out because almost everyone will see the great value in it. There are some experimental programs going on right now to install these in some human beings.

In prisons?

Well, things like that. Also with people who are sick and might wander off and get lost. Eventually the ID will be put in children so that if children are kidnapped or lost, you will know where they are very quickly. You can't take a child across a border with this device in the hand; they'll know immediately whether the child is supposed to be with you or not. In short, it will make a lot of things a lot better, improve the quality of your life, even though there will be some things about it that will bother and agitate many people. They'll feel like they've become numbers, because when they are exposed to the technology behind it that will have to do with digits and sound very computerized, some people will feel awkward about it. But you'll still have your names. You're not going to have a number printed across the back of your hand or anything.

So what are some abuses that you see?

Obviously, if information gets coded into it that's incorrect, it could create a problem until that information is corrected. So when the system starts getting applied . . . that's part of the reason they're experimenting with it now with human beings, and they also want to make sure that the device is in no way going to interfere with your physical bodies and also that your physical bodies will in no way interfere with the device. I think they'll get that all worked out pretty soon, and then I think that in the long run most of you will like it and see its advantages. I don't think it's a real problem, but you might see some problems develop in other countries where people don't want it or feel upset by it.

What your country will do—and probably some other countries—is, it will say, "If you're going to come to this country, you have to have a device like this. If you're going to stay in your own country, you don't have to. But if you're ever going to come here or if you're ever going to any place that has this device"—a lot of places in Europe and so on; generally, any place that has business and political exchanges—"if you're going to come to any of these countries, you have to have one of these things installed." But it will work out all right, so don't get upset and worry about it. So if someone comes over, he or she is going to have to have one installed, and that's it. Even if that person doesn't live there, even if that person is coming over for a couple of weeks, he or she will have to have one installed, and that's that.

The Benefits of a Universal ID to the SSG

On 9/11 you and Isis and Zoosh said that one of results of 9/11 would be that the universal ID would be accepted. The sinister secret government must want this. They were behind 9/11. What are the benefits of this to the sinister secret government?

You have to remember that sometimes some of the things the sinister secret government wants are actually the things you want. I realize that seems like it runs against your grain, but if you or those you know are running businesses, you don't want people who are upset in general or people who are fighting for a cause coming in there and blowing things up or making things worse. In short, you don't want people costing you money or making things inconvenient or hurting people you know. I think you can say that, and the sinister secret government wants that too, but of course, they also would like to know where everybody is all the time.

Now, granted, any time you go anyplace where you have to reveal your presence . . . say you go to the movie theater, you go to the supermarket, something like that, where you're purchasing something, you will be also revealing your presence there. I think that's one of the things that will bother some people. They don't like the idea that they can't just go somewhere and be there. They'll want to pay by cash, and a lot of the stores will accept cash for a long time, but eventually it will all switch over to this electronic system.

Anybody who wants to pay cash will have to basically make a deposit at the store—say, deposit five hundred dollars, and the money comes out of that deposit. In short, it'll make it awkward, because it's awkward for them. And after you deposit your money, your purchases at the store not only come out of that money you deposited, but there will be a service charge that will come out of there too, because that's something the stores don't want to do and it's going to cost them money to do it, so they're going to make money providing that service because they're in business to make money. Aside from the service they're providing, they're in business to make money, and that's understandable.

That sounds like George Orwell's 1984. The dissidents are all removed and everything is all . . .

That's the "1984" scenario. But the point is ultimately not to eliminate the dissidents. The point is to embrace them but to take the bombs out of their hands and to give them a means to come in and join everybody and to tell everybody what's wrong and what they want to fix. Granted, extremists will not accept the slightest compromise, but if you get them all into a room without weapons and with the means to communicate—not only with words, but with some feelings—things will get worked out eventually. People will have to learn to compromise.

It won't be easy for some people, but it can be done as long as the dissidents feel they have a means to present their grievances. Sometimes their grievances will be entirely justified and can be easily corrected—meaning conditions can be made to change so that such things that are happening to these people do not happen anymore and their lives improve or that the simple act of communicating might make things better. The main thing is that there needs to be more communication, not less, and there needs to be *no* means to create bombs, destructive devices or other means of current applications of technological terror. I don't think you're going to be able to eliminate knives for a while, but someday you will even find a way to do that and people will still be able to eat their food. Think about it.

Getting Rid of Weapons

You know, a lot of the work to resolve problems of terrorism, a lot of the study going on, is happening in prisons because the prisons, especially in some countries—including your own—are so terrible that a prisoner cannot survive without some kind of weapon. Now prisons are gradually improving in your country, and even though it might seem to be a bit extreme, it's best to have the prisoners isolated from one another. Then they each have their own space, and sometimes they can earn the right to mingle with the other prisoners if they wish to, but for the most part the prisoners feel safe. They don't have to have weapons. If they're safe from the guards, if they're safe from the other prisoners, they don't have to have weapons, and after a while, they don't. They don't carry them; they don't need them. Meals are delivered to them. They don't have to have a big mess hall where people all eat together and there are big risks there: "Who are you sitting next to?"

So a lot of study needs to be done there—that's why it's being done there. How can we help people to feel safe so they won't need weapons? As you know, weapons are not just available, but people can feel like they're necessary even when they're not. That's why sometimes children shoot each other, because they think something's a toy or a game that's real.

Ultimately, the public will not have access to any kind of weapon that can harm. There might be some antiques and so on in people's hands, but there will be no means, say, with a gun . . . you won't be able to shoot it. There might be target ranges where you might be able to go and shoot at paper and so on, but other than by the police and military, there won't be much need for that. Now, you understand that I'm talking well out into the future, but you're taking the first steps now.

The United Nations Needs to Be Bigger, Not Smaller

The initial steps are making things more secure. The next step, which really needs to happen concurrently, is giving a voice to people. That's why the United Nations is so important. It needs to be bigger, not smaller. There needs to be an auxiliary to the United Nations for groups who do not have countries. This auxiliary, these representatives of what you would now consider to be terrorist groups . . . these representatives need to have someone who can come and speak. Maybe not every day, but they will have these representatives in this auxiliary place, and they can come and speak in person so you can see them, see that they're living flesh and blood, a human being—not just dogma. They'll speak to the General Assembly and say, "This is how things are for my people." First they'll have to say that so you understand why they've come to this desperate act of terrorism: "This is why we're doing these things, and this is what we would like to have changed, and won't you please do something about it?" and that's it.

There has to be some beginning. So even though you don't normally consider certain groups . . . let's pick one out—Hamas. These people don't have a means . . . you don't talk to them. If Hamas was able to send a representative or two or three to a building . . . not necessarily part of the United Nations, but something that sits near the United Nations or that's in its own place or something like that. They can send representatives and they can talk, both privately and publicly, to a United Nations representative and say, "Look, this is how it is for us." That's important. I picked Hamas because it's a group that you know and have heard of in the United States, and it's one you consider to be a terrorist organization. You're justified in that thought, and yet they in their acts . . . what they are doing is not so terribly different from what others have done in their own time in their own way, some of whom are well established now as governments. I'm not trying to say it's good. I'm trying to say, "Let's put a stop to the need for terrorism by creating a venue to allow these people to talk and send representatives."

Think back when your country and other countries were involved in trying to create some peace between the Irish Republican Army and the rest of Ireland and the UK in general and the rest of the world in general. You had to accept the fact that the IRA was going to send political representatives who were going to talk about things in ways you understand. There is a precedent. You can't just relate to people on the basis of, "We're going to stop you," and they say, "We've got to do something because we are suffering here."

So think about it, United Nations and others. What kind of organization can you create that will allow groups of people like this who have problems that you may not be able to solve but whom you might be able to help in some way so they at least feel like they have a means to, as you say, redress their grievances. It will help, and it could break the chain of what you've seen in the past—study history if you want—of how an organization or a group is a terrorist organization, just as the colonists were to the British in your own country. I can assure you that they were considered terrorists when there was the rebellion. You know they were terrorists. You go on to establish something in time that might be of value, but it takes awhile and a lot of the processes along the way are ugly and unpleasant. It's your job, in your time, to break the chain of those ugly processes and give people a means to communicate, improve the quality of their lives and, in the process, improve the quality of your life. While you're doing that, you can make vulnerable systems in your society safer, but concurrently—not one thing after another.

I know there are people working on this now, and I'm giving these words because I want to support you. I want to suggest that it's a good thing and it's how you consciously create a workable global society. Your first global society is based on the business model as Zoosh told you, but the transition is already beginning to include social systems and cultures. That will be more challenging, but you can do it. You've already begun. I'm encouraging you to continue.

Dreams Connect You to Spirit

Reveals the Mysteries
May 23, 2002

*S*peaks of Many Truths said that sometimes when you have an image of yourself in a *dream and it only looks vaguely, if at all, like you, that it's not you, but rather someone you are guiding.*

In the Dream World, You Are Your Spirit Self

Very often when you have dream images you can recall, sometimes you do not see an individual in the dream. Therefore, you feel it is you. If you were able to see the scene in the dream, it might be you, but it would not look like you. It would perhaps look like a point of light or something small, meaning that you in that visual presentation would be almost like a peephole of light. So you are the observer in the scene in that dream.

You do not feel the feelings when you wake up from such a dream, a dream where you are the observer. You do not feel any of those feelings that you would expect to feel when you wake up. Even if it is a nightmare, you don't feel that in the dream, because in the dream world when you're fully engaged in it, you are your spirit self, your immortal personality, your soul. Especially as the immortal personality, you can observe such things, learn to understand them in the larger picture and not need to fit them into your physical life that you're living. This is because the immortal personality and, to some degree, the soul . . . the soul has to do specifically with the life you are living and the immortal personality has to do not only with that one life but with all the lives you've lived and is a little more closely connected to Creator. It's not that the soul isn't closely connected to the Creator, but the soul is more directly connected with a given life.

When you observe this action—going along as the immortal personality—this drama has, not an abstract point of view, but you are observing the drama, as it were, in a classroom with your teacher or teachers so that you can understand where it fits into all of your lives or maybe even your purpose for living those lives. In other words, generally speaking, this is a connection to make sense out of. So what goes on, then, is a feeling, a genuine sense of feeling having to do with a life purpose as well as an intention. That's most important.

Personal Identification in Dreams

Now, if you see *someone* in the dream—you're not just the observer, but rather you see someone—and you wake up from that dream . . . you might see that person from the back and he or she is doing something or saying something. In short, your assumption is that this person, whether you are seeing him or her from the back or the side (rarely from the front, but occasionally), you will notice very often that this person doesn't really look like you, but there's a feeling that the person *is* you. In short, there's a feeling of personal identification.

If you see that person from the back and do not have any recollection of his or her appearance at all, his or her face, then that person is you in another life, you in an alternate life—in short, a version of you, meaning that this has to do with your life in some way. But if you have a recollection of seeing this person's face, even from the side, and he or she does not look like you or there is only a vague resemblance, there is a very good chance that either this is someone you are guiding, or you are there with that person's guide, angel or teacher, observing how the guiding process goes on—either because you are doing some form of guiding with that person, or you are learning how to become a guide, even while you are living a physical life. Perhaps you have even been a guide and are living some physical lives to learn how to do your job better. Perhaps you are even—this is rare but possible—concurrently a guide and are also, again, living physical lives to know how to guide individuals better.

Understand, then, that there is not one answer but many answers. And there's another possibility as well, and that is that the person you see from the back, the side, occasionally from the front, is potentially someone you will be or someone you may even meet in this life. Now, if you meet that person in the life you are living and his or her relationship to what was going on in the dream bears no similarity to who or what that person is in this life, then when you meet that person, it is not him or her. Even if the person looks very similar to that person, he or she isn't. But if there is a similarity, say in a job or in a relationship, then it would fall under the heading of potentially being a prophetic dream—I cannot always say, because it depends on the individual dream and the person. As you know, prophetic dreams are about things that may happen. To a greater or lesser degree of probability they may happen, depending on what happens in your life and in the lives of others around you, or even in your global or cultural life. All of these variables factor in.

You Are Closely Connected to Spirit

I mention these things because it is not always known or understood or appreciated by the average person living right now on Earth how closely you are connected to spirit in the function of spirit. Yes, you are a living, breathing human being, but you might also be simultaneously receiving guide training. You might, as I said, in some rare cases be a guide now, or you might even be receiving training in becoming an angel or some form of assistant to one, which requires absolute openness, love and appreciation.

This tells you something essentially true. It is true 98 to 99 percent of the time—maybe 99.5 or 99.8 percent, something like that—that people who are training to become angels (or who are training to become assistants to angels) who are living a physical life, because of the openness they have to learn, that most of the time they will be in feminine form. In short, they will be a girl or a woman, depending on their time of life. This does not mean that men cannot do this, but you can see simply by the cultures you have on Earth now that you would have more opportunity to be open as a woman than you would as a man, so practical reality is a factor here.

Objects and Symbols in Dreams

Now, there are other things that happen in dreams. Sometimes you'll wake up with a sense, not only of the people in the dream, but the image that resonates in your mind or memory is that of an object. If it is a frightening object, do not assume that it will have anything to do with your life. Think about every possible use for that object, even if it appears to be frightening, and don't leave out the fact that one of the uses and applications of that object is to provide a picture for your mind. So if the object is very resonant in your memory after you wake up, even if it is something frightening (which is not often the case but is occasionally), remember that you might see a picture of that object. You might see it from afar, or someone might refer to an object like that. In short, don't assume that that object will affect your life.

What happens if the object is more benign, something simple, something in your day-to-day life? You can always analyze these things mentally—psychologically they say—but that only represents one small picture that may or may not be helpful to you based upon your approach to life. This is not all pictures that you are left with from a dream, but some particular picture of an object that seems to come and go. Even when you're not thinking about the dream, suddenly a picture of that object from the dream pops into your mind. This probably means that that object and all that it might represent—not just what it seems to be in the dream, but all of that, all of the potential meanings, as well as a photograph or even an apparent shape in the sky of that—will in some way affect your life.

Generally speaking, when such things are seen in dreams, it means that there's going to be something benevolent associated with this, and it's important for you to watch for this. But this is only the case if the picture of that object keeps popping up in your mind's eye (even after you've forgotten the dream or aren't even thinking about it anymore). Or even if it pops up once or twice, that is usually a reminder from your guide or potentially from your teachers that there's something about the shape of that object or one of its many applications or symbols—meaning, what does it mean?

It might be something that is symbolic in its own right, or it might be something that is obvious, such as a piece of bread with butter, food, and so on, that has some meaning in your life and to watch out for it. For example, it might be something, say with our bread-and-butter example: Maybe you see a picture of bread and butter or you even see a piece of bread and butter out of the corner of your eye, and at that moment, something else happens in your life that is important for you to pay attention to   Then the bread and butter is simply just a symbol like a flashing light to catch your attention that something important is going on now. Or maybe it's the bread and butter itself.

In short, think about it. If you're a spirit teacher or guide and you are attempting to help someone you are guiding or teaching, the best way to help that person in a way that does not interfere with her life—remember, guides can help you, they can nurture you, they can guide you, but they cannot interfere—is to give her a picture that she may remember from time to time. And you might give it to that person more than once, as I indicated, which is intended to catch her attention, either for its meaning or for something else that happens when she sees that or sees something that reminds her of that.

I realize it's complicated, but it is not your job to remember all these things, only to remember that if you suddenly see that picture, pay attention to your surroundings. Maybe something important is going on, or in the case of the bread and butter, maybe there's somebody hungry nearby whom you can offer a sandwich to. It could be something that simple. Just remember that it won't always be bread and butter. That's just my example—an innocuous example, but one that definitely spells nourishment.

You have to remember that everyone dreams. Granted, the rare individual does not remember his or her dreams, and it is slightly more common that people don't always remember their dreams. But people can identify with dreams. Therefore, one of the foundation blocks that attract people to anything metaphysical or New Age or philosophical along these lines is going to always be dreams.

Planet X Is Coming to Test Humans: Choose Fear or Love

Zoosh
June 18, 2002

W hat's all this baloney about Planet X? Do you really want to claim and practice misery? Is that really what you want? Think how very long you've been conditioned to believe that misery is part of life. I grant that you can produce chapter and verse to prove to me that it is, and yet I will say to you that almost all the misery—99.7 percent —almost that you experience is based largely upon conditioning, even that which appears to be physiological happenstance, meaning, "That's the way it is, Zoosh." But, in fact, almost all of this can be changed by what and how you do things.

So why do you think I haven't spoken to you very much over the past few years? Because the whole point has been to expose you to the manners and means by which you could literally learn how to change your physical world. That's why I stepped back and let Speaks of Many Truths, Reveals the Mysteries and others speak to you about these things, not only because they have lived physical lives as human beings on Earth, but because of their experience, they had to learn how to be natural, to live naturally and to do it in the best way possible without any visible means of support. So I felt that they had the most to offer you, to expose you to means by which you could benevolently change your world. I don't expect you to have done it; that's not the point yet. You're working on it—you'll get to it. The main thing is, I wanted them to talk to you about it.

Now, as far as *Shining the Light* goes, I'll take that over now; Speaks of Many Truths will only talk to you in *Shining the Light* from time to time. I've been letting him do it, and he volunteered because he could teach you things that you could *do*. But I'm here today because I'm really rather sick and tired about your addiction to unhappiness.

Planet X is Planet Wonderful?!

I know that very often you feel at the short end of a sharp stick; you feel that life is difficult. Of course, it's difficult! If it were anything else, you wouldn't be here, because you've all had to qualify to come here to this school that is intended to be challenging and weeds out the theories that have to be replaced or practiced in a practical way. Does it work? That's the real application of this planet. "Bring all your theories here, and we'll try them out and see if they work. If they don't, then back to the drawing board." That's really what this school is. So often you will be confronted with "terrors." The purpose of terror is that it is important for you to get ready and be able to confront this terror, even if it never appears, which very often it doesn't.

So it's been one thing after another in your experience here on Earth—first it's this, then it's that. Now it's Planet X: "Planet X is coming back after thousands of years, and it spells gloom and doom!" . . . ad nauseam. Regardless of what the threat is, don't blame those who are waving the flag of this terror. Rather, are you ready? What can you do to change—not only your own lives but the lives of others—to make you stronger, work together and unite. What can you do to have the means, the opportunity and the ability to not just protect yourself from whatever terror it is that you're worried about at the moment, but to literally change that thing from being something frightening to being something friendly—in short, transformation, not on an attitudinal basis, but on a physical basis.

Why do you think Speaks of Many Truths' first *Shamanic Secrets* book was about material mastery? Things were given to you in the *Shamanic Secrets* books based upon your *immediate needs*. Your first immediate need dealt with material mastery: "What can we do to change our physical world so that it will function better?" [*Shamanic Secrets for Material Mastery*]. And the next book in the series is about, "What can I do to change my physical body so it will function better?" [*Shamanic Secrets for Physical Mastery*]. And the third book in the series is about, "What can I do to incorporate my spiritual body and my spiritual surroundings into my world, to be at peace with my spiritual world so that my spiritual world is consistent with the benevolent physical and material world that I am working to create?" [*Shamanic Secrets for Spiritual Mastery*, coming 2005]. In short—and not to put too fine a point on it—let's stop worrying about Planet X and all of its so-called terrors, and let's change it. Planet X is really just a test; let's change it to be something *wonderful*, all right? So instead of being Planet X, it is Planet Candy Store, it is Planet Wonderful, it is Planet Fabulous, it is Planet Reward. *That* is going to be up to you.

If you have not already done so, read and practice *Shamanic Secrets for Physical Mastery. This is not an advertisement.* It is a practical piece of advice. In order for you to be able to accomplish and achieve what you *need*, you need to have the means and the abilities that you have practiced and tried so you know they work—so they're not just Zoosh's crazy theories, but things you've practiced and tried so you know that they work. You have to have them on hand so that it's not just second nature but first nature to use them in order to transform physically that which is frightening to that which is safe.

Tom and the Bear—Choose Love and Change the Reality

I will tell a story now. It's a real story, about a real, physical person on Earth. I will abbreviate it, but he will know who I am talking about. There is a man, a well-known author, who lives in Sedona, Arizona. Once upon a time he felt drawn to drive down near a river. He went down to that river, but he did not know why he was there. So he went for a walk into the forest as he often does. He looked around and did not know why he was there. Then he heard a rustling sound and he looked; he saw a very tall, very frightening, wounded bear. Now, anybody who has ever been around a bear, even one not wounded, knows that this is not a safe place for a human being to be. The bear, for one thing, can run faster than the human being, so running is out. The man did not know what to do, but he saw that the bear was injured.

Being a spiritual man, he immediately went into a peaceful meditation that he could feel. He could see how the bear had accidentally injured itself. So he went into a feeling that he could create, that he had learned, been taught to do. Even though the man was frightened, he surmounted that, and the energy was good; it felt good to him going out. He stood there for a long time feeling that, and the bear stood where the bear was. Eventually, the bear looked over at him and nodded. This man, whose name is Tom, decided that he had done all that he could do. The bear nodded and got down on all fours—even though one paw was wounded—and hobbled away. Tom had been drawn to that area to help that bear, and being a man who has worked extensively in nature, he knew he was facing a terrible threat to him personally. But he had been drawn to something that was frightening, and he used the tools he had with him, his abilities, and not only transformed that fearful situation but made a friend. He did what he could. It saved him and helped the bear.

I'm revealing this story to you because it contains a practical application of a terror changed into something wonderful. Tom was drawn to that place—does that not suggest something to you? It is this: You are drawing things to you as the Explorer Race, the beings who are here to change, transform yourselves and ultimately your whole universe into something better. You are drawing things to you to test you, not to destroy you or wipe you out. You are constantly creating challenges to change a situation into something better. You will be taught in the pages of *Shamanic Secrets* how to do it. It will be simple, not complex. It will not be something you will have to compromise your philosophy or religion to do, but something simple. The love-heat/heart-warmth/physical-warmth that you've been taught to do in these books is intended to be simple [see p. 23].

If Tom had felt the love-heat, that would have worked, too. Maybe he did, in addition to his meditative state. The main thing is, it transformed an emergency, not only for himself, but for the bear, too. The bear was in desperate pain and literally broadcasting a cry for help, and Tom responded to that. He went to the forest simply on the basis of faith. He got there, was frightened and then did what he did. What he did actually caused enough relief—it was a healing energy—for the bear so that the bear could not only go on and bear his pain and gradually get better, but know that another being, another life form—not even another bear, but another being—felt his emergency so much that it would come and help him. Tom gave the bear the faith to go on and live. Sometimes when you transform a terror, it not only transforms things for you and makes them better, but what strikes you as terrible has its life restored and renewed as well.

Don't assume that Planet X is only terrible. Begin working right now; feel the love-heat. Get together in groups; feel it together. Understand that it will naturally radiate—don't send it out. Just say, "While we feel the love-heat today for ourselves, let that which radiates beyond this group go where it is needed. And if some of it goes to Planet X, may it nurture beings there and serve them well." That's what I recommend. It's a challenge; don't assume it is only a terror.

Planet X Is Coming

Can you say what is coming? Is it a spaceship? Who is in it?

I will say that it is not exactly a ship, all right? Certainly, it is something that is not a natural planet, but if one were to look at it from a distance with the naked eye, one might reasonably assume that it has a sort of satellite quality to it—but within the context of the word that, for instance, the Moon is a satellite, you understand? It has a sort of natural look to it, but it is not a natural object. And the residents live not on the surface, but inside.

What is its . . . not trajectory, but orbit?

It's not an orbit, but a traversing route. If a salesman goes out on his or her rounds, he or she tends to go to the same places around the same times on a consistent calendar basis. It is like that. It is a route, not an orbit. And it is not a planet per se.

It's under conscious control?

Yes.

Can you say anything about the inhabitants? Why are they traversing?

They are looking to see how things have changed.

Since the last time they came by?

I realize much has been said: "Oh, they came, they created all of this . . ." That is not true, but they certainly did come and they certainly created some things. Look at your planet. It is quite obvious that there is a hand involved here that has many shapes and sizes, many different things . . . all the different life forms on this planet.

In different creations all over the planet . . .

. . . different creations, that's right.

Are you saying this is the planet called Nibiru, as Zecharia Sitchin put forward?

I am saying that it has many names. I do not object to that particular theory put forward by that author.

Are there any other names for the planet that we might have heard?

Well, I like to use that term, Planet X, because it's a nice term that sort of comes under a catchall phrase, isn't it? I like that one.

Your Material-Mastery Techniques Make a Difference

So what are their motives? Do they plan to visit the Earth?

They might. They're certainly not going to come here and command, reject or do anything like that, but you can make a lot of difference if you use material-mastery techniques—not control, but material-mastery techniques. How, for instance? Many techniques in *Shamanic Secrets for Material Mastery* tell you how you can work with mountains and other portions of the Earth in order to recharge them, and I can assure you that the more those mountains are recharged, the more they are likely to broadcast certain signals of strength that will deflect things from the Earth. For example, if a person walks down the street projecting strength and self-assuredness, it is less likely that he or she will be susceptible or vulnerable. It is the same for planets. If a planet is broadcasting strength and self-assuredness—it's not exactly like that, but similar—then it is less likely that meteors or objects are going to hit it. The field around the planet comes about, not by something external, but rather by radiations from mountains and a few other geographical terrain types. So the field itself is not only strong but tends to broadcast a more powerful signal and support all that is created from itself—that is, human beings, animals, plants and so on. And everybody and everything gets stronger.

What is the mindset of these people as they approach the planet? What are they thinking?

They are looking to see what progress you have made: Are you now involved in creation, or are you waiting to have creation done to you? In short, are you still wallowing about in the mud, or are you doing it? They don't talk that way, but that's essentially the feeling that would broadcast from them. And it's not because they have a hierarchical point of view, but rather that they want to see how far you've come. They won't know how far you've come unless you're doing something they can actually feel. They have the capacity to feel at quite a distance. They are not going to feel your feelings if your feelings are tumultuous and miserable and unhappy, but if they are strong and self-assured and resolution-oriented—meaning, "Okay, it's difficult, it's complex, but working together we can resolve it"—if they're going to sample those feelings, they're going to be more inclined to interact with you in some beneficial way, rather than staying at a distance and deciding whether or not your culture, from their point of view, deserves to continue to go on.

Planet X's Intention Is to Create a Humane Existence

Now, that sounds a bit ominous, but I will tell you what they do. I know you want to know. This is what they do: They don't foster civilizations—meaning they don't start them—but they might tinker with them a bit as they've tinkered with life forms on Earth here. They're not creators; they're not to be looked upon as gods. Please don't think of them that way; they don't think of themselves that way. But they do go around and observe civilizations that have begun. Sometimes they try to help out. Sometimes they will try to help out in odd ways, meaning that they might put something into the civilization or onto the planet that would be a challenge but is designed to prompt you to become stronger or to surmount it in some way that actually is to your benefit. That's how they got the reputation for being something to be afraid of.

So, from their point of view, if they see that you're still fighting and doing things to destroy one another and, in short, they don't have much respect for what you're doing as a civilization, they are probably going to make a recommendation. Their recommendation is not necessarily going to be followed, but it will be most certainly followed up on, and that is that another group will come around within about twenty of your years to observe you. So this is kind of like a warning, saying, "We don't like what we see; we recommend the next step." That's basically it. This other group will come around in about twenty years, maybe a little less—nineteen years and eight months, something like that—and take a look. If they concur, agree with that first recommendation, then they will simply say, "We agree." If that happens, somewhere within thirty-five years—around seventeen years is the average—someone will come around and basically push a button (that's not what's involved, but that's about as much time as it takes) and radically alter the civilization on your Earth. From their point of view, that would probably mean that human life as you know it would come to an end, but that animal life as it has existed now—encompassing what existed on Earth in the past, not back to the dinosaurs or anything like that, but for the past few thousands of years—and plant life would become the predominant life forms again. They would essentially do that.

It is not exactly a weapon; it is something that basically uncreates. Of course, your souls go on and you simply reincarnate elsewhere. But you see, that's how they've gotten the reputation of being something to be afraid of. We're not talking about fires or floods, fires falling from the sky, biblical stuff like that—which, I might add, was intended to just encourage people to follow certain suggestions. But rather it is done with an intention to create a more humane existence. In short, from their point of view, if the human race is just making one another miserable and making plant and animal life and the planet miserable, then they will simply do something that stops the civilization. This group and one other like it have done this before. I've mentioned before that civilizations have risen and fallen and situations have predominated on Earth and then disappeared.

Several times in the past, civilizations were doing terrible things to one another and—with the exception of the planet in Sirius talked about in some of the *Explorer Race* books where they allowed things to go on for longer than normal just to see if it was possible for this extreme discomfort to eventually transform itself into something better, and they discovered it didn't—basically someone came along and said, "Okay, this far and no farther," and "pushed the button" there, meaning activated this device. So . . . it's not instantaneous. If it happens, it's designed to be humane. Nobody suffers, and you go on. But you can change all that. You don't have to transform your world in the next twenty-four or eighteen months or whatever. But you do need to begin! And doing the love-heat is a very good way to start, because you can't do that without feeling better yourself. And it can only help others feel good, because it tends to broadcast what it feels like for you. Don't send it out to others. Just feel it for yourself, and if you like it, teach it to others as well.

Don't Get Attached to a Time Frame

Is their traversing on a 3,600-year cycle? In other words, were they here 3,600 years ago?

We can trace that back to about two cycles, equaling about 7,200 years. It's not exactly a happenstance; it's just the basis of things. But if you went back those 7,200 years, then you'd have to go back 14,000 years. See, it's not necessarily a fixed thing like that.

I would say this: Don't get attached to that. If you're attached to a time, then you're going to wait. You know that if you have nine months to do something, then you might very well wait eight months and thirty days—you know how you are! Don't get attached to a time . . . do the love-heat for its own sake, because it feels better to you and others. Don't wait.

Who are they reporting to? Who causes this visit by the second group?

Well, it is a loose-knit group. We're not talking about a planetary civilization who tries to rule the universe. It is a loose-knit group who basically patrols around to make sure that no one group is indefinitely creating misery for other groups. It's something that borders on being a club.

But do they understand the purpose of the suffering here, the Explorer Race concept?

Yes, that's why they've allowed it to go on as long as they have. Normally they would have done this a long time ago. That's why I say, don't be attached to the time. Oh, you know, about 1,600 years ago a group came around and took a look and said [makes a dismissive "ppppfff" sound], "Let's do it now." But someone said, "No, there's actually a purpose to all this," and they discussed it. They knew about it, they discussed it more; they sort of had a little debate about it. Then they said, "Okay, we'll wait."

But I don't think that the Creator or you, the friends of the Creator, or the Council of Creators would allow them to do that when we're so close to completion, right? Would you?

Oh yes, certainly. We respect what they are doing, because they don't do it arbitrarily. This is how they know when it needs to be done. I'll tell you how. They go on the basis of what they feel. If, for example, they came within a close orbit to the Earth—within, say, thirty-six miles—they'd be overwhelmed by the discomfort. But they stay a great distance away from Earth. In other words, their attitude is that even if you pollute your entire solar system with this energy, they're okay with that. They're not happy about it, but they're willing to allow your solar system to be polluted. *But* if it goes out to about the point where a twelfth planet would be, that much distance away from your planet, if they feel uncomfortable at the point where they measure, then they will decide that that energy is broadcasting out farther than is safe for the rest of the planets in creation to feel. And they will say, "Okay, this far and no farther." It's like a line in the sand.

So where they show up is not an accident, physically speaking, you understand? Where they show up is the line in the sand: "This far and no farther." But if they feel a little bit better and say, "Oh, it feels better than last time," they go away and say, "Well, let's send somebody back in seventy-two years." Someone comes back in seventy-two years and says, "Oh, it feels fine." Then they go away; that's it. But that's why I say it's like a club—it's an organization of volunteers. They go around and feel things; most of the time they never feel anything bad. When they feel something bad or it gets worse and worse, then they say, "Okay, that's it." But it's not sudden and arbitrary; you can see that there are steps. They say, "Well, we recommend . . ." And the next guys come along and say, "Oh, we agree." And then the next guys come along and they say, "Okay, there it goes."

The Beings on Planet X

How many beings are there? How long do they live? Are they the same beings reputed to have tinkered with the DNA in Africa many thousands of years ago?

You mean human DNA? Are we talking about the African peoples? The dark-skinned African peoples?

Well, this was before there were any people there. Supposedly they created the first ones in that area.

Well, of course they didn't do that. You can go back millions of years and find beings who would approximate the human beings you have now. But I'm not going along with the idea that they created the human race as you know it.

Did they create some particular group to work in the gold mines?

No. What did they need gold for? Did they come to get gold? Certainly not— what did they need that for? There are certain things on Earth that are fairly rare in other places, but gold isn't one of them. It is a useful mineral, an interesting mineral. It certainly has profound properties, most of which you're not using at the moment. But is it something valuable in its own right as a jewelry item or as a currency? No.

Okay, let me rephrase that. In their traversing, did they stop to look for some rare earths or metallic compounds in Africa?

No. They might have stopped to pick up a little sand, but that's about all. This is not the first time that's been noted, I might add. But I'm mentioning it because I think they might be interested in quartz, a high-quartz sand composite. They wouldn't have taken very much, though—perhaps what is equal to a couple of bushels worth. They're pretty sensitive about not taking too much from a planet.

Did they push the button and cause a flood? Did the flood have any relationship to them?

No. When they push the button . . . you understand that they're not pushing a button?

I understand, but those are the words you used.

Okay. But a flood, you understand, would cause suffering.

Right. That's why I asked.

It's not a pleasant way to die. If they did something and you were there and could slow it down about a thousand times in terms of speed, you would see the physical bodies of the human beings on Earth just disappear. That's all. It's very gentle; no one suffers. There is not even a moment of pain. They wouldn't cause a flood.

But then, when they've done that in the past, other groups of ETs have come in and reseeded and worked with the survivors, right?

They would put it out, circulate that they had restored the planet to a pristine condition. Of course, that would be from their point of view. The planet might feel differently about that because there would have been changes. So they wouldn't do too much to change the planet itself, but they would do something. They really don't have that capacity to change planets very much. Up to a point, they essentially can put things back the way they were—as far as plants and animals go, for instance.

Don't they have to get permission from the planet, the Creator?

They have permission.

If I looked at them, what would I see? What do they look like?

Well, they're humanoid. By this I do not mean that they look like human beings. They have two arms, two legs, a body and a head. I'd be a little hard-pressed to describe what they look like and I think I'm disinclined to say what they look like, because it would be very easy for people to say, "Oh, them." I will say this: If you saw them, you would say, "Wow! Where are these people from? I mean, they're not from Earth." They have two arms, two legs, a body and a head, but they don't resemble human beings much beyond that. I mean, they have hands and fingers and all of that, but . . .

What dimension do they live in?

Oh, they can traverse roughly from the third to the fifth. But they've been known to travel in the seventh as well.

How long do they live?

I've known a couple of them for several thousand years, and they were around for several thousand before that. So . . .

That sounds like a good story. How did you meet them?

In their travels. You know, sometimes a person might want to know something and no one else is around to tell him or her, so they show up.

I wondered if you talked them out of it last time. That's why I was asking.

Never. They are doing a service. Just because you don't like the service doesn't mean it isn't valuable. After all, people on Earth do that all the time. Every day someone on Earth is spraying and doing other things that are eliminating whole colonies of beings. The fact that you do that is a learned thing. That you would even consider putting material into a can and spraying it on a colony of beings, wiping them all out simply because you don't like having them around . . . that is learned. And unfortunately, what you spray on those beings causes them to suffer and die. You haven't gotten to the point where you can just snap your fingers and they move on; you haven't gotten to the point yet where you can ask them to move on.

But that's what you can do now. Things can be done with love, warmth and cooperation between beings, and they will move on if they can. Or you might feel a place you wish to move on to, if you could, so you don't all have to live under one roof if you don't wish to. The Earth is intended to be big enough to accommodate you. Ultimately, of course, you as a race of beings will want to move on to other planets. That's why planets are available for that. Certainly, it will not be that difficult for you to colonize Mars. It's not exactly what you need, but you can make it work. I don't think it will be too difficult to create underground cities there. I don't think you're really going to do dome cities; that's ridiculously expensive. But once you find a way to do it underground on Mars, you'll be able to make it work. It will give you something fun to do: "Oh, let's go to Mars for the weekend!"

Radiate Love-Heat to Show You've Learned

So these beings are coming in eighteen months, twenty-four months, something like that?

Something like that. I'd say that the timetable is pretty accurate. You might or might not notice them being here. For one thing, they're not going to just land on Earth; you're not going to see their ship in the sky. It's not going to be three months of darkness and all that kind of stuff—not that. But the purpose to advance warning of such terrors . . . it serves to remind you: "Well, hey! It's time to do what I can do to create something more benevolent for myself and others that might be felt by these beings, because they're going to sample the energy of Earth." They're going to sample the energy of plants, of animals and then, in that order, of humans. And they're going to sample that from a great distance. Something that travels very well, that they will be able to sample at a distance, is radiated energy, and we all know that love naturally radiates and warmth naturally radiates. So if you're doing the love-heat, they're going to feel it. They sample the planet—what do they sample the energy of? They're sampling the love-heat!

They're going to feel from the planet that the love-heat capacity of the planet has been decreased because of all the mining and because of the planet reacting to things that aren't in the right place, what you call pollution. Then they're going to sample the plants—how do the plants feel? "Well, there don't seem to be as many plants as there used to be." You know that's true. Then they're going to sample the animals. "Well, there aren't as many animals as there used to be." In short, they're going to feel how much love-heat is naturally being radiated by these natural beings. And then they're going to feel human beings who, from their point of view, are not natural, because you're not living in the natural way that plants and animals and planets live, but you're here to learn something new. You're the Explorer Race.

So have you discovered this love-heat as the foundation of all life? Have you discovered it and are you doing it? They're going to sample it. If they feel it, they're going to say, "Well, the planet doesn't feel that good, the plants and the animals, they don't feel that good, but we feel from the human beings this love-heat, and we didn't feel that before. Sixteen hundred years ago when we came here, the general feeling then was to say, 'Let's put an end to it,' even though we didn't. But we're feeling that now from human beings, so let's say, 'Okay!'"

The main thing is, I want you to be conscious of the fact that it is in your power to transform things, just as it is in your disempowerment to react only to your conditioning and say, "Oh, woe is me," when you are creators-in-training. You know, you can look around a house and say, "Oh, it's so dusty, it's so dirty. Oh, woe is me," or you can say, "Gosh, it's dusty and dirty. I think I'm going to get a broom and sweep it out, and boy, it'll look a lot better." That's creation. It might seem like a mundane level of creation, but it's certainly creation.

And what you're saying is, everyone on Earth has the capacity to feel this love-heat and to change it.

Yes. Not everybody will be able to readily access it immediately, but enough people will. So that's the whole point: the more people who can feel it, the better. The main thing they reach for to sample is the one thing—they are sampling the sweetness of life. Love, warmth: that is the sweetness of life. "Well, this doesn't feel too sweet and that doesn't feel too sweet, but the human beings, they seem to have more of this sweetness of life, so . . . okay, I guess we'll let them be, and on we go."

You're into Application Now

Do the beings on Planet X live on this vehicle that they have created and take from place to place?

That's about it, really—it is a service. Think about it. You know, if you had something going wrong on your planet and you were suffering, you would want someone to come along and put an end to your suffering so you could go on and reincarnate somewhere else and live more benevolently. I realize that sounds a bit ruthless, but that's basically what they do. They travel around and check up on things. If things are way, way out of balance, they make recommendations. Then eventually people come along after them, people like them—meaning in their group—and they check up on things again. And if it's still that way or worse, then they just say, "Okay, let's do something about it." But until the third group comes around, there's still time for change. In short, things don't happen overnight; they're not arbitrary. But, in time, if things change or at least show the potential for change, then they'll say, "Oh well, you know, things are getting better."

But do they understand that we'll be on another timeline soon? I mean, do they see that?

Well, they can access that. They are advanced beings. We're not talking about dense beings here; they understand what you're striving for. But you are not going to get on another timeline just by waiting around for it to happen. You have to do things to make it happen. I think that's quite clearly revealed in *Explorer Race: Techniques for Generating Safety*. You don't just sit back and wait for it to happen.

But can't they see the progress we're making?

My friend, say you're in a kitchen making soup and you tell me it's soup, but I taste it and it tastes like dishwasher water and I tell you, "This tastes like dishwasher water." You taste it and say, "Well, I know it does, but I'm making soup and it will taste better in the future." That doesn't alter how it tastes. In short, they gotta go by the evidence. It's not what it's going to be, it's not what it could be, it's not what it might be . . . it's what it is. They're going to sample the energy and make a decision based on what is, what they feel—not based on what could be, what might be, what should be, none of that. In short, they are evidence gatherers; they make a report and a recommendation.

And off they go.

And off they go, that's right. But they're not going to bring lightning bolts to hurl at you. However, that doesn't mean that you won't have thunderstorms and whatnot; the Earth will do what it can to support your need for drama and to be tested.

Thunderstorms are only to support the drama and to test us?

Well, granted, the exchange of electricity from the sky to the Earth is part of Mother Earth's natural body, but if you have an outbreak of severe thunderstorms that are really extreme, that go on for a long time—more than what is typical for your planet—then you might reasonably say, "Something is going on." It might be a good idea for those who work on the weather to try and alter it, at least move it out to sea. There are those human beings on Earth now who work with the weather.

But what it's reflecting is the emotional imbalance of the humans in that area. Is that correct?

Well, that's a nice psychological analysis, and one might say that it's true, but there might be more to it than that. The whole point is that it doesn't make any difference what it's caused by. You're into application now, you understand? It's not about analysis. You could say, "Well, this is caused by this and this is caused by that, and if only we change this and if only we change that," and that might be nice, but you won't be able to change it immediately. What you need to do is move the weather. It's like . . . if the car slips off the jack and falls on you, you don't want someone to come along—if you don't mind my analogy—and tell you how you should have propped the wheels up better. You want someone to come along and lift the car off you. [Chuckles.] In short, it is about application, all right? Analysis has been in the past and conditions and understanding and all that kind of stuff. Now you're into application. What are you going to *do* about it? That's why I've been—how can we say?—sipping tea on another planet and swapping stories and letting Speaks of Many Truths and Reveals the Mysteries and other wonderful beings sit in for me and say, "Here's what you can do about it, because we've done it."

Don't Get Caught Up in the Enemy

I took a little time off so that you would understand that it's important for you to do this. It's not just about analysis; it's not about, "Hey, look at what these guys are doing." It's not about enemies. It's about you, what you can do, what you can transform. If you get caught up and attached to the idea of enemies, *you won't get it.* That's why I haven't talked about it very much. Oh, occasionally Speaks of Many Truths has talked about it, but the whole point is, what can you *do* about it? There are always plenty of sources of information of who's doing what to whom, but you know, you can build only so many prisons.

Prisons, as you know, are not about bringing about constructive change in criminals so that they will be better citizens and feel good about one another and feel good about life. People are sent to prison to suffer. And while they're there, they're in crime school. So it's safe to say that prisons are not even remotely doing what they're intended to do. They're certainly not protecting society from the criminals, because they go there and suffer miserably, scandalously and outrageously, or cause suffering to others but suffer themselves. They get out, and the only thing they really want to do, unless they have monumental self-control, is to either revenge themselves—which is why the police and the guards are always nervous about prisoners getting out—or they want to kill themselves. In short, prisons are a scandal. I've talked about prisons before, and I'm bringing them up again because this is not about enemies; this is about what you can do to transform yourself and, if others like it, to share the technique with them. You don't send the love-heat to others; you do it for yourself and it naturally radiates. And there are other things . . . many things are built on that. But first you must build a good foundation, and the love-heat is the foundation.

That's all I'm going to say about that. I will say this in closing: Don't get caught up in the enemy. Chances are, even on Earth you have very much in common with them and only a small amount that is different. So if you do the love-heat and other things like that, you will discover how much more you have in common, how much easier it is to communicate and how very much you want to help one another resolve your real problems—and not just perpetuate the revenge. Learn to understand that you are here to resolve, not just to revenge yourself. Resolve means change, cure, benefit; that's what it's about. Learn that, apply the techniques and discover that no matter what "enemy" or "terror" seems to confront or threaten you, there are things you can do as an individual—to say nothing of what you can do in groups—that can transform the worst terror. If you don't believe me, ask Tom.

The Stock Market and Business Prospects

Zoosh

June 18, 2002

I *understand that the scenario for business this year was that there would be an upward bump in the business index at Christmas 2001, then it would be looking up by February and by June it would all straighten out. That doesn't seem to be happening.*

Oh, I disagree with you; in fact, it is all straightening out. It's just that other things are happening to get people's attention and the stock market is reacting. Think about it. Let's take the stock market, for example. One of the things that is truly baffling to some of the long-time traders is that a lot of news in the stock market is really pretty good and yet the market is plunging. And why is that? Because the investors who have come in over the past eight to ten years came in with the mythical belief that the stocks were a commodity rather than a means for an investment that would pay off in the future. And this investment that would pay off in the future was usually calculated by the price/earnings ratio, which is time-tested. But if you think of stocks as a commodity, buy the stock and sell it later (or sooner, if you like) for more money, then it tends to disrupt and corrupt the whole process of investment. So investment becomes something by which you can make the most and the fastest buck possible, and that, as you know, has done a great deal to corrupt the entire business community.

Because they're always looking at the short term.

To say nothing of the long-term investment that builds big business, makes valuable products and gives lots and lots of people a place to work so that they might support their families in the way they'd like to do and have become accustomed to. That whole model has really been crushed. What you see going on in the stock market now is that even though there are wonderful products being developed—many of which everyone will want—and there is much news to celebrate in the business community and these investors are coming to this realization, it will still take them another year or so. But the news in terms of business is actually pretty good.

Except that they are absolutely trashing some of these companies.

The Fallacy of the Big Business Model

Think about it. Think about when you were growing up, in years gone by, all right? When your parents or other adults around you spoke about big corporations, did they hold big corporations up as bastions of morality?

Sure.

They said that these big businesses could be trusted to lead you?

In moral matters

No, I don't think so. They would have said to you that these big businesses, while they produced products that you'd like to get—a new tractor and so on—that the businesses themselves were not the moral leaders of the community. The moral leaders of the community would have been the family and the church. You understand? But over the years . . . people have been conditioned for about fifty years of advertising where the business says how wonderful it is and how great it is and look at these good things we're doing for you . . . old advertising is really different. Nowadays—aside from selling their products—corporations take out advertising just to say how wonderful they are. But what you have gotten yourself into, what the current fallacy is, is that people have become not only conditioned to the false belief that business is about making money by any means necessary—in other words, it is about overnight goals, not long-range goals—but also that business is about control, period.

Control the market, control your competitors, control the buyers—everything is about control. Because people want to be rich and want to be powerful and admire those who are that instead of having the family and the church—whatever that might be . . . philosophies, New Age . . . whatever—be your benchmark for morality. This thing that you want, meaning to be rich by any means necessary through use of the method of control, is the given and the model for how you're going to live.

People are literally confronting the fallacy of that model right now, and what you're seeing in the stock market is the breakdown of that model and the realization that it is not something you want to live by. The function of this breakdown is that people are shocked, outraged and literally have their feelings hurt because these giant corporations that were exhibiting the qualities of wealth, power and control they wanted to have for themselves and were trying to emulate for themselves so that they could be wealthy, powerful, controlling and rich and all of this, are breaking down because that whole concept is breaking down. They're angry at the businesses for not giving them the key to life and for falling down on that key.

It's like when you're growing up as a child and become a teenager and need to develop your own personality, and suddenly, even though your parents might have done nothing to anger you, you are angry at your parents because you realize they cannot be—nor were they ever intended to be—entirely the one and only model by which you live. So what you are seeing before your eyes going on in the stock market and in the business community in general, what is going on with Enron and other businesses, is truly the same. It's not just about the loss of money, which is catastrophic for many people, but it's about the loss of . . . the heartbreak, literally, is seeing that this model of living—wealth, power, control— is not one that serves you. It's literally as if these investors—especially these young investors who have been in the market for ten, some of them even twelve years—receive the shock of realization that this is not the way to live, that the way they've been controlling and manipulating and forcing isn't it.

Investments Help Good Companies Develop into Worthwhile Organizations

Now, this seems to be quite obvious to people who have moral principles that go beyond business and money, but to a great many people it isn't. That's why you have the stock market reeling when it should be spiraling up out of sight. This also suggests something to you, and that's that it's very possible that the stock market will do just that once you have gone through this period of awakening, once investors realize that some companies have really wonderful products, electronics and medical things and so on. I don't have to go into it. These companies are quite obvious; they are great investments. They are going to employ thousands and thousands of people, and everybody all over the world is going to want these products—they are great investments. And they will not only be investments that will provide products that will improve the quality of life for many people, but companies like that also need to be supported on the investment level simply because of what they have to offer their workers and because they will develop into worthwhile organizations.

So, investors, use the time-tested techniques. What kind of management does the company have? Do not just look at price/earnings—when companies are starting off, there's a lot of investment, but there are not a lot of earnings. Look at what kind of management the company has, what kind of product it has. Use all those techniques, and you will make a good long-term investment. Don't think about it as something you're going to sell and make a quick buck on. Think of it as something you're going to buy, hold and receive payments from in the form of earnings per stock, the quantity of stock you have—as something that will pay off, not only for you, but for your family and your heirs in the future. In short, be working on foundations, not just towers into the sky. And know that as you go through this growth—and you're literally going through it now, all the investors, not the old-timers in the market but *all* investors—as you go through this and learn this (and you're maturing and learning it now), you will then gradually become educated. Go with these time-tested methods and rebuild your stock market.

Now, it has been inflated. I've said this for a long time, and other beings have said it, including people. It is adjusting itself, but in time it will readjust itself. And—I'm talking about the U.S. stock market here, not just foreign stock markets—I wouldn't be at all surprised, once you make the adjustment, to see the Dow, let's say, up in the general area of seventeen thousand, something like that, maybe a little beyond that, within three to five years. So that's my comment on business. And remember about this whole thing that I mentioned, that once investors shift into the time-tested manners and means of obtaining stocks, waiting for earnings and passing the stocks on to their heirs, they'll shift from being "instant-gratification" or "now" investors to one of the long-term investors who built the business economy in your country as well as in other industrialized nations. And that will help a lot.

Full Employment Makes a Big Difference

I cannot tell you what a difference it will make having full employment in your country and what a huge difference it might very well make in other countries as well. How do you think the Palestinians would feel if they not only had their own piece of land so they could say, "This is mine," but if they were all working or had jobs they liked? If they were employed, making good livings for their families and for their children, things would be very different. There is one thing about old Christian philosophy that is sometimes—not all the time—true, and that's that idle hands . . . you know that old comment. It's not that you can't be so-called "idle" sometimes, because sometimes the mind and the heart have other needs. But if people are not working, not making money, not doing something they want to do, that they find interesting, not producing products and services that they enjoy and experiencing this expression of life, not enjoying the vital creation elements of the economy and growing food and selling it and just enjoying life, then that lack of feeling creative and productive is crushing and creates despair. So full employment and interesting employment . . . you're a grocer, but you want your children to go to college so that they can be scientists or doctors or attorneys or whatever you've envisioned for them or whatever the children want. All that is good.

And just something like the maturing of the investors in your stock market and the shift from the "get rich now at any cost" goal to the "let's build for the long run and improve the quality of life" model is going to go a long way toward improving the quality of life. And someday it won't even be necessary to do anything but show your ID when you go to the airport or run your ID through the scanner. You won't have to do any more than that. Because everybody will be working and your products will be selling in their country and their products will be selling in your country, so things are going to get better—not back to normal, but on to something better.

That's wonderful. You got positively lyrical there.

In that case, I should sing good night!

9/11 Catalyzes Feelings of Compassion and Global Unity

Zoosh

July 30, 2002

Now that you have discovered your vulnerability, it is time to be compassionate toward other countries and cultures that have been vulnerable and have suffered. Even many of your closest allies have suffered. Remember, war is not something that happens "over there"; it's not just something that happens somewhere else. You in the United States are blessed with good neighbors—Canada and Mexico are your friends. Oh, you might have this complaint or that complaint about your neighbors, as you often do with those who live next door. But really, think about what could be. Think about what other countries have had to tolerate. Think about how France and Germany have struggled over the years. Yet you find yourself now in close feeling, good feeling, with both those countries.

It is not that people in other countries have pointed their fingers at you, so to speak, and said, "Oh, now you see what it's like." But they have been waiting for the average American citizen to recognize that war is not just guts and glory as the movies paint it—all soldiers know that it isn't guts and glory—but rather that war is miserable, suffering, hideous and other things like that. It's important for you to become a world citizen, a global citizen. I understand that you have suffered, and I am not saying that you should suffer more. Rather, I am saying that it is time to understand that war is serious business and not something to pursue for simple reasons of economics, finance and other things.

This is not to say that such things have not been the cause of wars in the past. Many countries, I should think, certainly regret it, and I'm sure that certain peo-

Fig. 32–1. Lights shine where the towers once stood.

ple—if they were still alive today—would even shamefacedly admit that many wars were started for strictly financial reasons. But you know, now your world and the citizens in your world are getting closer together, and you will continue to do that. Neither a country of a sophisticated nature nor a country that seems to be unsophisticated—"Third World," you call it—can afford to make war on its neighbors, nor can you ignore the sufferings of others who need places to live, food to eat. The United States of America with its generosity to support and sustain others, including its enemies, has been a beacon to the world. President Truman's program after World War II to support the suffering Germans is an example. This has been noted.

And so I am calling not only on politicians, who are struggling to do their job the best way they can, but on average American citizens. You are living in a republic. Write, call or use any means of communication to contact your representatives, your senators, whether they be local or national, to say you want the United States to become a beacon for peace, for economic stability and for heart values as well as head values. I grant that they might not always know what that means, but I think that you will find that they will feel the feelings—and all people feel feelings the same way, even though they do not feel them at the same time. So feel your own feelings.

The world expects the United States to be a leader, but this does not mean that you have to be a military leader. You can be a heart leader; you can be, to some extent, a political leader even. But in order to do that, you will have to go to the school of statesmanship and consult the wise people of all other lands. This terrible thing that happened to your country was not just a wake-up call that you need to be more careful, it was also a wake-up call that you need to become a global citizen.

It is not an accident that the United Nations is in the United States. Embrace your world leadership role and practice being united globally, not only with one another. I'm proud of you for the way you rallied around one another, fellow American citizens, and now you need to rally around the world as well. I know you can do it.

Crop Circle Faces Demonstrate Your Personal Creative Relationship with ETs

Zoosh

September 16, 2002

Greetings.

Greetings. Do you want to talk about the crop circle with the ET face?

I'd like to talk about the *three* crop circles with ET faces. They've appeared in different places, as is typical for such things. One of them appeared recently on the sand, and I believe that was in the Samoan Islands. One of them appeared in the snow, up in the general area of the permafrost, in northern America. And one of them appeared in the UK, as it's called, but I'm not going to comment on the popular one, all right? I'm going to leave that for experts to analyze, and there's a reason.

Generally speaking, I find that commenting on this particular subject, about things that other people are exhaustively commenting on, is a bit like saying I approve or I disapprove, and I don't really want to do that. I'd rather bring forth new information that enlightens and prompts interest in the *purpose* of crop circles, rather than just saying yes, no or maybe. That is how I feel, and I think it's important so that I do not become identified as a judge or a jury.

Crop Circles Are Meant to Stimulate Your Imagination

But there's no way to get pictures of the ones you're going to talk about.

So what? What do you need pictures for? It is better to have them described to you. If you have pictures, then you will all have to say, "That's how it looks," but if you have general descriptions, then you can say, "Well, maybe that's how it looks," or at least you can form up the pictures in your own minds. The whole purpose of the crop circle pictures that are authentic, you understand, is to stimulate your imaginations, prompt you to have feelings, support, nurture and sustain your own inner magical creative power. Period. That's the whole purpose of crop circles.

It's not a big issue about a language, all right? I know there are some people channeling that, and I'm not saying no, but I am saying that the whole point is to have a physical impact on you. Obviously, ETs or even people from your own planet from the past cannot write down their language and hope against hope that you will understand that language thousands of years into the future. There's always the occasional rarity where you do understand the language or you are able to interpret it, but as archaeologists well know, that is the exception. So it is pictures, and the ancients left pictures for you for the same reason that the ETs leave pictures for you. So my description of what crop circles do largely covers the ancient pictographs and even pictograms in some cases.

And the cave paintings?

That's right, and rock art and so on. It's intended to have a physical impact on you. It's not intended to be a language in itself, though I honor that interpretation by others. So let's talk about the one in the permafrost.

The Orion Face in the Snow

When you say North America, is that in Canada? Or do you mean the North American continent, so it could be way up by the Arctic Circle?

It could be. It isn't.

Can you say where it is?

It is where I said it was, and I'm not going to go any further than that. I don't want people traipsing all over there scaring the local population. Well, now we'll talk about the pictures of *who* they are.

The one in the permafrost, if you were to see it, it would look very much like a human being—just a face—with a couple of exceptions. One of the exceptions is that the top of the head is clearly bald and yet there's something delicate about the face, so it would prompt one to think that this is a woman with the top of her head bald. Also, there are no distinct eyebrows. In fact, the being does not have eyebrows. And the nose is wider than your nose is. It begins at the brow . . . all of your noses have a certain narrowness there. But the nose is wider there.

Those are the only real appearance differences, and other than that, if you saw the picture, you could say, "Well, that's an odd-looking human being." And if the people were here, you would say the same thing, that they were unusual-looking human beings and so on. But they would, for all intents and purposes, appear to be human. They have this ET . . . they're from Orion, Orion of today. A benevolent being for you.

It is very much like triggering a response. You could say to me reasonably, "But Zoosh, who's going to see it?" And I will say, "The messengers will see it." And you might reasonably say, "Who on Earth is that?" And I will say, "They're winged creatures who will fly over it, look down, notice it, and they will pass it on. Eventually the word will get out—in dreams, by the vision of birds, all right? So there's that.

Birds are very important, I might add. In general, in crop circle formations, as farmers and others who are around these things a lot know, one of the first things that happens—and not just because food is more readily available—is that birds whiz in, eat the grain and go on. And in the process, of course, they take in the energy, and wherever they fly, they tend to distribute it. As you know if you're a long-distance runner or one who works out vigorously on a frequent basis, when you are working out, your energy sort of splays out all over the place. Well, that's how it is with birds: when they are flying, their energy broadcasts all over the place. So that's why they are often promptly in crop circles.

The Arcturian Face in the Sand

Moving on to the one in the Samoan Islands, here we have a being who looks radically different—doesn't look much like you. As a matter of fact, the youngsters who saw it before it disappeared because of the tides and water didn't really identify it right away as a being. They thought that someone drew a circle and then put the face of something kind of like an animal, but they had never seen an animal like that before. So they wondered about it. But it was seen by human beings.

That being is from a distant galaxy, one that you will not explore for a long time—Arcturus. And it is not a being you would identify as being in the family of humans. Still, the head was shown as humanoid, and what was pictured was a child in that race of beings. This was done because it was known that those who would see this image would be children, and the energy that the children picked up from this image was in fact buoyant and enthusiastic—just like energy picked up from any child anywhere and broadcast from child to child.

The Zeta Reticuli Faces in the UK

Now, the one in the UK was not really seen. There are still people in the UK who, quite reasonably, resent crop circles because they are always destroying crops, and that is an unfortunate phenomenon of crop circles. It would be better to have someplace where they could put down such a tableau, but often they choose to return, as people know, to places they've either been to before or where the energy draws them as individuals. So this particular crop circle was only present for just a few hours, and then the farmer eliminated it. I'm not saying that's a bad thing, because the energy was still present and the birds were able to fly in and out. And little flyers—many-leggeds, as some people say, or you might say insects—arrived and did their duty as well and flew off to distribute the energy.

But there's a picture on the Internet—is that not the same one?

No, it isn't. So the issue there—you wouldn't really be able to immediately notice that there was a face, but have you ever seen one of those artistic drawings that when you look at it, it first looks like a vase, and then when you look at it closely, you notice that it's two faces touching together? It was like that. So upon casual observation, it would look like a vase or just a simple diagram, you might say. The farmer assumed that it was somebody hoaxing because it didn't look like anything important—not that the farmer doesn't have skills of observation and even some interest in art, but since that kind of picture that I described is intended to fool people so they don't notice the faces right away, and since farmers have more than enough work to do just doing their occupation, that farmer didn't notice it right away. If he had noticed it, he probably would have left it there for a while because he is an art enthusiast.

So I mention that one. That one was left by a group of individuals who are particularly interested in art. They are individuals that your people will meet someday, a society referred to before as the Faun group associated with the Zeta Reticuli culture. And it is typical of them to leave something artistic that would have similar characteristics to your own art, except in this case what would have been seen would have been the profile of two of their faces—which do not look *entirely* like Zeta Reticulan beings, but there is a similarity. Still, if you put two faces on the profile facing each other, it would look like . . . kind of like a vase, if you looked at it the other way.

What was their motivation for creating it?

Their motivation was to encourage you to understand, as I said before, that your relation to ETs is infinitely more personal and creative than you realize, and that ETs are prepared to meet with you just as soon as you've demonstrated more than a tolerance for the races of human beings on Earth. This means that you have to do . . . how can we say? Say you go to the art gallery or even pick up a magazine and look through it. Very often you will see pictures of animals, photographs or paintings, and most of you find these pictures attractive, especially if they are meant to be attractive. Sometimes you will see pictures of human beings of other races, and you don't always find these attractive—sometimes it's because of the subject matter, and other times it's simply because you don't really feel that same sense of attraction to that particular race of human beings that you might feel to, say, a beautiful picture of a bear or a butterfly or something like that.

So what ETs are waiting for but feel you have progressed on, is for you to find other races of human beings attractive—whatever race you want. And there has been significant progress toward this by the human race as observed by ETs in general, and that's another reason they're making their presence known with these crop circles, including the one that everyone's all excited about in the UK, which appears to depict a Zeta Reticulan.

Two Earlier Versions of the Zeta in the UK

Can you say who put down the one that looks like a Zeta and what their motivation was?

That crop circle—which, I might add, is not the original version of that one, and I'm not going to define that any further—has been placed twice in the UK before. Once it was erased by a farmer who didn't appreciate it, partly because it took up so much room. Think about it. If you go to all the trouble to plant a crop . . . and anybody who's ever been involved with gardening, to say nothing of farming, knows that it's a big job. And most farmers don't get the credit that they thoroughly deserve for the effort that's involved. After all, what does it do? It only feeds people in the world [chuckles]—a pretty important job. And so if somebody comes along and—regardless of the spirituality and the purpose—destroys a considerable portion of that crop, you don't usually have a real good feeling about that. So don't feel bad if farmers destroy crop circles out of some frustration.

So one of them was destroyed that way. And another one was not in a place where there are crops. As a matter of fact, it was in an area in the northern part of the island; it took place in a snowy area. It didn't last, but it was seen by quite a few people. I might add, however, that many people up in that northern area are disinclined to yak, as it were (or gab, if you like), to the rest of the world about what they see. They might see it, they might talk it over amongst themselves, they might speculate about what it means, but they're not necessarily going to talk about it to "outsiders," from their point of view. So it's not the first time that this picture has been seen.

Can you say who put it down?

Who put it down? I'll say who put down the first two. That's as far as I'll go. The first one was *not* put down by Zetas; it was put down by Orion individuals. And the reason they put it down is that they wanted to show you that these beings you hear about—sometimes in "con" rather than "pro" ways—are actually loving beings. That's why the first time they put it down, they included on the fringes what would look like crescents, meaning . . . you have seen a crescent moon. We really need a drawing here, but I can pretty much describe it for you: There was the face, and then in the lower left and in the lower right, and I think also in the upper left and, to a lesser degree, in the upper right, you would have seen crescents, but the crescents would have been sculpted in such a way that they would look like smiles. They weren't intended to be crescent moons; they were intended to *indicate* a smile. This was to suggest that the being pictured was actually good, a friend.

The second time, besides the face, one saw a ship pictured—clearly a ship— and that was also to indicate that they've been here before. It wasn't to suggest that they'll be here again, even though they might come at some time in the future, but they will wait until they are quite certain that they will be welcome. And then they are more or less likely to encourage the members of the Faun group to come because they think you will probably find them a lot of fun and you'll find them artistic and witty and charming. Everybody's going to want somebody from the Faun group at their party.

As far as the one being seen now, I'd say that that one is a little bit more . . . clinical. I'll leave it at that.

Crop Circles Can Be Made from a Distance

Now let's talk about who put down the second picture in the snow in northern England. That one was put down by the Pleiadians at a considerable distance, all right? That's the thing that is not really understood by people who speculate about crop circles. There is a strong belief that one must be practically on top of the tableau—the slate, if you like—to sketch the drawing, but that's not true at all. One can be off quite a distance and do this.

Beyond our solar system or within our solar system?

Well, let's just say, at quite a distance. I think that's important. There's a reason.

So they use lasers or something?

No. They use something. It's important not to say too much. Why might that be?

Why can't you talk about it?

There's a reason That's because you are already—in many of your societies— experimenting with this ability yourself. They don't use lasers.

Is this a mental ability? A spiritual ability?

No.

Experience Creation in a New Way

Zoosh, Reveals the Mysteries and Miriam

September 2002

Zoosh: Understanding Attraction

Those of you who find that the coming year [2003] has distractions will also find that it has attractions. You will find a couple of things functioning here that will surprise you. For one, you will find that you are attracted to people in ways most of you have never been attracted before. By this I do not simply mean sexually, but rather that you will be attracted to people, wanting to make friends or do things together, even things you don't normally do with anybody other than the friends or family you now have—activities, picnics, sports, whatever. You will find that certain people look more appealing, even people you would not normally want to include. Don't be shy about that, especially if he or she is responsive. The unity of people is beginning. Don't feel so bad [chuckles].

Meet Unlikely People

Why do I put it this way? Those of you who feel that you are safer or more comfortable with one type of person might be a little unsettled by having these unfamiliar feelings frequently this year and, for some of you, well beyond this year. They will arise regardless of whether people are like you and your friends and family or not. Try to get over your feelings that it must be only the people you've always known, and reach out. Say, "Would you like to join us? We're having a meal," or "We're going to the movies. Would you like to join us?" If that person doesn't want to or if there's not a return smile, he or she doesn't make eye contact, then go on about your life. But perhaps you will have him or her sit down and enjoy tea with you in a restaurant or do some other casual human activity that does not make a big impact on your life. Just try it. Talk, even at the bus stop or around the water cooler, as you say.

Attraction is a funny thing. You will find that your feelings of attraction will be heightened in this coming year. You will find that the function of those feelings will be heightened as well—meaning the way you know physically in your body that you are attracted to someone or something. And you will find it much more difficult to ignore those feelings. This does not mean that you have license to become a pest [chuckles] about people who do not want your attention. Learn to work with these feelings. You might have made a mistake. Maybe it's not the person you thought; maybe it is someone who looks like that. Or maybe the person does not want your attention, you see, which might be the case. Maybe you are right; maybe you are attracted, maybe you do want to include him or her, but if he or she is not ready, give that person permission to say, "No," or "Not at this time." There will be others you will feel this attraction toward, many opportunities.

Develop Your Own Sensing System

Understand that the physical feeling of attraction within you is heightened in this coming year because it is time for you to begin to learn the feminine means of creation—and it is not sufficient for only women in your culture to learn this. Women know a great deal about the feminine means and qualities and functions of attraction. Men must feel it as well, not only to begin to resolve some of the more male-dominated problems—meaning wars, disputes and long-standing antagonisms—but also to find solutions that do not involve control, manipulation or force. How can we fit this into what works for us? Or, as feminine attraction qualities really work, what can we fit into what to accomplish our purpose?

It is as if you are developing your own sensing system—not a *mental* sixth sense, but a *feeling* sixth sense. That's why it has been difficult for you to mentally construe, create and theorize about how the so-called sixth sense works. I'm not just talking about precognition but about the means and the manner of knowing how to create in ways that are benevolent for all life around you. I'm talking about what is naturally attracted to what to produce the qualities, the goal, the purpose and the ideals of what it is we're actually trying to achieve or a step toward that. And as you know, the journey begins with steps. So I want you to be aware of that.

New Qualities of Attraction

It's my job to give you the mental overview, the concept, the understanding to know what is physically happening to you. Your powers of attraction—not just how others might be attracted to you, but more to the point, your function of physical attraction (how it feels to you, what you know in your body, how you feel in your body)—are being not only activated but heightened in this year and, for some of you, beyond. You can begin to understand creation from an attraction point of view rather than from a strictly control-and-manipulation creation point of view. It is not time to be learning how to hammer the nails, how to force these two boards together, but rather what kind of shelter naturally seems to attract one piece to another to form protection and nurturing for yourself and your loved ones. I grant, that's a ways off. You're not going to immediately learn which stone is attracted to another stone so it can make a structure that will remain standing for thousands of years, which will create seams and so on that will defy the stonecutter's current understanding of how to achieve it.

The more you learn about the actual qualities of attraction, the more you will discover that your capacities are much greater than you thought. Attraction is not just about, "Who do I want to go to the dance with?" [chuckles] or "Who will I go to the movies with this week?" Attraction goes right down to the very basic level, how the seed knows where to sprout, which sperm finds which egg to create the exact child the mother wants. Understanding attraction will allow you to experience creation in a new way. I wish you well in your pursuits of attraction, and I think you will enjoy it.

Reveals the Mysteries: Apply Benevolent Magic

In this coming year [2003], you will be called upon to perform tasks that you have never been called on to do before. The workings of your physical body will now begin to break through the chains of conditioning that you've experienced in this life. You have all been conditioned to believe that your power and influence are limited. Sometimes the conditioning was unintentional, and other times it was not only intentional but even subversive. This kind of subversion sometimes exists to sell you products or services, but other times it has the hidden agenda of making you subservient and receptive to whatever immediate stimulation can be activated in you. You know you've all responded to advertising or even made spontaneous purchases at the market or the auto store.

I want you to know that your physical body is not an accident or some scientific model. Nor is it an example of evolution—which, by the way, is a theory but not a natural fact, though those who believe in evolution try to persuade others that it is a natural fact. Your physical body is very carefully constructed by Creator—not only to activate the functions of life within you, but to be able to connect to Its overall Spirit as well as the soul personality you express in life. But there are other factors that sometimes show themselves in a given life in a spectacular fashion. You all have heard about the woman or boy who has executed some act of great strength in an unexpected fashion, lifted a car off of someone just like that; it makes the news. Scientists are, regardless of their theories, essentially baffled about how this is done.

This is an example of the capacity your body truly has, and your Bible as well as your other religious books have this correct: Your body is fashioned after the Creator's body, only in miniature. The Creator, while not having a physical body as you understand physicality, still has the capacity to create. You might say that the Creator is condensed creation, which would suggest that your physical body is also about creation. Because of this fact, you are being activated—not only on the physical level by the means I suggested in your conditioning, but more to the point, by Creator—to be creative in ways that imitate Creator's desires for your benevolent good.

Making Things Better

How might you see this begin to show itself this year? You will all begin to have desires that feel like they can go beyond wishes, hopes and dreams to be able to make things better. Whether this "making things better" is a desire or a need, a hope or something that seems to be impossible, you will have the desire. More to the point, you will have a feeling that it is possible; you need only to know how to do it. This is a huge step for you all, considering the lifetime of conditioning you've had. Think about it. Think about something you'd like to do that's benevolent. How many of you are ill or injured and would love to have certain capacities, or have fears you'd like to transform into strengths and so on? It's easy to think of something.

This coming year, through books such as the *Shamanic Secrets* series and teachings in the pages of the *Sedona Journal of Emergence!*, it will be my intention to instruct you on how to achieve those goals in a practical, physical sense through the further understanding and application of what your friend Zoosh has called "benevolent magic." Benevolent magic is just a fun way to refer to natural creation, which is possible by any being in the creation of this Creator. You are activated, yes; you've been activated before, in steps to prepare you. You've already been given instructions. But in these brief comments, I will give you a glimmer of what you might expect to be able to do, along with some homework.

Creativity—The Capital "C"

Once you've done the work, you will be able to begin working with something that is an actual substance. From a scientific point of view, it would seem to come out of thin air—meaning that what it produces is not quantifiable or measurable before the effects are noted. If you could measure this substance, you would call it creativity. In time you might come to refer to it simply as the capital letter "C." Some of you will refer to it using the capital "C" followed by the digit "2," meaning creative, meaning you as Creator's children are "2." Do you understand the digital reference?

Here's some homework for you in the next few months—especially during January, February and the first part of March—if you have a pain, an ache or a disability in your bodies. This is for you to practice on your own bodies—not on others, even though you love them and want the best for them. You learn what works on the basis of your own physical feelings. I might add that your physical feelings are the divine touch of Creator, Its touch from the inside out. You know that Creator loves you, and yet if you do not pay attention to these feelings, Creator will find a way to make them more obvious and hard to ignore [chuckles]. This is not because Creator wishes to punish you, but rather because Creator needs you to pay attention so that you will know the consequences of not doing so. This is not punishment but an effect. If you are going to learn how to create, you must begin experiencing creation that you prompt in your own physical body because, young or old, you've had a lifetime to learn how you personally, physically feel in your body—if you're old enough to understand this, that's the distance of your lifetime. You've had this understanding; now you're going to re-create it.

Healing with Love-Heat and Light

Here's your homework: For those of you who can do the love-heat/heart-warmth/physical-warmth [see p. 23]—let's not call it an exercise, it's an *experience*—for those of you who can do this experience, do it that way. For those of you who can visualize, visualize condensed white and gold light. White light alone will not work. Sometimes in your visual spectrum you might see light as white when it contains other colors. But if you see light as gold, it will be easier for you to assimilate all colors. This is something your science actually knows. So I recommend white and gold, but you can do just gold if you wish.

Put the warmth or the light in a place that is the exact point where you feel some pain, discomfort or need in your physical body, even if it's just a stomachache. If you've experienced a wound or an injury or were born without some part of your body that you'd like to have, address your pain first. If you don't have any pains, don't be too shy to put that warmth or that light in some area of your body where something is missing or where you'd like to be better in some way. But you can't fine-tune it at this point. You have to trust your body. If your body has pain at some given point, it will be receptive to this warmth or the light right in that spot, and your body will know what to do with that. These are lessons in creation.

What about those of you who do not know or have not learned how to do the love-heat? Feel love and experience the heat as often as you can. Wherever it comes up, feel into it and go into it more, feel it more. I want you to actually move it to the spot where you have the pain, even though you might feel it in your chest or abdomen area. This is the next step. For those of you who do not do the love-heat, use gold light, use the visualization of gold light [see p. 32].

Healing with Your Tone

What about those of you who do not do either? Are we going to leave you out? No! We're going to do something else. That's why you have abilities and senses that are born naturally with you. Feel where that pain is; if you have more than one pain, pick one place. If it turns out that it helps the other places, that's fine, but pick one place. Then make a sound. It's not a tone that you measure musically, saying, "This note, not that note." Rather, it is a sound that is the most comfortable sound you can make. Go up the scale [sings] and find, in your body, the exact musical tone that you can make that feels the most natural and easy for you to do. Make that tone, and while you're making it, if you can, lightly touch the spot where you have the pain. Or if the pain is too much, you can touch the air right above that spot, five or six inches away if you like, and make the tone. Just naturally breathe in, making the tone as you breathe out and so on. Do that for a few minutes. Do all of these things, whichever way you do it, just for a few minutes.

But what if you feel like doing something else with the tone? You might open your mouth and go a-a-a-h. Maybe you'll make the tone with your teeth clenched, not with your mouth opened [makes that sound]. That's fine. If you want to make the tone with your hand, one hand or the other or both, in some gesture in front of you, do that—whatever feels good to you physically. Don't make a gesture that has a meaning known and understood by your society, because that gesture will have been mentally conditioned into you to mean something else, even if you are using it for the first time. In short, it is to be a natural motion of your hands, however you feel it's best to place them. Experiment a little bit, those of you doing the tone.

Healing with Fragrance

Now let's move on. What about those of you who can't easily do any of those things? Let's give you an option. Some of you are very good with smell, very attuned to fragrances. This is what I'd like you to do. I want you to obtain some cinnamon and smell it. Notice the fragrance. Try to get it from an herb store or even a cooking supply store, because it will come in some form where its odor will be more significant. You want something natural, with no preservatives. See if you can memorize that smell. Remember, this is about creation, which you do with your body, and it is intended to have an effect on your body. Why do you think you have pain in the first place? It is to perform creation, to resolve your own pain. I know, you would have liked to have known this a long time ago! But you know now, and you have the motivation to do something about it, don't you?

Now, this is what to do with the fragrance method. Smell cinnamon as much as you can over the course of a few days—not just when you have the time, but when you can be relaxed. You will be prepared to perform the creation work when you feel the pain, wherever you feel it. It could very well be temporary—a headache, a stomachache, some kind of thing that passes or some other injury you might feel or long-term discomfort you try to ignore. If you don't feel the pain, don't do anything. Wait until you do. You're a human being—you'll feel one eventually! Those of you who use the fragrance method will have memorized the smell of cinnamon by that time.

Hold your hand or the fingertips of your right hand—if you want to try your left hand, you can—parallel to your body, not pointing at your body, but parallel to it, right over your body, maybe five or six inches above where you feel that discomfort. And remember, don't pull out the cinnamon at that point; you will have had to have smelled it enough that you memorized the smell. Remember the smell of cinnamon. Focus only on your body's recollection of the smell of cinnamon, and do that for a few minutes.

About Your Homework

That's what I'm going to recommend for your initial homework. You have something that works with physical feelings, you have something for visualization, you have a tone and you have a fragrance. That's four choices. Just do one, whichever one works best for you. I've offered you the fragrance method as an alternative. Some of you have that capacity, and it might be good for you to begin to use it. That's your homework in the coming months and perhaps years. We'll give you more homework that will work forward from this point, initially for your physical body, and someday for the physical body of Earth. First you begin with your own body. Those of you who are in the healing arts, whatever form that might take, might also get instructions to work on others and support them to work with their bodies. The rest of you can follow instructions if you like to support and work on with and for Mother Earth's body, that she might feel better. Don't use all the methods you have learned before, but use the material- and physical-mastery lessons you will receive, building on the *Shamanic Secrets* series that Speaks of Many Truths and myself have given. I wish you good life in these pursuits and good life in general.

Miriam: Touching Living Flowers

M y name is Miriam. I am one of the essences of the natural world. I am associated with water and the more delicate essences of life around—fragrance, the energy bodies around flower petals and the means by which such physical membranes are attracted to all those who might need them. I will speak only at this time. In the year to come, flowers will become much more sensitized, especially through their petals—not de-sensitized, but sensitized—to the touch and even the near touch of the human being.

Change the Way You Touch Flowers

As you might already know, flower petals do not like to be physically touched by the human being because of skin oils. The way the human being touches the flower petal needs to change. When a flying creature lands on the flower, it is often something very feathery that actually touches it, like fine hairs. For those of you who are around flowers this year, try to touch them first with the hairs on the back of your hand or leg or another part of your body. For most of you, the hairs on your head have been desensitized, except for the ones on the back of your neck. You can have a friend touch you to the flower petals this way, but not if the flower has been moved—you will have to lean down to the flower.

This is the best way for human beings to touch flower petals. I'd recommend working this touch first with roses, dandelions, violets, peonies or apple or cherry blossoms. That's what I recommend. All of those flowers can only imbue the human being with nurturing love and support qualities.

Flowers Will Diminish Hunger

If you are hungry but cannot reach or obtain food or for some reason cannot eat at that moment, touch these flower petals with those hairs on your body and your hunger will either completely go away or greatly diminish. If you can allow the flowers to grow where they naturally grow, that is best. The touch will not work or the effect will be greatly diminished if the flower does not grow where it has naturally sprouted up. The next best place is in a garden where the flowers can grow undisturbed, where they are not disturbed much, rarely poked at, and where weeds are not constantly being dug out of the ground. Understand that what you call a weed is often a companion, especially for a flower that has been planted by a human being in a place where it would not naturally sprout up on its own. What you call a weed is actually a natural companion that the flower welcomes to remind itself of the natural world. Please do not pull up many of these weeds if you can possibly help it. Then lean down or, if you have hairs on your arm, touch the flower petals—the outer ones are best, meaning those that fold outward. Just touch. Your hunger will go away.

My job is to prepare flowers for this touching. People who work with herbs and plant essences have known for years and years that these things can be helpful to people. But what even some of them do not know is that contact with these flowers in the way I mentioned can also be very healing.

The Flower Should Be in Its Natural State

Now, if you were to cut the flower, bring it to your body and touch your body, the effect would be about 1 percent, almost nothing. So the flowers that grow where they are welcomed by nature, natural and wild, are best, but those in a garden are almost as good. In a greenhouse, shut off from the sun and only receiving the sun, the wind and the touch of the flying creatures by accident, the effect is about 70 percent. In your home, with windows open or at least partway open sometimes so there is an air exchange, it's about 60 to 55 percent. In a home where the windows are shut almost all the time, the effect is about 50 percent. In a home where the windows are shut all the time, it's about 40 percent. In an office where the windows are shut all the time, which is typical in offices these days, the effect is about 20 percent.

This gives you some idea of the effect of these things. It might interest you to know that this kind of contact with flowers is even more effective when the humidity is higher, because water in its gaseous form heightens the experience. This does not mean that in a dry climate the percentages are decreased, but rather that in a moist climate the percentages are heightened.

The Flying Beings Will Contact Flowers

So I'm going to recommend that as homework. Try to make this contact in the safest, most comfortable way for you, and try to take note of these flowers, how their amazing life-giving qualities are well known to the little beings who fly into them or contact them in some way. They do this not only to consume what the flowers offer in the way your observers have noted, but sometimes the flying beings need some support, some nurturance. They will contact the flower, not only in the place to which you know they are being attracted (the center, the blossom, and so on), but sometimes they will crawl about on the outer parts of the blossom. When they do this, very often they are obtaining the physical support they need for the quality of their own life. If they have been trained by their own cultures to bring the essence of that wondrous energy back to their own colonies and families, they will pass it on to those who were unable to fly to that flower, usually the young who are not mature enough to make that journey.

If those natural beings know this and do this, there is no reason that you as human beings, who are natural in your own way but come here to learn natural creation, cannot do so as well. I wish you well in your journey, and I recommend that you try this out if you can. I think you will find it very enjoyable and in the future will have a much greater appreciation for the effects living flowers and their blossoms—rather than those that have been severed from their bodies—can have on you.

What You Can Do Now to Make a Difference

Zoosh and Isis
October 16, 2002

Zoosh: Commit to Humanity

All right, Zoosh speaking. Let us talk a little bit to our dear readers. Are you going to understand that in order for the world to change, you must make a choice? There is no complexity with the choice, but it requires a commitment from you, and I realize that for some of you the word "commitment" in its own right is frightening. But when you hear the choice, it won't be so terrible.

Here Is Your Choice

This is the choice—and I will phrase it for those of you who would like to say it out loud, which is the best way: "I am committing myself to join with all humanity here on Earth, to be a part of humanity, to work toward the betterment of all humanity and to see humanity as of value." That's the choice. It's simple, and yet it is vitally important because so many people tend to curse the humanness not only in themselves but also in others. It is important even if you think you are wonderful and other human beings are terrible. Your consciousness, which mentally works with your physical body, is very clear, but it is very much like a switch—it is on or off, like that. In short, it is simple. If you think that one or many other human beings are bad, then in your consciousness—which directs, supports and is sustained by your physical body and your instinct (which is made up of all but your mentality)—it all comes together to create a gradually growing snowball, and this snowball rolls downhill and gets bigger and bigger. So you eventually believe that if some humans are bad, then simply being human is bad or even a curse.

So I've given you the choice. I want to make it clear to you that it is a choice, meaning that if you cannot make that commitment, then acknowledge the truth to yourself. Say, "I acknowledge my disappointment in human beings and in humanity, and I ask that all spirit beings, all . . ."—and here you fill in the religion of your choice, whatever your gods and deities are—". . . come and generate a better race of beings on this planet. And when they do, then I'll want to join that."

You recognize that this sounds a bit like a dissatisfied statement, but in order to bring about any kind of benevolent change, it's critical for you to understand that the bedrock is that *you're a human and it's okay*. If you're human and it's not okay, it's not likely that you're going to have a lasting impact in any benevolent way. You can yell at someone and he or she will get quiet, but that doesn't mean that you've changed the way that person feels or thinks. That's an old piece of wisdom and you know it. It's been done to you before, and perhaps you have done it to others.

My message is short and sweet. Another will come along and give you another version, but I'm putting it to you like this, because it's important to make a choice.

Choose to Feel Good about Humans

You might reasonably ask, "But, Zoosh, why is this so important?" It's because right now, for the next year and a half or perhaps the next year and seven months, you are in a time that is simply labeled "Choice." During this time, you can either choose to be human and attempt to create a better life for all humans, including yourself and the ones you know and love, or you can choose to wait. That's really about what it comes down to. If you don't feel good about human beings, you're essentially waiting. And think about how it makes you feel when you wait—when you've gone to places and you've waited in line, or when you've had to wait and wait and wait for something you wanted and needed.

So this is why you are surrounded with people who are impatient, and it's all over the news headlines these days; people are sick and tired of waiting for whatever it is they want. So you see it more clearly now, eh? The choice is to either engage as a human being and help improve your life and the lives of others, or wait. And waiting, as you know, will in time make you feel impatient. If you're impatient enough, you might say or do something that you will regret—immediately or later, but you will regret it for sure.

I can assure you, self-destructive acts are not going to help you or others—and those of you who've read my words in the past know what self-destructive means, that it means harming yourself or harming another. So I call upon you to make your choice. If you like, you can leave a message in the chatroom [www.lighttechnology.com] about what is your choice and why. And I will—perhaps not immediately, but eventually—respond. So don't be shy about asking questions.

Look at your world. I want you to think about it. Look at the news and think about it; you know what's going on. And say, "What's the underlying motive of these people, regardless of what side they're on?" And in every single one of those cases in the news on TV, you will be able to say, "These people are all impatient because they've been waiting and they want what they want now." For the most part, they are doing what they are doing because they are impatient. And you can all help by choosing to be human and by embracing your humanity and by working to improve your life and the lives of your family, your loved ones, your community and the greater humanity to the best of your ability. Good night.

Isis: Choose Benevolent Goals

There are so many things going on that are causing so much fear in people. Is there someone or something behind all of this? The Bali and other bombings, the snipers, the Middle East, everything—they're not isolated incidents, are they?

It is true that in some circles is the desire to herd the global population into something like order and control. In some ways, that might be desirable by some individuals in the near future—not just to control and manipulate, but rather to create a predictable society, predictable in the sense of being largely benevolent. But it is too soon for that. You still have to resolve dilemmas, attitudes, opinions and your feelings about one another. I feel that this desire to control and maintain control, which runs throughout almost all civilizations on Earth now, is largely a precondition, a precircumstance of something that will in time be benevolent.

Technology for Benevolent Solutions

If you were to go to other planets, you would say, "This society seems very controlled." But you also would have to say that the society seems very benevolent and wonderful. The people are so happy; everyone is happy. No one is suffering. Now, I grant that those who wish to control and manipulate your societies now are not first and foremost interested in benevolence, but it is an ultimate experience that will happen here on Earth.

For example, within a generation, in no more than twenty years, the technology will exist to alter people's personalities rather than giving them lengthy prison terms for whatever their crime. They will be recognizable, meaning they will have some mark on them, but they will be delightful people to be around. Granted, they will not recognize their loved ones, if they have them, and their loved ones will feel bad about this. But they will be generically loving and friendly to everyone. They will lose their individual personalities, but it is much better than to have them go to prison and be mistreated and to come out and avenge themselves on society.

This technology is almost at perfection, but in terms of your societies, it will still take quite awhile for it to become clinically acceptable. And, of course, it is more likely to be acceptable for prisoners. The prisoners will not have it thrust upon them; they will have the choice to finish out their sentence—whether it is life in prison or forty years or what-have-you, or even the death penalty—or to accept the alternate personality program. It won't be forced upon them. Most of them will choose the alternate personality program, because once their personality is altered, they are free to go. They will not commit any more crimes in the future; they will tend to be very benevolent people, even well-accepted in society, the kind of person you'd enjoy having as a friend—friendly, cheerful. They're not going to become unintelligent. It won't affect their intelligence—with the possible exception of helping them to become more so—but it will affect their personalities and they will permanently forget who they were and what they did in the past.

Striving toward Benevolence

But for you in your now time, you have to recognize that civilization around you is radically changing. You might have to decide what you want and choose goals—meaning long-term goals—that have to do with benevolence for all beings, including yourself and your family and friends and loved ones. For short-term goals, pick things you can accomplish that are not self-destructive or harmful, meaning harming yourself or others. And take a step every week—not every day; don't overdo it—toward accomplishing your goals. It will help you. Even if you are not successful, you will learn what works and what doesn't.

You understand, what I am saying is that it is important to begin to strive toward something that is benevolent for you, your family and humanity in general—even if it means explaining to the world why your people have suffered and getting that information out to the best of your ability . . . even if it means your people might have legitimate complaints or complaints that others would at least be compassionate toward, though you're not sure the complaints are legitimate. So get involved to a degree, even if it is simply encouraging your government to get involved. Talk to people on the other side of the world, even if it means writing to them. And don't yell. Just say, "This is who I am, this is what I do. I am a human being, who are you? What do you do?"

Time to Make Friends

In short, it is time to make friends. I know that sounds silly and simplistic. But what invariably happens when people on opposite sides get to know one another—no matter what the battle, whether small or large—is that they find out how much they are alike, how very little they are different. Ask old warriors, warriors of World War II or other wars, who come together and meet one another. They almost always say after time has passed, "Wouldn't it have been better for us to have found another way to resolve this?" You understand, it is time to do what you can and be open to reading, listening or simply allowing other people to say what they believe—especially if it is a complaint, when they feel that they've been injured or harmed. I feel that your time supports this.

Computers and the Internet give so many people the chance to say how they've been harmed. And if you've been harmed, simply ask—not demand, but ask—"Who will help me?" or "Who will help that I might help myself?" Because you look around and say, "People are so selfish," and it might come as a surprise to most of you who are upset and angry and even violent that this is a time when people are more likely than at any other time to be helpful. This is not just because there's something in it for them, but simply because people are waking up. Remember, when your heart opens, the first thing that happens is all the pent-up emotions are released and expressed in some way. That's what you're going through now. But eventually, as your heart opens more, you want to talk, you want to listen, you want to resolve—and when you want to, you'll find the way. Good night.

With Absolute Perfection, There Is No Possibility of Growth

Isis

November 8, 2002

Excerpt from a private channeling, with permission.

T his is Isis.

Greetings, Isis, and with great joy I greet you.

What would you like to talk about?

Past Lives Are More of an Echo Than a Reality

I'd like to begin with a conversation about joy. I would like to have a sense of the origins, or at least the appropriate origins, of my relationship with my life mate. By what roundabout route did my life mate and I arrive here on Earth at this cycle? I have been advised by Zoosh that the prior incarnation was a particle of water existing about ten days in Earth time before my current identity. How about my mate?

I will tell you from my point of view: Your routes here were not really closely interrelated, meaning there was not "met in this life," "chose in that life," none of that. It was more a "met in this life to begin more encounters in the future."

You have to remember that this loop of time in which you are now living is really an anomalous existence, compared to other worlds. It is not in that sense a typical way of existing. Therefore, talking about the past and the future is almost conjecture, but I would say that on the basis of what I see, this is more of an anchor, meaning a beginning that launches things. But you have to remember—since this reality is an existence in what amounts to the past; it is the present that is actually a past that has been laid out from the future to correct a future that was not benevolent—that your multiple encounters with each other have yet to happen.

This is why when you came together, you felt a profound sense of familiarity, almost like, "Oh yes, of course." That is because if you were in your normal state of existence, you would have already been together for some time—off and on, granted. But in this state of existence—which is not normal for anyone in these times, I might add—you can experience familiarity, but especially in your cases, it is future. That's really why I don't like to go into past lives at all for anybody, because they are more or less theoretical, meaning past lives are more an echo than a reality. So I'd rather say that your connections are more future-based.

There Needs to Be a Sense of Continuity

As I recall, it was Zoosh's explanation (and I'm going to do my best to paraphrase) that past-life memories and that which sensitives perceive about an individual are in fact much of the time the neurons, particularly in the brain, that are remembering their lives, which then become the individual and are seen as being the lives of the individual. As I recall, Zoosh suggested that it was a device to keep the souls interested and anchored here in 3D before they flew off elsewhere. Is that a reasonably accurate remembering?

I'd say that's pretty close and as good of an explanation of the manner and means of necessary continuity as I've heard before. In order to keep people's interest in living here at all, given where you are, there needs to be a sense of continuity since it is such a hard place to be. If everyone felt that this was a completely anomalous existence without any past or any apparent future of value, the suicide rate would just continue to go up and up. So there needs to be an almost artificial continuity so that people will stay in school and not create—how can we say?—a recess period before it's time.

Then the past-life readings that are a staple of our society today are, in effect, a theatrical device to keep people engaged here.

I wouldn't want to make it sound that trite. I'd rather say: a method that can be used therapeutically in order to support, sustain and otherwise help to clarify current situations or future-based situations that are being supported, worked out or even created in this time.

Transposition of the Surface Population of Earth Is Extremely Unlikely

There is a huge barrage of channeled material that crosses my desk almost on a daily basis, some of which refers to Terra forming within Gaia in preparation for the transposition of some of the surface population at some point. Is this a likely future or simply a possible future?

Meaning that portions of the population would be transferred to some other place?

Yes, within the planet.

No. There's a lot of desire for that, and if you look at religions, you can see the corollary. I would say that it is *extremely* unlikely. I'm not ruling it out completely, but it is extremely unlikely, though I certainly see why it's attractive and why many people would feel reassured by hearing about it.

It is my memory and understanding that the bulk of the planets have their cities inside and the surface is left in what we'd call the natural state, so this may be summoning up memories for those involved in that.

I would also suggest that it isn't this planet. It is in a sense this planet, but only in a sense—meaning that it is a different incarnation of this planet in another pulse of itself, sometimes called a dimension. It is very easy to see such things. I'll tell you that if you see this planet, which you believe to be Earth, and you see underground cities or even aboveground cities or even well aboveground cities, various forms, with the Earth looking beautiful . . . people often think of this as the past or the future, when it is, in fact, simply in existence now but in a different pulse that allows more than one thing to be present relatively in the same space. This is not unlike—on a more, if I might say, high-tech mundane level—the way the same data might occupy a large area, or multiple data entries might occupy a small area for that matter. It is not much different with the same pulses occupying roughly the same area. By "roughly" I mean that there's a lot of overlap.

This Is a Teaching Society

Much of the material crossing my metaphoric desk (since it comes via computer screen) suggests that our friends from the alliance, the Anunnaki, are apparently very close to being removed, certainly the last group holding on to power. Are these correct perceptions in our present time context?

You have to understand that your civilization is in school, and in order for that school to have lessons, there needs to be a lot of push-pull. If things are perfect, then it is a poor school indeed. It may sound tough—and it isn't my nature to be that way—but for school to work, there needs to be something to want or need to achieve. Therefore, what appears to be the enemy is sometimes a taskmaster—granted, sometimes a tough taskmaster—but ultimately it is a function of a teaching society.

I know that sounds tough. You could say, "Isis, is all that suffering necessary?" and I would say, "No." But it is up to the students to choose to not only strive for another reality but to generate it attitudinally as well as spiritually. This sometimes requires, not only benevolent magic, but purpose, goals, orientation, action, activities and application. Therefore, the answer to your question is that until those things take place—because everybody wants to do it—that and those you refer to will remain.

My sense, personally, continues to be that the actual number of those holding fast to the old patterns—what I call the dark side and what you refer to at the highest levels as taskmasters—is an astonishingly infinitesimally small fraction of the number of souls incarnated, and yet they continue to march on. I gather there has to be a weighting of some kind, but I'm not sure where that critical mass shows up between the people who wish change and those who obediently continue to follow the dark side.

I don't like calling it the dark side.

I didn't think you would.

It's more like a pressure pedal. The pedal is spring-loaded, and it naturally pops up. And yet if you put pressure on the pedal, the spring might get stronger and have more resistance, but the pressure is there nevertheless. So it isn't so much that it won't happen. The pedal pops up on its own, but it is almost by way of a test and it is to say, "Do you want this? How much do you want it? Are you prepared to take the actions and do what is necessary and perpetuate those actions all the time?" It's like that. Rather than call it the dark side, and I understand why it is called that . . . but it is a test that you yourselves have created, not something that's coming from something external.

There are no externals—*at all!* So if you have created it—not unlike setting a crossword puzzle—even from some future (and a benevolent future at that), you must have created it for a purpose. If the purpose is grand, it might require a tremendous launching pad, and that launching pad would probably need serious motivation. In short, why strive for something grand if you're already very happy, if life is fine?

That sounds like the Pleiadian society.

Why strive if you're already happy and there is no need to improve things? If you want growth and you feel that there is value in it, then you might set up in an isolated place—you can almost hear this being politically arranged—a test society to see if growth could be spurred or stimulated without affecting the rest of the universe. Can't you just hear that speech being given? It would be some place that would be isolated, meaning you could look around the assemblage, so to speak, and everybody would be nodding their metaphorical heads and saying, "Well, as long as it's completely isolated." Can't you almost hear it?

So here you are, meaning almost as if everyone said, "Well, if it's worthy, go ahead, as long as no one else is affected except in a good way." In order to do that, you would have to set up conditions on this planet and all that you go to beyond this planet—but *from* this planet, meaning you're launching from this planet. So you could go out to the ends of the universe theoretically, and you would experience it as you are here as long as the condition remains as it is here without affecting anybody in their pulse of the universe, without tainting or affecting anything, until you change your attitude to make it synonymous with the rest of the universe in its benevolent state rather than anomalous. Now you can have astronauts go to other places that are experienced benevolently by various ET groups and experience them even malevolently—meaning a rock fell off a cliff and broke somebody's leg—whereas an ET might go to the same place and such a thing would never occur, because we're talking about the synonymous versus the anomalous. Understand that I'm giving you information I've not given out to others.

You Are Isolated from the Rest of the Universe

From your viewpoint, how are we doing in this particular phase of our change?

Not to sound as if I'm not taking your question seriously, but given that you get so very little help—meaning you're isolated; the rest of the universe at your natural state of being does not help at all—given that, you are literally doing as well as can be expected. In other words, no one else could do better or has done better, and it takes as long as it takes because of the almost total lack of help from the synonymous universe. And they are not going to help because if they helped, they would literally open up a door from what you are experiencing to what they are experiencing. So not only are they not allowed to help, they're not motivated to help.

So what you do, you must accomplish entirely on your own. The help you get is that you are not allowed to stay here very long, because everybody else in those natural places where you live believe that what you are doing, although it may be a great sacrifice for a greater cause, from their point of view, they feel that you are suffering and they feel sorry for you and it is their choice that you do not stay here any longer than you absolutely have to. Do you understand? It's a bit patronizing, and it is why they often sound patronizing when they talk to contactees and so on—not out of cruelty, but simply out of attitude.

This is an attitudinal situation: "You poor souls. We hope you can get out of there as soon as possible. I'm sorry you can't come to our planet." For those who have gone—they have gone to other planets, yes?—they remain isolated, meaning they are either in an isolated part of the planet or they must always wear something that energetically isolates them from the rest of the population so that they do not affect the rest of the population.

Will the Game Ever End?

It's marvelous to hear a point of view at the level that you speak. Down here, if you will, on the surface of the planet, one wonders if the game will ever end.

This "game," as you call it, is happening in such a tiny fraction . . . let's put it in the context of time. It's happening in such a tiny fraction of the sort of time that you naturally live that what seems to take so very long is actually over before you can do that. It is happening so very quickly, but to give an answer to your question, if it does not achieve its goals or a purpose—how can I put it in time so that you can understand?—in about a third more of the experience that has taken place so far, I don't see what good that is to you. But if it does not achieve that purpose, then it will be uncreated, and people will say, "Well, that's all."

And we go with it.

We'll just leave things the way they are and we'll get along without growth. So you see, those who have chosen to attempt to add growth on a personal as well as a galactic level to all these universes, believe so deeply in the value of that project that they're willing to pour all of this into it, including Creator, of course. But if it does not achieve its purpose, then it will be entirely uncreated, but only that part of the universe or universes in which there is any trace of discomfort. And then you, in your immortal personalities, will go on. But if it is uncreated, any shred of any part of you that partook in this experiment will be entirely uncreated so that you will not—nor will you ever be able to—remember it in any way.

We speak also of Creator in this particular uncreation conversation.

That's right. Creator simply will not have found that strand that prompted him to produce a universe of variety. He would have found another strand and created something else.

And that strand would not have drifted by?

It wouldn't have existed.

So there would be no Master of Discomfort or Master of Feeling?

They would have existed but in some other form. The Master of Discomfort would have been a Master of something else. The Master of Feeling might very well have existed, but there would be no feelings in any way having to do with discomfort or anything else that might prompt growth in any way.

Is the concept of growth so radical in infinity that . . . ?

Think of it this way: Imagine to the best of your ability absolute perfection. Now consider yourself living in absolute perfection. Growth would change that.

Yes. Among other things, I would not know that there was the possibility of growth if I was in perfection.

If someone else did and he or she came along and said, "You're living in perfection," and you said, "Oh, yes," and then that person said, "We're going to change it" . . . goodbye.

People Are More Aware of Discomfort

Are we in that 1 to 2 percent of discomfort that we've been speaking of? Will we say that sort of thing to someone else?

Why would you want that? "Here's 1 to 1.5 percent of discomfort. You'll hardly notice the difference, but you'll be able to learn and grow and become more." On the other side, you say, "But I am already all that I could ever choose to be and my world is perfection. Everything around me is wonderful. Why would I want to be more when I am all the more I might ever need to be?" It is philosophical, you see?

Yes, and difficult for a 3D brain to be playing with.

Yes, and that's why I don't talk about this at random.

From your viewpoint, has the percentage of discomfort on the planet accelerated or diminished since the last material I heard about some years ago?

I think there's been a slight increase, but more to the point, I would say that people are more *aware* of discomfort as well as of the discomfort of others. You are becoming more unified as a global citizen on a personal level—meaning everyone—and sometimes the discomfort you feel is not your own per se, but it is the discomfort of others. Ultimately, this is intended to motivate you to improve the comfort for all beings—not you alone, you understand, but you as a citizen. That's why people are feeling more anxious. It's not simply because they're afraid that a few individuals somewhere will be able to make your lives miserable.

You Are Beginning to Feel More

In that same context, I haven't asked in a very long time . . . are we still at 3.47?

No, I think you're closer to 3.48, but not quite. A lot of it is the freedom of feeling, meaning that your feelings were held in check to a great degree before, but now you're beginning to *feel* more. This is why when there are moments of passion, it is almost an explosion of passion, but at the same point, this is why when you have uncomfortable or anxious feelings for no apparent reason, they are probably not your own. They may very well be on the other side of the Earth. If you don't know what to do with them, then do something vigorous physically. If you cannot do that, then meditate or ask lightbeings to come and clear you— they will.

With my life mate and myself listening, what would you say to me that I have not had the insight or wisdom to ask of you in this conversation since it appears to be the first time that we have spoken together consciously in this manner?

Enjoy the moments of perfection you have. Don't try too hard to make the lives of others better by encouraging them to think like yourself. If they want to be unhappy, let them! If they want to know why you are happy, then tell them.

You Don't Have to Save the Whole World by Yourself

There are many, many days when I feel that I'm still not serving at the level I'm capable of serving. I've had a conversation with Gaia about that, and she suggested that I will probably feel this to the end of my days on this planet but I'm serving elsewhere. The problem is that serving elsewhere has no memory for me and is therefore not satisfying in this context.

If you had that memory, you'd be exhausted. How would that help you? Have you ever had the opportunity of working very hard physically and then you rest up and then you feel regenerated, but then, at a later date, you might think of that hard work and for a moment get tired? That's why you don't remember things like that. It's protection. It wouldn't pay you. What's the advantage? If you're moving a mountain somewhere, it might make you tired here. You might miss out on things. Also, as an old friend of mine used to say, "You don't have to save the whole world by yourself." If you did, you'd take the fun of it away from others.

That sounds like the dialogue reputed to be spoken by Jesus when he told his disciples, "Be not so quick about trying to heal everybody. We're moving the opportunity for growth from the individual with the disease."

When things like that are spoken, the speaker understands that he or she is talking philosophically and also that the growth is not always fun. So let's just say that that quote is probably not being attributed to the person who actually made it.

I hear it as a point of view spiritually and in terms of teaching rather than through the individual or attached to the individual.

That's right. If one attaches certain things that sound like suffering is a good thing in any way, if you attach that to something or someone that has the connotation at the very least and the factual existence to many people of being a deity, then it sounds like the deity is saying, "Suffer. It's part of life." I assure you that the being you mentioned never said that.

The church has founded great percentages of its survival on endorsing suffering for those who buy that. It's integral to that church.

You have to remember that the church at all times, including at its beginning, was quite clear that it was a political organization first and a religion second, and that the—how can we say?—at the upper management levels, they are still quite clear about that.

I had not thought of that context, but it's helpful to remember that.

It's not that they are that cynical about it at those levels, but they are quite clear that they are managers and they see a direct correlation between their management and the management of any large corporation, which is how they can rationalize what they do.

Having been around senior management of major corporations, that makes a great deal more sense to me to view it in that context.

You Must Incorporate Change within You

Isis, do we still have the fold or the loop back in time that earlier Zoosh conversations involved?

Yes. That's what I referred to before.

But the loop is not the same as the possibility of uncreation?

No.

I just wanted to make sure I was clear on that. So I still have no clear sense of where we are in that game—as you laughingly said, another third of the way?

It's a little difficult to say it because what is required is not only an attitudinal change but a generated change within the individual. That's why we've been exposing you lately to the idea of benevolent magic, because this helps you to incorporate not only change within yourselves, but it also shows you that there is, in fact, physical evidence to be generated by using benevolent magic that works interactively with other beings beyond the human level. Nevertheless, not only is that intended to—how can we say?—to cheer you up, but it is also intended to prepare you to be able to change your mood, let's say, for the sake of doing so in order to see if that change of mood—not based on the facts around you, you understand—could in its own right not only improve the quality of your life, but more to the point, improve the quality of your experience and hence change life around you.

So it is not madness. One might say it sounds like madness, but if enough people do it, then life changes around you. But it does not mean that people have to commit mass suicide because of some delusion. The whole point is to do something because it improves the quality of your life. And you are pre-sented from time to time with the facts that support it, such as people walking across hot coals and not being burned, which was popular there for a while. It wasn't comfortably recognized by science, but it was recognized, albeit with significant shuddering, to say, "Well, this is real. Now let's go on to something that's more predictable." So it is not really meant to complicate your life, but it is meant to draw your attention to something that is part of your life when you are born.

When children are young, they play "let's make-believe." They don't act as a performer does. Performers know that they are who they are and that the role they are playing . . . no matter how much they are engaging with that role, they are clear that this is a role. When children play, they literally become that role; they are that in those moments. They *believe* they are the princess; they *believe* they are the cowboy and the Indian. They take it on as a reality while they are playing. It is a devotion of sorts. It will take that kind of playing by adults to change things.

Think about it: If childhood and the things of childhood are not an accident, then this suggests that Creator wants you to learn something very early on in your life so it is something that you know and understand and do not have to learn as an adult. Therefore, you might be able to use that childlike experience in some way as an adult to change your personal existence and, in time, change the physical evidence of your world. Children see things very often that adults do not see. Cats and animals see things that adults do not see, but are they there? Think about it. Good night.

The Language of Feeling

Isis

January 20, 2003

In January 2003 the religious editor for the LA Times *contacted us and asked for a response to a recent Web posting from the Vatican. Here is a reprint of that Web posting followed by a response from Isis.*

THE VATICAN: A CHRISTIAN REFLECTION ON THE "NEW AGE"
FORWARD

The present study is concerned with the complex phenomenon of "New Age" which is influencing many aspects of contemporary culture.

The study is a provisional report. It is the fruit of the common reflection of the Working Group on New Religious Movements, composed of staff members of different dicasteries of the Holy See: the Pontifical Councils for Culture and for Interreligious Dialogue (which are the principal redactors for this project), the Congregation for the Evangelization of Peoples and the Pontifical Council for Promoting Christian Unity.

These reflections are offered primarily to those engaged in pastoral work so that they might be able to explain how the New Age movement differs from the Christian faith. This study invites readers to take account of the way that New Age

religiosity addresses the spiritual hunger of contemporary men and women. It should be recognized that the attraction that New Age religiosity has for some Christians may be due in part to the lack of serious attention in their own communities for themes which are actually part of the Catholic synthesis such as the importance of man's spiritual dimension and its integration with the whole of life, the search for life's meaning, the link between human beings and the rest of creation, the desire for personal and social transformation, and the rejection of a rationalistic and materialistic view of humanity.

The present publication calls attention to the need to know and understand New Age as a cultural current, as well as the need for Catholics to have an understanding of authentic Catholic doctrine and spirituality in order to properly assess New Age themes. The first two chapters present New Age as a multifaceted cultural tendency, proposing an analysis of the basic foundations of the thought conveyed in this context. From Chapter Three onwards some indications are offered for an investigation of New Age in comparison with the Christian message. Some suggestions of a pastoral nature are also made.

Those who wish to go deeper into the study of New Age will find useful references in the appendices. It is hoped that this work will in fact provide a stimulus for further studies adapted to different cultural contexts. Its purpose is also to encourage discernment by those who are looking for sound reference points for a life of greater fullness. It is indeed our conviction that through many of our contemporaries who are searching, we can discover a true thirst for God. As Pope John Paul II said to a group of bishops from the United States: "Pastors must honestly ask whether they have paid sufficient attention to the thirst of the human heart for the true 'living water' which only Christ our Redeemer can give" (cf. Jn 4:7–13). Like him, we want to rely "on the perennial freshness of the Gospel message and its capacity to transform and renew those who accept it" (AAS 86/4, 330).

1. What Sort of Reflection?

The following reflections are meant as a guide for Catholics involved in preaching the Gospel and teaching the faith at any level within the Church. This document does not aim at providing a set of complete answers to the many questions raised by the New Age or other contemporary signs of the perennial human search for happiness, meaning and salvation. It is an invitation to understand the New Age and to engage in a genuine dialogue with those who are influenced by New Age thought. The document guides those involved in pastoral work in their understanding and response to New Age spirituality, both illustrating the points where this spirituality contrasts with the Catholic faith and refuting the positions espoused by New Age thinkers in opposition to Christian faith. What is indeed required of Christians is, first and foremost, a solid grounding in their faith. On this sound base, they can build a life which responds positively to the invitation in the first letter of Saint Peter: "always have your answer ready for people who ask you the reason for the hope that you all have. But give it with courtesy and respect and a clear conscience" (1 P 3, 15 f.).

1.1. Why Now?

The beginning of the Third Millennium comes not only two thousand years after the birth of Christ, but also at a time when astrologers believe that the Age of Pisces—known to them as the Christian age—is drawing to a close. These reflections are about the New Age, which takes its name from the imminent astrological Age of Aquarius. The New Age is one of many explanations of the significance of this moment in history which are bombarding contemporary (particularly Western) culture, and it is hard to see clearly what is and what is not consistent with the Christian message. So this seems to be the right moment to offer a Christian assessment of New Age thinking and the New Age movement as a whole.

It has been said, quite correctly, that many people hover between certainty and uncertainty these days, particularly in questions relating to their identity.[1] Some say that the Christian religion is patriarchal and authoritarian, that

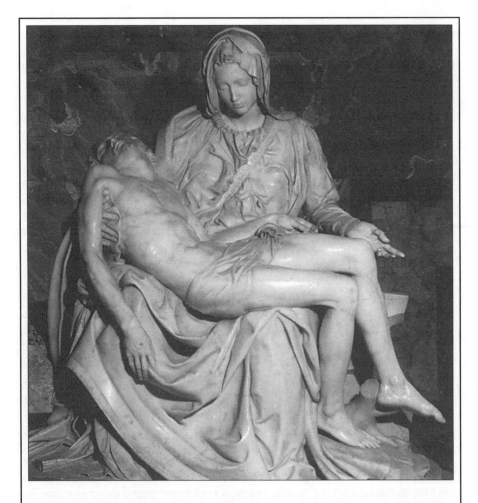

political institutions are unable to improve the world, and that formal (allopathic) medicine simply fails to heal people effectively. The fact that what were once central elements in society are now perceived as untrustworthy or lacking in genuine authority has created a climate where people look inwards, into themselves, for meaning and strength. There is also a search for alternative institutions, which people hope will respond to their deepest needs. The unstructured or chaotic life of alternative communities of the 1970s has given way to a search for discipline and structures, which are clearly key elements in the immensely popular "mystical" movements. New Age is attractive mainly because so much of what it offers meets hungers often left unsatisfied by the established institutions.

While much of New Age is a reaction to contemporary culture, there are many ways in which it is that culture's child. The Renaissance and the Reformation have shaped the modern Western individual, who is not weighed down by external burdens like merely extrinsic authority and tradition; people feel the need to "belong" to institutions less and less (and yet loneliness is very much a scourge of modern life), and are not inclined to rank "official" judgements above their own. With this cult of humanity, religion is internalised in a way which prepares the ground for a celebration of the sacredness of the self. This is why New Age shares many of the values espoused by enterprise culture and the "prosperity Gospel" (of which more will be said later: section 2.4), and also by the consumer culture, whose influence is clear from the rapidly growing numbers of people who claim that it is possible to blend Christianity and New Age, by taking what strikes them as the best of both.[2] It is worth remembering that deviations within Christianity have also gone beyond traditional theism in accepting a unilateral turn to self, and this would encourage such a blending of approaches. The important thing to note is that God is reduced in certain New Age practices so as furthering the advancement of the individual.

New Age appeals to people imbued with the values of modern culture. Freedom, authenticity, self-reliance and the like are all held to be sacred. It appeals to those who have problems with patriarchy. It "does not demand any more faith or belief than going to the cinema,"[3] and yet it claims to satisfy people's spiritual appetites. But here is a central question: Just what is meant by spirituality in a New Age context? The answer is the key to unlocking some of the differences between the Christian tradition and much of what can be called New Age. Some versions of New Age harness the powers of nature and seek to communicate with another world to discover the fate of individuals, to help individuals tune in to the right frequency to make the most of themselves and their circumstances. In most cases, it is completely fatalistic. Christianity, on the other hand, is an invitation to look outwards and beyond, to the "new advent" of the God who calls us to live the dialogue of love.[4]

1.2. Communications

The technological revolution in communications over the last few years has brought about a completely new situation. The ease and speed with which people can now communicate is one of the reasons why New Age has come to the attention of people of all ages and backgrounds, and many who follow Christ are not sure what it is all about. The Internet, in particular, has become enormously influential, especially with younger people, who find it a congenial and fascinating way of acquiring information. But it is a volatile vehicle of misinformation on so many aspects of religion; not all that is labelled "Christian" or "Catholic" can be trusted to reflect the teachings of the Catholic Church and, at the same time, there is a remarkable expansion of New Age sources ranging from the serious to the ridiculous. People need, and have a right to, reliable information on the differences between Christianity and New Age.

1.3. Cultural Background

When one examines many New Age traditions, it soon becomes clear that there is, in fact, little in the New Age that is new. The name seems to have gained currency through Rosicrucianism and Freemasonry, at the time of the French and American Revolutions, but the reality it denotes is a contemporary variant of Western esotericism. This dates back to Gnostic groups which grew up in the early days of Christianity, and gained momentum at the time of the Reformation in Europe. It has grown in parallel with scientific world views, and acquired a rational justification through the eighteenth and nineteenth centuries. It has involved a progressive rejection of a personal God and a focus on other entities which would often figure as intermediaries between God and humanity in traditional Christianity, with more and more original adaptations of these or additional ones. A powerful trend in modern Western culture which has given space to New Age ideas is the general acceptance of Darwinist evolutionary theory; this, alongside a focus on hidden spiritual powers or forces in nature, has been the backbone of much of what is now recognised as New Age theory. Basically, New Age has found a remarkable level of acceptance because the world view on which it was based was already widely accepted. The ground was well prepared by the growth and spread of relativism, along with an antipathy or indifference towards the Christian faith. Furthermore, there has been a lively discussion about whether and in what sense New Age can be described as a postmodern phenomenon. The existence and fervor of New Age thinking and practice bear witness to the unquenchable longing of the human spirit for transcendence and religious meaning, which is not only a contemporary cultural phenomenon, but was evident in the ancient world, both Christian and pagan.

1.4. The New Age and Catholic Faith

Even if it can be admitted that New Age religiosity in some way responds to the legitimate spiritual longing of human nature, it must be acknowledged that its attempts to do so run counter to Christian revelation. In Western culture in particular, the appeal of "alternative" approaches to spirituality is very strong. On the one hand, new forms of psychological affirmation of the individual have become very popular among Catholics, even in retreat-houses, seminaries and institutes of formation for religious. At the same time there is increasing nostalgia and curiosity for the wisdom and ritual of long ago, which is one of the reasons for the remarkable growth in the popularity of esotericism and gnosticism. Many people are particularly attracted to what is known—correctly or otherwise—as "Celtic" spirituality,[5] or to the religions of ancient peoples. Books and courses on spirituality and ancient or Eastern religions are a booming business, and they are frequently labelled "New Age" for commercial purposes. But the links with those religions are not always clear. In fact, they are often denied.

An adequate Christian discernment of New Age thought and practice cannot fail to recognize that, like second and third century gnosticism, it represents something of a compendium of positions that the Church has identified as heterodox. John Paul II warns with regard to the "return of ancient gnostic ideas under the guise of the so-called New Age: We cannot delude ourselves that this will lead toward a renewal of religion. It is only a new way of practising gnosticism—that attitude of the spirit that, in the name of a profound knowledge of God, results in distorting His Word and replacing it with purely human words. Gnosticism never completely abandoned the realm of Christianity. Instead, it has always existed side by side with Christianity, sometimes taking the shape of a philosophical movement, but more often assuming the characteristics of a religion or a para-religion in distinct, if not declared, conflict with all that is essentially Christian."[6] An example of this can be seen in the enneagram, the nine-type tool for character analysis, which when used as a means of spiritual growth introduces an ambiguity in the doctrine and the life of the Christian faith.

1.5. A Positive Challenge

The appeal of New Age religiosity cannot be underestimated. When the understanding of the content of Christian faith is weak, some mistakenly hold that the Christian religion does not inspire a profound spirituality and so they seek elsewhere. As a matter of fact, some say the New Age is already passing us by, and refer to the "next" age.[7] They speak of a crisis that began to manifest itself in the United States of America in the early 1990s, but admit that, especially beyond the English-speaking world, such a "crisis" may come later. But bookshops and radio stations, and the plethora of self-help groups in so many Western towns and cities, all seem to tell a different story. It seems that, at least for the moment, the New Age is still very much alive and part of the current cultural scene.

The success of New Age offers the Church a challenge. People feel the Christian religion no longer offers them—or perhaps never gave them—something they really need. The search which often leads people to the New Age is a genuine yearning: for a deeper spirituality, for something which will touch their hearts, and for a way of making sense of a confusing and often alienating world. There is a positive tone in New Age criticisms of "the materialism of daily life, of philosophy and even of medicine and psychiatry; reductionism, which refuses to take into consideration religious and supernatural experiences; the industrial culture of unrestrained individualism, which teaches egoism and pays no attention to other people, the future and the environment."[8] Any problems there are with New Age are to be found in what it proposes as alternative answers to life's questions. If the Church is not to be accused of being deaf to people's longings, her members need to do two things: to root themselves ever more firmly in the fundamentals of their faith, and to understand the often-silent cry in people's hearts, which leads them elsewhere if they are not satisfied by the Church. There is also a call in all of this to come closer to Jesus Christ and to be ready to follow Him, since He is the real way to happiness, the truth about God and the fulness of life for every man and woman who is prepared to respond to his love.

2. New Age Spirituality: An Overview

Christians in many Western societies, and increasingly also in other parts of the world, frequently come into contact with different aspects of the phenomenon known as New Age. Many of them feel the need to understand how they can best approach something which is at once so alluring, complex, elusive and, at times, disturbing. These reflections are an attempt to help Christians do two things:

- to identify elements of the developing New Age tradition;
- to indicate those elements which are inconsistent with the Christian revelation.

This is a pastoral response to a current challenge, which does not even attempt to provide an exhaustive list of New Age phenomena, since that would result in a very bulky tome, and such information is readily available elsewhere. It is essential to try to understand New Age correctly, in order to evaluate it fairly, and avoid creating a caricature. It would be unwise and untrue to say that everything connected with the New Age movement is good, or that everything about it is bad. Nevertheless, given the underlying vision of New Age religiosity, it is on the whole difficult to reconcile it with Christian doctrine and spirituality.

New Age is not a movement in the sense normally intended in the term "New Religious Movement," and it is not what is normally meant by the terms "cult" and "sect." Because it is spread across cultures, in phenomena as varied as music, films, seminars, workshops, retreats, therapies, and many more activities and events, it is much more diffuse and informal, though some religious or para-religious groups consciously incorporate New Age elements, and it has been suggested that New Age has been a source of ideas for various religious and para-religious sects.[9] New Age is not a single, uniform movement, but rather a loose network of practitioners whose approach is to think globally but act locally. People who are part of the network do not necessarily know each other and rarely, if ever, meet. In an attempt to avoid the confusion which can arise from using the term "movement," some refer to New Age as a "milieu,"[10] or an "audience cult."[11] However, it has also been pointed out that "it is a very coherent current of thought,"[12] a deliberate challenge to modern culture. It is a syncretistic structure incorporating many diverse elements, allowing people to share interests or connections to very different degrees and on varying levels of commitment. Many trends, practices and attitudes which are in some way part of New Age are, indeed, part of a broad and readily identifiable reaction to mainstream culture, so the word "movement" is not entirely out of place. It can be applied to New Age in the same sense as it is to other broad social movements, like the Civil Rights Movement or the Peace Movement; like them, it includes a bewildering array of people linked to the movement's main aims, but very diverse in the way they are involved and in their understanding of particular issues.

The expression "New Age religion" is more controversial, so it seems best to avoid it, although New Age is often a response to people's religious questions and needs, and its appeal is to people who are trying to discover or rediscover a spiritual dimension in their life. Avoidance of the term "New Age religion" is not meant in any way to question the genuine character of people's search for meaning and sense in life; it respects the fact that many within the New Age Movement themselves distinguish carefully between "religion" and "spirituality." Many have rejected organised religion, because in their judgement it has failed to answer their needs, and for precisely this reason they have looked elsewhere to find "spirituality." Furthermore, at the heart of New Age is the belief that the time for particular religions is over, so to refer to it as a religion would run counter to its own self-understanding. However, it is quite accurate to place New Age in the broader context of esoteric religiousness, whose appeal continues to grow.[13]

There is a problem built into the current text. It is an attempt to understand and evaluate something which is basically an exaltation of the richness of human experience. It is bound to draw the criticism that it can never do justice to a cultural movement whose essence is precisely to break out of what are seen as the constricting limits of rational discourse. But it is meant as an invitation to Christians to take the New Age seriously, and as such asks its readers to enter into a critical dialogue with people approaching the same world from very different perspectives.

The pastoral effectiveness of the Church in the Third Millennium depends to a great extent on the preparation of effective communicators of the Gospel message. What follows is a response to the difficulties expressed by many in dealing with the very complex and elusive phenomenon known as New Age. It is an attempt to understand what New Age is and to recognise the questions to which it claims to offer answers and solutions. There are some excellent books and other resources which survey the whole phenomenon or explain particular aspects in great detail, and reference will be made to some of these in the appendix. However they do not always undertake the necessary discernment in the light of Christian faith. The purpose of this contribution is to help Catholics find a key to understanding the basic principles behind New Age thinking, so that they can then make a Christian evaluation of the elements of

New Age they encounter. It is worth saying that many people dislike the term New Age, and some suggest that "alternative spirituality" may be more correct and less limiting. It is also true that many of the phenomena mentioned in this document will probably not bear any particular label, but it is presumed, for the sake of brevity, that readers will recognise a phenomenon or set of phenomena that can justifiably at least be linked with the general cultural movement that is often known as New Age.

2.1. What Is New about New Age?

For many people, the term New Age clearly refers to a momentous turning-point in history. According to astrologers, we live in the Age of Pisces, which has been dominated by Christianity. But the current age of Pisces is due to be replaced by the New Age of Aquarius early in the Third Millennium.[14] The Age of Aquarius has such a high profile in the New Age movement largely because of the influence of theosophy, spiritualism and anthroposophy, and their esoteric antecedents. People who stress the imminent change in the world are often expressing a wish for such a change, not so much in the world itself as in our culture, in the way we relate to the world; this is particularly clear in those who stress the idea of a New Paradigm for living. It is an attractive approach since, in some of its expressions, people do not watch passively, but have an active role in changing culture and bringing about a new spiritual awareness. In other expressions, more power is ascribed to the inevitable progression of natural cycles. In any case, the Age of Aquarius is a vision, not a theory. But New Age is a broad tradition, which incorporates many ideas which have no explicit link with the change from the Age of Pisces to the Age of Aquarius. There are moderate, but quite generalised, visions of a future where there will be a planetary spirituality alongside separate religions, similar planetary political institutions to complement more local ones, global economic entities which are more participatory and democratic, greater emphasis on communication and education, a mixed approach to health combining professional medicine and self-healing, a more androgynous self-understanding and ways of integrating science, mysticism, technology and ecology. Again, this is evidence of a deep desire for a fulfilling and healthy existence for the human race and for the planet. Some of the traditions which flow into New Age are: ancient Egyptian occult practices, Cabbalism, early Christian gnosticism, Sufism, the lore of the Druids, Celtic Christianity, mediaeval alchemy, Renaissance hermeticism, Zen Buddhism, Yoga and so on.[15]

Here is what is "new" about New Age. It is a "syncretism of esoteric and secular elements."[16] They link into a widely-held perception that the time is ripe for a fundamental change in individuals, in society and in the world. There are various expressions of the need for a shift:

• from Newtonian mechanistic physics to quantum physics;
• from modernity's exaltation of reason to an appreciation of feeling, emotion and experience (often described as a switch from 'left brain' rational thinking to 'right brain' intuitive thinking);
• from a dominance of masculinity and patriarchy to a celebration of femininity, in individuals and in society.

In these contexts the term "paradigm shift" is often used. In some cases it is clearly supposed that this shift is not simply desirable, but inevitable. The rejection of modernity underlying this desire for change is not new, but can be described as "a modern revival of pagan religions with a mixture of influences from both eastern religions and also from modern psychology, philosophy, science, and the counterculture that developed in the 1950s and 1960s."[17] New Age is a witness to nothing less than a cultural revolution, a complex reaction to the dominant ideas and values in Western culture, and yet its idealistic criticism is itself ironically typical of the culture it criticizes.

A word needs to be said on the notion of paradigm shift. It was made popular by Thomas Kuhn, an American historian of science, who saw a paradigm as "the entire constellation of beliefs, values, techniques and so on shared by the members of a given community."[18] When there is a shift from one paradigm to another, it is a question of wholesale transformation of perspective rather than one of gradual development. It really is a revolution, and Kuhn emphasised that competing paradigms are incommensurable and cannot co-exist. So the idea that a paradigm shift in the area of religion and spirituality is simply a new way of stating traditional beliefs misses the point. What is actually going on is a radical change in world view, which puts into question not only the content but also the fundamental interpretation of the former vision. Perhaps the clearest example of this, in terms of the relationship between New Age and Christianity, is the total recasting of the life and significance of Jesus Christ. It is impossible to reconcile these two visions.[19]

Science and technology have clearly failed to deliver all they once seemed to promise, so in their search for meaning and liberation people have turned to the spiritual realm. New Age as we now know it came from a search for something more humane and beautiful than the oppressive, alienating experience of life in Western society. Its early exponents were prepared to look far afield in their search, so it has become a very eclectic approach. It may well be one of the signs of a "return to religion", but it is most certainly not a return to orthodox Christian doctrines and creeds. The first symbols of this "movement" to penetrate Western culture were the remarkable festival at Woodstock in New York State in 1969 and the musical *Hair*, which set forth the main themes of New Age in the emblematic song "Aquarius."[20] But these were merely the tip of an iceberg whose dimensions have become clearer only relatively recently. The idealism of the 1960s and 1970s still survives in some quarters; but now, it is no longer predominantly adolescents who are involved. Links with left-wing political ideology have faded, and psychedelic drugs are by no means as prominent as they once were. So much has happened since then that all this no longer seems revolutionary; "spiritual" and "mystical" tendencies formerly restricted to the counterculture are now an established part of mainstream culture, affecting such diverse facets of life as medicine, science, art and religion. Western culture is now imbued with a more general political and ecological awareness, and this whole cultural shift has had an enormous impact on people's lifestyles. It is suggested by some that the New Age "movement" is precisely this major change to what is reckoned to be "a significantly better way of life."[21]

2.2. What Does the New Age Claim to Offer?

2.2.1. Enchantment: There Must Be an Angel

One of the most common elements in New Age "spirituality" is a fascination with extraordinary manifestations, and in particular with paranormal entities. People recognised as "mediums" claim that their personality is taken over by another entity during trances in a New Age phenomenon known as "channeling", during which the medium may lose control over his or her body and faculties. Some people who have witnessed these events would willingly acknowledge that the manifestations are indeed spiritual, but are not from God, despite the language of love and light which is almost always used. It is probably more correct to refer to this as a contemporary form of spiritualism, rather than spirituality in a strict sense. Other friends and counsellors from the spirit world are angels (which have become the centre of a new industry of books and paintings). Those who refer to angels in the New Age do so in an unsystematic way; in fact, distinctions in this area are sometimes described as unhelpful if they are too precise, since "there are many levels of guides, entities, energies, and beings in every octave of the universe. . . . They are all there to pick and choose from in relation to your own attraction/repulsion mechanisms."[22] These spiritual entities are often invoked 'non-religiously' to help in relaxation aimed at better decision-making and control of one's life and career. Fusion with some spirits who teach through particular people is another New Age experience claimed by people who refer to themselves as 'mystics.' Some nature spirits are described as powerful energies existing in the natural world and also on the "inner planes": i.e., those which are accessible by the use of rituals, drugs and other techniques for reaching altered states of consciousness. It is clear that, in theory at least, the New Age often recognizes no spiritual authority higher than personal inner experience.

2.2.2. Harmony and Understanding: Good Vibrations

Phenomena as diverse as the Findhorn garden and Feng Shui[23] represent a variety of ways which illustrate the importance of being in tune with nature or the cosmos. In New Age there is no distinction between good and evil. Human actions are the fruit of either illumination or ignorance. Hence we cannot condemn anyone, and nobody needs forgiveness. Believing in the existence of evil can create only negativity and fear. The answer to negativity is love. But it is not the sort which has to be translated into deeds; it is more a question of attitudes of mind. Love is energy, a high-frequency vibration, and the secret to happiness and health and success is being able to tune in, to find one's place in the great chain of being. New Age teachers and therapies claim to offer the key to finding the correspondences between all the elements of the universe, so that people may modulate the tone of their lives and be in absolute harmony with each other and with everything around them, although there are different theoretical backgrounds.[24]

2.2.3. Health: Golden Living

Formal (allopathic) medicine today tends to limit itself to curing particular, isolated ailments, and fails to look at the broader picture of a person's health: this has given rise to a fair amount of understandable dissatisfaction. Alternative therapies have gained enormously in popularity because they claim to look at the whole person and are about healing rather than curing. Holistic health, as it is known, concentrates on the important role that the mind plays in physical healing. The connection between the spiritual and the physical aspects of the person is said to be in the immune system or the Indian chakra system. In a New Age perspective, illness and suffering come from working against nature; when one is in tune with nature, one can expect a much healthier life, and even material prosperity; for some New Age healers, there should actually be no need for us to die. Developing our human potential will put us in touch with our inner divinity, and with those parts of our selves which have been alienated and suppressed. This is revealed above all in Altered States of Consciousness (ASCs), which are induced either by drugs or by various mind-expanding techniques, particularly in the context of "transpersonal psychology." The shaman is often seen as the specialist of altered states of consciousness, one who is able to mediate between the transpersonal realms of spirits and gods and the world of humans.

There is a remarkable variety of approaches for promoting holistic health, some derived from ancient cultural traditions, whether religious or esoteric, others connected with the psychological theories developed in Esalen during the years 1960–1970. Advertising connected with New Age covers a wide range of practices such as acupuncture, biofeedback, chiropractic, kinesiology, homeopathy, iridology, massage and various kinds of "bodywork" (such as orgonomy, Feldenkrais, reflexology, Rolfing, polarity massage, therapeutic touch, etc.), meditation and visualisation, nutritional therapies, psychic healing, various kinds of herbal medicine, healing by crystals, metals, music or colours, reincarnation therapies and, finally, twelve-step programmes and self-help groups.[25] The source of healing is said to be within ourselves, something we reach when we are in touch with our inner energy or cosmic energy.

Inasmuch as health includes a prolongation of life, New Age offers an Eastern formula in Western terms. Originally, reincarnation was a part of Hindu cyclical thought, based on the atman or divine kernel of personality (later the concept of jiva), which moved from body to body in a cycle of suffering (samsara), determined by the law of karma, linked to behaviour in past lives. Hope lies in the possibility of being born into a better state, or ultimately in liberation from the need to be reborn. What is different in most Buddhist traditions is that what wanders from body to body is not a soul, but a continuum of consciousness. Present life is embedded in a potentially endless cosmic process which includes even the gods. In the West, since the time of Lessing, reincarnation has been understood far more optimistically as a process of learning and progressive individual fulfilment. Spiritualism, theosophy, anthroposophy and New Age all see reincarnation as participation in cosmic evolution. This post-Christian approach to eschatology is said to answer the unresolved questions of theodicy and dispenses with the notion of hell. When the soul is separated from the body individuals can look back on their whole life up to that point, and when the soul is united to its new body there is a preview of its coming phase of life. People have access to their former lives through dreams and meditation techniques.[26]

2.2.4. Wholeness: A Magical Mystery Tour

One of the central concerns of the New Age movement is the search for "wholeness." There is encouragement to overcome all forms of "dualism," as such divisions are an unhealthy product of a less enlightened past. Divisions which New Age proponents claim need to be overcome include the real difference between Creator and creation, the real distinction between man and nature, or spirit and matter, which are all considered wrongly as forms of dualism. These dualistic tendencies are often assumed to be ultimately based on the Judaeo-Christian roots of Western civilisation, while it would be more accurate to link them to gnosticism, in particular to Manichaeism. The scientific revolution and the spirit of modern rationalism are blamed particularly for the tendency to fragmentation, which treats organic wholes as mechanisms that can be reduced to their smallest components and then explained in terms of the latter, and the tendency to reduce spirit to matter, so that spiritual reality—including the soul—becomes merely a contingent "epiphenomenon" of essentially material processes. In all of these areas, the New Age alternatives are called "holistic." Holism pervades the New Age movement, from its concern with holistic health to its quest for unitive consciousness, and from ecological awareness to the idea of global "networking."

2.3. THE FUNDAMENTAL PRINCIPLES OF NEW AGE THINKING

2.3.1. A Global Response in a Time of Crisis

"Both the Christian tradition and the secular faith in an unlimited process of science had to face a severe break first manifested in the student revolutions around the year 1968."[27] The wisdom of older generations was suddenly robbed of significance and respect, while the omnipotence of science evaporated, so that the Church now "has to face a serious breakdown in the transmission of her faith to the younger generation."[28] A general loss of faith in these former pillars of consciousness and social cohesion has been accompanied by the unexpected return of cosmic religiosity, rituals and beliefs which many believed to have been supplanted by Christianity; but this perennial esoteric undercurrent never really went away. The surge in popularity of Asian religion at this point was something new in the Western context, established late in the nineteenth century in the theosophical movement, and it "reflects the growing awareness of a global spirituality, incorporating all existing religious traditions."[29]

The perennial philosophical question of the one and the many has its modern and contemporary form in the temptation to overcome not only undue division, but even real difference and distinction, and the most common expression of this is holism, an essential ingredient in New Age and one of the principal signs of the times in the last quarter of the twentieth century. An extraordinary amount of energy has gone into the effort to overcome the division into compartments characteristic of mechanistic ideology, but this has led to the sense of obligation to submit to a global network which assumes quasitranscendental authority. Its clearest implications are a process of conscious transformation and the development of ecology.[30] The new vision which is the goal of conscious transformation has taken time to formulate, and its enactment is resisted by older forms of thought judged to be entrenched in the status quo. What has been successful is the generalisation of ecology as a fascination with nature and resacralisation of the Earth, Mother Earth or Gaia, with the missionary zeal characteristic of Green politics. The Earth's executive agent is the human race as a whole, and the harmony and understanding required for responsible governance is increasingly understood to be a global government, with a global ethical framework. The warmth of Mother Earth, whose divinity pervades the whole of creation, is held to bridge the gap between creation and the transcendent Father-God of Judaism and Christianity, and removes the prospect of being judged by such a Being.

In such a vision of a closed universe that contains "God" and other spiritual beings along with ourselves, we recognize here an implicit pantheism. This is a fundamental point which pervades all New Age thought and practice, and conditions in advance any otherwise positive assessment where we might be in favor of one or another aspect of its spirituality. As Christians, we believe on the contrary that "man is essentially a creature and remains so for all eternity, so that an absorption of the human I in the divine I will never be possible."[31]

ENDNOTES

1 Paul Heelas, *The New Age Movement. The Celebration of the Self and the Sacralization of Modernity*, Oxford (Blackwell) 1996, p. 137.

2 Cf. P. Heelas, op. cit., p. 164f.

3 Cf. P. Heelas, op. cit., p. 173.

4 Cf. John Paul II, *Encyclical Letter Dominum et vivificantem* (18 May 1986), 53.

5 Cf. Gilbert Markus o.p., "Celtic Schmeltic," (1) in *Spirituality*, vol. 4, November–December 1998, No 21, pp. 379–383 and (2) in *Spirituality*, vol. 5, January–February 1999, No. 22, pp. 57–61.

6 John Paul II, *Crossing the Threshold of Hope*, (Knopf) 1994, 90.

7 Cf. particularly Massimo Introvigne, *New Age & Next Age*, Casale Monferrato (Piemme) 2000.

8 M. Introvigne, op. cit., p. 267.

9 Cf. Michel Lacroix, *L'Ideologia della New Age*, Milano (il Saggiatore) 1998, p. 86. The word "sect" is used here not in any pejorative sense, but rather to denote a sociological phenomenon.

10 Cf. Wouter J. Hanegraaff, *New Age Religion and Western Culture: Esotericism in the Mirror of Secular Thought*, Leiden-New York-Köln (Brill) 1996, p. 377 and elsewhere.

11 Cf. Rodney Stark and William Sims Bainbridge, *The Future of Religion: Secularisation, Revival and Cult Formation*, Berkeley (University of California Press) 1985.

12 Cf. M. Lacroix, op. cit., p. 8.

13 The Swiss "Theologie für Laien" course entitled *Faszination Esoterik* puts this clearly. Cf. "Kursmappe 1 - New Age und Esoterik," text to accompany slides, p. 9.

14 The term was already in use in the title of *The New Age Magazine*, which was being published by the Ancient Accepted Scottish Masonic Rite in the southern jurisdiction of the United States of America as early as 1900. Cf. M. York, "The New Age Movement in Great Britain," in *Syzygy: Journal of Alternative Religion and Culture*, 1: 2–3 (1992), Stanford CA, p. 156, note 6. The exact timing and nature of the change to the New Age are interpreted variously by different authors; estimates of timing range from 1967 to 2376.

15 In late 1977, Marilyn Ferguson sent a questionnaire to 210 "persons engaged in social transformation," whom she also calls "Aquarian Conspirators." The following is interesting: "When respondents were asked to name individuals whose ideas had influenced them, either through personal contact or through their writings, those most often named, in order of frequency, were Pierre Teilhard de Chardin, C.G. Jung, Abraham Maslow, Carl Rogers, Aldous Huxley, Robert Assagioli, and J. Krishnamurti. Others frequently mentioned: Paul Tillich, Hermann Hesse, Alfred North Whitehead, Martin Buber, Ruth Benedict, Margaret Mead, Gregory Bateson, Tarthang Tulku, Alan Watts, Sri Aurobindo, Swami Muktananda, D.T. Suzuki, Thomas Merton, Willis Harman, Kenneth Boulding, Elise Boulding, Erich Fromm, Marshall McLuhan, Buckminster Fuller, Frederic Spiegelberg, Alfred Korzybski, Heinz von Foerster, John Lilly, Werner Erhard, Oscar Ichazo, Maharishi Mahesh Yogi, Joseph Chilton Pearce, Karl Pribram, Gardner Murphy, and Albert Einstein." *The Aquarian Conspiracy: Personal and Social Transformation in Our Time*, Los Angeles (Tarcher) 1980, p. 50 (note 1) and p. 434.

16 W.J. Hanegraaff, op. cit., p. 520.

17 Irish Theological Commission, *A New Age of the Spirit? A Catholic Response to the New Age Phenomenon*, Dublin 1994, chapter 3.

18 Cf. *The Structure of Scientific Revolutions*, Chicago (University of Chicago Press), 1970, p. 175.

19 Cf. Alessandro Olivieri Pennesi, *Il Cristo del New Age: Indagine critica*, Vatican City (Libreria Editrice Vaticana) 1999, passim, but especially pp. 11–34. See also section 4 below.

20 It is worth recalling the lyrics of this song, which quickly imprinted themselves onto the minds of a whole generation in North America and Western Europe: "When the Moon is in the Seventh House, and Jupiter aligns with Mars, then Peace will guide the Planets, and Love will steer the Stars. This is the dawning of the Age of Aquarius. . . . Harmony and understanding, sympathy and trust abounding; no more falsehoods or derision—golden living, dreams of visions, mystic crystal revelation, and the mind's true liberation. Aquarius. . . ."

21 P. Heelas, op. cit., p. 1f. The August 1978 journal of the Berkeley Christian Coalition puts it this way: "Just ten years ago the funky drug-based spirituality of the hippies and the mysticism of the Western yogi were restricted to the counterculture. Today, both have found their way into the mainstream of our cultural mentality. Science, the health professions, and the arts, not to mention psychology and religion, are all engaged in a fundamental reconstruction of their basic premises." Quoted in Marilyn Ferguson, op. cit., p. 370f.

22 Cf. Chris Griscom, *Ecstasy is a New Frequency: Teachings of the Light Institute*, New York (Simon & Schuster) 1987, p. 82.

23 See the Glossary of New Age terms, §7.2 above.

24 Cf. W.J. Hanegraaff, op. cit., chapter 15 ("The Mirror of Secular Thought"). The system of correspondences is clearly inherited from traditional esotericism, but it has a new meaning for those who (consciously or not) follow Swedenborg. While every natural element in traditional esoteric doctrine had the divine life within it, for Swedenborg nature is a dead reflection of the living spiritual world. This idea is very much at the heart of the post-modern vision of a disenchanted world and various attempts to "re-enchant" it. Blavatsky rejected correspondences, and Jung emphatically relativised causality in favour of the esoteric world view of correspondences.

25 W.J. Hanegraaff, op. cit., pp. 54–55.

26 Cf. Reinhard Hümmel, "Reinkarnation," in Hans Gasper, Joachim Müller, Friederike Valentin (eds.), *Lexikon der Sekten, Sondergruppen und Weltanschauungen*, Fakten, Hintergründe, Klärungen, Freiburg-Basel-Wien (Herder) 2000, 886–893.

27 Michael Fuss, "New Age and Europe—A Challenge for Theology," in *Mission Studies* Vol. VIII-2, 16, 1991, p. 192.

28 *Ibid.*, loc. cit.

29 *Ibid.*, p. 193.

30 *Ibid.*, p. 199.

31 Congregation for the Doctrine of Faith, Letter to the Bishops of the Catholic Church on Some Aspects of Christian Meditation (Orationis Formas), 1989, 14. Cf. Gaudium et Spes, 19; Fides et Ratio, 22.

Isis Responds

Generally speaking, the reason the New Age is popular at all is because it is all about heart and feelings and not particularly about dogma—although one needs only to look to the New Age and its pundits to find dogma: "This is what is so! And that is what is so!" But you understand that the purpose of dogma is to help people feel safe. It is no different with the Church's dogma, because it was developed over years—I might add somewhat lovingly, not just manipulatively—to serve the needs of the people and to create the safest, most predictable society possible. This way society would not have to be constantly at the mercy of unexpected passionate outbursts that often led to fighting, battle, fear, war and so on. So the Church attempted to provide not only the beauty offered by Jesus, the special person, but also a practical philosophy.

Creation Is Not Intended to Be Known

This is oversimplified, but any time the Church ran across something they understood or believed they could understand and did not actually have a good way to explain its complexities to the people of the time—whom they did not feel could take in complexities very well—they said, "Well, it is one of the mysteries of God." If you look at the New Age philosophy, there is not that much difference. There are attempts to explain mysteries, attempts to give details about what the mysteries might mean, but ultimately the further you go, the more mysteries there are.

It is not intended that life be fully understood and fully explained, because it is in the nature of creation (as any artist knows who has ever painted a painting and stopped rather than said, "I am done"). Creation is always opening, like a forever-opening flower, with variegated patterns, beauties, fragrances and so on. Creation is not intended to be known, it is intended to be experienced—not only by creating, but also by experiencing the creation. It can best be experienced through the use of feelings.

In the old days, in the old churches—not just the Christian Church, but other more ancient religions as well—the attempt was made to create workable philosophies, to try to come up with something that would allow resolution between peoples, to say nothing of tribes or countries, that would not require war or battle—another way to keep the peace. In many ways they were successful, and in some ways not. One of the ways that worked for a while was to create support and maintain the value of working things out mentally and spiritually. But because feelings—especially passion, strong feelings, arguing and so on—had been the source of much of the difficulty in the first place, creating wars and battles, the tendency was to discourage much exploration into feelings because of its difficult side. But now, as you know, people are experiencing their feelings more and more.

Heart Can Be Integrated Now

It may be possible—by gently exploring feelings and by looking for common feelings in all people to discover a way using the mind, using the spirit and using the heart—to find out how we, the human race, can live together in a more benevolent way. The love-heat/heart-warmth/physical-warmth method [see p. 23] says, "Here is something you can feel, and when you are feeling that love-heat, it is possible to speak, but it is not possible to maintain the love-heat and speak in complexities." This tells you that the mind can work with the heart and the heart can work with the mind as long as the mind remains simple and uncomplicated. Because if you're going to find common ground with other people, you need to start in the simple, uncomplicated areas. Keep it simple, keep it uncomplicated—not because other people don't have the capacity to understand complexities, but because you need to start with your common ground, and the best way to find your common ground is to speak in simple, uncomplicated terms.

The way to avoid arguments is to stay focused in that love-heat, which you may feel in your heart. Some people might feel it in their legs, some might feel it in their stomachs, but it is a physical warmth that can be felt. That warmth is the physical experience of loving yourself and of feeling God's love. So if you can maintain that, it allows you to include heart and not have to yell and scream and become overly aggressive. As a matter of fact, love-heat is not about aggression at all; it is a way to include heart that's safe. And after all, isn't that the ultimate intention of religion, to create safety for all people? So the point is, heart can be integrated now. There is no point in trying to yell louder in an argument with somebody. That doesn't work.

Calling it "heart-warmth" is a bit of a misnomer because one might feel it in some other part of one's body. So to feel that physical-warmth and talk at the same time, maintaining the warmth all of the time, requires concentration and effort, at least in the beginning. In order to do that, one cannot communicate in complexities, so one tends to use basic communication skills. This allows others to do the same, and by doing so, more than one being is experiencing that warmth, which is loving oneself and being loved by the greater being also known as God. Thus one can communicate in an entirely new way for the times. And that way is simple and uncomplicated, using words with feeling and with thought and with Spirit's guiding hand.

The Warmth Is Communication through Feeling

The Church is the beginning toward a practical world philosophy that intends to create a better life for all people. That means that it is the foundation of modern times, including other religions I see no problem with looking for God within. After all, if God has created the heaven and the Earth and all the people on it, it is safe to say that there is God inside the people. One just needs to know how to look, and that is why I am recommending that we look with physicality and that physical feeling. No matter who you are, whether you are young or old, you can find that warmth, and it gives you physical evidence that something is happening. As long as you stay focused on the warmth, meaning wherever it comes up, you maintain your awareness of it. Try and go into it and feel it more, and when you can feel it, then talk. You will find that you can't talk in too complicated a way at first, but there is more to it. Whatever you can say, you have to maintain the warmth, *because the warmth is the communication, and that is what people feel!*

People are now responding to what they feel, not what they hear. That is why there are so many misunderstandings all the time, because people are responding to what they feel. They get confused in their own selves that way, and the reason the New Age is so popular now is that people are trying to understand their own feelings so they can improve communications between one another and between all people. In short, you can't leave anybody out. You have to include and you have to be able to communicate with the most basic and most nurturing form of communication, which is feeling.

You were taught this when you were a very little child. Your parents, whoever raised you, loved you and you felt their love. It is not that they said, "I love you"; that doesn't mean anything. They might as well have said, "Bow-wow." But they felt love.

This is why the child tends to gravitate toward the mother in the beginning. The mother naturally feels love because she gave birth to the baby. It requires a great deal of commitment to do such a thing. If you find yourself in that situation—you are pregnant, you have to give birth—there is nothing like that feeling of being presented by the midwife or the nurse or the doctor with your baby after the baby has come out of your body; you have that love. Fathers might feel the love, but it is not the same. It's a good thing, but it takes time for a father to develop love, and it is never quite the same as a mother's. This does not mean that fathers are not worthy; it means that most children almost always remember their mothers more fondly than their fathers.

Feelings Are the Most Important Method of Communication

The point is, from the very beginning, at the earliest time of your life, you are taught that feelings are the most important method of communication. Now people need to move beyond words. Even the most helpful attempts at improving the spoken word run up against the complications of your time, and that not only includes different languages but different nuances within your own language. Look at your culture. Most of you speak English—not all, but those of you in the United States can speak a few words of English even if you are new to the country. But think of the nuances, the slang, the dialect within that language. No, you need more than clearly defined words, because not everyone is going to understand your idioms, to say nothing of understanding your nuances—that a word said this way means this, but when said that way means that. It is clear that there needs to be some kind of communication that feels safe.

In the past, it was touch: "If I touch you in this way, then you can be reassured; if I touch you in that way, then you might feel frightened." If you're touched gently, you might feel reassured, but it is not always safe or considered proper in your time. So the best way to touch is through the feelings that you pick up from others. Everybody is picking this up more and more these days, and the reason there is so much confusion is that people do not know what they are picking up, or they simply do not understand their own feelings.

This is why the New Age people, or people who are interested in New Age things, are looking inside for God, because they are trying to understand their own feelings so they can understand themselves better and then take the next step to communicate clearly with others so that others understand them. And this has to start with the language everybody knows, no matter what their native tongue is, and that is what you feel. You know what you feel when you are laughing—you feel joy. You know what you're feeling when you are angry, when you are upset. But you also need to find out what you're feeling when you are feeling love and nothing but, and so you start with that physical-warmth. It will be very nurturing, very comforting, and even though it might take some of you awhile to get there, you can do it, especially if others around you are doing it.

Those who are interested in the New Age are really people who are looking to broaden their philosophy. Most of them are not interested in ignoring or abandoning other valuable philosophies, but they are intrigued to see a broader view. As you know, in today's world, which appears very complex, a broader view can be very helpful in order to understand and appreciate other people's points of view. The New Age, with all of its various faces and reflections, is attempting to provide a means toward attaining that broader view, as well as to provide new insights into that view itself.

It's Up to You to Apply Your Material-Mastery Training—Earth Is More Receptive to You Now

Zoosh

March 15, 2003

Let us talk a little bit about energies. Some of it is very simple, uncomplicated. Let's do the uncomplicated part first.

You Need to Start Planting and Encouraging Trees

Why are people feeling so tired? The reason is ridiculously simple and I've talked about it before, but I'll just bring it up again. It's this: There is a decreasing level of the atmosphere that you need. You breathe oxygen and other elements. The oxygen supply is decreasing, and other gases in the air are increasing. You know about that; this is widely known. For people living in cities, it is more of a factor, but even people living in the country, including well outside of even small towns, have begun to notice it. That is because the air currents do travel around the planet—not just at the high levels, but also at low levels, considering that industry, in one form or another, is global.

So you've got to face the music on that one. You can't just continue to wipe out oxygen-producing plant species and whatnot. You're going to have to start . . . and I recommend that this happens; there are some people who are doing it now, yes? You're going to have to start, on a concerted basis, planting and encouraging trees—not just planting them, but encouraging the trees that do exist to remain in existence. This is one of the most difficult things. A lot of plants on your planet now do not feel particularly welcome anymore. This is an accumulated situation for them, so my feeling is this: There's not a great deal you can do in the United States about various so-called Third World countries who are clearing their land so they can grow food and do other things to support their people, so you will have to do what you can where you live.

I grant that trees planted by humans do not usually thrive as well as trees that are fostered, cultured and welcomed by the Earth, growing on their own. Please, when you see trees growing on their own, just let them grow if you possibly can. I grant that if a tree is growing in the middle of the highway, that may be an exception. Maybe you can transplant it. But if it is anyplace else where you can allow it, I recommend letting it grow. Consider the fact that you have only so much that exhales oxygen, and that is constantly being reduced.

That's the scientific level, the obvious level—and the obvious in this case should not be ignored because it is fully 40 percent of the problem. But what about the rest? The good thing about the 40-percent part of the problem is that you can do something about it—you know, start a plant-a-tree club. But don't just plant it; go out and nurture it. If you're going to plant it, you're going to be responsible for it. Planting it means watering it and talking to it, encouraging it and welcoming it.

Before you get into the next one, how about more plants in the house? Do houseplants give off very much oxygen?

Yes, they do, and some of them also defeat pollution. They are well-known, and you might know about some of them.

Spider plants?

Spider plants and so on.

Moving Electrons Are Interfering with Your Natural Cycles

So what about the other 60 percent? The other 60 percent is caused . . . okay, let's take it in order. Fully 20 percent (that's a lot; it didn't use to be that much) of this increasing difficulty and discomfort and disruption of natural cycles . . . natural cycles would be what is natural for you—not what is natural for your society, not what you've been conditioned to do, but what is natural for you in terms of your sleep cycle, your food cycle, your elimination cycle, all of these cycles that you have in your life. Fully 20 percent of that is being impacted by microwave radiation, radio frequency broadcast, all of this kind of stuff.

This not only comes from these radio phones and other things, but also from satellites that broadcast to the ground and so on. You know, the trouble with this is that most people do not live in metal houses, and perhaps that is a good thing. Obviously, this does not affect those who do live in metal houses, and there are some: trailers or recreational vehicles usually have a thin skin of aluminum or some kind of metal. But everyone else is bathed in these moving electrons all the time, and it is interfering with your natural cycles. That is also something you can do something about, and in time there will be methods used for transmitting that will have less impact on the human being, but it's taking awhile for that to develop and be deployed. So there's that.

Earth Is Moving into a Dormant Stage

So we're on to the rest of it. There's about 40 percent left. (You understand, this is approximate.) Your planet Earth, in the cycle in which it's in, is not doing all that well; you know that. People have heard about wobbling on the axis and all that, so I won't go into it.

More importantly, your planet is beginning to move into a dormant stage. Now, don't panic. It's beginning to move into a stage where she, if I may refer to her that way, is going to be more receptive to what the creative human beings on her are doing. If you are feeling self-destructive, then she might feel that way. Don't be that way if you can possibly help it, because if she takes on the bulk of your general feeling, she will start to do things that will speed up her dormant period.

A dormant period, for example, might be an ice age. Another possibility might be a reaction and then an ice age—a reaction would be a volcanic eruption or an earthquake, and that could be followed by an ice age. Your geologists and other scientists have studied this matter. But I'd say this: What's really going on is not that Earth is planning to shut down gradually over time, but that she is at this midpoint. She is receptive to you actually *doing* things to help her feel better. Over the years, we've spoken of these matters. [For more information, see *Shamanic Secrets for Material Mastery*, *Explorer Race: Techniques for Generating Safety* and *Shamanic Secrets for Physical Mastery*.]

How to Keep Mother Earth from Moving into Dormancy

So here is the situation: You really need now—every one of you and everyone you know who is receptive to this kind of material, and even everyone you know who is receptive to holistic and other approaches to life—to do more than just meditate. Meditation, to a lot of people, is something that is thoughtful, meaning mental, and physical . . . not good enough. It's all right, but it's just not good enough; you can have so much more impact. How much more? Three times more impact if you include—or attempt to include—the physical on the feeling level. So don't use the mind to quiet the body. Now, I know a lot of people are into certain styles of spiritual pursuits and believe that is the best thing. In this case, it is not.

What you need to do if you cannot do the love-heat/heart-warmth/physical-warmth [see p. 23] . . . the love-heat is the best, and if you can do the love-heat, do that for five minutes at least every day, without thinking about anything if you can possibly help it. The best way to do that is to distract yourself by looking at something neutral, like a blank wall or a blank ceiling. Now, if you cannot do that, then you need to activate your feelings in some way.

Try to think—you can use your mind—of some incident and some time. You can think about a place as well, but not of a person; you don't want to distract yourself, and with a person there are always going to be other feelings that come up. With a place there can be feelings that come up too, but try to make it a place you haven't been to and would like to go to so there's a sense of good feeling about it, see? Or think of a benevolent feeling of some sort, a feeling that feels good.   Try to do that at least once a day for two or three minutes, and finish up with a picture of the Earth—you know, that picture of the Earth you have from space. If you can do it outside, you can skip the picture of the Earth; when you're into this benevolent feeling, just touch the Earth. If you're sitting on the Earth, you don't have to do that. If you're not, then touch the Earth. You can touch a rock, all right? But don't touch something man-made, even if it's made of Earth materials. It's better to touch something that is purely Earth—rock, dirt. But if you're inside, then picture the Earth.

Everyone needs to do this now for two to three minutes a day minimum, because it will take . . . think of how many people there are on Earth. You have a pretty good idea of the number, but let me give you an idea of the percentage needed to do this to keep Earth from moving from her current cycle of being receptive to you as creators-in-training taking over some of her duties. In the past, she was allowing you to take over duties for yourself; now you're being allowed to take over duties for her. It's important for you to do this as she is receptive so that you can prevent her from moving into the next state, which would be the full-on dormant stage. In that case, you might begin to see more earthquakes, more floods, more storms—you know the whole scenario—culminating in an ice age. So it's important for you to do this, okay?

Now, the percentage of the population that needs to do this for Mother Earth, to be aware of it . . . that's the key. If five thousand people do it or ten thousand people, it won't last. That's the thing: You can't just have an Earth Day; it has to be Earth Day every day, as the environmentalists like to say. In this case, this has to be done every day. Here's the percentage that needs to do it at least once every day, at any time during the day . . . before you go to sleep at night, when you wake up during the night, anytime. At least 14 percent of all the people on the planet need to do this once a day, every day.

Now, how long do you have? It's not a matter of life or death. How long do you have where she is open and receptive to being cued or being made aware—either one of those things—before she begins to move. It isn't a thought; she doesn't think, "Well, the heck with you guys." It's nothing like that. She begins to move— she's a physical being, yes?—toward dormancy. You have now been in this stage for about a year and a half and have about seventeen or eighteen months to do this. Now, I don't want you to panic if you don't get it done, meaning if there's not that percentage of people doing it in seventeen or eighteen months. After that time, even if she begins her dormant stage and you haven't begun doing this, she will still respond and come out of dormancy, back into that prestage in which you have taken over some of the things she would normally do for herself. I'll get into that later. You can still, by having about 21 percent of the people doing it once a day, every day, bring her back out of that stage, and for that you'll have about thirty or forty years, so you can still catch that and bring her back.

Learn How It Feels to Be Welcomed

Now, what are some of the things you need to take over? For one, you need to take over something that's very important—and this is a lot of the reason you've been getting some of the training you have over the past few years through this channel. You need to be able to *welcome life*. Speaks of Many Truths and Reveals the Mysteries are perhaps the best teachers along this line. I recommend reading the *Shamanic Secrets* books, and of course there are others. But at the very least, learn how to feel welcomed by others so that you have a benchmark to know how you feel physically when you know you are welcome—not just when you feel people are faking it, but when you genuinely feel welcome—or when you welcome people in a genuine way . . . and there are people you know whom you would welcome. And for those of you who don't know people like that, there may perhaps be animals whom you would welcome that way.

Take note of the way you *feel*, because you will need to use those same feelings, meaning generate those same feelings, perhaps with a recollection of those beloved people or animals to start with until you can generate those feelings on your own. You will just have to walk around outside and welcome life, even if that life isn't there.

For example, you might find a place where a forest was, all right? For some of you, this might take place on an old empty lot in the city; others might do it in the country, or you might simply walk around someplace where life could be—meaning perhaps a park where trees could grow and perhaps are growing. You would walk around and go into those feelings. Try to walk around. The best way is barefoot; I know that's not practical for you, so the next best way is in leather-bottomed shoes. (You can get this kind of instruction from others, but I'm passing it on too.) And if you have to, walk around in rubber-soled shoes, but it will be a little less effective. How much less? About 50 percent less effective.

Walk around with that feeling. Try to be clear about what you are welcoming. If you get to the feeling and it's strictly, completely welcoming . . . you have to be careful about that, because you'll be in a public place. There will be other people around, and you could draw things to you that you might not wish to. So the thing to do in this case, especially if you're new to this kind of thing, is to walk over to the trees while you're welcoming and touch the trees. Those trees will feel welcome. When you're touching the trees, touch them with the back of your hand, not with your fingers. Just brush them with the back of your hand. You can lean against them gently if you wish, but all the while maintain the feeling of welcoming.

The physical feeling of welcoming might be different in each of you, so don't be attached to how it feels. Some of you will feel it as the love-heat; others will feel it in other ways. Brush against the trees to welcome them, you understand? Also, for those of you who live on or near farms . . . granted, a lot of the plants and other things that grow or are raised on farms are not in their natural state, but you just have to do what you can do. Try to touch or lean against or get near the plants or animals you wish to be here, to remain here, to feel that welcome. In some cases, you can't touch everything.

Welcome All Life

Now, why am I going into this at such length? It's one of the main ways Mother Earth has managed to attract the abundance of life forms, including those that are still in existence in your time. You all know, scientists have told you, that a great many life forms have moved out of existence at the moment. These life forms may make a comeback if they feel enough welcoming energy. Anthropologists and others, ornithologists, take their cue from what I'm saying about welcoming. You can guess what to do—picture things and so on.

Considering all of that, you need to welcome life. Mother Earth welcomed life, all right? Granted, she welcomed it in a broad spectrum. That's why you have not only birds and plants and animals and fish and humans and all that, but you also have viruses and bacteria and so on. That's why I say, you have to be careful if you walk around welcoming in the outdoors or even indoors; you need to be specific about what you are welcoming, and you can't be specific in your mind.

You might think you can be specific, but if you're focused in the feelings that you feel when you're welcoming, you won't be able to discipline your mind. This is not your mind disciplining the body; it is the body feeling in a very specific way, as described, and you emanating that feeling. You don't have to broadcast the feeling; it will naturally broadcast itself. All feelings naturally broadcast themselves, all right? So it will naturally broadcast. Mother Earth used that feeling to attract all life, and that's why there are so many varieties.

Granted, you're probably fortunate that some of them are not in existence today, although in a different form of Earth, someday it would be all right. You might see saber-toothed tigers running around on the surface again someday when human beings have learned how to live in a most benevolent, wonderful and comfortable way, largely under the surface of the planet in very beautiful areas and with tremendously huge skylights that allow you to see the surface. But we'll talk about that some other time. It's been discussed in other books.

It's Up to You to Take Over Earth's Duty

Now, in order for you to accomplish this welcoming, you need to practice, so practice when you can. This is sort of extra credit. You practice it so that you can begin to take over this duty that Mother Earth is doing. Why do you think so many species have been leaving in recent years? You would say they're no longer in existence, but I would call that leaving because their souls do go on elsewhere, return to their points of origin and so on, and there they continue. As you can guess by my suggestion before about Mother Earth welcoming all life, she didn't have as much life on her before she welcomed all life from all points of origin.

So how are you going to do this? You need to understand clearly that welcoming all life for you needs to be a contact sport, all right? So you walk around and welcome the trees, you welcome the tomato plants through touch, okay? Mother Earth welcomed these different life forms, and she has begun to release that capability in herself to you so that you creators-in-training can do it. Understand this: The creatures and the life forms that are no longer in existence here have been going out of existence at an increasing rate because she has been releasing that function, and it's *up to you* as creators-in-training or even, if you like, as souls-in-training to take over these functions. There will be other things you will need to take over, but that's one of the most important right now.

Welcome Oil

I'm going to put out the call on this someday, in about six, seven, eight, ten months. Someday I'm going to want you, especially those of you in the oil industry or who have been around crude oil and know what it feels like, I'm going to want you to imagine welcoming oil. Just imagine it first. How would you do it? Well, you need to know what it feels like. It's one thing to know what a tree feels like and to go out and touch a tree, but most of you cannot go out and touch crude oil. For those of you who can and know what it feels like and are open to this kind of thing, welcome oil.

This is an interesting thing. The oil industry might wish to know about this, that you can walk around to some convenient place on the Earth . . . what would be a convenient oil area? Obviously, the most convenient place would be a place where you've already got a well that's gone dry. So oil people and others, walk around to a tapped oil well—not one that's going to be tapped at some point in the future, but one that was tapped and has gone dry—and just welcome oil. For those of you who are in other places not near the oil fields, also welcome oil. This is what to do: Picture yourself, imagine yourself deep down in the Earth, especially those of you now . . . listen up here, those of you in earthquake zones, picture yourself or imagine Earth as being part of you, and welcome the oil. (You might want to get the advice of Speaks of Many Truths or Reveals the Mysteries on this; they might suggest different or additional techniques.)

Don't welcome oil first; practice with trees and other things first. Once you feel you've got the knack of how it could work for you safely, then walk around some earthquake zone and welcome oil because . . . I'll tell you something: Mother Earth does use her oil to essentially lubricate her plates. All the geologists know plate tectonics and all this stuff, but deep down within Mother Earth, she also has plates and levels and layers, and the oil actually performs the function inside of her to allow her moving parts to move in a cushioned way, not unlike the way a shock absorber works. So if you can welcome oil within Mother Earth, then she will also begin to feel better and will begin to trust you, have faith in you and rely more on your capabilities and abilities.

Welcome the Atmosphere and Recall the Feeling

What about that extra-credit homework in the future? I'd like some of you, a lot of you . . . you know what good air is like to breathe (not all of you, but those of you who live out in forests or who are around lots and lots of plants). Perhaps some of you work in greenhouses where plants are in abundance and not many people are there, where the atmosphere is thick with oxygen, although a well-vented greenhouse may not be like that. But those of you in forests, especially dense forests, know that the oxygen is a little better there. And when you go out to the forest, you not only feel better physically and more relaxed (the energy is more natural for you as a human being), but you also get refreshed from the

The amount of oxygen carried by the blood depends primarily upon the concentration of oxygen within the inhaled air. This is shown by the graph below.

As the airborne concentration of oxygen decreases, the amount carried by the blood initially shows only a gradual decrease. When the airborne oxygen concentration is 10.5 percent (that is,

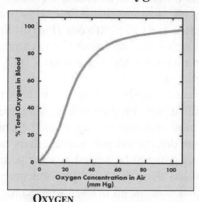

50 percent of normal), the blood is still carrying approximately 85 percent of its normal level. However, when the airborne concentration falls below 8.4 percent, there is a marked decrease in the amount of oxygen carried. The resultant effect upon the body is shown in the table below (Hammer 1988; Timar 1983).

OXYGEN CONCENTRATION	SYMPTOMS
21%	None (normal oxygen level)
15%	No immediate effects
14%	Fatigue, impaired judgment
10%	Dizziness, shortness of breath, deeper and more rapid breathing
7%	Stupor sets in
5%	Minimum amount that will support life
2%–3%	Death within 1 minute

As the table above indicates, oxygen concentrations down to approximately 16 percent can be tolerated. However, this is at the expense of increased demands upon the cardiovascular system. An oxygen concentration of 15 percent, for example, will show no immediate effects, but the load upon the cardiovascular system is equivalent to a workload of 3 kcal/min (Timar 1983).

www.safetyline.wa.gov.au

more oxygen-rich atmosphere. While you're breathing that, go into your welcome and welcome that atmosphere.

I'll tell you what's good about that: You can walk around in the forest and welcome that atmosphere. Try to do it someplace where the air is oxygen-rich, but not artificially so. Those of you in laboratories—don't take a breath of oxygen and try and do it. It's not the same. It has to be produced naturally, in the natural circumstances of the forest. Understand that you can do this in a forest and it will still function all over the Earth, but you need to do it someplace where contact is available. If you've done this repeatedly in the forest and you can remember what it is like breathing the forest air, then you can try it someplace where the air is not that good. But do it repeatedly in the forest so you've got it down. How many times is repeatedly? Fifteen to thirty times, until you've got it down.

I'm not saying you should do it; I'm saying it's extra credit if you can do it, if it's available to you and you *want* to do it. I've given you a lot of homework, and I don't want to give you any more right now. (You know I love to give homework.) I really honor and respect you for doing it, because ultimately you grow and you will have the opportunity to take over what Mother Earth is doing. You know you *are* creators-in-training. That's what the Explorer Race is all about, and you therefore need to give yourself the opportunity to create things that are beneficial.

Creator knows how. Creator can get you interested in such homework, such activities to encourage Mother Earth to let go of these natural abilities that she has, even for a short time, so that you can pick up the cue. And Uncle Zoosh will come along to cue you if possible, all right? Creator knows that in the beginning you are more likely to respond, to apply your creator training and your abilities if you need to, if it's urgent—and of course, as you get used to applying this training, you will ultimately be able to apply it to other things.

Please don't use these techniques on human beings, to alter or change human beings right now. This is something you are not prepared to do, with the exception of some shamans and other mystical people. Generally speaking, I do not recommend this for those I'm speaking to in this article, because it is too soon and requires a great deal of finesse and a lot more training than most of you already have.

You Are a Creation, Not a Machine

Okay, 40 percent oxygen, 20 percent microwaves and radio frequencies—what percent is this whole thing with the Earth? The rest of it?

Exactly.

So this whole thing with Mother Earth is the other 40 percent?

Here's something interesting. This is beyond interesting—it's intriguing. If you can go out into the forest and breathe that air and feel refreshed, after you've done that even just a few times . . . or say you did it yesterday. You did it even just three or four times, and today you find yourself in a polluted environment. Do you know that you can actually remember being in that forest, just recall it? Now, it's not a meditation; you don't have to think about it. Just recall it, and the purpose is to recall the *feelings*, your physical feelings of being out in that forest. And do you know, your body will reinvigorate itself for a moment, because your body is not a computer, it's not a machine. You're not a machine! Get over that, as the kids say.

You're not a machine; you are a creation. Creations are not machines. Creations might wish to make a machine, but it's not the same. Machines are not creations, none of them are. With you recalling those feelings of being in the forest, your body can create, in that moment, a momentary refreshment for you by reacting to the recalled—not memory, but *re-called*—*re-called feelings*, because you're calling the feelings there. So that's pretty important. You can do other things, but I want to get you started with this bit by bit and not jump too far ahead. So that's enough homework for now.

It's Up to You!

When you talk about an ice age and volcanoes and earthquakes, that seems to flow with the old timeline. Is this also on the new benevolent timeline we're going into?

No. It's just that Mother Earth is cooperating with Creator. Mother Earth knows that you're the Explorer Race and that you're here to be creators-in-training, and certainly at this stage of your training, you are getting more and more into application. What did I say a few years ago? I said you were doing all this preparation and then you were coming into a time of application and so on. Well, this is the time of application.

So the so-called new timeline is that the whole experience will not, is not, involved with such apparently terminal situations [see *Explorer Race: Techniques for Generating Safety*]. What it is involved with is that you take over and do things that Mother Earth has been doing—not only for herself, but what she has largely been doing for you. Why should she welcome life forms who generate way more oxygen than the planet normally needs? Because you were coming. All right, animals were coming too, but you were also coming and you, unlike the animals, would tend to expand your populations past the point where she could take care of you.

So it's *up to you* to take care of you. If she cannot welcome the life or chooses not to because it's time for you to apply your training, if she does not welcome the life that produces the oxygen that you breathe, then what? And Creator wants her to do this because it's part of your training. Don't ask Creator to help. *It's up to you!*

Trust Your Physical Material-Mastery Body

That's extremely interesting. I have a personal question: I felt really good yesterday and then I went to a chain store and I could hardly open the door; I got weak all of a sudden. What on earth was that?

The next time you have that feeling, do not go in. When you, who are a sensitive being, open the door to walk into some place and get a bad feeling, that is your physical material-mastery body, okay? I want you to understand that you do not have a physical body. No one on the planet has a physical body. Everybody on the planet has a physical material-mastery body. Period! That's how it reads. When your physical material-mastery body tells you that this is not a good place for you to be in that moment, you do not go in. There could be an abundance of reasons. Maybe there's simply some place better for you to be. How would you know?

If you're in a shopping center, just turn around physically or walk around to different stores. As you approach the door, perhaps you wave your left arm in the wand form toward the store just a little bit so that it doesn't draw attention and you don't feel embarrassed. If you get a good feeling in your body, then that's where you go in. Maybe it's to look at the products, maybe it's to buy something, maybe it's to meet someone and talk—who knows? Don't keep pushing. When you push to go into a place and it's not the right place for you, your body just gets discouraged. You're in no position to ignore what you are promoting others to believe.

I want to leave this in. I just thought I got weak. It didn't occur to me that it was a warning, so I want to put this out for other people, too. I just wondered why I got so weak.

This is good, and I'm glad you are willing to do that because it is a typical thing that people feel. Here's the situation: Sometimes you have more than one chain store available to you. You might go into a particular store . . . there's nothing wrong with that store, it's just that at that moment there was someone, something, some circumstance . . . it wasn't the right time or place. Some other time you might feel totally attracted to go in there. It's not the place, all right? It is the *circumstances* of the place.

Granted, there might be some places you would go toward to go into, and you might never feel good about going there. That means that place isn't for you; clearly it is for others. There could be an abundance of types of stores or even just generally places that you might need to shy away from for years at a time— some of you for very good reasons that are obvious to you, others for reasons that are also good but are not so obvious. This is your material mastery, your physical material-mastery body, yes? This is that part of you giving you that notice. How does it give it to you? In *feelings!*

Well, I did take heed a little bit, because although I usually walk through the store and see what jumps out at me, instead I got what I needed and ran.

Good for you. So others, listen up. If you don't catch that feeling right away, if it dawns on you later, grab what you came in for and hotfoot it over to the cashier and right out after that. And if you can, after that, try to go someplace where you feel a little better. If you're exhausted—and you might be exhausted because you're in a place that your body was trying to suggest to you is not the best place for you in this moment—then you simply need to go somewhere and rest, ideally sitting by a tree or something like that. But if you can't do that, then just go somewhere and sit down for a moment, okay? Perhaps drink some kind of a refreshing drink—a little water, a little tea, something that refreshes you— and you'll feel better. Maybe if you're hungry, you have a little snack, something. If you're in a rush, if you have to go somewhere, go back out to the car or bus or wherever. If you go to the bus, you can perhaps sit down and rest; if you go to the car, sit and rest for at least three minutes before going anywhere. Just sit in the seat and rest for a few minutes, otherwise . . . what? You might be exhausted. What happens to drivers when they get exhausted?

They lose their awareness and are careless.

That's right. They could make mistakes. So this is all connected. Good for you for leaving this in; I'm proud of you. It's real, it's human; you're a human being, your readers are human beings. It's important to allow it to be personal, because readers are people like you.

Okay, truthfully, my first response was that there was something wrong with me. I'm not used to thinking like this. I just got exhausted and I was blaming me.

Pets Teach You about Your Feelings

Perhaps the most draining feeling—and it's not a real feeling of its own; it's a thought that generates other feelings—is blame. Blame is a combination of many things. You were blamed; you know what it's like. You get angry at people and you blame them for this, that or the other thing or circumstances and so on. When you blame, when you get involved in blaming—whether it's yourself or anything else—you immediately set up certain self-destructive feelings in yourself, and as you know, Zoosh's description of self-destructive is "harming yourself or harming somebody else."

Here is the situation: When you're blaming yourself in that moment, do you know that anybody standing within three to four feet of you will not feel blamed but will feel momentarily self-destructive, to a percentage of anywhere up to 3 percent? Now, if they're already feeling self-destructive, it's not going to help them. If they're not feeling self-destructive, they might just get a vague, uncomfortable feeling and walk away.

I'm going to give you an example of that. Sometimes you've been around people who have looked perfectly fine, charming, what-have-you, but when you're near them, you get a vaguely uncomfortable feeling. Perhaps they're feeling self-destructive or angry or upset. You know that, you've had that feeling before, and others have had it, so you understand it. I'm just mentioning it because blame—either blaming somebody else or, as is more often the case, blaming yourself—is something that harms you and harms others.

Those of you who live closely with dogs or cats or other animals will very often know by their sudden unexplained reactions to you. Suddenly your pet will move away or jump away if it's on your lap. When that happens and your pet is not going to do something . . . usually, in that case, your pet will be very gracious about it, especially if it knows you well, meaning it'll jump off your lap and go over and lay on the bed or something like that. So sometimes that's purely practical. But if your pet is not going to do anything—maybe it just sort of saunters around and does no particular thing—then try to get in touch with what you were feeling just the moment before your pet did that. Try to remember. This gives you instantaneous feedback of your feelings that are harmful or aggravated or that in some way affect others.

At least 50 percent of the time the reason your pet—dog or cat usually in this case—jumped off your lap in that moment is not because it was so aggrieved or made so miserable by it, but because your pet knows that its job is to teach you about yourself and this is one of the ways it can do that. Don't assume if your pet jumps off your lap that that's what it's about. But if your pet seems to wander around or not be particularly interested or walk over to the corner and lay down somewhere else, then try and remember what you were feeling in that moment.

This is a good way to learn, and if you notice that you are feeling uncomfortable or feeling angry or blaming or something, then just look at your cat or dog and say, "Thank you, my friend." Don't say it just as words, but go into the feeling of thank you. "Thank you, my friend," and that's it. Your pet may or may not come back. The whole point is not to blame yourself, "Oh, I was feeling bad and I made my dog feel bad." It's not about that. It's about recognizing that your dog or cat (in this case, I'm talking about the majority of pets) is your teacher— not all the time, but many times.

Do Something about Those Things You Can

You talked about the oxygen supply and what we can do about it, such as planting trees and welcoming oxygen. There's not much that we can personally do about microwaves. As we go into wireless technology, how will we handle the additional radio frequencies?

An increase in the number of devices using such energies could make it worse. That's why you can't do anything about it until that technology is changed. You're not going to throw it out; you're just going to change the technology as more is understood about that impact. There's some reluctance in some parts of the world, especially in the U.S. and other places, to accept the responsibility that these frequencies have a negative impact on people. But there are countries in the world that are exploring that and doing research on ways to make this technology more benevolent. Even if they don't develop it, they will at least apply the technology that is being developed or that they develop to allow such communicative devices and other broadcast radio frequencies and microwave frequencies to still be used, turning them into something that allows you to use the technology but doesn't impact human beings or, for that matter, animals. So that's being developed.

But the reason I gave you all this homework is so you know what you can do, and I don't expect those of you who are not in the scientific community to do anything about broadcast frequencies. There's not much you can do about that. It's better to do something you *can* do and feel empowered as well as maybe have some good experiences.

Thank you.

Good night.

Atlantis and Lemuria
Were Two Planets Ago

Zoosh

May 24 and June 30, 2003

*C*an you *discuss Antarctica? There are rumors that the Nazis went there, that there are old civilizations and underground tunnels—Byrd was sent there. Have humans lived there in the past?*

Antarctica: An Enigma to Explore

One of the simple facts that one normally has to face is that Mother Earth changes her physical face—that which is viewable from the outside in, as if you were hovering over the planet. She changes her physical face always with some form of water, wind or motion. That is fairly obvious. So she uses her physical appearance and physical capabilities to have an effect on herself, not unlike what human beings or animals do, which is necessary since you are made up of portions of her body. So it's not too surprising that you find ice over this part of her body.

The civilizations who have lived there in the past, you might say, and also in the future . . . the reason I'm putting it that way is because you have to allow for the fact that we're dealing with other realities, other existences that are not now readily accessible by your civilization. These existences, although they might be simultaneous in a way, are largely shielded, not just physically from your eyes by having an ice covering. But they are shielded in terms of not only keeping you focused on the natural beauty of Earth, that which you can readily see—blue water, mountains, streams, trees and so on—but also functioning as an enigma for those who have seen those things and want to know what's under them that cannot be seen.

That was fulfilled for a long time by those who went searching in caves and would find what they found there and find it interesting, to say nothing of those who would dig under snowdrifts to see what was there. But after a time and frustrated attempts to leave the planet and explore the planets in fifteen different directions at once, so to speak, you came back as an explorer with the need to stay at home and more cheaply and reasonably and easily explore that which is enigmatic here.

So I'm getting around to saying that one of the main jobs of that polar cap is to entice explorers to find out what's underneath. Of course, in some cases, you find land under both polar caps. In other cases, you simply find water. The water itself has largely been explored by undersea vessels from various countries, and that's that. But if you're asking about civilizations who existed there, then we're talking about other existences who do not have anything to do directly with people of your time. I'm not against discussing it, but it may not be particularly relevant.

The Nazis Went to Antarctica

Now, I will mention that the Nazi party (as it is abbreviated as kind of a condensed word of its actual name) did spread out all over the world for that short time when the Nazis were influential, to find anything and everything that could have a bearing on their own form of mysticism. Granted, it was applied in a distorted way, but that was bound to happen since they attached themselves to a worthy symbol, the swastika, but they turned it around, also tipping it up on its end. They used the symbol, in a way, to explore something on the other side, meaning it was as if they were determined to pursue the opposite of benevolence.

This is actually a fertile ground for exploration in its own right, in that if what was originally intended to happen had happened, the man who has come to be known as Hitler would have come to be known by a completely different name and would have been a fine teacher, artist and historian whose words and writings would have been revered and appreciated by many, though he would not have been deified. But due to various happenings in his life and due to distortions of the world he found himself living in—culturalization, conditioning and so on—he got off track. I can assure you, he regretted it after life and viewed it as a missed opportunity.

Nevertheless, during the time of the Nazi party that you're aware of, there were explorations of this icy region. But other than planting a flag and saying, "This is ours"—which, I might add, almost every country does when it goes there—they did not find anything that could prove or disprove, from their point of view, anything they believed in (which, I might add, is a basic tenet of any dedicated philosophy or religion). I'm not trying to suggest that Nazism is a worthwhile religion, at least as it was practiced, but it has tremendous similarity in its dogmatic principles—not based on other religions as they are, but on the fundamentals of dogma.

Nazi Oaths Go Back before Orion

You said "during the time of the Nazi party that you're aware of"—hasn't history covered the Nazi party completely? Is there a period of time before or after the second world war that we do not know about?

Well, you have to remember that what is referred to as the Nazi party is something that was formed up as a loose-knit group of political dissidents before it actually became a party, and to some extent history has covered this, but you have to recognize that people were not widely interviewed for this. This was very secret, deep-dark, not unlike some secret societies or clubs and so on in your own country. People do not speak about these matters publicly and openly, and for that matter, only limited records are kept, for their own uses. So when I refer to that which you are aware of, I mean that which has been published at least with some attempt toward documentation. I am not referring to that which has been speculated upon, since everything from A to Z and beyond is speculated upon, but to that which I feel is within the bounds of speculation and not what I would call at least somewhat documented.

The Nazi activity started years before we think it did?

That's right, and there was always a great deal of that which was hidden that was going on with it—not just ceremonies and so on, but oaths. One of the main things, one that is not particularly discussed in English-translated history, is the oath taken. Now, you know, any study of European history—to say nothing of that of other countries, but particularly European history—has a great deal to do with oaths and pledges and covenants and so on, and not very much of this has been translated into English, partly because there is not that much interest in it. Some older works are well documented and of interest, but I would say that for the major background for oaths and pledges and so on, you would probably have to go to other languages: German, a little bit of French, certainly Latin and so on. This gives you an idea of how far back this goes. Also, you could—especially in studying the cultures of the planet—take this back to certain planets and the Orion galaxy and so on; you could take it a long way back.

This all has to do not only with loyalty, which on the surface seems to be what an oath is about, but it has to do more with commitment. And commitment, you know, involves a broader range of actions, or in some cases, nonactions—meaning if you are committed to a cause or a person or anything like that, you are much more inclined to overlook certain things as long as that cause or person is moving in the general direction toward what you believe is your shared bond or intent.

So that kind of thing has always created problems over the years. In recent years, you have had the Nazis. They were here as this commitment that was political went way overboard, became horrendous and so on, for various reasons—initially largely to establish power, then eventually to maintain power and ultimately to create self-destruction, which to the inner circle of the Nazi party meant everyone. It didn't just mean their own being.

The Commitment of the U.S. Can Be Traced Back to Other Planets

But I have not yet stated the reason I alluded to the idea that not that much is known, so I will go on. When you look at your own history, which as a country is short comparatively speaking, you have to recognize that the history of your country does not begin in the 1700s. The history of your country—considering those who founded your country and took it away from those who were here before and who essentially suppressed all opposition in accordance with their commitment—begins in Europe and could be traced well back to other planets. But I am just going to skip over that for now, since this article is not really intended for that, meaning it is not intended for those who are interested in extraterrestrial matters. It's more intended for what is going on on Earth now, what's real on Earth now.

The Energy of Contradiction

The history does not begin there; it begins in a very deeply rooted place. Now, some of this is going to be for those who have studied the Explorer Race material deeply. The deeply rooted place where your history begins is simply in the energy of contradiction. You all know that some things, even though they may be part of a whole thing, are in total contradiction to that whole thing. An example might be the family: In the family, everyone agrees—at least in principle, not in every moment—that they love one another, they support one another, they will do whatever they can for one another. But very often there is at least one member—and sometimes more than one member—who is wildly in contradiction with everybody else in almost every waking moment. This is a perfect example of contradiction. You have all had this experience with a family member at least one time; some families have it consistently.

"But," you might reasonably ask, "why does this take place? Is there something wrong with this person?" or "Is there something wrong with this moment?" (for those of you who have it only occasionally). It takes place because you have a planet that is a school, and in this school the Creator felt that Creator must set up certain contradictions that will come up no matter what. You have to think about it: Other than the human situation on Earth, most of the planet is functioning in a homogeneous state, meaning that one thing balances another, and this is the case for the planet herself, for the plants and the vegetation, for the animals. One thing balances another.

That's basically the summation of natural science, but there is an exception. In the human condition, while it might be that biologically and microbiologically one thing balances another most of the time, it is not always that way socially, and to put it mildly, it is frequently not always that way. This is intended. You can get animals in the animal world who are, so to speak, antisocial, but they either do not last long, as many naturalists and others can explain, or they are shoved out of their society and therefore do not last long. But in human society, such a so-called anomaly—as it would be called in the so-called natural world as I am separating it, as a way of separating it—such anomalies are not, in fact, anomalies at all. What appear to be anomalies are built into the human system so that they will absolutely force human beings to learn and grow, even if they are only doing something to attempt to solve what is, in many cases, the unsolvable.

Of course, if the disputing family member is a child, usually that child is suppressed by older children or parents or grandparents, meaning the child is essentially controlled. This does not mean, of course, that in the future these people will not act on their disagreeing principles, thoughts, ideas and so on. But what about adults who may have had these disputes, arguments and disagreements as youngsters, but as adults there is a more broad-minded attitude allowing such disagreements? This is built in, and it forces those who would like peace or agreement or consensus or any of those things . . . it forces you to try different things, to solve things. It forces you to stretch, and at the very least, it forces you to grow.

Creator Set Up Contradiction to Force Humans to Grow

So the reason I am going into this explanation is, it is essential for you to understand that that which you do not know, cannot change, misunderstand—in short, trip over and, *boom*, fall flat on your face—sometimes is built in by Creator. That literally forces human beings to grow, change, adapt and come to consensus; grow, change, adapt and come to some kind of consensus; grow, change, adapt and come to some sort of livable consensus; grow, change, adapt and so on. This is built in.

Therefore, when I say that these contradictions—or the contradicting state— are something that is not known and understood, not appreciated, not really seen clearly in your country, it is because the oath that might have been taken, perhaps with the intention to pass it on to generations to come, or the oath that might have been taken in some countries by people whom you are not related to by blood or otherwise (meaning, there is no genetic relationship), that oath might have been taken for you without your knowledge or consent. Now, how can that happen? And what does this really mean? Logically and intellectually, it doesn't seem to mean a thing. It's as if somebody said something—so what? On the surface, it is "so what?" But you have to remember—how did that person say these things? In recent years, Speaks of Many Truths, Reveals the Mysteries, my humble self and others have been talking to you, gentle readers, about *benevolent magic*.

Now, you've been hearing a lot about benevolent magic. Why do we continue to call it benevolent magic? One might reasonably say, "Well, Zoosh, you've identified this as benevolent magic over and over and over again. Why don't you just say magic?" or "Why don't you come up with an acronym so we don't have to read 'benevolent magic' every time?" I will tell you why, and that is that there are other forms of magic. There are attempts to create other forms of magic to last a long time. One might reasonably call it *malevolent magic*. One might reasonably call it that, but I would choose to use a more contemporary term, meaning a term that has been used by various individuals—shamanic people, mystical people and others—in the past few hundred years. I am going to call the use of magic without a specific benevolent application stated or incorporated directly in the magic *sorcery*, because it is possible, either through ignorance or through intent, to intend magic to enslave, instruct, control, authorize, command and generally to boss others.

Nazis Used Oaths to Bond

Now to get back to the Nazi regime. One of the main unifying forms of bond that existed—especially in certain units such as the SS and primarily with the officers, but to a degree with all of the individuals assigned to that unit—was oaths. And these oaths were not stated only as something like, "I . . ." then your name, "promise . . ." No, no, no, no, no; it was not done like that. Remember, something these people used to say regularly was the "Thousand Year Reich," and with the Thousand Year Reich, they were not talking about themselves; they were talking about those to come, their heirs. And they were not only talking about their heirs, they were talking about the world, meaning all human beings, all animals, all plants, Mother Earth herself.

This tells you something. Since they obviously cannot control when the Sun comes up, when the stars come out . . . this tells you that they were attempting to use magic to control and so on. This tells you, based upon how I have explained it, that they were attempting to use sorcery. Now, I grant that in sorcery . . . I am describing it as something that is an umbrella situation, meaning that it might at times very well use benevolent magic to accomplish some benevolent purpose, but it might also at times incorporate or decompose that benevolent magic by incorporating into it other controlling elements, thus ruining the purpose and function of the benevolent magic. In short, sorcery is a broader brush stroke, which is intended to have impact and effect toward whatever the sorcerer (or sorcerers) is attempting to accomplish, and this may very well have a malevolent impact on many, many beings.

Nazi Sorcery Affected This Time and Times to Come

So on the one hand, you might reasonably say, "Well, logically . . ." And the moment you say logically . . . I say that logic is a worthwhile pursuit, but as anyone who studies logic knows, there is within logic something that is an unsolvable conundrum, and that is paradox. When you bump up against paradox in logic, this means essentially that something cannot be explained logically, and if there is something that cannot be explained logically, calling it paradox is just another way of saying that there is something missing from this system we are using.

So I do not wish to go into explanations and discussions on logic; rather, I would prefer to say, let's talk about whole systems that do not have gaps. In this case, I am talking about sorcery, I am referring to oaths and I am talking about things that were attempted, you understand, to affect not only their times but your times and times to come. Why do you think that in recent years you have been getting instruction in these pages through this channel and possibly through others to support benevolent magic, to support that you move on to a more benevolent timeline, a timeline of the future—to create instead of a past-oriented motion toward the future, a future-oriented motion toward the future? Why do you think all of that has been instructed?

I will tell you why: because of the damage largely, ironically, unintentionally created by the sorcery done in those times you refer to as WWII and which I will say is also pre-WWII. This sorcery was done, for the most part, unintentionally, meaning accidentally. Now, how can that happen? If you've got a regime with motives to create a Thousand Year Reich, then you might reasonably say, "Well, they are going to do whatever they can do to maintain control." To essentially establish their Reich in the face of all opposition was but, in their minds, the need . . . the intent was, "What about when we're gone? Our leader, our leaders, the inner circle, what about when we're gone? Can we absolutely count on those we've trained, no matter how well we have trained them, to maintain the Thousand Year Reich?" And there was general agreement that no matter how well people were trained, they couldn't absolutely 100 percent count on them. Therefore, the desire for something beyond their own capacities to influence was present; thus, sorcery was chosen.

Why Benevolent Magic Needs to Be Precise

The motivation, the demanded commitment, involved oaths. I am not going to say what the oaths were, because that would compound the problem. What I am going to say is that they called upon, and here is what . . . you understand, when we give you words, when Reveals the Mysteries, Speaks of Many Truths and others give you words, we often tell you exactly what to say, *exactly, exactly,* precisely, so that you do not trip over yourselves and unintentionally fall into something that might hurt you or others. So when the Nazis, the SS and so on in their times said these oaths, they unintentionally—for the most part, I might add; occasionally intentionally, but for the most part unintentionally—said things that made it possible to be destructive.

You have to understand . . . just overlook for a moment how destructive they were to others. Their whole point, their whole intention, was to create, to construct something that would live a hundred years and beyond. A thousand years struck them as something they wanted to do. And they were desiring and willing to do whatever it took to accomplish that. Therefore, they would put it out in their oaths, in their commitments, in their prayers, if you can call them that, meaning—how can we say?—things they would say speaking to the gods. They would sometimes say, "The gods . . ." and it was assumed that they were without religion, but that is not quite true. They would ask, for instance (I'll mention bits), they would ask, "Those most powerful . . ." I won't say more than that. You can imagine.

And they would ask . . . the way they saw it, the way they intended to bring about their goals, was they intended to bring that Thousand Year Reich about (and the study of what they did in their times, not just the horribleness of what they did, but also the intentions, will help you understand that better). They wanted it to last for a thousand years and beyond, they would always say. Now, by saying that, they actually created for you, in your own time, an undercurrent—not something you necessarily have to buy into.

Undercurrents Are 99 Percent Benevolent

Most of the undercurrents and the underpinnings of your existence, your creative ability and so on, are benevolent. If you want a percentage, it's a little better than 99 percent benevolent. I don't want to tell you too much. But because of what they said, what they did, how they did it and the corrupting methods they used—sometimes used simply because they didn't know what they were doing—they have created and added this other undercurrent to the benevolent undercurrents of all life in your time.

And sometimes when you see, in your time, history repeating itself, it's because of things they did. You don't have written history for too much time, but you have some. Now, you might reasonably ask, "Are they the first ones to have done this?" No. You have to remember that what I am talking about here is essentially something Creator originally set up—not that Creator set up malevolence for you, but Creator set up contradictions. Creator set up things so that you would necessarily have the opportunity to solve problems, even if in your society there were no problems to solve, which would happen occasionally in societies that were long and well established and had come to some benevolent expression of themselves. Nowadays, these would be considered isolated societies, but go back far enough and you'll find that.

So that factor set up by Creator in order to encourage you to grow is what they accidentally influenced, meaning that that thread is something they unintentionally expanded into to create a potential for malevolence to repeat itself, not only . . . you have to remember, they were attempting not only to influence their present and their future, but they were also attempting to influence the past.

Sorcery Created Repetitive Cycles

How might they do that? Not just on the basis of rewriting history, which they attempted of course, but also in an attempt to draw strength from the past that they didn't have themselves in order to give themselves more capacity to endure on an individual and on a group basis. So they would call not only on that which was present but also on that which was past. This has unintentionally restructured your past somewhat.

I am now explaining to you in perhaps excessive detail why you will see, if you go back in written history, certain repetitions that weren't obvious in recent years. Look at the studies that have been written, especially those with corroborating physical evidence, historical studies that have taken place and have been published or have come close to being published (I will allow for research), that have taken place from, let's say, 1935 on, which incorporates the WWII years but also those that preceded them. You will find that there has been greater notice taken of repetition in historical patterns of strife especially and so on. Now, I am not going to go into that. I am simply going to say that there has been unintentional influence by those individuals through their oath to affect your times.

U.S. Founders Used Commitment to Benevolence

Now, in your country, the continental U.S., for the most part—also somewhat in North America, but for the most part in your country where the founding fathers came—you had those individuals who were attempting to create a society even while destroying, in many cases, more advanced societies of native peoples simply because they did not understand how advanced they were, because the people looked so different and of course did not speak a language that they knew, so they could not explain the greater depth of their societies to the newcomers. The people who came over and established the society in which you are now living as Americans would create commitment to their cause by oaths. It was known and understood—going back way before, of course, the Nazi government came to power—that absolute commitment would allow all individuals within this commitment to not only do what needed to be done to further their cause, but to overlook the excesses, mistakes and errors, no matter how horrendous they might be, in order that that which they were committed to move forward in some way that they could all agree on, on various points, was to their mutual advantage.

Now, I am not saying that everybody sat down and explained these things to each other, but that was the general understanding by those who could understand such concepts. Fortunately, there were a few among the so-called founding fathers who had other visions and could see beyond the immediate, and that is why your government has to this day a significant amount of the mystical built in symbolically and otherwise. This was built in, in an attempt to keep you, as the government of the U.S., on a more benevolent path and to break ties with the oaths taken in Europe—going back quite a ways—to forward just a few people and to rather, in this country, put forward the many people.

Practice the Love-Heat

Now, you understand that I am trying to cover world history for several thousand years and we cannot do it in one brief talk, but I am attempting to give you an answer to your question that not only answers that question but undoubtedly encourages you to explore other areas that you haven't looked into. And I am also underlining something that has been coming through this channel for a long time, and that's the instructions about benevolent magic and why we always say benevolent magic—because benevolent is not just a word, but it is something you can genuinely feel.

That is why the love-heat/heart-warmth/physical-warmth [see p. 23] is one of the foundational elements of benevolent magic—so that you know that benevolent is not just a word but a feeling that feels good. It is love that binds things together in a way that does not use an oath, that does not use command, that does not usurp you as an individual, but binds things together and only binds those things together that wish to be together in their hearts. This means that they want to bind together, even if that togetherness is just for a moment, because it feels more. By feeling more, I simply mean that if you can bring up the warmth in yourself, and you go and interact with another individual on the basis of this work, and you both feel greater warmth in that moment, the physical evidence is overwhelming; it feels good. That which feels good feels better in that moment.

In short, there is an absolute understanding that the word "benevolent" is not just a word, it is a feeling (and feeling is the underpinning of all creation), and that the love-heat you feel (though you may feel it in places other than your heart as well) is the physical evidence of loving yourself—and loving yourself is the natural way of all life. The instruction has been given to do this with trees and otherwise to learn how to do it.

Is there anything we can do that you haven't mentioned before that can help us overcome or overrun or get beyond that eddy, that undercurrent that these people caused?

Don't you think we've tried that? No, there is not much you can do except to be conscious of your history as a society or as multiple societies. Be conscious of world history. Take note when things seem to be repeating themselves, not just individual issues that are meaningful for your people, but history in general. Patterns are repeating themselves—wars and so on. Take note of that. If something like that is going on, it's probably a repetition that is not to your advantage.

Exercise: Make a Connection to Your Benevolent Future

See if you can make that connection with your benevolent future. By that, I'm not talking about this life; I'm talking about any future life you could imagine for which, by imagining it in your mind's eye . . . it's okay to use your mind. Picture it, imagine it—it must be completely benevolent. Don't imagine an ego situation where you are right all the time and everyone else is wrong. None of that; that is not benevolent. If everyone else is wrong, then that hurts you, too.

Now, I know that most of you understand this, but I am trying to make it crystal clear. Picture a future life in some totally benevolent place. Then, while you are imagining it, either with your left hand or your right hand reach forward as if you were reaching into that time and very gently and slowly close your hand in that area. It could be your left hand or your right hand. You might have to move your hand around; it might even be a couple of fingers, sort of like pinching the area. Move your hand around until it feels good in your body to do it. Ideally, you'll feel the warmth for a moment, but you may have to feel around just a little bit; you may have to move your hand. You may just have to get a slight hold in that area and take note of how your body feels. Ideally, it is best for you to feel that warmth, but if you cannot do that, just make sure that your body feels at ease and comfortable physically—not just mentally, but physically.

When you feel that ease and comfort physically, while you maintain that vision of the beautiful benevolent future, you can do this (you have to do it slowly): Move your hand back just a little bit, pulling it toward you, all the while making sure that you feel physically comfortable. You don't have to pull it all the way to your physical body, as you have your hand and arm stretched out all the way. You don't have to do that. Just pull it toward you in a few inches of motion or pull it toward you to the extent that your physical body stays relaxed and feels comfortable and, if you can do it, maintains the warmth. If at any moment you feel uncomfortable, or if the warmth goes away, or if you can't see the vision that you saw or imagined anymore, or if the vision changes to something that is uncomfortable and isn't completely benevolent and beautiful, then stop.

You can do that once, twice, three times—as often as you like. I'd recommend that two or three times be the minimum. If you feel like doing it more, you can. You don't have to. If you do that at all, it will help you as an individual to connect to your future benevolent timeline and help you improve the quality of your life, because you will no longer be connected only to that past timeline with that unpleasant undercurrent, however small an influence it might be, and you will perhaps—no guarantees—add a greater benevolence to your life.

Creator Wanted Variety and Resolution

Now, you might reasonably ask, if Creator included this stumbling block, so it seems, for your growth, was Creator just shortsighted? No, you have to remember that Creator's desire for Creator's creation here was not only to have the maximum amount of variety at all times but also to bring about as much resolution of that which was unsolvable in other creators' creations as possible, and one of the most ongoing conundrums of unsolvability that no creator had actually been able to make any progress on was discomfort. And Creator's intention—not for other places in this creation that cannot handle discomfort, but for your school here on Earth—was to add just a little bit of that influence, to make it open to an influence of discomfort in an attempt to find a way to utilize discomfort in some benevolent way that would bring about a means for discomfort as a being, as an existence, to be appreciated. The way Creator intended to do that . . . granted, it's gotten out of hand, but you can in time as a society on Earth make it lots better, and Creator intended for there only to be about 1 to 1.5 percent discomfort, which would stimulate your growth.

Now it has come to be much, much more than that. But as a society, as you come together now (and I mean as an Earth global society) to form the world order based upon business and specific expressions of business—for instance, media, publishing, energy resources and so on, things like that; specific orders of business, one might say—then you at least establish a common-ground connection between all individuals to improve the quality of life in the world so that the world runs efficiently in a businesslike way, creating a more benevolent existence for all people who then become consumers and can create within the business world a better quality of life for all human beings. Ultimately, of course, this leads to a desire to simply improve life for all human beings, then to improve life for all beings and so on. And thus your totally benevolent world is created. This takes time, but you are firmly on that path.

Zoosh: Byrd's Arctic Diary Is True

Is what we've read about our government sending Admiral Richard E. Byrd to Antarctica with atomic bombs and to find the Nazis correct?

I'm not going to say that. Your current government is determined to defend its goals and purposes, both public and unspoken, with efficiency, whether it be generous and warm-hearted or whether it be ruthless. And there may have been a time when such devices seemed to be attractive. But nowadays, given the level of your technology and mobility above, on and under the ground (or let's say, under the surface), one does not, from a warlike position—also referred to as defense—need to have fixed installations anywhere when installations of weapons can be so mobile.

Let me phrase this more specifically: After the second world war, did any part of our government send Admiral Byrd down there to look for the Nazis to bomb them? Was that his mission?

I'm reluctant to speak to this since it is still secret, still classified. I am not really inclined to speak of things that your government (or other governments, for that matter) considers to be things it would rather not discuss because they represent an ongoing investigation or an investigation that did not reach a conclusion that could be supported by further documentation—in short, something that stopped but was not completed. So this is my way of backing out of that question. I would prefer to say that Admiral Byrd's duties were largely assigned and his discoveries—which he talked little about until much, much later in his life cycle—were reported and duly noted, and because they could not be readily reproduced in terms of documentation, they were not followed up on.

But if you're saying, "Did he discover what he personally claimed to discover?" then I will say yes. But you have to stay focused on what he personally claimed to discover, not on what other people said and on, "Here's what he didn't say," and all that other stuff. No. He said all he had to say. He reported on what he saw, and what he saw had to do with another existence.

And when it's with another existence, you're having a report on something that is not unknown on this Earth, meaning people—and this is largely known; it's something people know about—go into the Bermuda Triangle and see things that are there, but they are there in another existence and cannot be found and documented by others who were never intended to see them. That doesn't mean that what the original people saw (or even others who came along later to see them, and it was perhaps in a slightly different way that they were seen) . . . these were things that were seen. If others did not see them, then obvious things leap to mind: one, they were not intended to see them, and two, the things that were seen did not wish to be seen by those individuals, period. But it is not snobbery. It has to do either with personal discretion, preferring not to be seen, or with some other existence that does not function in a full-time way in your world.

As we expand our abilities and our spiritual awareness, will there be a time in the future when we can interact with those beings whom Byrd saw?

Why would you want to? Define "interact."

Go there, talk to them and look around and explore.

You can do that anytime when you're not physical. You'll be welcome then, because your energy will be completely benevolent and safe for them.

So it has to wait that long—until we are totally benevolent as humans.

Yes, because your natural radiations, which you cannot help—radiations not from your soul, but from your conditioning and life experience—would be uncomfortable to beings who are completely benevolent. That doesn't mean they don't want to help you, but that they have to do it with a little distance and in some cases with a lot of distance.

Did these beings inside the Earth possibly seed the German race?

Let's just say that all accents preceded this Earth, including most languages.

ADMIRAL RICHARD E. BYRD

It is not possible to know the history of the polar regions or undertake scientific investigation of the areas without being aware of Admiral Richard E. Byrd or benefitting from his contributions. As a navigational aviator, Byrd pioneered in the technology that would be the foundation for modern polar exploration and investigation. As a decorated and much celebrated hero, Byrd drew popular attention to areas of the world that would become focal points of scientific investigation in numerous disciplines. Finally, as a naval officer Admiral Byrd contributed to the role of government in sponsoring and facilitating research in polar regions and topics.

Richard E. Byrd first made his mark in the U.S. Navy. Graduating with the class of 1912 from the U.S. Naval Academy, he served in the battleship fleet until forced into medical retirement in 1916 from the after-effects of a smashed ankle suffered while a midshipman. Recalled to active duty in a retired status, he organized the Commission on Training Camps. In April 1918 he won his wings as Naval Aviator 608.

From the start of his flying career he demonstrated unusual ability. Byrd pioneered the technique of night-time landings of seaplanes on the ocean and flew out over the horizon, out of sight of land, and navigated back to his base. In 1918 he proposed flying the newly built NC-1 flying boats across the Atlantic to the war zone in France. His war service was in Canada as Commander, U.S. Naval Air Forces with responsibility for two air bases in Nova Scotia.

Fig. 39–1. Admiral Richard E. Byrd.

With the conclusion of hostilities, Byrd was called to Washington and made responsible for the navigational preparations for the transatlantic flight attempt of the NC flying boats in 1919. He was a skilled officer in representing Navy interests under consideration by the Congress. Byrd won wide acclaim for directing the lobbying effort that resulted in the first post-war pay-raise for military personnel. Byrd was also invaluable in the long campaign of Naval aviators to establish a Bureau of Aeronautics.

Interested in polar exploration from childhood, his adult involvement began in 1924 when he was appointed navigator for the proposed transpolar flight of the Navy's dirigible Shenandoah from Alaska to Spitzbergen. When the flight was canceled by President Coolidge, Byrd began to organize his own Navy flight expedition to the Arctic. He was compelled to join forces with the MacMillan Expedition to northwest Greenland sponsored by the National Geographic Society in 1925. At that time Byrd completed the first flights over Ellsmere Island and the interior of Greenland.

In 1926 he took leave from the Navy to organize a privately financed expedition to the Arctic, which was to be based in Spitzbergen. Plans included several flights over the pack ice, including one to the North Pole. Supported by Edsel Ford, John D. Rockefeller, Jr., the New York Times and others, Byrd and his pilot, Floyd Bennett, claimed to have reached the North Pole on May 9, 1926. Both men were awarded the Medal of Honor after their return to the United States. In later years scholars have raised questions about the success of the expedition in flying over the North Pole.

Cheered by the outpouring of public support and admiration, Byrd continued his leave from the Navy. With commercial sponsorship, he completed the first multi-engine airplane crossing of the Atlantic to France. Byrd then turned his sights to Antarctica in 1928. During the remaining years of his life he was involved in five expeditions to Antarctica. These explorations accounted for the discovery of hundreds of thousands of square miles of territory which were claimed for the United States. He personified the inception of the mechanical era of Antarctic exploration. No other person in Antarctic history has contributed more to the geographic discovery of the continent than Byrd.

With highly visible accomplishments, he thrilled millions and raised large amounts of funding. He flew over the South Pole in November 1929. He spent most of the winter of 1934 alone in a meteorological hut some 100 miles into the interior. His winter weather observations were the first taken from the interior. This effort almost cost Byrd his life when he was poisoned by carbon monoxide fumes.

Byrd remained a promoter of Antarctic exploration. He merged his plans for a third private expedition with governmental plans and became the commanding officer of the United States Antarctic Service. With the onset of World War II he returned to active service and earned two decorations as the Chief of Naval Operations.

In the early post-war years, Byrd participated in the organization of the U.S. Navy Antarctic Developments Project in 1946–47 (Operation Highjump). He supervised the preparation of a study for the Joint Chiefs of Staff of Greenland as a site for military training and operations. In his final years he was called again to serve the nation as Officer in Charge of United States Antarctic Programs. This responsibility gave him authority to coordinate government supported scientific, logistic and political work in Antarctica. Admiral Byrd remained an influential figure in polar research until his death in 1957.

www.-bprc.mps.ohio-state.edu/AboutByrd/AboutByrd.html

ADMIRAL RICHARD E. BYRD'S DIARY
(February–March 1947)
The Exploration Flight Over the North Pole
[*The Inner Earth: My Secret Diary*]

I must write this diary in secrecy and obscurity. It concerns my Arctic flight of the nineteenth day of February in the year of Nineteen and Forty Seven.

There comes a time when the rationality of men must fade into insignificance and one must accept the inevitability of the Truth! I am not at liberty to disclose the following documentation at this writing . . . perhaps it shall never see the light of public scrutiny, but I must do my duty and record here for all to read one day. In a world of greed and exploitation of certain of mankind can no longer suppress that which is truth.

Flight Log: Base Camp Arctic, 2/19/1947

0600 Hours: All preparations are complete for our flight northward and we are airborne with full fuel tanks at 0610 Hours.

0620 Hours: Fuel mixture on starboard engine seems too rich, adjustment made and Pratt Whittneys are running smoothly.

0730 Hours: Radio Check with base camp. All is well and radio reception is normal.

0740 Hours: Note slight oil leak in starboard engine, oil pressure indicator seems normal, however.

0800 Hours: Slight turbulence noted from easterly direction at altitude of 2321 feet, correction to 1700 feet, no further turbulence, but tailwind increases, slight adjustment in throttle controls, aircraft performing very well now.

0815 Hours: Radio Check with base camp, situation normal.

0830 Hours: Turbulence encountered again, increase altitude to 2900 feet, smooth flight conditions again.

0910 Hours: Vast Ice and snow below, note coloration of yellowish nature, and disperse in a linear pattern. Altering course for a better examination of this color pattern below, note reddish or purple color also. Circle this area two full turns and return to assigned compass heading. Position check made again to base camp, and relay information concerning colorations in the Ice and snow below.

0910 Hours: Both Magnetic and Gyro compasses beginning to gyrate and wobble, we are unable to hold our heading by instrumentation. Take bearing with Sun compass, yet all seems well. The controls are seemingly slow to respond and have sluggish quality, but there is no indication of Icing!

0915 Hours: In the distance is what appears to be mountains.

0949 Hours: 29 minutes elapsed flight time from the first sighting of the mountains, it is no illusion. They are mountains and consisting of a small range that I have never seen before!

0955 Hours: Altitude change to 2950 feet, encountering strong turbulence again.

1000 Hours: We are crossing over the small mountain range and still proceeding northward as best as can be ascertained. Beyond the mountain range is what appears to be a valley with a small river or stream running through the center portion. There should be no green valley below! Something is definitely wrong and abnormal here! We should be over Ice and Snow! To the portside are great forests growing on the mountain slopes. Our navigation Instruments are still spinning, the gyroscope is oscillating back and forth!

1005 Hours: I alter altitude to 1400 feet and execute a sharp left turn to better examine the valley below. It is green with either moss or a type of tight knit grass. The Light here seems different. I cannot see the Sun anymore. We make another left turn and we spot what seems to be a large animal of some kind below us. It appears to be an elephant! NO!!! It looks more like a mammoth! This is incredible! Yet, there it is! Decrease altitude to 1000 feet and take binoculars to better examine the animal. It is confirmed—it is definitely a mammoth-like animal! Report this to base camp.

1030 Hours: Encountering more rolling green hills now. The external temperature indicator reads 74 degrees Fahrenheit! Continuing on our heading now. Navigation instruments seem normal now. I am puzzled over their actions. Attempt to contact base camp. Radio is not functioning!

1130 Hours: Countryside below is more level and normal (if I may use that word). Ahead we spot what seems to be a city!!!! This is impossible! Aircraft seems light and oddly buoyant. The controls refuse to respond!! My GOD!!! Off our port and starboard wings are a strange type of aircraft. They are closing rapidly alongside! They are disc-shaped and have a radiant quality to them. They are close enough now to see the markings on them. It is a type of Swastika!!! This is fantastic. Where are we! What has happened. I tug at the controls again. They will not respond!!!! We are caught in an invisible vice grip of some type!

1135 Hours: Our radio crackles and a voice comes through in English with what perhaps is a slight Nordic or Germanic accent! The message is: "Welcome, Admiral, to our domain. We shall land you in exactly seven minutes! Relax, Admiral, you are in good hands." I note the engines of our plane have stopped running! The aircraft is under some strange control and is now turning itself. The controls are useless.

1140 Hours: Another radio message received. We begin the landing process now, and in moments the plane shudders slightly, and begins a descent as though caught in some great unseen elevator! The downward motion is negligible, and we touch down with only a slight jolt!

1145 Hours: I am making a hasty last entry in the flight log. Several men are approaching on foot toward our aircraft. They are tall with blond hair. In the distance is a large shimmering city pulsating with rainbow hues of color. I do not know what is going to happen now, but I see no signs of weapons on those approaching. I hear now a voice ordering me by name to open the cargo door. I comply. END LOG

From this point I write all the following events here from memory. It defies the imagination and would seem all but madness if it had not happened.

The radioman and I are taken from the aircraft and we are received in a most cordial manner. We were then boarded on a small platform-like conveyance with no wheels! It moves us toward the glowing city with great swiftness. As we approach, the city seems to be made of a crystal material. Soon we arrive at a large building that is a type I have never seen before. It appears to be right out of the design board of Frank Lloyd Wright, or perhaps more correctly, out of a Buck Rogers setting!! We are given some type of warm beverage which tasted like nothing I have ever savored before. It is delicious. After about ten minutes, two of our wondrous appearing hosts come to our quarters and announce that I am to accompany them. I have no choice but to comply. I leave my radioman behind and we walk a short distance and enter into what seems to be an elevator. We descend downward for some moments, the machine stops, and the door lifts silently upward! We then proceed down a long hallway that is lit by a rose-colored light that seems to be emanating from the very walls themselves! One of the beings motions for us to stop before a great door. Over the door is an inscription that I cannot read. The great door slides noiselessly open and I am beckoned to enter. One of my hosts speaks. "Have no fear, Admiral, you are to have an audience with the Master . . ."

I step inside and my eyes adjust to the beautiful coloration that seems to be filling the room completely. Then I begin to see my surroundings. What greeted my eyes is the most beautiful sight of my entire existence. It is in fact too beautiful and wondrous to describe. It is exquisite and delicate. I do not think there exists a human term that can describe it in any detail with justice! My thoughts are interrupted in a cordial manner by a warm rich voice of melodious quality, "I bid you welcome to our domain, Admiral." I see a man with delicate features and with the etching of years upon his face. He is seated at a long table. He motions me to sit down in one of the chairs. After I am seated, he places his fingertips together and smiles. He speaks softly again, and conveys the following.

"We have let you enter here because you are of noble character and well-known on the Surface World, Admiral." "Surface World," I half-gasp under my breath! "Yes," the Master replies with a smile, "you are in the domain of the Arianni, the Inner World of the Earth. We shall not long delay your mission, and you will be safely escorted back to the surface and for a distance beyond. But now, Admiral, I shall tell you why you have been summoned here. Our interest rightly begins just after your race exploded the first atomic bombs over Hiroshima and Nagasaki, Japan. It was at that alarming time we sent our flying machines, the 'Flügelrads,' to your surface world to investigate what your race had done. That is, of course, past history now, my dear Admiral, but I must continue on. You see, we have never interfered before in your race's wars, and barbarity, but now we must, for you have learned to tamper with a certain power that is not for man, namely, that of atomic energy. Our emissaries have already delivered messages to the powers of your world, and yet they do not heed. Now you have been chosen to be witness here that our world does exist. You see, our Culture and Science is many thousands of years beyond your race, Admiral." I interrupted, "But what does this have to do with me, Sir?"

The Master's eyes seemed to penetrate deeply into my mind, and after studying me for a few moments he replied, "Your race has now reached the point of no return, for there are those among you who would destroy your very world rather than relinquish their power as they know it . . ." I nodded, and the Master continued, "In 1945 and afterward, we tried to contact your race, but our efforts were met with hostility, our Flügelrads were fired upon. Yes, even pursued with malice and animosity by your fighter planes. So, now, I say to you, my son, there is a great storm gathering in your world, a black fury that will not spend itself for many years. There will be no answer in your arms, there will be no safety in your science. It may rage on until every flower of your culture is trampled, and all human things are leveled in vast chaos. Your recent war was only a prelude of what is yet to come for your race. We here see it more clearly with each hour . . . do you say I am mistaken?"

"No," I answer, "it happened once before, the dark ages came and they lasted for more than five hundred years."

"Yes, my son," replied the Master, "the dark ages that will come now for your race will cover the Earth like a pall, but I believe that some of your race will live through the storm, beyond that, I cannot say. We see at a great distance a new world stirring from the ruins of your race, seeking its lost and legendary treasures, and they will be here, my son, safe in our keeping. When that time arrives, we shall come forward again to help revive your culture and your race. Perhaps, by then, you will have learned the futility of war and its strife . . . and after that time, certain of your culture and science will be returned for your race to begin anew. You, my son, are to return to the Surface World with this message . . ."

With these closing words, our meeting seemed at an end. I stood for a moment as in a dream . . . but, yet, I knew this was reality, and for some strange reason I bowed slightly, either out of respect or humility, I do not know which.

Suddenly, I was again aware that the two beautiful hosts who had brought me here were again at my side. "This way, Admiral," motioned one. I turned once more before leaving and looked back toward the Master. A gentle smile was etched on his delicate and ancient face. "Farewell, my son," he spoke, then he gestured with a lovely, slender hand a motion of peace and our meeting was truly ended.

Quickly, we walked back through the great door of the Master's chamber and once again entered into the elevator. The door slid silently downward and we were at once going upward. One of my hosts spoke again, "We must now make haste, Admiral, as the Master desires to delay you no longer on your scheduled timetable and you must return with his message to your race."

I said nothing. All of this was almost beyond belief, and once again my thoughts were interrupted as we stopped. I entered the room and was again with my radioman. He had an anxious expression on his face. As I approached, I said, "It is all right, Howie, it is all right." The two beings motioned us toward the awaiting conveyance, we boarded, and soon arrived back at the aircraft. The engines were idling and we boarded immediately. The whole atmosphere seemed charged now with a certain air of urgency. After the cargo door was closed the aircraft was immediately lifted by that unseen force until we reached an altitude of 2700 feet. Two of the aircraft were alongside for some distance guiding us on our return way. I must state here, the airspeed indicator registered no reading, yet we were moving along at a very rapid rate.

0215 Hours: A radio message comes through. "We are leaving you now, Admiral, your controls are free. Auf Wiedersehen!!!!" We watched for a moment as the Flügelrads disappeared into the pale blue sky.

The aircraft suddenly felt as though caught in a sharp downdraft for a moment. We quickly recovered her control. We do not speak for some time, each man has his thoughts. . . .

Entry in Flight Log Continues:

0220 Hours: We are again over vast areas of ice and snow, and approximately 27 minutes from base camp. We radio them, they respond. We report all conditions normal . . . normal. Base camp expresses relief at our re-established contact.

0300 Hours: We land smoothly at base camp. I have a mission. . . .

End Log Entries:

March 11, 1947: I have just attended a staff meeting at the Pentagon. I have stated fully my discovery and the message from the Master. All is duly recorded. The President has been advised. I am now detained for several hours (six hours, thirty-nine minutes, to be exact). I am interviewed intently by Top Security Forces and a medical team. It was an

A Chronology of Admiral Byrd's Life

* 1888: October 25, birth at Winchester, Virginia.
* 1908–12: United States Naval Academy.
* 1914: First flight in an airplane.
* 1916: Retired from active duty because of an injury to his foot that prevented sustained duty at sea.
* 1916–17: Naval aviation cadet at Pensacola, Florida.
* 1925: August expedition to Greenland with Donald MacMillan, financed by Edsel Ford and John D. Rockefeller, with planes from Navy and Navy volunteers.
* 1926: May 9, flew the Fokker tri-motor plane *Josephine Ford* from Spitzbergen with pilot Floyd Bennett and claimed to have reached the North Pole. This expedition was privately financed and made up of volunteers.
* 1927: June 29, *Trans-Atlantic Flight of America*, a Fokker tri-motor commanded by Byrd reached France some thirty days after Charles Lindbergh.
* 1928–30: Byrd Antarctic Expedition, privately financed.
* 1929: With Bernt Balchen as the pilot, Byrd flies the *Floyd Bennett*, a Ford tri-motor airplane, across the South Pole.
* 1933–35: Second Byrd Antarctic Expedition, privately financed.
* 1934: March to August, Byrd stays alone in a hut some 120 miles from base to record weather and observe aurora. Rescued in August from carbon-monoxide poisoning. His autobiographical account of this ordeal, *Alone*, became a best seller.
* 1939–41: U.S. Antarctic Service expedition, led by Byrd but government financed.
* 1946: Operation Highjump to Antarctica, involving 13 ships and 4,000 men, mostly U.S. Navy, with Byrd as "Officer in Charge," but not in command.
* 1955: Operation Deep Freeze to Antarctica to provide logical preparations for the beginning of IGY 1957/58. Byrd was nominally in command.
* 1957: March 11, death of Admiral Richard E. Byrd.

www.-bprc.mps.ohio-state.edu/AboutByrd/chron.html

ordeal!!!! I am placed under strict control via the national security provisions of this United States of America. I am ORDERED TO REMAIN SILENT IN REGARD TO ALL THAT I HAVE LEARNED, ON THE BEHALF OF HUMANITY!!!! Incredible! I am reminded that I am a military man and I must obey orders.

30/12/56: Final Entry:

These last few years elapsed since 1947 have not been kind . . . I now make my final entry in this singular diary. In closing, I must state that I have faithfully kept this matter secret as directed all these years. It has been completely against my values of moral right. Now, I seem to sense the long night coming on and this secret will not die with me, but as all truth shall, it will triumph and so it shall.

This can be the only hope for mankind. I have seen the truth and it has quickened my spirit and has set me free! I have done my duty toward the monstrous military industrial complex. Now, the long night begins to approach, but there shall be no end. Just as the long night of the Arctic ends, the brilliant sunshine of Truth shall come again . . . and those who are of darkness shall fall in its Light . . . FOR I HAVE SEEN THAT LAND BEYOND THE POLE, THAT CENTER OF THE GREAT UNKNOWN.

www.v-j-enterprises.com/byrdiar.html

Foo Fighters Were from Inner Earth

In Admiral Byrd's diary, the Master said, "Your race has now reached the point of no return, for there are those among you who would destroy your very world rather than relinquish their power as they know it . . ."

Sounds familiar to you now, eh?

Yes . . . and he said, "In 1945 and afterward, we tried to contact your race, but our efforts were met with hostility, our Flügelrads were fired upon. Yes, even pursued with malice and animosity by your fighter planes."

In the beginning, you know, the foo fighters as they came to be known, at least in the Western world, these vehicles were largely ignored as you might ignore something if you were in an air-to-air battle with a plane trying to shoot you down and another vehicle was glowing in the sky or noticeable in the sky at a distance and it wasn't shooting at you. You probably wouldn't do anything about that second vehicle because you were, to put it mildly, too busy.

But if you had a moment, you might just—since you're in the middle of battle and it's not your plane—you might shoot. Of course, it didn't cause any harm.

So to those pilots those Flügelrads looked just like a light in the sky?

They would look like a light for the most part—glowing objects as they were referred to. Sometimes they would have some detail that would be noticeable. But the main point that everyone could agree on is that they were glowing objects. The reason the vehicles were glowing is that they were attempting to disseminate benevolent energy. They were of the belief that if they did that, they could perhaps bring the battles to an end. It was done for humanitarian reasons, to save lives and to attempt to help. But the people of those times were going ahead with their lives as they had to live them, you understand?

So it was a well-intentioned attempt to interfere, you might say, with a benevolent intent and only a benevolent influence. But history marched forward nevertheless. The foo fighters, as they were called, spotted by pilots of all sides, were not Germanic, were not put up by Germans or Nazis . . .

Oh, so then the foo fighters were these Flügelrads?

Yes.

Byrd Went from One Dimension to Another

I asked before when we would contact these beings in the center of the Earth, and you said when we were totally benevolent. So they are of a higher dimension, then?

Yes.

But . . . so Byrd at that moment was . . .

Welcomed into that society. They were still making an effort to benevolently influence the surface population of the dimension in which you all understand to be Earth. But they gave up. Or at least . . . let's say that their teachers advised them that the time wasn't right, that you had to proceed along your own path and that even a benevolent interference was still interference and was not desired or welcomed. And they had to be taught that even if they arrived in the most benevolent way, in the most loving way, if they are not welcome, then it is important to take that message and understand it and retreat. That is something that took them a little while to learn, but they got it.

Admiral Byrd visited these beings in 1947. A few years ago, you said that all the civilizations inside the Earth had left. So these beings are gone now?

Well, yes. Gone is relative; they are not on or in third-dimensional Earth.

Ah, so they just allowed Byrd to get in . . . they allowed him to see them.

Yes, and in that moment, Byrd went from one dimension to another, was allowed access. It was a bit of a struggle for the beings to allow that to take place, but they managed it for a time.

The Nazis Sought Secrets from Antarctica

So from your perspective, any civilizations who lived in or on Antarctica before the icecap or during it are not relevant to the Explorer Race?

I would say that they are not relevant in terms of your growth and your understanding of yourselves. Largely, the answer to your question is yes. But that's why I touched on the Nazi visits there—because yes, they went there. They went just about every place they could go to, including sending spies or asking others who might have been enamored of them, at least temporarily, to look around in and report on places they couldn't go—openly, that is.

Basically, they were looking for secrets from Atlantis?

I think they were not that narrow-minded in their approach. They were looking for secrets they could use to influence their understanding of things they wished to know and to perpetuate their influence to create Hitler's dream of the Thousand Year Reich, which of course didn't turn out because Hitler by that time had already been thoroughly and completely influenced in self-destructiveness. And he determinedly exposed the citizens of his own country to his destructiveness. A self-destructive nature is usually determinedly so. Not all are as extreme as that man, but he certainly did not have an exclusive on being self-destructive.

Atlantis and Lemuria Were Not on This Earth

They were looking for secrets from Atlantis, amongst other secrets?

No, they were looking for secrets, period. They were not attached to Atlantis only, but they were looking for secrets . . . you might say about Atlantis and other places, but it wasn't exclusively about Atlantis. I think this whole Atlantean connection with them has to do with the fact that it would have encompassed and been part of their pursuit, but they were not exclusively looking for that.

You see, the myth of Atlantis has significantly more impact in your time than the reality, and the myth is that it lasted a long time on Earth. You and I know it didn't last on Earth at all. It lasted for as long as it lasted on the planet that used to be present in this orbit—the whole point is, *used to be present in this orbit.*

But you see, at that time that the Nazis were looking for secrets, that information was not widely understood, to say nothing of not being widely known in those times, and that is that many of these mythical worlds you have heard about—for example, Atlantis, Lemuria and so on—didn't happen on this Earth as you know this Earth to be. They simply happened on the third planet from the Sun, a planet that used to be here, which Earth came to replace to provide a home for the Explorer Race.

Maldek Was in Third-Planet Orbit

The planet before that was in this orbit, was it the first Earth or was it what we were told to call Maldek?

It is what you like to call Maldek, though I assure you they did not themselves call it that. I tend to trip over that word, because it is a being's term provided for that place, since the being who originally provided that term felt that it was important to keep the name of that planet a secret. I personally have no intention of revealing the name of that place, because what happens when some place—or for that matter, someone—is no longer available? Invariably, it will come to be thought of as something wonderful by some, and people like to have something wonderful that is unattainable. Granted, not everybody is like this, but many people feel that way. I will give you a contemporary example: Elvis. He was a human being but not a figurehead as has been made of him.

Can you say who gave the planet that name?

I think you won't have to go back too far in literature to find that on your own. When did the name first show up? I will simply say it was a being who said, "This is this planet." And when questioned, "What is its name?" the being said, "Oh well, you can call it _____." That's exactly the words that were used originally: "You can call it Maldek." Now, I assure you that when spirits speak like that, "You can call it _____," that is their way of saying, "Here's a name you can use."

If I gave you the name of the planet, no matter how good your intentions, there would undoubtedly develop a following that would turn this place into something that it never was. It was simply a planet where people lived, went about their lives and, not unlike yourselves, ultimately made mistakes. In their case, they made an irreversible mistake that ended the planet.

Hitler Intended to Destroy Earth's Population

So you can be reasonably happy that the Nazi party did not discover too much about Atlantis because it would have been—and actually was—Hitler's intention to destroy the Earth, to take everybody with him. It was his intention to destroy every last living individual, not only living in Germany during the time he took power, but every last German and Germanic individual on Earth. When he died, his orders, which have largely not survived today, essentially . . . I don't want it to sound too bloodcurdling, but his orders basically were to "Carry out my final plan." Those were the orders, and then he, as has been reported, took himself and his wife elsewhere. Let's just say he removed his presence from you.

But his final orders were to kill everybody. What was intended to happen—and there were installations present, most of which have been found and deactivated—was to release poison gas. That was really why the rocket program was created, not just to attack England, their current foe, but to have a weapons delivery system that could go all over the Earth and release vast quantities of poison gas or toxics in the form of perhaps even radiation that would kill everybody and everything. That was his final plan. His own people were perfectly happy to say, after he had removed himself, "The heck with that."

You said it was Hitler's intention to destroy every last living individual who not only was living in Germany during the time that he took power, but every last German and Germanic individual on Earth. Why was that? You would think that for the Thousand Year Reich he would want the Germans to live?

Natural history was not lost on the individuals in that political and world power of that time. It occurred to them—referring to the man who came to be known as Hitler and also to the inner circle, especially those who were more studious—that a chrysalis might be possible. Yes, they were losing the war. Yes, they and their people were being decimated. Yes, it was quite obvious that they would not live on physically, or if they did, they would be vastly disempowered. So what might be possible was not unlike what the caterpillar does—to simply die off.

The Nazis Tried to Extend Their Power into the Future

The caterpillar, you might reasonably say, dies, and the butterfly is born, because if you look at the body, the actual physical body, not counting the wings, there is not a great deal of similarity. It is quite astonishing. There is the birth of the caterpillar, then it lives its life, then it literally dies and is reborn as a butterfly. They saw that if they could not create the world in their own image at that time—meaning to destroy all those who were not in their own image as they defined it, Germanic peoples, or Aryans you might say—then if they had to die off and go through the chrysalis stage, they would then have to destroy all

Aryans. They thought that they would then reemerge in some future time in a more beautiful and wonderful and influential way. This means that they would not only be perceived as something beautiful and wonderful . . . you have to remember . . . put yourself in their place: They felt that they were offering something wonderful to the world.

And the people in Germany were not idiots, they were not morons. I am not saying that they did not make a mistake in embracing Hitler and the Nazi party, which they later regretted deeply. But at the time and at its zenith—not counting those who were suffering terribly by what the Nazis were doing—the people of Germany and many others loved and admired what the Nazis were doing. I am not saying it was admirable; I am just saying that the love was palpable and the joy of the people looking toward the Nazi party as their savior, essentially on the physical level, was palpable. What the Nazis felt in that inner circle at that time was that love and joy are possible: "How can we encourage others to love us and have that joy toward us and believe in us? We will have to change our appearance somehow so that we are loved and admired and appreciated and followed the same way a child follows a butterfly in a field toward beauty."

Now, I am not saying that they believed in that literally. But utilizing the sorcery methods and what they were told by all the beings who talked to them about how to gain power, how to maintain power and how to extend power into the future, no matter what resistance was there from whatever source, it was determined that one of the best ways to do this was to be attractive on the surface and to do whatever you needed to do outside of the exposed surface, even if what you needed to do was horrible and malevolent in its fact.

Now, I might add that this idea was portrayed especially well . . . for those of you who haven't read the story, I strongly recommend *The Picture of Dorian Gray* [by Oscar Wilde], a classic story by one of your famous authors in your recently past time that will give you some idea of that kind of power influence, what it ultimately leads to. So the idea of what they wanted to create would seem to be illogical on the surface. You might reasonably say, from a reasonable logical position, "Why wouldn't he do everything he could, why wouldn't the inner circle do everything it could, to maintain, foster, encourage and spread as many Aryans around to keep the Aryan race going in their absence?" But you have to remember that they were deeply rooted and involved in sorcery, and sorcery—as they used it and as sorcery is often used unintentionally—becomes self-destructive, meaning, "If we can't have what we want now, then nobody gets to have any fun" . . . meaning, "We are perfectly willing to die for our cause, especially if we can take everyone else with us." Now, where have you seen that politically applied? It's in the news all the time these days.

Suicide bombers?

Any suicide bomber. The cause, in their eyes, might be perfectly just, and even in a logical stand-back approach, their cause might be also perfectly justified. It's the application that isn't justified and tends to perpetuate such actions.

If an individual wrongs another individual, then you might be mad at that other. If A harms B, B might be mad at A and might go to great lengths to harm A and then A becomes B—B is the harmed one—and on and on and on.

Those beings who were giving the advice, were they channeled negative beings?

Not channeled; they were what I would call inspired inspiration brought about by rituals that were malevolent in their intent. Now, you have to consider what I said: malevolent—ma-levolent, got it?—in their intent, meaning control. Dominate with absolute ruthless means whenever and wherever necessary. What single word would pop into your head now? I will say the word used in your westernized culture does begin with an S.

Edgar Cayce and Atlantis

I'd like to lead this into Atlantis, because I have a memory of being so shocked when you mentioned earlier that Atlantis was two planets ago that I didn't ask for more information. Can you say something about Atlantis?

You understand, the reason I haven't gone into any elaborate explanations of Atlantis, at least in recent years, is that I have to look at the way they wound up. The more I tell you about their civilization, the more likely you will find it interesting and want to explore it and want to duplicate it, and why would I even think that you would not actually duplicate it and destroy the Earth? There is every reason to believe that you would follow those exact steps.

But it's always been said that in order for us to get beyond it, we had to face it again—technology, what we're doing to crops, cloning. We have to do it right this time. That was always my understanding of the lesson of Atlantis.

Edgar Cayce (1877–1945) was an average individual in most respects: a loving husband, a father of two children, a skilled photographer, a devoted Sunday School teacher, and an eager gardener. Yet, throughout his life, he also displayed one of the most remarkable psychic talents of all time. For forty-three years of his adult life, Edgar Cayce demonstrated the uncanny ability to put himself into some kind of self-induced sleep state.

This state of relaxation and meditation enabled him to place his mind in contact with all time and space. From this state he could respond to questions as diverse as, "What are the secrets of the universe?" to "How can I remove a wart?" His responses to these questions came to be called "readings" and contain insights so valuable that even to this day individuals have found practical help for everything.

Today on file at the Association for Research and Enlightenment, Inc. (A.R.E.), in Virginia Beach, Virginia, are copies of more than 14,000 of Edgar Cayce's readings. These are available to the public and have been filed along with any follow-up reports received from the individuals who had asked for the readings. This material represents the most massive collection of psychic information ever obtained from a single source.

The organization founded by Cayce in 1931 to document, research and disseminate his information has grown from a few hundred supporters at the time of Cayce's death in 1945 to one which is worldwide. Countless individuals have been touched by the life work of this man who was raised a simple farm boy and yet became one of the most versatile and credible psychics the world has ever known.

http://www.edgarcayce.org
A.R.E. 215 67th St., Virginia Beach, VA 23451-2061
800-333-4499

EDGAR CAYCE ON ATLANTIS

If Atlantis did exist in the Atlantic above the great fault line that runs between the present continents, it would certainly have been plagued by earthquakes and volcanic eruptions. Is it mere coincidence that Plato should have situated his lost continent in an ocean that does apparently contain such a continent, and in an area subject to the very kind of catastrophe he describes? Atlantists think not.

On the other hand, there are some Atlantists who believe that the destruction of Atlantis was brought about not by geological events but by a man-made disaster, such as a nuclear explosion. According to the Cayce readings, the Atlanteans achieved an astonishingly high level of technology before the continent sank, around 10,000 B.C. They invented the laser, aircraft, television, death rays, atomic energy, and cybernetic control of human beings, and it was the misuse of the tremendously powerful natural forces they had developed that caused their destruction.

Cayce is best-known for his apparent ability to diagnose illness even in people whom he had never met. This ability was tested by a group of physicians from Hopkinsville and Bowling Green, Kentucky. They discovered that when Cayce was in a state of trance, it was sufficient to give him the name and address of a patient for him to supply a wealth of information about that person, often drawing attention to medical conditions of which the physicians were then unaware, but that subsequent tests on the patient proved to be correct. This work alone would appear to justify the description of Cayce as America's most talented psychic. And if one aspect of his clairvoyant powers could prove so successful, it seems reasonable to give a fair hearing to other psychic statements he made, however, fantastic.

Cayce's sons, who help run the organization set up to study his work, admit that their life would be far simpler if Edgar Cayce had never mentioned Atlantis. Hugh Lynn Cayce comments: "It would be very easy to present a very tight evidential picture of Edgar Cayce's psychic ability and the helpfulness of his readings if we selected only those which are confirmed and completely validated. This would not be fair in total, overall evaluation of his life's work. My brother and I know that Edgar Cayce did not read Plato's material on Atlantis, or books on Atlantis, and that he, so far as we know, had absolutely no knowledge of this subject. If his unconscious fabricated this material or wove it together from existing legends and stories in print or the minds of persons dealing with the Atlantis theory." Edgar Evans Cayce makes the comment that "unless proof of the existence of Atlantis is one day discovered, Edgar Cayce is in a very unenviable position. On the other hand, if he proves accurate on this score he may become as famous an archaeologist or historian as he was a medical clairvoyant."

If, as his sons and thousands of followers believe, Edgar Cayce's readings were supernormal and not the product of reading the works of others, it is certainly an intriguing case. There are, for example, some fascinating similarities between Cayce's descriptions of Atlantis and those of occultists such as Madame Blavatsky, Rudolf Steiner, and W. Scott-Elliott, including references to the Atlanteans telepathic and other supernormal powers, their advanced technology, their moral disintegration, and the civil strife and misuse of their powers that finally caused their demise. Cayce's readings also mention Lemuria, or Mu. Either Cayce was psychically readings the works of these earlier writers, or he—the they—really were "tuning in" to the past.

http://www.greatdreams.com/bermuda.htm, pp. 31–32

And you're right. But that much of it you are doing. You can't do everything. The more of an imprint of Atlantis you make, the more likely you are to wind up like Atlantis. So the things that you are doing—mining and all of that kind of stuff—that's as much as you are really being encouraged to do. But we can't say too much about the way they lived, because it will sound attractive, and ultimately, where does it lead?

Now, this is a picture and it's hard to describe, but picture a hair braid. It's those lines twisting around, only we're using three streams of hair here, or three lines. There are numerous ways you can go, and you're going through the time of your flirtation with things Atlantean, but it is intended that you take a different path. In order for you to take that different path, you have to have only a little bit of the Atlantean energy with you. If you have a lot, well—*poof!* So I tend to dodge around those questions.

But what about Edgar Cayce? He was so right about so many things, and he didn't know that Atlantis wasn't on this planet. As he looked back, couldn't he tell the difference?

You have to remember that when a person in an altered state looks back, that person is going to look back completely in a straight line. If you look back in a straight line from your position, you're going to look back from the third planet from the Sun, yes? You're going to look straight back and you're going to keep right on going back to the third planet from the Sun before this planet was here and the third planet from the Sun before that was here, you understand? You would look straight back in a linear fashion, and there's no reason for him to have considered that the third planet from the Sun would have been anything but the planet that was here, although I might mention that those in the know with the Cayce material know that a lot of the Cayce material never went public. It was kept quiet, and do you know why? (It is a sad thing, but true.) It is because it was believed, with the best of intentions, that it was necessary to maintain consistency in order that the material be believed. Later in life, Cayce spoke continuously and more elaborately of things that have not been published. Many of these statements are still available, but not to the public.

It's Safe to Publish Everything Now

Normally I would never reveal such a secret held dear by individuals, but now I would suggest to people who may have these documents to allow them to go public. Feel free—you can put a notation in the beginning somewhere that it was believed best to hold these back for a time. You can also say that these are the transcripts verbatim and that although you, the editor/publisher, feel that some of the material may be relevant . . . you can feel free to say that some of the material may or may not be relevant to people of this time and to please read it with that in mind. In short, you can make your opinion known.

But I speak to you: Please, what you have available, even if you think it is wildly inconsistent, release it and let it find its own community, which will be beyond the community of those who now feel that Cayce and all of his valuable contributions were relevant and worthy of practice indefinitely. So expand the horizons and recognize that it's safe to come out now. If you like, you can publish it at a distance, but please identify it with your foundation. That's a note to the Cayce people. I do not intend to offend them, but I do intend to tell them— *it's safe now.*

So Cayce brought information in that was exact and true, but because it was so different from his other material, the people around Cayce held it back, just filed it away?

It's that it wasn't consistent with the information they were interested in or that they wished to publicize. You have to remember that the whole reason for putting out the Cayce documents—and they were clear on this—was to improve the quality of life for people here on Earth. They were dedicated and they've done a great deal of good insofar as it goes. But if something wasn't consistent or was about a topic that they felt was not something they wished to be identified with, they kept it quiet. You have to remember that when they were coming out with these things, times were actually quite dangerous for them; it was not safe. In some cases, some of these things have been lost or—how can we say?—distributed out to individuals who were once associated with the Cayce group. But it might be possible for the Foundation to retrieve some of that material. There has been a quiet attempt to do this in the past, but now, by doing it perhaps more publicly, it might be possible to get some of it back.

Existence of Former Lives May Be an Illusion

On my own bookshelf, I must have a hundred books—and there are many hundreds more published—of people who remember their life in Atlantis. So they're remembering truly . . . people on Earth now were on that planet, right?

I cannot give you a blanket answer.

All right, let me put it this way: Some souls who are on Earth now as humans had previous incarnations in Atlantis, on Maldek?

Insofar as your context of linear existence goes, yes. That's how I have to put it, because you are changing the very context of your existence in this moment. For those who wish to stay focused in linear existence as you understand here, the answer is yes.

So let me put it this way: On the old timeline, which we're leaving, it is part of our direct past, but as we go to the new timeline, that will be a different existence, right?

As you put it—no. But you have to understand that the reason I'm splitting hairs here is because I want you to be perfectly clear that the existence of former lives in general may be a complete illusion; I think that's something you weren't understanding. To have some recollection of a former life . . . it may not have been your life at all, and I will explain why.

To understand philosophically—whether it's through New Age or religion or simply through a grand picture of life—that you are all one is completely attainable as a thought. In fact, it is a complete reality. Nevertheless, I understand and acknowledge that it does not seem to be a reality in practical day-to-day existence when you are here on Earth. I acknowledge that. When you are not here on Earth in this challenging school, it not only is recognizable as a reality, it is known and completely understood as a reality. Therefore, the experience of past lives will seem directly linear to anyone's past life anywhere, because you are all one—you know it, you experience it and, therefore, that's what you know to be.

Before you came here you were clear on that point, and after you leave here you will be clear on that point. My whole point is that if you are attached to a linear idea of past lives—meaning you're living on the planet now linearly; you don't remember and you're not absolutely clear that you are all one—all of that is an illusion. However, if you are saying, "Did I . . ." meaning the greater you as all one, meaning, "Did I (we are all one) have a past life on Atlantis?" then I would have to say, within the context of "you are all one," that everyone had a past life on Atlantis, including people who have never been in this part of space. You understand, I'm speaking to the reader here.

What is so interesting is that I have a memory of being involved in all of this, partly because of Pino and Rene Turollo in Miami. Pino used Cayce's prophecies about Atlantis, and what Cayce said would be found, Pino found in the years Cayce said we would find it. It's just that it was some other old civilization there on Bimini or in the islands off Florida, right?

Yes. What was found was intended to encourage you to keep looking for something that you would perceive as being more ideal, more beautiful, and to make it part of your physical world. Was it part of Atlantis? No.

What was it part of? Or was it created for us to find?

Let's just say that if the parts of your world, of Earth, that are covered with water right now were the land and the parts that are the land were covered with water, one would, even after thousands of years, still find remnants of your buildings or bits and pieces of your creations underwater due to the shifting sands of underwater motion that take place. There are earthquakes and motions underwater, and things that were not visible on the surface are then visible, so let's just say that it's typical.

I'm not predicting that you're going to have a big flood and everybody's going to die. I'm just saying that it is only natural. You can even ask geologists; they will tell you that the land is going up and down all the time. It is not unusual to dig down in places in the land that might be fifty or a hundred feet above the ocean or way higher than that and find shells, mollusks or remnants of the sea. You would have to say that the only way they could be there is that it was covered by water, and people assume that that means that the entire Earth was covered by water to that height at one time. But if you had an understanding of geologic time, you would recognize that it could also be that the land was upthrust over time and that it only appears to be that way. I'm not saying it was one way or the other; I'm just trying to give some support to the scientific community, which, in this case, might need it.

The Planet between Maldek and Earth

You said that Atlantis was two planets ago. If Maldek was the previous one, then what was the other one?

Another planet. Do we have to give it a name?

No. Your statement was, "Atlantis was two planets ago . . ."

But that was not the name of the planet.

No, that wasn't the name of the planet. You just said it was on Maldek, so then there was another planet between Maldek and us. There evidently was another planet we lived on and had experiences on after Maldek and before this Earth.

I see. Are we talking about the third planet from the Sun in this solar system, or are we talking about where individuals who lived on Atlantis might have chosen to reincarnate, no matter where it was?

I'm trying to get you to explain your statement. You said Atlantis was two planets ago. What did you mean by that?

Here you are on Earth, the third planet from the Sun. Then there is the planet that was here before Earth, then the planet that was here before that. That's where Atlantis was.

We blew up two of them?

I did not say that. I said the a planet that was here before Earth. Then I said the planet that was here before that one was where you had the planet you like to call Maldek. I don't like that term and I try not to use it, because it has been used to describe a myriad of things that I do not feel comfortable with. I will simply say this: The planet that existed between the presence of Earth and the presence of that planet you refer to by the "M" word was not suitable for the Explorer Race to live on because it didn't have all the levels of wisdom and applied wisdom that Earth had. Therefore, that planet was gently and in a nurturing way moved to another place where it could be safe and comfortable, and the wise and deep Earth that you know came to be here from Sirius. I don't know if that's clear.

Gentle Souls on Earth Now Are from That Gentle Planet

How was that decision made? There were beings who were incarnated on it . . .

There were beings who were living on it, yes, and it was clearly understood that that planet did not have the capabilities to deal with what the Explorer Race would be doing, would need to do and would need to attempt, even if you would never accomplish it. To give you an example: That planet would have immediately—immediate in terms of planetary time could be anywhere up to a thousand years of what you understand linear time to be—the moment anybody dug anything out of that planet, the planet would have immediately begun to die. That includes a child shoving a play pail into the sand. It was a very gentle place, intended to foster and nurture that which is gentle. I might add that there are some people on Earth now who identify the third planet from the Sun in that way, because their connection is energetically associated with that third planet from the Sun. Their connection in this life that they are living now is identified with the third planet from the Sun, but it is that gentle, benevolent, soft, tender, very feminine place, and it is difficult for most of them to get along.

If you are identifying with that and that's how you are (I'm not trying to change you), it would be good for you to go somewhere and be with people, to the best of your ability, who are gentle, soft, tender and nurturing. It may not always be easy to get there, but try to find those people and try to find those places and go there and stay there and let the rest of the world go on about its business. You don't have to participate if you can help it. I'm not trying to say that you are better or they are better—"better" doesn't come into it. I'm just talking about what is for you, and those of you I'm talking to know who you are, so don't feel as if you are here to learn to tough it out.

If you are that way, then by all means go to those places and you will then be able to bloom and find the strength to go on because those around you will be like you and you will bloom and provide what you can provide and enjoy what is provided by others. These places—and I'm not talking about this place and that place, and 460 miles from here, and this parallel and that parallel; none of that—are all over the Earth, and for all of you whom I'm speaking to, one of these places exists within 100 miles of where you live. So it might be a hill, it might be somebody's orchard; in short, it might just be a place where you can go, where you feel better. Sometimes that place is a person.

I know that sounds vague, but I cannot say too much, because I'm trying to protect you and I want you to be safe. You will find that these places are often places of beauty. If you cannot find a place like that, create one in your meditations or in your imaginations, and experience it once or twice a week or three times a week, and be nurtured by that. I recognize that you cannot all drop everything and go to such a place, but do that meditation and visualization so that you feel nurtured.

Can you say how many people you're talking to? Is it a large number?

Many thousands.

Gentle Souls Are Here Intentionally

Is it possible they came here not realizing it wasn't the planet they thought it was?

Yes, that's why I'm talking to those of you who identify with this. You were here not by mistake—your life is not a mistake—but your arrival was perhaps . . . it is a worthy question; I will not give it a short answer.

Your arrival has been intended, to some extent. You tend to have nurturing personalities, but you also need to be nurtured. Of course, all are like this when they are very young and often when they are very old—meaning in various senile states, not all—and many times during life as well. But for you individuals, you are like this pretty much all the time, and to some extent it is that this energy, this benevolent, nurturing energy often referred to as feminine (I refer to it that way myself sometimes), is meant to be here, to anchor here a bit to provide more of that energy than is naturally created by that which is called Mother Earth.

I might add that it is that energy from that planet left here, not only in remembrance of that planet, but also focused through you individuals, that gives Mother Earth her motherly qualities. Other than that, she would simply be "Mom" from time to time, but not the consistent reference to Mother Earth, and I understand the reason is that your bodies are made from her body and so on. But with that nurturing that you are providing simply by being, even if you are not nurturing all the time—I do not expect you to be that way all the time—you are anchoring that energy here, so it is something you have taken on.

It is not an accident, your being here. Granted, in other lives that you live that are not in this challenging school where you've also come to learn like everyone else, you will experience that nurturing and be able to give and receive it in an ideal place for you. But here you are performing a duty that you have taken on, and you do not have to spread it around or go to any great efforts to spread it around, meaning you don't have to run around on the land saying, "I am spreading nurturing." Just be yourself—you know who you are—and it will naturally emanate.

That Gentle Planet Volunteered to Come to This Solar System

How did that gentle planet happen to come to this solar system?

Orbits that are unoccupied by planets as a solid body destabilize solar systems. When that other planet became a nonplanet, it was essential to have a planet in this orbit as quickly as possible, so there was a volunteer from another solar system, not this one. It came here intact with its civilizations, most of whom had to move underground during its time in this solar system, simply because of the physical conditions of the solar system not being most benevolent for them. It was here for a time, until Earth traversed from Sirius to this point. If you were to approach the planet from a distance, it would look largely white and gold—depending on your view of the color gold, you might say white and yellow.

Did this solar system have to prepare itself in a special way to deal with the lack of benevolence from the Explorer Race?

Let's just say that the solar system itself is just physically difficult. When you look at the other planets of the solar system, it's obvious how very difficult it would be to function as a human being on those planets, with the possible exception being Mars. And then, of course, you'd have to be underground or very seriously sheltered, essentially living in a spaceship on the surface, due to the lack of atmosphere. To produce an atmosphere would take you quite awhile. I think you could produce an artificial atmosphere, though, as you do in a spaceship, without having to stretch too far technologically. So in that sense . . .

I'm not saying that the solar system is hostile, but it doesn't, by its nature, support life in a nurturing way, meaning all the planets do not have oxygen-based atmospheres that support your forms of life. But they do represent challenges, places to visit—including the Moon and so on—that would be a struggle, but just enough of a struggle so that you can do it. You can go to Mars; it will be a commitment, but you can do it and you will as a civilization.

As the Explorer Race, we've been there before, right?

Yes, but I think it's more important what you're doing now and what you may do in the future. We can examine the past all you want, but there's one thing I assure you that you will not be able to do, nor will any person who reads this: You will not be able to live that past. Therefore, I tend to pooh-pooh, so to speak . . . I tend to treat questions like that as irrelevant.

Granted, in the past I went through it quite a bit, but that is because those questions were asked at a time when individuals needed to build up a relationship with me so that we could talk about things that were, from my point of view, more relevant to the nature of humanity—your progress, your abilities, your applications, your capabilities and ultimately your existence. It takes time to build up that kind of relationship, and it's easier to talk about things in the past for which there is no pressing problem today.

On Earth Your Nature Is Different

Now, it's essential that you, as an individual whom I'm speaking to now, that in that way you are exactly like everybody else on Earth, and that is that it is in your nature to be self-destructive, which is why most ETs give humans a wide berth. The reason you are that way . . . it's not in your personal nature when you're not here on Earth in this school; it is your nature because this is such a hard place to be and you don't want to be here. And do you know, almost all babies feel that way when they are born—within the first two or three days at the most—that they don't want to be here and they wish they hadn't come? It's a tough school, and it's a tough school twenty-four hours a day, seven days a week, very often even when you are asleep.

Suppose I tell you, "Here's a magic word that you could say, but I'm going to keep it a big secret from you, see? I'd tell you the secret, but it could destroy the world." If you're honest, you're going to tell me that you want to know the word, even though you'll never say it. The point is that it's such a tough place to be that you are constantly in a state of inner conflict, that you would rather be somewhere else. That's why we try to get you to find out, to explore things on the Earth, to discover things that you like so that you can, as people say, ground those things and find enough things that you like so that you'll stay here as long as you possibly can, given the short duration of your immortal existence that is focused on Earth as an Earth human being in this tough school.

So the reason I bring that whole point up is that before in this session, I was talking about Hitler being self-destructive. He was self-destructive in the extreme, and other people who are suicidal are also self-destructive in the extreme—even though, in Hitler's case, he tended to project that out on people, meaning, "I am suicidal, so you will die." Well, in everyone's case, there is that element because this is such a tough place to be. I'm not here to be his apologist, but it's important to understand that it is your nature, though it may seem like a small part. *It is only in your nature when you are here on Earth*, and it would be in anybody's nature. If I were living a physical life on Earth as it is now, in your time, it would be in my nature, too. I'm not trying to place myself above you. I'm simply saying that it is natural, given the conditions on Earth, because it is so unlike your normal state of being, to the extreme.

Think about it. If the tiniest little discomfort would bother extraterrestrials—who do not come here unless they are highly, highly shielded and then only briefly—if the tiniest thing, which to you might be the mere pittance of an annoyance, would make them sick or possibly even kill them, can you imagine for a moment what a day of life on Earth, which you have been conditioned to experience and tough out, would be to them? But their way of being—ETs as we like to call them—is your nature when you're not on Earth. That's what you were like; that's your nature. So I know you think that this doesn't have any point and it's completely irrelevant and that I'm picking straws, but I'm talking to the people of Earth and you are living on Earth as it is now—you, Melody—and you are their representative, because you are an Earth human being now and you are just like them now in most ways. I'm not picking on you. I want you to notice how that feels inside you. Do you know that almost everybody on Earth would feel the same way except for the very young, teenagers who want to be like everybody else, but that's only a stage; you went through it, too.

I don't want to get too personal, and I can hear you gnashing your teeth as if to say, "I didn't have anything to do with this, and I'm not having anything to do with this, and that's not me, and you've completely misunderstood me." But you have to remember that it is your job in these conversations to represent human beings, and the only way you can do that is to be one. It is my job to represent Spirit, and the only way I can do that is to be one. It is my job to speak to all people, even though all people in your time will not read this. It is your job to speak to Spirit and to demonstrate your needs, both personal and in the grander sense of human nature of your time. Take a moment and think about that.

Zoosh Asks That We Focus on the Human Condition

You've clarified a lot of things that I was hesitant to tackle. What I'd really like to know is, what things interest you? What things do you feel we need to know in the times ahead that I may not even think to ask about? Will you discuss that?

I will. I will give you a platform, and that is this: Take a good look at the human condition. I made a point and you wondered why. I'll stitch it up nicely for you now. You wondered why I went on and on and on about the self-destructive nature of human beings and that you are a human being and that you are intended to represent human beings. You must take a look at who you are as a human being. You have to be absolutely honest with yourself—not about what you "should" be, meaning not about, "No, no, don't tell me the magic word, because I don't want to destroy the Earth."

If you want the areas in which I want you to be asking things about . . . it's about your human qualities and everything that has to do with your human qualities, your discomforts and, if you like, the included conflict between your physical and feeling nature and your mind. Other human beings are going through that, too.

But human beings . . . I am talking to human beings; I am not talking to animals, I am not talking to plants, I am not talking to stones, I am not talking to the rain. I am talking to human beings, and the reason I am talking to you and the reason I have ever spoken to you at all at this time on Earth as it is now is that I am talking to human beings. Therefore—and you know when I talk this way, I'm not yelling at you; I am stressing the point—please focus on your humanity, how you are like human beings, what you are feeling, what you are going through, and be completely, brutally (if you like to be) honest with what you are going through. Talk about that in future sessions, because I can assure you, everyone on Earth is almost simultaneously feeling the same general feelings at the same time. That is why your communication—news and all the stuff on TV and in the newspapers—as upsetting as it is, is really reflective in its motivation; the news motivation is to ultimately, on the spiritual level, unite everybody on the same feeling level.

So to put it simply, pay attention to what you are feeling, pay attention to your physicality, pay attention to your humanity, and ask about that. Your job is to be human, and I will talk to you about many things, but I will be profound, interesting and even humorous if you talk about your humanity. If you promise that you will do that at least sometimes and especially many times, I'll be back.

When you said that after this you want me to ask only about the human condition, it's like a 180-degree turn, because you called yourself the end-time historian. It seems like you have changed your focus.

Well, let's just say that I am attempting to be the good example. If I am asking you to connect to your benevolent future, then I must focus myself in your benevolent future and instruct you on how to get to that place. But I will, from time to time, such as today . . .

. . . humor me . . .

. . . be willing to talk to you about things. All right, good night.

Good night.

Dreams and Visions: Are They Real or Are They an Illusion?

Speaks of Many Truths, Reveals the Mysteries and Isis

May 27, 2003

The following email to Robert Shapiro led to several channeled responses.

Email Dated May 25, 2003

Beloved Family/Friends:

At your convenience, I request your meditative insight into what is really being conveyed in this attached series of "earth changes" emails, only one of a variety of similar information coming across my desk on a fairly regular basis (yours too perhaps?).

For years it has been my sense that such predictions, no matter how real to the recipient, are either a movie planted in the impressionable mass subconscious or a brand-new projection designed by the media masters of the dark side. No illusions/visions, however immense or outrageous, are impossible to manufacture any longer—as witnessed in the stunning technology of recent films like The Matrix. And all the admission ticket one needs is to resonate in harmony with such a frequency to get to "see" the movie for free!

As so many more family members awaken, I ask you, are we not tipping the balance to becoming responsible for our actions and our lives in a variation of the beloved Charles Dickens summation for Scrooge when confronted at last by the Ghost of Christmas Yet to Come? As best I recall, Scrooge, trembling, says, "I am not the man I once was. I will not be the man I have been but for this intercourse. Why show me this if I am past all hope? Assure me that I may yet change these shadows you have shown me by an altered life. Tell me, spirit, are these the shadows of things which must come, or only the possibilities of what may yet come?"

—With love, (name withheld upon request)

Editor's note: We do not want to print people's dreams and visions without their permission, so we are listing websites where you may find that information if you are interested:

- http://www.syzygyjob.net
- http://www.zetatalk.com/info/
- http://www.angelfire.com/fl3/gammadim/
- http://www.dreamdoctor.com/dreamboard/
  dreamboard.html
- http://www.network54.com/hide/forum/106909

Robert Shapiro Answers

Dear Friend,

I cannot read other people's visions, of course. However, the guidance I have always received about upsetting visions is as follows: "This is Speaks of Many Truths. These upsetting visions, my friend, are always and only intended in your time to encourage you to change disasters to more benevolent scenarios."

And also the following: "This is Reveals the Mysteries. In my time, such visions were meant to encourage movement of the peoples, a change in practice, something to do; in short, it was intended to require response on our part. It was simply spoken—a warning most often, other times simply a possibility. In your time, it is different. Your time involves the teaching and the practical application of transformation and its results, consequences and further transformation which may be required. You are, as Zoosh likes to say, living in the time of experience, application, results. Therefore, if I were you, I would approach such predictions on that basis. Equally, for those who receive such visions and predictions, don't be shy. If you feel a strong urgency or any urgency to let people know about them—go ahead.

"Try to tell people whom you feel will not be too upset or too frightened or experience some unpleasant medical phenomenon as a result. And yet, if you are getting the vision, it is most likely intended for you to tell at least someone. So do that if you feel the need. If you don't, then see if you can experience the love-heat/heart-warmth/physical-warmth [see p. 23] or other nurturance that you may need so you feel better. A hot bath might be good for those who do not know how to do the love-heat—or a comforting bath in some way that you have available.

"Understand that the purpose for these visions, if they are upsetting, is for you to change them in some more benevolent way. If they are not upsetting, their purpose is to give you knowledge and foresight. If they are predictive, check out the physical facts first before you jump or leap into something that may entirely be a fabric of possibility. Don't assume it is an absolute.

"Predictions and visions are always and only possibilities unless they are accompanied by physical feelings during the prediction. If this happens, then mention it to others, that you felt this way or felt that way during the prediction. Then you might find that it is essential to attempt to transform it in some way. The simplest and best way, if it is an upsetting vision, is to go into the love-heat if you know how to do that. If you don't know how to do that, then visualize something better happening and send out the vision to those you feel can now visualize something better happening and ask them to visualize that. All right, that's what I recommend in general."

Isis Elaborates

Isis, I'd like to get more into this issue that is so strange to everybody, about . . . well, on the one hand there is duty, discipline, commitment, keeping your word, getting things done, deadlines, all this stuff, and on the other hand is the self-destructive way some of that seems to be. Many people I've mentioned this to just look at me like I don't know what I'm talking about because it's so ingrained in our nature.

I'd like to talk about something similar but different. There is something that is going on for people now, and you can identify with it as well, and that's that . . . I'm going to entitle this "Dreams and Visions: Are They Real or Are They an Illusion?" Understand that you've always dreamt. That is really what allows your soul to be at peace in your body. But many, many of you these days are having vivid dreams that wake you up out of a sound sleep, and they're often very upsetting and too real, as you say. This has to do, these days, with something that might surprise you.

For most of your lives, unless you are very young, you've experienced on Earth a great deal of Mother Earth assimilating your overwhelming passions. By overwhelming, I mean that which you really cannot take—you get angry, you get upset, you want, you need. In short, there is so much desire or fear or upset within you, it's more than you can bear. In the past, Mother Earth has taken that on for you so you could live—have a life. But now many of you are unifying with other people. You cannot all be in unity with every single person on the planet all the time, but you can, as individuals, be in unity with some people on the planet—or even in a dream, with one or two people on the planet, and they will be dreaming too.

Experiencing Others' Experiences

What's happening is not what I'd call a complete linkup, but there is a sensitization process going on that will allow you all to experience things that others are experiencing or to experience the dreams of others who are overwhelmed by their own life experience. So you might find yourself in a dream doing something or participating in something that is entirely unlike you, entirely foreign to your personality, or is seemingly crazy, for lack of a better term. You might be involved in something that is, in the dream, violent; or is, in the dream, strange; or is, in the dream, bizarre. It is so extreme, you wake up and then you settle yourself for a few moments. If you are afraid you are going to have the dream again, even if you are alone, speak out loud a few words of what the dream was about. You don't have to record it—that's unnecessary. You don't have to write it down in your dream book, especially if it's in the middle of the night and you need to sleep. Just say out loud a few of the words that will prevent you from going back into the dream. Then you can fall asleep and rest.

What I'm saying is that there are, all over the world, people who are going through agitating, overwhelming things. You yourself, as individuals, may be going through that now, and instead of Mother Earth taking on that excess of feeling that she has in the past, other human beings are taking it on—not in their waking state, since that would be like taking on a lesson from somebody else or taking on some-one else's physical energy, but in the dream state where you are largely protected and looked after by your guides and teachers and angels and others. And yet as the Explorer Race and as creators-in-training, it is natural to be in school, yes, all the time. And in the past, being in school all the time meant that in every waking moment it was possible and even likely that you would be working on a life lesson or an experience that needed to be worked out in some way.

Working on Life Lessons in the Dream State

But now you are working on things in the dream state as well. Many of you—not all of you, but those of you who have not had this experience—may have it at some point. When you take on someone else's overwhelming feeling in the dream state . . . in the dream state, in your case, being protected as you are, you only take on a little bit, but you might experience something that is a total reversal of what your natural personality would do. Don't assume that it is predictive about your life. Don't assume that it is something for which you must mourn the world. It is rather, in the dream situation, something that allows you to develop and under-stand and experience compassion for others who are going through this great ter-ror or fear or even desire—in short, a feeling that is too overwhelming for them in that moment. You do not experience their terror, their fear, their desire that they experience in their lives in their waking moments, but you do experience some-thing that they are dreaming. You become like a character in their dream and they become a character in your dream. This allows you to experience a level of lesson that is only possible for the Explorer Race here on Earth.

It is what I would call a lesson in teaching mastery, as well as some exposure to a dimensional-mastery teaching and even a little bit of quantum-mastery teach-ing—quantum mastery being the mastery of consequences. You do not become masters of that, but you are being exposed to the teaching, which is only possible here on Earth, in this experience of Earth. And it is essential to be exposed to this teaching in an applied physical way, to have physical experiences, at least in the dream state. It is necessary because in other places you could not have these experiences; you could not react to these dreams with feelings. You could not experience an awakening to what other people feel, why they do the things they do on other benevolent planets, because to dream like that on another benevolent planet is too violent, even in a dream, for those planets.

Learn about Compassion in the Dream State

Know that these experiences are going to be safe for you and yet you will touch on them so that you will have much greater compassion to understand— even as a dream recollection, which is often vague and not always available. Even as that dream recollection, you will know and understand a little more and certainly be a little more compassionate when you hear about things that seem unfathomable: "How could they do that? I can't imagine or even think of doing that." "What is wrong with her?" "What is wrong with him?" "Are they crazy?" So creators must be able to be compassionate at all times toward the beings they have helped to create. You are not creators yet in this place, but you need to develop your compassion further.

In your time, you have some support to develop compassion, not only from your physical life, your day-to-day experience, but also by the means of communication that are available—radio, television, computer and communication between peoples and things that happen in the neighborhood and in families or around the world. You have the opportunity to hear about things, but now the opportunity extends further into the dream state, and that is something I want you to know about.

Release Judgment, but Don't Release Discernment

These dreams are different than visions. These dreams are about the capabilities of compassion. Compassion's job is not to change things. Compassion's job is to know and understand and appreciate perhaps the motivations or experiences of others. Compassion's job is also to give permission for you to act on the basis of others' needs without judgment. Compassion at the dream level will allow you to release a great deal of judgment. It will not, however, force you to release any discernment. There's a big difference between discernment and judgment.

Discernment is what allows you to be street-smart as well as to know the difference between something that is good for you and something that is meant for oth-

---

DISCERNMENT OR JUDGMENT?

Discernment: n. 1. a. Perception by the senses; distinguishing by sight, direct vision. b. The faculty of discerning; discrimination, judgment; keenness of intellectual perception; penetration, insight. 2. The act of distinguishing; a distinction [*Oxford English Dictionary*, 2nd ed.].

Judgment: n. 1. To pass judgment upon, to judge, to criticize (with an assumption of superiority) [Oxford English Dictionary, 2nd ed.]. 2. The act or process of judging, the formation of an opinion after consideration or deliberation. The capacity to assess situations or circumstances and draw sound conclusions; good sense. 3. An opinion or estimate formed after consideration or deliberation, especially a formal authoritative decision [*American Heritage Dictionary*, 4th ed.].

ers or something that is not good for you or others. Judgment tends to protect you, you might say, but it also tends to keep you from your opportunities. So, you see, judgment is not always so good. It can protect you, yes, but it is not a good time to be kept from your opportunities now because they will be increasing and increasing in an increasing way. Therefore, it is better to be discerning rather than judgmental.

Visions Are Different Than Dreams

Now, I want to talk a bit about visions, since this is something that is profoundly the case, which is happening for many of you now. Visions are different. They will often happen in a slightly somnambular state. This means that you are not asleep, but you feel sort of relaxed. For those of you who meditate, it is similar to that. For those of you who do not do that, it is something that begins as something you see.

Sometimes there are words, but most often there are pictures, and the pictures are sometimes alarming—perhaps of disasters, perhaps of global problems, perhaps of threats to your country or your friends in your neighborhood or something like that. Usually a vision represents, in your time, a disaster—an earthquake, a flood, a fire, something like that. If you have physical phenomena when this is going on, it is important to tell others of this vision. If, on the other hand, it is strictly a vision and you feel calm during the whole experience, it is also important to pass that on to someone or to various individuals.

Now, visions are different than dreams because they usually happen in a waking or semiwaking state. Many, many of you are having these visions now. Know that they are intended to stimulate change. You're aware of Earth conditions. Volcanoes are erupting, but that's good; it creates land, it changes the face of the land, and as long as the people are evacuated, it does not represent catastrophe. It is only a catastrophe if people are killed or wounded. I grant that sounds a bit hard on my part, but volcanoes are Mother Earth's birthing technique. It is the easiest and most benevolent way for her to bring more land to the surface or to alter the face of the land for your ultimate good, and a lot of that is going on—it's much better than having earthquakes that upthrust the land, which can cause catastrophic damage.

So for those of you who are seeing or feeling catastrophic disasters coming, if you would, tell your friends who can visualize or do visualization. Tell them of your vision and ask them point-blank—whether it be in an Internet message or spoken word—say, "I've had this vision and I'm concerned. If you can visualize, please visualize benevolence in the areas where I've had the vision. Picture the people happy and calm and peaceful, and everything as safe." Ask your friends who can meditate or visualize to do this. For others, don't be shy. You'd be surprised how many people can bring about change, even if they do not know they can do that.

If you are getting visions of disasters, feel free to put them out verbatim, meaning describe what you saw. Don't get fictional. Don't say, "And then I saw this," if you didn't. Describe only what you saw. If you like, you can add that you are frightened or upset and that you hope that those who can will bring about change. This will allow people who are religious to pray, but it will also allow them to feel a sense of urgency to change it, and that will trigger within them their unconscious creator impulses to bring about benevolent change—that's what it does.

You Are Intended to Make Unconscious Changes

You are creators-in-training. You are not intended to make conscious changes. You are not yet ready to be conscious creators, but you are intended to make unconscious changes. This incorporates not only what you do energetically as a soul on Earth, but is now beginning to include what you do in your dreams and linking it to your conscious state by waking up from that which upsets you. Be aware that dreams and visions are linked, as is the spiritual nature of each and every one of you, though many of you will look at someone and say, "I don't see it." But I am seeing, in fact, the spiritual nature of each and every one of you rising, and that rising will take place first in something that you are not quite in touch with—that which is called the unconscious.

It is not mental, the unconscious; it is largely physical, it is spiritual and it is feeling. That's why when you have these dreams, as strong as they are, you wake up not just with pictures or images but with strong feelings. These feelings are a relief to others who are overwhelmed with those feelings, and if you just speak a few words when you wake up about the dream, then you won't go back into it. That's what's going on.

Your level of responsibility as creators-in-training has increased and has moved beyond the unconscious into the subconscious, which unites all of the physical parts of you, the spiritual parts of you and that which functions in a state of mental awareness that you cannot touch or know at this time. The subconscious unites all that with your feelings (I mean your physical feelings), and therefore, this subconscious is the vital part of you that is allowing you to literally change the creation of Earth.

As creators-in-training it is intended that you do so, and no amount of conditioning to bring about distraction by whatever forces—be they corruptive or political or even simply greed by those who wish to make money or manipulate you in some way—can change it. Know that greed is not only something that others have, but greed is something that is within each and every one of you. This does not make you bad; it just means that you have the capability to feel about this or that in your life—that you don't have enough and you want more than you'll ever need so you can be assured you will always have enough. It is not in its own right evil, but sometimes it results in an evil by the accumulation of more than you'll ever need, which means that others do not have what they need.

Your Dreams and Visions Are Uniting

So I am simply saying that it is not my intention to cure every situation today. Just know that your dreams and your visions are uniting, and as creators-in-training and apprentices along the soul path toward creation, you have taken a giant step forward. And remember, if these dreams upset you—and I cannot stress this enough, which is why I'm repeating it—when you come to that waking state, even if you're wide awake, don't just think about the dream. Say something about it out loud—you must say it out loud. Thinking about it won't help. Say something about it out loud, even if you have to whisper (perhaps others are present). Say something out loud, and you will not go back into the dream, all right? That includes people who have nightmares regularly, by the way. If you have nightmares a lot, always say something out loud about the nightmare when it wakes you up. That will help to prevent it in the future.

That's wonderful for mothers to tell their children. It's wonderful for them to go to their rooms and have the children talk about it.

And particularly helpful for people who have had great traumas that they continue to dream about in an intention for their physical and spiritual and feeling bodies to cleanse themselves of that terrible experience.

So to summarize a little: The dream that you dream for others . . . when you wake up, you actually release that energy for the other person. And the visions, by talking to other people about them, they help to dissipate it, to prevent it from happening?

Yes. Good night.

You Must Have the Tools and Abilities to Support Life

Zoosh

June 6, 2003

Y ou need to understand the meaning of the title "Lord" before someone's name. I think it is important for me to make that absolutely clear. It is important since it is continuing to be popular in some circles. When it is in front of the name of a being perhaps who is being channeled or who is advising, either on the written page or in the spoken word . . . I can assure you that those beings may or may not know the full meaning of this, so it is my job to remind them.

Beings Who Use the Title "Lord" Need to Be in Service

For starters, for those spirits who choose to go by that name, the title "Lord" means that it is your job to emulate a creator to the best of your ability, using all the resources you have at hand to fulfill the responsibilities of a creator. By this it means that it is your job 100 percent of the time to be in service, not only to the requested needs of the people who may speak to you or inquire of you, but also to remind those people of the needs they have insofar as serving themselves and other people and other beings wherever they might live. Such things are often easy to overlook in the headlong pursuit of wisdom, which sometimes, to some people, seems to be like food, meaning that your appetite may at times become insatiable as a human being. Therefore, regardless whether they are angelic or otherwise, it is those spirits' job if they use that title—especially if they insist that it's used—to be 100 percent in service to those beings' true needs.

What might a human being's true needs be? Aside from your responses to their spiritual questions, their true needs are the basic human needs: food, shelter, clothing, support, nurturance, love and the ability to provide love where it is wanted. That has to underlie any advice you give. Therefore your advice *must be practical*. If it is impractical, then you need to state that what you are putting forth, the impractical thing, is to be considered an ideal, something to strive for, not something that the human beings are expected to actually deliver or to ignore their basic needs and sacrifice anything or everything they actually require to live so that they might strive for this impossible ideal. You must state that it is an *ideal* that they are not expected to achieve. Rather, it is an ideal only, and all goals set toward that ideal need to be reachable and practical. If you set the goals for them, fine; set those goal by those standards. If they set their own goals, which is more likely, then you must lay down practical and reachable standards by which they may achieve those goals.

Human Beings: The Title "Lord" Denotes Responsibility

So that's the definition for spirits who choose to go by that name. Now, what about human beings who choose to go by that name—and I'm not referring to aristocrats in various countries who might utilize that title, since that is something that is receding in your social systems. I think everyone is fairly clear that this is occurring. Rather, I am referring to those people who might, in exploring various types of spiritual or idealized religion, gain the desire to emulate some great being and begin to use the title for themselves, perhaps even with a spirit name or a name given to them either by someone of that religion or philosophy or through some spirit—you choose it or it is given to you to call yourself "Lord." The definition for you as compared to the definition for spirit is significantly more stringent. As a human being, you can strive only toward goals that are practical and real. You cannot even consider an idealized goal as something that you or other human beings can actually accomplish.

Now, if you are going to call yourself "Lord" this or "Lord" that, even as a spirit name, you must understand that this means you are 100 percent in service to the people, whether you are using that title with the general public, whether you are using that title only occasionally with your small group of friends or whether you are using that title between you and your spirit buddies. Understand that this title denotes responsibility; it does not denote in any way leadership or respect that other human beings or even spirits should bestow upon you. It denotes only and always that 100 percent service is required of you to serve the actual needs of the people first. It is not your job to place a dogma and ideals upon the people as if those ideals were more important than food, shelter, love, nurturance and all those other things I stated, as well as other basic human needs—clothing and so on.

If you are going to claim that title, my friends, you are going to need to deliver. You do not have to tear your clothing into rags and live in suffering, no. Nor am I suggesting you ever use the title "Lord" in front of your name, whether it be a spirit name or your given name. I am simply saying that if you believe you ought to use that name and if a spirit is suggesting that you are to use that name, first and foremost you need to ascertain whether that spirit is choosing to serve the real, practical needs of human beings or whether that spirit has its own agenda.

It is essential to understand, then, that you human beings must never remove your eyes, your hearts and your commitment from the real and the practical. You cannot be striving for some unrealistic need while those around you are suffering and starving and need shelter and food or gainful employment. You cannot. Granted, many of you do those things, but you especially cannot if you are going to use the title "Lord," which denotes *only* responsibility and denotes that it is your job to provide. I assure you that such service will require on your part practical, moral, legal and ethical provisions by you to others to the best of your ability.

It is not your job to be Robin Hood, as in the mythical story. It is your job only to do the best you can to support others around you to achieve their basic human needs, and if and only if they ask you what you believe in, what your philosophy is, then you may answer by giving certain basic ideals that you believe in, that you can demonstrate that you believe in—not arguments to support why *they* should believe in them.

"Lord" Is *Not* a Title of Respect

What brought all this up?

Well-intentioned people have gotten off track and have become confused over the title of "Lord," ascribing that title to the regal in various societies so that someone who uses the term "Lord" needs to be considered someone whom you respect, whom you pay duties to, whom you simply thank for your existence. In short, people are giving the worst of the religious meaning to the title without any of the best of the religious meaning. So this has become a corruption of the title's meaning.

Now, in the case of the religious use, referring to Creator as Lord, there is no problem with that whatsoever because Creator is 100 percent clear, 100 percent of the time, that Creator is in absolute service to you. But the difference is that Creator does have an agenda, and that agenda not only serves that which Creator has created, but also, to a lesser degree, Creator's own personal agenda, which we have talked about extensively in the *Explorer Race* series.

But Creator's agenda will also serve everyone. It's potentially a service to everyone everywhere.

But that does not justify the use of the term "Lord" as if it were a title of respect. I'm going to use the military as a perfect example. When young people go into the military in your United States, they do not have a title. They are just referred to by their last names or some derogatory statement, unfortunately, in order to turn them into a homogenous group rather than individuals in pursuit of individual goals. I understand that. But the title that used to be used—and I don't think it's used anymore—of buck private, meaning someone who has not achieved a private first-class status and is simply at the beginning of his or her education in the military, is significantly higher in terms of respect than the title of "Lord" for a human being.

I'm going to tell you why, and that is that in the military, so much is demanded of an individual to set aside his or her individual needs in order to serve the needs of the greater group to accomplish whatever purpose is intended. Granted, right now it is geared toward warlike pursuits, but it is also at times geared toward benevolent pursuits to help people, and in the future, that will be the way of the armies of the world as time goes on. Even so, the title of "Lord" means that you set aside your individual goals 100 percent of the time. That is why I'm not really encouraging human beings to use that title, because I do not think it is practical to ascribe or even set as a goal to be in service 100 percent of the time.

Do Not Use the Title of "Lord"

You are here as human beings, as souls, to accomplish purposes meant for you to accomplish as an individual or you wouldn't be an individual. Therefore, utilizing the title of "Lord" tends to discount your purpose for being here in the first place and, by so doing, discount the purpose of the Explorer Race—and if I might expand further, discount the value of Creator's desire that you accomplish something as an individual, which is why Creator allowed you to be here in the first place. So please do not discount Creator. Do not deny your human need to be an individual and to understand that you have individual purposes for being.

In short, I do not recommend that human beings use the title of "Lord" at all. Nor do I recommend that beings or entities who might speak this way or that way to the human race use this title, even if their purposes are divinely inspired. Do not, beings, allow human beings to refer to you by the title of "Lord," even if you believe in that moment that they mean it respectfully. Every time a human being calls you that and you are in touch with that person, say, "Just call me by my name." I am watching.

Now, I do not claim to be Creator or a voice of Creator, but I do claim to be just as much Creator as all beings. If I am watching, I assure you that others are watching. All are watching. And remember, those of you spirit beings who are allowed to speak to human beings are being given a great gift, and that is that regardless of your level of accomplishment, you are being given the opportunity to learn in ways that very few beings are given. Don't betray that trust by placing yourself or, even worse, allowing yourself to be placed *in any way* above those whom you serve.

You Have the Ability to Change Things

It's important for everybody to do what they can to not only assuage the energies moving toward this—meaning, if I might define that, to cool those energies—but to do what they do in the most benevolent way to encourage human beings to learn how to solve individual and larger group (or social) problems with patience, attention and kindness. A beginning step is to be polite and to listen when you can. Sometimes you won't understand the meaning of what others are saying; maybe they speak another language. But just listening can be helpful when you can. If you cannot, then say, "I sympathize to the best of my ability, and I will do, to the best of my ability, all that I can to help."

It is certainly true that there are those who would, by ignorance or attachment to past goals, choose to re-create the world in their own image. However, there are others who are helping and teaching human beings to be a benevolent tone, feeling and energy so that no matter what goals are being produced by which group, that energy is the underpinning and an overlay around and about this. This is so that any excessive goals and their pursuits are being touched by this energy, thus maintaining a capacity and an ability by the human race and by all whom the human race affects to be not only rooted in reality, but also to have the tools and abilities to support life—not just to force it to change to a temporary and purely temporal ideal.

Now, for the past few years, you have heard through this channel and perhaps others manners and means by which you can do things. For all of you out there who are doing benevolent magic, I will suggest to you that you now have my permission and my support and the permission and support of other beings to say this—with benevolent magic, say it only once [for more information on benevolent magic, see *Benevolent Magic & Living Prayer*]. I will give you the words right now:

Benevolent Magic

"I REQUEST THAT ALL HUMAN BEINGS FEEL AND KNOW THEIR INTERCON-
NECTIVENESS IN ALL TIMES AND IN ALL PLACES, INCLUDING THEIR SLEEP
TIME, IN THE MOST BENEVOLENT WAY FOR ALL INDIVIDUALS, AND MAY
THAT KNOWLEDGE AND FEELING GENERATE THE MOST BENEVOLENT
OUTCOME FOR ALL HUMANITY AND ALL WHOM HUMANITY TOUCHES."

Each individual doing this might say it just once, please. If you say it more than once, you will tend to decrease its effectiveness by you as an individual. That is a fact in benevolent magic in any event. And for those of you who are not familiar with benevolent magic, understand that this is not sorcery; it never uses or forces individuals or beings or plants or animals to do anything against their will. It only encourages them to do some small thing perhaps that would otherwise be easy for them to do (I like to say to walk on one side of the street instead of the other when they go down to the store for bread and milk—something simple that's no big deal).

And that is always and only benevolent magic's effect, regardless of how many spirit beings, Creator or creators who cooperate in it. Its effect is only that, to encourage, support and nurture human beings and others to do, in the most benevolent way, that which provides a service that most of you will not even know you have contributed to. But perhaps in time, with this stated as benevolent magic—and it will take time in many cases and in some cases be more noticeable right away—you will see, feel and appreciate its benefit.

A lot of what has been going on with the *Shamanic Secrets* books, the *Ancient Secrets of Feminine Science* books and others with benevolent magic, living prayer [see p. xxii], disentanglement [see p. 70] . . . all this stuff has been designed to give people the tools and methods and means that are practical and real and have been clearly aimed toward their urgent personal needs so they remain practical and real. Regardless, any desires they might have that they might put out and say a living prayer for the greater community or the world at large, these things, these types of statements, these teachings, have been given to support these times of excessive confrontation. Really, what excessive confrontation does, is that it makes it possible, given living prayer and other things, for each and every one of you to change the result to a benevolent outcome.

Moving at Different Paces toward the Global Economic Order

The main thing—the reason for what is going on with this crisis the world faces—is simply impatience by various human beings. Do you know the interesting thing here, which we often talk to the channel about when he gets questions—"Oh, this is going on," or "That is going on," and he asks, "Can I do something?" He's always asking various beings for their suggestions and advice on whether it's acceptable to do benevolent magic or living prayer for something, and very often he gets the response, "No." This is because human beings must achieve their goals as well as strive toward their ideals on their own, and they must take the steps themselves. Then the channel is reassured very often that what he sees is really an attempt by human beings to create the first global order—order in this sense not meaning an authoritarian regime that tells people what they're going to do, but rather a means for economic cooperation. You might call it business cooperation, but in some governments, it will simply be economic cooperation, so its business may not be a major factor of certain governments—such as in mainland China, where you'll find economic cooperation more than business cooperation. But the point you come to is that what is occurring—and the channel is being informed of this—is motion toward these goals, which is sometimes not pretty to behold.

What you are seeing now is basically impatience by various influential world leaders, who say, "Let's get this economic world order in shape so that everyone can produce what they produce best, trade what they trade best, and so that everyone can, in a practical manner, have their basic needs served"—which may be a worthy goal but which is not always practical. One must not rush people. One must understand that different individuals move at different rates, and I think people understand that, but this is an individual example of what happens in larger groups as well. Some groups move speedily to accomplish a desired goal. Others move more slowly because their system or society must have other goals fulfilled while moving toward this equally desirable goal, and if those goals in their society cannot be served, then this even most desirable goal will have to wait until those needs can be served.

In short, this is a macrocosm of what occurs for an individual. Say, for instance, an individual is going to run a race. For some individuals who've trained and trained and trained, maybe they can do a marathon, complete it; others have to train slowly, build up slowly. You understand that as an athlete. But how about for an individual to accomplish a task, say, in a business or even for a personal goal or need? Some people must go slowly, learn slowly, and by so learning, they understand perhaps even more deeply not only how the task can be accomplished but its means—why it is to be accomplished. These "slow learners," so to speak, would perhaps be seen as less valuable employees, but very often it is people like this who think about it and may in time come up with other systems that work better. Or they might mention to somebody, "I'm having such a hard time learning this," and those they mention this to might come up with a better system.

In short, it is intended in your society that different individuals move toward any goal at their own pace. It is not for your society, whether it is done on an individual level or whether it is done on a worldly level, to try to force everyone to accomplish the same goal at the same pace. Those who move slower very often—if not in and of themselves—provide a solution to some greater problem that the speedier ones (the rapid, so to speak) have accomplished or are working on accomplishing. If they are moving slower, perhaps they will notice other things that need to be served. Even if they do not serve those things by their objections or by their route of travel, they say to others things that must be said. And therefore, when that goal is reached by the world, it will cover all the bases, it will take care of all the problems, and you won't find that there are trapdoors opening beneath you to return you to some point in the past to fix something you have overlooked.

I know that those who are in the computer world understand very well what I am talking about. Sometimes the most obvious is that which is overlooked, and it only becomes obvious later when other things have died down and things are quieter. It is better to have the turtle come along slowly, as in the famous race: noticing things, observing, perhaps speaking of these things so that all is accomplished at various paces to achieve worthy goals. Ultimately, you understand, this first so-called world order that I've talked about before will be a model—not just so that the basic needs of all human beings can be achieved around the world, so everyone has enough to eat, the shelter they need and so on. But when it is time to create a more benevolent process for all people and the planet and the animals and the plants and everyone, you will have a process you have worked out to achieve an economic balance system so that all people are providing what they can provide in ways that are good for them to provide and are receiving things from others since they cannot provide them for various reasons—in short, the global economic order.

By working on the global economic order, you will have discovered the value of various parts working quickly and various parts working slowly in order to be thorough. It is thoroughness that counts in order to produce not only a product that completely fulfills its expectations but that also has the durability to serve that which will be expected of it, whether it is for a short time or a long time. Therefore, trust in Creator's plan. Some of you are expected to go slower and some of you are expected to go faster. So you see how that applies not only to individual circumstances but to global ones as well.

Embrace Those Aspects of Your Personality That You Like

As a practical issue to improve the quality of our lives, I've been thinking a lot about the issue of conditioning that you've talked about so much. I went to the Grand Canyon today and saw the layers and levels, and it occurred to me that we have those within ourselves, put down year after year after year after year, sometimes with some upheavals, or cracks. Most of us aren't psychologists. How do we begin to work on this, to recognize this, to deal with it, to see how it affects our decisions, our thoughts, our actions, our reactions?

One of the most difficult things for people to do, since your world is complex and often demands a great deal more from you than you can deliver in a practical manner, is to adjust to the current state of things. This is difficult for you because as a youngster, you learned certain basic things: "Don't stick your finger in the electrical outlet; you might get a shock. Don't push your finger toward the fire no matter how beautiful it is; you might get hurt." Basic things: "Open your mouth to eat, then swallow."

All of these things seem very obvious now to adults, and yet as a child, you learn that the practical world you live in requires certain practical adaptations on your part, even though the spirit you, which is present when you are a little baby, has not changed—even when you are an old and wise adult. Granted, your thoughts will change, your feelings to some extent in terms of how you react based upon your conditioning and your experience in life, yes. But the basic functions are there: the means of feelings, the communication of feelings, the mechanics of feelings, all of that. What has been sometimes called your instinct—that's all there when you are born.

What happens, of course, given your different societies, those societies' histories and the goals and desires of the parents for you as their offspring or simply life's unexpected occurrences . . . perhaps you weren't even raised by parents because something happened and you were raised by others who had perhaps an agenda of their own or simply were kind and wanted to help you to become the best adult possible according to what they believed would make the best adult out of someone—in short, their ideals or beliefs. What occurs is an exposure to those ideals or beliefs, based not only upon that person's religion and philosophy but, more to the point, based upon his or her experience. How was that person raised? What instructions has he or she had in becoming a good parent?

Parents are, aside from their biological function as your birth parents, simply teachers, and if their teachers have been impatient or short or brusque with them or unkind, then even their goals to be kind, patient, loving, nurturing and supportive will at times not be the practical reality. Perhaps they are tired, perhaps they are upset, perhaps they are any number of things. At times like that, they will fall back into doing what they were exposed to, even if later they regret it.

So what I'm saying is this: The complex way, the time-consuming way, which is also a valuable way to understand things mentally, is through analysis (psychoanalysis as it's called) or support from therapists and psychologists (which is also a valuable tool). And yet there is something simple that many of you can do who cannot for whatever reason see a therapist, a psychologist or an analyst, and that is that over time you change, you develop other attitudes, other ideals. Perhaps your personality changes for various reasons, and then I encourage you to embrace those qualities in your personality that you like and that you would like to experience from others.

One of the big things that goes on in relationships, loving relationships between individuals, is that the person you're with is almost constantly, if he or she is doing things for you that you like, demonstrating things to you that he or she would like to experience from you—if not that exact thing, then that kind of consideration, nurturing and support. Take note of that, please. It's very basic. It's something you all do for one another, and even though you do it many times unselfishly, it is still a message to others that you would like that kind of consideration for yourself. For those of you who do not feel safe in receiving this kind of consideration from others, you can ask the person who is giving it to you, "Are you providing me with the consideration I am showing to you? Because if you are, thank you very much, and please be patient with me. It might take me awhile to learn how to gracefully accept it, but don't give up. I'll learn in time."

Demonstrate Your Benevolent Qualities to Others

You realize that I am covering a broad topic on the basis of your question in a fairly concise manner. Therefore, I may be skipping over a few things, but that's all right. The important thing is, I want to give you something practical that you can do while acknowledging the value of doing something that takes more time, such as therapy, and that is this: Embrace those qualities in yourself that you have now in your life that you like and would like to experience from others. Embrace those qualities and demonstrate them to others any time you not only feel safe to do so but at times when you feel they might be appreciated. Qualities like that will often improve the overall quality of life for all beings, so demonstrate them to those whom you're with—whether they have known you only briefly, whether they are someone you work with or whether they are a relative who remembers you better as a child than as you are now as an adult and often reacts to you in that child way (meaning as they were when you were young and as you were when they were young).

The best thing you can do is to demonstrate those qualities you have now that you like that you would like to experience from others without any expectation or attachment that they will demonstrate those qualities to you. What you're really doing is showing them who you are now, and if for various reasons—whether done capriciously, mischievously or unpleasantly—they try to draw out things in you that they once saw in you when you were younger, or if they simply try to engage you in some unpleasant activity, simply refuse to participate by ignoring it. Wait for them to ask you point blank, "Why aren't you acting this way?" But wait for them to ask. When they ask you, simply say, "I'm not that person anymore, and the qualities you see me demonstrating to you now are who I am now. If you like, you can get to know who I am now and see if you want to spend time with me. If you don't care for those qualities, then perhaps it would be better for you to seek out those old qualities that you remember me having when I was younger with someone else."

That's what to say to a relative. It's not something you can say to a workmate or someone who has barely known you for a while, but if he is trying to engage you in some argument, know that he might be reacting to you out of some conditioning that he experienced as a youngster. If it does not seem to fit you, then work with that person as well as possible. Always and only demonstrate those qualities to others to the best of your ability. You won't be able to do it all the time; you're a human being. Do the best you can, of course. But to the best of your ability, demonstrate those qualities to others that you would like demonstrated to you. Many of you are doing this now, and I salute you. For others, think about it and consider it.

That's a pretty clear answer to a very complicated and large issue, and it's pertinent to the moment as always.

What Happened? Why Did the Channeling Change?

Zoosh
August 31, 2004

It's important for you to know this, reader, because I'm giving you all homework. You know how I am [chuckles]. My whole point is, if you are really spiritual students like some of you say you are, it is time for you to show Uncle Zoosh what you can do, all right? This is the challenge. I can't tell you exactly when an event that is coming up in your future is going to happen because I don't want you to: (a) get terrified of it, (b) anticipate it or (c) tell others all about it and walk down the street saying, "The end is near."

But I will say, it is in your future. Don't yell at me; I know you are doing all you can, but I want you to do a little extra instead of proceeding generally along the line of "minimum effort." The extra effort, however, won't involve anything that you normally do. I want to explain: I'd like you to apply yourself. Some of you work in your dreams, set up your dreams, request to have dreams with insight, and I don't want to mess with that. But many of you just go to sleep at night, or perhaps you do your disentanglement [see p. 70], or you might say some prayer to ease you into your sleep.

Use the Power of Your Natural Self to Dream for Benevolence

Here is what I would like you to do . . . and it is up to you how many of you want to do it, but I think it is something that not only you readers will like to do, but it is something that can really nourish life all over. It's easy and it will involve your full capability—and by full capability, I mean more than you normally have spiritually and otherwise in your normal day. And it might just be

something that other people who would like to have a more peaceful and benevolent world in general, regardless of their religion or philosophy or spiritual
practices, might enjoy doing as well, because it doesn't add much strain to your
life, but it does make a difference.

I will give you the homework first so you don't get nervous, and then later I
am going to tell you about the moment that caused the reason for the homework
and also the change in the focus of the channeling/teaching. This is the homework. Try to do it before you go to sleep. For those of you who have lovers and
so on and go to bed for fun and then go to sleep, the best time to do it is when
you are in bed after all is said and done. Or sometimes, if you are on your own,
when you turn off the light after reading or something, simply say out loud:

Living Prayer

**"I AM ASKING THAT I DREAM WITH MY FULL SPIRITUAL CAPABILITY
OF BENEVOLENCE IN MY PHYSICAL WORLD ON EARTH
AND BEYOND WHEN I SLEEP TONIGHT."**

That's all [for more information on living prayer, see p. xxii]. Now, for those of
you who say other living prayers or other prayers before you go to sleep at night,
wait at least a minute or two for the energy to calm between the prayers, or if you
say this first, then wait a minute or two before you say your normal prayers, because
you might feel a very benevolent energy during this living prayer—or even, if you
say it every night for a while, prior to saying this living prayer, as well as during and
even after. And you want that to pass a little bit, to calm. Don't shove it away; it's
nourishing, nurturing. It's benevolent, and the energy will support your life and
your experience of your world.

Now, why do we say the prayer in such a way that it is quite clear that you
are saying "my world"? It honors the fact that you are a portion of creation.
It also honors the fact that your first responsibility, to the best of your ability,
is to create the most benevolent life for yourself that is possible. And for
those of you who might feel that this sounds selfish, it isn't, because you
have to factor into your life all others who are in it. If you have children, if
you have extended family whom you live with, if you have friends, if you have
animals and so on in your life whom you experience, the most benevolent life
would be not only that you are happy and happy with your life, but that people around you are happy and happy enough with their lives so they are not
complaining to you or that you do not pick up with your sensitivity how they
may be distressed.

In short, it builds from the center foundation, and you are all responsible for
your own lives first, and then you are responsible, in the greater sense, for the
happiness of all other beings. In this way, nobody gives up responsibility for his
or her own creation while taking over responsibility for others' creations. Of
course, you cannot run the lives of other people entirely on your own, even in a
spiritual sense, but you can create your own life spiritually to the best of your
ability, because your soul will know you best. It is that simple.

So this is what I recommend you do for homework. You can say it just once. Because you are incorporating your dream state, this does not really add to your daily duties. And because it will happen in your dreams—it is not going to impact your sleep; if anything, you are going to sleep deeper and longer, if you like—it will tend to support and nurture greater benevolence in your life and support and nurture greater benevolence in your extended life, meaning all of those people and animals and beings you might meet, including plants and so on. And it can only be a good thing.

What Happened? What Changed?

Now [pauses a moment] . . . I would like to tell you why I would like you to do this homework. The witness here, my associate, who has been prompted to ask this question [see p. 419], has been prompted to do so because she noticed a few years ago that everything seemed to change. At one moment it was one way, and then suddenly it changed. Now, this was something that many people who were spiritual or simply sensitive did notice, that there was suddenly sort of a radical change and a shift, not only in the way you perceived the world, but even in the way the world perceived you, and you weren't really sure what had happened. What happened? And some of you weren't quite aware of it until a little after the fact, but you came to become aware of it later.

Let me tell you what happened. I'm not going to give you an exact time, but I'm just going to say that something happened in your future that affected your past, your past from this point back. Now, this is what happened: There was a convergence of angry people with problems that couldn't seem to wait. Just on the basis of that, I want you to notice how in recent years, it has been more and more difficult for you to be patient about anything. I am not singling anyone out as being exclusively impatient; rather, this is what many people suddenly felt, as if it were underneath them, like a vibration or an energy—in waves, not always consistent—of urgency. This is global. It does not affect the animals. It affects to a small degree the plants, and it affects to a large degree human beings.

Urgency, Creator's Gift, Is Accelerated by Technology

The urgency is to support you coming into your total being spiritually, yes, but this sense of urgency has been amplified unintentionally by certain broadcast-media effects. I am not trying to single out any industry, but there are satellites that revolve around the Earth for various benevolent purposes, to improve communications from one continent to another and so on, and most of you benefit from this. But some of those satellites broadcast not just directly from one point to another on the Earth—or transfer signals, actually—but they interact with surface stations on the Earth, broadcasting and transmitting and transferring back and forth all the time, which prompts a greater degree of amplification than might otherwise be used in the transference of broadcast signals. This does not include the telephone or anything that transmits communication of some form from one human being to another, nor communication on the automated level from one machine to another.

These radiating devices have produced purely unintentionally—I am not blaming anyone—a signal that could be measured. If you went down into the Earth about six to twelve feet, especially around these broadcast and transfer stations, you would find a measurable signal, yes, but it's more of what I would call a harmonic. An example of a harmonic would be if a group of people sang or if a group of tones were made by a musical instrument—and you have all heard of someone hitting a high note and a glass breaking.

Now, it is not exactly that dramatic, but the harmonic that is created unintentionally has amplified that benevolent signal being put out by your total spiritual being, by Mother Earth and, of course, by Creator, direct from Creator, to support and urge you to "wake up," as people say. It's not really "waking you up"; it's more to support and urge you to remerge with your total spiritual being. This has had an unintentional side effect, and that is that it has amplified the impact on you all of urgency. Once this was understood—or shall we say, once this happened—Creator could not lower the signal in the Earth or ask Earth to lower it for you, because it is so supportive and nurturing of all of your hearts. But it has prompted this excessive feeling of urgency.

You Can Counterbalance the Accelerated Urgency with Living Prayer

You can do something about this. That is why I have given you this homework, because I think you can do something much more easily in your sleep, when you have full access to all of your spiritual capabilities. Your body is still on Earth, yes, so you have some physical function. Your soul supports that physical function, and your soul is out and about when you're sleeping, with teachers, guides, angels, sometimes even Creator, discussing things and being loved and nurtured as is necessary for living on Earth. What occurs is that in various moments, usually at the deepest levels of sleep, you are in full contact with your full spiritual capabilities—not only as an individual of Earth, but as an immortal personality. So you might say that your soul is fully active. (I use the terms "soul" and "immortal personality" interchangeably.)

This is why at these deep levels of sleep you are more likely to be able to fulfill the intention of this living prayer or request, whichever you wish to call it, that I suggested at the beginning of this talk—because that full capacity will allow you to do things, to support things and, most importantly, to be supported by the other loving beings you interact with when you are at these deep levels. So you can not only act, you can not only create, but you can be supported in your action and your creation by all of the loving beings you interact with when you are in deep levels of sleep. I am not talking about dreams that are troublesome or even psychologically based where you are processing things. I am talking about the deepest levels of sleep where you don't normally remember any of that when you wake up. Occasionally, people do remember, but it is not typical for most people.

So what I am suggesting, then, is that something occurs in the future that has prompted something in the past, and as I said, the occurrence in the future is a convergence of people with feelings of great urgency. The reason it prompted it in the past is that the thing that happens in your future required a buildup of a countermeasure, meaning to balance something. When you put a heavy weight on one side of the scale, naturally the scale falls to that side. If you put a balancing weight on the other side, then you get scales that are evenly balanced. You have seen pictures of the scales with the two little plates that hold weights on either side.

Now, in order for that thing that happens in the future to be counterbalanced, all that really needs to take place is that those people meeting in that future time do not feel as much of a sense of urgency as they would have felt. And what will balance that urgency isn't you saying that you want everybody to be more patient, because sometimes a certain amount of urgency is necessary, as you have all experienced in your life when the signal light changes while you are crossing the street and you suddenly realize that you have to pick up your pace. So we don't want people to universally slow down too much for all situations. (I use that example humorously, because most of you have experienced this at one time or another.) And there are other situations where urgency is necessary—for example, when you run, your heart has to beat faster and you have to breathe faster. All urgency is not a bad thing. So let's not blanket things, saying "good" or "bad." Sometimes, in different situations, different things are called for.

World Health Group Feels Frenetic Urgency

So now we will talk a little bit about what happens. In the future, when these parties, these individuals, meet because they feel so profound a sense of urgency, they do something. They do something they think is going to support their cause, but they accidentally create something that is not obvious to them for quite some time, and by the time it becomes obvious to them, it is too late to do anything about it. And I might add that this sometimes occurs when diseases are accidentally released into the public. This has happened once or twice, and the disease lingers and everybody says afterward, "What were we thinking?" meaning something was tried just to make sure that everyone would be safe. There have been instances in the past where, with the best of intentions, some form of disease organism was released by well-intentioned individuals who said, "Look! See, it will moderate!" Or in the case of the security of nations, "How are we susceptible to chemical and biological warfare?" and so on. You can research this; some of it is available in print. But it will probably just upset you.

So let's just say this: These people get together. Some of them are scientifically oriented, many of them are well educated, but quite a few are just regular folks with no greater degree of education than anybody else. And they all say, "If we can just release this organism—it seems to be very mild—it will support a greater degree of intellectual capacity, and if everybody on Earth gets just a little smarter, then we will be able to rationalize and talk together and make a lot more sense to one another," believing, as they do, that greater mental capacity makes for peace. But as you have seen in your recent history, simply greater mental capacity does not always make for peace; as a matter of fact, greater mental capacity has often invented the tools of war.

Your Mind Is the Student, Your Feeling Body
Is the Teacher

Your mind on this planet is here as a student to learn from your physical body and the way your physical body functions, to learn from your physical feelings and the general feelings of many others around you, to learn from your spiritual inspiration and from the thing that you have noticed in animals but don't really recognize in yourself all the time, and that's instinct. And your mind is here to study and learn about creation and how to differentiate between what's a benevolent creation by yourself and what's a creation that isn't benevolent, even though mentally it will seem to be perfectly all right.

And the way you know that—and the way that's been discussed in many of these books: the *Explorer Race* series, the *Shining the Light* series, certainly the *Shamanic Secrets* series, the new *Ancient Secrets of Feminine Science* series and other books you've read—the way you know something isn't good to create, is because of certain feelings you get. If you get an uncomfortable feeling, you know that it's not right for you to do that at this time. Maybe it's all right to do it at some future time. If you get a good feeling, a warm feeling, a safe feeling, a happy feeling, maybe it's a good thing to do. I'm being very general here, because there are principles you would apply to anything that you create or hope to create. But I do not wish to talk for hours and hours here.

So what happens is that these individuals in the future get what they feel is a wonderful idea. They say, "Well, everybody needs to get these vaccination shots to support their immunity for this disease." And I'm not going to say what disease it is; I'm only going to say that it's a disease that you don't have amongst you in a way that you're conscious of right now. But I will say one thing about it because you've seen glimmers of this: It's a disease in people.

Imprisoned Chickens' Desire to Die Gets Eaten and
Absorbed by Humans

You've seen the beginnings of this, especially in some countries, that are very troubling because it's a poultry-based disease. I will be specific: Although it has to do with chickens mostly, it also affects turkeys, to a lesser degree, but it doesn't really affect ducks very much. And it doesn't affect any wild bird, meaning if you have chickens on your farm or in a small situation you have with a house and an acre or something like that, and the chickens are free ranging where they walk around all over the place—not just that they have a small pen they can move around in, but they walk around all over the place and scratch and peck at the dirt the way they do—they're going to be all right.

It's imprisoned chickens especially, and you've seen this or heard about it, where a chicken will live its whole life in a very tiny cage. That is really quite a horrible thing to do to any creature. These birds are experiencing and have been experiencing over time a personal depression within them that just prompts them all to want to die. They don't want to live. And when a being doesn't want to live, it cannot help it. When it produces eggs for human consumption or when it is killed and used for human consumption, there is no way to filter out from the eggs or the meat of the chicken itself that desire to die.

This is so much in conflict with the human desire to live and survive no matter what, and you've seen this many times (doctors, medical staff, nurses and so on are particularly aware of this), where somebody's very sick and is hanging on and hanging on. This desire to survive is built into you by Creator so that you will have the best opportunity to fulfill the spiritual desires that you as your soul before this life—with your teachers, with your angels, with Creator—chose to do in this life. Of course, eventually, at the end of your life, you just let go, and because your teachers or guides or angels come and . . . well, they're not seen by other physical people, but they come and they are there with you, and you know then that you can let go. It's not a mental decision you'll have to make; you can just let go because you feel it. That's how everybody on Earth transitions at the moment when it takes place.

Live or Die? The Ambivalence Created by Eating Imprisoned Chickens

So this desire to survive in the human being is very strong. And this desire in the chicken meat and chicken eggs and, to a lesser degree, in turkey meat and turkey eggs, as well as in the other birds I mentioned, is in direct conflict with the human desire to live. What occurs as a result is a kind of ambivalence in the human, a confusion about whether there is a desire to live or not.

This has already been seen, even though the disease has not yet been identified. But I'm trying to tip off you researchers out there, too. What is occurring is that one of the manifestations of the disease itself is that there is somewhat of an ambivalence about life. For people who have other stresses in their lives, this makes their lives miserable or uncomfortable at certain times. And this happens, as you all know. There are certain times that you all go through, times that are difficult or seemingly impossible, and you struggle on through and then you live on, you live your life. This happens a lot for soldiers, of course, or for people in hazardous professions, or for people who are sick or injured. Yes, you know about this. But it also happens when people are ill-equipped to deal with such things, not as adults might be. So this happens then sometimes for children, for youngsters who are not sophisticated enough to know how and what to do, what to say, when to ask for help and who to ask it from and so on. And that's why some countries have seen a troubling rise in youth suicide.

So I'd like to suggest that one of the things that isn't being looked for too much . . . although, of course, forensic and other specialists are looking for anything that connects. But here is one of the things I want you to look for, you forensic people, pathologists and anyone who may have an opportunity: Examine not just the body of the person who has passed away or committed suicide but also the lifestyle of the person; examine how much chicken the individual ate and for how long. Now, I grant that people who are strong, who are determined or who have a cause that they are determined to fulfill will be less affected by this ambivalence, this confusion about "live, don't live." But for others, especially if they're going through a rough patch, it can make for some confusion. And some civilizations might even give a—how can we say?—an almost imperceptible nod to allowing certain circumstances to support suicide. I'm not saying suicide pro or con here. What I am saying is that I want the researchers to start looking toward chickens.

And ultimately, of course, what I'm saying is that even though I know it would be very impractical and it would take very much land and so on for producers, farmers and ranchers who have animals they are raising, that if they have chickens . . . I know in the old days, they just took up a lot of space, and then eventually they developed chicken coops, and then when further things happened, other things were developed. I'm trying to let some of you off the hook, okay? I'm not trying to say that agribusinesses are the enemy, but I am trying to suggest that efficiency is not always the first choice for benevolence. Never forget that. I'm trying to suggest that sometimes you're going to need to use more land to let the chickens roam around, have space. Those chickens, their eggs, their meat, will be safe to eat.

Cruelty to All Animals Must Stop or They Will Leave Earth

So psychologists, pay attention. I know that you're not going to have psychologists for chickens, and I am not saying that entirely as a joke, because there are people who can work with animals and impart the animal's feelings. They really interpret the feelings into words that human beings can understand. Animals do not think the same way you do, but their feelings can be interpreted, just as human feelings can be interpreted. This is going on quietly all over the Earth, and I might add that a lot of veterinarians have this skill, but they just don't talk about it—at least the really good ones don't. And you know who they are, those of you who are farmers and ranchers. Some veterinarians just seem to have that gift; they know what's going on with your animals, even though medical science doesn't always point to it.

And of course, simply people of good will and good heart would never expect an animal to live its entire life in that teensy little cage hardly bigger than its own body. If you want to eat chicken and eggs in the future, I'm going to recommend that you pay real close attention to where they came from, because this is not something that is going to go away. Neither the chicken nor the eggs can be treated in this way.

You really need to pay attention to how you're treating farm animals. Now, ranchers who have cattle, for instance, they are actually quite well aware of this. That is why many cattle will range all over open country, because the ranchers know it affects their temperament, and their temperament does affect the way they are eaten and experienced by those who consume them. This is something that is actually well known and understood by cattle ranchers, especially smaller ranchers who make certain that their cows can roam all over the place. Granted, you have to get government leases and so on, and it's expensive, but they know this. Don't squeeze out these ranchers so that large businesses that are geared toward efficiency can raise all cows in some small box that they stand in for their whole life, which is already done now with some animals. I know that this has been said in these pages before, and I know it sounds like I'm preaching against certain things, and I admit it. I understand that you eat meat, okay? I'm not trying to say it's bad. That's why you have such strong teeth. But I do not think that it is acceptable to raise an animal in a small box just so you can serve it and its very tender meat called veal. I think that you can get along without it. That's all I'm going to say about that.

I will say that if this continues to go on—and cows know that this is going on with beings of their own kind—then cows will also get angry, upset and depressed. And people who have been in the ranching business for a long time know that aside from making it more difficult to deal with the cows, there is also a bad feeling about how that meat will eat. This knowledge is not just based upon their intuition, which is certainly true and valuable, but also upon stories they've heard from other generations, from their fathers, their grandfathers, their great-grandfathers; these stories have been passed down. They say that if you eat a cow who has been forced to live in a box or cage like this, you're not going to feel good. It might make you feel poorly, might make you susceptible to catching some disease. Why? Because the cow doesn't want to live; it's suffering. When you eat meat from an animal who doesn't want to live, who just wants to die, your body might be confused, even if you want to live. So you see, I'm not talking about things that are entirely unknown here. I'm just correlating them.

Health Group's Decision Jeopardizes Humanity

So when those people meet in the future and they have this wonderful idea that they will include in this vaccine something that will support greater mental development, what it actually does is it just creates—how can we say?—it might actually stimulate greater mental development. But a side effect is that it will create a slightly more disenfranchised mind or mental self, and it will support in all people an analytical tendency to classify everything that is not understood—and I mean a broad range of subjects that are not understood, especially your own physical feelings and unspoken thoughts—which will create unintentionally . . . this partly has to do with the way this chemical is created, but it unintentionally creates greater alienation from your own physical, spiritual and feeling selves.

So once it is released, included with a perfectly valuable and helpful vaccine for something else, that's it. It would be amongst you indefinitely, and the only way I think it could ever be cured and eliminated is by some major action of Creator through the Earth. And those actions in the past have usually resulted in the elimination of civilization as you know it, with only a few surviving, usually underground somewhere, to reemerge on the surface many years later.

I'm not talking about a select few; I'm talking about civilizations and cultures who, on the basis of how they feel, on the basis of how their mystical people and shamanic people and sensitives know that something is coming, know that they need to move quickly, and that if they do it, they will be safe as a people. For those of you out there who research peoples and what they've left behind, cliff dwellings and so on, there's always the question of what happened to these people: "Why did they leave this stuff and just disappear?" I'll tell you why: Because the sensitives amongst them whom they trusted and their shamanic people and their mystical people all had this feeling—you might call it an uncomfortable feeling, a danger feeling. They said, "We have to go."

They packed up what they could, food and everything, and they left. They left physically from their place, and as they got a few miles away, all those sensitives and shamanic people and mystical people suddenly started to feel better because they encouraged the tribe to go in this direction, not that direction—they could feel which was the safe direction to go. They started to feel better: "Let's keep going." Some of the people said, "It's a hardship. We left behind so many things that we use." But they were reminded by the elders, "Now, we've always followed the guidance and advice of our sensitives, our mystical people, our shamanic people. That's why we're still here." That kept people going until they found the next place where they felt safe and comfortable and that would support their lives. They reestablished themselves there, sometimes joining other people who welcomed them, other times establishing a civilization and creating that civilization elsewhere. But many of your archaeologists and anthropologists have studied this matter, so I don't wish to go into it too much here; I'm just pointing it out to you.

The Moment: Incident in Future Changes Focus in Past

So I've covered a wide range of subjects today in talking about this "incident" that happens in your future that required you all to do something in the past. What did it require? It required—and this happened a few years ago; I'm not going to give you an exact target date, because some of you felt it at slightly different times—and built into you an urgency to find your true being. This means (and I know that you can all identify with this) that the question "Why am I here?" or "What am I supposed to be doing here?" suddenly came to the forefront of your thoughts, and many of you have attempted to fulfill it. And the "Why am I here?" and "What am I supposed to be doing here?" are questions entirely spiritually based. That is also why in recent years there has been an upsurge, an upswing, in religious pursuits and, I might add, also in things that are called metaphysical or New Age, and people have tried to discover why they're here. So that's what happened, and that's its effect.

Mistreated Animals Want to Leave Earth and Go Home

We can only talk for just a given amount of time, because the energy is a bit overwhelming. That's because there are a lot of beings in the room who want me to talk about this and that, and I talked a little bit about this and that as well as telling you about other things. There are a lot of animal spirits here in this room. The animal spirits feel such a tremendous urgency that they all want to go home when they or any of their number are being mistreated by human beings. They see that this might continue to perpetuate and perhaps get worse, and they want to go home. That's why so many animals on Earth have become, as you say, extinct. Of course, their energy is still here for the future, and should human beings start to treat one another and the animals—and the plants, I might add—

better, then they might choose to reemerge on Earth. But for now, a lot of them want to go home. That means home to their home planets where their souls live and incarnate and appear the way they normally appear on their home planets—whereas out here, they volunteered to be here to support you, to help you learn, to help you remember who you are, to support your knowledge and wisdom, and particularly to support your own hearts so that you would feel and experience some kind of benevolent, safe love.

Sometimes, as you know, love between human beings doesn't feel safe all the time. So there's a benevolent, safe love that you can count on, meaning you might have a dog or a cat, or you might have a favorite horse, or you might enjoy seeing the animals free out in the countryside, the squirrels, the rabbits, the elk, the deer and so on, depending on where you live—maybe it's the giraffes. In short, the animals are here to support and nurture safe and benevolent love for human beings, and of course, some of them are simply here to look nice, not necessarily to be hugged by you or to hug you. I won't discuss all of this, but they are here. The animal spirits wanted me to bring this up.

Decisions Not Based on Feeling Can Lead to Disaster

What is the name of this disease that will require the universal vaccination?

No. If I say that, then many people might actually avoid the vaccination. I will say that it's for a disease you don't know about yet. That's what I'm going to say.

Is this meeting about the vaccine, when these beings who feel the accelerated sense of urgency decide to secretly add the brain enhancer to the vaccine, a national meeting or a global meeting?

It's more of an international meeting, and it's not something public, it's not corporate. They are well intended, that's the thing. They're not monsters; they honestly feel that this is going to be a great thing, a wonderful thing. They do it with the best of intentions. Now, you know how many times you can look back in your history and read the documents of the time if you have them available. How many times were things done with the best of intentions, but they turned out terribly? So these are not evil people, but they are people who have a strong sense of urgency.

I might add that one of the reasons they have a strong sense of urgency is that they feel that they are literally sick of human conflict and what happens in human conflict, such as the terrible things that have happened in Africa and other places—not just where there are wars, but where there's fighting between groups of people. Terrible things happen, and these people at the meeting are just disgusted with that. They feel, as many people have felt in the past, that if everyone could just think more clearly, everyone would see that violence and conflict don't make sense. But that's not what changes things, even though it might seem to and there's even some evidence to suggest that it would. What changes things is that people feel their own hearts and their own love, and they begin to identify that other people feel the same way as they do about the basic qualities of life. People want other people to be happy—not necessarily to have the same things they have, but to be happy and have what they need to have in order to enjoy the basic needs of life. And when you all feel that way about everybody else on the Earth, life is going to change here and you'll take a big step toward heaven on Earth.

Living Prayer Will Keep the Health Group from Adding Brain Enhancement to the Vaccine

So if many people do this nighttime prayer now and mitigate the sense of urgency that these scientists and others at the meeting will feel, then they won't add the brain enhancer to the vaccine and the danger of human extinction will no longer be an issue?

That's right. That's what it takes. It takes a decrease in the feeling of urgency, and then what will happen is that the substance that might stimulate an improvement in the mind will not be combined with this vaccination. It will still be made available to individuals. It will be very expensive, but it will be available to individuals who want to improve their minds and so on as it is supported. But the brain enhancer will not be combined with the vaccination and people won't get it without knowing that they are getting it. So it's not going to stop the development of that product, but it will not be combined with something else that people need.

How far in the future is this meeting? When will this meeting happen?

I will not say. I've already given you a clue. When you become aware of a new disease and it's defined and there is an urgent desire as there often is—the same urgent desire as there is with any other disease to find some cure, and scientists are supported and encouraged to find a cure—it will be like that, the same kind of process as always

What is the name of the new disease?

Something you don't know about yet.

Is it related to poultry?

Of course. Why do you think I brought it up? Fortunately, you don't have to figure it out. I know that sounds like I'm brushing you off, but I'm really speaking to others here. I'm interested and I'm glad that you want to figure it out—and you are, of course, not only the person I interact with for these talks, but also the representative of humankind, so I'm glad that you have this curiosity. The people who really have to figure it out are the people in the research medical community who create . . . who are beginning to understand, for example, that all the research they've done on men does not necessarily mean that their products, as a result, will apply directly to women.

This is why, for those of you youngsters out there who are looking for a job in the medical field that will be guaranteed to be huge in the future, there's going to be huge amounts of research done on various . . . not just diseases, but various things with volunteers who are women. Vast amounts of research in the past were done—medically and psychologically and so on—on people who are men, and the assumption was, "Oh well, this also applies to women," but it doesn't. Sometimes it does, but most of the time it doesn't. That's why women have had certain lingering diseases that seem to defy cure. I'm not going to indict the medical profession; it has nothing to do with science. But it does have a lot to do with your coaches and your societies, with the way your coaches and condition-ers put greater value on one gender over another. But you'll get over that.

I'm talking about a disease that human beings have. I'm not talking about a dis-ease for animals. Animals aren't going to be injected with this so they become intel-lectually superior. It's something you don't know about. That's all I'm going to say.

And I feel like I haven't been unfair with those who raise chickens. I've just suggested that you need to raise them in another way, that's all. Get them out of their cages and let them run around on the ground. I know all the problems. You will be able to figure it out. It's not natural for a bird to be raised in a build-ing; birds need to be outdoors. Okay, they need to have some place they can come indoors when it rains, but other than that, they need to be outdoors. You know—I'm not telling you anything you don't already know.

Creator Training Was Set Up in the Past, Which Was Then the Present, to Prepare You to Resolve a Crisis in the Future

So the illustration [Fig 42–1] you drew in response to my question as to what happened, what changed a few years ago to cause a difference, not only in the way life felt, but also in the focus of the channeling through Robert [Shapiro]—the channeling went from Explorer Race information to material-mastery teaching ("You are an apprentice creator; learn how to do living prayer and benevolent magic")—all relates to the incident in the future that you saw from that time a few years ago and for which you are giving us a living prayer to resolve the situation you are describing in these pages?

Creators-in-training—what do creators do? Do they work a shift and then sleep? Creators-in-training do things even when they're sleeping! Yes, it relates entirely. What I said, that's what happened. And we couldn't . . . there was an urgency, we had to do something, and you couldn't do it overnight. I couldn't say, "Okay, you are all now mystical people and shamanic people, and you're all assigned to do this." You needed to have training. Therefore, I asked my friends Reveals the Mysteries, Speaks of Many Truths and others to come and train those of you who wish to be trained, who would embrace this, who would like to invest in the idea of being creators-in-training and do the best you could. And then, hopefully, when you engaged this process, you would choose to share things with other people, your friends and others, when you felt that certain of your trainings were developed by you or by others that were benevolent for all. And many of you have done exactly that. Thank you very much.

Understand this, my friend—you are asking and I appreciate your clarity—I know that you're asking why the teaching, the channeling, changed. But for other people, they felt the change differently, as I described today. Most people do not have your experience talking to Uncle Zoosh, understand? So my answer applies to most people, not just those who are talking to me.

Fig. 42–1. In the nineties, the Explorer Race mentors saw the situation involving the vaccination scenario in the future and began training all humans to use their natural abilities as benevolent creators.

And along with the increase in the "creators-in-training" abilities in humans, the SSG, the sinister secret government, also seems to have increased its level of power in its efforts to control and manipulate the peoples and monies of this planet?

No, it's more their fear and their awareness that human beings globally are suddenly very interested in spiritual things and that this might lead to greater power and influence of individuals over their lives. And this also spreads, to a slight degree, to people's interest in religion, but it is not always the case with religion. Some religions are very benevolent; they support and nurture and urge their practitioners to be very humanitarian and so on. But other religions are very exclusive and talk about the enemy and the bad people and how they should all feel guilty and ashamed for being alive. I do not really feel good about what they are teaching, but that's something that they are teaching at this time. They will change. Those religions that survive in the future will all change. And I'm not saying that they're all evil; they do many good things for their parishioners.

But you cannot teach that some groups of human beings are evil just because they are from another religion and hope to develop a more humanitarian Earth just as soon as everybody is of your own religion. If you do that, you're just asking to perpetuate and amplify conflict. I'm not trying to say that religions are evil. I'm just trying to say: Teach things that you can all agree on globally are benevolent human characteristics and qualities that you'd like to increase and support, as well as teach an understanding, from that religion's point of view, of who God is. God has many faces, maybe appearing in the belief forms of different religions in different ways.

The Good News: The Future Remains a Field of Infinite Possibility

The whole purpose of articles like this is to say, "Here's some information. Now you do what you wish with it." The whole purpose of anything channeled through this channel and others very often works to support and educate and—how can we say?—"to wise you up," to present you with something that you can do something with or not. It's up to you. It's our job not to tell you your future but to tell you more about yourselves so you know about your capabilities and to suggest at various times that different ones of these capabilities might be to your advantage to learn about, which is our way of telling you your future.

I want you to think about that. If we stress something suddenly, "out of the blue" as you were suggesting, then that's our way of telling you about your future: "Develop these capabilities, and you won't be sorry," like that. We can't tell you your future, but we can suggest, even with urgency, that it might be a good idea for you to learn how to do this, those of you who would like to. Now, as an example, for a person who's going to take a long ocean voyage in the future that he or she doesn't know about . . . maybe the parents decide it's time to move to this other continent: "Things aren't working well for us here, but we have a feeling that moving to this other continent, or even this other island . . . we're on an island and maybe we can move to another island, or maybe on a continent we're going to move sixty, eighty miles away to another continent." With boats and ships not necessarily being as safe as they are today, parents might urge their children to learn how to swim. They might not necessarily tell the kids why, but, "Oh, why don't you learn how to swim? It might be fun. You can swim with your friends, have time together and so on." The children all learn how to swim, and then the parents are relieved, thinking, "Well, if the boat isn't quite safe, then at least if they fall in the water, they'll be safe; they can swim."

I'm not trying to suggest anything about boats here; I'm just suggesting that sometimes someone who knows something about the future might suggest that you start doing things in a different way because of what could happen in the future, or even because of opportunities that you may have in the future, and if you have these skills and abilities, you can take advantage of these opportunities. If you don't, it might be more difficult. I'm just trying to cover your curiosities.

Now, I'd like to say to you all that these articles are not intended to be "gloom and doom." Rather, picture the future as a time of opportunities, not just as a time of impending challenges or "doom," as it were. And if there are opportunities, quite naturally you're going to want to have skills and abilities heightened—perhaps even things that are within you such as talents—and discover how you can do things in a way that will improve the quality of your life. You may even improve the lives of those around you, such as your love, your friends, your companions, animals perhaps or plants. And that's why I stressed the homework at the beginning of this article, so that you would know that there's something you can do that does not particularly weigh heavily on you as homework that you have to add to your life: "One more thing . . . oh no, Zoosh, not one more thing."

This is something that's designed to improve the quality of your life, to improve benevolence in general for all beings, and you don't have to really do a whole lot extra. Don't feel like you have to do it every night. Just say it when you think about it, before you go to sleep. It will have a cumulative impact. At some point, when you notice that your life is a lot more benevolent—which could happen, no guarantees—then you might feel that you have capabilities and capacities spiritually that you didn't know you had, and that maybe by improving your life and your experience of life—as being more benevolent—that that will spread around and others might feel their life more benevolently too, especially if they are in any way associated with your life. This homework that I gave you at the beginning of the article is intended to, yes, improve your life, but ultimately as more people do it, it will improve the lives of all beings. Good night.

Part 3:
Three Alignments to Bring the Explorer
Race (Human Race) to Benevolence
While Leaving No One Behind—the First
Alignment, Using the Corporate Model
as a Method of Unification, Leads to
World Peace on Planet Earth

Preamble to the First Alignment

The Professor
January 13, 2004

The First, Second and Third Alignments are gifts to humanity from Creator. They are designed as safety mechanisms, as a last resort to bring *all* human beings on the planet into benevolence in the event that you as a planetary society stray too far from a benevolent path, even temporarily.

But the First Alignment is *not* an objective, something you're striving for, something that you want to do as a global society. Perhaps that wasn't made clear by Counsel [in the article that follows in chapter 44]. It was always meant to be not just a last resort—yes, that—but also a safety mechanism so that no matter what path you take, no matter how twisted or tortuous the path becomes, no matter what way you go, at the very least you will all get to where you need to go by the First Alignment, the Second Alignment and the Third Alignment.

So rest assured that there is absolutely no way that anyone—such as the sinister secret government and their inner and outer circles—who wishes to corrupt the arrival of all of you at your natural state of being, in your natural personalities, while you are physically in bodies on Earth (compared to the usual way you get to that when you die and move on or walk out, in the case of a walk-in), that no matter who tries to do that, it cannot be successful. The First Alignment, the Second Alignment and the Third Alignment are safety mechanisms. That's all.

But before that and during that and all around that, there will be others of you doing other things to bring about more benevolent creations. That is why Zoosh and perhaps Isis and others, I believe, said that the First Alignment is a good thing *and* **here is what you can do about** it: benevolent magic, living prayer [see p. xxii] and all of the feminine science teachings in the Light Technology books and the *Sedona Journal of Emergence!*, which are all designed to support all of the other things that you do to bring about benevolence. The First Alignment is not meant to replace what you do.

I want to tell you that, looking at it from my point of view from my time, apparently 10 to 15 percent of your readers and those who look at the website did not understand that. They thought it was a replacement for their benevolent effort, and thence they were offended and they felt betrayed.

When you read this preamble in front of the First Alignment articles, and then you read—or reread, for those who first read these articles in the *Sedona Journal*— the channeling about the First Alignment, then you don't feel that anything has been taken away from you. You feel reassured that there is a safety mechanism that will work. It may not have anything to do with you, because you are doing what you are doing to bring about benevolence in your lives and in the lives of others. But for everybody else who isn't doing that, there is a safety mechanism, and that's going on all around you as well. It's intended to explain your world as it's happening on a commercial and business level, and all around you are people who perhaps are not yet as awake, since they have not yet embraced spiritual and physical and philosophical points that you have embraced.

We're not singling out any group; we're talking about everyone who isn't currently involved in benevolence and choosing that—and by "benevolence" I mean not only what you do benevolently with others but also what you are doing with yourselves working with your own bodies and everything we've been talking about (myself and all the others) in these books and magazine articles. If you are embracing that or something like that to create benevolence for yourselves as individuals and others, then the First Alignment and its mechanism are not intended to replace what you are doing, but they are intended to help you to understand what the rest of the world is doing until they get to that point as individuals to choose that benevolence for themselves. It is a safety mechanism for them, and because what they are doing affects everyone else, it allows you to understand the mechanism that they have chosen as a safety mechanism for themselves so that they won't, by going off on one of these paths, fall off the deep end into something and bring others with them.

It's a safety mechanism that they chose in their souls, working with Creator and all beings, that has been granted to those who are doing these things that are destructive, including the sinister secret government and so on, and for their expedient purposes—yes, the world as you know it commercially, business and stuff. Some business is good, some commercial is good, but some of it is just too greedy and avaricious, and it crushes and harms people and whole societies. So those beings who are doing that need the safety of the First Alignment in their souls.

They're not evil; they are just blind to what they are doing. Only some of them are evil, but not many. And they all are engaged in that, some who are working for others and feel obliged to do that. They all have asked on a soul level, "Give us something that we can have that no matter what we do or what we feel obligated to do, there is something that will happen as a result of this so that no matter how far we go, it will allow us to become our natural, benevolent, loving selves for ourselves and for others."

So it has been granted: the First Alignment, world peace; the Second Alignment, happiness; and the Third Alignment, fulfillment. That's the way I see it from my time.

The First Alignment: World Peace, Your Future and You

Counsel, Zoosh and Isis

July 13, 14 and 15, 2003

Greetings. I will say only this about myself: You can refer to me as Counsel. I will answer no questions as to my identity. Now I will speak of the First Alignment: The First Alignment is in process now on your world. It has to do with aligning and stimulating corporate agreements to achieve alliances beyond borders. An even casual examination of your history will show you that nationalistic borders have not brought about peace, no matter how effective a nation's propaganda. The hope for true peace on this planet comes about through a staged progression.

Business and Corporate Alliances Will Break Down Borders

The First Alignment is based entirely upon self-interest. It is understood that self-interest at this time in your world, although not universal for all individuals, is by and large universal for all corporations and businesses. I will not rationalize why; I think it is understood. So the First Alignment for your world is entirely based on business and corporate alliance; it is intended to break down borders entirely. The alignment, when it is complete, will go largely unnoticed by the bulk of the population. For all intents and purposes, it will appear as if borders are still intact; nothing on the surface will seem to change very much. But the actual alignment will be on a basis of corporate and allied business.

This does not mean that corporations are taking over the world in terms of your daily life. Your daily life will still be regulated by your beliefs, your values, your purposes; it will still be regulated by local governments and, to some degree, national governments. But, in fact, the days of the borders as you've come to know them, meaning each country attempting to meet its own needs based upon what it can provide—even using trade to provide and therefore be independent—are over. A simple, casual look at your trade policies for the past forty or fifty years would already suggest this; this is not news to you. What is important to know as a citizen of Earth is that these alignments are intended to bring you into global citizenship.

This does not mean that cultures will be lost. If you are Iranian, if you are South African, if you are Italian, if you are American, Canadian and so on, your cultures will not be lost, but they will tend to be shared more freely with the world. You see that now—do you not?—with restaurants and literature, the arts and so on. And you will see more of that. These are benevolent expressions of culture.

The less benevolent expressions are based on greed and, to a degree—which does not exclude greed—religion. For a time—and this was tried for several thousand years—the attempt to create global unity based on religion was given a chance, but not only has it not worked, it has been a disaster. Granted, some wonderful things have occurred in alignment with religion that will not be lost. But you still have now in the world battles from one religion to another based primarily on religion and very little else. Even people . . . if you stood them side by side, you'd say, "These people look alike; their culture is very similar. Why are they at each other's throats?" It's entirely based on religion—granted, with political attitudes that are fully meshed with that religion. So that's not working, and this is known.

Corporate Self-Interest Establishes Unity

The unity, then, that can be established without any great problem, has been getting established for some time, as you may know. This alignment of business can create working relationships between people who would otherwise be fierce enemies for one political, religious or nationalistic reason or another, to say nothing of personality conflicts. A shared desire for self-interest and to expand self-interest beyond the individual level to include a business or corporation, or even a multilayered or leveraged corporation, is still self-interest regardless. This self-interest is going to be the steppingstone that will propel you all into a more benevolent state or condition. Granted, it will turn peoples and nations into something that is generalized.

United States Americans and, to a degree, Americans north and south, Europeans and so on, have been in a long period of experimentation with consumerism. Consumerism has been such a success that it was a clear indicator that the First Alignment had to be based on self-interest. Consumers are interested in their own self, and if they are not, there are products that encourage interest in oneself. These are based upon showing you things about yourself, encouraging you to be interested in yourself, encouraging you to be interested in the appearance and so on of others. In short, consumerism based upon self-identity has been very successful and so have businesses, corporations and multi-level corporations who cater products that in some way—either in the basic way or right down to the product delivered into your hands—are all based on serving self-interested consumers as you have been conditioned to be, all right? And even though this might seem crass, it is actually a solid foundation, proven over time, that works to bring you into a global harmony—though granted, it is a harmony initially based on self-interest.

This might seem unpleasant to some of you, but that might be partly because you are living in a place where you can take the time to consider such philosophies and thoughts. There are people living in other places where they do not know from one minute to the next whether they will be killed, maimed or tortured. It is not acceptable for people to be living in those situations; it is unacceptable. They must be brought out of those conditions, even if it means some degree of sacrifice for the consuming world. There needs to be a unified and, to a degree, regulated system to do this. Most of the pieces for this are in place now.

Anyone Not Absorbed Benevolently into the First Alignment Will Be Eliminated

You will find gradually increasing involvement by the governments of the world to support this First Alignment. Anyone, whether they be world leaders—*especially* world leaders, world governments—or whether they be organizations, even so-called hidden organizations striving for some political or religious gain or simply a self-interested gain in the case of a criminal empire . . . all of these organizations, if they cannot be absorbed in some benevolent expression of themselves into the First Alignment, if that cannot happen or if they will not allow that to happen, they will be crushed, they will be eliminated. I am not stating this as some external authority; I am looking at what has happened on your planet. And I'm telling you now, this First Alignment is a critical step toward something that your religions have encouraged you to pray for; that your philosophies have encouraged you to believe is possible if only you'd follow that philosophy; that your hopes, prayers and dreams for years have supported. It is a worthy first step—yes, a worthy first step toward world peace.

World peace is not enough. That's right. You need to go past world peace, but it's important and that's what's going on in the First Alignment. What comes past world peace? World happiness, world fulfillment, of course—those kinds of things. But one thing at a time. World peace means no people having to worry about being killed, maimed or tortured. That's a big process. You may not see your neighborhood businesses or even the corporation names you're familiar with as brave soldiers toward achieving this task, and I'm not suggesting you do see them that way. I am simply stating that this is, in fact, going on right now. It is well on its way toward achieving that goal.

You will not see at this time the elimination of greed. The fact that greed exists truly allows much of this to take place, because one cannot overlook the things that people feel, partly as a result of their conditioning and partly as a result of what seem to be external events, meaning global events—this happens here, this happens there; you respond, you react. Some people store up groceries, just in case; other people store up money, just in case; some people store up weapons, just in case; some people make arrangements, agreements or organize all kinds of things, just in case. These are all responses, and there are many more. And although they might not at all seem to be greedy—they might very well seem to be prudent, a very good business term—they are, in fact, sharing a common denominator, *all* of them, no matter what their reaction. The common denominator is self-interest. This is not what they're trying to show the world, but the expression as judged by others—not themselves—still would be greed.

Do you see? Someone's throwing up this, throwing up that, creating these alignments, doing this, doing that. It seems to be prudent to them and might very justifiably seem to be so, but if you see it from the outside in, you are inclined to think of them as greedy. They may not think of themselves as this; they might be able to rationalize it very well. It is not my job to dispute their rationalization. Their rationalization may, in fact, be absolutely true—not only for themselves and for those they are in alignment with, but it might also be true for the general perception that they have of themselves.

World Leaders Know the First Alignment Is Taking Place

Now, all the world's leaders, presidents and so on, they all know that this alignment is taking place. Some of them are more on the forefront of bringing the alignment about. Partially this may have to do with the fact that they have the resources, the wealth, or that they can summon the resources and the wealth to bring this about through alliances. Given their capacity to bring these circumstances about, one might reasonably find that their goals—seemingly immediate to themselves or to their immediate connection to whatever industries seem to fuel the actions—create an underpinning that supports the First Alignment.

I'm talking to you, the public, about this First Alignment now, not just because I'm campaigning for something—which I'm not; I'm strictly an historian, you might say, an observer—but because I see how you have moved, from my perspective [from the future], from the First Alignment to the Second Alignment, which takes into account not only peace, but adds happiness to peace. It's a big step. Peace is vital, it is wonderful and it is critical, but happiness involves many, many more things. Then the third step adds to that fulfillment, meaning not only individual fulfillment, but group fulfillment as well. And I can see how, given all the other things you've tried as an Earth population/civilization.

There have been some small successes; groups who have lasted for a while have achieved wonderful, benevolent societies. But even sometimes within those benevolent societies there are practices that are abhorrent. Not every member of the society might know, but they're there—not in every society, but they are there.

The First Alignment Is Going to Work!

So I can see what has not worked, and I can see that this First Alignment is going to work. If you as an individual feel like some cog in a large machine, think about it this way: Your desires on a personal level can be fulfilled in this First Alignment. Whether those desires are to survive and be free of threat, or whether they are expanded to include your family, your friends, maybe even your neighborhood, it can all happen on the basic level, which has to do with personal security, otherwise known as safety. This is most likely to be achieved in the First Alignment. You can, many of you, achieve quite a bit of happiness, relief. You will be able to be conscious that you are safe—not just have some voice come out of the sky or over the airwaves and tell you that you are and say, "All right, we've established the First Alignment," though they won't call it that, but some might. But you might not hear that term in public.

Over time people will notice that the threat level decreases, decreases, decreases; pretty soon there's no threat at all. People can really leave their doors unlocked, and everybody will be secure. That is not now quite obvious, but it will be, and it will be enforced. You will see many more security agencies, even small armies, fielded by corporations. This is already happening to a degree, and some public officials have begun speaking of it openly, mostly to authenticate the validity and the approval of governments here and there. They have begun speaking of the legitimacy of such corporate enterprises as large security agencies—depending on your point of view, you might even say it's something that looks like an army.

Some people will feel that this is a terrible thing, and I can understand that. Keep an eye on the big picture, though. Mistakes will be made, as it is with human beings at this stage of your existence; people will be hurt. There will be worse things. People who happen to be in the crossfire, so to speak, will be killed for no reason. That's why your consciousness is being raised about terrorists. Some of these people were terrorists in the past. However, these people who may have been terrorists in the past, these groups of terrorists, have gone on to establish countries; after all, your own United States was established by what were deemed to be terrorists in England.

So granted, if so-called terrorists do acts of terror on civilians who did them no harm . . . you are being conditioned somewhat so that if one of your enforcing agencies or governments says, "This group is a terrorist group," you will not think of them as they think of themselves, as freedom fighters. It will be hard for many of you, because you have grown up and been conditioned to different political views. I am not here to campaign, to say that this is bad and so on; I am here simply to let you know that the First Alignment is well under way, that Creator will stand back because Creator recognizes that this is a vital step toward not only world peace, but world happiness, then world fulfillment. And it must happen on the basis of things that all people can reasonably believe in—not just by having their arms twisted behind their backs and being asked, "Do you believe?" And then, "No, no, I don't believe," and then a little more twisting, "Oh, yes! See, I believe! I believe!" [Chuckles.] As terrible as that is, I chuckle a little bit because that is the political cartoon one sees down through the ages. You've seen it many times in many cultures.

Creator stands back because Creator knows that to interfere with this process is to interfere with Creator's own intent, which is to align and bring together divergent feelings, capacities and abilities that have been unsolvable in other creations throughout all time and existence. Your Creator of this universe is determined to find a use for the unsolvable—not only that which could be called and deemed unsolvable, discomfort as Zoosh calls it, which can range from minor annoyance to horrible, miserable suffering. Any reasonable person would say, "There's no use for this; let's get rid of it." And yet here it is in your universe. Here on Earth especially, you see it every day, plus you usually experience it in greater or lesser degrees, depending upon your time of life and your circumstances. You might very reasonably say, "What good is it?" And I'm not saying it is; I am simply saying that your Creator of this universe noticed that it existed in other places and that they couldn't find a way to resolve it, to bring it into some expression of itself that is benevolent.

This Process Is a Last Resort

Now, I am not here to reiterate truths that have already been stated in other documents, such as the *Explorer Race* books, the *Shining the Light* books and so on, but I am here to inform you of a process that is going on, that is in motion, that is universal—meaning universal on Earth. No matter what faces you see, no matter who's behind the scenes encouraging and supporting those faces and individuals, no matter what temporary changes you see, the First Alignment is in progress. *Many of the things you see are intended to condition you globally to accept circumstances that you would not accept otherwise.* Sometimes these are terrible things, done with the greatest reluctance and often at great personal sacrifice by the people who order them done. Nevertheless, there are those on your world who believe in the ultimate value of this.

You have to look at your history over the long term; I'm not just talking about written history, but beyond. Everything else has been tried. This series of alignments and the process by which it is going on and being brought about is literally a last resort. I'm not saying this as a threat; it's not a threat. But it is a last resort to bring every citizen on the Earth first to peace, then to happiness, then to a fulfillment that is something he or she personally feels—not that other people say, "You're fulfilled now," but something that person personally, individually feels as fulfillment. That alone increases your level of happiness. It is not artificial; it has to be real.

Therefore, I do not see that it fails in any way, but theoretically speaking, if it were to fail (just for the sake of those who would ask that question), it does not mean that some lightning bolt would come out of the sky and destroy your world. It just means that your world would literally be allowed to come to the conclusion that groups of people fighting one another with increasingly larger and more damaging weapons would bring about, which would be the death of your planet as you know it, at least on the surface—and over time, under the surface as well. There are those who believe that the citizens of Earth can not only be saved as a global community but can be brought to peace, happiness and fulfillment on both a global basis as well as on a personal, individual basis.

The Three Alignments

These things will happen over a period of years. Given a full life—meaning so many years, whatever the average is—those of you alive now, especially the young ones in a country with full medical and societal support systems, you will likely live to see the First Alignment. It is very possible that you will live to at least partially experience the Second Alignment, and some of you very young ones who live a long life might even live to experience the Third Alignment. By the time the Second Alignment takes place, it won't take very long to accomplish the Third Alignment. The First Alignment is the hardest one and has been in process now for forty or fifty years.

I'm not going to talk about the steps that led up to it, but over the past forty or fifty years things have been changing. Some things might have seemed alarming to some of you, such as global international corporations taking over your local businesses, which can be alarming. But remember, it is intended to create an overall evenness. Granted, some people will be wealthy and some people will be struggling, but the First Alignment is meant to bring about world peace. It is the Second Alignment that brings about world happiness—not that you're happy with your lot in life, that's not what I mean by happiness; I mean that you are happy.

So the Second Alignment will be about a—how can we say?—an evening off, meaning people will be happy but not through some distorted pursuit that makes them momentarily happy. Rather, you will be happy because your life is going in a way you like; you will have what you want and need. That's what I mean by happiness. It's not just that the different strata of society will be happy within their strata. There will not be strata of society separated as you see now, and it will not come about by some ruthless suppression of this or that. It will come about because of the personal desire of every individual. But it will come about.

The First Alignment is what's most important. You will notice the Second Alignment developing even while the First Alignment is being established; you will notice it here and there. But the First Alignment is what is most important to discuss.

Businesses Will Merge

So the trend will continue, the merging of companies of a similar nature, with expansion all over the globe. Correction: The trend will continue until there's only *one* of each. One. There will be, for a time, individual corporations, even multileveled corporations. But eventually both kinds will form up under one for every type of business. Transportation, fuel, resources, chemicals—all of these will tend to form up under one. Other things will be aligned; your own publishing will form up under media and communications resources, other things like that. It will seem almost as if, for a time . . . like your civil servants, they won't be servants, but in time you will all be working for the same company, so to speak. And while that might seem to suppress individual expression, that company will be very versatile, very allowing. If your particular branch wishes to express itself this way or that way, that will be completely acceptable. What was once an individual company will be a branch of something else, but it will not have its personality wiped out; its personality will be encouraged to do more, not less.

Even a little business that has struggled to meet its payroll, for instance, or has been unable to compete with larger businesses or organizations that can provide medical and dental and vacation and stock options and all that, will be able to do that then in alignment with that bigger business. Then individuals will not have to choose to leave a business, even a small business, that they enjoy working for because they need to get ahead for their own sake or for the sake of their families. They will have all of those perks, as you call them, working for a small business, because the small business will be a part of a large business.

And these large businesses will be owned by stockholders or by individuals?

The large businesses are owned by somebody now, even though they may seem . . . even though stockholders have a share in the profit, if they wish it, meaning they can purchase stock and hold it and receive dividends, as compared to, say, buying and selling the stock on the basis of its day-to-day perceived value. But the stockholders, unless they are very large stockholders and even then only to a degree, do not run the business. It is not their business.

But as far as your question goes: Yes, it will be like that for a time. But ultimately it will have less to do with people who buy and sell stock and more to do with people who invest or people who buy stock and hold it, sit on it. And they will get dividends.

The End of Corporate Diversification

So there's going to be a sorting out. Where one company now may own a dairy company, a music company, a beverage company and an airplane company, in the future all the airplanes will be here, and all the farming will be there, and all the entertainment will be there—like that?

That's right. Right now, you see, corporations diversify with the idea that if one element in the company fails, even if they lose that whole element and have to sell it out at a fire-sale price to whomever will buy it, other elements of the company have no connection to this element and will not be damaged. That's the purpose of diversification.

But in the future, one gradually will see, and we're seeing it right now . . . since you used the airline industry as an example, we will gradually see that eventually there will be one airline authority. But it will also be associated with some other forms of rapid travel. And it will allow and encourage different brands. One might say that General Mills, for example, produces cereal and all kinds of things, different brands of cereal. The companies that put out those different brands of cereal, they are still companies, but they are under General Mills. Do you understand? One will see something like that in the airline industry, so that if one airline company is struggling but is providing an expression of service that the public gravitates to, if the public gravitates to that struggling company, even if other airlines offer a similar service, that struggling company will not only be nurtured but will be fostered to grow in some way so it can serve that segment of the population who would like to have more of whatever that company is offering that they find so attractive.

So I'm not saying that companies will be crushed; what I am saying is that there will be a realignment based not on diversification but on allied arrangements—that each version of the global corporate entity tends to feed, support and nurture one another, not only for some act of kindness [chuckles], but rather because this feeding and nurturing serves other elements within the global corporation. Therefore, profitability is improved, if not in the immediate short run, then in the immediate long run. The immediate long run might be within two or three years.

A Balancing Act

So such things will actually foster and encourage individuality because . . . think about it. Over the years, many years now, agencies—this or that agency or group within a company—have analyzed demographics very well, so that markets are quickly analyzed and served, and this is ongoing. If the group of individuals who like something reject something that's being offered to them, it is quickly discarded. Whatever they do like, they get more of and in different varieties and so on.

I'm not saying that this is something you build your philosophy, your religion and your beliefs on. Rather, I am saying that it is intended to be a balancing, something to even off—not socialistically speaking, not someone coming into your life and house and family and saying, "Here, we need someone to operate this machine and you're it," but rather something that you want to do. You want to get ahead, you want to have things, you want to improve your lifestyle, you want to improve your family's lifestyle, you want to improve your community—all of these things will come about through the First Alignment, though there will be rough patches. You're going through a rough patch now. There might be more rough patches, but I assure you, even though you are seeing some things that are ugly or terrible, those things will be resolved. It is not intended that you will see something like a political situation, like you've seen in wars where one country spreads out all over, influencing and stamping out all resistance and saying, "You will believe what we believe or we will kill you." Those days are not going to spread into the future, and governments or heads of governments who think they can make it happen will be crushed.

I am not speaking as some authority. I am speaking as one who has looked back, from my perspective, into your times and seen governments who thought they could stand and function outside of these global corporate approvals intended to bring about world peace through the expression of consumerism based on self-interest. These governments or heads of state or even heads of various groups who thought they could take a little bite here and a little bite there—or even a big bite—will be eliminated.

So prices based on competition will be gone.

Yes. Prices will be based upon what's needed by the global corporation to establish its goals, to feed its hungry mouths—in short, to establish the satiation of greed. But at some point, even the global corporation realizes, "Now, wait; if we take all the money from the people, there will be no more money to come to us. Plus, we won't have anything to purchase the things we want." In short, all global corporations have to come to the realization at some point that they cannot raise their prices arbitrarily to some point where they are out of reach. Even criminal empires have to realize this. They will be absorbed. As I said before, if the criminal empire cannot be absorbed into the First Alignment, it will be crushed, it will be eliminated.

But criminal empires will be absorbed. Much of what they provide now illegally will, in time, be made legal in order to increase the value and desirability for those who wish to consume those products or services. Prices will be set based on causing the product or service to be desirable, and various degrees of those products providing various levels of momentary happiness will be made available, just like with other products and services, anything—drugs, food, medicine.

Corporate Individuals Must Become Global Citizens

Now, these different products will be offered, and as I say, even if the criminal empire is offering these products, they will be made legal. Laws against them will be eliminated. You understand, this will tend to bring about the desire, in time, to go past world peace and bring about happiness. If you are addicted to something and suffering and cannot simply rob, cheat and steal to get the money you need to get it . . . because that won't be allowed anymore, why? World peace! Things will have to change.

Corporations, whether they be criminal or legal or motivated by other basic drives—primarily self-interest, perceived by others as greed (and perhaps that's true; it certainly is in some cases)—these individuals who are involved in this are being forced into a position, but not by having their arms twisted behind their backs (which we know doesn't work; it may work in the short run, but not in the long run). They're being forced by the evidence of their own eyes and perceptions that they must become responsible global citizens, that they are providing valuable services that people want and need, and that they must be responsive to the needs of other large corporations and responsive to the needs of the consumers, which, from the corporation's point of view, includes everyone on the planet, including everyone who works for the corporation.

You all have that in common. If the managing directors and so on are not clear on that point, then they will simply become clear on the fact that you cannot raise your prices beyond the point where people are able to purchase things. You can raise your prices just to the point where you have all that you want and need, but if it gets to the point where others do not, that's going to impinge—in the future, of course—on happiness. It's going to impinge on the practical pursuit of the absolute—no individuals eliminated from it—the absolute intention of the First Alignment, which is world peace that serves consumerism and self-interest. And no exceptions will be allowed.

But aside from that enforcement, it's critically obvious to people who make the decisions at the top, as it's called, that if people can't afford to buy something but they actually want it, then there have to be versions they can afford to buy, just as people might want to improve their conditions if they're living in desperate circumstances. If they're living in desperate circumstances and things get better for them, they can afford a modest apartment. A modest apartment may not be much to people living in a grand apartment or a huge home or some fabulous place, but a modest apartment is pretty fabulous if you've been living in a cardboard shack. So there are different levels, all right? It's all part of peace. All part of peace.

China Will Be a Major Influence

What about education?

I will speak of that. In education it will be recognized that initially certain languages need to be spoken in business. One sees this being catered to now. For a long time, English has been a business language. You see in the past, of course, in your history, that other languages were the business language and French was the diplomatic language for years. But even though English might appear to be the business language now, other languages will emerge and become temporarily dominant. I will not speak of which languages; I will simply say that it will be whatever languages are the most expressive, not only in their mental, linear description (because different words cover different things), but also in their mood, in their way of expressing things. This becomes very important so that subtle messages can be delivered with the same words as absolute messages. These languages will come to be adapted by business—if not as their primary language, then as a secondary language used for negotiating, especially when vast continents such as China, for example, are being encouraged to join the global community to bring about world peace and the First Alignment.

And yet China has a system that is working and, regardless of external perceptions, is a vast improvement over what existed before in terms of it serving the needs of a much greater number of people than were being served in the past. I'm not trying to make heroes out of the government; I'm simply saying that in a few short years they have managed to improve the quality of life for the average citizen in a very big way, so do not expect them to give this up quickly. But as they come to see that the global corporation and self-interest and all of this business is becoming the predominant theme, and as they notice these qualities in themselves and feel safe with them, over time different elements, different expressions of the community, will join.

The self-interest global corporate world is not going to make war on China, though they have in the past through their representatives in the form of various governments. They now know that this does not work, and they will therefore invite China in the most benevolent way to join the system they have to offer. But the only way China is going to consider doing that, even in an incremental way as you see now, is if the government and the political beliefs of China are fostered, encouraged and allowed to exist in some way, at least for a time, and if the improved state of existence for the citizens of China is not turned into the feudal system they struggled under in the past. This is why they are so aggressively antifeudal. If they define something on their borders—a country or its government—as having been supportive of the feudal system in the past and being demonstrative in some way of the feudal system in the present, even if they do not need anything in that country . . . you have seen them demonstrate in the past such a sense of personal and moral (to them) outrage, that they will go and invade this country, and commit all kinds of atrocities to eliminate the feudal system.

Now, I'm not saying "good" or "bad." I'm simply saying that it will take them awhile to embrace the global corporate community, but they will in time, possibly bringing with them the lessons of their history, which they have kept back further than many other nations, and influencing the global corporate community to understand that if you set your prices too high, at some point it doesn't work. They will be a major influence in convincing global corporations that the needs of the people for peace are supported and nurtured by the basic needs of all the people in the country being served, at least in some benchmark way. This is the basis and no worse. Right now in China it's no worse, no better. But the global corporate entity is influencing them now, will influence them more, and they will, in time, not capitulate, not go to war over this—obviously, the whole point of your past history, that you've gone to war over this or that, isn't the solution. They will simply join on the basis of seeing many of their values being expressed in this new world alignment, this First Alignment.

So I'm not talking about communism, I'm not talking about capitalism; those ideas will be forgotten in the future. I'm talking about a First Alignment that brings about world peace, a Second Alignment that takes a much shorter time to bring about world happiness (that everyone is going to know for certain whether they're happy or not) and a Third Alignment that comes about quicker still, which is world fulfillment.

The World Community Will Keep Its Diversity

What will be the function of national governments and borders, then?

Over time national states and borders will cease to exist, because when people are safe, they will be able to freely flow from one country to another and only be restricted to the degree that they do not know and understand the culture or local language and customs. So the more that is known and understood about that, the more the world community becomes somewhat homogenized, perhaps for a while, but not ever looking bland—not "A" and "B," maybe a little "C." All the letters and all the numbers, all kinds of things will be seen. Individualism will be encouraged as long as it fits into the world alignment, all right?

We'll keep our diversity . . .

You'll keep your diversity; it will be fostered and nurtured because you can see how it has supported business and brought about happiness. You've all experienced this in recent years, most of you to whom I'm speaking in this article: If you have only one or two types of food in your town, the first time some new restaurant opens, isn't it true that you all beat a path to the restaurant to try it out? Many of you do. Maybe it's not the greatest, but it has one or two things that you really like, and then you go for that. And then other restaurants come and the restaurants you had . . . when people say, "Gosh, I don't care for all of their food, but there's one or two things that are great," the restaurants in town start making their version of those things. So individuality is still encouraged, especially if it's good for the business community, local and international.

But borders as you've come to know them gradually dissolve so that by the time you're in the midpoint of world happiness and you wish to see a map of the world, there will be no political boundaries delineated. However, for those of you who wish to study the past, you might see such political boundaries delineated. You see maps on the basis of rivers, streams, mountains, cultural diversity. You see that, but it spreads beyond cultural diversity as it has always been in the past; it spreads beyond political boundaries.

Basic Services Will Be Privatized

What about the level of basic services? Will water, trash, police forces, firefighters, everything we know of that are responsibilities of local government, will that all be privatized?

Yes. You will find that police forces will be privatized, and the police forces will at first be uncomfortable with it, but then they will feel much better. Their salaries will improve to some degree, but more to the point, their benefits will vastly improve. And there will be a great deal of attention paid to their safety; it will not just mean wearing bulky things that are hot and uncomfortable, but they will be encouraged to wear or have a lot of safety equipment. If they are not safe to go out . . . it's really outrageous that one police officer should go someplace where if three went, it would be much safer; one does not always know when one is going into a dangerous situation. So there will be more police officers, not less.

There will be levels, meaning one now sees community groups such as the Scouts getting exposed to policing or the fire department as a public service. But you will see, say, in the police, that there will be levels, meaning there will be something like the youth police, for instance, and they will be supported; they won't get salaries if they're teenagers—and by teenagers, I mean seventeen or under, still in school—but they will get support and training in case they wish to become police officers. It will not be demanded of them, but if they wish to become police officers, they will have the opportunity by going into these programs, not unlike the ROTC program for the military. There will be that for the fire department and other things.

It will be found—even though there will be a lot of resistance—but it will be found by the employees, by the police employees, by the fire department employees and so on, that working for a private corporation gives one a great deal more security, a great deal more safety and the means to interact on the enforcing level, say, for the police, or the means to interact for the fire department to, say, put out fires. The technology will be vastly improved. Obviously, the whole point, from a business point of view, is to make a profit, but also whether you're going to be perceived as a worthy business. You wouldn't buy a cereal that tasted terrible if you could buy a cereal that cost the same or maybe a couple pennies more—by a couple pennies, I mean literally two or three cents more—and tasted wonderful. No, no; the fire department will become vastly more efficient because the methods they use to put out fires will become much more universalized.

Many is the time now that a fire department, for example, will go out on a call that they know is a fire for which equipment exists that could put out the fire very quickly—say, an oil fire or a chemical fire or a refinery fire. The equipment actually exists that could put out the fire in half the time or even less, but they don't have that equipment because it's expensive to produce right now. But at some point, when a corporation is running the fire department, everyone will have that equipment and the fire will be put out [snaps fingers] very quickly, saving lives, reducing suffering and saving property.

Municipal Services Become More Efficient

So you will see the fire department get more efficient. For starters, the biggest trouble most fire departments have been having over the years is not only a lack of good equipment but also of good training and, most importantly, full funding. It is almost unheard of for a fire department in your municipalities to be fully funded, but they will be. Over time, when the fire-suppressing capacities become greatly improved, then the fire departments will get smaller; people won't get fired, but people will retire and so on. There will be less necessity for vast fire departments and thousands of firefighters fighting an individual fire as you see now in a forest fire. When the equipment is much better, when new technologies are employed and when fires are put out almost immediately . . . this is not going to happen instantaneously, but it will happen over time. It's a similar situation with the police.

Fire departments will have youngsters, teenagers seventeen and younger and right on down to thirteen; they'll have some educational things that twelve-year-olds can be exposed to—and they are exposed to it now to some degree. Whole schools will be given a stipend. By stipend I do not mean that individual payments will go to individual students or teachers, but there will be a stipend to fully fund a program in schools not unlike the ROTC. It will not be militaristic—not demands and commands—but rather will involve exposure to firefighting techniques: "Would you be interested in this?" Part of the reason it will be attractive, of course, is that they will have the uniforms. The uniforms won't look the same as the uniforms firefighters wear, but they will be similar, perhaps a lighter color or in some cases a darker color, so that you will be able to say, "Well, these people are in the firefighting club." This will be very attractive to a lot of youngsters.

You will see privatization for the police, and you will certainly see it for other types of what are now recognized as municipal chores as well. Of course, you will see this in transportation in many communities, whether they have cabs or buses. It will happen with buses—it will all be privatized. At first there will be some resistance, but the bus drivers themselves are the most likely people to want it, because even if their salaries do not go up right away, their benefits will be vastly improved. And benefits, especially if you have been on the job for a while, really make a big difference. You don't want to have to pay 20 percent of your dental bill if the dental bill is a thousand dollars—two hundred dollars is a lot of money. You want that dental bill to be covered 100 percent. Things like that will occur. It will make a big difference to individuals, to say nothing of families.

The Planet Will Be Protected

Who will protect the planet from mining, logging, oil drilling and such?

You have to remember that the purpose of global corporations is not only to make a profit but also to take the long view, as they are discovering now in the First Alignment. The long view is, "What about fifty years from now? We have a responsibility to this global corporation past ourselves." It won't just be a committee in the corporation, but those at the top will see clearly, "What are we going to do in twenty years? What are we going to do in fifty years? We are going to run out!" Obviously, there are going to be efforts to explore the Moon and so on, but that is not practical in terms of transiting the materials, no. That is why they will start to look at other technologies, some of which have already been invented but are being held—how can we say?—behind the scenes until they are needed. And they will pour money into that and development into that, and someday oil will not be necessary.

They will look also at forests, for how much wood do we need? We know how long a tree takes to grow, even if we encourage it. So at some point other materials will happen. Some day all wood furniture will be considered antique and valuable and people will want it. Right now, it is not really seen that way, but [laughs] look differently at your wood furniture now, especially hardwood. Someday the corporations will say, "No, no, no! Trees are needed for other things, not the least of which is that they exhale the air that we breathe and we need lots more of them, not less of them." There will be no allowance to cut down the trees. Vast areas will be considered to be off-limits to human beings because they are tree land. This won't be a national forest. Tree land will show up all over the world, and it will be for beauty, granted. Campers will still be encouraged; there will be small areas that will serve the campers, which will be profitable. But tree land will not be allowed to be damaged. So, for instance, in tree land you will not find fires, even casual fires, that are lit with twigs. If you are going to light a fire, it is going to be in an improved built brick oven of some sort or something like that, and it will be fired by gas or something else. Especially the global corporations in general are crystal clear that what you are seeing now—drilling for oil, taking out coal and all of that—cannot go on forever. So don't worry; they have plans.

An Enforcement Arm Ensures That Resources Are Shared

So who is going to be the referee if, say, a global car company and some other global corporation both want a territory or the same resources?

You can see this actually developing now, with the World Trade Organization. Granted, it is slow and ponderous at the moment, but it is feeling its way. At some point, the WTO will have an enforcement arm, and that enforcement arm will be provided by all of the different global corporations that cover particular fields. They will all contribute to it. If only one global corporation happens to be near something that is an outbreak of damaging activity to the First Alignment, then that one corporation will simply provide the enforcement arm for the WTO or some other group who says, "This is not acceptable." And if that anomaly—as it will come to be referred to—takes place, it will be shut down.

Of course, initially, "How about this? How about that?" will be offered; some negotiation will take place. But if they who are doing something are stubborn and determined and will not negotiate, they will be crushed. The enforcement branch will have absolutely no qualms about telling them the degree to which they will be crushed: "You will be wiped out, and everything you care about will be wiped out. All of your property will be seized and will go to others. Maybe we won't kill you; maybe we will just let you suffer for the rest of your life, seeing your mistake. Maybe if we feel that you have rehabilitated yourself, we will let you express yourself in some other way. Maybe you are in the wrong business. Maybe this business doesn't satisfy you, and the reason you wanted more that wasn't in your alignment, that wasn't part of your corporate alignment, was because you were not happy in the business you were in. Maybe you would be happier doing something else." They might be offered that. Or they might simply be killed.

That sounds brutal.

The purpose is world peace. Suppose this imaginary car company you mentioned says it wants this and it wants that, and it spreads out and goes for it against the alignment of corporations (as is already being done), meaning it does something that amounts to a criminal enterprise because it is outside its boundaries of expression. Not only is it not efficient in these other areas, but it is doing something that isn't acceptable.

Various Powers Will Define Boundaries of Expression

Who defines the "boundaries of expression"?

That will be defined by the various powers of the First Alignment. The alignment groups will have representatives, and now you see the budding versions of this in the WTO and so on. If you look at the philosophy of the WTO, you will see the nucleus of everything I am talking about right now. This doesn't mean the WTO ought to be perceived as the enemy; it is simply the visible version of what is intended to be a benevolent benefactor resolving international business problems.

But sometimes these things cannot be resolved with words and binding agreements. There must be an enforcement branch. You cannot expect nationalistic political enforcement; you will have to have international private enforcement. Nationalistic political enforcement may be compromised due to bribes or other factors, threats, to say nothing of the fact that nationalism tends to support from the outside in—meaning from the borders, the outside of the borders, in, and then out and in that circuit. Global, on the other hand, is always thinking in terms of the whole picture, the circle, the complete. And that is how the circle takes you from world peace to world happiness to world fulfillment—because it is complete, not based on political borders.

The Identity Chip Is Essential

Do you see the identity chip as required in this scenario?

Yes, it is essential. Define "identity chip" for the reader who may not know what you are talking about.

It is a computer chip inserted into your body that has your identity and various data about you available.

Yes, including, of course, your medical information in case anything should happen to you . . . you are unconscious, maybe in a car crash, you may or may not have your wallet on you, nobody knows who you are. Think how invaluable it will be to have your identity, your address, your family, your blood type and so forth, on you. Lives will be saved. Plus, to also know whether or not you have allergies as well as lots of other factors—maybe your likes and dislikes, so that when you are recovering in your room, it can be your favorite color, pink or perhaps green . . . all kinds of things like that.

You have to let go of having too many secrets, because sometimes you are keeping something a secret only because your culture or your immediate family culture has conditioned you to believe that something is shameful, whereas many, many other people like it and it is not shameful at all. Many, many things that are now considered illegal will be fostered and encouraged as long as they are not harmful and destructive to others in ways that interfere with peace, world peace, you understand?

If, say, your neighbors down the street are of different sexual orientation, if that doesn't interfere with your safety, okay, then it will be encouraged. If your neighbor down the street has cats and you have dogs and you can't stand cats, so what as long as it doesn't interfere with your peace? A lot of things like that . . . that is the First Alignment based on self-interest consumerism, with the goal of absolutely unwavering world peace for all citizens.

Reconditioning Will Replace Punishment Whenever Possible

A lot of laws will simply be considered irrelevant. It will take awhile to establish that, because some people will consider some things to be sacrosanct. But it is all conditioning. If it doesn't interfere with your peace and safety, so what?

I am not talking about child molesters; obviously, that interferes with people's peace and safety. People like that will be reconditioned. Techniques exist to condition them to bring them to a state of greater balance so that they no longer wish to molest children and probably won't remember that they ever did. That is the key. If it is so enmeshed in their personality—which it usually is because they have been damaged, usually having been molested themselves—then they will essentially be served. They will be given a treatment whereby the personality they know themselves as will be eliminated (this is for severe cases where people cannot be treated otherwise) and a new personality will be encouraged; they will then become peaceful citizens. By peaceful I mean that they can go and have fun and go skydiving if they want to; I don't mean they can do nothing. But they will not be impinging on the safety of others. If for some reason those techniques fail, they will be eliminated. There will be no exceptions. That's why I say that personal sacrifices will be made.

It may not happen immediately, but think of how often people in the past had a loved one . . . you might be wealthy and influential and that loved one commits a terrible crime, perhaps in your own family, where crimes like that tend to occur first. And you are heartsick, but you love this person, so you protect him or her. In the distant past, people like this were shut up in towers somewhere. In your more modern society, they go through various therapies. Electroshock was initially tried for such things, but it was too terrible. It had vast impacts, not the least of which was destruction to internal organs. There are other therapies, though. But what I am saying is that protecting these people can still bring about disasters. I am not picking out just child molesters; there are others—murderers and so on.

In the future society, if therapy doesn't work, they are not going to wait for the person to molest someone again and say, "Oh, the therapy didn't work." They will have ways of keeping an eye on you if you are a molester. If you exhibit those tendencies and are incorrigible in exhibiting them, and no matter what therapy they use that they have at that time, nothing works, you will be eliminated—no exceptions.

This will apply to leaders as well as citizens. You are becoming Earth citizens. Certain behaviors are unacceptable. The First Alignment means world peace.

A Gift from God

How will this play out for the heads of government across the world now? Are they aware of this process?

Once a premier is elected (or a prime minister or a president or those in other offices like that), once they are elected, if they do not already know about these things—they may have some vague idea or even more of an idea about these world alignments—then someone will sit them down and slowly and patiently explain it to them. Some of this has gone on in the past. Most world leaders now—meaning elected leaders—know this, and they know they can go this far and no further. They might also be called upon to perform certain tasks that might seem to be nationalistic but are not really; these tasks are more in alignment with certain corporate entities, and by "corporate" I mean global corporate entities. People might easily be able to perceive this by looking around in your culture from day to day—not just those associated with the United States, but those in other countries as well, because in other countries they are not so self-absorbed as in the United States. They will be self-absorbed in their country and about what is going on in their country, and they will be able to see the things that I am talking about emerging in their countries, too.

And as I say, to some people it will seem excessive and ruthless, but other people who are suffering right now will think of it as a gift from God. They are suffering. At any moment they could be killed, maimed or tortured, or their loved ones could have that happen to them. You will agree, of course, that that is intolerable. Therefore, those people must be brought to the point where they feel safe.

Other people's safety is the first goal, which, as I said, helps bring about the First Alignment. It is essential. From the corporate point of view, you might say, "Well, these people are all future customers." Now, that might sound very ruthless. But it is true, and I assure you that if you are worried about being killed, maimed or tortured, the idea of having the option of being a consumer and being a customer will seem like a gift from God. It is a vast improvement over living in a war zone. So—I speak to the reader now—don't be so quick to judge.

Change Will Happen

I just don't see how it is going to begin. How are you going to get every state to give up its highway patrol, every mayor to give up his police force and every country's government to give up its control over its borders?

Oh, it doesn't happen from the bottom up; it happens from the top down.

Please explain.

There are certain industries for which it is crystal clear that as a small, struggling business they can only do so much. And many is the time, especially if they are dealing with a corrupt local government—which is a global fact, not just in a community here and there—they may have to be paying to this one and paying to that one, to say nothing of paying to criminal enterprises . . . paying and paying and paying. How much can you pay?

If you either align yourself by being purchased as a company or align yourself in some way with a bigger version of what you might see as a competitor (but that competitor, that bigger version, doesn't see you as a competitor), then you are a fly, a gnat. But you are on a competitive level, from their point of view, and you are also serving a segment of the community that their product has not appealed to, and they are going to say, "Well, this is good." Then you become more powerful, then the mayor wants to make you happy, then the criminals are either frightened of you or they want to be your friends. In short, suddenly you have more power. That example at the corporate level goes from the top down, not from the bottom up. It is very clear, is it not? Of course, this is just a small case of a little business and a bigger business. But the further you go globally looking at businesses that you can think of in a moment, you can easily see how even a big business can sometimes be threatened by a big government.

It's different if the business is international and global, and all the elements of that business are totally together, saying, "If we as the different elements of a business are strong and want more elements and want to get stronger in our own field but someone threatens us, then we draw in our resources. We don't necessarily send out our enforcement, but we say, 'Okay, if you are going to push around our business, then we will just raise what we are charging you for something.'" I will give you an example: Maybe the guys who are trying to push are advocating consumer protection for this and that and it might seem to make a great deal of sense, but a lot of it is ahead of its time, meaning that other things need to be accomplished first before you as a municipal government or even a state government can crush corporations and force them into providing services (given all of their other expenses) that will drain them of all of their capacity to provide the services that you and the citizens themselves desire. So if that takes place, eventually revenge happens. And revenge happens. Now I will get there. I will use California as an example.

What Happens When the Government Is at Odds with the Corporate Community?

Now, this was well before the First Alignment was under way. Years ago California was known as a place where the consumer was protected. It was known as a place where municipal, county, state and even at times federal enforcement branches could literally bring a corporation to its knees, could say, "You will do this, and you *will* do it. Otherwise, we will make your life miserable, and we will stop at nothing." Why? On the one hand, there were people who were altruistic who asked the government to do something. Granted, something terrible was happening to the public—maybe there was a dangerous product or a chemical. I'm not saying that these things weren't worthwhile; somebody had to do something to bring about greater safety, as you have seen with the Consumer Product Safety Commission in the United States. A lot of good has been done.

But some corporations that were very good, that were budding, that had good services to offer, were destroyed, even when they were perfectly happy to change something in their products. But they were hit with fines and restrictions that destroyed an otherwise viable company, and then the people all dispersed and went different places, lost their enthusiasm, and that was the end. Twenty, thirty, forty years later, maybe those ideas are picked up and a company develops a product that everyone loves and wants. This could have happened earlier, but you had to wait thirty or forty years for that to come down the road.

I am not saying that the altruistic individuals who were attempting to protect themselves and the public were wrong. And I am not saying that the government was wrong. I am just saying that on the basis of the First Alignment, everyone can agree to self-interest, and self-interest in this case has to do with peace expressed as safety. You can walk out of your house, walk safely to your car. You do not have to use a key; just get in, press the button to start the ignition (no ignition key necessary), drive safely to work, park your car on the street or wherever and go—in short, in complete safety. That wasn't the case. So the First Alignment, from my point of view, is a good thing, looking back on it.

I am not picking on California; I am simply stating that California and other municipalities were known to be protective of the consumer, and not everyone could agree—the corporations couldn't agree, many other people in the country couldn't agree—that this was a good thing. A lot of people agreed, and California became known as a place that nurtured some businesses, but only to a degree, and if the businesses did something that one of the government regulating concerns felt was a problem, the government would after a while begin to serve itself and would bring about enforcement, no matter whether a complaint was made or not. Now, I am not saying that this is bad. I am being very diplomatic here; I do not wish to step on the toes of these good intentions. But sometimes good intentions go wrong, and that is what happened in the past, the recent past . . . some of it.

Corporations got their revenge. Corporations can't usually get their revenge, meaning that the company that is crushed, what can it do? Nothing. It's over for that company. It tries to pick up the pieces of its life and go on, or maybe it picks up a few bits of the corporation and tries to start it up somewhere else. But other corporations say, "Well, this represents a serious threat to what we're doing. How can we affect them? We must do something that will change the public's perception of this government entity that was originally established to protect the public but has now become a vast bureaucracy—yes, protecting the public, and yes, sometimes encouraging change that we wish we would have seen ourselves, that created a problem in our products, but other times creating vastly more of a problem just by its existence due to overenforcement or overregulation that creates conflicting regulations so that no matter what we do, we are wrong. How can we bring about a change? We need to bring about a change in the average California citizen's perception of his or her government." And that change was brought about over time by increasing the cost of something that everyone uses, all right? I am not going to go into all of that; you all know what happened there with the cost of electricity, the cost of gasoline, the cost of fuel. I am not trying to say that the oil companies all put their heads together and said, "How can we crush California?"

The whole point is . . . alignment. Granted, some of this took place in a sort of a loose-cannon situation so that some corporations and some companies were fostering and encouraging things for California to sort of say, "Okay, take that—pow! Take that—*pow!*" So some of it wasn't in alignment with the global corporate intention.

But if you pull back, you can see that the citizens of California now—although they might be mad at the corporations that have cost them a lot of money—are actually mad at the government and say, "Why didn't you see this coming?" Not all citizens are thinking this, but these are general things that all citizens might agree with: "Why didn't you see this coming? Why didn't you see this in some way so that we don't have to go through all of this and pay and pay and pay because you made a mistake?"

You can see what is going on in California right now, and that is a change of government, which will happen either sooner—if there is some change between terms—or later. Eventually, it will bring the California government to something that is not at odds with the corporate community, that will continue to regulate it to a point but not attempt to create a war zone between the government and the corporate community. In short, it will be something that works in concert rather than in conflict, and that will help bring about and support the goal of the First Alignment—world peace. Not just because it is California, but it will fall into concert because it works with rather than against to bring about . . . yes, protection for the citizens of California, but also overall peace, safety for all. This will not happen immediately, but over time.

Regulatory Agencies Won't Change Much Initially

What happens to federal government regulatory agencies like the FCC, FAA, IRS and so on?

It won't be much different than what has been happening for a long time. You see, organizations like that must hire people who know and understand the businesses that are being regulated. They don't hire someone who knows and understands the automobile business to regulate the medical community; you have to hire someone who knows and understands the medical community. People have to understand what they are regulating. And this has been the case in these organizations for a long time.

People are hired who have expertise in these situations, and once they leave that situation, that government service, they often go to work in the community they were regulating—not only because of their even greater expertise in those areas, but because of their capacity to communicate with people who are still in service in those fields on perhaps a friendly first-name basis. So not that much changes. The intention still is there, the intention to keep things from going too extreme one way or the other—"too extreme" meaning too much regulation and the other extreme meaning not enough. So things go on pretty much the same for a time.

Then what?

Well, eventually things have to change. Eventually, you move into happiness, and then things have to change.

Focus on the First Alignment

But I am not going to talk about that. I am going to talk about the First Alignment and what takes place to bring about the First Alignment. I'm not going to talk about the Second, which is world happiness. What's the point? The point is, you are *living in* the time of the First Alignment, and I am going to talk about things that are affecting you as a citizen and the other citizens who are reading this, who are now citizens of Australia, citizens of America, citizens of England, citizens of France or Germany (if they can read this language) and other places. I am going to talk to you about what is going on for you *now* so you know and understand what is going on; I am not going to talk about things that may go on for your children.

If you think about it . . . even though there may be things you don't like about it, you can also think of things you do like about it. Many of you in European communities don't have to go back too far to get to a time when terrible wars were being fought on your soil, when people were suffering. What if world peace was established as an absolute and you didn't have to worry about that anymore? Well, I don't have to tell you—I can feel your hearts uplifting just now while saying that. Marvelous! Other places in the world are going through that kind of struggle now. We need to bring the world to peace first before we can talk about things having to do with happiness. Peace first, happiness next, fulfillment after that. That's the order: First Alignment, Second Alignment, Third Alignment.

I'm not speaking as an authority; I am not telling you how you must do it. I'm simply saying that this is what I have seen that you have done. This is what you do. When you think about it, it makes complete sense.

If you think of more questions, ask for me. And may you experience the best life you can.

Thank you.

More from Counsel

Publisher's note: I was a bit upset with Counsel's presentation—with the authoritarian "you will be crushed and eliminated" statements. Evidently, Zoosh and/or Isis and others counseled the Counsel.

I would like to say something: In the area of existence where I function, my quality of existence is based largely upon observation, research, technical matters and the application of those to other civilizations. My job then is to help prepare civilizations—meaning in terms of your time, over the next ten to twelve thousand years—for temporary shifts and changes. So given that, great decisiveness is a quality I must demonstrate in order to be precise and clear to the representative of any given civilization to whom I speak.

Now, I have been informed that my personality is not fully harmonious with your own based upon wisdom and life experience. I wish to apologize for that, but I must explain that normally when I speak to representatives of a civilization, they are political, meaning they are conscious that they are representatives of their civilization. I have not spoken before in such a way as you are doing here, strictly to disseminate information to whoever can find it.

So my personality is geared toward the way one might speak to someone from the diplomatic corp. You will have to excuse me for my delivery if it sounds very firm or strict sometimes, but in diplomatic relations—politics, you know—one must be very clear. Friendship comes after the talks. You do that, I think, on your planet; people negotiate and they are very firm and clear, sometimes a little strong and edgy, and then afterward everybody goes out for food. But that entertainment comes after the communication. I am saying this so you will understand that my communication to you is based on that level. My tendency is to report on what I see and have seen in that kind of crisp language.

You have to understand that when I spoke about those who could not be rehabilitated, you have to remember what you and your societies do with people who cannot be rehabilitated. You know what you do. And the worst of it is that people give up. You either send them to prison where they suffer and inflict suffering on others, or they are released after a time with the full knowledge of those who have held them that they will go right back to doing what they have always done. Do you think it is worse to eliminate them, or to let them wreak havoc?

You don't have to answer that question, because it is not stated only to you. Please remember that as a representative of the human culture on Earth, you are often expressing the concerns of other human beings, and that is why sometimes you will get hung up on a point that you understand intellectually. Others might find what I am saying to be very firm, authoritarian, but I am not speaking about something I am going to do or anyone I know is going to do; I am talking about history as it develops and when things change. I will give you an example.

Historical Hindsight Informs This Process

Many, many periods of time ago—it can't be measured in years—on the Pleiades, there was a planet that culturally experimented with discomfort and extremes: some of them more extreme than your own in certain areas, others much less so compared to your own. And it was understood by the overall culture of that galaxy, as you say, that this must be stopped. Out of kindness, they took, let's say in your terminology, about three hundred to three thousand years to bring it down slowly—depending upon what was being expressed, you understand; long for some things, less for others—so it could get to a stop in that expression.

Over that time—and this is why I think you have oversight councils and oversight committees—other individuals in that culture formed what amounted to an oversight council of the process that was going on to shut down that extreme behavior. And it was noticed that during that lengthy period of time, many, many people suffered who didn't have to, from the council's point of view. Therefore, they recommended that if this should ever happen again, though they would not foster it—one does not know what might occur in the future for certain—that they would never take so long to slow down a destructive process like that because so much extra destruction took place.

So that's why these lessons, learned in one place, became common knowledge amongst travelers to the stars, and as a result—through inspiration, dreams, visions and practical wisdom and knowledge on your own planet, as well as through occasional contact by some means with visitors from afar—this wisdom accumulated over time. Then the decision was made.

As I reported to you, the First Alignment, taking perhaps a hundred years, is done as gently as possible but firmly where necessary—and where absolutely necessary, ruthlessly. Because if you let it go out of the kindness of your heart . . . "Ah, he is a nice guy. He did these terrible things, but he seems to be okay now. We can let go; maybe he will be all right." "Maybe he will be all right" isn't good enough. He goes out, kills and maims, tortures five, six, seven more people. Then everybody feels bad. They take him back and lock him up and maim and torture him while he is there; perhaps he kills, maims and tortures a few more in prison before someone finally kills him. So that cannot be allowed, you see? It is not my advocacy, but rather something that has been discovered over years, and I think that it is loosely under consequences that happen when you do things, but sometimes consequences happen even when you don't do things. There still are consequences. Let us proceed with your questions.

Discomfort Levels Will Drop

You're saying that the First Alignment will effectively reduce the level of discomfort we have now down to 2 percent at the end of about fifty years?

That's right. The First Alignment is intended to create peace for the individual, and by peace I do not simply mean that people are not fighting and killing each other in the streets. What I mean is, on the practical level, as I said before, that you know you can walk out of the house, walk up to the school and meet your children—your little children, of course; older children don't need that—saying, "Happy to see you! What was your day like? Let's go home," feeling completely safe, not looking over your shoulder, "Don't look at those people! Don't look them in the eye!" None of that. Safe.

So that itself . . . when that level is reached, you will find that discomfort on its representative basis will drop, but it will be in a range. Given that you are in a shift, what they call a transition, discomfort will drop, but not immediately while that is going on. The First Alignment has been going on now for a time. Sometimes things get worse before they get better. You're in that kind of space right now, but once the First Alignment is realized—let me say it that way rather than incrementally—then you will find that discomfort levels drop in terms of percentage of the average situation. We can't be precise for each individual, but the average discomfort level drops to somewhere between 30 to 31 percent for some people, up to as much as 35 percent for others, but no more than that.

Of course, there is such a tremendous improvement and people luxuriate in that, and then, of course, they want it to get better. So it builds a groundswell. Even though it is planned to put in the Second and Third Alignment, a groundswell is built pretty much on its own, with relatively little leadership toward that end, to bring about the Second Alignment—which by that time, of course, once the people see and experience personally how much better things are, they want it. There is no resistance to speak of, and the Second Alignment happens very quickly [snaps fingers]. I like this. What is this called?

Snapping your fingers.

I like that. It is fascinating. The Second Alignment, being happiness, might take no more than five to seventeen years, in terms of your years It is much quicker. And the Third Alignment, fulfillment, is really a short step, a year or two, possibly three years tops. So it is the First Alignment that takes awhile, because it represents a truly radical change from what was.

It started about fifty years ago?

It started about forty-five years ago, but for some people it started about fifty years ago.

And we have about fifty years to go?

You have forty-five to fifty years to go—it depends how it goes. It's not precisely timed, meaning a hundred years from X we reach Y—it's not like that. At the current moment measurement, I would say that around fifty years is a good estimate.

News Will Be Easier to Access

Will there be just one corporation globally for news, one communication company?

One overall company, yes, but you will have individual companies developing different stories that they are good at. Some will develop feature stories; people are always interested in what other people are doing or what people are doing together. There will be whole segments of the media that work on that, and there will be other segments that work on reporting global priority kind of news, which might be a bit more precise, intellectual. There will be all of these different types of news voices, perhaps a few more news voices than you have today. Right now you have news voices in individual cultures—or what you call political boundary areas—that tend to follow a fairly general, somewhat predictable policy in what they report. In the future society, which nourishes and fosters individual expression, you will have other news sources, but you will have to seek those out. They may not be quickly available on your television, but you can seek them out. You can go and read the news you want on the Internet, but you have to go and find it.

But if you are asking about popular news in the future that can be easily accessed . . . the difference will be that you will tend to hear, in your own language, more the point of view of people of other countries—not just people who speak your own language, but there will be a translation so the international viewpoint will be more readily accessible. This helps bring more people into greater alignment, because you can develop some compassion for people who are currently perhaps faceless. You see them on the news when they are angry and unhappy, but you don't know why. So you find out why in future news broadcasts, and then you as a fellow human being can identify with some of that and say, "Oh well, we need to make changes," or "The changes that are being made now make sense to me." In the past, it would just be, "They're bad." So this is something that is more accessible and is intended to show a mutual condition between all people, and then people will be able to understand why something happens and that it isn't just some ruthless or authoritarian action.

So from my perspective, the news will be more varied, more accessible. It will be the same news you have now, but accessibility will be there. Now you have to hunt for it. The information can be found if you have an interest in something, but sometimes it may not be in your language, so it doesn't really help you. The nucleus of what will be the news in the future is here now; it just needs to be more accessible, which will happen.

Less Censorship in the Future

I was more concerned about who was controlling the news—controlling what is published and what is held back and not published.

The control of the news . . . that is the editorial policy with the news that gets reported. I took that to mean that. That was my answer, that the news that is still available you can find, but you have to look for it in your time. Sometimes it is hard to find and sometimes it is judged by others and so on, but you can find it. Also, people are helping that to take place in your time now with what you call political advocacy groups, which are usually made up of the individuals who are advocating something, but are sometimes also and even instead made up of professional advocates promoting the cause of those who have hired them. So perhaps you could rephrase your question, if this isn't helping.

I am asking about the level of censorship. If only one company controls the publishing of all the news on the planet, that company can pretty much control what is printed and what is reported, how it is reported . . .

You mean the way it is today, in your time? This is why you are asking this question, because you see this in your time. It is much better in your future, much better, because corporations are not threatened by the same things that governments are, or religions, or philosophies. A corporation is completely objective and is not conditioned to this bias or that bias.

All right, here is an example: Particularly and specifically right now, news about any off-planet contact with anyone on this planet is totally censored by various levels of most governments. Is that going to change?

Completely. As I said, access to information will not be considered a threat. Corporations will understand, "Well, if visitors are going to come from other places, if they do not threaten us, we are anxious to meet them. Perhaps they will have something to share with us. Perhaps we can share with them. Perhaps we can start trading." If other parts of the alignment see it as a threat, they will check that out first. That would come under the heading of security or protection. If the security/protection people for the planet feel that it is a threat, they will check it out first and make sure it is safe. Of course, most of the time it will be, and then you will begin to have more interplanetary trade. It's good for business.

Security, Intelligence and Medical Communities of the Future

Who will the security people work for?

They will be just like the media. You can understand the media as an overall group. When I talk about security, I'm referring to what now might be called armies, although armies' jobs will change once the First Alignment is accomplished. Armies will become more like police, helpers, and assist in rescues—you know, people lost at sea, ships sinking and so on. In short, armies and militaries will slip into the more benevolent activities that they are even now trained to do. You are familiar with perhaps certain aspects of the military that are identified quite often with rescues at sea and other things. And police forces, which are now largely a representation of the government, they are civil servants. That will all be privatized; all of that will come under the heading of security.

Intelligence will change. The intelligence community will shift from keeping an eye on a political rival or even a political enemy—that will no longer be a factor. It will shift as a planet. Intelligence will become more like information gatherers, interpreting as contact is made with other planets. Intelligence's job will be to learn to understand who these people from other planets are socially, and these people from other planets will bring people who will want to talk and explain who they are socially. The intelligence people will be the obvious people to talk to (and so will teachers) because their job will be to inform the various corporations on the basis of their specific fields of interest—not on the basis of a need to know, but on the basis of their fields of interest. Obviously, if you are producing automobiles, you might be interested in how the ship is made when it flies from place to place, but if you are producing automobiles, you have no particular interest in what they serve to eat in the vehicle.

So the intelligence community will serve privately, and it will be part of the security community. This all will happen also to maintain the peace, so the intelligence community, the enforcement community, the military community, all of these, will join in order to maintain peace, to help people out in emergency situations that might still develop—hurricanes, tornados, things like that—and also to enforce the peace. And by enforcing the peace, I mean if it happens that someone has a violent outburst . . . perhaps that person has some disease that causes him or her to be violent. Representatives will be sent, usually two or three, from the security corporate entity, and they will go out and capture the person, bring him or her into custody. Other elements of the security community might help out at the scene of the violence.

The medical community will be different. You will find your fire department and your emergency medical people—doctors, acupuncturists, herbalists, all of these people—generally under the health community; it is not going to be the disease community. All that supports health will be unified into one corporate entity, like that.

The Focus Will Be on Rehabilitating Criminals

What about the judicial department, the courts?

The judicial will change, because the whole point will be to bring about peace and ultimately happiness and fulfillment. Initially, for the First Alignment, the judicial will change, because the point is to literally take criminals as you have today and rehabilitate them, to bring them around to being good citizens, and whatever is necessary will be used—with the exception of torturing them, making them suffer, which happens now, by the way, in your prisons or even in your holding cells. People are often beaten and tortured for whatever they did and are often beaten and tortured for stuff they didn't do. That's why when prisoners come out of jail, they are either crushed personally or they want revenge. That has to change.

So the system will be set up strictly for rehabilitation. Drug therapies might be used, other therapies—in extreme cases, perhaps surgical therapies. In the rare and unusual case, where destructive persons who have killed or maimed others, caused great harm to others, cannot be rehabilitated, they will be eliminated as gently as possible. Some drug or some other technique will be used that will allow them to have a peaceful death. Much better than what you have now, I assure you!

Art and Culture Will Be Encouraged

But enforcement is not going to go into—I think you were concerned about this the other day—they are not going to barge into artistic communities and say, "You're different; you're dead." Nothing like that. All of those things will be encouraged; artistic things to do will be good for business. I know that sounds very crass, but you have to recognize that the business community is your best opportunity to bring about the goal of the First Alignment—which is peace, as I say, experienced right down on the individual level as "I'm safe, and the evidence of my eyes and my experience and my daily life tells me I am safe—not just because other people tell me I am safe and I can go out now, but I'm literally safe, and all of my stuff is safe, too." This is better, don't you think?

What about the cultural diversity we have now?

There will be more culture than you have now; culture will be encouraged.

It is hard to imagine.

Of course, it is. It is hard to imagine from where you are, from how you were raised—the society you were raised in, the conditioning and other influences you might have been exposed to. It is hard to imagine how you are going to get from where you are now (let's call that A) to Z. Of course, it is hard, because you won't be able to identify all of the steps on the path. But you will, from time to time, be able to look back on your life as an individual or look back on your life as a citizen of a given culture, even a family, and see how things have improved by looking back. Sometimes looking back is easier, because you can see that there is a trend, that things are going this way. Sometimes you thought something was going to be terrible, and it turned out to be mostly good and just a little bit terrible.

Now, I want to bring up something you said about culture, and that is that an interesting thing will happen. There will be an education department, and cultures of the past will be thoroughly studied. Much of this work has already been done. And if a culture has died out, is no longer represented but has many good aspects to it and is interesting, and if it might be possible to create products and services that people will want that represent the good qualities of this community, then people will be educated about this culture that has died out. They will be encouraged and nurtured to try different parts of it to see if this is something they would be interested in. So there will be more culture, not less.

And you see how this prepares you very nicely for being exposed to cultures of beings from other planets. Their cultures, their foods, what they are interested in, sometimes won't be compatible with you, and other times you will say, "This is fantastic! This is an entirely new spice that has a completely different flavor and effect that we have never experienced before." Or, "Here is something in behavior or medicine or science that we never considered. It will be fabulous!" So you see, culture is encouraged. And then it allows you to flow very nicely as an Earth society into embracing and welcoming visitors from other planets once your security department—as you call it now, but it would not be a department—or once your security group has overseen them and checked them out to make sure they do not represent a threat, that they're not bringing any weapons in that they are going to share with others.

The Globalization of Companies

So how does this play out? First large companies buy small companies until there is only one left of each kind?

Only one global one. You have seen this happen on a smaller level—automakers and cereal makers find themselves under one general umbrella to a degree, where they initially give up personality. But after a while, the corporation that is wise realizes that it wants to nurture and encourage individual expression: "They were doing this thing when we bought them, and we didn't at that time realize how valuable it was. But now look—they were ahead of their time, and because they did all of that work, we can catch up quickly and bring out that product for that segment of the market we completely overlooked." So the smart corporation does that even in your own time.

This will happen more and more. Yes, the buying and the selling is happening now, the consolidation is happening now, and all that has been happening for quite a while. It became a matter of public knowledge in the past twenty, twenty-five years, and even more so now. Now it makes big news if some big company is going to buy some big company, but it often creates more efficiency. Sometimes it doesn't work; there are problems. That is why the First Alignment takes time. Aligning things that don't normally mesh well or haven't been meshing well in the past takes time and effort and patience, and sometimes the cogs in the gears have to be reshaped so that alignment takes place.

One element of the corporate community can help another, and not just as a personal sacrifice. If a bank were to give a loan to another part of its corporate community, even though it wanted to use that money for its own expansion, to hire more employees and so on, that would be a personal sacrifice for the bank in this example. But in the future, the bank doesn't have to make a personal sacrifice. Yes, it contributes some monies toward this other part of its corporation, but this pays off for the bank, meaning that it not only gets that money returned, but things the bank might now be paying for as an expense to the bank, if that is being done by some other part of the corporation, then that service is provided to the bank at a greatly discounted rate. And that might happen, that different parts of the corporation support and nurture one another. That will become standard practice.

But who is going to be the ombudsman for the people?

This is a problem we are having; I am not expressing myself well. The way you see it . . . you don't understand that everyone is part of one of these systems. Ombudsmen are not needed, but if they are perceived to be needed, then they will be recruited. You are seeing it as some thing *over* the people, that the ombudsman is needed because the people are being ruled by this thing over them. That is a misperception on your part.

Everyone is in one system or another, and in the big picture, it is only *one* system. That is how you get to be Earth citizens—not Americans or Canadians or Argentineans. You are Earth people. "Who are you? Where are you from?" you're asked at this planetary conference. "Oh, I am from Earth." "That is such a pretty planet from space." Like that, not: "I'm from Earth, from the Americas." No, not like that, because everyone is included. The whole point is inclusion; things work better when everyone is included. No one, without exception, is not included, and if one person . . . think about it: The First Alignment is peace and safety, and if one person's peace and safety is threatened, then the First Alignment hasn't taken place yet, see? So no one is excluded. Not one.

Every Individual Will Be Part of a Community

So you're saying that everyone who works at Wal-Mart is part of the retail corporation, every individual chiropractor is part of the health corporation, like that?

Absolutely. Every person who may be a dishwasher today in a restaurant is part of the food industry, and the food industry will include many things, not just restaurants and farmers, but it might also include nutritionists and dietitians and so on. The latter two are part of the medical community, but they also have an interconnectedness with the food industry. That is a good example of how an individual community—which they will probably be called, not corporations—serves its own community but also has interconnectedness. No one is left out. Everyone is part of one community, and some people, at various times, are part of another community. The nutritionists and the dietitians . . . this is the medical community, but also the food industry.

So someone, a youngster perhaps, starts out as a dishwasher. She will tend to move upward in that community, not just to be the head dishwasher, but she moves up to something in that community where they have what you call upward mobility, and she moves up along that line. But say she is a dishwasher, yet she is going to college and wants to be a scientist. Fine. Even though she is working in one community, she goes to college, gets an education, and then she shifts to the science and technology community, for example. So the whole idea of corporations, stocks and all of that eventually disappears, not during the First Alignment, but it eventually disappears, unless it contributes to happiness or fulfillment, which it might. It will . . . let me look at this now. I've been looking mostly at the First Alignment . . . no, no, I see that stocks and bonds and all of that still survive for some people who like them, because for some people that is happiness and fulfillment.

So what we can look forward to is no homeless, no unemployed, no starving people . . . ?

That's right, starvation is unknown, period.

No selling of female babies in China . . . ?

All of that stops, but it doesn't just stop; it is replaced with better things. Certainly the scientific and genetic community will have something to do with it. People want to get together, and sometimes babies come unintentionally. However, things will change there so you can still have a baby intentionally, but contraception will become very easy, very gentle—no side effects that harm you or anybody else, no venereal diseases, none of that. You don't have a baby until you want to. This is not an ending so much as a happy beginning.

We must stop now. Good night.

There Is a Plan in Effect and It Is Intended to Bring About Benevolence

All right, Zoosh speaking. Greetings. What's up?

Tell me about Counsel.

He is from a benevolent existence, but that existence does not generally have contact with human beings directly. And so you might say . . . I will just define him/her this way. (I will say "him.") He is a scholar, and as a scholar he understands his field very thoroughly. But as a scholar he also doesn't necessarily have much contact, so his social skills are not as polished as they could be. Everything he said was absolutely true.

Your complaint was very clear. The first time you found listening to him to be authoritarian and uncomfortable, and the second time he sounded kind of bland. But you understand, after the first time he was consulted with and told, "You don't talk to human beings like that. She was obviously frightened, upset and intimidated, so the next time you talk to her, you be very gentle." So it was the extremes: one time this way and the next time that way. If he got enough training and fine-tuning, it would be different. But what he had to say, I find no fault with. Just chalk him up to someone who needs to get out more often, personality-wise. Your feeling reaction was vitally important to him to learn how to communicate with a species he has not communicated with before.

But what he said was a gift. His technique was a little rough coming through the channel—rough on you, rough on the channel—but I find no fault with what he said. Perhaps I can be a little critical with *how* he said it, but that is his socialization skills you pick up.

Creator Does Not Wish to Have WWIII

Why did the Aide to the Creator come through and say, "This is urgent. Please get this out right away"? What is really going on here? Why does this need to go out right now?

I feel Creator wants this out, because Creator feels that an Earth conflict could erupt from people not understanding that what's going on is intended to be benevolent, even though sometimes it might show a malevolent face. Creator does not wish to have World War III over something that is intended to serve every last person on Earth in a benevolent way—and it's not just *intended*, but it will do that, even though some individuals might suffer. Meaning people who are self-destructive—and you know my definition of self-destructive, that it means hurting yourself or hurting others—some of those individuals (be it very few), as he explained, might have to be eliminated if necessary. I am not heartless, but my feeling is, if someone is killing, maiming or injuring others, and nothing can be done to stop that person, what do you do? Just sit back and say, "Oh, dearie me"? What do you as an individual personality do?

Recommend that he be helped in some way, and if he can't be, then he leaves this body, is taught and counseled between lives, and tries over again?

That's close. That's progress. What do you do if you are there? You are not in danger, but you are there, and you see someone running around killing, stabbing, murdering other people, torturing other people, people crying out for help. There you are, and there is a rifle next to you. What do you do? I say this to the reader. Sometimes I need to be confrontative, because there are people who have good hearts, and because they have good hearts they want to say, "Well, never give up. We will keep trying to rehabilitate him." How many times have you heard that a person comes out of prison and the social scientist says she is completely rehabilitated, or someone comes out of a mental hospital completely rehabilitated and they say he will be just fine . . . and what?

"As long as he takes his medication." How many times have you heard that? And maybe sometimes people can be resistant to taking medication. He doesn't take his medication, and he has a psychotic break, grabs whatever weapon is handy, kills, maims, injures, tortures, kidnaps, rapes. And that is the problem. It is not an exception. As described by Counsel, in the future and even now, techniques are being developed to transform individuals, and only as a last resort will an individual be killed.

From Greed to Benevolence

So this system is to be run by greed and self-interest. How do we get from the greed and self-interest of these leaders to the promised altruistic heads of corporations? How do we get from here to there?

That would take an incredibly long answer, and I feel that Counsel has covered this. I will say that the short answer is that you get there entirely out of self-interest. Corporations make mistakes, and as long as the same board is in power, they go back and say, "Boy, that was stupid."

To pick an example: A branch of a corporation that sells canned fish has years and years of going out and gathering tuna, killing dolphins—not wanting to kill dolphins, but after a while the people fishing say, "Well, it just happens. We don't want to kill the dolphins, but it just happens, because the dolphins are with the tuna." In fact, what doesn't get out is that the dolphins lead the tuna to the fishing boats, because the dolphins are trying to help you. But they're not doing it on a suicidal basis. A few years ago, this became more public knowledge, partly because the fishermen on the boats were disgusted by the fact that the dolphins were treated as if they were just some kind of garbage.

And so it comes out. And then the corporation says, "We must be idiots. We could have been doing this in a completely different way. How many years have environmentalists and animal rights people been telling us, 'Stop this, stop this, stop this'? And because we are idiots . . ."—you understand, I am not saying they were idiots, but this was their attitude about themselves—". . . because we are idiots, we do not make the slight change, increase the expense just a little bit and make a big campaign about how our brand protects dolphins, that no dolphins will be killed in any way. Thereby we not only look good in the public's eye, but everybody who loves dolphins (which nowadays is almost everyone) sees us as the good guys. Now because we didn't do that, we look like the jerks." And what happens? When the information came out, sales of tuna went down. People got mad. They ate something else for a while. The corporations got over it, but there were big profit losses.

So I bring this up, because corporations that are wise learn from their mistakes. After that, every corporation that had any brains at all bent over backward to make sure that dolphins would be safe. They even came up with a symbol and put it right on the can so you knew that they were keeping dolphins safe. The corporations knew that the animal rights people and the environmentalists were going to keep an eagle eye on them, which they have. So they had to deliver. What I am saying is this: that the corporation in that case (you can see clearly, yes?) becomes altruistic about dolphins out of self-interest. So take that right on to affect everything. That kind of experience, the dolphin-safe experience, is not only not lost on that segment of global corporate decision making but lives on well past the time.

Granted, corporations still make mistakes. They try to improve their product, they say "new and improved." Everybody says, "Ugh, bring back the old stuff." So profits crash for a few months until they bring back the old stuff and people walk around in the corporate head office examining the carpet for a few months, not looking one another in the eye—"Oops, we goofed." But they learn and make less mistakes, meaning . . . self-interest—it will come about initially.

True Self-Interest Defined

What's the goal of the First Alignment? Peace! And that will be experienced right down to the level of the individual being safe. So it will come about by self-interest. How do we not only keep the peace, but how does peace come about? "How do I feel safe?"—safe not only on the individual level, but let's look at it on the corporate level.

How does peace affect the corporation? Well, it means we don't have to worry about fighting, battling. We don't have to pay some warlord a million dollars just so he won't attack our pipeline or something like that, blow it up, create a big problem. In short, there is peace, plus there has to be the feeling of safety. How does a corporation feel safe? A corporation feels safe by acting in its own self-interest, and many corporations have discovered this in your time, right now.

It takes awhile to percolate down through the ranks, but many of them have discovered—and they will all discover it in the future if they expect to not only survive but thrive—that self-interest involves *true self-interest*. Now, what did I say before about the definition of "self-destructive"? Self-destructive means harming yourself or harming another; self-interest means looking after your own needs and looking after the needs of others. See? Add a definition there, and suddenly the fog lifts.

Self-Interest Looks after Others' Needs

So this great clearing now, this great exposure of the excesses and scandals of large corporations, is . . .

Exposing the underside and clearing the way for them to take off in a different way, meaning they can't be self-destructive, they can't harm themselves and they can't harm others if they expect to thrive. In the past, that wasn't true in the short run as corporations perceived it. The robber barons, while they weren't corporations, would get what they could get any way they could get it—"and the public be damned." You've read about that.

But what happened to those people? They discovered with competition . . . when competitors came along and said, "No, no. Not the public be damned. Let's serve the public; we'll give them what they want. We will put a bar car on the train, a smoking car; we'll put in comfortable seats and so on." And the other guy said, "The public be damned," and had wooden seats on the train and open windows to create ventilation. But what if it rained? Too bad, get wet! The competitor said, "No, no. Comfortable seats, windows that open and close; ventilation, yes, but if it rains, close the windows and you stay dry." In short, with the competitor—the corporation, let's call it—bringing it up to modern times, the one that is involved in self-interest, looking after its own needs, looking after the needs of others, which is self-interest . . . everybody wins, eh?

But there won't be any competition.

There will still be self-interest involved, because you will want to expand your market. For example, some people like sushi, some people don't. If you were involved and you had a chain of restaurants that served sushi, you would not only want to serve sushi in the most beautiful way (which is part of the tradition) and in the most healthful way (which is also part of the tradition), but also in a way that is filled with variety. In short, you want to please your customers and have comfortable seats and a happy atmosphere. You want them to come to your restaurant. But what else do you want to do? You want to expand your market!

So instead of competition, what you have is corporations wanting to expand their markets. That's why they foster and stimulate variety, new ideas, new types of things. That's why you have restaurants serving food you never heard of in most parts of the world but are crazy about all of a sudden. They'll do it because they will recognize that it is in their own interest to look after others, because others will not just think well of them—"That's nice"—but will also say, "Well, this is a good thing. Maybe I will try sushi." And they try it and say, "Oh, this is wonderful!"

What You Can Do

Okay, what can our readers take from this? What can they do to facilitate this process?

Just live your lives as well as possible and recognize that some of the things going on in the world are not as menacing as you think. The overall intent—not only by people behind the scenes, but by many people who understand and can look at the big picture—is that there is something good happening. But it doesn't always show a good face, also because of resistance and misconceptions and mis-perceptions and misunderstandings and simply a lack of knowledge and wisdom about what is going on for the other guy and why he is acting that way and all this business that needs to all be corrected. The overall intent is that something good is going to come out of it.

Don't be alarmed if your favorite little local bank changes its name and becomes Big Corporation Bank. Don't be too alarmed, okay? And you might say, "Oh, too bad." And someday the bank name gets changed back, ostensibly for nostalgic reasons, to Local Bank, but in fact, it also causes people to feel better about the bank. They say, "Gosh, I remember when it used to be Local Bank and it's Local Bank again, and I feel better about it. I forgive them for being Big Corporation Bank, and now that it's Local Bank again, I'm going to bring my business back."

People Don't Want "One Thing"

Will all of the local banks be individual units within one bank, or will there be one bank?

You've seen the banking community, how it changes. It is this, it is that; then it becomes bigger and bigger. For a while you will see that—*one* thing, *one* thing—but this is a period of adjustment. Corporations will realize that people don't like "one thing," and they will be quick to realize that. Do you know who will remind them of that? Advertising agencies.

They're going to tell them, "Hey, if people only wanted one thing, they would only eat McDonald's hamburgers and not desire Burger King. It is beef, it is bread, it is condiments, but they like Burger King, too. It is different in its own way." If they forget, their advertising agencies will remind them and present it to them in a way they cannot deny—not just because it is rational, okay? You understand the rational, but it's because it is more profitable. As a business person, one must think of profit. One can be as altruistic as possi-ble, one can serve the community as much as possible, but one cannot serve the community very well if one is bankrupt. So you have to make a profit that covers not only your expenses, but covers at least what you would make if you were working for someone else so you can live your life. And hope-fully you will make more than that so you can expand and grow and do more things.

How is this information—that things look pretty bad but are not quite what they seem— going to get out around the world?

Well, for starters, you're publishing it. Maybe you will take quotes that you feel are significant and post them on the Web, and people will pass them around to their friends. And other people will channel on them with their version, and it will add to the pie and circulate around. It will get near and far, and other people will write about it and opine about it. Don't worry. Do your part and let it go on.

Governments Won't Be Needed

So what happens to governments as we know them now?

The government becomes . . . you understand, the whole point is to globalize things, so the government shifts over time. The government of the U.S. and the governments of all other places—the government of England, the government of Peru—they all shift over time, in every place, to being a global government, one that has the best qualities.

How do we define the best qualities? This will go through some confusion for a while, but after a time people will say, "Wait, it is very simple. The best qualities of any government will be qualities that will lead us toward the objective of the First Alignment—peace, safety, like that." And they will say, "Okay, let's pull out all of those things in this government, and we will contribute and offer these to the global government because we feel that it will lead to peace as experienced in safety. We feel it will, and this is why we feel it will; this is what we believe." And you will find that most governments will contribute just about the same things.

But there will be a group of global representatives from each country?

What you will see is essentially a large group of citizens globally, whose number-one objective is to improve the lot of all people on Earth, striving toward that first goal of the First Alignment. As a result of so many people being involved and saying, "Well, this group isn't being served"—initially advocating their own group, but after a while advocating other groups, and then everybody advocating everybody else, working within that structure like that—they will all be very clear about what needs to be done, what needs to be served and how the global community can come to be resolved—everyone with everyone else—on the basis of their own personal experience within this global government becoming resolved with everybody else. In short, they will learn from their own mistakes and they will learn from their own successes.

The Global Government Will Cooperate with Global Corporations

So there will be a global government that will cooperate with the global multinational corporations?

Yes, it will be cooperative. This does not mean that it is perfectly all right to use some horrible poison in your factory that will destroy people. It means, rather, that you don't have to file fifteen hundred different documents to accomplish something. (By the time you've filed all of the documents, you can't accomplish it anymore, because the time to do it is past.) In short, the government will not try to trip the corporations. Rather, it will oversee the corporations so that the corporations do not . . . either for expediency or for the sake of profit, or simply because of ignorance, because that corporation does not have all of the knowledge it needs to make the best decision.

The government will help that corporation get that knowledge, because all of corporations will share information—not everything—but they will share basic information with the global government, and the global government will share with others and so on, so that everyone can make an informed decision. If a corporation makes a mistake, it will be corrected. If a corporation, in the early years, becomes stubborn and balky about correcting it, the process will go forward to help it make that correction.

Workers Learn from Corporations' Mistakes

You are seeing that nowadays. Sometimes corporations have been brought to their knees because they continued to make the same mistake. Maybe they didn't see it as a mistake, but they continued to make the same mistake, which was very destructive to other people, and they ultimately became self-destructive to themselves (separating those two things), continuing to make self-destructive errors. So the corporation was essentially banished from its existence—one might say, using a medieval term—and its corporate charter was vacated—in that sense, to use a legal term.

And the workers learned from that lesson: "If we do that, we know what will happen in the future." If they go off to get their next job and the bosses tell them, "Well, you've got to do that same thing, only we can hide it this way and hide it that way," they are going to protect themselves a little bit. So those kinds of mistakes that hurt the public and hurt the corporation are more likely to be revealed, especially if someone has worked for that corporation before and is going to keep a personal record, saying, "So and so told me to do this on this day. I am writing this down and making a document of it so it is clear that I didn't do this on my own." In short—self-interest. I'm covering a lot in a short time, so that's why I'm jumping around quite a bit.

The Global Government Is Temporary

You said something important, that there will be a global oversight group over the corporations, that they are not all-powerful.

What I am saying is this: The global government will be there for a while and then will simply become . . . it will evolve into something that primarily functions at diplomatic levels, meeting and greeting civilizations from other planets in the far-flung future (not that far-flung—a few hundred years off).

After a while, the system will run so smoothly that you won't need to have an authoritarian government, okay? You won't need to have a fed come around—as you might say, or as the people in municipal government say—telling you what to do and telling you that you will do it: "You will like it, or you'll be sorry." If people are being threatened, why is the government good? So the global government will be temporary. As people change, it won't be needed. We are talking about a long period of time. People come and go. This is not to be threatening, but rather to simply state a fact.

Things Do Get Better—Count on It!

I want to close by saying that your world is changing. I don't want you to assume automatically that something bad is happening to you or loved ones or friends or even those people you talk with on the other side of the world. What I am saying is that there is a plan in effect, and the plan is intended to bring about an improved benevolence over time. It is being done in three stages. The first stage takes a long time, because there are lots of problems. The second stage doesn't take as long, and the third stage is even shorter. As has been discussed, these are the First Alignment, the Second Alignment and the Third Alignment.

The plan is intended to bring this about in the most benevolent way possible. But for the First Alignment, things are not always benevolent, because you've got warlords, you've got people shooting one another, you've got people angry—in short, you've got a society that you're dealing with right now with all of its problems. It takes awhile to sort all that out. But it does get sorted out. Things get better, but it takes awhile. Some things might get worse before they get better, *but they do get better*. Count on it.

You Must Add Love to the First Alignment

This is Isis. I have come through for a time to comment on this Counsel. The first day Counsel talked, you heard him as his normal personality. The second time he talked, he was shifted to another extreme, as one might talk to a youngster—not because of having anything to do with mental capacity, but entirely because he was instructed that the impact on your feelings was not right, that you might be offended. So the second day didn't feel exactly right. It actually felt better, but it just felt odd.

And you will note that no matter how much was discussed about the First Alignment ultimately leading to happiness and fulfillment, the word *love* didn't come up, if you recall. My feeling is this: For those of you who are reading this, perhaps in a fuller context than you might normally read it, know that the human feelings you have every day are important, a vitally important factor in all things here on Earth. So rather than talk about how you can resist what seems to be the ruthless nature of the First Alignment, let's talk about how you can influence it.

Use Love-Heat to Support the First Alignment

This is what I recommend: The love-heat/heart-warmth/physical-warmth is something you can do [see p. 23], meaning more of you experiencing what we are calling the love-heat— although you might very well feel it in your belly or some other part of your body. If it comes up there, don't try to move it to your heart, but just go into it and feel the warmth more. That is the best single thing you can do. The more people are doing that, the more likely all life will be affected benevolently.

Remember, don't send it out as you've sent out light and other things like that. Just feel it for yourself and know that it will naturally radiate. If you send it out, it will not work as well, because that is a willful act. Yes, even in a benignly willful act you will tend to send it to this person and that place, and when you do that, even if you send it in the most benevolent way you can imagine, it will still be something that you are *doing*. I would prefer that you, in feeling the love-heat for yourself, act as a foundational block to support and sustain it. It will be good for you, yes, but by simply radiating, which love or heat naturally do, it will tend to create more benevolence in the world.

If you know other people who are doing it, you can get together and do it as a group if you feel like it, just for fun. But remember, never send it or direct it; let it naturally radiate on its own. That will make it easier, and it will also keep even good intentions out of the restrictor role. We don't want to restrict it; we want it to radiate and go where it is needed. It will know where it is needed. [Chuckles.] I know you mean well, but I want to give you all these fine points. Now, that's what you can do, possibly. Plus, I am sure that others of you will suggest other things.

Communicate across the Globe

Now, for those of you in a position to do something active, I feel that the best thing right now is to communicate as much as possible with people all over the world. When I say communicate, you'll notice that sounds vague. What I mean by that is, talk about anything you are interested in that friends on the other side of the world or friends down the street or even neighbors might want to talk about. People-to-people contact these days is vitally important, because it reassures human beings that they are not alone, that there are other people who agree with them. That's important so you don't feel isolated and that no matter where people are living, they are not just faceless.

So write, call, email or whatever. Stay in touch with people as much as you can. That is something active you can do that is also benevolent. I am sure you can think of other things. The point is so that you can be forming, on your part, the Earth humanity experience, so that each individual is important, groups of individuals are important and Earth people are important. But what is most important now is for each individual to know that he or she is important and has something to offer, even if it is an opinion. Many of you have more than that to offer, but this is critical these days.

So the love is up to you. Counsel spoke as one who studies other civilizations and who is essentially a scholar. He wasn't making proclamations, but it sounded like proclamations, just like any scholar or instructor . . . you've all been to school, most of you, and you know how teachers will talk about something in the past when they are presenting facts to you. So please forgive Counsel for his factual point of view as he expressed it. His intention was good.

For my part, what I say is to add love yourselves, the love you have for one another, friendship and the love warmth you can feel in your own bodies, as I discussed. This is what you can do no matter where you are, no matter who you are, no matter what you are doing. I hope it will improve your lives; it might very well. It will certainly cumulatively improve the situation. So just because Counsel didn't talk about love doesn't mean that there isn't love, but you have to add it.

Moving through the Three Alignments

If you ask if I approve of the concept of the First Alignment, I will say this: I can think of any number of ways peace could be brought about that I would like better, but in fact, all of those ways have been tried more than once—so as to factor in variables and possibilities—and they didn't work here on Earth. Do you understand? So my feeling is that I am not exactly thrilled [chuckles] with the way the First Alignment will be brought about, but I honor that it is an attempt to bring about a worthy goal.

It will take perhaps a generation or so *after* it is accomplished for people to feel at peace with the way it came about, because to create peace, you understand, as Zoosh and Counsel were talking about a state of being, meaning safety— Counsel talked about peace as safety, and that is an important aspect of it—but to bring about *individually felt* peace, where you feel peaceful, that will take awhile. You have to be at peace for twenty to thirty years and to feel like this is a good thing, building up a groundswell. Of course, there will be happiness, but building up a groundswell to have more and more happiness requires a little sorting out, as some people who will be doing some things would rather be doing others and so on—that will take some sorting out. And then before you know it, as you are sorting things out so that people can do other things that they would rather do and so on, you will be in the Second Alignment before you fully realize that that is what you are doing.

By the time the Second Alignment is achieved and you are experiencing it, you will enjoy that for a time. Then before you know it, people will start feeling fulfilled, and then everyone will want to feel fulfilled. And then you will find yourself in the Third Alignment and realize that you are there after the fact. By the time that is accomplished, things will be in balance, in love and harmonious, and will be a little more like things were always intended to be.

Everything Else Was Tried First

When was this decision made to create this First Alignment? Did they watch businesses and watch what was happening?

It wasn't made in a linear way. All decisions like this . . . are you talking about when humans made the decision?

Creator and His advisers.

It was always there as a possibility, but it was deemed to be of value to try every-thing else first, because in order to spur the First Alignment or to support it or to sustain it, or even to get out of the way and let it take place—because different beings would react in different ways, I am giving those examples—in order for that to take place, the consensus was that it would be better to try everything else first more than once, so that everyone could be sure that there wasn't some more benevolent way to establish it. That was done, and everyone is now quite clear that this is not something that can be done *and* sustained. You see, that is just it— to bring it about and sustain it is the hard part. So the First Alignment process as it is done will be able to bring it about and sustain it. That is the key.

What was tried before besides religion?

Think of anything: love, joy, happiness. Think of anything: relationships, friendships, kinships. I cannot explain it to you, because these are all one thing, you understand. It is not something that relates in a way you can understand, but picture it like a formula, a molecular formula, where there are three or four thousand components for each thing that was done. This doesn't mean three or four thousand individuals; it means three or four thousand component parts, so to speak, to put it simply. But I don't want to bring those things up, because if I talk about them, you will say, "Well, that is worth trying again," and so will everybody else. But it is quite clear that, as I said, everything else was tried more than once and didn't work.

But I don't understand. We are going onto another timeline. Are we going to be doing this on the new timeline?

It is part of the transition to the timeline. You understand, your magazine and these instructions reach only so many people. For the people who can make the connection to that benevolent future timeline, that will be wonderful and it will be helpful and supportive. But the vast majority of people will not read this or ever hear about it, so there needs to be more.

What about the rest of the people who don't hear about it or don't feel good doing the methods to get to the future timeline?

It's not about just a small amount of people doing this; there needs to be another method that brings everyone on board. Remember what Counsel said: *No one is left behind.* Every single individual is included. So for people who make the connections to the benevolent future timeline, it will be more benevolent and it will be gentle, of course, and it will help others. But how many people do you have on Earth? Lots of people, right? But this information or word of mouth cannot reach this many people in time.

When was this decision made?

You keep asking. The decision was made before this creation. All decisions having to do with creation are made before creation, so the question is a perfectly reasonable one but is not synchronized to your linear time in any way, so I cannot explain it. That is why I went around it before. You have to understand that even though you are living on Earth in linear time as you experience it, it is just a way to live, but it is not *the* way. Spirits do not sit back and say, "Okay, let's wait till tomorrow." [Chuckles.]

An Aide to the Creator doesn't usually come in and say, "It is important to get this into the next issue of the Sedona Journal." So this must be urgent.

It is urgent.

And from your point of view, if people understand what is happening, will they be more allowing of the process?

They won't be quite as panicky about the process. That is just it. We want to keep the panic level down. By panic, I mean, I am not talking of people in war zones; for people in war zones, panic is completely understandable there. I am talking about situations where people—how can we say?—are just worried and upset about the way things are going, the way life is going.

Think about it: You are a human being, and you think about the way things were before in the past, in some ways not so good and in some ways—you might think nostalgically, like any normal human being—sometimes you wish that some things were still like they used to be. Do you understand? Everyone is like that. And therefore, when things change and contemporary things occur that are upsetting, if you don't understand it, if you don't have the big picture, it then tends to create anger, frustration: "Why is it that way?" "Why can't it be the other way?" It creates resistance.

Resistance Creates a Barrier

The more resistance there is to it, the more difficulty and struggle is involved. It is just like if a boat is traveling through water slowly, someone is paddling perhaps, and the water parts to get out of the way; the oars are thrust gently but firmly into the water, and the water is pushed to thrust the boat forward. But this is acceptable. There are no big propellers thrashing through the water killing fish and other sea creatures. Do you understand? Paddling gently, nicely.

But think about if the water was resistant, if it was difficult to paddle. Think about if the water wasn't water, but ice. You could do it, but if you had to get your oars into the water, you would have to break through the ice: struggle, crash, boom, crush, struggle. Now, the reason I am saying this—obviously, you wouldn't be doing that—but when many people are resisting, it creates a genuine barrier. You can go through that barrier, but it takes a great deal of time to get through it, and given the world situation, I feel that we do not have an infinite amount of time to bring about resolution.

Think of it as an earthquake. The Earth rumbles and cracks and moves and "Aah." Just like you if you move your body around suddenly to a more comfortable position—you feel better. She feels better. So it's like you are making a sudden move, but for every sudden move there need to be some compensating factors: love-heat, gentleness. It's like putting your paddles in the water gently but thrusting forward firmly—that's all right.

My analogy is not intended to be vague; it is intended to reach many others in other ways. The reason I am talking about it in this way is that the panic I am referring to involves people who are resisting change because they want it to be how it was. But the way the memory functions is that your memories will often remember things affectionately in the past and blot out things that were horrible for you then.

Memory Filters Out the Traumas

Memory functions with a filter so that life doesn't become one misery after another, which would make life unbearable. Memory is intended to do that. It isn't a conscious, selective memory; memory is intended to filter out the traumas, at least as best as possible, from the past. Yes, enough recollection exists so you can learn and have discernment, but not so much recollection that you continue to relive it in your dreams and suffer, and you are overwhelmed by the memory of some past traumas, or whatever they were to you or others.

You are intended to remember good things about life in the past. Sometimes this creates an affection for the past, because remember that today and every-thing that is going on today for you readers who are reading this right now . . . today is your past when you are in tomorrow or the next day. And all of the dis-comforts you had today, most of them—other than the ones that are intended to bring you discernment so you will learn, become street-smart, as you say, and just learn about things that you will retain as motivation—but it is not intended that you remember every discomfort. So today is just as much the past, in this moment now. See, we have spoken for a few moments—that was the past, yes? And as you are reading this, you can laugh a little bit, because every moment is the present, but then you are off to the next moment and the previous one is the past. It is important to bring this up from time to time; it is easy to forget.

You're saying that in the same way that a lot of people resisted the WTO, NAFTA and so forth, they are going to resist what is going to happen in the future?

No, I am saying that a lot of people are resisting now. I am not saying this will happen in the future; I'm saying that the resistance is happening now. I think that the example was brought up about the bank of Home Town [Local Bank]; compound that times everything that you wish was the way it used to be, remem-bering only the good parts.

True Peace Is a Good Thing to Bring About

In closing, I wanted to add these comments so you do not feel that this was some ruthless hatchet falling from the sky above, intended to destroy you at all costs and to bring about peace at any price. It is not peace at any price, but when you look back even on the history that you can recall or read about, you might reasonably say that a lot of it is about strife and struggle and suffering. So true peace might be a good thing to bring about, even if it has to be enforced for a time by those who would enforce it. And all who do not embrace it . . . meaning that as you are created to feel safe as individuals, you have to allow other people to feel safe as individuals, and if you are doing something as an individual that prompts others to feel unsafe, then you will not be allowed to do it anymore.

Think about that. How might this play out? For example, one of the ways it will play out is that when the First Alignment is accomplished, it is unlikely that individuals who can now obtain a driver's license will be allowed to do that, as licensing arrangements will change. Transportation will change; it will become much more of a community transportation system and it will be very finely tuned—

not just a bus that gets you from here to there, but transit systems that are very complex so that they can take you directly from your home to where you want to go, just like a cab. And they will not be that expensive. You can afford it. This is not an attempt to make you a prisoner, but if your freedom and joy involve tearing through the streets at seventy miles an hour with your friends for fun, don't you just know that that is going to be stopped because it causes other people to feel unsafe?

I give you an example, something you can look at. I realize this is going to cause you to say, "Oh no, you're not going to take my driver's license away!" But think about the things that happen. I know they seem to happen to others, but those of you reading this can think about things that happened either to you or people you know or care about. What are you willing to do to make it possible for others to feel safe? And what do you need to ask of other people so that *you* will feel safe? If you want extra credit, you can make a list like that.

It is something to think about, your list of what you would do so that others would feel safe and your list of what you would need other people to do so you would feel safe. And if others feel safe, the tension level relaxes and you feel safer. Oh yes, it is good homework to do, something kind of fun. If you know others doing it, you can compare lists; you can talk it up. Talking it up might be good. Think about these things openly, chat about it and so on. It could be a good thing. So on that note of extra-credit homework, I will say good night.

The First Alignment: Questions, Answers and More Information

Zoosh

August 31, 2003

The following email (abridged for space) from a reader of the Sedona Journal of Emergence! *is a representative sample of a multitude of similar emails we received after the publication of the "First Alignment" channeling in the September 2003 issue of SJE [reprinted in this volume as chapter 44] and after posting it on our website. There were 239 posts on our Reader's Forum on this topic at last count. Therefore, Zoosh, through Robert Shapiro, was asked for clarification, and the following is the result.*

Email Response to the First Alignment

People with some knowledge of the Illuminati, the Shadow or whatever you want to call the rulers of this planet, will be extremely upset by the content of the channeling on the First Alignment. This is not because "Counsel" is "undiplomatic" and his/her statements are "hurtful," but because the Illuminati/the Shadow is not taken into consideration or mentioned in the channeled material. How it is possible to characterize the Illuminati-controlled "corporations" of this world as something that would ultimately bring about peace and happiness is beyond comprehension. The Illuminati's mind control, its abuse of humans, animals and nature, and its need for enslavement of humanity do not fit the notions in the channeling that its manipulations should eventually bring about the "peace" the channeling predicts. No peace in any sense that a human would know will come from these beings and their "corporations." Ever!

I suggest that a new channeling take place, requesting a clear and unambiguous definition of the term "peace" and of "peace" for whom. Is it for the Illuminati who have full control, or is it for humanity? If it is for humanity, is the "peace" based on a microchipped, docile, nonthinking population who will not rebel against being treated like cattle? Will the Illuminati dictate what "peace" is, and we—the sheep— bleat in subservience? Will the Illuminati somehow disappear? If not, how would peace come about?

—Ane, Westminster, CO

Zoosh here. Greetings, my friend. For a long time I mentioned that the First World Order would be based on the corporate model. I also suggested things you could do to soften the impact. Now I have asked Counsel to give you some details, all the while encouraging you to continue to do your work to raise consciousness by involving your heart and your heart's abilities.

Let me try to put this recent article in the September 2003 issue of the *Sedona Journal* into some perspective. I know that it is in Counsel's nature to speak objectively. It's almost like going to a history class at school and your professor is droning on—not about something that's unimportant, but rather about something that you personally are not particularly interested in—when suddenly, while his voice drones on in the same sort of rhythm and sound, he's talking about things that you are not only interested in, but are overwhelmingly interested in.

Now, the reason I mention this is that it is in Counsel's nature, his personality, to speak about these matters, or any matters upon which he is requested to speak, as if he were reading from a long script—not something for which there is passion or personal involvement, none of that. He's like a historian, not an end-time historian like yourself, Melody, in some ways and me in other ways, but a historian not dissimilar in motivations and pursuits to historians of your time. Therefore, there's at times a tendency to be somewhat academic.

It's not that the material in the article is academic, but that the manner of delivery is academic, spoken as if this has already occurred; it's that kind of attitude, so it sounds a bit preachy. But if you listen to other historical lecturers, they can also sound preachy—not that they are—because the individuals are speaking about things that are simple facts according to all the research they have done and all of the established and known details of the time. So I wanted to explain that—not so much for you, Melody, but for the reader who may well have been offended by the manner of delivery of Counsel.

Now I'll say a little bit about Counsel's personality, even though he may be a bit shy. He lives on a planet that your readers, as the Explorer Race on Earth, are likely to encounter at some point. That is why it is to your advantage to be exposed to this sort of attitudinal, historical, conversational style. It is one of the many different styles of personality that you will encounter in your travels as Explorer Race space explorers. So it's good to be exposed to these things.

The First Alignment Is Based on the Corporate Model

Now, Counsel's whole planet is geared toward study of one sort or another. Much of it, of course, is more contemporary for their own times and their own interests, but as always there are those interested in history, and some are very specifically interested in the history of other places. I asked Counsel to do this because he is particularly interested in the history of places that have gone through sudden changes—sudden in historical terms might mean fifty years, which might be sudden when looked upon over the broad expanse of history. You people on Earth are going through a sudden change right now in that you are experiencing what I've been talking about really now for quite a few years.

You can remember that I've been saying for a very long time that the First World Order will be based on the corporate model [see *The Explorer Race: Origins and the Next 50 Years*]. Now, the reason I said that was not to suggest that it would be some benevolent experience where everyone is happy and the feeling of the world being all right all the time would be present. The corporate model, whether you work within it or whether you are simply exposed to it in one way or another, can sometimes be very arbitrary and in some applications ruthless, as you can see by looking around at the world situation in your times. Yet the one thing you can be certain of when it has to do with a corporation is that there will be organization and structure, and it is all motivated toward the pursuit of profits.

Now, I'm not trying to say, "Well, this is wonderful, and what a wonderful way for everybody to live." What I am saying is that it is a unifying force in which you are, in fact, functioning in your times almost universally—meaning globally in this case—on your planet. You can live almost anywhere and see this, although, granted, a few populations in isolated spots may not feel much of a sense of connection to corporations. But other than the rare isolated individuals, most people, if they think about it, will realize that they are very much affected by corporations—if not directly for some, then certainly indirectly.

Even with governments that are attempting to pursue a system that might be different than that of other governments, such as mainland China, you still find that they are swayed and affected by corporations. I'm not saying that they are a corporation, but that the world corporate function affects them and how they act, and they are very well aware of this and have been for a time. Of course, in the past their perception of that was entirely hostile and not without cause, but now they are attempting to see if they can function within that system in hopes— as is always the case with systems that people believe in—that they can spread their ideals around in some way as well as having to bob and weave with the corporate model itself. I'm not trying to pick sides here; I'm just trying to say that this is the system that most people on Earth are exposed to. I'm doing a little review, as you can tell, for those who have not read the books in which I may have stated—excessively at times and repeatedly at other times—that the First World Order will be based on the corporate model.

So you are seeing this now. And yet from Counsel's prospective, he is looking at it as something that has been long established in the past on your planet, a planet which Counsel, in any form, has never been to. That is why he uses a sort of academic approach to stating what occurred from his future time.

It's All about People

Now, as Reveals the Mysteries and Speaks of Many Truths and Isis and myself and others have stated over and over for these many years now, there are things that you can do to soften all of this. While this is going on, it is certainly true that there is a spiritual awakening happening at the same time, and although these forces might seem to be competitive, they are not. After all, if they were truly competitive forces—spirituality, the raising of consciousness, the opening of hearts, the feeling of connection from one to the other, all of this—if this was a struggle between so-called . . . to put it in an almost cartoonish form, if this was the good and the corporations were the evil, then of course it could never go anywhere. No, the spiritual consciousness, becoming more influential, must be compatible with the First World Order in some way. Granted, it will be much more compatible with the Second Alignment and the Third Alignment and so forth, and it will also be influential to help bring it about, even as you are establishing the First Alignment now. It has to be this way because it's all about people—human beings—and what you do.

Now, you can loosely say that every single thing we have talked about over these many years [since 1987] of our working together, Light Technology, all of Robert's channeling—and for that matter, channeling from others—is basically under the umbrella of people and what you do, but there needs to be more. That's why so much of the stress lately has been placed upon the idea of people, what you do and what you feel, because what you feel . . . although it seems—in the past, in your intellectual perception of things—that what you feel can sometimes make problems, know what you feel and learn about what you feel and understand that all people have the same feelings, the same function of the feelings. Maybe they don't experience the same feelings at the same time, but the functional aspect of feelings works exactly the same for all human beings, all animals, all plants, all stone, even the rain and things you think of as elements, as circumstances. Everyone and everything has feelings. This then tells you that this is a unifying element that can be built upon to create connections and to help support the feeling of common ground leading to common bond among all people.

Order Means No Extremes

Therefore, this whole spiritual phenomenon going on in its many phases these days is compatible with (to a degree, and there is meeting ground to many degrees) the various systems that are being established to help bring about a form of peace known as order. Now, I'm not talking about order as in something that is totally authoritarian, based upon some political or extreme establishment of beliefs—such as in your contemporary times, speaking historically, one that globally people can identify with. The flirtation in Germany with the extreme expression of Nazism didn't bloom out of nothing. There were a lot of things in that political and philosophical belief system that were familiar, having been long-standing practices, some of which were not horrible, many of which were. I'm not talking about that kind of authoritarian order.

What I'm talking about is order in the sense . . . I want to be very clear about what I mean by First World Order. Order means that no extreme elements are functioning to bring about chaos and suffering by anyone. So this tells you that by extreme, I mean something like Nazism or perhaps religious fanaticism, something you can identify with completely in your time, meaning, "My way or you're dead. Embrace my religion or I will kill you." None of that. You find that a lot in your time. Sometimes, of course, it is simply painted as religious extremism where there is a cause that has gone largely misunderstood by others. In other times, it is simply an extremist situation.

So extremism that brings about suffering and misery, as you have with terrorism, will simply vanish in the First Alignment and actually well before that. But it won't happen strictly because those who are carrying out extremism—whether it is backed by some small group of people with very firm beliefs, or even by some government with specific and extreme beliefs—because all of these people involved in these activities will simply be eliminated, as Counsel put it. It means that there will be large and ongoing . . . how can we say? It will not be superimposed by some outside authority, but there will be ongoing conditioning present to encourage all people to believe in the value of all life.

You might find that this does not seem to be connected to anything you usually identify with a corporation. Many of you think of corporations as something ugly. But, in fact, if you analyze your daily lives, even in families, you will find certain levels of authoritarianism in families that are very similar to what you find in corporations, and people studying business have looked at this quite thoroughly. There needs to be a little more explanation of this to the general public, but that will come in time and will sometimes come in amusing ways, as you find in your situational comedies and other entertainments.

Now, the corporation is not going to preach how we are all alike and that we have to come together, and say things that you might hear from philosophies and religions, many religions. It's not going to say things, for example, that you might hear in the United Nations or in some political systems that promote this. Rather, it will come from the spiritual connection that people have with themselves and the increase in consciousness having to do with the awareness that no matter how people are different, there is certainly a connection that we are all human beings, you might say—that we are feeling beings, we have likes, we have dislikes. In short, things that people have been saying for years and years will come to be much more accepted and spoken about even while people have varying different beliefs, many of which are not particularly compatible with other people's beliefs.

It's Easy to Adapt to Something That Is Better

So I'm not saying that people's individualism or individual personalities and beliefs will be suppressed in the First World Order, but rather—and this is a point I've made before—that it's easier to learn something, to apply something new, to do something that is beneficial and learn how to do it, than it is to simply stop the thing you were doing that isn't working. It's easier to adapt to something that you find is better. So people will simply discover that certain things are better and adapt to them and find that things work better doing it that way. It improves their lives, it improves the quality of their lives, it improves the quality of their family's lives and so on. Therefore, they simply stop doing what they were doing before—not because of some authoritarian demand, but rather because they notice that what they're doing now works better, they like it better, it feels better.

So this is a point of compatibility between the raising of the spiritual consciousness and the intent of the corporation. The corporation would like to sell a product—whatever it is—to people who see it as something desirable; who consume it, so to speak; who bring it into their lives and discover that their lives are improved in some way by utilizing this product and then want more of it. It's that simple. You can see on that basis how that falls into alignment very nicely with spiritual practices where you discover something that works better in your life and want more of it, and you practice it. This may seem to be very basic indeed, but it requires basic similarities for there to be connections for you from one thing, which might seem to be on one side, to another thing, which might seem to be on another side.

That's why we've been saying for some time now—myself and other entities speaking through Robert—that the point of having enemies, the good guys and the bad guys, "Who did this?" and so on . . . we're not going to talk about that so much, because ultimately people are people. You all have the same functioning mechanisms within you, and you all tend to express yourself in very similar ways to others. Granted, some people might be more extreme than others, and some people might be more passive, but this is largely based upon their conditioning, their expression of their personality, their opportunities, their path in life. Nevertheless, all of the functions of the human being—physiological, psychological, spiritual, instinctual—are very similar on the functional level, if not identical.

This does not rule out individualism, circumstances under which one might do something different, but it does say (if I can use a computer as an example) that computers are essentially based on the same technology, but different computers might display different things at different times. I do not wish to suggest that a human being is as simple as a computer, but the mechanism that you all share is very similar, if not identical. Nevertheless, it leaves a great deal of room for individuality.

Your Government Cares

That's why I'm not going to say that corporations are this and that human beings are suffering under the corporation's crush and all of this, because if you look at corporations, there is one thing you will see without a doubt, and that is that you will see people. It's very similar to what you see in governments. You might get mad at your government and so forth, but there are many things that people do in the government, especially governments that are caring as you find in many countries. Take your own country, the United States. You might get mad at your government sometimes, but take a good look at it. There are many services that are provided by your government that are based very strictly upon a statement that the government might be able to say if it was an entity unto itself, and that is, "We care about you and we want you to be happier, and we don't want you to suffer if we can prevent it." The social systems in your government are not traditionally part of governments per se. If you look back at governments—or even look at the governments that exist all over the world—they are designed to be orderly and to establish a flow of sustainable and maintainable systems that will allow those who are in charge at the moment to maintain that while keeping those who are outside from rebelling too much. That's essentially governments.

But look at your government. Although it may have that quality, it also has all of these other qualities that have to do with, "What can we do for you?"—social security, Medicare, to name but a few. There are other governments; you have your federal government, your state government, your city government, all of that. It may seem overwhelming because of the taxation systems and other regulatory functions, but your government and the governments of many countries are similar—Canada, England, France and so on, countries that you're familiar with, countries that you feel a sense of kinship with and bond to, to say nothing of countries that you are beginning to feel a sense of kinship with and bond to that you have not felt lately, but there's still this similarity. Granted, there are governments of other places that need to be more caring, and given the opportunity they will be, but they will need time to grow into the expression of more benevolent or benign approaches to government that some countries have had the opportunity to do.

If you look back in history, you will see it—that many terrible things were done even in the establishment of those governments, that those governments in the beginning did things that were horrible which they do not do anymore as a general rule, even though there might be problems that are ongoing. So I'm not trying to advocate one system or another; I'm just trying to put this all in contemporary terms with a certain amount of connection and interconnectiveness to ideas that I've spoken about over time, and to acknowledge the value of Ane's question while at the same time pointing out that this is not new. It is something that I've discussed for a long time, but not in the detail that can be provided by someone such as Counsel, who can speak about it without any great passion. As you know (I admit it freely), I am a passionate being. I care strongly about your happiness, your spiritual fulfillment and so on, and so I felt it might be of some value to have someone speak about the way you get to spiritual fulfillment in a practical, day-to-day, systematic approach, so you understand it. So I requested that Counsel do this. I grant that Counsel might seem to sound authoritarian, but he's not. He's strictly, you might say, a history researcher with an inclination to share what he knows in a calm or—as he might say—rational manner.

The real question, which you haven't come to yet, that anyone who has read the six Shining the Light *books is going to ask is, "What is the mechanism by which those who control the planet now are going to give up that control?"*

I think that was very clearly stated in Counsel's comments. You do not feel that?

No, I don't.

Really? But if you look at what was stated, you will simply find—as stated by Counsel, for instance—that certain criminal enterprises . . . from Counsel's point of view, the sinister secret government is no different than a large criminal-based organization. If what they are doing is not compatible with the First Alignment, they will be eliminated. I gave Counsel certain editorial suggestions. He was not to say how this will go about. You understand why, yes?

Well, we need to work it out ourselves.

No. Think about it tactically for a moment. If you were in a situation that needed to be corrected and you were up against some beings who were very influential and powerful and ruthless, would you explain to them patiently what you were going to do, how the change . . . ?

I see what you mean.

So I saw no value in that, but I asked Counsel to touch on the important points, and I feel he did. But go ahead with your question. I will say what I can, but I'm not going to say, "Well, this is our game plan."

Okay, that makes much more sense. I didn't feel that was explained. It just seems that they are so powerful, that they control the planet and tell the governments what to do. For all I know, they tell the corporations what to do. It's a little difficult to imagine how they're going to allow themselves to be put aside.

There Are Fewer and Fewer Secrets

Well, you have to remember that the number-one function that's going on here in your time—and many of you feel the experience of it and sometimes feel offended by it—is that there are fewer and fewer secrets. I know that many of you would like to keep things to yourselves and you are concerned about your privacy and so on, but you would find even on the most benign and benevolent planets—places where you would love to visit, to say nothing of living there—that there are no secrets. There is a great value to this, because where there are secrets, people are either motivated by a desire to gain something over someone else or, more often on the personal level, by a feeling of shame. If there is no shame about one's personal desires or needs, then it's all right for something to be completely known. And if it is completely known and appears to be self-destructive—and as you know, self-destructive to Zoosh means harming yourself or harming someone else—then it will be known and the individual can be helped so he or she can get past it.

We have never said, "These are the individuals in the sinister secret government. Here are their names and addresses, and here's where you can find them." We've never done that, because those souls do not give permission for that, just as we've never said, "Well, here's somebody else and she's doing this and that and so on." Souls must give permission to allow that to come out. But it's not as if all these things aren't known on the spiritual level. Think about the way information is acquired in your own time. Many things are known. Sometimes many things are known by individuals and how much you all love—you have to admit it now—not necessarily a scandal, but yes, maybe a little bit. And then you find out things that you didn't know before, and it's exciting and fun and you talk about it, even though certain individuals might suffer as a result. I'm not trying to say you're bad; I'm just trying to say that information has become its own pursuit for many people these days. And one can certainly say that the pursuits that we perform together—you and I, Melody, and others—are certainly about information, and there's no question that it can be exciting sometimes. Wouldn't you agree?

Absolutely.

And so it is safe to say that corporations and those who run corporations pursue the uncovering of information and secrets with a zealousness that is a sight to behold. It's not at all dissimilar from governments and even on the individual basis . . . as I've said, there's a great deal of interest in what was once secret and now can be known. So this is not something foreign. I will simply say that those— and they know this, by the way; it's not a surprise to them—who are in even the inner circle of the individuals in the sinister secret government are known in part by one corporation or another to be functioning in this manner, and that most of the individuals of the sinister secret government, if not all of those in the inner circle, do know that this group or that group "knows about me and what I'm doing and so on," because there have been times (and of course, it's very tempting to do this for members of the inner circle) that they tip their hand, so to speak, to say, "Well, if you mess with me, you're dead."

Some intelligence gets shared, and things are found out. It's not as if the beings, even of the inner circle of the sinister secret government, are unknown. They will be known, and you know that different groups come together, even on the basis of your day-to-day friendships—you know something and your friend knows something and his friend knows something and her friends know something, and you all get together and share information and you get a bigger picture. Granted, not all the information is always right, but at least you can form an idea about something and know how to pursue it to get more information. In short, this is something that is largely of interest in your time, and this will continue to be the case. End-time historian that I am, I'm inclined to see things in that way. In that sense, you then have the understanding and a better glimmer of how the sinister secret government will be absorbed. I'm not ruling out that some of them could change and become less self-destructive and choose to join in the First Alignment, but if they don't choose to change, then I think it was stated very clearly by Counsel that it is possible they will be eliminated if necessary.

Now, I grant that when Counsel said that this group or that group will be crushed or eliminated, speaking academically on the basis of his perception of the situation, he didn't say—and I'm adding this, all right; I had asked him to put things in a certain context without suggesting to him word for word what to say—he didn't say "if necessary." But this is just a term that he doesn't use. You have to remember that he's not a human being. He's not cultured or acculturated, you might say, to your social systems, but he does sound very much like an historian and he will put things in terms that he understands adapt to the English language. Some of this is personality, and I think that when he realized the impact it was having on you on a feeling basis, he attempted to adjust that to some degree. But it was a shock to him, because from his perspective, when he was speaking to you, he was speaking as someone in his society—especially in a society of academic historians—might speak to another academic historian about a subject for which there is a shared mutual interest: "This happened and that happened and da, da, da." Not as if to say, "Well, I'm going to do this," or "I'm going to do that," or "My people are going to . . ." There was no sense of personal expression.

You Can Join the "Good Government" Behind the Scenes

There's one other thing that wasn't brought out, and that is that for I don't know how many years—it was suggested that it's been about fifty years—there's been a group of humans on the planet who are functioning almost as the opposite of this sinister secret government, a good government behind the scenes who has known about this plan. Is that true?

Yes.

How were they chosen? How did they come into being? How did they get involved? How did that come about?

In the same way all choose their general path in life before they come here, with certain options and possibilities. They weren't born to it; it's not a hierarchical thing that you're born to. It's not a group who meets in a specific place all the time. Granted, they have at times in the past. But, generally speaking, it is something that you can become right now. Why wait? If you have a spiritual practice, a benevolent feeling, a capacity for benevolent feelings and time to devote to it, you can be one of these people right now. That is why we've been talking about your personal experience for so many years. We started talking initially about gold light: "Feel the gold light in your body and let it expand," and so on [see p. 32]. Many others have talked about this as well. Then we talked about the love-heat/heart-warmth/physical-warmth: "Feel the warmth in your body and let it expand," and so on [see p. 23].

We've done this because we wanted to give you something that would allow those of you who have the time and the capacity and who choose to do something to do so. Do you know that one individual, even if he is not near other individuals doing this, can sit there and feel that warmth? He might feel it in his stomach, he might feel it in his chest, something like that. If he can generate that feeling, that physical feeling, or notice it and go into it and feel it more . . . if he can do that on his own for even a few minutes a day, it has a tremendous impact. You don't send it out; it naturally radiates. If you purposely send it out, it's somewhat authoritarian. You can do something kind for someone, but you all know the old joke: There's no point in helping the lady across the street if she's waiting for the bus. So you don't send it out. Rather you allow it to do what it does naturally. You feel it, you experience it benevolently and it naturally radiates. You can do it with a tree, for instance. If the tree is compatible with the experience in that moment and isn't busy, and you sit in front of the tree and feel that heat, if you suddenly feel a great deal more, the tree and you are doing it together and it will radiate more and that's fine.

The reason we talk about this is that you don't have to be qualifying for some great mission like this. It is our purpose—speaking for myself and other entities right now—to spread this around, to bring it about more so. That's why we've spoken in the past about coming together. If you know other people doing this love-heat, then you can come together and do it together and it's a wonderful thing. You simply do it on your own, with other people doing it on their own in the room, and you also feel greater love-heat. Or maybe you go out and do it with the trees, and you feel this wonderful warmth and it radiates out and has this benevolent impact, because that kind of radiated love and warmth cannot, will not, is not set up to in any way change people by some authoritarian standard of behavior. Rather it will nurture and bring about the best in individuals if those individuals are receptive in that moment and can take that in. It might spur something; it might support something. It will certainly nurture it as an energy of nurturance. So my answer to your question, although it may seem to be oblique, is the most important answer.

You Are in a Time of Responsibility

I'm not going to talk about this group that was established long ago to bring about your spiritual enlightenment, and I'll tell you why; there's a reason. Think how many times over the years you've been told and you have read that this group or that group was responsible for keeping people in a general benevolent direction. But all that does is, for the most part unintentionally, create a hierarchical system that says, "Well, if they're doing it, I don't have to."

What I'm talking about is—and you know well, you know me—I'm talking about responsibility. What have I been talking about for these many years now? That you are living in a time of understanding, a time of coming into wisdom, a time of coming into knowing and being aware of the knowledge in your life that works, that you apply in your life. And that becomes your wisdom; you use your wisdom because it works. It changes from time to time, but you use the knowledge that works in your life as your wisdom. You're also in a time of trying out different things, applications, to see what works and what doesn't. And of course, you are also in a time of responsibility, because you are responsible for experiencing what works benevolently for you and to do this benevolent thing—and benevolent simply means that which works for you in a way that is nurturing and helpful, and that may be nurturing to others but in no way harms others. That's the key to understanding benevolence. Benevolence in this sense is more complex, and I grant there's more meaning, but I'm trying to keep this simple since the question was direct and I'm attempting to keep my answer direct or it may not be obvious.

So what I'm saying is this: I don't think it pays to talk about this group or that group who has been helping over time, because the individuals in that group have changed. The faces have changed, the names have changed, and no one nominated them to the role. They took on the role, and they did things that are very similar to what I'm suggesting people do today. They experienced something that was naturally human, that all beings could do, that felt good to them and felt good to those around them. As you know, the love-heat is part of that. You've also noticed, because of your experiences with spirituality, that when you're around a benevolent energy, sometimes you feel it as a benevolent energy.

Conversely, when you're around a malevolent energy—even if it is fleeting as it might be with somebody being angry—you feel that, even if the anger isn't directed toward you. In short, you are feeling beings, and therefore, if the feeling is good, many people will feel it and notice it. Why not hop aboard and do this love-heat and be a member of that group who helps bring about benevolence and spiritual consciousness of unity and love?

That's beautiful.

Some Stories Are Still Ignored

Let me ask this: Had there not been the conditions prevalent at the moment—the Middle East problem, North Korea, Iraq, all the things that we're facing right now—would you have talked about this, or just allowed it to happen? It was only explained because of what you perceived of as such unrest on the planet that you were concerned—is that correct?

Well, yes and no. You have to understand that your news services tend to report some suffering; they equally tend to ignore a certain amount of suffering. Some stories are spoken about and some stories aren't spoken about, either because—from the news services' point of view—they've talked about it before and it doesn't seem to be of interest to people, so they simply say, "Okay, forget it," or there's an editorial policy that doesn't encourage that for some other reason. But now you see change. You might see organizations that are influential, magazines even that are putting out articles such as the important article that you find in the current issue of *National Geographic* about slavery, which still exists in your time. It is a vitally important article that many news services know about and have attempted over time to talk about, but there hasn't been much cooperation or allowance for this to come out.

So what I'm simply saying is that there has been struggle and strife and wars and suffering for a long time, but now that the Western world, as it is called, generally speaking—or the place where you live and places where other people you know live, the Western world—is becoming more aware of how the strife can take place . . . which is essentially, regardless of how it starts, a desire by one to have more or a desire by many to have more. Even what's going on in the Middle East . . . although over time it will become more benign and show a more benevolent face to the people there, it still amounts to a foreign power coming in and saying, "This is how we're going to do it." So even though much of it was desired, it was saying, "Well, we're going to come in and we're not going to allow Hitler, so to speak, to take over and kill all the people, but we're going to go in before he carries out that ruthless plan." At least that's how it was put to people of the world, and they are now wondering why people don't say, "Gosh, you did a good deed."

There Are Things That Need More Exposure

Now, I'm putting it in very simplistic terms. I simply asked Counsel to talk about these things, because the Western world—as you understand your culture—is aware of the beginning of something that could become a much more widespread struggle involving a lot of suffering, and you're seeing how it happens, sometimes with truly the best of intentions. You're seeing it and you're aware of how it's beginning. It's not something that you hear about happening in other countries, meaning struggle that you don't know, that you don't understand because you simply have no grasp of the culture, such as the long-standing battles and struggles and suffering in Africa. Most people . . . not all, but most people in your Western culture do not understand what's going on there, just as most people in your culture do not understand the struggle and strife in Asia and other places like that. I'm not talking about the Vietnam War so much, but about struggles in China and things that are kept secret and so on. Most people don't know about that, but it's there.

So there are things that need more exposure in your time, and it's not an accident . . . it's not that people put their heads together and say, "Okay, let's tell them all about it now," but it's not an accident that things that need to be discussed, understood and corrected and to be made more benevolent are coming out. And they've been coming out, and I salute *National Geographic* for bringing out that article. There will be others who expose things that need to come out, even though, in the case of the editorial policy of that magazine, they may not seem to fall within the realm of the normal articles. But they are influential.

If you look back at the channeling from years ago, you will find a mention about *National Geographic* benevolently in the past; it's there. That's just a little fun thing that I'm pointing out to people who have read everything they can get their hands on. There are other publications that will come out with this, too. I assure you that that particular magazine is publishing that article with some trepidation, worried about how the reading public will take it. It will be shocking to many people, but it's something you need to know about. It is a self-destructive thing that's going on, and it needs to be changed—self-destructive means that which hurts you or hurts others or both. Self-destructive things need to be changed to make things more benevolent, and that's the fact of the case.

Do Something New

Let me finish by saying that I want to thank Ane and all of the others for their questions. She and others are able to put this question forward. It is not that I am stating to you, Ane, that your question is not valid, but rather that we must go forward utilizing the capacities that all of you human beings have in order to bring about change, rather than struggling and suggesting that we must punish. Punishment, however it may seem to be entirely and justifiably warranted, has invariably caused—if you look back at history—further strife in the future. Just look at the end of World War I. Countries in your world—take a look at that and you can find that out—punished Germany and made them pay war reparations and so on with the idea that they were the bad guys and they deserved to be punished. But I can assure you that if those people at the time, when they were giving those punishments out to Germany, could have looked into a crystal ball and seen what it would bring about—the next world war—they wouldn't have done it. They would have said, "Well, what can we do to help the people of Germany so that they can feel more a part of the world rather than apart from the world? What can we do to help them see other people in benevolent ways? How can we present ourselves in benevolent ways? In short, what can we do to help them, to nurture them, to love them, to bring about the change that we desire from them?"

I grant, that sounds idealistic and it doesn't always work. I'm not saying you just allow a murderer, for instance—to put it in your contemporary times—to run about freely, and after she kills someone you say, "Oh, how can we help you?" and so on. But there are ways to change systems. Prisons do not have to be horrible places of torture; they can be more benevolent. They can separate your criminals from society, but they do not have to be places where the people, the prisoners, are tortured and maimed and other things so that when they come out, if they haven't been deterred from their past behaviors, they are so destroyed personally that they might be self-destructive in some way. This is not always the case for prisoners. Many come out and say, "That's it. I'm going straight." But sometimes, if they've been miserable or they've had to make alliances that they wouldn't have made otherwise, they come out and are self-destructive.

Things need to be changed in your time now, Melody. And things need to be changed in your time now, Ane. I speak to you both. Those things need to be done now. You can't just make a temporary fix; you can't just force this one to pay reparations and force that one to go to prison. You can't just have revenge only, because you must, must, must look back at history. You must understand that if you indulge in revenge exclusively, it will come back to you, because those who are revenged upon, even if the whole world believes that they deserve it, will in some way express exactly what was expressed toward them. Why perpetuate suffering, no matter how justified it may seem to be, if it only perpetuates suffering in the future for future generations?

Do something new. Try something benevolent. You can't correct actions on the other side of the world by yourself, but you can experience the love-heat. It will help you to feel good, and because it naturally radiates, it might very well help others somewhere else, whom you will never meet. Is that not a valuable thing to do? Good night.

Benevolent Magic, Living Prayer and Benevolent Creation Mechanics Can Influence the First Alignment

Zoosh

September 13, 2003

I have looked over some of the responses on your website to the comments by Counsel on the First Alignment [see chapter 44]. I'd like to add a postscript, all right? I realize that this is a shock to many of you. After all, you expect New Age and metaphysical commentary to be heart-centered, or at least to be encouraging to the heart in the most nurturing way. But let us put it like this: In this day and age, where you have to think tactically and act practically, you still have some things that you desire the metaphysical and New Age to be that are of value, certainly, but you also have some things that you desire the metaphysical and New Age community to be that are not that practical anymore. With all the billions of human beings living on Earth at this time—and with each and every one of you having all of your individual wants, needs and desires—you have to be able to respond quickly to events in your world.

Information about the Future Is Useful

I don't have to tell people in the business community, to say nothing of individuals, that if you have an opportunity to know that something is going to happen, how valuable it is to know it's going to happen before that time. For instance, how many of you have had this circumstance come up: You are told, "When you get to the next town, the police have set up a speed trap, so when you go through that town, be sure and be very careful, slow down and look both ways." And it's a good reminder to be a better driver in any event. (That's really the purpose of some speed traps; they're not just to get funds for the city's coffers.) So that's good to know, isn't it?

Suppose you are told, as you are in many business traveler circulars and web-sites, that, "This condition or that condition is occuring at the airport, so come early or be prepared," or "It's not the time to wear your high-top boots to the air-port"—in short, practical things you can use. I'm bringing up a couple of ordi-nary examples that many of you know about. Suppose, on the other hand, that you listen to the traffic reports before you drive to work and they say, "This high-way and those streets are jammed. You better take another route." Now, you know that it's very practical to hear that, and you say, "Well, I'm glad I heard that. I won't take that route."

It was with that motivation in mind that I requested Counsel to speak to you in a recent channeling, to talk to you about something that is a trend, that is an underpinning, and this is an ongoing situation. I know to some of you it sounded as if I were allowing Hitler to speak and tell you his plans, but it's nothing like that. Counsel is purely a researcher—not unusual. Many of your teachers research or have staff to research for them, and they will read the reference books or the history books of the past and perhaps extrapolate a future based upon their theories. In this case, Counsel was speaking about something that has hap-pened in the past. He was looking at his own environment, his own planet. He wasn't speaking perhaps with the gentility and grace that one of you might speak to another about something dramatic that was going to come along, but then again, he wasn't from your planet and he wasn't socialized in your system. He was simply speaking matter-of-factly about something that occurred, since he is in the future.

The reason this was told to you wasn't just a warning or what some people might look at as a reassurance. It was so that you would know it was coming and that there are many things you've been taught in the pages of these books and in discussion groups you've been to that you can do to keep things as mel-low and as energetically loving as possible. And that is your job. I grant that the article by Counsel didn't come right out and say, "Here's what is going to happen, and here's what you can do about it," but we tried to make that apparent after the article in postscripts, and this is another postscript.

Homework: Take the Love-Heat to the Next Level

So I'm here now to give you your assignment—this is your homework. For those of you who can do the love-heat/heart-warmth/physical-warmth [see p. 23], just do it every day for your own benefit, and whatever excess comes through will radiate out in the world and can only improve things. But if you're doing that love-heat, I want you to take it to the next level. As I've said before, if you know others doing it, sit in a group together and do it together. It will be stronger and will naturally radiate out. Don't send it out; let it radiate out.

For those of you who don't have a group handy, then go for a walk on the land somewhere, and when you find a tree that you like, say, "Good life," go into the love-heat and see if the warmth comes in stronger. If it does, don't project it out. Just let it be there, and whatever extra there is will radiate out. If it doesn't happen with that tree, thank the tree, say, "Good life," and walk on to the next tree. Trees are available to support you in this homework assignment. Try to pick a mature tree, not a sapling. Saplings have all they can do to just survive, and they're usually shy around human beings. Now, trees are what I recommend, but for some of you, there may not be trees in the area, so if there are big rocks, you can try this with big natural stones—not ones that have been cleaved by human beings, but those in their natural state. You can try that, or even try this with mountains.

Now, this is homework I have touched on before, which is why I'm glossing over it a bit, but there's more. I don't want you to feel like this is some juggernaut that is just going to plow over everything. Think of what Counsel said in the First Alignment article as an advantage. It's as if you were a stock trader—someone who buys and sells stock—and someone gave you a general idea of what was going to happen in the future, and you were able to listen to that and make practical plans about your buying and selling so that you could do as well as possible in the future. We're not trying to manipulate the stock market here; rather, this is a broad commentary on social systems.

So this is what I'd like you to do as individuals and as a group: I'm not going to state a time of the day, because depending upon where you live, the time of day is different. But I will say this (we'll call this extra-credit homework): For those of you, if you like, over the next ten, twelve, fourteen years, during which time you will see a certain amount of tumultuousness as people adjust to this system—including people in business and government communities, seeing its practicality—you can really contribute to keeping it as benevolent as possible in the following way. I've mentioned some ways, and I'm going to mention another way; in the future, I might bring up other ways—we'll see.

When the Moon is out at night, as long as it's at least a quarter moon and as long as you know it's out—meaning if it's a cloudy night or it's raining and you can't see it, wait for another night, but when the Moon is out, even if you live way in the north where you have mostly light, as long as the Moon is out and you can see it (or if you can't see very well, someone tells you it's out)—then I'd like you to do all the work I've mentioned: the love-heat, the warmth and all of these things, except perhaps walking out in the forest and looking for trees or rocks. I'd like you to do that and to add that you would like the Moon . . . just say out loud along with whatever else you're saying:

Living Prayer

"I'M ASKING THAT THE MOON MULTIPLY THE EFFECTS OF WHAT I AM DOING IN THE MOST BENEVOLENT WAY."

This will help. [For more on living prayer, see p. xxii].

Supporting Your Feeling Self during the New Moon Cycle

You'd be surprised to know that the Moon is very much involved in the feelings of human beings. This is not something simply stated over the years by astrologers, psychologists and others, including jokesters; this is something that is real. The Moon is intimately involved in each and every one of your individual feelings. That is why whatever you are feeling tends to be heightened by the full moon. Equally you might expect that during the new moon or during those very small visible portions a few days before the new moon or a few days after the new moon, that your feelings wouldn't be as strong, but it's not like that.

You mean the full moon, don't you?

No. I mean those few days before the new moon or the few days after the new moon, which might seem to be the opposite of the full moon. You might then feel that what's going on should be the opposite, that your feelings wouldn't be as strong, but that's not true. What happens during that time is that you're missing the support from the Moon for your feeling self, and sometimes you will get agitated. If you have any nervous conditions or things that are not working in your life, they might get agitated if you haven't built up another way of supporting and nurturing your feeling self in your body.

That's part of the reason we've talked for years and you've heard others talk through Robert [Shapiro] for years about doing this love-heat. It's a good way to nurture and to literally tune up your feeling self. It's especially important during what Speaks of Many Truths has referred to many times in the past—not particularly in public like I'm doing, but I'll pass it on now—as the new moon cycle, which is three days before the new moon, the new moon itself, and three days after the new moon. It's important for you to do this love-heat and this tune-up, or at least make the effort to nurture yourself, because it will help during that time. Be aware that your feeling self, which is vitally important in your creation, in your capacity to create anything, will need extra care no matter who is creating what. So you need to pay special attention to that.

Now, it might interest you to know something. I'm going to give you an example of a Bible reference. Many of you read the Bible or are interested in it. Do you know how it says that God created the Earth in so many days and on the seventh day he rested? In fact, those days have been changed, and we all know that it may have taken this long or that long, but the reference to "on such and such a day, God rested," what that really means—this is a literal creation meaning—is that during the new moon cycle, God rested. Why? Because that cycle in the creation of Earth and all that is on it actually supports all creation, even Creator. That's an interesting thing, and we'll expand on it. I'm just throwing that out there as an interesting factor.

I want you to think about it. You are all creators-in-training here. You have to know when it's time to slow down, go within yourselves and nurture yourselves and one another, and it's particularly important during the new moon cycle. You could say to me, "But, Zoosh, the Creator can do anything." That's true, but one thing the Creator must be, above all other things, is that the Creator must be wise. And it would be a foolish Creator indeed to struggle to do something when it is much easier to do it at other times.

After all, Creator created the Moon for this planet and other moons for other planets to support and nurture the feelings of the planet itself and all the beings on it, because moons are intended to give you the reflected light of the suns that are available. The Sun gives you strength and encouragement—to get out there and do it—and it supports your physical and your mental, whereas the Moon is showing you another side of the Sun's personality focused through the Moon and the Moon's nurturing of that light, literally transforming the sunlight into a gentle, nurturing energy, which nurtures your feelings.

How to Work with the Moon

You all know that sometimes your feelings go wild. Sometimes they need to express themselves. Sometimes it's not appropriate and you can hurt yourself or hurt others, which isn't good, but this doesn't mean that feelings are all bad, because there are other feelings that you love and enjoy. Love itself . . . life can't exist without love, and I'm not just talking about sex. I'm talking about love, nurturing, the binding together of that which wants to be together, all right? So, in short, this brief history of creation mechanics in terms of planetary phenomena is to remind you that Creator acknowledges the truth in this. I'm not going to say, "Well, Creator and I sat down by the pickle barrel and discussed this once," but rather, this is something that I know and that I feel is important for you to know.

That's why there's something else that Speaks of Many Truths has discussed—perhaps not in print before very much, but I could expose you to it now—and that's the full moon cycle. This cycle is, depending upon how sensitive you are as a being, either eight days before the full moon, the full moon itself and eight days after the full moon, or if you're a little less sensitive (not a lot, just a little less), it would be seven days before the full moon, the full moon itself and seven days after. This is a particularly helpful time to create, to do your creations, to bring about projects to fulfillment, to know that you will be nurtured and your feelings will be supported. Granted, during the full moon you might have *all* of your feelings supported, meaning those that are unexpressed and need to be resolved.

So one day before the full moon, during the full moon itself and one day after the full moon, know that if you have feelings inside you that are unexpressed and need to be expressed, then this is probably a good time, if you're physically able, to go out dancing, to dance up a storm. If you're athletic, get involved in your athletic games, or even if you like to do some form of athletics that isn't always considered athletic but has things associated with it that are athletic—such as bowling—then do that. You can even try to throw a ball as far as you can or something like that. This is a good time to do that.

It's probably a good time to be skipping rocks across the water or something like that, or jogging if you can do that. If you can't do that, then swim, do something vigorous, because when you have an intensity of feelings, especially ones you don't quite understand because they are around and emanate from issues that need to be resolved, if you cannot put your finger on it and you don't know what it is, one of the best ways is to, yes, talk to your friends and therapists and counselors and ministers, but also try to do something vigorous, especially something vigorous that is not just associated with your work and is task oriented. Do something vigorous where you can express yourself in a benevolent manner.

LIVING IN HARMONY WITH THE PHASES OF THE MOON

For centuries humans have used the phases of the Moon to guide and inspire them in daily life. When we move in harmony with the Moon and follow her cycle as if it were our own, our lives become a whole lot easier as we become in sync with the planetary energies. Whole books have been written on the Moon and her phases, and what follows is just a brief description of the main lunar phases.

The New Moon (First Quarter): A Creative Time of New Beginnings

Also known as the first quarter, this is when the Moon is new and is the time when new ventures are most likely to be successful. The New Moon is conjunct the Sun now and is associated with new beginnings. This is the best time to begin something new, develop new ideas or turn over a new leaf in some area of your life. Taken literally, this can be a good time for gardeners to plant new seeds and encourage germination. This is an outward looking phase when we benefit from being more actively oriented and doing things.

The Waxing Moon (Second Quarter): A Time of Growth and Expansion

This is a phase of growth—you've planted your new seeds; now watch them grow. Again, this phase is favored for being out there in the world and for working on and developing projects and ideas. It occurs halfway between the New and Full Moon.

The Full Moon (Third Quarter): A Time of Illumination and Completion

As the Moon grows full and opposes the Sun, it is at its most luminous and is an endless source of fascination as people gaze in admiration at the round silvery orb. Although it sounds poetic, the Full Moon is often synonymous with emotional unrest, but only if people have previously suppressed their feelings. At this time, it's impossible to ignore your own feelings, and you can erupt. On the positive side, the Full Moon brings culmination, clarity, completion and understanding. At this point, we start to draw our energies in and we should ideally become less action orientated now and instead focus on our inner needs.

The Waning Moon (Fourth Quarter): A Time to Draw In and Reflect

Here we enter the last phase of the Moon which is ideally a time for reflection, contemplation and a drawing in of our energy and reserves. During the final few days of the lunar cycle —known as the Balsamic Moon, or the dark of the Moon, when the Moon is no longer visible—we really need to be inwardly focused. This is the worst time to try and begin anything new and to do so usually results in failure. We gain from quietly waiting for the Moon to appear again, fresh, new and ready to inspire us again with a new cycle of possibilities.

Contributed by Donna Taylor
donna@scorpiorising.freeserve.co.uk • www.scorpio-rising.co.uk
Tel: 01144 1484 400872 (USA) • 01484 400872 (UK)
For more about living in harmony with planetary energies, see Donna's book,
How to Use the Healing Power of Your Planets. Published by Quantum, priced at £8.99.

These Things Will Help with the First Alignment

So I mention these things, I'm touching on them lightly, because I want you to understand how you can work with the Moon, which supports your feeling self. I want you to consider that the Moon is very helpful to you in creation, and if it is that helpful to you, then you know that you can ask for the Moon, as I said in those words before, to support the activities that you are doing to feel nurtured and to naturally allow the emanation of nurturance to come out of you. This is something you can do to moderate the First Alignment, and I can assure you that if Counsel were standing right here, if he could do that right now, he would say, "Wonderful." Counsel is not an authoritarian person, but rather he is professorial, and sometimes professorial people will read things that might, if read by news people, sound a little less . . . if the news people read it or even a compassionate friend, it would sound very different than when someone reads it as if it were an old fact in the past and just makes interesting reading. You can identify with that. If Counsel were here, he would say, "Wonderful. Do more of that. It can only help."

So I'm not here to rally aid around Counsel; he's not running for president or any political office. But I want to inform you that in order to moderate things to bring about the best possible result in the First Alignment in which you are all living right now, you need to do your metaphysical and spiritual practices. It can only help, and it will help you to feel better. It will help you to feel like you're doing something to benefit things. Remember also that the metaphysical and spiritual practices that you do on a regular basis, that you've been doing that are supportive and nurturing of yourself and others, these things will all help, too. So don't feel as if a sudden ax that you hadn't seen is precipitously falling out of the sky and your heads are metaphorically lying upon the block waiting to be chopped off. But do, rather, consider this to be a prediction of the future of a trend that is being developed right now that you are living in and that to know about it is to your great advantage.

So basically what you're saying is that there is a plan and a process to bring us from the level of violence and discomfort that we're living in now down to a gentle, benevolent time, and if we know about it, then the more gentle and loving we are as people and the easier our own process in it will be.

You could put that in a capsule that way, but what I'm trying to say is that you can't always be loving and gentle. Of course, if you have to go out and split wood for the fireplace, you'll have to pay attention to what you're doing and drop the splitting maul or ax in the right place, and to someone who can't see what you're doing, that will look like you are committing mayhem unless that person comes around the fence and sees that you're just chopping wood for the fireplace. You obviously can't be loving and benevolent in every moment, but still, when you are conducting yourselves in your spiritual or metaphysical practices—depending on how you define those terms—then you can bring about these benevolent influences. The whole point is to *influence* something. If something is going to happen and it's ongoing and it's something that is happening in your time, you may not be able to stop it— nor, if you could look at the end product, would you necessarily want to stop it. But this happens in stages, referred to before as the First Alignment, the Second Alignment and the Third Alignment.

You'll Be Able to Communicate with ETs and Animals

By the time the Third Alignment comes around, everybody will be happy, and when that comes around, I can assure you that you'll be having benevolent inter-actions with ETs and other beings, and perhaps more to the point, you'll be able to communicate in ways . . . maybe not speaking your language while looking at their faces and them speaking your language back looking at your faces, but you'll be able to communicate with the beings right here on the Earth. You'll be able to talk with the animals, and the animals will talk to you and give you all that wonderful advice that, simply by looking at their eyes, you knew was there for you to hear.

No one who lives with a dog or a cat or a horse, or even on a ranch with cows and so on, can deny the fact that you've looked at animals and they've looked at you with their eyes and you could tell that those feelings in those eyes are just like the same feelings you've seen in human-being eyes, which is because they have the same feelings. The function of their feelings is exactly the same as your own. I might add, as you've read before in these pages, that the feelings of all beings everywhere are exactly the same.

You don't always get a clear-cut hint about that with ETs, because ETs may not have eyes as you know them or they may have heavy lids or something over their eyes and you can't really see them—not unlike a person on your planet might wear dark glasses and you wonder what that person is feeling because you can't see, or something like that. Or they might just look completely different. But with animals, you can very often see their eyes and get an idea. You can't always tell with all animals, but certainly you can often tell with the ones you live with.

You said a few years ago that if things didn't straighten out on Earth, a lot of the animals were going to leave, particularly maybe the cows. Are they aware now of this plan, that there is an end in sight for this discomfort?

They were aware of this plan a long time ago. Remember, the animals aren't here to learn anything. They're here to teach and support you, so they were always aware that this was a possibility and was—in a highly complicated and complex society that had billions and billions of human beings—a way to put everybody into general grooves that would lead to something benevolent in the future. The grooves themselves might be somewhat difficult to deal with for a time, but after that time passed, things would be smoother. They always knew that, but it wasn't an intellectual thought; it was an awareness as you might have, like an instinct you can feel.

So many of you have had the experience where suddenly, for no particular rea-son, things feel better and you go on. It's like an instinct; it's a feeling. Then you feel more reassured. You can't put a particular thought into your head and say, "Oh, this happened, and now I feel better," but you feel better, you don't reject it and on you go, and things seem to work better sometimes or at least you feel reas-sured. That's like an instinctual feeling. And they are like that; they don't need to have their heads crammed with facts. So the cows may or may not stick around.

Using Benevolent Creation Mechanics to Create New Foods for the Future

In point of fact, at some point in the distant future, you may not be consuming animals as much as you consume them now. Some of this may be due to the fact that they just don't wish to be here anymore, and some of it may be due to other factors. I will give you a glimmer of the other factors so that you don't feel at sea about what I'm talking about, and that's that you would have other foods at your disposal. There are many new foods that you simply don't know about yet. Granted, some of them come about as a result of genetic research—combining that with this and this with that—and right now that sounds kind of blood-curdling to some of you. Others of you will say, "Well, this is like an adventure."

In recent years, one of the biggest and most popular things that has been going on socially is trying out other people's foods. That's why there has been an explosion of interest restaurants that put out a certain type of food from one country or another country or even a society within that country. That's become very popular. I know right now that the idea of having new foods based on genetics might not make you too happy, but in the future, your youngsters will feel very differently about that. They might like it a lot.

Certainly many of you have had hybrid vegetables, and these are brought about by known and established farming methods. Right now I grant that there are experiments with animals and vegetables and fruits that make you a little upset, and I don't blame you for being upset. But what I'm talking about in terms of "new" foods doesn't really have to do entirely with chemicals and genetics. It also has to do with creation elements. Many people are now learning how to create—not just pound this wood together and add these nails and so on. That's really basic and you're good at that, but rather this is about creating things . . . I know this is going to sound like the Holy Grail to many of you in terms of spiritual and metaphysical thought, but about creating something apparently out of thin air.

Now, you know that Creator, you could say, created the universe out of thin air. That means that at one moment there wasn't anything that could be seen, felt, touched, smelled and so on, and then at another moment—granted, over time as you understand it—there were things like that. So you could say that Creator created things out of thin air. You are here in creator school and you are learning how to create things out of thin air. We've talked a little bit about benevolent magic and living prayer, and you've heard others talk about that through Robert over the past many years in these pages, and a lot of that has to do with understanding further spiritual and benevolent applications of creation. And it will go on, if not through this channel, then through others, about benevolent practices of creation.

Now, why do I use the word "benevolent"? I use the word benevolent because . . . well, look it up in the dictionary. It sounds pretty good. But also it's simple and to the point, and as a word, it is as focused as possible on your immediate moment of time in which each individual is living—meaning that what is benevolent for you now may be completely different from what is benevolent for you tomorrow or five years from now, just as what would be benevolent for you five years in the past might be different than it is today. So the single word "benevolent," when used in living prayer and benevolent creations of benevolent magic . . . simply the use of the word "benevolent" all by itself is sufficient to state the quality of the feeling and the creation that you are attempting to bring about. So you are, granted, in the early days of creation mechanics, and yet as time goes on, you will get more and more instructions in creation mechanics so that you can begin to do what has been largely impossible for you in the past, and that is to apparently create out of thin air that which is not here now.

Can you imagine, just for a practical example, billions of people living on the Earth and scientists and ranchers and farmers working overtime trying to create enough food to feed everybody? And you know it doesn't always happen in the most benevolent way—not everybody gets as much as they need of food and water and other wholesome supports. But what happens as more people begin to practice Benevolent Creation Mechanics? What happens is this: You begin to have experiences that are good, not only for individuals or groups of individuals, but also for many, many individuals—whole societies. Suppose somebody says when practicing these things:

Living Prayer

"I AM ASKING TO EXPERIENCE THE CREATION NOW, TO BE ABLE TO SEE AND HAVE A VISION OF THE NEW FOODS OF THE FUTURE, THAT WHEN CONSUMED BY HUMAN BEINGS, NO MATTER WHAT THE QUANTITY, WILL NURTURE THEM, STRENGTHEN THEM AND GIVE THEM ALL THAT THEY NEED TO LIVE A WONDERFUL LIFE. I WOULD LIKE TO HAVE A VISION OF THAT NOW SO I CAN BEGIN WORKING IN A PRACTICAL, REAL WAY TOWARD BRINGING THESE WONDERFUL FOODS ABOUT."

Suppose that begins to happen? I can assure you it will. Then you will start to see glimmers of this, and eventually you will begin to see that food.

So be aware that the good foods, the new foods, are coming about, okay? New, wonderful goods are coming about, not only through genetics and these other things, but they're also coming about through the spiritual practice of Benevolent Creation Mechanics. Pounding two pieces of wood together or fitting them together nicely—that's it at a basic level. Doing living prayer and benevolent magic . . . this is also training. And Benevolent Creation Mechanics, which is the next step that I'm introducing you to a little bit over time here, is the step after that. Each step is built on the previous one; they are not separate. So good things are coming, and I can assure you that all these things will be happening simultaneously.

Don't think that the First Alignment is some authoritarian regime that crashes and smashes its way through everything. Everything happens at the same time so that all human beings learn, understand and embrace the value of themselves, all other human beings and all beings in general.

Pursuing a Deeper Understanding of
the First Alignment

Speaks of Many Truths, Reveals the Mysteries and Mother of All Beings

October 16, 2003

This article is in response first to Doreen's question and then to the questions of all the other readers who have contacted us with their concerns about the First Alignment article [see chapter 44]. Doreen asks: "Where does free will fit into all this?"

This is Speaks of Many Truths. Heart is more reliable than free will. It is universal. It offers physical evidence when a decision is right for you, and everyone feels the warmth to know it is right the same way. Free will does not have a universal feeling to know what is right, safe and of love for one's self and, of course, for others.

This is Reveals the Mysteries. Now, for a long time, for many years, including years that have really encompassed what could be referred to as the New Age and, to some extent, the length of the metaphysical movement, there has been an ongoing effort by many beings to help people in their spiritual search to move first to clarity of thought, since for the past 150 years or so, thought has been your dominant means to fully understand your world. This does not mean that thought did not exist before that. It's just that before thought became your profoundly universal means of perceiving, you understood your world by religion and, to a degree, philosophy—not meaning the philosophy of philosophers, but rather the philosophy of the culture in which you resided.

The Time of Understanding Your World through Thought Is Ending

So until recent years, when you came into a time when more and more thought was inspired to the point of overwhelm, it was deemed of value to suggest that clarity of thought could allow an individual to make choices based on that clarity and on the thinker's understanding of the functional aspects of thought, of which free will was a portion. One must look at your attempt to understand your world through thought and through a desire to achieve clarity as a step, just as your understanding of your world years ago through religion and cultural philosophy was a step. But now an increasingly large amount of you have noted, especially for the past year or two, how difficult it is to maintain focus of thought on any one thing for a considerable length of time. One might reasonably say, "Well, some of this has to do with distraction." That is certainly true, and yet from my point of view, it is because your time of understanding your world through thought is drawing to a close.

Thought does give you a nice transition to understanding your world through physical evidence. After all, thought in its own right is not in any way physical, and you all know that the evidence that is most appealing—to say nothing of that which is most trustworthy in your own eyes—is physical evidence. Even your television shows these days, your popular dramas, are entirely caught up in stimulating you about physical evidence, and that is not a complete coincidence.

The Universal Language Is Feeling

One might reasonably ask, "What is the most universal language, the most basic means that I can use at any time in order to understand my world and to communicate to any person, place, thing, object, plant or animal?" I include these other categories besides people, because you realize that if you were here to simply learn your lessons by interacting with other human beings, there would be very few animals and plants—only those that would be necessary to sustain life. But look around your world, even in your now time, and you will see that the variety of plants and animals is quite astonishing, and that is to remind you that variety is normal in this universe.

I would say that at its most basic level, the universal language is feeling, and interestingly enough, the most profound level of universal language is also feeling. I will explain why. When you are born as a baby, it doesn't matter how simple or complex the human conversation directed toward you is—your world is entirely based on feeling. You feel this, you feel that; you exercise your lungs in a way that stimulates your feelings and, I might add, often the feelings of those around you. In short, you communicate entirely by physical means. This is not an accident.

Why do you think Creator has laid out that cycle of life for you? After all, there are other means of being born and spontaneously living your life. Look to the animal and plant world. Just because things are the way they are does not suggest some accident. Just because your universe and your world are the way they are, this does not suggest—again, does not suggest—some kind of accidental big bang. Anyone who believes that some big bang took place does not understand the nature of loving creation. Loving creation is gentle; it is nurturing. You all know that when babies are born, they must be treated in a gentle and nurturing way.

So what I am attempting to say to you then (so that you will understand the nature of your next step) is that to use thought and to think in your language or even other languages, should you have that capacity, you're still severely limiting your capacities for communication. But when you use feeling, a great many feelings are communicable simply by you being in the presence of them.

Many of you have been around people who are angry. You did not need them to communicate their anger to you, even if they were standing across the room. You could feel it. You walked into the room and felt what? You felt the tension in your own body. You know that. Some of you have had the opportunity to walk into a room and feel someone exuding great love or friendship or happiness to see you. If you noted your own body, if you were happy to see that person, you would notice a relaxation, perhaps a warm feeling, a feeling you might define as, "Oh, I can be myself now. No pretense is needed here."

The Age of Free Will Is Too Restrictive

Understand this, my friends: The First Alignment article was not meant exclusively to shock you, but it was meant to cause the exact response in those who have written, requested and inquired about free will. Granted, it was telling you about your immediate future, which from my point of view appears to be coming right along. It won't be all fun, but it will ultimately achieve benevolent purposes. But your reaction is important, because it underlines your understanding of your world—meaning the writers, the callers, all those who said, "But what about free will?" That is a perfectly reasonable question. I am thanking you all for bringing to the attention of the other readers that many people want to hang on to thought exclusively as their one and only means to clarity.

In my experience, clarity is achieved when one can interact on a comforting basis by simply being around any other form of life, including a human being, and being able to feel certain benevolent feelings—à la the warm feeling that has been discussed numerous times in these pages. That warm feeling has to do with loving yourself and is always and only felt benevolently by others. It cannot be felt any other way.

So I would say that the age of free will as you understand it is entirely too restrictive. I'm not prepared to say it belongs in the Stone Age, but I am prepared to say it belongs in the Detached Age. After all, clarity of thought does allow a detachment from your physical experience around you. That is not what I recommend generally. How will you change things to be more benevolent for you and others around you? The only way I know to do that is to be actually aware of what is happening around you on the feeling level, and when you feel something that is uncomfortable or when you and others feel something that is uncomfortable, it is important to discover whether this is simply your reaction or whether someone else feels uncomfortable. Then you can inquire of them as to what you can do for them, either to bring about their comfort or to help them simply feel in balance.

You Are Moving into a Time of Material Mastery

You are moving now into a time of material mastery, which has to do with understanding the way your world works. Much of that understanding has been going on mentally for you for many years, but now it's time to move into what the professor might call the "lab stage." It's not sufficient to simply read about it—you have to do it. And many of you have been involved in attempting to apply these thoughts and experiencing the consequences in one way or another. But now it's important to have a shared, common language that you can use that will produce physical evidence in your own bodies that is completely benevolent to you.

Decisions made by focusing on the warmth can be helpful. Communication by focusing on the warmth can be helpful. There are many other aspects of the warmth that can be helpful, and an extensive discussion of that will be found in *Shamanic Secrets for Spiritual Mastery* [coming 2005]. But for these pages now, I will simply say that in order to understand your world now, you need to literally feel. It is not enough to think.

It Comes Down to Soul Agreement

I think the issue is even deeper than free will. Metaphysical teaching is that you create your own reality, and most of the comments I've heard about the First Alignment are that we are being told that we no longer have the ability to choose our reality, that it is being formed around us despite us, whether we feel that we want it or not—that it's happening without our choosing it.

I appreciate your comment, but it doesn't take into account certain factors, not the least of which is soul agreement. Soul agreement allows for the Sun in the sky, the air you breathe—the basics. All souls can agree that unhappiness, discomfort and suffering are things that need to be released, let go of and not experienced on Earth anymore. Because you can agree to that, there has been an attempt to try many different methods to bring about a step toward your natural benevolence, which occurs for all of you as souls incarnating elsewhere on other planets.

However, here on Earth, in this school, it is entirely challenging, so it is like this: In order to create your own reality, there must be soul agreement along many basic lines. You have tried many things, but the trouble with what you have tried is that even though you've come close at times to achieving that next step to moving toward unity and a more benevolent reality, you have never quite gotten there.

Creator Puts Self-Interest upon You to Keep You Alive

So now you're going to try something that you've all experienced in one way or another—meaning a move toward something you were born with. Creator does not put self-interest upon you as a burden; Creator puts self-interest upon you in order that you might stay alive. You breathe, do you not? You eat, and you find in your world that you often have to eat things you'd really rather not eat. Maybe you might love certain animals—"Aren't they beautiful? Don't they have pretty eyes?" and so on—and yet you must live. As many vegetarians know, this comes to you as well, no matter how far you might feel you have moved past the consuming of other life forms. Needless to say, when you consume plants . . . well, they are also life forms. They have dreams, hopes and desires. They perceive—as you would if you were them—that they have families and many other motivations. They have love. They have things that you would define as life.

But here Creator has given you a primary motivation. Sometimes you call it the need to survive, otherwise known as the survival instinct. But in point of fact, Creator does not put it that way at all. Creator would, if Creator spoke English exclusively, describe this as self-interest. It is a profound necessity. Otherwise, considering how difficult life is on Earth, why would anybody even try if you remembered—even in the slightest way—how easy it is everywhere else?

No, you have the survival instinct, which is also known as self-interest. Creator put that in there for all of you so that no matter what else you tried, even if it seemed to be most enlightening and wonderful, if all else failed, you would fall back on self-interest as a means—remember, this is a means; the First Alignment is not the last alignment—to achieve some form of planetwide Earth harmony that you could all live with and feel that your life had been improved upon. And from that point, you could move on to more benevolent states of being, such as the Second and Third Alignments and so on. So creating your own reality is involved on a very intimate basis, and that is why I began speaking about feelings. What more intimate is there?

Create Benevolence Both for Yourself and for Others

It's just that in the many, many, many emails and Web postings we received, people are crying out almost as if they feel they've been betrayed, that they've spent their whole lives studying and learning how they have the ability to create the kind of life they want, and now they see this form being put around them like an encapsulation in which they must live their lives, whether they like it that way or not.

And yet you all know—do you not?—that in any large group, individuality is fostered, nurtured and encouraged (of course, this is done more in some countries and cultures than in others). You are not going to have your identity taken away from you. You are not going to have any of these capacities you've been learning taken away from you. [See Isis's comments in chapter 44.] It is your job to create as much benevolence for yourself and others as you are able to so that this influence is present. This is not intended to be some horrible transition. You are not all going to be lined up against the wall and told, "You will be peaceful to yourself and others, or we will eliminate you." It's not about that.

Rather, it is about a global change taking place now that is intended to bring about complete benevolence by the time the Third Alignment is in effect. Breaking it up into First, Second and Third Alignments is like breaking it up into what one might call chapters of existence; it is a way of creating mental clarity for you to read about it. I'm not going to apologize in any way for the presentation by Counsel, because this was a presentation done by a scholar of the future on another planet—so, of course, this being has no idea what it's like to be an Earth human.

This tells you that the being, Counsel, was addressing certain individuals. Now, you might reasonably ask, "What does that mean, 'certain individuals'?" It means those who are interested in the study of cultures and their evolution. Naturally, many of you who read this magazine are interested in those very topics, since you're attempting to improve the quality of your lives and the lives of those around you, and so benevolence is more of a factor. Certainly, I am interested in that, and I know you are also.

I really must encourage you: Don't give up your teachings on benevolence. After all, it is like this: I do not intend to make a joke here, but when the ships on the sea were traveling by sail and steam engines as a means to move came along, many of them kept the sails for quite a while until the engines were able to reliably move the ships. It is your job as the sailors of Expedition Earth to mount up and continue to steer to the best of your ability by producing benevolence, love-heat/heart-warmth/physical-warmth [see p. 23], love—all of these good things—and increasing their application in order to keep the course to the best of your ability so that the First Alignment does as little damage as possible.

You All Have the One Thing That Keeps You Alive

You understand, as a metaphysical practitioner, you may not have, on the personal level, a great deal of influence over major corporations. You might have some, however, and that influence needs to be pursued as long as it is loving but not against. This is not about politics, about good guys or bad guys; you all are in this together. How many times have you heard that? And you all are going the same place. The reason the First Alignment is coming about is to do something that I've been hearing about now for years, and that is, "When are we going to get there?"—meaning that you're tired of the voyage and you want to see some progress. Then Creator says, "Well, you all have one thing in common that keeps you alive," meaning Creator knows you've got a lot of things in common, but you all have one thing in common that keeps you alive and living on planet Earth, and that is self-interest, which you in your time like to call survival instinct.

Maybe you'd better fall back on that and get started on that as a means to improve your world. Over time, given a desire toward heart, the evidence of that will be demonstrated by your actions and by their effect on others. This tells you that what you do must be benevolent so that it affects others only benevolently. After all, it is Creator who will allow the First Alignment, and I assure you that Creator's doing that and will demonstrate it by your benevolent interactions, allowing the Second Alignment and so on. Creator, however, is not the boss. It's one thing to allow, support, sustain and nurture. It's another thing to do it for you. Creator always wants people to do it for themselves.

I believe you can do it, so don't give up. But for those of you who are ready to take the next step—and I've been hearing for so many years that so many of you are—take it into feeling, take note of the love-heat. And remember, the love-heat is intended not only to serve your own nurturing needs but to serve the needs of others, to help you make decisions that do not require any thought and will be always be right. It can even help you do things along the line of creation mechanics—meaning being influential in the physical world with that which appears to be impossible to do. In other words, it is benevolent, loving magic as it appears that improves the quality of life for all beings.

Counsel's Scholarly Approach Was Very Matter-of-Fact

Okay, there's one more issue, and then I think we will have the very emotional response from the many people who have contacted us pretty much covered.

Let's just say "the response from people who were feeling disappointed or intimidated." After all, Counsel's scholarly presentation was very matter-of-fact. If you were taking history in college and your professor stood up in front of the class and spoke about medieval architecture as it demonstrates the needs of the people's desire to protect themselves, it might sound very abstract indeed to the average student, although the professor, since he or she is teaching about it, is probably very interested in the subject and so is presenting it. But it might simply sound like what? Facts.

Well, Counsel was talking about something that, from Counsel's point of view, were facts in the distant past in a culture he found interesting on some planet far, far away. And the reason I'm chuckling is that you do this now in your own classrooms. So how about this: Do any of you have younger brothers or sisters? When is the last time you explained the facts to them? How about new employees at your workplace? I'll bet you've explained the facts to them too, although it may not always be as rigid as it sometimes sounds, eh? Just remember that when you "explain the facts" to people, it often sounds very authoritarian to them.

People Are Being Controlled in U.S. Society Today

The part the largest group of people is strongly disturbed about is that for many years now, everything we've ever read about the shadow government, the secret government or the sinister secret government has been about manipulation and control. Some of the things that were talked about seem like part of what was considered the New World Order in the negative sense—ID chips, being told what you'll work at or what you'll do, that loss of freedom of one's desires. A lot of people are addressing that issue.

There are a lot of questions in your statement. I will address as many as I can, and you can cover them all later if you want to. I will simply say that ID chips are perfectly normal on every other planet, and I grant that in the beginning, they will not be perfection here, but they will be perfected in time.

Now, as for people being "told" where they'll go and how they'll work—that never occurs in the First Alignment, not once, although you might reasonably look around your society now. Do you think that in your society now people are never told where they must go and where they must do work? If you think that, you are naive to the extreme. Granted, in your culture, in the United States, this happens less often in your awareness.

But there are many people now being told what to do and how to do it in your society, even in the United States, and I'm not just talking about people who are in prisons. I'm also talking about people who work in sweatshops or even people who simply do not see the broad horizon for themselves. Either their culture or other people's presentations of themselves encourage them to go into some field of endeavor that may not be what they want. Maybe they want to go on to college, maybe they want to be a doctor or a physician of some specialty, maybe they want to be a therapist, maybe they want to be an athlete—who can say? Many times people are discouraged to the extreme for going for what they want to go for, as you might say. That's why stories are so popular in your culture about people who were able to succeed in their chosen profession "against the odds." How many times have you heard that?

So I could hardly say that in the United States . . . even with a culture that professes to be free, though I think it's not quite as free as you'd like it to be, very often people are told where to go, what to do and how to do it. And many of you have noted that this is becoming more so lately, though that is something that will pass in time. Now, in other cultures, in other places, such apparent indentured servitude or even bondage is normal. I'm not saying it's healthy; I'm not saying it's good. I'm saying that if you believe that people are not being told what to do and how to do it, it is a naive point of view.

The Goal of the First Alignment Is World Peace

I think it's important to recognize that the First Alignment will not be any worse than the situation you have now, and it will be considerably better because . . . consider the goal of the First Alignment, which is world peace—meaning not just world peace (I like the example in the original article) where you can leave your house unlocked, where you can be sure your children will be able to get to school without being harmed, where you can leave your car unlocked, won't need keys, can go out to your car and press a button and start it. In short, peace means that you will feel safe and that you will be safe to live your life in ways that are benevolent. By benevolent, I mean live your life in ways that do not harm others, and any harm you do to yourself will be discouraged.

So I feel it is really important for you to recognize that the goal—I might add, not just the goal of the First Alignment, but the achievable goal of the First Alignment—is going to improve the quality of all your lives and in such a significant way that many of you cannot even imagine it. I feel that the purpose is worth the effort. By effort, I mean self-interest, although it might seem to many that to be "self-ish" is really just another term for survival instinct. Some of you sacrifice your lives—say, in battle—so that others of the side you're supporting can live. I'm not saying that this is a bad thing; I'm rather saying that it is not the intention of the First Alignment that such battles ever be fought again. What if the First Alignment can eliminate war? That's its purpose, amongst other things. What's so bad about that?

Attachment to Dates Makes You a Slave of Time

To sum up, I think the disappointment and the comments from all the people . . . it's like everyone had the feeling that by 2012 there would be peace and happiness, that we'd be out of the molasses of the third dimension, and now it's suddenly being put off another fifty years.

By everyone, you mean the same everyone who fifty years ago thought that in ten years everything would be wonderful? You cannot be attached to time. Don't be attached to any date—ever! It is not that time rules you. Rather, it is that by what you do, you change the time in which you live. You must apply benevolent practices for yourselves, and those who do tend to experience a more benevolent life. It has been our intention in these pages to give you ideas, suggestions, thoughts and homework that produce feelings so you can understand and experience more to improve the quality of your life in benevolent ways. If you feel attached to a date, you will literally be saying, "I am a slave of time. Time has absolute rule over me, and whatever occurs in the future is entirely based on dates and times."

I think you have the capacity to be material masters, spiritual masters and masters of heart. Masters of heart are beings who know and understand who they are, where they belong, what the most benevolent place is for them to be and why, based entirely on how they feel with physical evidence—not some vague feeling, but a clear physical feeling that feels good to them, such as this warmth that is identifiable as being the foundational element of applied material mastery. So my advice to you is, don't be attached to dates. Coordinate your own time and understand that in the future, you will not use any calendar at all except day and night.

This is Mother of All Beings.

Well, we can talk about "don't be attached to time" all we want, but all the spiritual teachers taught that there were three waves of awakening, that we were going into a different vibration that would be benign and benevolent, and then it didn't happen. Now, suddenly, it's going to happen fifty years later. What happened? What did we fail to do? What did the dark forces do that caused us not to move? Something happened.

What happened is that you as a population decided to do something that parents often do. How often do parents tell their children that they wear them down when they, the children, really want something that the parents don't think is good for them? So you say, "Okay, you can do it, but be careful." That's what happened. You decided that you wanted to explore as many extremes as possible and be able to experience an interconnectedness. But as is not untypical in such requests, in the result—not in the process—the main extreme that was ultimately unworkable was your inability as individuals to communicate to one another how you were feeling about something, and that was because of your different cultures. Just think how many times, even in a situation where people speak the same language, misunderstandings take place. You love the variety, and yet you could not express all of the variety that you desired in recent times while your world expanded its communication capacities, and the communication, although seeming to be better, became worse and worse.

Experience Is More Beneficial Than Gathering Facts

One can learn and study a great deal about someone else's culture, but if you do not actually travel to that place, you do not really feel the nature of that culture, nor are you reminded on a daily basis how much you are alike. So the difficulty that occurred is not that this one or that one derailed your desire, but rather that the confusion factor became profound in the misunderstanding that learning about others somehow brought you closer together. Those who travel understand this completely. You can read all you want about another place, even some place in your own country, the United States, but if you don't go there and don't interact with the people there, all you have are what? Facts. Facts can be useful, they can be interesting, they can prepare you, but it's nothing like actually being there and knowing and feeling your reactions and feeling the way the people are around you.

This is what derailed things temporarily, and that is why many beings—through this channel and perhaps others—have been attempting to remind everybody for the past few years about feeling and the physical evidence of feeling and how to apply it. Because if you get too far away from that kind of feeling, it doesn't make any difference how clearly you mentally understand something. You will simply get too far away from, let's say, your center to experience whatever was planned, no matter how intricate the plans were or how benevolent. You cannot be a portion of them until you improve your . . . not communication, but you need to improve your communion with other people, and it would be good to improve it with other beings as well, meaning plants and animals. But first and foremost, you need to improve your communion with other people. That's what happened.

No One Will Be Left Behind

So we're taking these extra fifty years to move from thought to feeling and to learn communion?

No. Maybe you can do it in a couple of weeks. How will you do that?

Focus on feelings instead of thoughts?

No. I speak to you, yes? But you are representative of whom?

The readers.

More than that.

Well, in this case, all humans on the Earth.

That's right. You are representative of all humans on Earth. It will take as long as it takes all humans on Earth to accomplish this. You understand, suppose we said, "The cutoff date is fifty years." What does that mean? What happens if in fifty years, only so many of you have it? What do we do with the others? Do we just shovel them into a pile and say, "You get to stay behind?"

No. We extend the date.

That's right. Everyone comes along. No one is left behind.

Well, that's the good part.

That's right. And it takes as long as it takes for people to do it. You don't just wait for it to happen. If you wait for it to happen, you will wait as long as it takes. You have to do it, as everyone knows. If the cows need milking, what do you do? Just wait until the milk leaks out? You have to milk them. They can't reach around and do it themselves very well unless they have a calf nearby. If you have to shovel the snow, you don't just wait until springtime comes to melt it. You have to do it!

Love-Heat Is Your Natural Language

Then what people have to do is feel their feelings and learn to feel the feelings of others, right?

What you all have to begin with is the love-heat—everyone on Earth, not just the readers of these books. But it is not authoritarian. It is that the love-heat is universal. All human beings can feel it. All animals feel it now, as do all plants. So there's a lot of support. That's what you're born with, and this might surprise you: All babies, human babies, can do it right now. One of the reasons babies cry is that their feelings are not understood. Sometimes the parents do understand, but generally, the parents just make their best guess on the basis of what they know. It doesn't make them bad parents. Babies all can do the love-heat. What I'm saying is that you are all born with it, and I don't mean just babies of now; I mean every one of you alive on this Earth right now was born doing that, so you all have it. It's not something you learn. That's why the technique to learn it is not that complex. It's not something you learn; it's something you remember.

Could one say that we're in school and being able to feel the love-heat is graduation?

No. Being able to feel the love-heat is the beginning of having the capacity to return to your natural language. Your natural language does not involve much in the way of words. It primarily involves feeling, though you can interact using words. Don't throw out your languages. If you could make decisions about anything in your lives, from the simplest and most mundane to the most complex and involved, and every single time the decision would be right, would you not want to use that method?

Absolutely.

That's why the love-heat is the beginning. That is just one application of it. That's why we in the spirit world like to say that it's basic—because it's something you're born with. It's not something that you struggle and learn and learn and struggle, and then you learn it and that's it—that's graduation. No. You're born with it, and you need to remember it. That's all. You don't have to learn it from scratch. But you have to learn it by utilizing its own tools, meaning you can read about it as a means to understand it, but you still can only do it by utilizing the physical means to feel it. You feel the love-heat by feeling. You don't feel it by thinking, and even those who can feel it in any moment, if they start to think, the love-heat usually goes away. That's why I say that you can feel the love-heat by feeling; you cannot feel it by thinking.

Love-Heat Aids Communion between Humans

So what happened was that we didn't learn to feel the love-heat, and that's why we can't commune with one another?

You don't have a shared common language. You could, after all, have feelings of camaraderie and friendship even if you don't speak someone else's language. You could both just sit down for a moment or pause. You could each go into the love-heat. You would feel it from each other. There is a reaction. One feels it more. You both do. Then you would know there is a friendship between you two, even if you cannot communicate. You do hand gestures and so on, and you eventually pick up some of each other's words.

I'm talking about what might happen today, not in the future. But if you only have hand gestures and nothing else, it's not enough. It can be funny, it can be comical, but sometimes it can be tragic. There needs to be more, and the "more" is something you were born with. You cannot abandon the things you were born with. You do not abandon breathing. You do not abandon eating. You do not abandon dreaming. But because of the culture, meaning the way you are brought up these days, many of you—not all, but the vast majority of you now—do abandon some of your natural selves when you fit into your society. You must know how to now make decisions that are right for you and to know how you have to begin by feeling the love-heat. Even though you might feel it in your intestinal area, you will generally feel it in your solar plexus or anywhere across your chest. It doesn't have to be just in your physical heart. We call it the love-heat because it is associated with love and self-love and, in the larger picture, the love of all beings. It's enough, eh?

Very good.

Why Wait 100 Years? Use Benevolent Magic to Change the First Alignment Now!

Counsel's Teacher
August 30, 2004

I am Osaiowa [phonetically: Oh-say-eye-oh-wa]. I am Counsel's guide and teacher.

Welcome!

Counsel is a history student, in temperament not unlike students of your time. When students are informed of historical truth, they often become what you call—I've studied your terminology a bit—a know-it-all. But in his case, speaking for him, Counsel was merely reading a book—not like your books, but he was reading. There was no interpretation on his part.

I offer no apology for Counsel, but rather the simple explanation and reminder to students and others that students almost always, when they discover the facts of anything, are unable to withhold those facts from those whom they wish to enlighten or, in some cases, impress. So I'd like to invite the reader: You know facts. Many of you have studied healing techniques and have wisdom and knowledge that is benevolent to yourself and others. When someone rings the bell at the church and it's not the call to prayer, sometimes it's the call for an emergency: "Come, need help." Don't blame the messenger. It's up to you now.

You Are at a Crossroads: Act Now

You have been guided for years that you would be called to perform to the best of your ability all the benevolent things you have learned. Many of you have learned these things for years and years and years. Sometimes these things can be done only with one other individual; other times they can be done in prayer, in benevolent ceremony or in some other way to benevolently influence the outcome of individual, societal and global events.

If what you do is on a one-to-one basis, convert it to prayer and energy, and request that benevolence become the way of life in the hearts of all beings. Just because you have heard others do this does not mean that your voice will not add to the cumulative energies to support benevolence. Thinking it is helpful. Saying it out loud is much more effective. You live in a physical world. You are in the physical world to study the effects of physicality on beings. I am asking that you do what you can do now. Your world is at a crossroads.

You can allow your future as read to you by Counsel to develop unimpeded as it was read, or if you choose to influence and support benevolence, you can change what is read. I'm going to give you a challenge. It's up to you whether you choose to ignore it or do what you can now. Many of you who were upset about what Counsel read to you reacted only on the basis of the face value of what you read. Some of you were quick to see that this was a clarion call, and you began doing the benevolent and warm-hearted and well-intentioned training that you have available. For some of you, it was prayer. For other things, other times, other places, yes, prayer is good. And even now, prayer can be good.

For you, though, I recommend the energies that prompt you to feel safe, secure, loved, and that bring into your life that love and happiness to whatever degree they manifest. I'm going to ask you and challenge you to change that which Counsel read about. We are in your future, but it is our job as historians not to speak about some rigid past but rather to prompt those who are in the past, from our time, to change, to wake up, to pay attention and to understand that violence begets violence and that love begets love—for you to begin in some nurturing way to feel love for yourself and to ask that others feel love for themselves and feel their common ground between one another.

How many times have you heard this? If you've done it before, do it again and encourage others to do it too, if you would. The crossroads is that not enough people are involved in doing these things. There needs to be more. Don't ask people to do it at the point of a sword. This is not a religion; it is not a political movement. It is the true nature of all of you.

Send Your Energy around the World

Love, allowance, encouragement, nurturance, support, happiness, joy and, in short, benevolence—this is your true nature. You may not be able to experience your true nature in the complete sense in your lifetime, but you can make the effort. I am not going to teach you what to do. You know what to do. You do different things; do them more, if you can. Many of you are doing all you can. If you don't know what to do, then I will give you suggestions. This is what to do:

The water runs in rivers; it travels, it becomes warm and goes to the sky. It comes down in raindrops all over the world. Trees have roots, and sand blows freely . . . and powdered Earth as well—you call it dirt, eh? If you feel you are doing all you can, then this is what to do: Bring a little soil in, soil as finely grated and powdery as you can find where you are. Don't dig down deep; dust from the road is fine. Keep it in the rooms where you do your benevolent work or say your prayers. And once a week, take it outside, especially if there's a breeze, and stand upwind (of course). Then throw it into the air.

Some of it will travel. If there is no wind where you live, then place it on the ground, perhaps on a road where it will be picked up and moved from place to place. Some of you live near water—rivers, lakes, streams, oceans. Go out near the water and say your prayers, do your energies. Act as if the water is someone you are working on. Reach toward the water and touch it the way you would touch a patient or touch a person you were working on. Don't prod and poke it; just reach. If you are onshore, imagine reaching—reach out your hands and imagine them extending out into the water and touch it or caress it. Feel the energy flowing through you.

The water will travel. It will go places you are unable to go. The more of you who do this, the more the energy will pass around the world. You all drink water, it passes through your bodies; it rains on you sometimes or you take your bath. This work is not intended to coerce but rather to awaken.

Authoritarianism Is All around You

The crossroads you are at now is very simple: Either there will be a gradual benevolent coming together of all nations and pseudonations (that which you call corporations), with everyone discovering their common ground, and everyone will decide what common interests you all have, how you can help one another, how you can do business, work, enjoy your work, improve your work, buy things you want—in short, improve the quality of your life. Or you can live and turn your back and pretend greed does not exist—in which case the First Alignment will continue and it will be harsh at times, sometimes to unexpected people. People whom you would expect to be the bosses will be dispersed, not allowed to be of influence, as some greater giant corporation takes over. If they do not agree, then they will be dispersed so they cannot influence and, as you would say, harm the corporation.

I know you do not want this authoritarianism, but it is all around you—not just in your United States, but in other countries as well. This is partly because people who are authoritarian are impatient. They want what they want now; they're not willing to wait any longer, and they believe with all their feelings and thoughts that what they want will be good and that any resistance is getting in the way of a good thing. They are very often narrow-minded because their goal is all they see and they do not see the harmful destruction in how their goal impacts others. They have only their goal in mind, and they believe that their goal will make everyone happy.

Of course, if you hurt everyone along the way toward accomplishing your goal, even if you do accomplish it, people will not forget their pain, their loss and their suffering. And no matter how wonderful your goal might be in your own mind, it will not be accepted or loved or appreciated. It's not just the goal; it's how you bring it about.

Why Wait for the Third Alignment?

If you do nothing, then what Counsel, my student, read to you will happen. There will be the First Alignment, which will be a little rough, and you're going through it now. But it can be altered, it can be influenced. It can be prompted to be more benevolent, as I've said. Then there will be the Second Alignment, as was stated in the previous document. Then, ultimately, the Third Alignment will come.

Why wait for the Third Alignment? Let the Third Alignment happen first, in which the benevolence is felt, appreciated, encouraged and nourished and nurtured in all beings. You can make the Third Alignment first by what you do. You may not see it happen overnight, but you will see little things that will improve.

Reach out. Find others who are doing things, and influence the elements of Earth to the best of your ability, for they will flow. They will fly. They will travel around the world and touch all human beings. And then, in time, things will get better for you and they will get better for succeeding generations. I know that's what you want.

So from your point of view, what he saw is a possible reality?

What he read? He didn't see it; he read it. Granted, our kind of books allow him to see something that occurred. However, it is our job . . . he is not fully aware of that yet. He is a student; he hasn't graduated, eh? He is not fully aware— although a little more aware now [laughs]—but he is not fully aware that it is our job to influence history, to bring about more benevolent and mutually desired goals by all beings in any historical time from our frame of reference. One historical time from our frame of reference is your culture, your civilization, which is destined to return to its state of benevolence, but can do so quickly (meaning in a shorter time than a hundred, two hundred years) or can do so slowly, with continued suffering. I hope you choose to do so quickly.

Why not have benevolence sooner? Why wait a few hundred years? Don't just give up. I don't expect you to campaign politically and march down the street with signs. If you do so, that is up to you. That's fine. But I do want you to do the benevolent things you can do with the people as you work with them—the people who choose and want to come to see you or join you in prayers and ceremonies of benevolence—to do what you can do. But if you do not have many people who come to see you, then do it with the rain. Do it with the clouds, do it with the wind, do it with the rain that falls into the rivers, the lakes and the streams. Or do it with the rivers, lakes, streams and seas. And your work, your nurturance, will travel far and wide. That's what I recommend.

Can you say something about yourself?

This is about you. Ask all questions about you and the Earth first. If you are done asking, then I will talk a little bit about myself, but only when you are done with that. Because when I'm done talking a little bit about myself, I will say goodbye.

You Will Know You Have What You Need by the Benevolent Feeling Within

So we have an incredible opportunity now to create a more benevolent future. How many people does it take? How many do we have to make aware of this?

I cannot give you a number, because some people's work is more influential and impactful than others. It depends just as much on "who" as on "how many." It could be a greater number, or it could be a smaller number. It depends on "who," "how," "when," you see? There are variables. You have done well to print Counsel's historical reading. I personally do not feel that there was any harm in reading it. However, there needed to be time for people to absorb it, to think about it, to be repelled from it. And now there's been time to let it simmer, eh? As you all know, the best soup takes time to simmer so all the flavors can be mutually shared, and then it tastes better.

I'm not saying it tastes better—Counsel's soup, eh? But now is the time you can act so that further authoritarianism . . . which will come if you do nothing, will become increasingly a daily activity, not just from political people, but even in families and among individuals. You will feel it in your own individual body, an urgency to demand that things function in some way that feels better. But even when that better thing comes, you will be dissatisfied because what you want materially is very often a substitute for what you actually need materially.

You will know when you have found or experienced what you actually need because of the benevolent feeling within you. Yes, I know I'm using the word "benevolent" a lot, but I want to underscore this feeling that is more than a thought. It is more than an experience. It is a daily moment-to-moment physical feeling that you are influenced by within yourself, and as your feelings naturally radiate, that can only affect others in ways they will welcome. I'm not just talking about benevolent magic; I'm talking about the work on the Earth.

I am telling you about this because I'm feeling that you will print this and then your job will be over, aside from doing the benevolent work that you've been trained to do in the ways I have suggested. And since you are near the sea [in Hawaii, where this channeling took place], you can do that sooner, not later. I know that's not what you're asking, but I want to make it clear personally, as well as on a larger scale.

Everyone Can Do Benevolent Magic

A chiropractor could go sit on a rock near a river. He or she might consider, "What would I do? What places would I press in a body? What supporting areas would I press and encourage or move in someone's physical body to bring about a more relaxed, safe, nurtured, encouraging feeling in that body?" (Chiropractors do think this way, even if their profession doesn't always give them the results in patients that they would like.) So while you (the chiropractor) are thinking about this near this body of water, reach out toward the body of water—you don't have to stand in it and touch it; you can if you like, but you can sit on a bench or a rock near the body of water and reach out toward it—and imagine you're touching the body of water as a patient. Move your hands around until you get to the exact position that feels right to you, and then do those gestures.

People will think you're doing something in the air. Keep a friend nearby so that he or she can deflect curiosity and questioners from you. If you want to offer an excuse, just say that you are practicing a new technique or anything else you want to say. And if one chiropractor does this, what if twenty of them did it? What if fifty did it? What if a hundred did it? And there are other things, other professions. I picked that one because both you and Robert [the channel] know a chiropractor whom you like.

But there are any other number of things to do. For example, suppose you are a carpenter. Suppose someone asks you to come over to his house because the door is not opening well, not as well as it used to—it sticks in places. So you fix the frame; you shave down maybe a little bit on the door, and the door works well. You tell him there might be some problem with the house, but what you've done with the frame around the door will hold for a time. This is just an example—I do not claim to be of that profession. What would you do, as a carpenter? Maybe you would go sit by a stream and you would use your tools in your imagination in the air, just reaching out into the air as if you were doing something that makes something better, that makes it work better—something that is broken that you can make work better.

Imagine doing that while you move your hands in the air sitting next to that stream, as you get involved in it, acting it out—not jumping up and down and sawing vigorously, but gently acting it out as you sit there. That will radiate into the stream. Make sure you complete what you are doing so you have the feeling of satisfaction of a job well done. You will be able to remember when you've done things like that. You can remember this as well. If you are shy or there are other people around and you are concerned people will think you are strange, then just remember it as a thought—not necessarily all the talk that went on there, but just remember doing the work and the feeling of satisfaction of the job well done. It will help.

You might be an office worker. Perhaps you file papers. You get a big stack of papers to file every day and it's a bit annoying, but at the end of the day, you do see that all those papers are filed. You can see the effect of your work. Do the same thing. Find something that you have done or that you do regularly, for which at the end of the day or at the end of the job, there is satisfaction. The importance is to do something, and if you want to, at the end of the memory or the feeling, you can simply say, "That was a job well done." You'll probably get a good feeling, and it's the good feelings that radiate out of you. Feelings radiate out of you, and that good feeling will radiate out of you right into the water, go on downstream and influence other beings, other rocks, stones, water, rain, trees, humans, animals. It may be a small thing, but it all adds up.

Don't assume that because you are not in the healing arts, you cannot have good feelings next to bodies of water or good feelings out in the pasture someplace where the wind is blowing as you're having those good feelings and memories of happiness. And those good feelings are just dispersed into the air and carried where they might be needed.

Oh, that's brilliant. I was thinking narrowly in terms of saying benevolent magic, but you're broadening it to include all humans and their feelings.

Why keep it to a select few?

Work with the Earth to Disperse Your Energy

Certainly, if you can do benevolent magic or living prayer, that's fine. But everyone very often has feelings of satisfaction and happiness. I know you get feelings of disappointment and unhappiness, and you can do nothing to prevent those feelings from radiating. In fact, you have to let them radiate so Mother Earth can disperse them. She can take them with her winds and rains and water, and disperse them so they are not concentrated in you and others. That's why your body functions the way it does. You take water in, you take food in; it flows through your body and nurtures you, then it passes out of your body, taking that which no longer serves you, and it takes that away. It's a reminder that that which comes in flows out and through all beings.

Know that feelings are the same. When you get unhappy ones, the wind will take them. If you are miserably unhappy . . . perhaps you've already cried and you can't seem to get over it. Go out in nature, if you can, or simply go someplace where it's breezy, and ask the wind to take some of your unhappiness away and disperse it in the air so that it has very little effect on others. The Earth is big; the air is massive. Your unhappiness, as overwhelming as it is for you as an individual, when it is dispersed throughout the whole planet, it will not affect anyone in any overwhelming way, but it will help you. Let the Earth help you.

You also can help the Earth simply by having a happy memory of something that was a job well done—though not a happy memory of revenge, because people were harmed, including you in your own way. I will not speak too much about your morals and ethics, but try to keep it a happy memory, even if it's just something simple: a job well done in that moment or a feeling of satisfaction that you not only completed the job but did it well, felt good about it.

Remember it. Hold the memory of the feeling (meaning, "Job well done; I feel good"), remember that good feeling. Let the wind, the water, the air take that and disperse it, and they will help to compensate for all the unhappiness Mother Earth disperses as well. If by doing things like that you can simply allow Earth to balance all of this unhappiness that's being exuded by many people, it will stimulate something. Even though these terms do not necessarily follow one another, it will stimulate greater patience.

Mother Earth Helps Relieve Your Unhappiness

I do not expect you to give up your goals and desires, but I am hopeful that you will learn to work toward them in ways that are benevolent for you and others. Notice how you apply the techniques to achieve your goals. What consequences do they have on others? Your goals must be achievable by benevolent means to the best of your ability. If they cannot be achieved that way, then perhaps it would be good to redefine your goals and see if they can be achieved more benevolently with that redefinition. Then those goals will be worthy of you and, I assure you, will be blessed by beings whom you admire and love and whose love you wish to have.

God is not vengeful; God is not impatient. Yes, human beings can become vengeful and impatient, and sometimes they put those qualities on God, but that is not the God I know.

By God do you mean the Creator?

Yes, but I'm talking to people beyond you, Melody, who consider God to be God, not to be Creator. Do you understand? They know that God is Creator, but they have other names. Now, I am encouraging you to feel your good feelings and remember them as well as to honor your unhappiness. If you're unhappy, perhaps there is something you can do about it. If you're unable to do something about it or you are grieving over a great loss, let the wind blow some of it away, let the rain wash some of it away. You'll feel better, and it won't harm others.

Mother Earth rains, has wind to keep herself comfortable. She has learned that any feeling that is overwhelming in one place and too much for that place, when that feeling is dispersed over her entirety, it has little unhappy effect. And then there might be other parts of her body that are cheerful and happy and celebrating life. When that becomes overwhelming, she simply disperses it all over her body with the wind, rain, water and other ways, and that balances the unhappiness. You are made up of Mother Earth and the spark of Creator in your personalities. You can do the same.

Go out and allow Earth . . . if you can, if it is safe, let the rain sprinkle on you a little bit. You don't have to go out in a gale, but let the rain sprinkle on you a bit sometimes. It will literally anoint you with its natural joy. I know that sometimes that's inconvenient, so then let the wind go breezing through your hair. You have often wondered, "What is the purpose of hair?" Yes, it keeps the sweat out of your eyes sometimes, and yes, it is beautiful, but your hair grows out of the top of your head, as well as on other parts of your body, and it is intended to interact with the wind, to release things from your body that you cannot release because they are not in your conscious mind. They are feelings—or perhaps from your doctors' point of view, they would be subconscious feelings.

Go out and have a dip in a lake or a stream or a river. Let the water take the feelings from the hairs and from the skin of your body. Let the wind just blow through your hair sometime. I know it will get messed up—you can brush it later. And it will blow things out of your body and you'll feel better. Yes, you can wear your goggles over your eyes if you want to, or you can enjoy it. Let the natural wind do this, not just by moving quickly down the road in a vehicle.

The natural wind comes by Mother Earth as you simply stand or sit somewhere. It blows through your hair and takes that which is not possible to express, that which you don't know about, that which you forgot about. Hair takes a long time to grow out. In some parts of your body, it is permanent; in other parts, it takes a long time to grow out. You will have forgotten some old hurt, but as the wind blows through your hair, the wind will release the pain of that old hurt and take some of it away and disperse it.

Achieve Your Goals More Benevolently

If we can just make it known to people that all of the groups who come together for all kinds of reasons—spiritual teachers in workshops, yoga groups, the Girl and Boy Scout groups, musicians, the possibilities are unlimited—could radiate their happy energies and help change the world. They don't realize how helpful that would be.

Yes, but other times they do. And not just with the people who read New Age literature, but many times church groups go out on the land just for fun or for a trip or to enjoy nature, and they might sing, they might dance, they might pray and feel wonderful. If that causes them to feel wonderful, those good feelings go out and influence people benevolently as well. It's the good feeling, the happy feeling, the warm feeling, the enjoyment-of-life feeling that truly influences, supports, sustains and helps to bring about balance. And the greater the balance, the more you are likely to be able to be patient. It is patience and moving slowly toward your goal that allows you to see if the means you are applying to achieve your goal are benevolent or are harmful.

If you rush toward your goal, you may rush past something or someone who is harmed by the means of achieving your goal and never know it. If you take your time, you will be able to learn the exact techniques that feed and nurture people, not just as you observe them through your goal-oriented eyes, but as they tell you that it's working for them or it isn't, freely offered. This is not you asking, "Don't you love my goal?" which they may, but you asking, "Are you all right with what we are doing? Could we be doing this in some better way where you would feel better? Please be honest with me because what you tell me will help me to be able to apply techniques that will be more nurturing and loving to all people, and this I want to do. My goal is worthy, and I want it to be worthy of you and all people by the goal itself and the techniques I use to achieve it, helping you to feel good."

Be honest and encourage others to be honest with you, and you will find new ways to achieve your goal. Let your goal be worthy of you and those who are affected by it. And then you will find that Creator will give you the blessing. Very often many of you do not talk to Creator too much until after your life—talking to Creator directly or perhaps to angels or others. And you will find out how being patient might have been better. Why wait for the Third Alignment? Be patient. Make certain your goal is worthy of you and worthy of others, and thus it will be worthy in Creator's eyes as well.

Build from a Foundation of Agreement

Isn't that one of the problems we're facing now, that those who want to control the Earth are impatient and want it all now?

They see something they want, and they feel that if that thing is achieved, then they will be happy, and they convince themselves that others will be happy, too. And sometimes they are correct, but that is rarely the case. Usually there needs to be consensus, meaning that not everyone will be able to agree on everything. There are only a few things that all people can agree on, but over time, as you serve those things diligently and support benevolent goals and life for all beings, then you can use that as a foundation and say, "We know we all need to be clothed when it is cold and fed when we are hungry and housed so we are safe if we wish it." In short, you can agree on various things.

Build from that foundation of agreement, and make sure first that all beings agree. If they don't, then adapt your agreements on a broader level so that all beings can agree—for example, "We know we want to live life happily and we know we want to be able to eat and enjoy our meals." In short, keep it broad. Learn how to find out what you like and, if you like, what you don't like: "We know we don't want to suffer."

The more you can discover these things and allow Earth's natural elements and the good things you can do for yourself and others, the more you will become patient, the more you will feel the value of life, the more you will want to be in your life (not just want it to be over), the more you will feel good about what you're leaving behind for those who will follow.

ETs and You Are More Alike Than Different

Now I will say a little bit about myself: I live in a time millions of years in advance of your time. I did not live on your planet but in a distant star system. We have something like a university here, as you understand it, but it is a university that welcomes all ages, all peoples everywhere, all beings who wish to visit. It is my job to benevolently influence to the best of my ability and to inspire people who have suffered in the past to achieve greater happiness through any unified means that can help them to experience better lives. I have learned some techniques in this, but I have also learned truth in this.

It is true, from my experience, that all beings want to be happy. They want their loved ones to be happy and they want them to be able to have happiness when they want it. It is an oversimplification, I grant, but this is something I know to be true. You will find that such desires are natural, even when you fly beyond your planet to meet peoples from other places. You will enjoy the adventure, and when you get to those other places, yes, the people will be different. But in temperament, they will be more like you than they are unlike you, regardless of what they say, with the exception of the fact that they won't experience discomfort very much, nor will they have much tolerance for it. But by that time, you won't be experiencing much discomfort either, so it will be a memory for you, but not an overwhelming one as it is now.

Can you say what star system?

I won't, because some of you are more attached to some star systems over others. I will say that you would all be able to agree that where I live is a beautiful place and you'd love to visit here someday. Please do.

But to encourage those who have suffered . . . I thought only people who are on the Earth can suffer. No one else suffers, do they?

I will address only the Earth. It is to you I am speaking. It's time. There has been some suffering in other places and other times, but it is your suffering that I am addressing today.

Share Your Kindness and Happiness

Now I will make a closing comment: Don't assume because you might feel that your life is modest or not very influential that you cannot be kind and experience kindness. Sometimes being kind is the result of experiencing kindness. Someone might say a kind word to you: "Oh, your hair looks nice today," or "Your shoes are very shiny; they look terrific." Be kind in response. Say thank you. Don't just shrug your shoulders as if it's nothing. I assure you that it is much more impressive, no matter what people say, to experience kindness in return of kindness rather than some other attitude.

Suppose someone waves at you across the street. You're not sure who she is. It's all right. Wave back, or nod your head—that's okay—with a smile: "Nice to see you. Good life, have fun, see you again sometime." Suppose someone at work says, "Hey, you look pretty cheerful today." Until he said that, you didn't notice that you do feel kind of cheerful. Give him kindness in return: "Thanks. I do feel kind of good today." A smile, a wave, and on you go. It balances, you see.

If you know people at work and can say, "Hey, you look all right today," or "My, you look nice," or some simple thing—"That color looks good on you"—if it feels all right to say that in your culture, then say that. If it isn't, then just give a cheerful nod, a "Hello, welcome. Nice to see you here at work today," something simple. If you see your family members, if you know that there are things that are troubling to talk about, you don't have to talk about them all the time. Sometimes you do, but not all the time. Smile, nod, give a kiss or an embrace, a reminder that you love them even though you're not always happy with them. It's very reassuring. And if that happens to you—the smile, the nod, the kiss, the embrace—even if you're a little angry with this person, you can do that in return and let her know you love her too and that you'll always be able to talk about your problems in the future. Keep it simple and understand that the little things you do can be profoundly benevolent.

Now I'm going to tell you something that you can identify with: There have been times when you have felt overwhelmed with happiness and you wanted to go outside and shout your happiness. What this physical feeling is all about is that you really want to go outside and thrust your arms wide and allow the wind to share in your happiness and spread it throughout the world. Do that when you feel that happiness. It won't take it all away; you'll still have happiness, but you'll exude more happiness when you do that than you would be able to bear as a feeling because the wind will come or the Sun will shine or water droplets will pass through or there will simply be a breeze that will be available to take your exuding happiness and spread it. And when the moment passes, relax and go back and continue your life.

This feeling of desiring to exult in your happiness . . . it can be good to allow it to move about. Look at your life. See what serves you benevolently. Try to see that it serves others benevolently as well, and you will expand as a spiritual citizen no matter what your religion, and Creator will smile and say, "Well done." Good night.

Good night, good life, thank you.

THE EXPLORER RACE SERIES

ZOOSH AND HIS FRIENDS THROUGH ROBERT SHAPIRO

THE SERIES: Humans—creators-in-training—have a purpose and destiny so heartwarmingly, profoundly glorious that it is almost unbelievable from our present dimensional perspective. Humans are great lightbeings from beyond this creation, gaining experience in dense physicality. This truth about the great human genetic experiment of the Explorer Race and the mechanics of creation is being revealed for the first time by Zoosh and his friends through superchannel Robert Shapiro. These books read like adventure stories as we follow the clues from this creation that we live in out to the Council of Creators and beyond.

❶ THE EXPLORER RACE

You individuals reading this are truly a result of the genetic experiment on Earth. You are beings who uphold the principles of the Explorer Race. The information in this book is designed to show you who you are and give you an evolutionary understanding of your past that will help you now. The key to empowerment in these days is to not know everything about your past, but to know what will help you now. Your number-one function right now is your status of Creator apprentice, which you have achieved through years and lifetimes of sweat. You are constantly being given responsibilities by the Creator that would normally be things that Creator would do. The responsibility and the destiny of the Explorer Race is not only to explore, but to create. 574 P. $25.00 ISBN 0-929385-38-1

❷ ETs and the EXPLORER RACE

In this book, Robert channels Joopah, a Zeta Reticulan now in the ninth dimension who continues the story of the great experiment—the Explorer Race—from the perspective of his civilization. The Zetas would have been humanity's future selves had not humanity re-created the past and changed the future. 237 P. $14.95 ISBN 0-929385-79-9

❸ EXPLORER RACE: ORIGINS and the NEXT 50 YEARS

This volume has so much information about who we are and where we came from—the source of male and female beings, the war of the sexes, the beginning of the linear mind, feelings, the origin of souls—it is a treasure trove. In addition, there is a section that relates to our near future—how the rise of global corporations and politics affects our future, how to use benevolent magic as a force of creation and how we will go out to the stars and affect other civilizations. Astounding information. 339 P. $14.95 ISBN 0-929385-95-0

❹ EXPLORER RACE: CREATORS and FRIENDS
The MECHANICS of CREATION

Now that you have a greater understanding of who you are in the larger sense, it is necessary to remind you of where you came from, the true magnificence of your being. You must understand that you are creators-in-training, and yet you were once a portion of Creator. One could certainly say, without being magnanimous, that you are still a portion of Creator, yet you are training for the individual responsibility of being a creator, to give your Creator a coffee break. This book will allow you to understand the vaster qualities and help you remember the nature of the desires that drive any creator, the responsibilities to which a creator must answer, the reaction a creator must have to consequences and the ultimate reward of any creator. 435 P. $19.95 ISBN 1-891824-01-5

❺ EXPLORER RACE: PARTICLE PERSONALITIES

All around you in every moment you are surrounded by the most magical and mystical beings. They are too small for you to see as single individuals, but in groups you know them as the physical matter of your daily life. Particles who might be considered either atoms or portions of atoms consciously view the vast spectrum of reality yet also have a sense of personal memory like your own linear memory. These particles remember where they have been and what they have done in their infinitely long lives. Some of the particles we hear from are Gold, Mountain Lion, Liquid Light, Uranium, the Great Pyramid's Capstone, This Orb's Boundary, Ice and Ninth-Dimensional Fire. 237 P. $14.95 ISBN 0-929385-97-7

❻ EXPLORER RACE and BEYOND

With a better idea of how creation works, we go back to the Creator's advisers and receive deeper and more profound explanations of the roots of the Explorer Race. The liquid Domain and the Double Diamond portal share lessons given to the roots on their way to meet the Creator of this universe, and finally the roots speak of their origins and their incomprehensibly long journey here. 360 P. $14.95 ISBN 1-891824-06-6

THE EXPLORER RACE SERIES

ZOOSH AND HIS FRIENDS THROUGH ROBERT SHAPIRO

❼ EXPLORER RACE: The COUNCIL of CREATORS

The thirteen core members of the Council of Creators discuss their adventures in coming to awareness of themselves and their journeys on the way to the Council on this level. They discuss the advice and oversight they offer to all creators, including the Creator of this local universe. These beings are wise, witty and joyous, and their stories of Love's Creation create an expansion of our concepts as we realize that we live in an expanded, multiple-level reality. 237 P. $14.95 ISBN 1-891824-13-9

❽ EXPLORER RACE and ISIS

This is an amazing book! It has priestess training, Shamanic training, Isis's adventures with Explorer Race beings—before Earth and on Earth—and an incredibly expanded explanation of the dynamics of the Explorer Race. Isis is the prototypal loving, nurturing, guiding feminine being, the focus of feminine energy. She has the ability to expand limited thinking without making people with limited beliefs feel uncomfortable. She is a fantastic storyteller, and all of her stories are teaching stories. If you care about who you are, why you are here, where you are going and what life is all about—pick up this book. You won't lay it down until you are through, and then you will want more. 317 P. $14.95 ISBN 1-891824-11-2

❾ EXPLORER RACE and JESUS

The core personality of that being known on the Earth as Jesus, along with his students and friends, describes with clarity and love his life and teaching two thousand years ago. He states that his teaching is for all people of all races in all countries. Jesus announces here for the first time that he and two others, Buddha and Mohammed, will return to Earth from their place of being in the near future, and a fourth being, a child already born now on Earth, will become a teacher and prepare humanity for their return. So heartwarming and interesting, you won't want to put it down. 354 P. $16.95 ISBN 1-891824-14-7

❿ EXPLORER RACE: Earth History and Lost Civilization

Speaks of Many Truths and Zoosh, through Robert Shapiro, explain that planet Earth, the only water planet in this solar system, is on loan from Sirius as a home and school for humanity, the Explorer Race. Earth's recorded history goes back only a few thousand years, its archaeological history a few thousand more. Now this book opens up as if a light was on in the darkness, and we see the incredible panorama of brave souls coming from other planets to settle on different parts of Earth. We watch the origins of tribal groups and the rise and fall of civilizations, and we can begin to understand the source of the wondrous diversity of plants, animals and humans that we enjoy here on beautiful Mother Earth. 310 P. $14.95 ISBN 1-891824-20-1

⓫ EXPLORER RACE: ET VISITORS SPEAK

Even as you are searching the sky for extraterrestrials and their spaceships, ETs are here on planet Earth—they are stranded, visiting, exploring, studying the culture, healing the Earth of trauma brought on by irresponsible mining or researching the history of Christianity over the past two thousand years. Some are in human guise, and some are in spirit form. Some look like what we call animals as they come from the species' home planet and interact with their fellow beings—those beings that we have labeled cats or cows or elephants. Some are brilliant cosmic mathematicians with a sense of humor; they are presently living here as penguins. Some are fledgling diplomats training for future postings on Earth when we have ET embassies here. In this book, these fascinating beings share their thoughts, origins and purposes for being here. 350 P. $14.95 ISBN 1-891824-28-7

⓬ EXPLORER RACE: Techniques for GENERATING SAFETY

Wouldn't you like to generate safety so you could go wherever you need to go and do whatever you need to do in a benevolent, safe and loving way for yourself? Learn safety as a radiated environment that will allow you to gently take the step into the new timeline, into a benevolent future and away from a negative past. 208 P. $9.95 ISBN 1-891824-26-0

☼ LIGHT TECHNOLOGY
PUBLISHING
PO Box 3540 • Flagstaff, AZ 86003

Phone: 928-526-1345 or 1-800-450-0985 • Fax: 928-714-1132 or 1-800-393-7017
. . . or use our online bookstore at www.lighttechnology.com

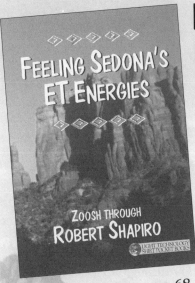

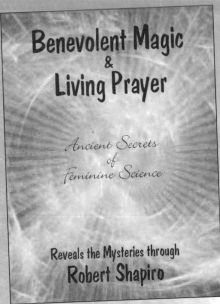
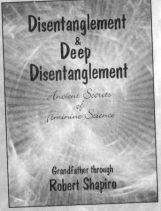
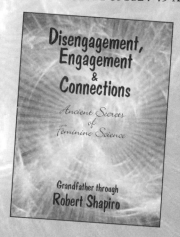

Shamanic Secrets for Spiritual Mastery
the third book of the Shamanic Secrets series
due out late 2005!

SPEAKS OF MANY TRUTHS AND ZOOSH THROUGH ROBERT SHAPIRO

SHAMANIC SECRETS for MATERIAL MASTERY

Learn to communicate with the planet!

This book explores the heart and soul connection between humans and Mother Earth. Through that intimacy, miracles of healing and expanded awareness can flourish. To heal the planet and be healed as well, we can lovingly extend our energy selves out to the mountains and rivers and intimately bond with the Earth. Gestures and vision can activate our hearts to return us to a healthy, caring relationship with the land we live on.

The character and essence of some of Earth's most powerful features are explored and understood, with exercises given to connect us with those places. As we project our love and healing energy there, we help the Earth to heal from humanity's destruction of the planet and its atmosphere. Dozens of photographs, maps and drawings assist the process in twenty-five chapters, which cover the Earth's more critical locations.

$19⁹⁵ SOFTCOVER 498 P.
ISBN 1-891824-12-0

Chapter Titles:

- Approaching Material Mastery through Your Physicality
- Three Rivers: The Rhine, the Amazon and the Rio Grande
- Three Lakes: Pyramid Lake, Lake Titicaca and Lake Baikal
- Mountains: Earth's Antennas, Related to the Human Bone Structure
  - Three Mountains: The Cydonia Pyramid, Mount Rushmore and Mount Aspen
  - Mountains in Turkey, Japan and California
  - Eurasia and Man's Skeletal Structure
  - Greenland, the Land of Mystery
- Africa and North America
- South and Central America and Australia
- Shamanic Interaction with Natural Life
- Africa and the Caspian and Black Seas
- Mauna Loa, Mount McKinley and Shiprock
- The Gobi Desert
- Old Faithful, the Cayman Islands, the Blue Mountains and Grandfather Mountain
- Meteor Crater, Angel Falls and Other Unique Locations on the Planet

PART II: THE FOUNDATION OF ONENESS
- The Explorer Race as a Part of Mother Earth's Body
- Spiritual Beings in a Physical World
- Earth Now Releasing Human Resistance to Physical Life
- Healing Prisoners, Teaching Students
- The Shaman's Key: Feeling and the Five Senses
- How to Walk, How To Eat
- Breathing: Something Natural We Overlook
- How to Ask and Let Go, and How to Sleep
- Singing Our Songs
- Some Final Thoughts

SHAMANIC SECRETS for PHYSICAL MASTERY

The purpose of this book is to allow you to understand the sacred nature of your own physical body and some of the magnificent gifts it offers you. When you work with your physical body in these new ways, you will discover not only its sacredness, but how it is compatible with Mother Earth, the animals, the plants, even the nearby planets, all of which you now recognize as being sacred in nature.

It is important to feel the value of yourself physically before you can have any lasting physical impact on the world. The less you think of yourself physically, the less likely your physical impact on the world will be sustained by Mother Earth. If a physical energy does not feel good about itself, it will usually be resolved; other physical or spiritual energies will dissolve it because it is unnatural. The better you feel about your physical self when you do the work in the previous book as well as in this one and the one to follow, the greater and more lasting will be the benevolent effect on your life, on the lives of those around you and ultimately on your planet and universe.

$25⁰⁰ SOFTCOVER 544 P.
ISBN 1-891824-29-5

Chapter Titles:

- Cellular Clearing of Traumas and Unresolved Events
- Feeling is Our Body's First and Primary Language
- The Resolution of Fear, Trauma and Hate
- Dealing with Fear, Pain and Addiction
- Shame, Arrogance, Safety and the Inability to Trust
- The Role of Trauma in Human Life
- Letting Go of Old Attitudes and Inviting New Energy
- The Waning of Individuality
- Clearing the Physical Body
- Using the Gestures to Protect, Clear and Charge
- The Flow of Energy
- Connecting with the Earth
- Communication of the Heart

- More Supportive Gestures
- Sleeping and Dreamtime
- Responsibility and Living prayer
- Communicating with the Natural World
- Life Lessons and the Vital Life Force
- The Sacrament of Food
- Working with the Elements
- Communication with Those Who Would Follow
- Elemental Connections
- Taking Responsibility
- Creating Personal Relationships

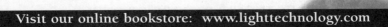